No Stress Tech Guide To Using Crystal Reports 2008 With ACT! 2010 Databases

By Dr. Indera E. Murphy

Tolana Publishing
Teaneck, New Jersey

No Stress Tech Guide To Using Crystal Reports 2008 With ACT! 2010 Databases

Published By:
Tolana Publishing
PO Box 719
Teaneck, NJ 07666 USA

Find us online at www.tolanapublishing.com
Inquiries may be sent to the publisher: tolanapub@yahoo.com

Our books are available online at www.barnesandnoble.com.
They can also be ordered from Ingram.

Quantity discounts are available for corporations, non-profit organizations and educational institutions for educational purposes, fundraising or resale. www.tolana.com/wholesale.html

ISBN-13: 978-1-935208-10-5
ISBN-10: 1-935208-10-1

Library of Congress Control Number: 2010920411

Printed and bound in the United States Of America

Cover by Mary Kramer, owner of Milkweed Graphics, www.milkweedgraphics.com

V1.0b

Who The Book Is For

This book is primarily for end-users that have never used Crystal Reports to create reports using an ACT! database. The second audience is people that have used a previous version of Crystal Reports and want to learn how use Crystal Reports with an ACT! database. This book does not cover how to use ACT! or how to use the version of Crystal Reports that comes with Visual Studio.

About The No Stress Tech Guide Series

The No Stress Tech Guide To Using Crystal Reports 2008 With ACT! 2010 databases, is part of the growing series of computer software training books that are designed to be used in a classroom setting, an online class or as a self-paced learning tool. The books contain an abundance of screen shots to help reduce the "stress" often associated with learning new software.

Tolana Publishing believes that the following principals are important when it comes to computer software training books:

⇒ The print should be large enough so that the reader does not have to squint.
⇒ The step-by-step instructions should really work and not leave something out.
⇒ Features or options that do not work as intended should be pointed out, not to bash the software company, but so that you do not think that you are crazy <smile>.
⇒ That there should be a realistic mix of theory, real world examples and hands-on exercises. It is important to know the past, because it helps you transition into the future with ease and dignity.

Titles In The No Stress Tech Guide Series

	ISBN-13
Microsoft Works 7	978-0-9773912-2-6
Microsoft Works 8 & 8.5	978-0-9773912-1-9
Microsoft Works 9	978-0-9773912-7-1
Windows XP	978-0-9773912-0-2
OpenOffice.org 2 Writer	978-0-9773912-4-0
OpenOffice.org 3 Writer	978-1-935208-08-2
ACT! 2007	978-0-9773912-5-7
ACT! 2009	978-1-935208-07-5
ACT! 2010	978-1-935208-09-9
Crystal Reports For Visual Studio 2005	978-0-9773912-6-4
Crystal Reports Basic For Visual Studio 2008	978-0-9773912-8-8
Crystal Xcelsius 4.5	978-1-935208-02-0
Xcelsius 2008	978-1-935208-05-1
Crystal Reports XI For Beginners (2nd Edition)	978-1-935208-00-6
What's New In Crystal Reports 2008	978-1-935208-01-3
Crystal Reports 2008 For Beginners (Revised)	978-0-9773912-9-5
Using Crystal Reports 2008 With ACT! 2010 Databases	978-1-935208-10-5

About The Author

Dr. Indera E. Murphy is an author, educator and IT professional that has over 20 years of experience in the Information Technology field. She has held a variety of positions including technical writer, programmer, consultant, web designer, course developer and project leader. Indera has designed and developed software applications and web sites, as well as, manage technology driven projects in several industries. In addition to being an Executive Director and consultant, Indera is also an online adjunct professor. She teaches courses in a variety of areas including project management, technical writing, information processing, Access, HTML, Windows, Excel, Dreamweaver and critical thinking.

Why A Book On Crystal Reports 2008 Specifically For ACT! Databases?

After reading the Users Guide that comes with Crystal Reports 2008, I felt that users, especially new users would prefer to have more assistance in learning how to get the most out of the software when using an ACT! database. More importantly, currently, there is no book for Crystal Reports that covers using ACT! databases in depth. There are differences when using an ACT! database then other types of databases.

I know that many books claim to have "step-by-step instructions". If you have tried to follow books that make this claim and you got lost or could not complete a task as instructed, it may not have been your fault. When I decided to write computer books, I vowed to really have step-by-step instructions that actually included every step. This includes steps like which file to open, which menu option to select, when to save a file and more. In my opinion, it is this level of detail that makes a computer book easy to follow. I hope that you feel the same way.

CONTENTS

GETTING STARTED WITH CRYSTAL REPORTS 2008

The easiest and fastest way to overcome an obstacle is to have someone that has been there, to be by your side every step of the way. That is the goal of this book - to be by your side every step of the way through learning how to use Crystal Reports 2008 with an ACT! database.

A hands-on approach is usually the best way to learn most things in life. This book is a visual guide that has over 95 exercises. There are over 575 illustrations that practically eliminate the guess work and let you know that you are doing the steps correctly. There is more to Crystal Reports than knowing how to open and print a report. Crystal Reports is robust and has a lot of features.

One goal of this book is to discuss report design issues and potential solutions on how to resolve them. The good thing is that you have taken a great first step towards learning Crystal Reports by purchasing this book. Now, all you have to do is use this book to learn how to overcome the hurdles. From time to time, I will point out functionality that may not work as expected. When I do this, I am not complaining, merely pointing out things that you should be aware of.

It is my sincere hope that whatever your current skill level is with Crystal Reports, that you will learn more about features that you are already familiar with as you go through this book and that you learn about features that you did not know existed. While you can jump to exercises that cover something you need to know now, I hope that you complete the exercises in the order that they are presented because you will get more from the book. Learning new tips and shortcuts will let you work faster and smarter. The more you know about Crystal Reports, the easier your day to day report design experiences will be.

So sit back and lets get started.

Thank you for purchasing this book!

About Crystal Reports

Crystal Reports is a software package that allows you to create reports. It is the report writing software that many companies use. Almost all businesses today that maintain data, have a need for reports to help them get their job done and to make business decisions. Reports allow one to be able to read and make sense of large amounts of information that is most often stored in a database. Most databases have limited reporting capabilities and only allow reports to be created in that "type" of database. Database types include Sybase, Microsoft SQL Server and Oracle, to name a few. These are often called SQL databases and are usually stored on a database server. Some of them do provide a desktop version that is used for learning purposes. If you need to create a report that has data (information) in both Oracle and Sybase databases for example, you would have to use Crystal Reports because neither database allows you to create reports that have data in other types of databases.

Crystal Reports provides the ability to use data from a variety of database types and combine the data in one report. Crystal Reports can use databases of any size. In addition to the SQL databases mentioned above, you can also use mainframe databases and what I call desktop or PC databases like Microsoft Access and Visual FoxPro. This type of database usually contains a lot less data than the SQL databases and do not have the capacity to support hundreds or thousands of end-users like SQL databases do. Crystal Reports also comes bundled with a lot of software development tools including Visual Studio. It also comes bundled with several leading software packages like PeopleSoft and JD Edwards. In addition to creating paper reports, reports can be exported to Word, Excel and PDF formats from Crystal Reports. You can create almost any type of report that you can dream up.

Normally, Crystal Reports is a read-only program, meaning that when you create or modify reports the data in the database is not changed. You can however, include SQL commands in the report, which will allow the report to edit, delete and add records to a database.

The primary goal of Crystal Reports is to allow a wide range of users to have the ability to work with the raw data in databases to be able to create reports that allow data to be interpreted and analyzed. Crystal Reports makes creating basic reports easier through the use of report wizards, which are similar to wizards that you may have used in other software packages. You can also create complex reports that include subreports, formulas, charts and much more.

What's New In Crystal Reports 2008?

What you will notice that's new, depends on the previous version of Crystal Reports that you used, if any. The older the version of Crystal Reports that you are upgrading from, the more new features you will notice. The following list does not include all of the new features, but it should be enough to make you want to learn more.

Single Edition

Prior to Crystal Reports 2008, there were multiple editions of the software. Now there is only one. It is the equivalent of the developer edition from previous versions. That means that you have all of the features of the software.

Sort Control

This option allows the person running the report to sort the data on their own.

Reduced Installation File Size

The installation file size has been reduced because the sample database and reports have been removed. They can be downloaded if needed.

Parameter Panel

The Parameter Panel allows the person running the report to select different parameter values without refreshing the data in the report.

Built-In Bar Code Support

Basic bar codes can be printed on a report by converting data in a field.

Enhanced Cross-Tabs

This feature allows calculations to be added to rows or columns of cross-tab reports and charts. There are also new functions for cross-tabs.

Save Reports Directly To CrystalReports.com

If you have an account on crystalreports.com, you can save reports directly to this web server instead of having to upload them.

Adobe Flash & Flex Integration

These options are used to link or embed a Flash (SWF) file into a report. They also provide the ability to create mashups (pulling different types of data from multiple sources) in reports, which makes the reports interactive.

Xcelsius Integration

This option allows Xcelsius created SWF files to be incorporated into a report. Xcelsius is used to create dashboards, which provide "What If" functionality. Xcelsius is another software package owned by SAP, who purchased the company Business Objects.

Flexible Pagination

This option allows more control over how reports can be printed and viewed online. Reports can have different page orientations (landscape and portrait) in the same report by selecting options on the Section Expert.

Other New Features

Integrated SalesForce.com drivers
Interactive Report Viewing
Enhanced Report Designer features
Enhanced Web Services data driver
Hyperlinking Wizard
Improved XML Exporting
Advanced Report Publishing
.Net Report Modification SDK

Objectives

This book is written to accommodate classroom and online training, as well as, to be used as a self-paced training course. While there are no required prerequisites to successfully complete the exercises in this book, having a general knowledge of any of the following would be helpful.

- ☑ Prior version of Crystal Reports
- ☑ ACT! data and database structures
- ☑ Database structures in general
- ☑ Basic programming
- ☑ Report design

Step-by-step instructions are included throughout this book. This book takes a hands-on, performance based approach to teaching you how to use Crystal Reports and provides the skills required to create reports efficiently. After completing the exercises in this book, you will be able to perform the following tasks and more:

- ☑ Create a connection to a database and link tables
- ☑ Utilize report design and planning techniques
- ☑ Understand database concepts
- ☑ Use the report wizards and create reports from scratch
- ☑ Modify existing reports
- ☑ Format and edit reports
- ☑ Utilize the Workbench to organize reports that you work on
- ☑ Create report selection criteria
- ☑ Sort and group data
- ☑ Create charts
- ☑ Create reports that have subtotals, counts, running totals and summary information
- ☑ Export data
- ☑ Add Special Fields to reports
- ☑ Incorporate drill-down techniques in reports
- ☑ Create mailing labels using a wizard
- ☑ Create Cross-Tab reports
- ☑ Use the Formula Editor and Formula Workshop to create formulas and use functions
- ☑ Use the Highlighting and Section Experts to format data conditionally
- ☑ Create If...Then...Else Statements

Lesson 1 Objectives

After completing the exercises in this lesson you will be able to:

- ☑ Understand the options on the Start Page
- ☑ Check for updates for Crystal Reports
- ☑ Use the Online Help file

Conventions Used In This Book

I designed the following conventions to make it easier for you to follow the instructions in this book.

☑ The `Courier font` is used to indicate what you should type.

☑ **Drag** means to press and hold down the left mouse button while moving the mouse.

☑ **Click** means to press the left mouse button once, then release it immediately.

☑ **Double-click** means to quickly press the left mouse button twice, then release the mouse button.

☑ **Right-click** means to press the right mouse button once, which will open a shortcut menu.

☑ Click **OK** means to click the OK button on the dialog box.

☑ Press **Enter** means to press the Enter key on your keyboard.

☑ Press **Tab** means to press the Tab key on your keyboard.

☑ Click **Save** means to click the Save button in the software.

☑ Click **Finish** means to click the Finish button on the dialog box.

☑ **SMALL CAPS** are used to indicate an option to click on or to bring something to your attention.

☑ This icon indicates a tip or additional information about the topic that is being discussed.

☑ This icon indicates a shortcut or another way to complete the task that is being discussed.

☑ This icon indicates a warning, like a feature that has been removed or information that you need to be aware of.

☑ NEW This icon represents a new or modified feature in Crystal Reports 2008.

☑ The blinking cursor is the marker that is in a field or document and appears to the right of where you are typing. This is also known as the **INSERTION POINT** or **KEYBOARD CURSOR**. This is different then the pointer that is controlled by the mouse. The **MOUSE POINTER** usually looks like an I-beam when not in use.

☑ When you see "**YOUR SCREEN SHOULD HAVE THE OPTIONS SHOWN IN FIGURE X-X**", or something similar in the exercises, check to make sure that your screen does look like the figure. If it does, continue with the next set of instructions. If your screen does not look like the figure, redo the steps that you just completed so that your screen does match the figure. Not doing so may cause you problems when trying to complete exercises later in the book.

☑ The section heading **EXERCISE X.Y:** (where X equals the lesson number and Y equals the exercise number) represents exercises that have step-by-step instructions that you should complete. You will also see sections that have step-by-step instructions that are not an exercise. Completing them as you go through the book is optional, but recommended.

☑ "L2.1 Report Name" is the naming convention for reports that you will create. L2.1 stands for Lesson 2, Exercise 1. You may consider some of the report file names to be long. I did this on purpose, so that it is easier to know what topic the report covers. If you do not like to type or do not want to type the full report name, you can just type the first part as the file name (Example, L5.8, L7.2 etc). That way when you have to find a report to complete another exercise, you will be able to find the correct report.

- ☑ [See Lesson 3, Database Concepts] refers to a section in a lesson that you can use as a reference for the topic that is being discussed.
- ☑ [See Lesson 6, Figure 6-8] refers to an illustration (screen shot) that you can use as a reference for the topic that is being discussed.
- ☑ "Clear the (name of option)" means to remove the check mark from the option specified in the instruction.
- ☑ "Save the My practice document as" means to open the My practice document and save it with the new file name specified in the instruction. Doing this lets you keep the original document.
- ☑ **FILE ⇒ NEW ⇒ CROSS-TAB REPORT** means to open the **FILE** menu, select the option **NEW**, then select the option **CROSS-TAB REPORT**, as illustrated in Figure 1-1.

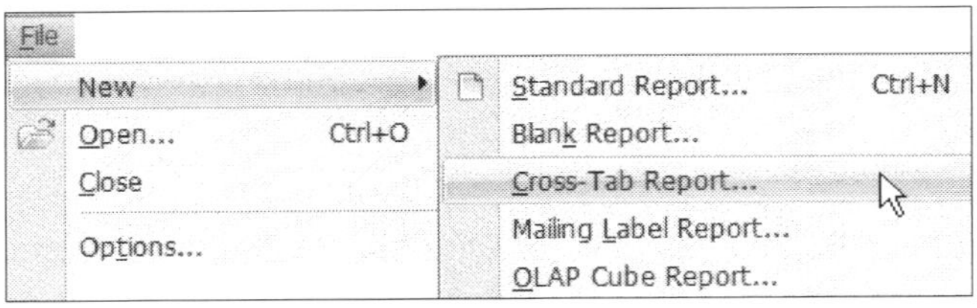

Figure 1-1 Menu navigation technique illustrated

Assumptions

Yes, I know one should never assume anything, but the following assumptions have been made. It is assumed that . . . .

- ☑ You have Crystal Reports 2008 installed on your computer. If you are not sure what version of Crystal Reports you have, open Crystal Reports, then select Help ⇒ About Crystal Reports. At the top of the dialog box shown in Figure 1-2 you will see the version that you have.

Figure 1-2 About Crystal Reports dialog box

- ☑ You have ACT! 2010 installed on your computer.
- ☑ You know that the operating system used to write this book is Windows Vista. If you are using a different version of Windows, some of the screen shots may have a slightly different look.
- ☑ You are familiar with the Windows environment including Windows Explorer and are comfortable using a mouse.
- ☑ You have Crystal Reports open at the beginning of each lesson.

- ☑ You have access to the Internet to download the practice files needed to complete the exercises in this book and to download any updates to Crystal Reports that are available.
- ☑ When you see <smile>, that signifies my attempt of adding humor to the learning process.
- ☑ Optional: That you have access to a printer, if you want to print any of the reports that you will create.
- ☑ Optional: That you have Microsoft Word and Excel installed if you want to view the reports that will be exported to these formats. If you don't have either of these software packages, other options are covered in the book.

Interactive Message Symbols

Like many other software packages, Crystal Reports will display interactive messages that require a response from you to confirm an action. Table 1-1 explains the three types of interactive message symbols and what they mean.

Symbol	Name	This interactive message type . . . . .
	Information	Provides information about an action that you just performed.
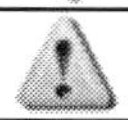	Warning	Usually requires you to make a decision.
	Critical	Requires you to make a decision before moving on to the next step.

Table 1-1 Interactive message symbols explained

Start Page Overview

The Start Page provides a lot of options that you may find helpful. The options on this page should save you some time because you do not have to remember which menu the option is on.

Open Crystal Reports

1. When you first open Crystal Reports you will see the Register dialog box if you have not registered the software yet. For now, click the **REGISTER LATER** button. You will see the window shown in Figure 1-3. (I scrolled down on the page to hide the logo on the screen shot.)

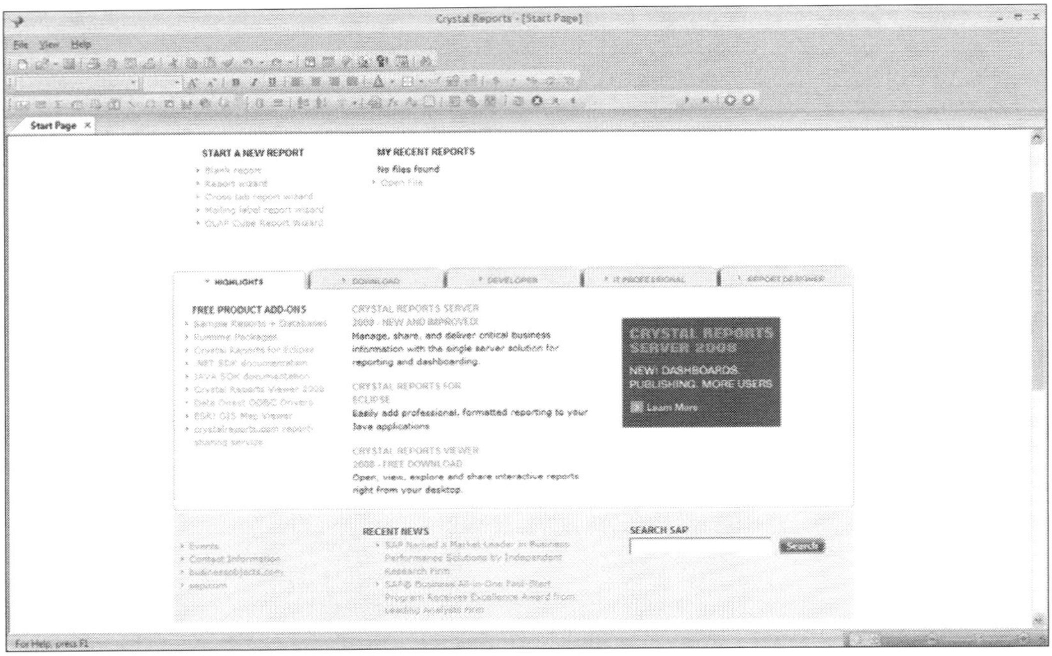

Figure 1-3 Start Page

NEW Start Page Tabs

There are five tabs on the Start Page. They provide information, help, updates and add-ons for Crystal Reports. Each tab is discussed below.

① **HIGHLIGHTS** Provides free product add-ons, updates and news stories.
② **DOWNLOAD** Provides free product add-ons, service packs, sample applications and reports.
③ **DEVELOPER** Has links to How To articles, forums and online documentation.
④ **IT PROFESSIONAL** Has links to How To articles, forums and online documentation.
⑤ **REPORT DESIGNER** Has links to How To articles, forums and online documentation.

Depending on the security that you have set in your firewall software, you may be prompted to grant Crystal Reports access to the Internet. It is probably a good idea to grant the access so that you can check for updates. Your firewall software may prompt you if you have the Check for Updates on Start Up option on the Help menu selected.

If you close the Start Page either on purpose or by accident, you can still get to all of the options on the Start Page through the menu, toolbar or shortcuts.

Crystal Reports does not have a spell checker.

Start A New Report Section Options

The options in this section are the report wizards. They are also on the File ⇒ New, menu option.

> The **BLANK REPORT** option is what you would select when you want to create a report from scratch (not use a wizard).

My Recent Reports

This section displays the last five reports that you opened, as shown in Figure 1-4. The first report listed is the most recent one that you opened. I think that it would be great if there was an option to display the last nine reports, like the bottom of the File menu does.

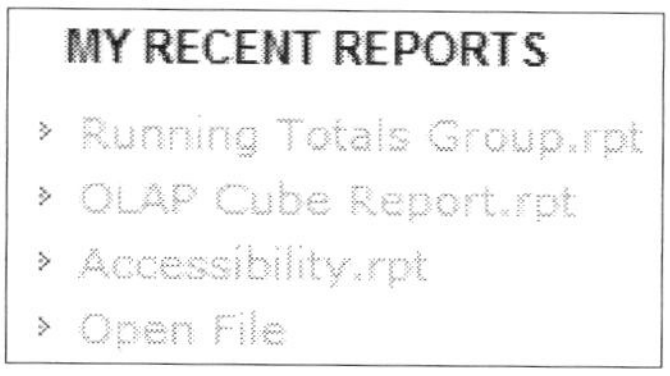

Figure 1-4 My Recent Reports section

The **OPEN FILE** link will display the last folder that you opened in Crystal Reports. Clicking on this link lets you look for the report that you want to open. You can navigate to another folder, if the folder that opens is not the one that you need.

Start Page Menu Options

The Start Page menu contains some of the options available in Crystal Reports. This menu is a subset of the menus that are available when a report is open in Crystal Reports. For example, Figure 1-5 shows the options on the File menu on the Start Page. Figure 1-6 shows the options on the File menu when a report is open.

> One difference in the location of items on the File menu that I noticed is the **LOG ON OR OFF SERVER** option. It is on the File menu on the Start Page shown in Figure 1-5. When a report is open, this option is on the Database menu.

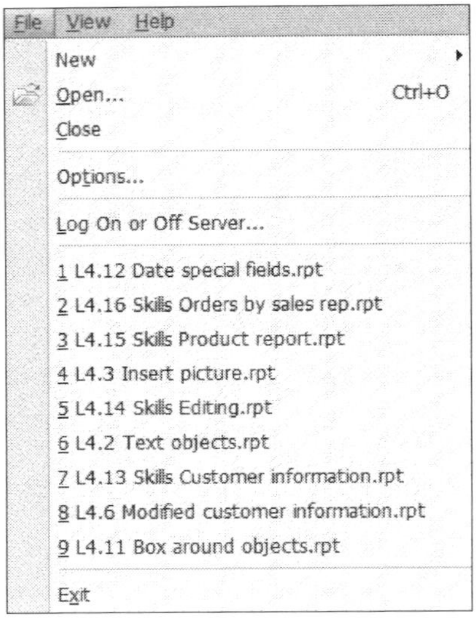

Figure 1-5 File menu options on the Start Page

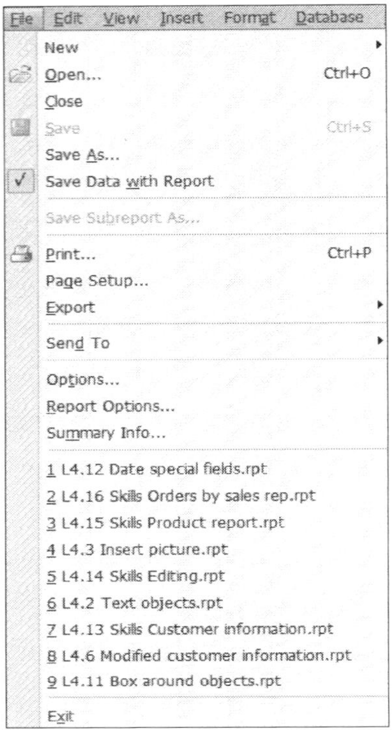

Figure 1-6 File menu options when a report is open

Checking For Software Updates

There are several ways that you can check for software updates as explained below.

① **Check for Updates on Start Up** If this option is selected, every time that you open Crystal Reports you will be prompted to check for updates. I don't know about you, but this would get on my nerves.

② **Check for Updates** This option lets you control when the check for updates will occur. This option is also on the Start Page.

③ Check for updates using the options on the Download tab on the Start page.

1. When a report is open and you open the Help menu, you will see the first two update options discussed above, as illustrated in Figure 1-7.

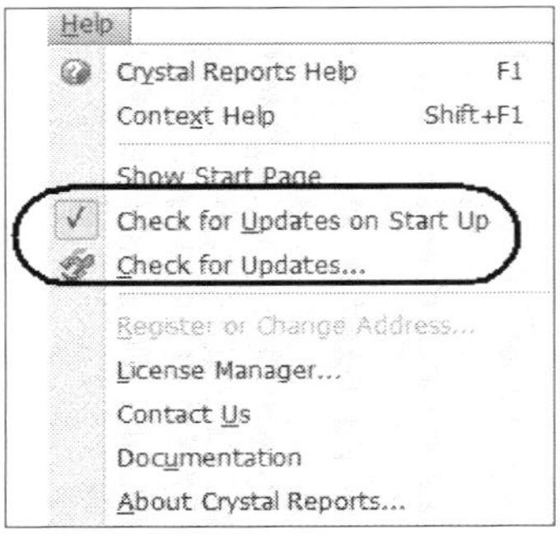

Figure 1-7 Update options illustrated

2. Clear the option **CHECK FOR UPDATES ON START UP**, if you do not want the software to check for updates every time that it is opened.

How To Manually Check For Updates

1. On the Start page, click on the Download tab. You will see the options shown in Figure 1-8.

Figure 1-8 Download tab options

2. Click on the first three links in the Service Packs and Fix Packs section.

3. Click on the Crystal Reports Service Packs link, then click on the Crystal Reports 2008 link.

Product Support Options

Below are some of the more popular support options for Crystal Reports.

Hot Fix Notification

If you want to receive the free monthly hot fix e-mail announcement for Crystal Reports, click on the link **SUBSCRIBE TO MONTHLY HOT FIX NOTIFICATIONS**, shown above in Figure 1-8. Signing up here will also allow you to post questions in the forums, which are explained in the next section.

Crystal Reports Forums

If you have a question about Crystal Reports you can post a message in the forum. On the Development tab, click on the Support Forums link in the Community section. If you do not already have an account, you will be prompted to create one. It's free. SAP does not provide staff to answer questions on the forum. The questions are answered by other Crystal Reports users.

Online Help File

The Help file in Crystal Reports is quite extensive. When you open the Help file, it opens in a new window instead of opening on the right side of the workspace, like it does in other applications. To open the Help file, follow the instructions below.

1. Help ⇒ Crystal Reports Help.

   You will see the window shown in Figure 1-9.

   The **CONTENTS** tab is the online manual. This tab is like a table of contents.

   Click on the plus sign in front of the topic that you want to know more about, to see additional topics.

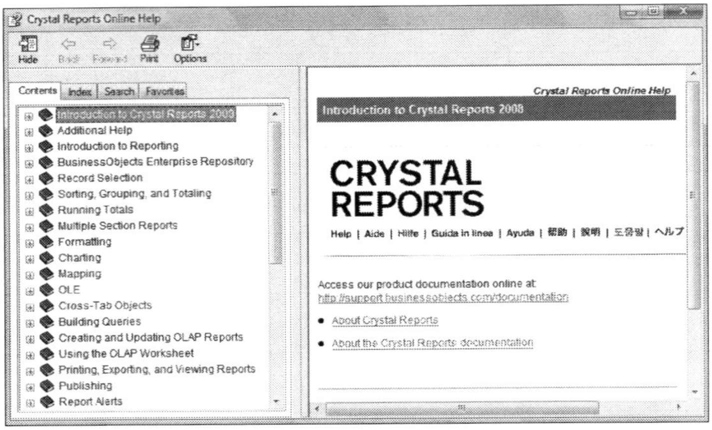

Figure 1-9 Contents tab options

You may have seen this style of help in other software packages. Each of the tabs (Contents, Index, Search and Favorites) provide help in a slightly different way.

Figure 1-10 shows the options on the Index tab. You can enter a keyword and click the **DISPLAY** button or scroll down the list of keywords and select the topic that you want.

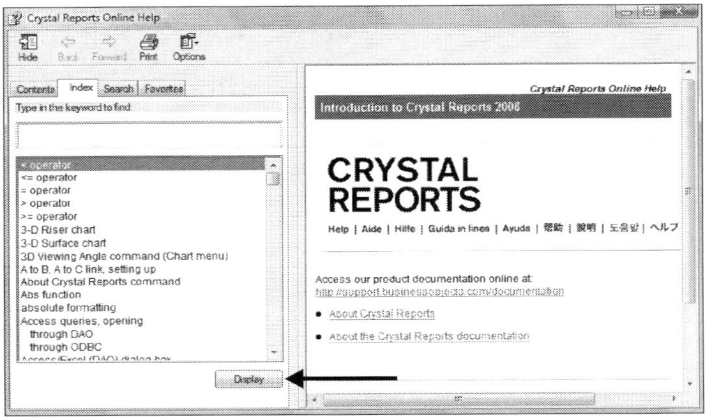

Figure 1-10 Index tab options

2. Click on the **SEARCH** tab.

   If you type in a keyword on the Search tab, then click the **LIST TOPICS** button shown in Figure 1-11, you will see a list of topics that relate to the keyword that you entered.

   Select the topic that is closest to what you are looking for, then click the **DISPLAY** button or double-click on the topic.

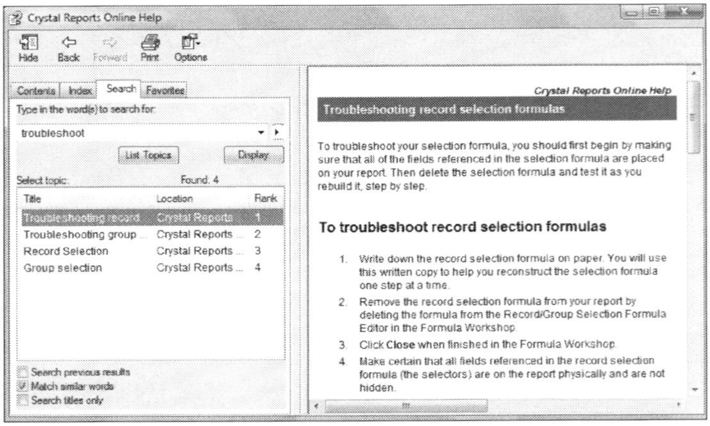

Figure 1-11 Search tab options

Error Message Help

Hopefully, you will not create a lot of errors, but if you do, the following files should help you decipher the error messages that you may encounter. On the Search tab, type `error message`, then click the List Topics button. You should see the results shown in Figure 1-12.

The **CRYSTAL REPORTS ERROR MESSAGES** topic lists each error message. To view the error messages, after selecting this topic, click on the right arrow in the topic window, on the right, as illustrated.

The **ERROR MESSAGES AND FORMULA COMPILER WARNINGS** topic lists the error messages and what may have caused them.

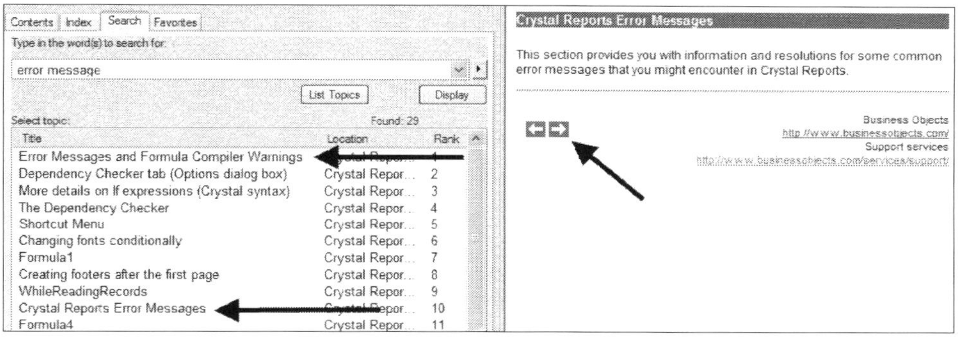

Figure 1-12 Error message topics

3. Click on the **FAVORITES** tab.

   This tab is used to view a list of the help topics that you have bookmarked, as shown in Figure 1-13.

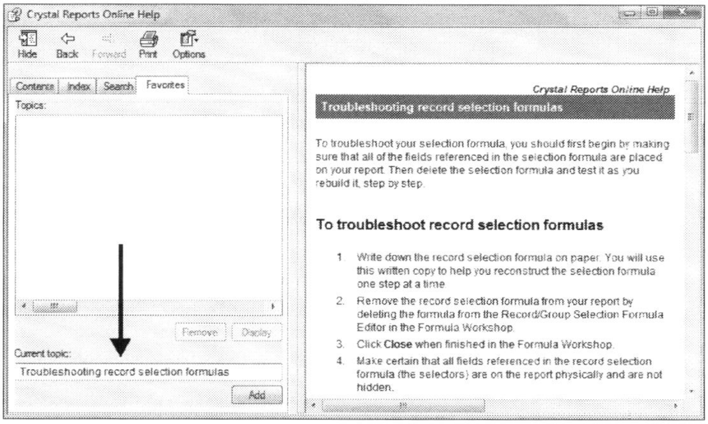

Figure 1-13 Favorites tab options

How To Add A Topic To The Favorites Tab

1. Display the topic on the right side of any help window.
2. Click on the Favorites tab. You should see the topic name in the **CURRENT TOPIC** field at the bottom, on the left side of the window, as shown above in Figure 1-13.
3. Click the **ADD** button.

There are five buttons at the top of the help window, as shown in Figure 1-14. The toolbar buttons are explained below.

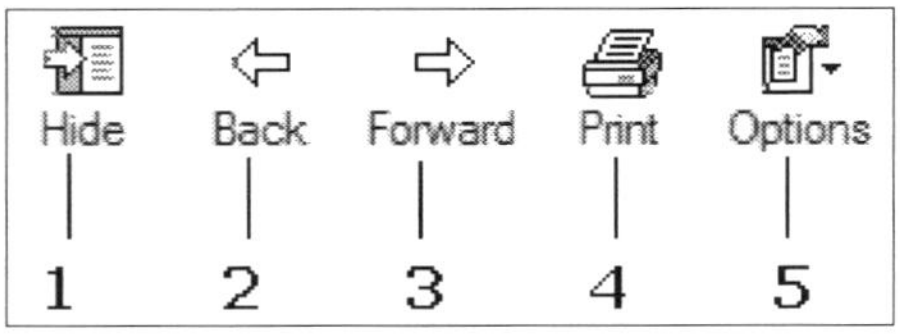

Figure 1-14 Help toolbar buttons

① The **HIDE** button will close the left side of the help window as shown in Figure 1-15. Compare this to the window shown earlier in Figure 1-13. To restore the left side of the window, click the **SHOW** button.
② The **BACK** button displays the previous topic that you viewed. This option is only available after you have viewed at least two help topics.
③ The **FORWARD** button works similar to the Back button. The Forward button also displays topics that you have already viewed.
④ The **PRINT** button will print the help topic that is displayed.
⑤ The **OPTIONS** button provides options to customize the help window. The options are shown in Figure 1-16.

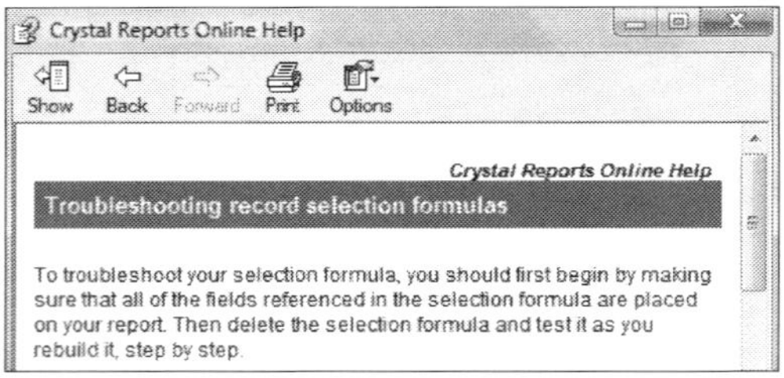

Figure 1-15 Left side of the help window hidden

Figure 1-16 Help customization options

4. Close the Help window.

Create A Folder For Your Reports

You will create and modify several reports in this book. It would be a good idea to store all of them in the same folder on your hard drive so that you can find them easily. I will refer to this folder as your folder. The instructions create the folder at the root of the C drive. If you want to create the folder in another location or under an existing folder, navigate to that location prior to starting step 2 below.

1. Open Windows Explorer and click on the C drive.

2. File ⇒ New ⇒ Folder.

3. Type `Crystal Reports Book` as the folder name. Press Enter, then close Windows Explorer.

4. The reports and files needed for this book are in a zip file named cr2008_act.zip. To have the link for the zip file sent to you, send an email to actcr2008@tolanapublishing.com. If you do not receive an email in a few minutes with the subject line Crystal Reports 2008 For ACT Files, check the spam folder in your email software.

5. Extract the files in the zip file to the folder that you created in step 3.

Backing Up Your Work

I cannot stress how important it is to back up your work frequently. Doing so will save you frustration in the event a power failure occurs or if your computer has a hardware failure. The majority of times that you lose work, it can't be recovered or if it can, it may cost you a few hundred dollars or more to recover it.

If you aren't already, you should also be saving a copy of your work to an external source like an external hard drive or USB drive. Windows has a backup utility that you can use. I tell my students this and it never fails that a student loses some, if not all of their work. Don't say that I didn't warn you <smile>.

TOOLBARS, MENUS & CUSTOMIZATION OPTIONS

In this lesson you will learn about the options on the toolbars and menus. You will also learn about the report design customization options.

LESSON 2

Crystal Reports Toolbars

There are five main toolbars in Crystal Reports: Standard, Formatting, Insert Tools, Navigation Tools and Expert Tools, as discussed below. They are right below the menu that you read about earlier in this lesson. Like toolbars in other applications, you can rearrange the toolbars by clicking on the dots at the beginning of the toolbar with the left mouse button and dragging the toolbar to a new location in the workspace. You cannot add or delete buttons on the toolbars, but you can turn off (remove) toolbars that you do not need or use. If you have used other Windows based applications, you are already familiar with many of the menu options. You will probably find that you will use the toolbar buttons more frequently then the options on the menu.

> Keep in mind that the buttons on the toolbars are available based on what you are doing and the object that is selected. There are some differences between the toolbar buttons and their menu counterparts. These differences will be pointed out.

Standard Toolbar

The Standard toolbar shown in Figure 2-1 contains options from the File, Edit, Format, View, Report and Help menus. Table 2-1 explains the purpose of each button on the Standard toolbar.

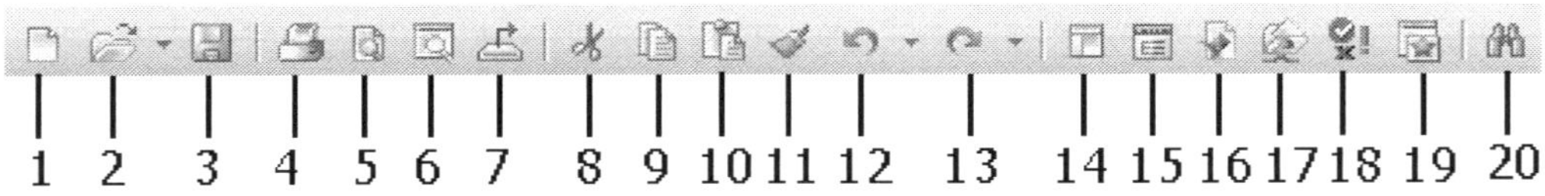

Figure 2-1 Standard toolbar

Button	Purpose
1	Creates a new report.
2	Opens an existing report. If you click on the arrow at the end of the button, you will see the last nine reports that you opened.
3	Saves the active report.
4	Opens the Print dialog box.
5	Displays the active report in the Preview window. This is the same as clicking on the Preview tab. You can click this button if the Preview tab is not visible.
6	Displays the active report as a web page in the HTML Preview window.
7	Opens the Export dialog box which is used to export the report to one of several popular formats.
8	Removes the selected object(s) from the report and places it on the clipboard.
9	Copies the selected object(s) to the clipboard.
10	Pastes object(s) from the clipboard into the report.
11	Copies (absolute or conditional) formatting properties from one object to one or more other objects. This is a shortcut to the Format Painter command.
12	Undoes an action. (1)
13	Redoes the last action that was undone. (1)

Table 2-1 Standard toolbar buttons explained

Button	Purpose
14	NEW Toggles the Preview Panel on and off on the Preview window.
15	Opens the Field Explorer so that you can add fields and other objects to the report. (2)
16	Opens the Report Explorer so that you can see the objects on the report in tree view. (2)
17	Opens the Repository Explorer so that you can see the contents of the repository. (2)
18	Opens the Dependency Checker so that you can check reports for errors.
19	Displays or hides the Workbench.
20	Opens the Find dialog box, which lets you search for information in the report.

Table 2-1 Standard toolbar buttons explained (Continued)

(1) You can select how many changes that you want to undo and redo from the drop-down list. This capability is not available from the Edit menu.
(2) Clicking this button a second time does not close the Explorer window.

Formatting Toolbar

The Formatting toolbar shown in Figure 2-2 contains options to format objects. Table 2-2 explains the purpose of each button on the Formatting toolbar.

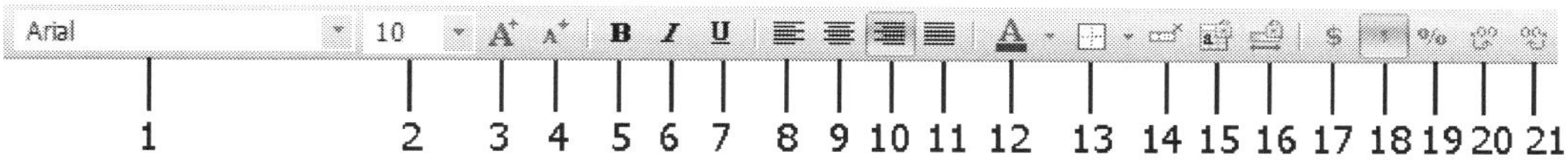

Figure 2-2 Formatting toolbar

Button	Purpose
1	Select a font.
2	Change the size for the font that is currently selected.
3	Increases the font size of the selected object one point each time this button is clicked. (3)
4	Decreases the font size of the selected object one point each time this button is clicked. (3)
5	Makes the selected object bold.
6	Makes the selected object italic.
7	Underlines the selected object.
8	Aligns the selected object flush left.
9	Centers the data of the selected object in the frame.
10	Aligns the data in the selected object flush right.
11	Justifies the data in the selected object between the length of the frame that the object is in.

Table 2-2 Formatting toolbar buttons explained

Button	Purpose
12	Applies the selected color to the object. This button is used to select or define colors in the Color dialog box. If you click on this button, the font color will change to the color that is on the line at the bottom of the button. Click on the arrow to change the color.
13	Applies the selected border to the object. You can select from several border style options. Click on the arrow to change the border style.
14	Suppresses the selected object. This means that the object will not print on the report.
15	Locks or unlocks the formatting of an object so that it can't be changed accidentally.
16	Locks the size and position of an object in relation to the object to its right.
17	Adds or removes the currency symbol in the selected numeric field.
18	Adds or removes the comma in the selected numeric field.
19	Adds or removes the percent sign in the selected numeric field.
20	Moves the decimal point in the selected numeric field one place to the right each time this button is clicked. (4)
21	Moves the decimal point in the selected numeric field one place to the left each time this button is clicked. (4)

Table 2-2 Formatting toolbar buttons explained (Continued)

(3) There is no menu option that has this functionality.
(4) Rounding is set to the number of decimal places in the field.

Font Size Tip

If the font size that you want is not in the drop-down list, highlight whatever size is showing in the font size drop-down list and type in the size that you want. You can also type in half sizes like 9.5.

Insert Tools Toolbar

The Insert Tools toolbar shown in Figure 2-3 contains additional report options. Table 2-3 explains the object type that each button will add to a report. These options are also available on the Insert menu.

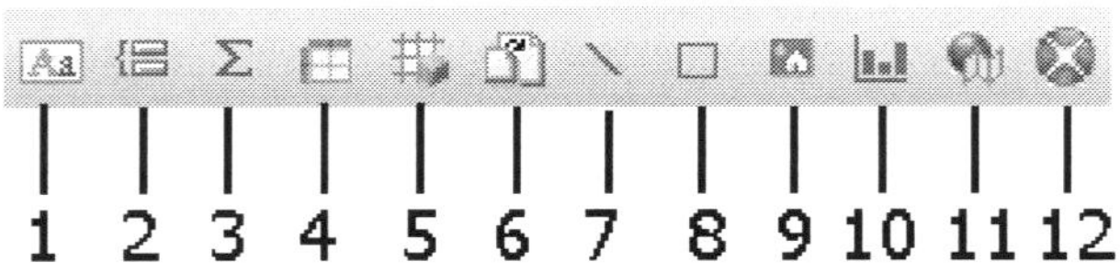

Figure 2-3 Insert Tools toolbar

Button	Is Used To Insert A . . .
1	text object
2	group
3	summary field
4	Cross-Tab object
5	OLAP grid object
6	subreport
7	line
8	box
9	picture
10	chart
11	map
12	NEW Flash object

Table 2-3 Insert Tools toolbar buttons explained

Navigation Tools Toolbar

The Navigation Tools toolbar show in Figure 2-4 contains options to navigate in a report and refresh data. This toolbar is activated once you preview a report. Table 2-4 explains the purpose of each button on the Navigation Tools toolbar.

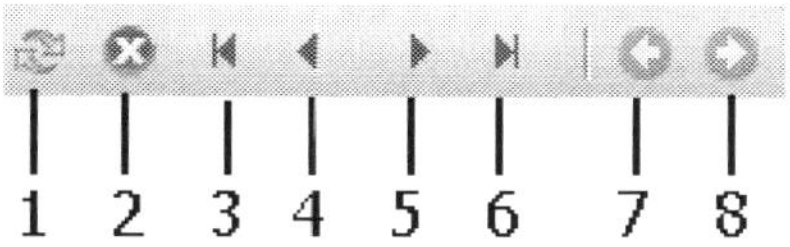

Figure 2-4 Navigation Tools toolbar

Button	Purpose
1	Refreshes the report data.
2	Stops the processing of data and only displays the report with the data that has been processed prior to clicking this button.
3	Displays the first page of the report.
4	Displays the previous page of the report.
5	Displays the next page of the report.
6	Displays the last page of the report.
7	Displays the previous page of the report. (5)
8	Displays the next page of the report. (5)

Table 2-4 Navigation Tools toolbar buttons explained

(5) This button is only available when you are using the HTML Preview option.

Expert Tools Toolbar

The Expert Tools toolbar shown in Figure 2-5 provides access to the experts, including the database, group and template experts. The buttons on this toolbar open dialog boxes that provide options to complete a task. Table 2-5 explains the purpose of each button on the Expert Tools toolbar. These options are also available on the Report menu.

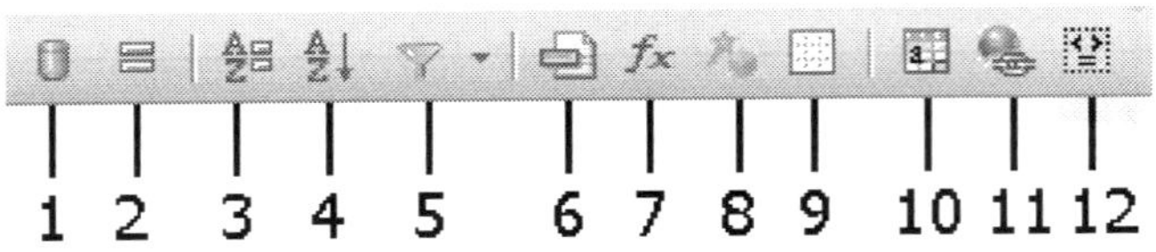

Figure 2-5 Expert Tools toolbar

Button	Purpose
1	Opens the Database Expert. It is used to add (or remove) data sources for the report.
2	Opens the Group Expert. It is used to create, modify and delete groups.
3	Opens the Group Sort Expert. It is used to find the Top or Bottom N records or sort the report on summary fields.
4	Opens the Record Sort Expert. It is used to select the order that the detail records will be sorted in.
5	Opens the Select Expert. It is used to create report selection criteria. (6)
6	Opens the Section Expert. It is used to format any section of the report.
7	Opens the Formula Workshop. It is used to create formulas and add functions to the report.
8	Opens the OLAP Cube Wizard. It is used to create a report that uses an OLAP Cube or **.CAR FILE** as the data source.
9	Opens the Template Expert. It is used to apply a template to a report.
10	Opens the appropriate Format Editor. It is used to modify formatting properties of the selected object.
11	Opens the Hyperlink tab on the Format Editor. It is used to add a hyperlink to a report.
12	Opens the Highlighting Expert. It is used to apply conditional formatting to an object.

Table 2-5 Expert Tools toolbar buttons explained

(6) **NEW** The Select Expert button has a menu, as shown in Figure 2-6.

Table 2-6 explains the Select Expert menu options.

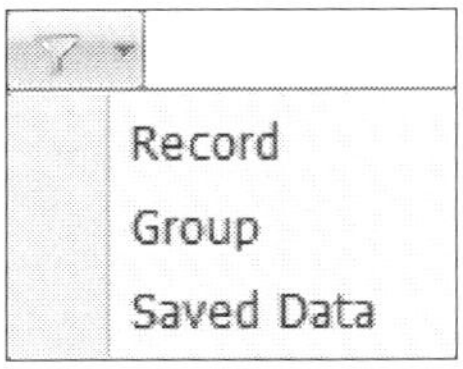

Figure 2-6 Select Expert menu

Select Expert Button Menu

Option	Description
Record	Creates selection criteria based on a field.
Group	Creates selection criteria based on a group name or summary field. Group processing is done after the record processing.
Saved Data	Filters data that has already been saved with the report. This option reduces the number of times a database has to be refreshed. This is helpful for reports that have parameter fields. When selected, this option only uses data that has already been saved with the report instead of retrieving data from the database.

Table 2-6 Select Expert button menu options explained

NEW External Command Toolbar

By default, this toolbar is not displayed because it is empty. After you have added an application to the toolbar, it can be displayed. This toolbar provides quick access to third party applications that you add to it. The **ADD-INS** menu can also be used to store custom controls. It is not displayed by default either.

How To Remove Toolbars

Like many features in Crystal Reports, there is more than one way to remove toolbars. There are two ways to remove a toolbar as discussed below.

① View ⇒ Toolbars. Opens the dialog box shown in Figure 2-7. Clear the check mark next to the toolbar that you do not want to be visible in the workspace, then click OK.

② Right-click near the toolbars at the top of the workspace. You will see the **TOOLBAR SHORTCUT MENU** shown in Figure 2-8. Click on the toolbar that you want to remove. Notice the **TOOLBARS** option at the bottom of the shortcut menu. Selecting this option will open the Toolbars dialog box shown in Figure 2-7.

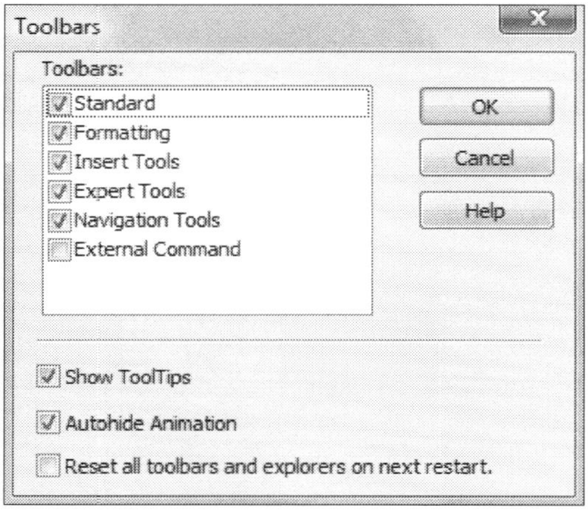

Figure 2-7 Toolbars dialog box

Figure 2-8 Toolbar shortcut menu

In prior versions of Crystal Reports, the Toolbars dialog box had a **VISUAL THEME** option, which was used to customize the interface. It has been removed.

Crystal Reports Menus

Tables 2-7 to 2-17 explain the Crystal Reports menu options. Many of the menu options will be familiar from the toolbars that you learned about earlier in this lesson.

File Menu Options

The options on the File menu are used to open, close, print and save files.

Menu Option	Description
New	Create a new report as shown in Figure 2-9.
Open	Opens an existing report. The default setting is to only display Crystal Reports files in the dialog box. You can change this setting and open other types of files. If checked, the **UPDATE REPOSITORY OBJECTS** option on the Open dialog box will cause objects in a report that are connected to the repository to be updated when the report is opened.
Close	Closes the active report. (7)
Save	Saves the active report. If the report is new, you will be prompted to give the report a file name. (7)
Save As	Saves the active report with a new name.
Save Data With Report	[See Lesson 4, Options For Saving Data]
Save Subreport As	Saves an existing report as a subreport with a different file name, even if it has already been inserted into another report.
Print	[See Lesson 14, Printer Options]
Page Setup	[See Lesson 14, Page Setup Options]
Export	[See Lesson 14, Export Report Overview]
Send To	Sends the active report via email using the dialog box shown in Figure 2-10 or to an Exchange mail folder. The first time that you use the Mail Recipient option, you may be prompted to insert the Crystal Reports CD to install the required components.
Options	Opens the Options dialog box, which is covered in detail later in this lesson.
Report Options	[See Lesson 14, Report Options]
Summary Info	[See Lesson 9, Document Properties]
Exit	Closes Crystal Reports. (7)

Table 2-7 File menu options explained

(7) If changes were made to the report before this option is selected, you will be prompted to save them.

As you learned earlier, the My Recent Reports section of the Start Page will display the last five reports that you opened.

The section above the Exit option at the bottom of the File menu will display the last nine reports that were opened, as shown at the bottom of Figure 2-9.

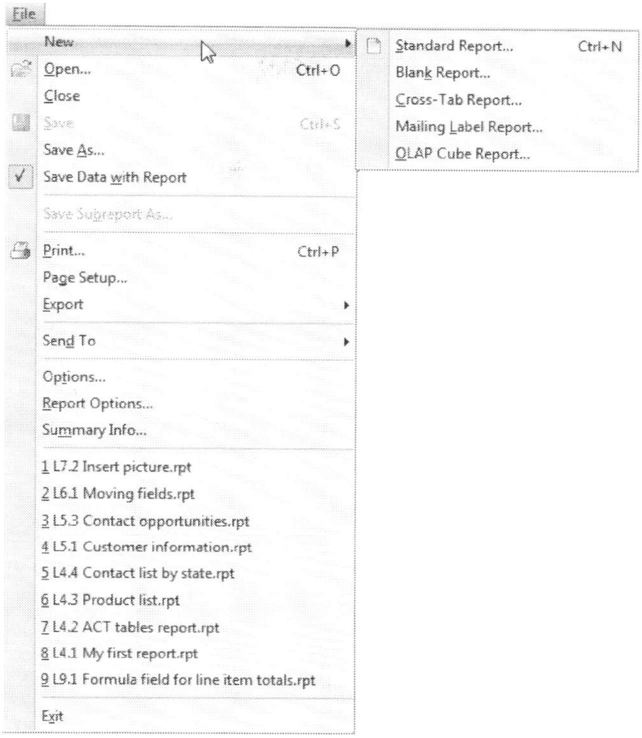

Figure 2-9 File menu options

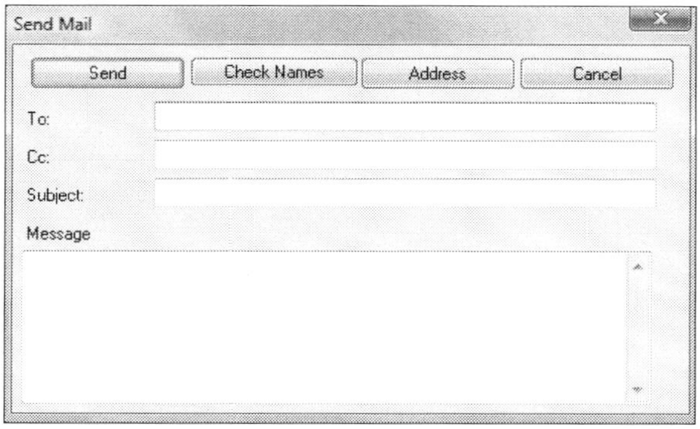

Figure 2-10 Send Mail dialog box

The **ADDRESS** button on the **SEND MAIL** window will open the default address book that is associated with the email software that you use. To send a report via email, you must use a MAPI compliant email software package. [See Lesson 14, Table 14-3]

Edit Menu Options

Many of the options on the Edit menu may be familiar, especially if you have used a word processing software package. Some of the options on the Edit menu require an object to be selected before it can be used.

Menu Option	Description
Undo	Undoes the last action that you did. If this menu option is not enabled, the last action cannot be undone. (8)
Redo	Redoes the last action that you did. If this menu option is not enabled, the last action cannot be repeated. (8)
Cut	Deletes the selected object(s) from the report and places them on the clipboard.
Copy	Copies the selected object(s) and places them on the clipboard.
Paste	Pastes object(s) from the clipboard into the report.
Paste Special	This option is primarily used for OLE (Object Linking and Embedded) objects because it gives more control than the Paste option on how an object is pasted into the report.
Delete	Deletes the selected object(s) from the report. Unlike the Cut option, the Delete option does not send the object to the clipboard.
Select All	Selects all of the objects in the report at one time. This will let you perform the same task to all of the objects at the same time.
Find	Opens the dialog box shown in Figure 2-12. The options are used to search for text in the report. The **ADVANCED FIND** button opens the dialog box shown in Figure 2-13 in preview mode. These options search for data (values in a field in the report). It is similar to the Select Expert because you can search in more than one field at the same time. These options work best from the preview window.
Go To Page	The dialog box shown in Figure 2-14 will display any page in the report. Type in the page number that you want to view in the field across from the Page field, then click OK.
Edit Report Object	The name of this menu item will change depending on the type of object that is selected. This option is only available for fields that can be edited, like summary and formulas fields. Editing a field is different then formatting a field. It is similar to right-clicking on an object and selecting Edit <Object Type>.
Subreports Links	This option is only available in reports that have a subreport. The subreport links dialog box is used to check and modify the link between the subreport and main report.
Object	Edit an embedded or linked OLE object.
Links	Modify the Link properties of the OLE object that is selected.

Table 2-8 Edit menu options explained

(8) The Undo and Redo menu options will change depending on the action (what you did) right before you opened the Edit menu. Figure 2-11 shows the Undo and Redo menu options after an action was taken.

Figure 2-11 Edit menu after an action was taken

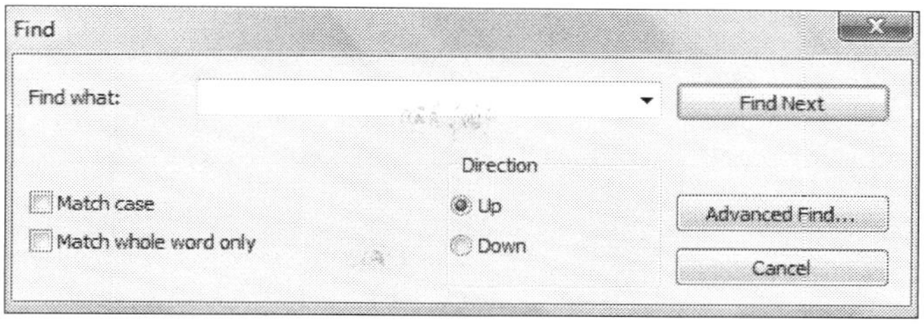

Figure 2-12 Find dialog box

> The difference between the Search Expert and the Select Expert is that the Search Expert searches through the data in the report. It does not search the records in the database like the Select Expert does.

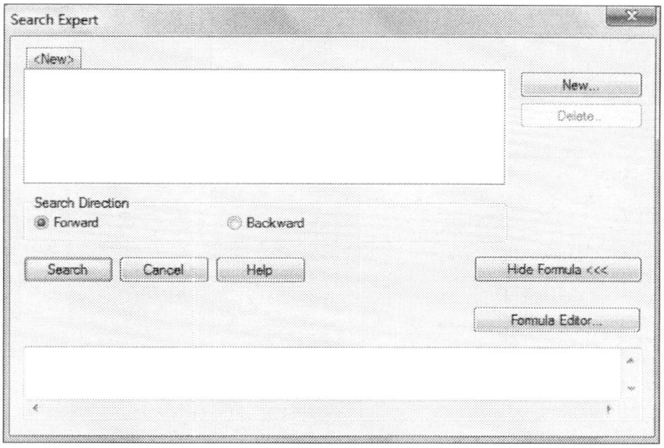

Figure 2-13 Search Expert dialog box

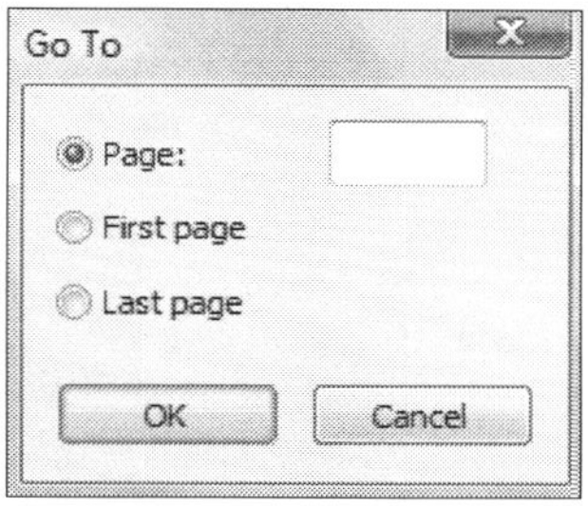

Figure 2-14 Go To dialog box

View Menu Options

The options on the View menu contain many of the tools in Crystal Reports, as explained in Table 2-9.

Menu Option	Description
Design	Displays the design tab.
Preview	Displays the preview tab.
Print Preview	This option is only available on the design tab. It is used to view the report. This is the same as clicking on the preview tab.
Preview Sample	Displays the report with limited data.
HTML Preview	Displays the report in HTML format. You may have to set some of the options on the Smart Tag & HTML Preview tab on the Options dialog box before you can use this option.

Table 2-9 View menu options explained

Menu Option	Description
Close Current View	Closes the active tab.
Field Explorer	Opens the Field Explorer so that you can add fields and other objects to the report.
Report Explorer	Displays all of the fields and objects on the report.
Repository Explorer	Opens the Repository Explorer so that an item from the repository can be added to the report.
Dependency Checker	Opens the Dependency Checker so that reports can be checked for errors.
Workbench	Displays or hides the Workbench.
Toolbars	Customize the toolbars.
Status Bar	Displays or hides the status bar at the bottom of the Crystal Reports workspace. The status bar provides additional information about the object that you are holding the mouse pointer over, as well as, other information about the active report.
Preview Panel	NEW The Group Tree, Parameters Panel and Find tab are stored in the Preview Panel.
Zoom	Sets the zoom level for viewing a report. You can change the zoom percent on the dialog box shown in Figure 2-15, or you can type the zoom percent in the Zoom field on the Standard toolbar.
Rulers	Displays or hides the rulers. (9)
Guidelines	Displays or hides the guidelines. (9)
Grid	Displays or hides the grid. (9)
Tool tips	Displays or hides the tool tips. (9)
Product Locale	NEW Change the language that the menus and commands are displayed in.
Preferred Viewing Locale	NEW Selects a language other then the one selected during the installation to display menus and commands.

Table 2-9 View menu options explained (Continued)

(9) This option works on the design and preview tabs.

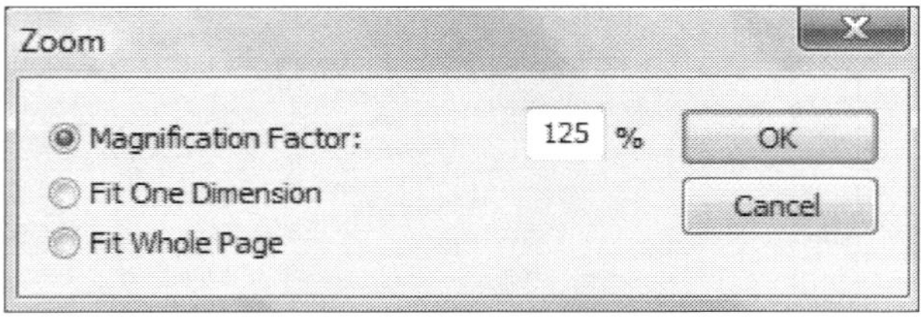

Figure 2-15 Zoom dialog box

Insert Menu Options

The options on the Insert menu are used to add objects to a report, as explained in Table 2-10. Many of these options are also available on the shortcut menu for the object.

Menu Option	Description
Text Object	Adds a text object to the report.
Summary	Adds a summary field to the report.
Field Heading	Creates a field heading for the selected field. If the **INSERT DETAIL FIELD HEADINGS** option is checked on the Layout tab of the Options dialog box, you will probably not have the need to use the field heading option because field headings will be created automatically for fields that are added to the details section.
Sort Control	**NEW** Add a control to a report that will let the person running the report sort it in a different order or on a different field.
Group	Adds a group to the report.
OLAP Grid	Opens the OLAP Expert, which is used to create an OLAP grid. (10)
Cross-Tab	Opens the Cross-Tab Expert, which is used to create a cross-tab object. (10)
Subreport	Opens the Insert Subreport dialog box, which is used to create a subreport or select an existing report to use as a subreport.
Line	Draws lines on the report. You can draw horizontal and vertical lines.
Box	Draws a box on the report. Boxes can also be drawn across sections of the report.
Picture	Add graphic files to a report. The supported file types are .bmp, jpeg, png, tiff and Windows metafile.
Chart	Create a chart using the Chart Expert.
Map	Create a map using the Map Expert.
Flash	**NEW** Link or embed a Flash (SWF) file to the report.
OLE Object	Add an OLE object to the report.
Template Field Object	This object is used as a placeholder for a field in a template. Template field objects are not connected to fields in a database.

Table 2-10 Insert menu options explained

(10)

There can be more than one OLAP grid or cross-tab object in the same report.

Format Menu Options

The options on the Format menu are used to change the appearance of the objects on the report.

Menu Option	Description
Format Field	Opens the appropriate Format Editor to modify the properties of the selected object.
Format Painter	Copies the formatting options from one object to another.
Hyperlink	Create a hyperlink.
Use Expert	Opens an expert, based on the object that is selected, so that the object can be edited. You may find it easier to right-click on an object and select the expert that you want to use, instead of selecting the object and then opening the Format menu.
Highlighting Expert	Opens the Highlighting Expert which is used to apply conditional formatting to a field.
Text Formatting	Apply formatting to a text field.
Move	Move a field from one location to another on the report.
Align	Line up objects.
Make Same Size	Makes two or more objects the same size by width, height or both.
Size and Position	Opens the Object Size And Position dialog box which provides you greater control over the size and position of an object, then you get if you size the object manually.
Pivot OLAP Grid	Change the row and column dimensions of an OLAP grid.
Pivot Cross-Tab	Change the row and column dimensions of a cross-tab grid.

Table 2-11 Format menu options explained

Database Menu Options

The options on the Database menu are used to interact with the databases that you use to create reports. They are explained in Table 2-12.

Menu Option	Description
Database Expert	Opens the Database Expert, which is used to add or delete data sources to or from the report.
Set Data Source Location	Select a different database for the report or a different location for the database that the report is currently using. This option is useful when you are using a copy of the database to create and test the report(s) and are now ready to move the report(s) into production (go live).
Log On or Off Server	Used to log on or off of an SQL or ODBC server, set database options and maintain the Favorites folder. Most of the tasks that you can complete on the Data Explorer window can be done another way.

Table 2-12 Database menu options explained

Menu Option	Description
Browse Data	View data in a field. This is the same as the Browse button that is on some dialog boxes.
Set OLAP Cube Location	Change the location of the OLAP Cube in the report.
Verify Database	Compare the structure of the data source that is used in the report to the structure of the actual database.
Show SQL Query	View SQL queries if the report is using any. Parameter fields are included if they are used in the selection formula. Figure 2-16 shows the dialog box.
Perform Grouping on Server	If checked and the report has a group and the details section of the report is hidden, the grouping process will be done on a server.
Select Distinct Records	If checked, duplicate records will not appear on the report. A duplicate record has the same data in every field in both records.
Query Panel	NEW Opens the Business Objects Query Panel, which is used to create queries that will be used in the report.

Table 2-12 Database menu options explained (Continued)

Each of the exercises that you will complete in Lesson 15 will create an SQL query, similar to the one shown in Figure 2-16.

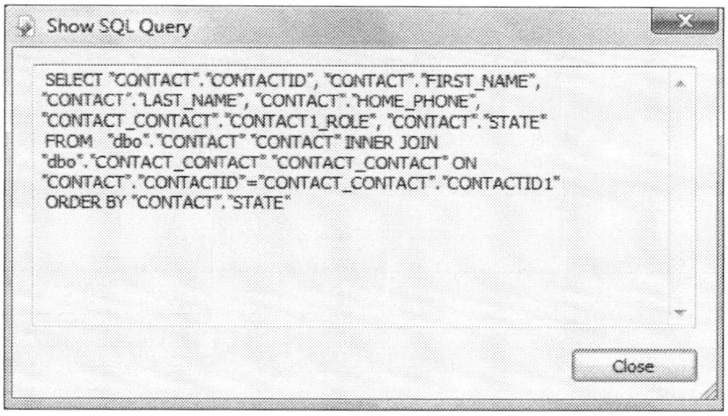

Figure 2-16 Show SQL Query dialog box

Report Menu Options

Many of the options on the Report menu will open an Expert. Some of the wizard screens look similar to some of the Experts.

Menu Option	Description
Select Expert	Opens the Select Expert which is used to create selection criteria to filter records.
Selection Formulas	The **RECORD** selection option opens the Record Selection Formula Editor, which is used to edit the record selection formula. The **GROUP** selection option opens the Group Selection Formula Editor, which is used to edit the group selection formula.

Table 2-13 Report menu options explained

Menu Option	Description
Formula Workshop	Opens the Formula Workshop, which is used to create, edit and view formulas and functions.
Alerts	Create and edit alerts.
Report Bursting Indexes	This option is only available on reports that have saved data. It is used to create indexes on the saved data. This improves the record selection process time.
Section Expert	Opens the Section Expert which is used to format any section of the report.
Group Expert	Opens the Group Expert which is used to create, modify and delete groups.
Group Sort Expert	Sort the groups in the report by group summary fields.
Record Sort Expert	Opens the Record Sort Expert which is used to select the order that the detail records will be sorted in.
Template Expert	Opens the Template Expert. You can create custom templates using this expert.
OLAP Design Wizard	Opens the OLAP Expert. This menu option is only available after an OLAP grid is selected in the report.
Hierarchical Grouping Options	Creates a hierarchical report.
Show Current Parameter Values	Opens the Current Parameter Values dialog box, which is used to view the parameter values that were selected the last time that the report was run.
Check Dependencies	Opens the Dependency Checker so that you can see the results of running the Check Dependencies tool.
Refresh Report Data	Refreshes the data in the report. If the report has parameter fields, you can select the parameter options that you want to use.
Set Print Date and Time	Overrides the values that would print if the Print Date or Print Time special fields are on the report.
Performance Information	Displays information similar to what is shown in Figure 2-17, which may help you troubleshoot report performance problems.

Table 2-13 Report menu options explained (Continued)

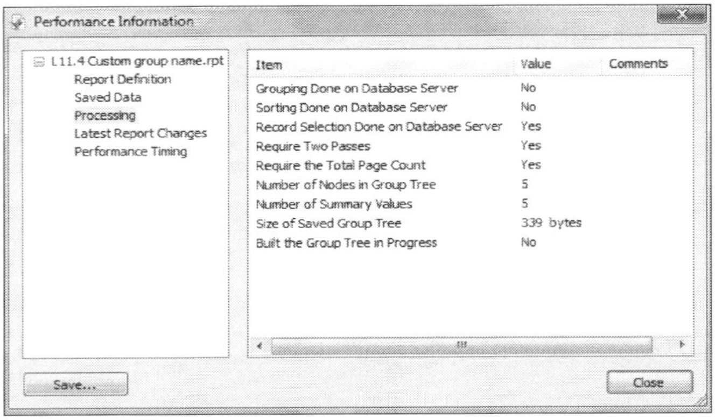

Figure 2-17 Performance Information dialog box

Chart Menu Options

The options on the Chart menu are used to customize a chart. This menu is only available when a chart is selected on a report.

Menu Option	Description
Format Background	Change the color or font of the selected item.
Chart Options	Opens the Chart Options dialog box.
Axis Options	Change the grid options.
Series Options	Change the options for the chart series that is selected.
3D Viewing Angle	Change the viewing angle of a 3D chart.
Edit Axis Label	Change the axis label that is selected.
Trendlines	Modify the trendlines.
Auto-Arrange Chart	Arrange all of the objects on the chart.
Apply Changes To All Charts	Apply the same formatting to all similar group level chart objects.
Discard Custom Changes	Delete all customizations that you made to the chart.
Load Template	Select a template to apply to the chart.
Save As Template	Saves the chart as a user defined template.
Select Mode	Prevents accidental zooming or panning on the chart.
Zoom In	Zoom in closer on the chart.
Zoom Out	Zoom out on the chart.
Pan	This option is only available when a chart has been zoomed in on. It is used to move through the data in the chart.

Table 2-14 Chart menu options explained

Map Menu Options

The options on the Map menu are used to customize a Geographic map. In order to use the options on this menu or view a map on a report, you have to install the Map DLL's. This menu is only available when a map is selected on a report.

Menu Option	Description
Select Mode	This option is enabled as soon as you click on a map on the preview tab. Once enabled, the Map menu is visible.
Zoom In	Zoom in closer on the map.
Zoom Out	Zoom out on the map.
Pan	This option is only available when a map has been zoomed in on. It is used to move through the data in the map.
Center Map	Center a map in its frame. You may need to use this option after you have used the pan option.
Title	Add or change a title on the map.
Type	Change the type of map.

Table 2-15 Map menu options explained

Menu Option	Description
Layers	Opens the Layer Control dialog box, which is used to change the order of the layers, so that the map can have more or less detail.
Resolve Mismatch	Opens the Resolve Map Mismatch dialog box which is used to select the map that you want to have the data values associated with.
Map Navigator	Turns the Map Navigator on and off. You can use the Map Navigator to center, zoom and pan on the map.

Table 2-15 Map menu options explained (Continued)

Window Menu Options

The options on the Window menu are used to change the default layout of the open windows in Crystal Reports. These options work the same way that they do in Windows XP.

Menu Option	Description
Tile Vertically	Arranges all open windows side by side.
Tile Horizontally	Arranges all open windows in rows so that they do not overlap.
Cascade	Arranges all open windows so that the title bar of each window is visible.
Arrange Icons	Arranges the icons at the bottom of the window.
Close All	Closes all open windows. You will be prompted to save any reports that have not been saved.

Table 2-16 Window menu options explained

Open Reports

At the bottom of the Window menu, you will see a list of all of the reports that are currently open, as shown in Figure 2-18.

The report that is active has a check mark in front of it. If you want to switch to a different report that is open, you can select it from the bottom of the Window menu.

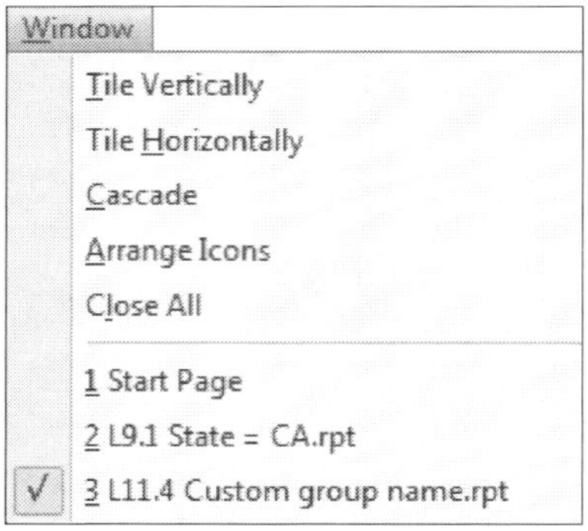

Figure 2-18 Open reports on the Window menu illustrated

Help Menu Options

The options on the Help menu are explained in Table 2-17. They provide several ways to get assistance. The other options are used to register and manage Crystal Reports.

Menu Option	Description
Crystal Reports Help	Opens the Online Help file.
Context Help	Displays help for windows, buttons and menus that you click on. After selecting this option, click on an item in the Crystal Reports workspace and a tool tip will appear that explains the item that you clicked on.
Show Start Page	Displays the Start Page if it is closed.
Check for Updates on Start Up	If checked, this option will automatically check for software updates each time that you open Crystal Reports.
Check for Updates	If checked, this option is used to check for software updates when you want to.
Register or Change Address	Opens the registration wizard which is used to register your copy of Crystal Reports or change your address.
License Manager	Add and remove Crystal Reports and Integration kit key codes and license information.
Contact Us	NEW Opens the Contact Us page on the SAP web site. This page lists several ways for you to get in touch with the company.
Documentation	NEW Opens the Product Guides web page on the SAP web site. This page has documentation for all of the software SAP sells.
About Crystal Reports	Opens the About dialog box which displays information about the version of Crystal Reports that is installed. Clicking the **MORE INFO** button shown in Figure 2-19 will display the Loaded Modules shown in Figure 2-20. This information could be helpful if you have to troubleshoot some types of report problems.

Table 2-17 Help menu options explained

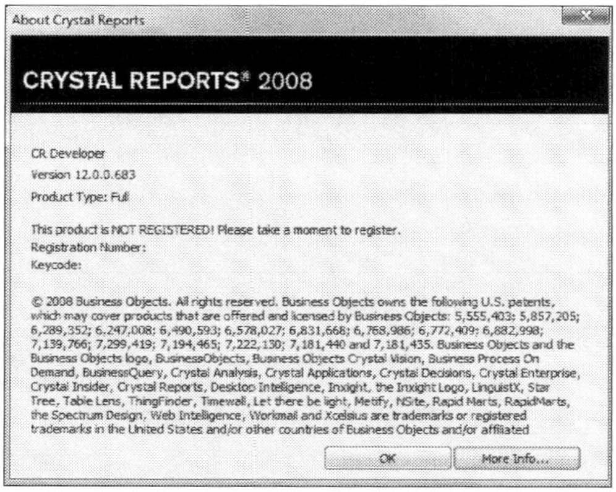

Figure 2-19 About Crystal Reports dialog box

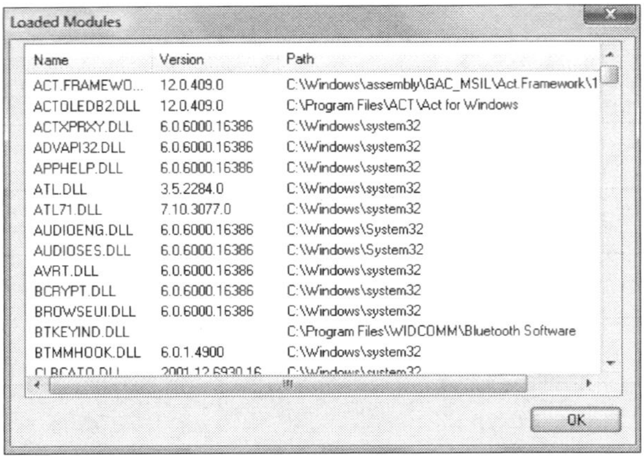

Figure 2-20 Loaded Modules dialog box

Customizing The Crystal Reports Design Environment

If you need to customize the design environment, you can, by following the steps below. These options are used to set the default properties for the majority of features that you will use to create and modify reports. An example would be if you wanted all date fields to use the same format. Once you have used the software for a while and find yourself always having to change an option, you should come back to this section and review the options on the Options dialog box and change the ones that you use, to better meet your needs.

While looking at the options, pay particular attention to the options on the layout, database and reporting tabs, as they contain the options that you are likely to need to change first, because they contain the options that most effect the functionality in the design window.

The changes that you make on the Options dialog box effect all of the reports that you create or modify once the changes on this dialog box are saved. Any changes that are made will not be picked up by reports that were saved prior to the changes made on the Options dialog box. If you want to apply changes that you make on the Options dialog box to existing reports, delete the object from the report that the change will effect and then add the object back to the report. It would be nice if there was an option to apply the change to existing reports.

1. File ⇒ Options. You will see the dialog box shown in Figure 2-21.

2. To find out more about a specific option, click the **HELP** button on the Options dialog box. You will see the Help window shown in Figure 2-22, which explains all of the options on the tab.

Notice that the Online Help file automatically opens to the page for the options on the tab that you have open. In this example, the help button was clicked on the Layout tab shown in Figure 2-21.

Options Dialog Box

The Layout tab options are used to select how reports are displayed on the design window.

The options in the Design View section are used to select the look and functionality of the design window.

The **SHORT SECTION NAMES** option provides more space in the design and preview windows because it abbreviates the section names. For example, page header becomes PH.

The options in the Preview section are used to select the look and functionality of the preview window.

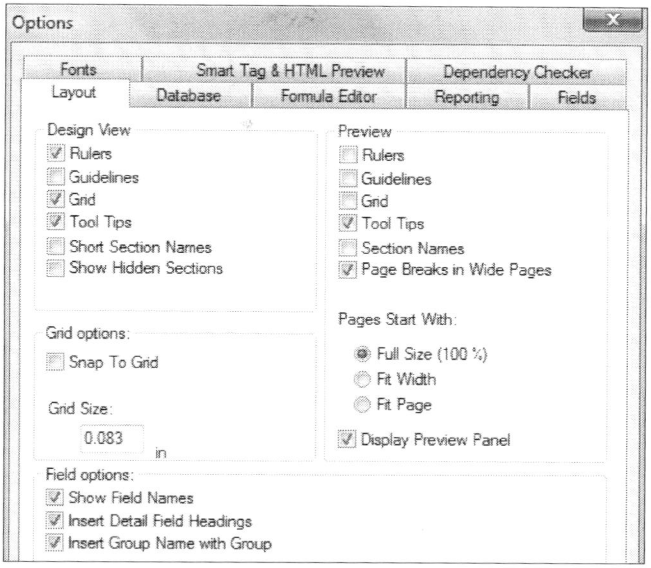

Figure 2-21 Layout tab options

The options in the Grid Options section determine how the grid will or will not be displayed in the design window.

The options in the Field Options section determine how fields are displayed in the design window. The **INSERT DETAIL FIELD HEADINGS** option is what causes field headings to be added to a report when you add a field to the details section. If the **SHOW FIELD NAMES** option is not checked, characters that indicate the field type will be displayed in fields in the design window instead of the field name.

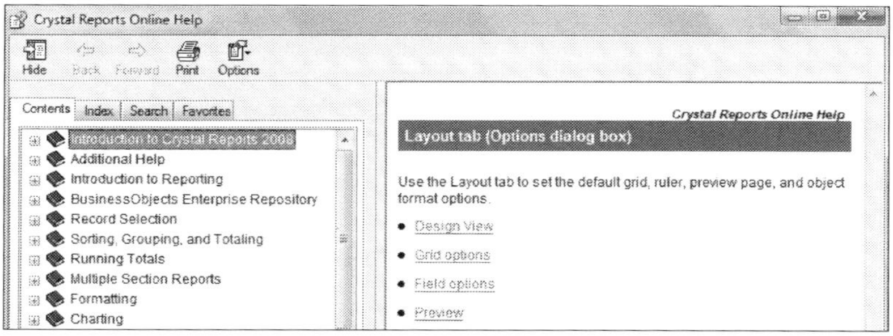

Figure 2-22 Help window

Figures 2-23 to 2-30 show all of the other options that you can change. When you are finished viewing the options, close the dialog box.

The Database tab options are used to select how data appears and how queries are processed.

The options in the Tables and Fields section are used to configure how tables and fields are displayed.

The options in the Data Explorer section are used to select how database objects are displayed in the Field Explorer.

The options in the Advanced Options section are used to help resolve performance issues like determining how queries will be run and when changes in the database structure will be checked. The first two options are only available for SQL tables, not queries.

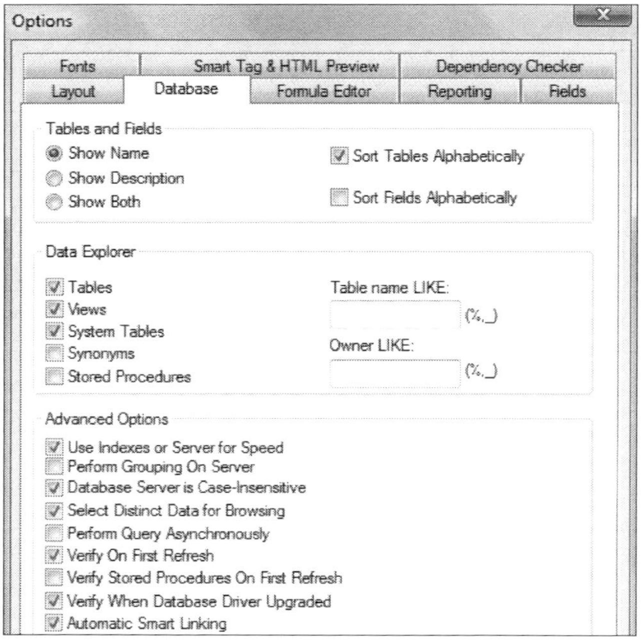

Figure 2-23 Database tab options

The Formula Editor tab options are used to customize the fonts and colors used in the Formula Editor.

The **DEFAULT FORMULA LANGUAGE** option is used to select the default syntax language for the formulas that you create.

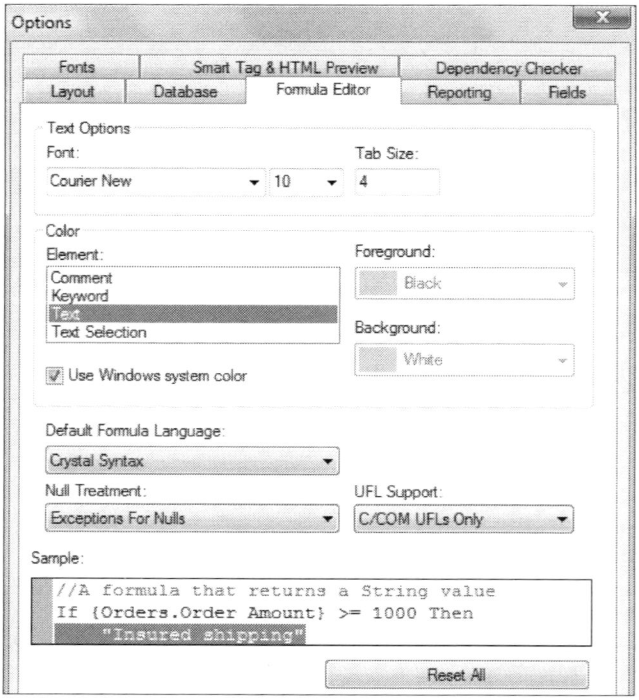

Figure 2-24 Formula Editor tab options

The Reporting tab options are used to select how data is stored and retrieved for the report. These settings can be changed on a report by report basis using the Report Options dialog box. [See Lesson 14, Report Options]

The options in the Enterprise Settings section are used to select report functionality in the Business Objects Enterprise environment.

The options in the Reading Data section are used to select how null values and sorting features will be handled.

The remaining options apply to a variety of report features.

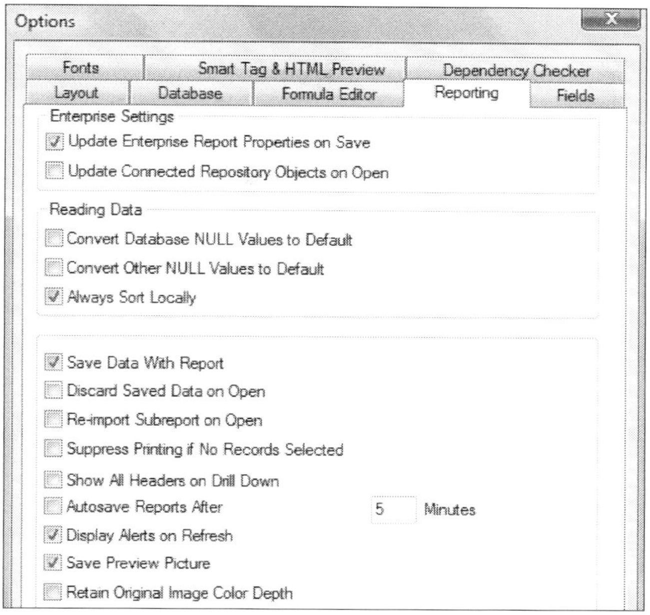

Figure 2-25 Reporting tab options

The Fields tab options are used to select the default options for the field types that Crystal Reports supports.

For example, if you want all string fields to have the Can Grow option selected by default, click the **STRING** button. You will see the dialog box shown in Figure 2-27. Select the option, then click OK.

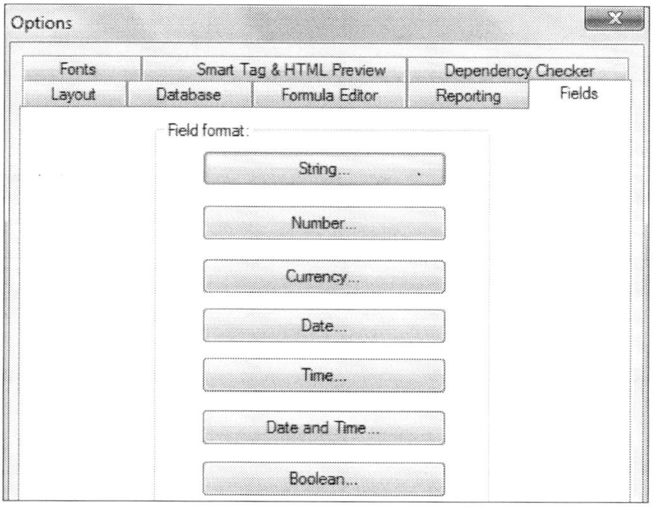

Figure 2-26 Fields tab options

You may want to click on these buttons now to become familiar with the default options. One option that you may want to change after completing the exercises in this book is the default date format if you think that you will use the same date format for the majority of reports that you will create. You do not have to change anything to complete the exercises in this book. (11)

(11) The options that you select will only be applied to objects that are added to a report after you make changes to this dialog box. The changes will not be applied to existing reports.

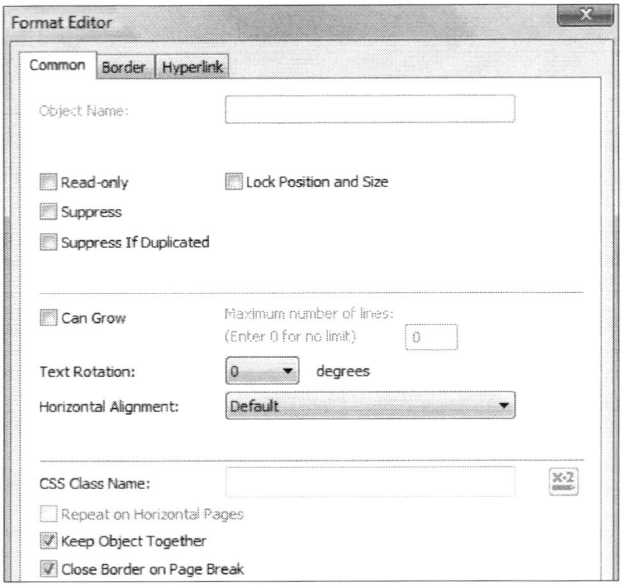

Figure 2-27 Format Editor string options

The Fonts tab options are used to select the default font options for a variety of fields and objects that Crystal Reports supports. (11)

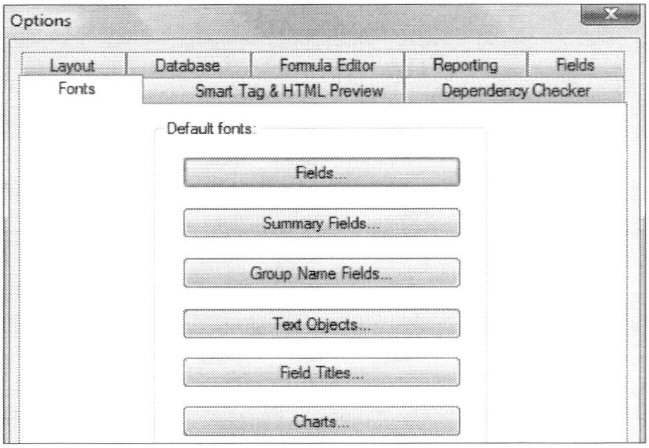

Figure 2-28 Fonts tab options

The Smart Tag & HTML Preview tab options are used to select how Crystal Reports Smart Tags will be used in Microsoft Office applications.

The HTML Preview Options are used to select and configure how reports will be displayed as web pages.

If your reports are not stored in the Business Objects Enterprise you may want to check the **ENABLE HTML PREVIEW** option so that you can preview reports as web pages

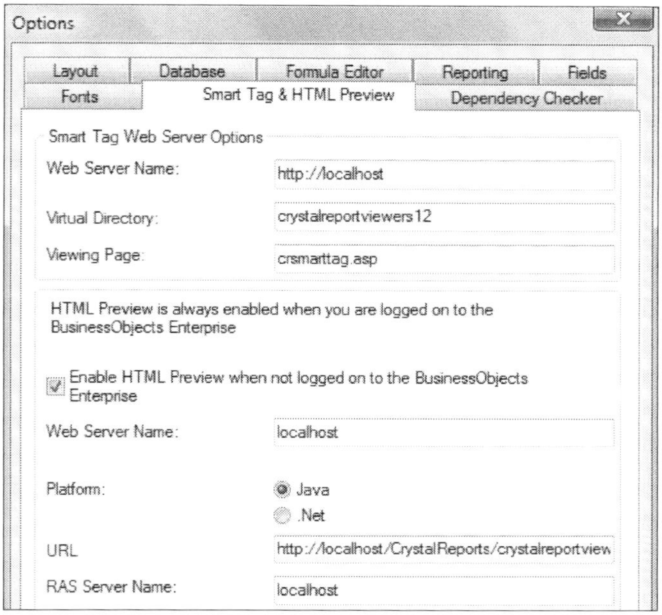

Figure 2-29 Smart Tag & HTML Preview tab options

The Dependency Checker tab options are used to select what conditions you want to verify when you check for formula errors, broken links and database issues in reports.

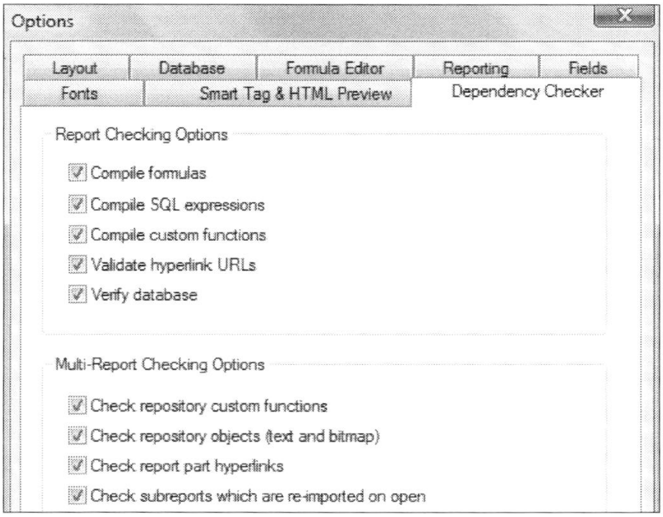

Figure 2-30 Dependency Checker tab options

CRYSTAL REPORTS TERMINOLOGY & WORKSPACE OVERVIEW

After completing the exercises in this lesson you will be able to:

- ☑ Have a foundation of database terminology
- ☑ Understand data types
- ☑ Have a foundation of Crystal Reports terminology
- ☑ Understand the report design process
- ☑ Understand the sections of a report
- ☑ Understand the report creation options
- ☑ Understand the save data report options
- ☑ Organize reports in the Workbench
- ☑ Use the Group Tree
- ☑ Use the design and preview tabs in the workspace

Database Terminology

Below are key terms that you need to understand about databases in order to work with them effectively.

① **Field** A field contains one piece of information and is stored in a record. Examples of fields include customer name and customer address.
② **Record** A record has one or more fields. Each of the fields in a record are related. A record looks like a row of data in a spreadsheet.
③ **Table** A table is stored in a database and is a collection of records. Most databases have more than one table. Tables are linked on fields. Tables may remind you of a spreadsheet when viewed, because SQL databases have rows and columns, which Crystal Reports refers to as records and fields. Each table contains information about a specific topic. For example, a customer table would only contain information about customers. The customer table would not contain information about products.
④ **Relational Database** A relational database is a collection of **RELATED** information that is stored in one or more tables in the database. It is important to note that there are different types of physical database structures.
⑤ **Database** A database is a collection of information that is stored in one or more tables.

Database Concepts

There are several database concepts that you need to be aware of. Having an understanding of these concepts is necessary to create reports effectively.

Data Source A data source is where the data is stored. Examples of data sources are databases/tables, views and spreadsheets.

Data Dictionary A data dictionary contains detailed information about a data source and includes the following types of information: database and table names, field names, types, sizes, indexes and related files. A data dictionary can be handwritten or typed. It can also be generated by some database software packages.

Relationship A relationship is how two or more tables are joined (linked). Tables can be joined when they have at least one field that is the same in each table. For example, an invoice table can be joined to a products table because each invoice record will have at least one item from the products table. Crystal Reports has a **SMART LINKING** feature that will automatically join tables that have related information. Crystal Reports also has a built-in visual utility that will help you link tables.

Length Is used to select the maximum number of characters that the field can have. If the length of a field is set to 20, the contents in the field cannot have more than 20 characters.

Null Any of the field data types discussed in Table 3-1 can be null (empty). Null means that the field does not have a value. Depending on the data source, an empty string may or may not be set to null. An empty numeric field is not equal to zero.

Index The purpose of indexes is to make the retrieval of records from tables faster. Knowing which fields in the table are indexed is important when you need to optimize a report.

Crystal Reports can indicate which fields are indexed in some types of databases and in other types of databases it can't. If Crystal Reports does not recognize the indexes in the table(s) that you are using, you can get the information from the data dictionary for the database.

PRIMARY KEY FIELDS should always be indexed. **FOREIGN KEY FIELDS** are usually indexed. Other fields in a table that are used frequently to retrieve (select) records should be indexed. Fields that fall into this category are fields that are used to sort, group or link data.

Databases that have too many indexes will retrieve records slower. Indexes are usually created by the DBA (Data Base Administrator). If you need to have an index created contact the DBA, unless you have the rights to create an index in the database.

Data Types

Each field must have a data type. The data type determines what type of information can be stored in the field. Table 3-1 explains the data types that are available in most databases. Crystal Reports recognizes all of the data types in Table 3-1. If you use a database that has data types other then the ones listed in Table 3-1, they will be mapped to a data type that Crystal Reports recognizes.

Data Type	Description
String	String fields primarily contain text. String fields can also have numbers, spaces and other special characters. String fields are also known as **TEXT FIELDS**. Numeric data that is stored in a string field is treated like text because there is no need to use the data in any type of calculation. An example of numeric data that is treated like text is zip codes. Numeric data stored in a string field cannot be formatted with any number data type formatting options.
Number	This data type can only contain numbers and decimal points. This data type can be used in a calculation like addition, multiplication and formulas.
Currency	This data type can only contain monetary data. You can use currency fields in calculations, just like number fields. Currency is a special number data type. By default, Crystal Reports will automatically display and print a dollar sign with this data type.
Date	Date fields are used to store dates, which can be stored in several formats. Date fields contain the month, day and year.
Time	This data type is used to store time, which can be stored in several formats. Time fields contain hours, minutes and seconds. Crystal Reports does not recognize fractional seconds even if the underlying data source has them.
Date and Time	Displays the date and time in one field, in this format - MM/DD/YYYY HH:MM:SS. You can hide the time portion of this data type on reports if you need to.
Boolean	Boolean fields are used to set a logical value of true/false, yes/no or 1/0.

Table 3-1 Data types explained

Data Type	Description
Memo	The memo data type is a free form text field, meaning that it can store almost any type of information. This data type may not be available in all databases. Memo fields can contain large amounts of data and embedded formatting. Crystal Reports can recognize **RICH TEXT (RTF)** and **HTML FORMATTING** in memo fields. A common use for memo fields is to store comments about the data in the other fields in the record.
Picture	This data type stores an image file or a link to the location of the image file. (This is known as the **DYNAMIC IMAGE LOCATION**.) Crystal Reports recognizes the following image file types: bitmap, JPEG, TIFF, PNG and Windows Metafile. Some databases refer to this data type as a **BLOB** (Binary Large Object). This field type can only be displayed on a report. It cannot be used in a formula.

Table 3-1 Data types explained (Continued)

ACT! Currency Values

When opened in Crystal Reports, ACT! currency values in the demo database have the Number data type, instead of the Currency format discussed above in Table 3-1, even if the field is set to currency in ACT!.

Crystal Reports Terminology

Below are some key terms that you need to understand about Crystal Reports in order to work with databases effectively. The four field types discussed below are not stored in a table like the data types discussed above are.

① **Formula Fields** Formula fields can include any of the 300 built-in functions that Crystal Reports has, or you can create a formula from scratch. The result of a calculated field is created on the fly, meaning that each time the report is run, the formula field will be recalculated.

② **Special Fields** Special fields contain information that is system generated. Examples of system generated fields include the date the report was printed and page numbers. There are 26 special fields that you can use.

③ **Summary Fields** Summary fields are calculated fields and like formula fields, they are also calculated on the fly, each time the report is run. You create summary fields.

④ **Text Object Fields** This is a free form field that is used to place information on the report that can't be added to the report by any of the field types discussed above. Text objects are often used to create a report title or a heading for fields that you create.

The Repository

The repository is used to store objects that you want to use in more than one report or share with other people. Examples of items that are commonly stored in the repository are SQL commands, logos, reports or functions.

Report Design Process

I know that you are anxious to create your first report, but there are several items that need to be addressed and worked out before you create a report, whether this is your first report or your 100th report. This section is an overview of the report design process and planning. Report design could be an entire chapter or two all by itself, but I am giving you the abridged version. The report design process is part of what is known as the "Business Requirements" phase of a project. As you gain experience, you will see that if you do not get the business requirements right, the project will be delayed, potentially be over budget and not produce the results that the business owner (requestor) or client is looking for. Many call this a "bad career move".

When you learn the concepts presented in this lesson, it will be easier for you to create reports. You should write down the answers to the questions that will be presented in the report design process. The more planning that you do before you create the report, the less you will have to modify a report after it is created. There are four primary steps to the report design process. Each step can have multiple tasks.

You will see how these steps come together through the exercises in this book. When creating reports, especially ones that other people will use, it is imperative that you fully understand the requirements, which often includes asking a lot of questions. This is not a task that you can be bashful about. Not asking questions or worse, asking the wrong questions will more than likely cause you grief down the road.

Step 1: Define The Purpose Of The Report

Yes, I know what you are saying - "How hard can it be to figure out the purpose of a report?". The answer is it depends on how well the person or group of people are able to explain what they want the report to provide and how well you understand what they tell you.

The majority of reports that you create will be used by someone other than yourself, which means that you should meet with the person or group of people that will use the report. These meetings are part of the requirement gathering process. Keep in mind that you may have to have more than one meeting to get a good idea of what the report needs to include, because the users may not tell you or be able to clearly articulate their needs in one meeting. Reports are often used as a decision making tool, which means that poor decisions will be made or the decision making process will be ineffective due to missing or incorrect data that is presented on the report. The data must be presented in a logical manner in order to be an effective decision making tool.

> Keep in mind that one report can be used by people at different levels in the company. This means that at each level, people can have slightly different needs. If this is the case, you will have to plan and design the report accordingly, so that it meets the needs for all of the users.

Your role as the report designer is to gather the information needed, which will help the user(s) of the report to be able to read it easily, as well as, understand the data on the report. If the information is not presented in a way that works for the users, trust me, they will let you know and you will be spending a lot of time modifying the report(s).

In my opinion and experiences that I have had, the more that users have you modify a report, the quicker your credibility goes down hill. That is not something that you want to happen. What I have discovered, as well as, many other Information Technology professionals, is that if you create a prototype (which is discussed later in this lesson) of the report for the users, they can discuss what they like and do not like about the prototype report. Usually, you will gain valuable information that is often hard to get users to discuss in a regular meeting. The worst thing that you can do in many cases, is give the users the impression that you know more about their needs then they do. I am not saying that in some cases that you won't know more about their data, just don't give them that impression, if you know what I mean.

To define the expected outcome of the report, write a descriptive sentence or two about the purpose of the report or what the report needs to accomplish. Below are some example purpose statements.

① The purpose of the report is to compare last years sales data to this years sales data by region.
② The purpose of the report is to show products that are low on inventory and need to be reordered.
③ The purpose of the report is to show the top 10 best selling products by sales team.

In addition to defining the expected outcome of the report you have to take into consideration who will be using the report. It is very possible that managers and their staff will request similar reports. In many cases it is better to create separate reports, even if there is only one field that is different, then to try and get multiple parties to try and come up with one report that works for both groups of users. As you gain report design experience, understand business requirements and know the requestors, you will be able to quickly determine which is the best option.

Step 2: Determine The Layout Of The Report

Now that you have determined the purpose of the report, you need to determine where each piece of data should be placed on the report. If you are creative you will like this step. In addition to determining where the data should be placed, you need to determine some or all of the following:

① Create a list of fields that need to appear on the report. If you know what database or table each field is in, include that on the list. If the data does not currently exist, include it on the list also. You will use this list to complete tasks in future steps in the report design process.
② What should the report title be and where should it be placed on the report. Should it only be printed on the first page or on all pages of the report?
③ Does the report need page numbers or dates? If so, what format should they be in and where should they be placed on the report - in the page header or footer section or someplace else?
④ Are any Special Fields other then the page number or date needed on the report?
⑤ Which fields or sections of the report need totals, summary, statistical information or some other type of calculated field? (**Hint**: Summary fields do not currently exist in a table).

⑥ An important question to answer during this step is what format the report needs to be in. This is known as the **DELIVERY METHOD** (for example, paper, PDF or web based). The way that a report needs to be distributed, can influence the layout of a report. You should find out if the report needs to be distributed in more than one format.

Step 3: Find The Data For The Report

This step is very important because without the data there is no report. As the person creating the report, life will be much easier for you if you are familiar with the data needed for the report and how it is organized. If you are not familiar with the data or are not technical, you may have to rely on Information Technology specialists like database administrators to help you with the tasks in this step. There are three tasks that you have to work on to complete this step successfully.

Task 1

The first task that you have to complete is to find out which databases and tables contain the data for the report. Use the list of fields that you created in step 2, to find the databases and tables. You may also have to find out what servers the databases are on. There are several types of databases that the data can be stored in. The data may also be stored in a Crystal dictionary, an OLAP Cube or something other than a database like an Excel spreadsheet. This task is known as finding the **DATA SOURCE**.

Task 2

This task involves selecting the actual fields in the tables that are needed for the report. Use the list that you created in step 2. Once the fields are selected, determine the formatting for each field and how the fields should be displayed on the report. You also have to determine if the field names in the table are the best choice for the field headings on the report. One example of when a field heading needs to be changed on a report is for fields that are known as ID fields, which you will learn about in Lesson 5.

Task 3

Now that you have found some of the data in the tables, there are probably fields left on the list that you created in step 2 that you have not found. Some may be special fields that you learned about earlier in this lesson. More than likely, many of the fields that are left on the list are calculated fields. This task involves writing out the formulas for the calculated fields. Some calculated fields may use a built-in function and others require a field that is in a data source, but will not be placed on the report.

In order to be able to create calculated fields, you have to become familiar with the database field types and the Crystal Reports fields discussed earlier in this lesson. Several of the Crystal Reports functions are designed to only work with specific types of data. Examples of calculated fields include:

① Sales price times quantity
② Number of days between the order date and the ship date
③ How long the person has been employed at the company

Step 4: Organize The Data

This step involves organizing all of the data. Many of the options that you decide on in task 1 below, will automatically dictate which section of the report certain fields will be placed in.

Task 1

To complete this task you have to organize all of the data, both from the tables and calculated fields, as well as, any other data source. Organizing the data means at a minimum, answering the following questions.

① Does the data need to be sorted? If so, which field(s) should the data be sorted on?
② Does the data need to be grouped? If so, which field(s) should the data be grouped on?
③ Does the report need summary data? Summary data is a calculated field, like grand totals, averages and counts.
④ Does the report need to have any data flagged? If so, how should the data be flagged? The primary reason data would be flagged is so that it can be easily identified on a report. Make a list of any data that needs to be flagged. Crystal Reports has several options including borders, symbols, changing the font size and other formatting techniques that you can use to indicate that the data is flagged.
⑤ Decide if the report needs any of the following: charts, cross-tabs, maps or alerts, which notify the person running the report that a specific condition has been met.

Task 2

To complete this task you have to determine which section of the report each field should be placed in. Task 1 had you make decisions on how to organize the data at a high level. There are several sections of a report that the data and objects can be placed in. The sections of a report are discussed later in this lesson.

Task 3

One way that you organize the data is by selecting which records will actually appear on the report. This is important because most reports do not require that all records in a table appear on the report. For example, if the report needs to display sales (orders) for a specific sales rep, you would create selection criteria that would only allow orders for the particular sales rep to appear on the report. Another example would be to display all customers that purchased a specific product or group of products.

In addition to record selection, it may be necessary to create parameter fields which will make the report more flexible in terms of record selection. Parameter fields allow the person running the report to select the criteria that will be used to retrieve the records that will appear on the report. Parameter fields allow one report to be run with a variety of selection criteria. An example of this would be an order report. If the report had parameter fields for the order date, order amount and sales rep fields, all of the following reports and more, could be run from the same report.

① A report to show all orders on a specific date.
② A report to show all orders for a specific sales rep.

③ A report to show all orders over or under a specific total order amount.
④ A report to show all orders in a date range.
⑤ A report to show all orders in a certain date range for a specific sales rep.

Task 4

Depending on the company, it may be necessary to have the person or group of people sign a document that states that all of the tasks discussed above will produce the report that they need.

Report Prototype

Even though you will go through the entire report design process, it is very possible that the users are still somewhat unclear or cannot visualize what the finished report will look like. If that is the case, creating a report prototype will be a life saver. A prototype can be hand drawn on paper or you can create a sample report that displays the data based on the information that you gather during the report design process.

Some report designers create this prototype as each of the steps and tasks that were discussed above are completed. Other report designers will create the prototype right after the report design process is over. The reason prototypes are helpful is because the users will get a pretty good idea of what the finished report will look like, based on the information that they supplied.

The feedback that you receive from the users about the prototype is invaluable because users get to "see" what they asked for. I have found this process to be a very effective way for users to tell me what they like, don't like, need and don't need.

Sections Of A Report

There are seven sections of a report that you can place data and other objects in. If you place the same calculated field in different sections of the report, it can produce different results (numbers, totals or amounts). It is important that you understand how each section of the report functions because they function independently of each other. Keep the following items in mind when deciding where to place fields and objects on the report.

① Not all sections are needed for every report.
② If you create a report using a wizard, the majority of fields are automatically placed in an appropriate section of the report.
③ All of the report sections discussed below except the group header and footer, will automatically appear in all reports, whether you use them or not. Grouping is optional.
④ The order of the default sections cannot be changed.
⑤ If a report does not need a section, it can be suppressed so that it does not display blank space on the report.
⑥ Sections can be resized vertically as needed.

Formulas, charts and cross-tabs will display different results, depending on which section of the report they are placed in. These differences are explained below in each report section.

> By default, the letters in parenthesis after each report section discussed below, is what you will see to the left of the report when it is previewed. These are known as **SECTION SHORT NAMES**. By default, in the design tab you will see the full section name. If you want to change either of these options, File ⇒ Options ⇒ Layout tab.

Section 1: Report Header (RH)

Data fields and other objects placed in this section will only print at the top of the first page of the report. It is quite possible that many of the reports that you create will not have anything in this section. Something that you may want to include in this section of the report is the criteria and parameters of the report. If the report needs a cover page, the report header section can be used for the cover page. If this is what you need to do, add a page break after this section so that the actual report starts on a new page.

FORMULAS are calculated for the entire report.
CHARTS and **CROSS-TABS** will contain data for the entire report.

> If the report header section requires more than one page, the information in the page header and footer sections of the report will not print until all of the information in the report header section has printed.

Section 2: Page Header (PH)

Data fields and other objects placed in this section will appear at the top of every page in the report except the report header page if it prints on a page by itself. This is where most people put the report title. Other objects that are commonly placed in this section include the date, page number and headings for the fields in the details section of the report. Report wizards will automatically place field headings and the system generated "print date" field in this section.

FORMULAS are calculated at the beginning of every page of the report.
CHARTS and **CROSS-TABS** cannot be placed in this section.

Section 3: Group Header (GH)

This section is only used if the data is grouped. Data fields and other objects placed in this section will print at the beginning of each group section of the report. Each time the data in the field the group is based on changes, another group header and footer section is dynamically created. This section is always right above the details section. If a report is grouped on two or more fields, a new group header and footer section will automatically be created for each field that the report is grouped on.

FORMULAS are calculated one time at the beginning of the group, based on the data in the group, not on all of the data in the report.
CHARTS and **CROSS-TABS** will only contain data or information based on the data in the group.

Section 4: Details (D)

Data fields and other objects placed in this section will print for each record that meets the selection criteria. The data fields and other objects in this section usually have field headings in the page header section. This section is automatically repeated once for each record that will be printed on the report.

FORMULAS are calculated for each record in this section, unless the record does not meet the condition of the formula.
CHARTS and **CROSS-TABS** cannot be placed in this section.

Section 5: Group Footer (GF)

This section is only used if the data is grouped. Data fields and other objects placed in this section will print at the end of each group. The group footer section often includes subtotals and other summary data for the group. This section is always right below the details section.

FORMULAS are calculated one time at the end of the group, based on the data in the group, not on all of the data in the report.
CHARTS and **CROSS-TABS** will only contain data or information based on the data in the group.

Section 6: Report Footer (RF)

Data fields and other objects placed in this section will print once at the end of the report. This is usually where grand totals and other types of report summary information is placed.

FORMULAS are calculated once at the end of the report.
CHARTS and **CROSS-TABS** will contain data for the entire report.

> If the report footer section requires more than one page to print the information, the page header and footer sections will print on the additional pages that the report footer needs. This is the opposite of what happens if the report header requires more than one page. If you think about it though, that makes sense because by the time the report footer section is printed, the "switch" if you will, for the page header and footer sections is turned on.

Section 7: Page Footer (PF)

Data fields and other objects placed in this section will print at the bottom of each page of the report. The page footer section is similar to the page header section. Page numbers are often placed in this section. Report wizards will automatically place the page number in this section.

FORMULAS are calculated at the end of every page of the report. This would be useful if the report needs to have totals by page.
CHARTS and **CROSS-TABS** cannot be placed in this section.

Report Creation Options

There are three ways (wizards, from an existing report and from scratch) that you can create a report. Each option has pros and cons. Once you understand all of the options, you can select the one that best meets the needs for the report that you have to create.

Wizards

This is the easiest way to create a new report. The wizards will walk you through the steps required to create a report. The wizards are helpful when learning the basics of Crystal Reports. Experienced report designers often only use the wizards to save time to create a basic report and then add advanced features manually. Keep in mind that the wizards do not provide all of the options that are needed to create the functionality that all reports need. The wizards are limited because they use default options which often do not meet the needs of the report that you are creating.

Based on your selections on the wizard screens, the fields are placed in the most appropriate section of the report. This does not mean that if you make a mistake when using the wizard, that the wizard will correct the mistake. It is possible to create a report that displays results that are very different then you intended when using a wizard. There are four report wizards that you can select from. What you will find, depending on the options that you select, is that additional fields are automatically added to the report, which you may not need. If this happens, you can delete the field(s) once you have the report open on the design tab.

Create A Report Based Off Of An Existing Report

If a report exists that is similar to the report that you now need to create, select this report creation option. Save the existing report with a new file name and make the necessary changes to the new report. An example of when to create a report based off of an existing report would be when two groups of people need to see the majority of the same fields and one group needs additional information that the other group does not need, or when one group needs the same fields in a different layout. You can also use one of the templates that come with Crystal Reports to format the report differently.

Create A Report From Scratch

This option provides the most flexibility to create a report. You start with a blank canvas so to speak and add the fields, formulas and other objects without any assistance. For many, this can be intimidating especially in the beginning, but being the fearless person that you are, I'm sure that when you get to the exercises that have you create a report from scratch, you will do just fine.

Wizard Types

As mentioned earlier, there are four report wizards that you can select from to create reports. They are discussed below.

① **Report** This is probably the most used wizard because it provides the majority of options needed to create a wide variety of reports. The report wizards discussed below create specific types of reports.

② **Cross-Tab** This wizard will create a report that presents data in a grid. Cross-Tab reports resemble spreadsheets because they have rows and columns. The grid often contains totals at the end of each row and column. An example of when a cross-tab should be used would be if you needed to know how many of specific products were sold by each sales rep. You should only use this wizard if the cross-tab will be the only object on the report.

③ **Mailing Label** This wizard will walk you through the process of creating mailing labels. While you can format a report created with the Report wizard to print labels, the advantage of using the mailing label wizard is that it has an option to select the label size that you need. This means that you will not have to manually format the report to match the dimensions of the label size that you need.

④ **OLAP Cube** This wizard is used to create a report that is similar to a cross-tab report. The difference is that this wizard connects to OLAP data. You can filter the data and create a chart. ACT! databases do not support OLAP functionality.

Crystal Reports Workspace

The workspace is where you will create, edit, preview and run reports. Therefore, it is important to know what tools are available in the workspace. As you will see, the workspace has a lot of options. The toolbars, menus and customization options were covered in detail in Lesson 2. The workspace has two tabs: The design tab and the preview tab. When a report is opened, these two tabs will appear below the Start Page tab. The majority of functionality available on the design tab is also available on the preview tab, including the menus, toolbars and formatting options.

Design Tab

The design tab shown in Figure 3-1 is where you will create and modify reports, as well as, see the structure of the report. Figure 3-2 illustrates the parts of the design tab. Table 3-2 explains the parts of the design tab.

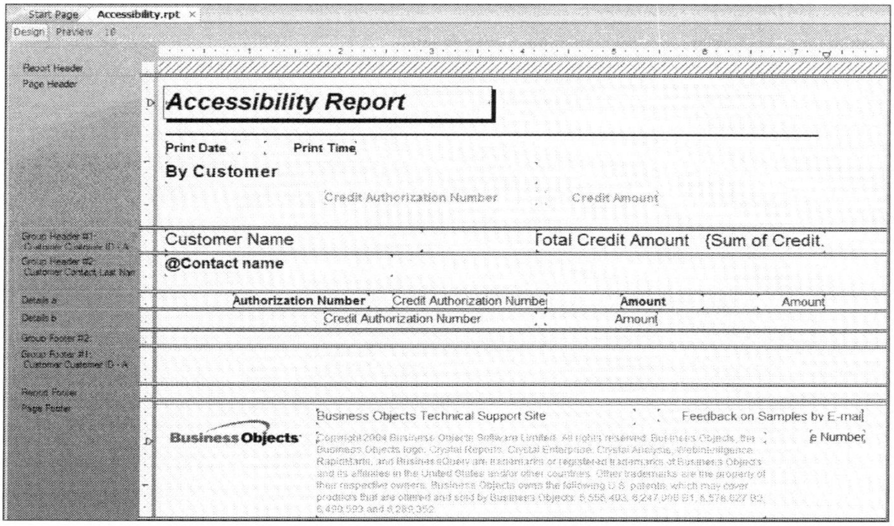

Figure 3-1 Design tab

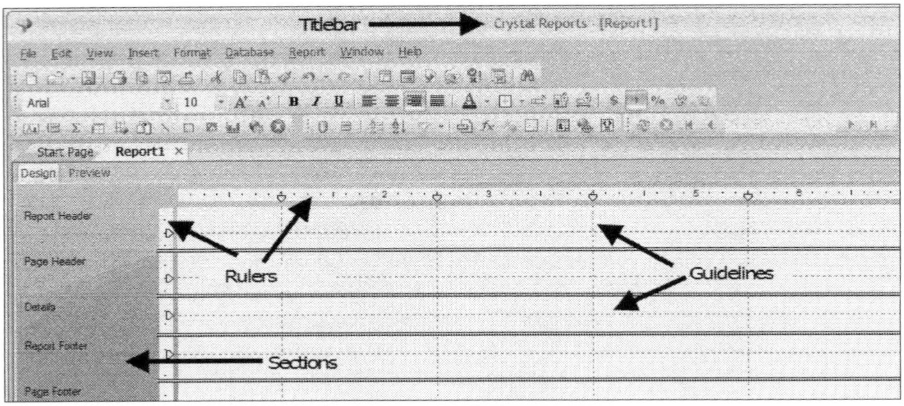

Figure 3-2 Parts of the design tab illustrated

Option	Description
Title bar	Displays the name of the software followed by the file name of the report.
Sections	Like other parts of the design tab, the section portion has a shortcut menu, which you access by right-clicking in the section that you want to work on. These are the same report sections that you learned about earlier in this lesson.
Rulers	The rulers help you place fields in a specific location on the report. The default unit of measurement for the rulers is set by the regional settings of your operating system.
Guidelines	The guidelines are used to line up fields and other objects in the design area.
Design area	This is where you will add, change and format fields and other objects. The design area is all of the white space inside of the rulers. You can place objects as close to the edge of this area as necessary because this area is inside of the report page margins.

Table 3-2 Parts of the design tab explained

> Everything on a report is an object. Each object has its own set of properties. Almost all of these properties can be modified. The properties can also be modified based on a condition that you set. You will learn about conditional formatting in Lesson 15.

Report Sections

As shown above in Figure 3-2, the design tab is divided into sections. The sections are divided by boundary lines, which are also called **SECTION BARS** and is how I will reference them. The sections can be resized by moving the section bar up or down. Figure 3-3 shows a smaller page header section and a larger details section, then shown above in Figure 3-2.

To resize a section of the report, place the mouse pointer over the section bar that you need to move, as illustrated in Figure 3-4. The mouse pointer will change to a double arrow, as illustrated in Figure 3-4. Drag the section bar up or down. If you do not need to display data in a section of the report, you can **SUPPRESS** (hide) the section and it will not appear on the preview tab or on the printed report.

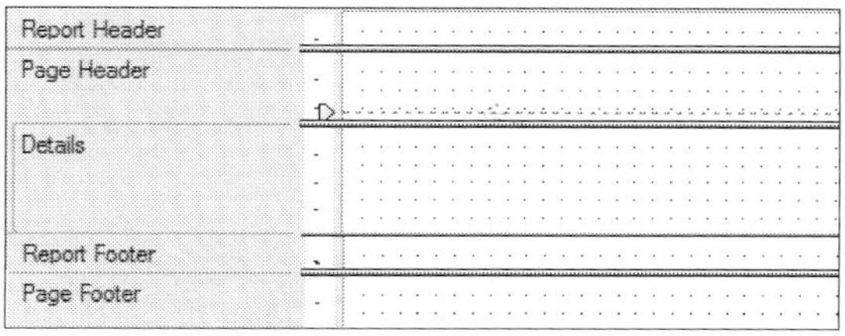

Figure 3-3 Sections of a report resized

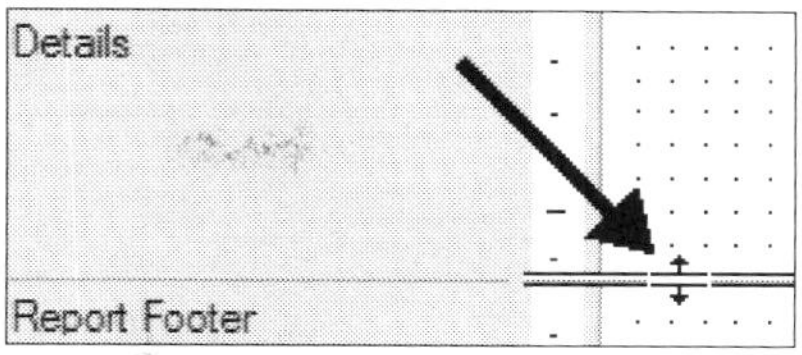

Figure 3-4 Mouse pointer in position to move the section bar

You cannot make a section of the report smaller than the objects that are in the section.

The Status Bar

NEW You can now see the number of records in the Status bar on the design tab.

The **STATUS BAR** shown in Figure 3-5, is located at the bottom of the workspace. It displays helpful information when you are designing and previewing reports. The information on the status bar will change, depending on what you are doing. It also displays tool tips when the mouse is hovered over an option on a menu or over a button on a toolbar. Like the toolbars, the status bar can also be turned off (View ⇒ Status Bar), but it can't be moved.

On the preview tab you will see the number of records in the report on the status bar.
If you do not see the number of records, resize the window. The date and time shown, 12/2/2004 9:15 AM in Figure 3-5 is the last time that the data in the report was refreshed.

If the data was refreshed or retrieved today, only the time will be displayed. If you click the **REFRESH** button, the date and time information will change. The percent shown in the far right is the zoom level percent of the report. If an object is selected on the report, its name will be displayed in the left corner of the status bar instead of the date and time, as shown in Figure 3-6. The object size and position are displayed on the right.

Figure 3-5 Status bar with report information

Figure 3-6 Status bar with field information

On the right side of the status bar are the **ZOOM** options as shown in Figure 3-7.
The first button displays the entire report in the workspace.
The second button displays the report so that it takes up the entire size of the available workspace. The slider is used to change how large or small the report will be displayed.

Figure 3-7 Zoom options

Preview Tab

The preview tab is used to view the report as it will look when it is printed. Reports can look different on this tab depending on the printer that is selected. Also notice the following:

① That some of the toolbars at the top of the workspace are now available.
② The report opened on its own tab. The tab name is either the report file name or the report title.
③ The blue area to the left of the report contains the "sections" of the report. Having the sections visible, lets you know which section of the report each piece of data or object is in. You learned about the seven report sections earlier in this lesson.
④ The options down the far left side of the report are the groups that the report has. This section is called the **GROUP TREE**. It is explained below.
⑤ You can modify reports on the preview tab. Unless stated otherwise, the instructions in this book are written to be completed in the design tab.

> The preview tab will not automatically appear for a report that was created from the **BLANK REPORT** option or for a report that is open, but the data has not been refreshed. If you need the preview tab and it is not visible, you can use one of the five options listed below.

① Click the **PRINT PREVIEW** button on the Standard toolbar.
② Click the **REFRESH** button on the Navigation Tools toolbar.
③ Press the **F5** key.
④ View ⇒ Print Preview.
⑤ View ⇒ Preview Sample.

NEW Preview Panel

The Preview Panel is a section on the preview tab. It stores the group tree, parameter panel and the Find tab, as shown in Figure 3-8. This feature adds more interactive options. This panel can be displayed or hidden by clicking the **TOGGLE PREVIEW PANEL** button on the Standard toolbar.

If the report has groups, a group section is automatically added to the preview panel. If you click on the groups button you will see the groups, as shown in Figure 3-8. Clicking on a group will display that section of the report.

If the report has a parameter field you will see options similar to those shown in Figure 3-9.

The **FIND TAB** is used to search the report for words or phrases. Clicking on this button opens the Search field shown in Figure 3-10. Type in the word or phrase that you are looking for, then click the magnifying glass button or press Enter to start the search.

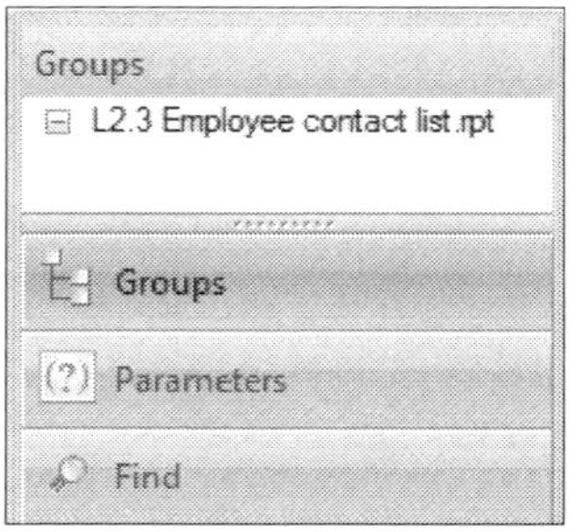

Figure 3-8 Preview Panel

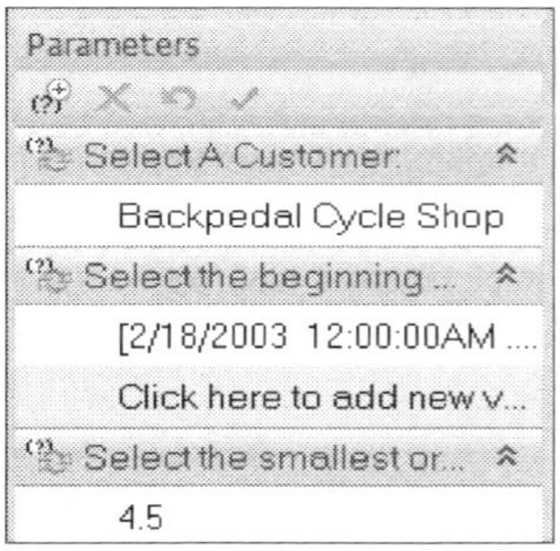

Figure 3-9 Parameter panel

You will see results similar to what is shown in Figure 3-11. Double-clicking on a search result option will display that part of the report.

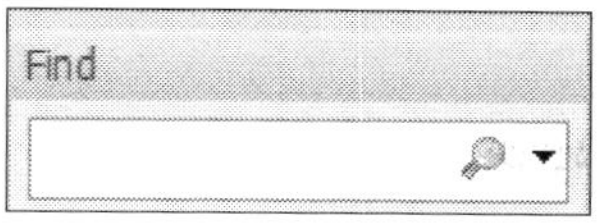

Figure 3-10 Search field

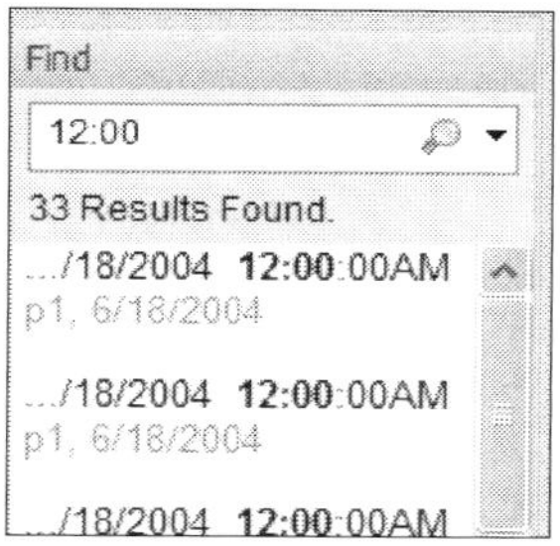

Figure 3-11 Search results

The Group Tree

This feature is helpful when you need to navigate through a report that has a lot of groups. The group tree is located on the far left side of the preview tab. It displays all of the groups and subgroups in the report. Clicking on an option in the group tree will display the corresponding section in the report. You can customize the group name.

If a group has a subgroup, you will see a plus sign (+) in front of the group name, as shown in Figure 3-12. Clicking on the plus sign will expand the group and display the subgroup, as shown below. The plus sign is also known as the **EXPAND BUTTON**. The minus sign is also known as the **COLLAPSE BUTTON**.

> To turn the group tree on or off, click the **TOGGLE PREVIEW PANEL** button on the Standard toolbar.

If you click on the plus sign in front of the number 4, then click on the name under the group, as shown in Figure 3-12, the section of the report for this group will be displayed.

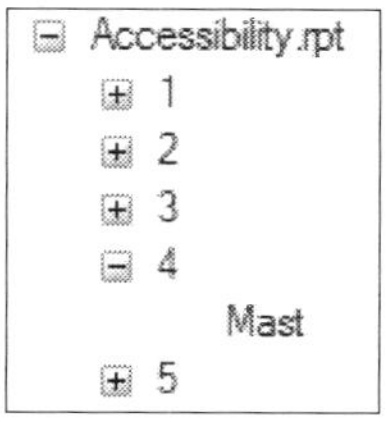

Figure 3-12 Group tree options illustrated

Group Tree Shortcut Menu

If you right-click in the group tree section of the preview tab you will see the shortcut menu shown in Figure 3-13.

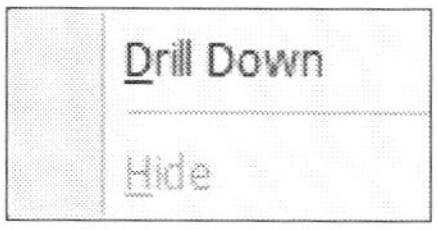

Figure 3-13 Group tree shortcut menu

The options are explained below.

① **Drill Down** This option will open another tab, as illustrated in Figure 3-14. In this report, the tab contains the detail information for the branch in the group tree that you right-clicked on. The number on the tab represents the heading in the group tree that was right-clicked on.

② **Hide** This option will hide the branch that was selected before it was right-clicked on.

Figure 3-14 Drill Down result

The Drill Down and Hide options are not available from a menu.

Previewing Reports

Figure 3-15 shows a report that comes with Crystal Reports.

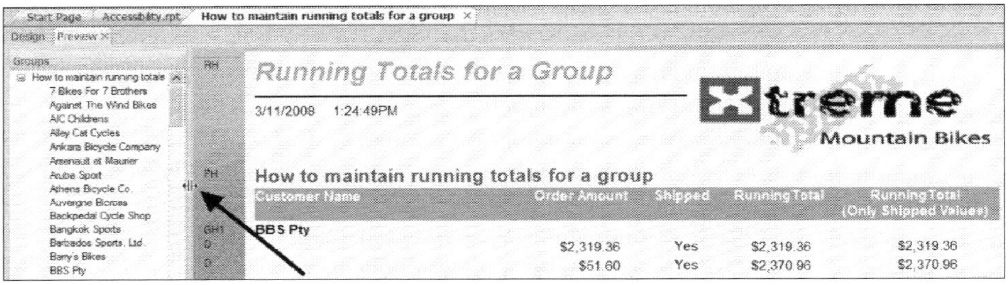

Figure 3-15 Preview of the Running Totals Group report

If you can't see the groups on the left side of the window, place the cursor on the bar, illustrated above in Figure 3-15 and drag the bar over to the right, as much as needed.

Notice that the report opened on its own tab to the right of the Start Page tab. You can have several reports open at the same time. Also notice that you do not see the file name of this report on the tab. Instead, you see the report title on the tab. You will learn how to create report titles.

The tab with the X indicates the active report window. To close a report click on the X. If changes were made to the report, you will be prompted to save them.

You can make some changes like formatting and moving objects on the preview tab.

Navigation Tools Toolbar

The **PAGE INDICATOR** section shown in Figure 3-16 lets you know what page of the report is currently displayed.

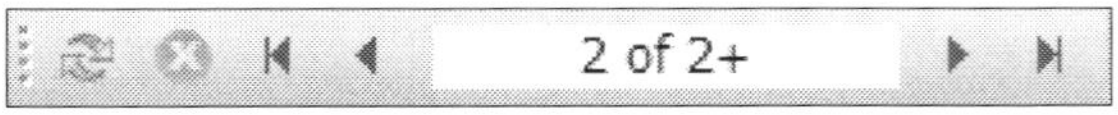

Figure 3-16 Navigation Tools toolbar

> If you see **1 OF 1+** or something similar and want to know how many pages the report has, click the **SHOW LAST PAGE** button on the Navigation Tools toolbar. The page indicator also lets you know how many pages are in the report. The plus sign shown above in Figure 3-16 means that Crystal Reports has not formatted all of the pages for the report. This means that the total number of pages that the report has is currently unknown.

If the **SHOW LAST PAGE** button on the Navigation Tools toolbar is checked, the last page of the report would be displayed, as shown in Figure 3-17.

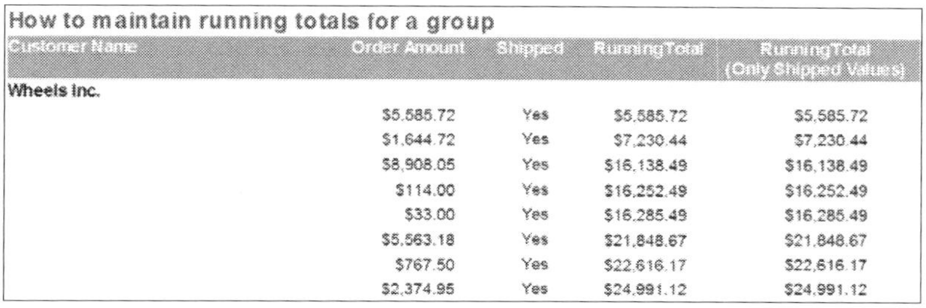

How to maintain running totals for a group

Customer Name	Order Amount	Shipped	RunningTotal	RunningTotal (Only Shipped Values)
Wheels Inc.				
	$5,585.72	Yes	$5,585.72	$5,585.72
	$1,644.72	Yes	$7,230.44	$7,230.44
	$8,908.05	Yes	$16,138.49	$16,138.49
	$114.00	Yes	$16,252.49	$16,252.49
	$33.00	Yes	$16,285.49	$16,285.49
	$5,563.18	Yes	$21,848.67	$21,848.67
	$767.50	Yes	$22,616.17	$22,616.17
	$2,374.95	Yes	$24,991.12	$24,991.12

Figure 3-17 Last page of the Running Totals Group report

You may see the warning message shown in Figure 3-18 when you close a report that you previewed.

Depending on what you have touched in the report, Crystal Reports will think that you have made changes.

Clicking **NO** on the warning message shown in Figure 3-18 will close the report window without saving any changes.

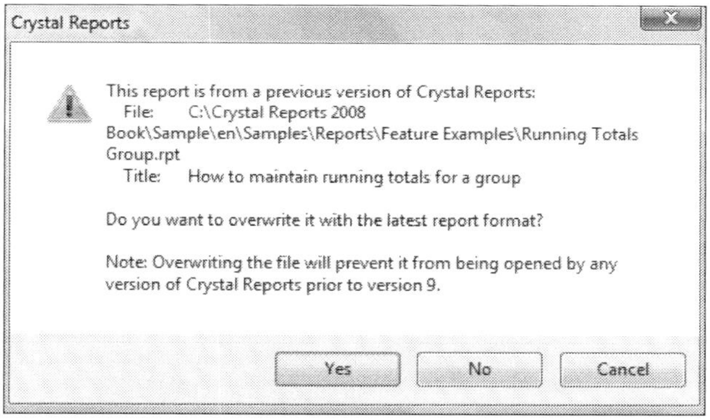

Figure 3-18 Modified report warning message

> File ⇒ Close, will also close the active report.

Design And Preview Tab Differences

As much as these tabs have in common, there are some differences between the tabs that you should be aware of, as discussed below.

① The section names display differently. On the design tab you can display the section names as long or short names. On the preview tab, the section names can be hidden or displayed as short section names, but not long section names.

② Only the preview tab has the group tree, page controls and refreshed data information.

③ If you select a field in the preview tab, every occurrence of the field in the report is selected.

④ If you modify a field in the preview tab, the report will take longer to be redisplayed then it will if you make the same change in the design tab.

⑤ The design tab does not display the page margins. On the preview tab, the margins are indicated by a black border around the page.

The Workbench

This tool is used to organize the reports that you create or are responsible for maintaining. By default, the Workbench is on the right side of the workspace. The way that you organize the reports in the Workbench is by placing them in folders which Crystal Reports calls **PROJECTS**. You can also add **REPORT PACKAGES** to the Workbench if you are using the Crystal Reports Server or the Business Objects Enterprise.

Project folders can only contain reports. Unlike other file management tools, you cannot create a folder under an existing folder in the Workbench. A benefit of using the Workbench is that you will be able to access reports without having to know where they are located on your hard drive or which server they are on. The downside is that you have to add the reports one by one to the Workbench.

Once you have added reports to the Workbench, you can move them from one folder to another by dragging the report. You can also rearrange the order of the project folders by dragging them to where you want them to be. When you need to go back to a report you will be able to find it easily, if it is stored in the Workbench. Placing the report files in the Workbench to complete the exercises in this book is optional.

> If you rename, delete or move a report, when you click on the link for it in the Workbench you will get an error message when you try to open the report. If this happens, you have to add the report to the Workbench again.

> The Workbench does not sort the reports in a folder. This means that they appear in the folder in the order that they are added, opposed to be sorted alphabetically. You can rearrange the order of the reports in the Workbench.

> You can publish an entire project to the Business Objects Enterprise.

Workbench Toolbar

Figure 3-19 shows the Workbench toolbar. Table 3-3 explains the purpose of each button on the Workbench toolbar.

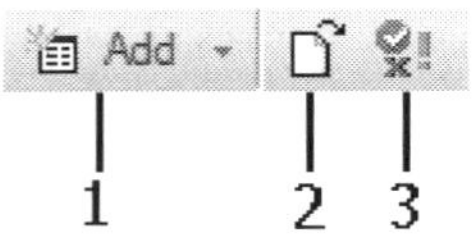

Figure 3-19 Workbench toolbar

Button	Purpose
1	The **Add Report** button is used to add three types of objects to the Workbench, as discussed below. ① **Add Existing Report** Select this option if you want to add an existing report to the Workbench. ② **Add Current Report** Select this option if you want to add the active report to the Workbench. ③ **Add New Project** Select this option if you want to create a new project folder.
2	The **Open** button is used to open a report that is in the Workbench. I find it easier to double-click on the report in the Workbench, then to click this button.
3	The **Check Dependencies** button will start the Dependency Checker. This tool is used to check one report or all reports in a folder in the Workbench for errors.

Table 3-3 Workbench toolbar buttons explained

Adding Reports To The Workbench

> If you need to add a report to the workbench it's easier to do it while the report is open.

There are four ways to add reports to the Workbench as discussed below.

① Add ⇒ Add Existing Report.
② Add ⇒ Add Current Report.
③ Right-click in the Workbench and select Add ⇒ Add Existing Report.
④ Drag a report from Windows Explorer to the Workbench.

Create A Folder In The Workbench

The Workbench has been discussed as a way for you to organize the reports that you create. In preparation for the first report that you will create in the next lesson, you will create a folder in the Workbench by following the steps below.

> View ⇒ Workbench, will display the Workbench if you do not see it in the report design window or on the Start Page. It is probably a good idea to leave the Workbench open all the time, because you can use it to quickly open reports that you have already created.

1. Add ⇒ Add New Project, as shown in Figure 3-20.

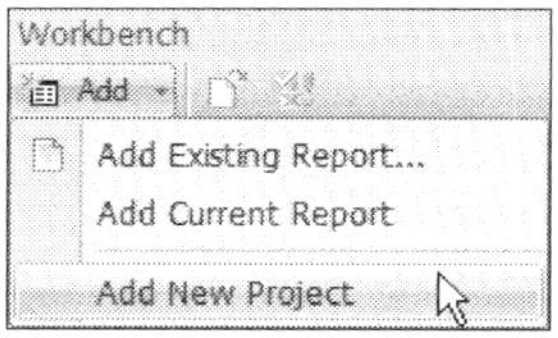

Figure 3-20 Menu option to create a new project folder

2. Type `Lesson 4 Reports`, as shown in Figure 3-21, then press Enter.

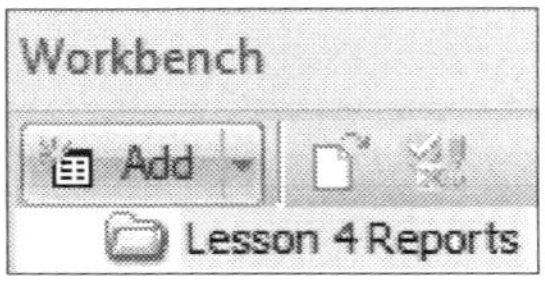

Figure 3-21 New project folder name

Report Packages

Earlier in this lesson I mentioned that Report Packages could be added to the Workbench. A report package is a group of related reports that are stored on a Crystal Reports Server or are in the Business Objects Enterprise. Report packages allow several reports to be viewed or scheduled as a single entity.

To add a report package to the Workbench, you need to have a login account to the Crystal Reports Server or Business Objects Enterprise system at your company. Right-click in the Workbench window and select Add ⇒ Add Object Package.

Selecting this option will prompt you to log into your Business Objects Enterprise System. After you log in, you can select an object to add to the Workbench. This option was removed from the Add Report button on the Workbench toolbar.

Deleting Projects And Reports From The Workbench

Deleting projects and reports from the Workbench works similar to how you delete folders and files in other applications. Reports deleted from the Workbench are not deleted from the hard drive or server that they are stored on. You are only deleting the reference (link) to the report in the Workbench. There are two ways to delete items in the Workbench, as discussed below.

① Click on the project folder or report that you want to delete, then press the **DEL** key on your keyboard.
② Right-click on the project folder or report that you want to delete, then select **REMOVE** on the shortcut menu.

Maintaining The Workbench

The information for the Workbench is stored in the file **PROJECTEXPLORER.XML**. This file is automatically saved in your personal folder under the Documents and Settings folder, which Windows XP creates.
(Documents and Settings\Your account name\Local Settings\Application Data\Crystal Reports)

If you have to reinstall Crystal Reports and want to retain your Workbench project folder and report links, you should copy this file to another location before reinstalling Crystal Reports and then copy the file back. If you get a new computer, you can copy this file to the new computer and you will have the same project folders displayed in the Workbench.

CREATE YOUR FIRST REPORT

In addition to creating your first report, you will also learn the following:

- ☑ How to create a connection to a database
- ☑ How to link tables
- ☑ Saving report data options
- ☑ Gain an understanding of the basics of the report processing model

LESSON 4

Learning To Create Reports

For some, learning to create reports can be intimidating. **LEARNING TO CREATE REPORTS REQUIRES TIME, PATIENCE, DEDICATION AND ATTENTION TO DETAIL**. Crystal Reports is a very robust package and has a lot of features and options. As you go through the exercises in this book, take your time and try to understand how the concepts that you are learning can be applied to reports that you will create on your own, once you have completed this book. It is possible to go through this entire book in a few days if you already have above average report design experience with another software package or if you have used a previous version of Crystal Reports and have a solid foundation of relational databases.

The reality is that you will make some mistakes along the way. If you have a fear of making mistakes, this is the time to let go of the fear because the fear will prevent you from learning. It is also normal to initially get confused on what to do next. Even though you may not understand why you are being instructed to do something, the steps in each exercise will allow you to achieve the expected result. This is how you will begin to build a foundation for creating reports and learning Crystal Reports.

The first time that a concept or technique is presented, a lot of information is provided. Each subsequent time that you have to perform the same task, less and less information (aka hand holding) will occur. As you will see, there are a lot of repetitious tasks involved in creating reports. These are the tasks that less and less information will be provided for as you go through the book. The purpose behind this learning technique is to allow you to rely more on your knowledge instead of flipping through this book to find the answer, which in turn allows you to complete an exercise in less time.

ACT! Demo Database

This is the database that comes with ACT!. It is the database that you will use as the basis for the reports that you will create in this book. This database contains the data for a fictitious company called CH Tech One. The database has tables that store the following types of information: Contact, Company, Opportunity and Activities.

While the ACT! demo database has a lot of tables, many of them are used to link to other tables.

The main tables, as I call them, like Activity, Contact and Opportunity, do not have a large variety of data, which made is somewhat difficult to use a wider variety of fields in the exercises.

Figure 4-1 shows the data model for some of the tables in the database. The fields with the arrows are the **PRIMARY KEY** fields. You will learn more about primary key fields in the next lesson.

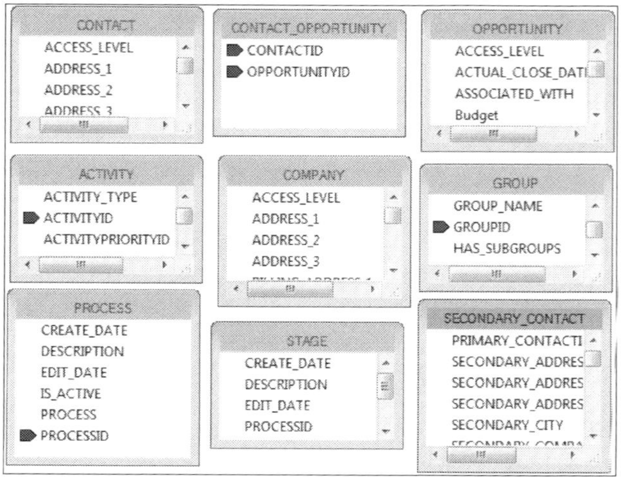

Figure 4-1 ACT! database data model

Why Do I Have To Connect To A Data Source?

First, I should explain what a data source is. A data source contains the underlying data for the report that you will create or modify. The most common data source is a database. In addition to there being several types of data sources that you can connect to, there are multiple ways to connect to some data sources. You connect to an ACT! database via the ACT! OLE DB Provider for Reporting 2.0 connection type that comes with ACT!. (This is why you need to have ACT! installed.) There are two reasons that you would need to connect to a data source, as discussed below.

① To view reports that do not have the data saved with it.

② If you want to create a new report or modify an existing report that does not have the data saved with it.

Exercise 4.1: Create Your First Report

I suspect that this is the moment that you have been waiting for - to create your first report. The first report that you will create is a report that only uses data from one table. The report layout is basic, but you will use almost every screen on the wizard dialog box so that you can become familiar with all of the options. You will use the Report Wizard to create the reports in this lesson.

Step 1: Create A Connection To The Data Source

There are several types of data sources that you can use in Crystal Reports.

Figure 4-2 shows the categories of connection options that are available.

Even though you see an option for ACT!, you will not use it in this book.

Table 4-1 explains some of the more popular connection options.

Figure 4-2 Available connection options illustrated

NEW The list of data sources have been rearranged. The more frequently used data sources have their own folder. Data sources that are used less, have been moved to the **MORE DATA SOURCES** folder. Some of the connection types have been renamed. For example, XML has been renamed to XML and Web Services.

You may see different data source options depending on the data components that were selected when you installed Crystal Reports. You will also see data source options that you have added.

Connection Option	Is Used To Connect To . . .
Access/Excel (DAO)	Access databases and Excel files.
Database Files	Standard PC databases including FoxPro, Paradox, Clipper and dBASE.
ODBC (RDO)	Any ODBC complaint database including Oracle, Sybase, Access and Visual FoxPro.
OLAP	OLAP cubes and **.CAR FILES**. OLAP stands for Online Analytical Processing. CAR stands for Crystal Analysis file.
OLE DB (ADO)	Data link files that contain connection information that is saved in a file.
Universes	Business Objects query and analysis tools like Web Intelligence.
More Data Sources	Databases through ODBC drivers including Btrieve, Informix, Sybase, Outlook/Exchange and Web/IIS log files.

Table 4-1 Connection options explained

If you haven't created a connection to any ACT! 2010 database, follow the steps below to create a connection. You can go to the section, Step 2: Select The Tables, if you already have a connection to the ACT! demo database.

How To Create A Connection To An ACT! 2010 Database

1. Click on the **REPORT WIZARD** link on the Start Page.

2. Click on the plus sign in front of the **CREATE NEW CONNECTION** folder, then click on the plus sign in front of the OLE DB (ADO) option.

3. You will see the dialog box shown in Figure 4-3.

   Select the **ACT! OLE DB PROVIDER FOR REPORTING 2.0** option, then click Next.

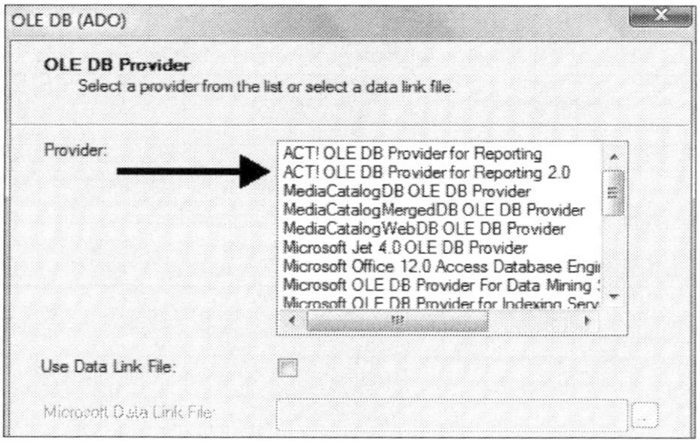

Figure 4-3 OLE DB (ADO) dialog box

The database that you will connect to is the demo database that comes with ACT! 2010. Depending on your computers operating system, the demo database is in a different location, as listed below.

Windows XP
C:\Documents and Settings\YourUserName\My Documents\ACT\ACT For Windows 12\Databases

Vista C:\Users\YourUserName\ACT\ACT for Windows 12\Databases

On the Connection Information screen you have to enter the full path to the database. It would be really great if the developers would add a Browse button to the **DATA SOURCE** field.

4. Type in the path to the database in the Data Source field. For Vista, you would type C:\Users\YourUserName\ACT\ACT for Windows 12\Databases\ACT2010demo.pad.

> In Table 4-1, you read that OLE DB (ADO) connections are used to select a data source that has the connection information saved in a file. That is why you selected the ACT! .pad file in the Data Source option instead of the actual database (.dbf) file. The connection information is stored in this file.

5. Type `Chris Huffman` in the User ID field, as shown in Figure 4-4, then click Finish.

You have completed creating your first connection to an ACT! database in Crystal Reports. That wasn't so bad, was it?

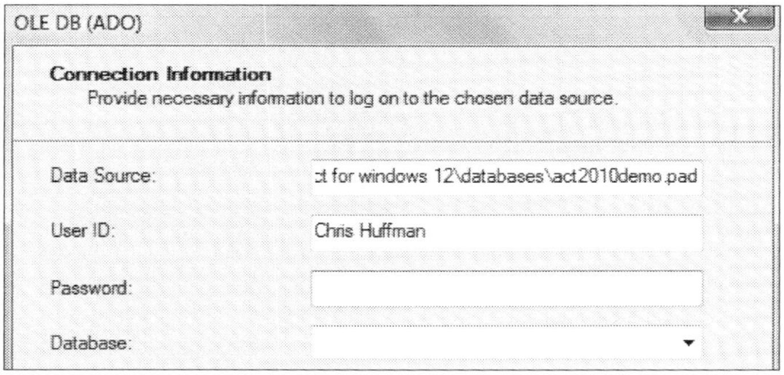

Figure 4-4 Connection Information screen

Step 2: Select The Tables

Under the OLE DB (ADO) connection option, you should see a connection to the demo database, as shown in Figure 4-5. The **DBO** and **SYS** nodes contain the tables in the database. The tables in the dbo node, shown in Figure 4-6, contain the data that you use in the ACT! demo database.

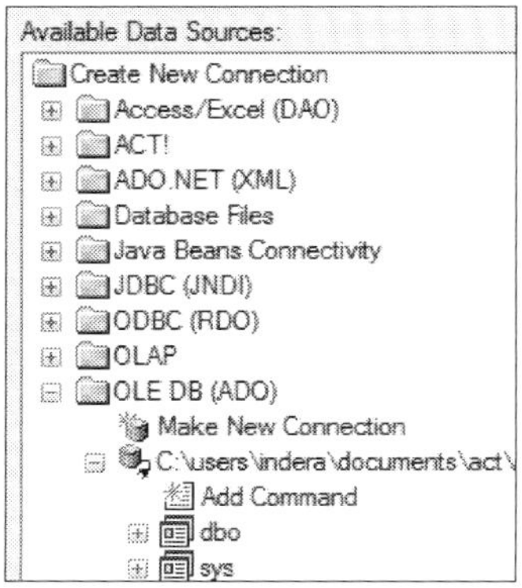

Figure 4-5 Connection to the ACT! demo database

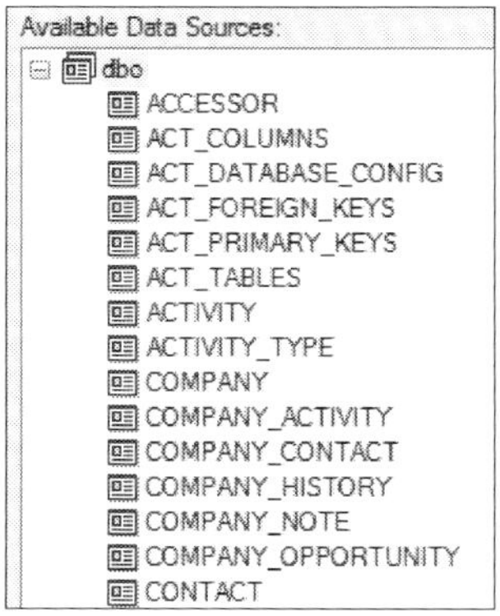

Figure 4-6 Tables in the ACT! demo database

The tables whose names start with ACT_ are similar to system tables, meaning that you probably will not have a need to use them for any of the reports that you create.

1. Click on the plus sign in front of the dbo node.

2. Click on the **PICKLIST** table, then click the **>** button.

   The Picklist table should now be in the **SELECTED TABLES** list, as shown in Figure 4-7.

   Click Next.

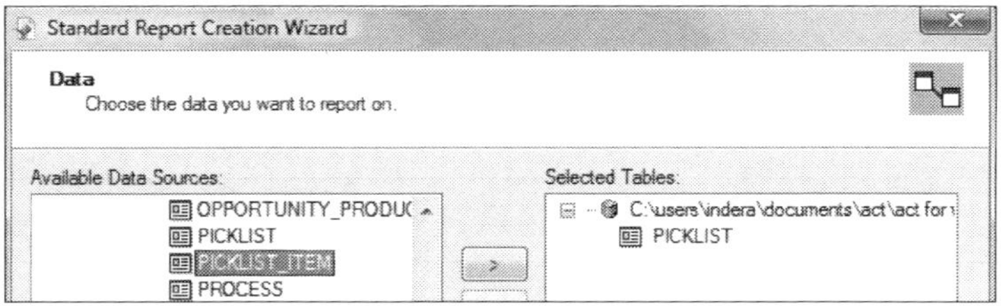

Figure 4-7 Picklist table selected

View The Data In A Field

The **BROWSE DATA** button on the Fields screen is used to view data in a field. This is helpful if you are not familiar with the data. This button is on several dialog boxes in Crystal Reports.

1. Click on the **DESCRIPTION** field, then click the **BROWSE DATA** button. You will see the dialog box shown in Figure 4-8. What you see is the data in the Description field.

   Click the Close button when you are finished viewing the data.

   If the dialog box does not display data, it means that no records in the table have any data in the field.

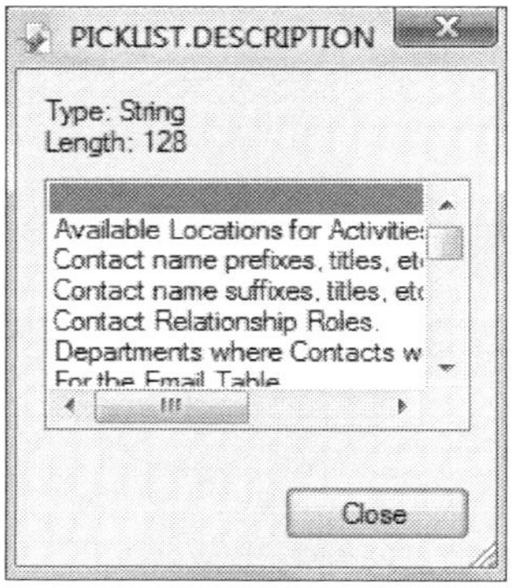

Figure 4-8 Data in the Description field

Notice that the field **TYPE** and **LENGTH** are displayed at the top of the dialog box. This information is helpful because it tells you the type of field and the length of the field.

You can also view the data on the design tab. By default, the first 500 distinct values in a field are displayed. The actual values that you see can be changed by clearing the **SELECT DISTINCT DATA FOR BROWSING** option on the Database tab on the Options dialog box or on the Report Options dialog box, if you only want the change applied the current report. OK, that's the way that it is suppose to work, but it doesn't. If this actually worked, it probably is not a good idea to turn this option off because you could see duplicate data in the Browse Data dialog box shown above in Figure 4-8. But since it doesn't work, turning it off has no effect. If you want to view a different number of records, you have to modify this registry entry: HKEY_CURRENT_USER\Software\Business Objects\Suite 12.0\Crystal Reports\DatabaseServer. Change the **MAXNBROWSEVALUES** key to the maximum number of records that you want to see.

How To Find A Field

The **FIND FIELD** button is used to search for a field in the table. You will see this button on a few dialog boxes in Crystal Reports. I'm not sure that I understand the purpose of this button because all of the fields in a table are displayed on this dialog box. It could be helpful if you don't know which table a field is in.

The Find Field button will only find the first field that matches the text that you enter in the dialog box shown in Figure 4-9. The first matching field that it finds depends on what field is currently selected in the Available Fields list. The search starts from the field that is selected and goes down the list. You can also enter a partial field name. If the same field name is in more than one table, the search does not continue.

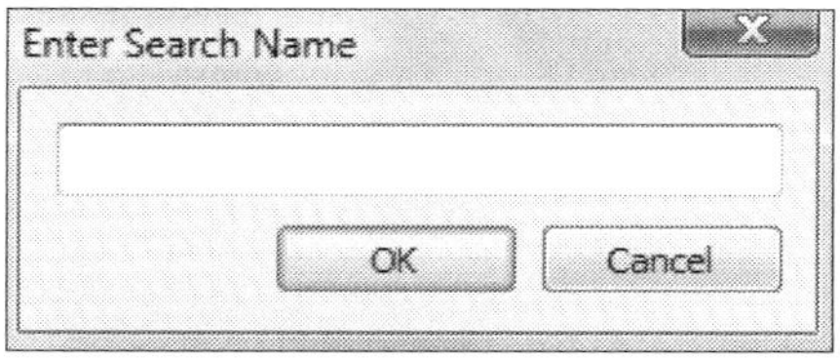

Figure 4-9 Enter Search Name dialog box

If you were creating a report on your own, in the report design process you would have already written down a list of fields and where they are located because you learned to do this in the previous lesson <smile>.

Step 3: Select The Fields

1. Click on the Create Date field, then click the **>** button. You should see the field in the **FIELDS TO DISPLAY** list.

2. Add the following fields to the Fields To Display list: Name, Description and Picklist Type.

All of the items in the **AVAILABLE FIELDS** list are the fields in the Picklist table.

Figure 4-10 shows the fields that should have been added.

Click Next.

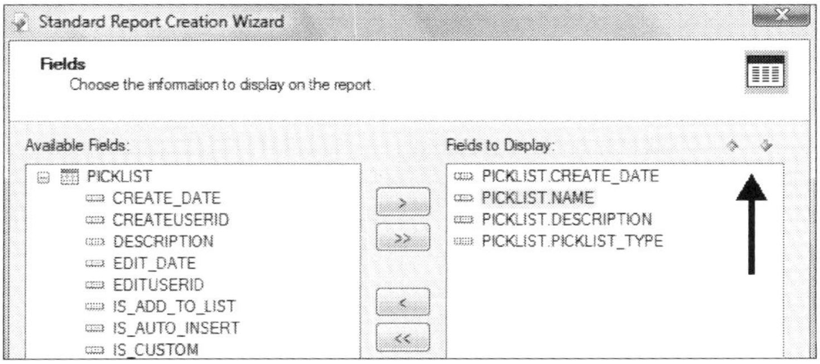

Figure 4-10 Fields selected

To add all of the fields in the table at one time, click the **>>** button. You do not have to select any fields before clicking this button.

To remove a field that you do not need on the report, click on the field in the Fields To Display list, then click the **<** button.

To remove all of the fields from the Fields to Display list, click the **<<** button.

You can add several fields at the same time by clicking on the first field that you want to add, then press and hold down the **CTRL** key and click on the other fields, one by one that you want to add. When you have all of the fields selected that you want to add, click the **>** button.

The order that you add the fields to the Fields to Display list is the order that they will appear on the report in the details section from left to right. If you discover that the fields are not in the order that you want them to appear on the report, click on the field in the Fields To Display section and click the **UP** or **DOWN** arrow buttons illustrated above in Figure 4-10 to move the field to where it should be.

When using a wizard to create a report, the order that the fields are in will change automatically if at least one field is selected to group on. Fields that are grouped on are moved to the beginning of the details section. You can rearrange the fields after the wizard has created the report. This does not happen when you create a report from scratch that has groups.

Notice in Figure 4-10 above that fields in the Fields To Display list have the table name in front of the field name. This is done to let you know which table the field is located in. This is helpful when you are using more than one table to create the report. Primary key fields in tables often have the same field name when the tables have related information. Without adding the table name, you would not know which table a field is in.

Primary key fields are fields that are used to link one table to another table.

Step 4: Select The Grouping Options

As you learned earlier, grouping is used to organize and sort the data. Grouping data forces all records that have the same value in the field that is being grouped on, to print together. Grouping data makes reports that have a lot of data easier to read. Grouping the data in a report is optional. You can group on more than one field. You can group on fields that have already been selected to print on the report, or you can select fields to group on that will not print on the report. The Accessibility report that you saw in the previous lesson uses the grouping option. That report is grouped on customer name and contact name.

1. Add the Picklist Type field to the Group By list. The default grouping option **IN ASCENDING ORDER** is correct. Figure 4-11 shows the grouping options that you should have selected. Click Next.

There are two options that you can select from to group the records by, as discussed below. This is how you sort the values that are in the field that is being grouped on.

IN ASCENDING ORDER This is the default grouping option. The values in the field being grouped on will be sorted in A-Z order if the field is a string field. If the field is numeric, the values will be sorted in 0-9 order.

IN DESCENDING ORDER The values in the field being grouped on will be sorted in Z-A order if the field is a string field. If the field is numeric, the values will be sorted in 9-0 order.

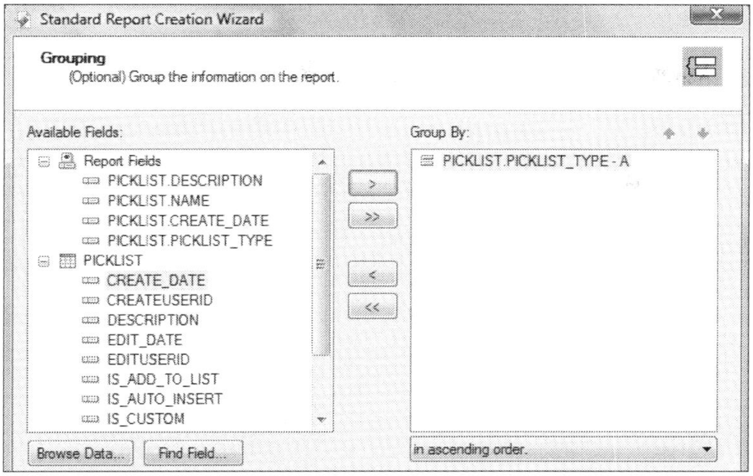

Figure 4-11 Field added to the Group By list

> The only reason that I can think of to click the **CANCEL** button on a screen in the wizard is if you decide that you no longer want to create the report. You will lose all of the options that you have selected if you click the Cancel button. It is better to use the **BACK** button to go back and make changes because you cannot reopen the wizard to make changes or pick up where you left off.

Step 5: Select The Summary Options

1. Add the Name field to the **SUMMARIZED FIELDS** list.

Creating summary fields is optional. Summary options usually involve calculated fields.

By default, the wizard will create a summary field for all numeric fields that were selected to print on the report. You can remove the ones that are not needed.

There are 25 built-in summary functions that you can use. Some of them are shown at the bottom of Figure 4-12.

The number of summary functions that are in the list depends on the data type of the field that you are summarizing on. Not all data types can use all of the summary functions. Many of the summary functions are only for numeric fields.

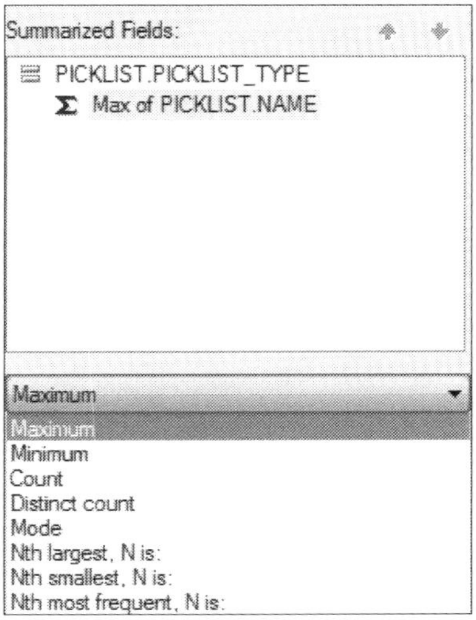

Figure 4-12 Summary function options

2. Open the drop-down list shown above in Figure 4-12 and select **DISTINCT COUNT**.

   Figure 4-13 shows the summary options that should be selected.

   Click Next.

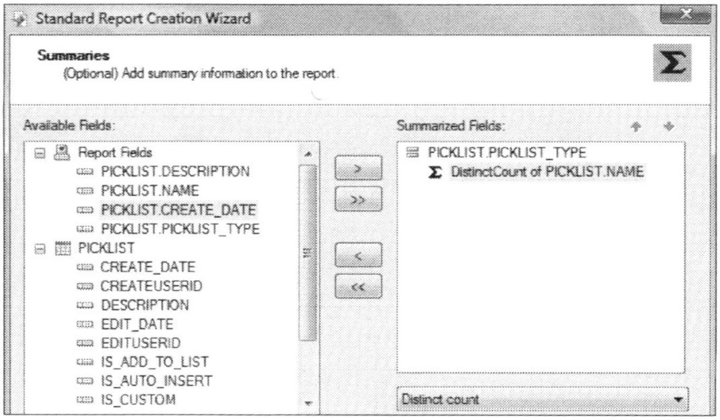

Figure 4-13 Summary options

3. Select the **TOP 5 GROUPS** option.

   Figure 4-14 shows the Group Sorting options that should be selected.

   Click Next.

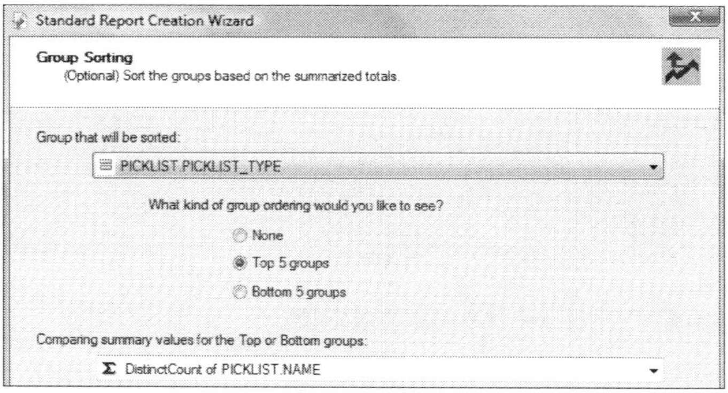

Figure 4-14 Group Sorting options

The Top 5 Groups option will only display data for the five groups that have the highest value in the field selected in the **SUMMARY VALUES** field. Selecting **NONE**, which is the default, will display all groups. It is possible that you will not get the five groups that you think should appear on the report. This is because of the way that Crystal Reports processes data. In Lesson 12 you will create a Top 5 group report that illustrates unexpected results because a wizard was used to create the report.

Step 6: Select The Chart Type

Adding a chart to a report is optional. Once you select a chart type, the wizard will fill in information for the other fields on the dialog box. If you are not sure what options to select, accept the defaults, preview the report and then decide which chart options need to be modified.

1. Select the **PIE CHART** option. Figure 4-15 shows the chart options that should be selected.

   Click Next.

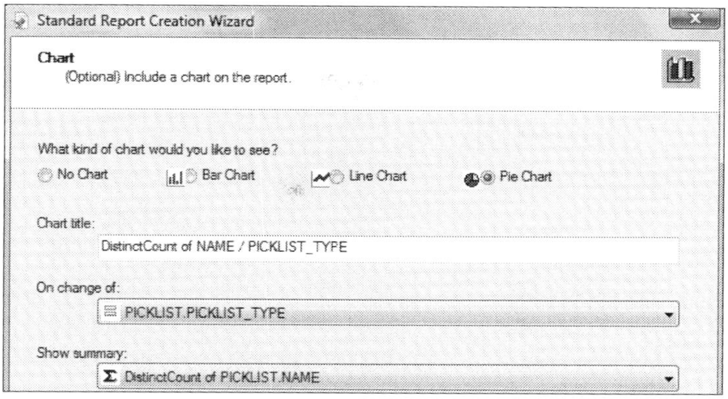

Figure 4-15 Chart options

Step 7: Select The Fields To Filter On

Creating filters is optional. Filters are another way that you can narrow down the number of records that will appear on the report. You can create more than one filter. In this step you will create a filter for the Is Add To List field to only display records that have True in the field.

1. Add the Is Add To List field to the **FILTER FIELDS** list. Open the drop-down list and select **IS TRUE**.

2. Figure 4-16 shows the filter options that should be selected. Click Next.

   The filter that you just created will only display pick list items that have the value True in the Is Add To List field.

   Click Next.

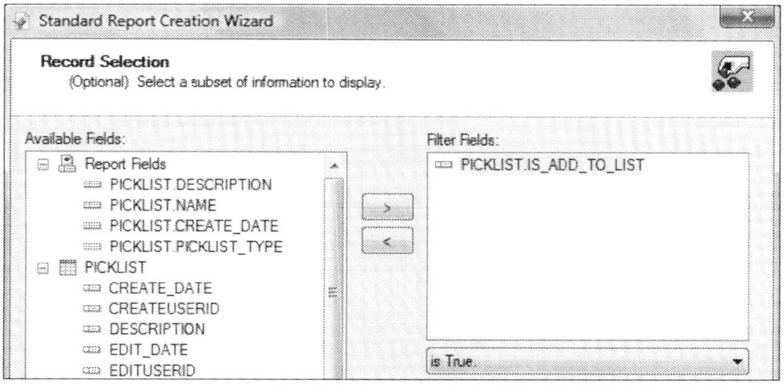

Figure 4-16 Filter options

Step 8: Select A Template

Selecting a template on the screen shown in Figure 4-17 is optional. If you do not want to use a template, select the **NO TEMPLATE** option. You can preview what the other template options look like by clicking on them.

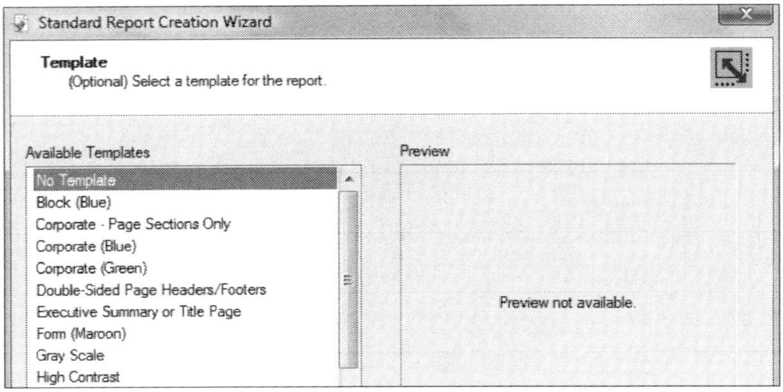

Figure 4-17 Template screen

1. Select the **CORPORATE (BLUE)** template, then click Finish. The first page of the report should look like the one shown in Figure 4-18. The top of the second page of the report should look like the one shown in Figure 4-19. As you scroll through the report, you may see things that you would like to change on the report.

In Step 4, because grouping options were selected, the **GROUP TREE** shown down the left side of the report in Figure 4-18, is displayed. Clicking on the options in the group tree will display that section of the report. If for some reason the group tree is not visible or you do not want to see it, you can click the **TOGGLE PREVIEW PANEL** button on the Standard toolbar to turn it on or off.

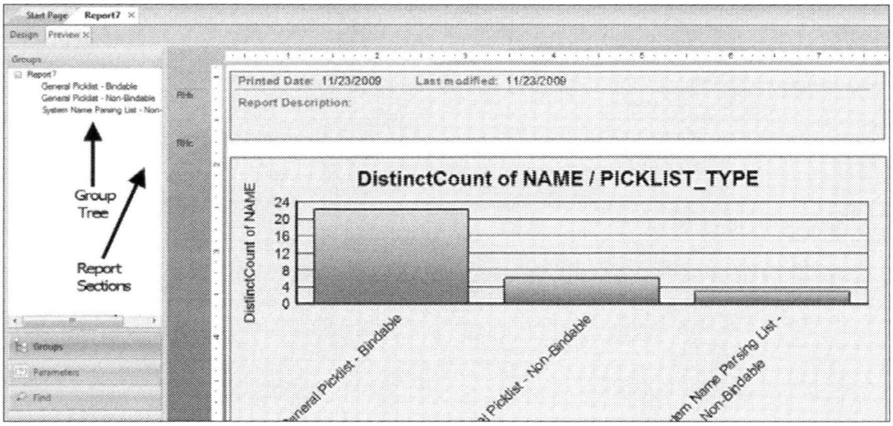

Figure 4-18 Page 1 of the report

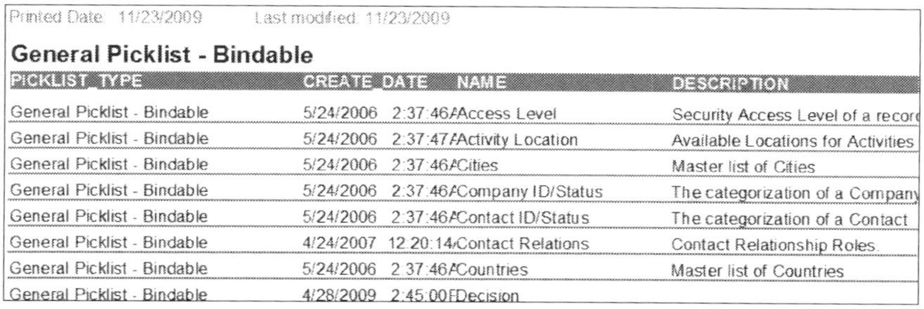

Printed Date: 11/23/2009 Last modified: 11/23/2009

General Picklist - Bindable

PICKLIST_TYPE	CREATE_DATE	NAME	DESCRIPTION
General Picklist - Bindable	5/24/2006 2:37:46A	Access Level	Security Access Level of a recor
General Picklist - Bindable	5/24/2006 2:37:47A	Activity Location	Available Locations for Activities
General Picklist - Bindable	5/24/2006 2:37:46A	Cities	Master list of Cities
General Picklist - Bindable	5/24/2006 2:37:46A	Company ID/Status	The categorization of a Compan
General Picklist - Bindable	5/24/2006 2:37:46A	Contact ID/Status	The categorization of a Contact
General Picklist - Bindable	4/24/2007 12:20:14	Contact Relations	Contact Relationship Roles.
General Picklist - Bindable	5/24/2006 2:37:46A	Countries	Master list of Countries
General Picklist - Bindable	4/28/2009 2:45:00F	Decision	

Figure 4-19 Page 2 of the report

Step 9: Save The Report

As shown earlier in Figure 4-18, the report was given a default name of **REPORT 1** which you can use. You should save the report with a name that is more meaningful. In addition to giving the report a meaningful name, you have to decide whether or not you want to save the data with the report, which is discussed below.

Options For Saving Data

Unless you changed the default options after Crystal Reports was installed, the data is saved with the report by default.

Figure 4-20 illustrates the **SAVE DATA WITH REPORT** option selected on the File menu. There are pros and cons to saving data with a report as discussed below.

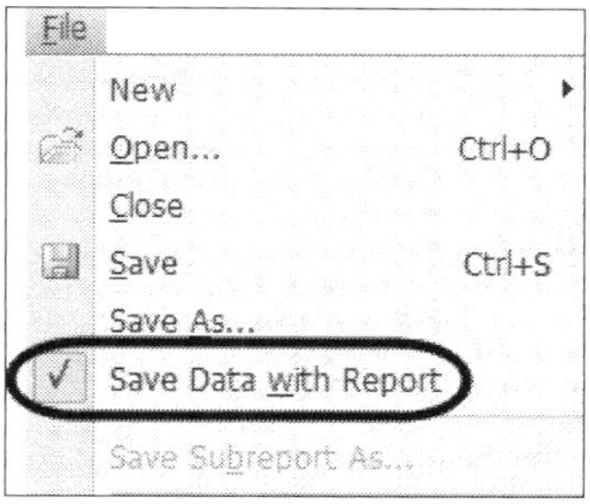

Figure 4-20 Save data option on the File menu

If you do not want the **SAVE DATA WITH REPORT** option set as the default, File ⇒ Options. Click on the **REPORTING** tab. Clear the option, **SAVE DATA WITH REPORT**, then click OK.

Save The Report With Data

As stated earlier, this is the default option. You can preview and print reports faster with this option selected because the data does not have to be retrieved from the database. This option is also useful if you need to send the report to someone that does not have access to the data. One downside to saving the data with the report is that the report requires more hard drive or server space. A second downside is that anyone that runs the report with saved data will not be using the most current data. A third downside occurs if the database has security. Unless the report has been published to a Crystal Reports Server, the security is bypassed and anyone that opens the report will have access to the data, whether they should or not.

Fields in tables are indexed to reduce the time it takes to retrieve the records needed to create the report. Fields that are used in the record selection criteria are often used as an index.

Indexes are not usually helpful in reports that use saved data. The exception to this is reports that have parameter fields that the person running the report can use to change the record selection formula. The **REPORT BURSTING INDEXES** command is used to create indexes in reports that are saved with data.

Save The Report Without Data

Selecting this option requires less disk space. With this option, the report will be using live data each time it is run. The downside is when you need to preview or print the report, it will take a little longer to process because the data has to be retrieved. Most of the time, you will not notice the delay.

From a report developers perspective if you have the space it will save time, a considerable amount of time if there are thousands of records for the report, if you save the data with the report while you are creating and modifying it. The danger that some developers have <not us of course> is that they forget to change the save data option before putting the report into production. Another danger is not testing the report with live data. Remember that most data is volatile, meaning that it changes frequently, is deleted and added to on a regular basis. Not testing with live data before putting the report into production could be a bad career move, if you know what I mean. Testing with live data before putting the report into production, also means that it won't go into production with the saved data.

Refreshing Report Data

As you just learned, you have to decide whether to save the data with the report or not. If you decide to normally save data with a report to save processing time while designing the report that's fine. Anytime that you want to work with the current data, click the **REFRESH** button on the Navigation Tools toolbar.

If the changes that you make to a report fall in the formatting category, like changing fonts, moving fields around on the report or adding titles to summary fields that were already saved with the report, you do not have to refresh the data.

Automatic Data Refreshing

If any of the options listed below occur after a report have been saved, the data will automatically be refreshed, regardless of the save data option that is associated with the report.

① A new field is added to the report.
② If a formula is added to the report that uses a field that was not already being used on the report.
③ If an existing formula is modified that uses a field that was not already being used on the report.
④ If any report criteria or parameter fields are added or changed that include a field that was not already being used on the report.
⑤ If the grouping is not done on a server, the detail record data will be refreshed.

> If you drill-down on hidden data, the data is not a full refresh. If the grouping is taking place on a server, drilling down in the details section will only retrieve the new data required by the drill-down for the details section.

Yes, I can sense that you are shaking your head about the save data with report options. Keep in mind that only the fields on the report and fields needed for formulas or functions that the report uses are saved with the report. Other fields in the table are not saved with the report. This is why you are prompted frequently to refresh data when the save data option is turned on. As you become more familiar with modifying reports, you will know which save data option is best suited for each report that you are modifying or creating.

Real World Data

Many companies have what is known as a "development server" that has a copy of "live data" and applications (Live data is also known as production data). This is done so that anyone that is creating new applications, modifying existing applications or testing software, can do so without putting the companies data in danger. If this is the type of environment that you working in, keep in mind while going through this book, the differences between "live" and "refreshed" data, when these terms are referenced.

When creating reports on a development server and you click the **REFRESH** button in Crystal Reports, you are not getting a copy of the data from a production server. You are getting another copy of the data from the development server. The same is true if you have placed a copy of the production data on your hard drive. Usually, data on a development server is refreshed from a production server at pre-defined intervals (ex. daily, weekly monthly). If you want to know when the data on a development server is refreshed, ask the DBA or the person that manages the databases that you are using.

Save The Report

> The default file extension for reports is **.RPT** in Crystal Reports. Report file names can have up to 255 characters and can include spaces and special characters. Reports can be stored in almost any folder on your hard drive or server. You should not store reports in operating system folders.

1. File ⇒ Save As. Open the **SAVE AS** drop-down list on the Save As dialog box and navigate to the Crystal Reports Book folder that you created.

> You can also click the **SAVE** button on the Standard toolbar when saving a report for the first time.

2. Type `L4.1 My first report` as the file name, as shown at the bottom of Figure 4-21, then press Enter or click the Save button.

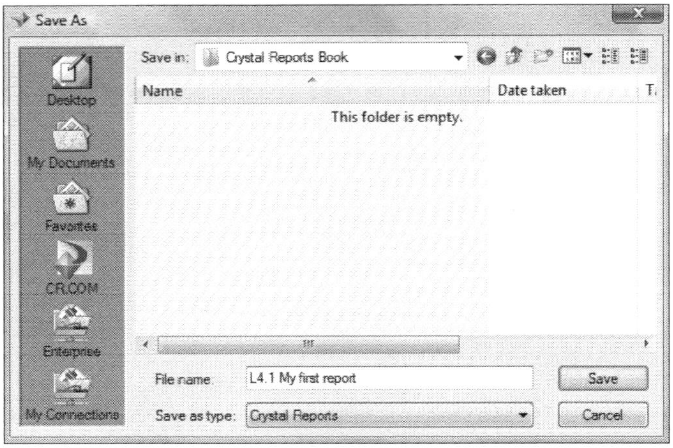

Figure 4-21 Save As options illustrated

> Report file names like the one shown at the bottom of Figure 4-21 are different then report titles. Report file names are what you save the report as. Report titles come from the **DOCUMENT PROPERTIES** dialog box.

The name on the design and preview tabs by default will display the report file name. If the report has a report title, it will be displayed on the tab instead. In the previous lesson, you saw the Running Totals Group report. The tab for that report displays, "How To Maintain Running Totals For A Group". This is the report title. [See Lesson 3, Figure 3-15]

Step 10: Add The Current Report To The Workbench

When you save a report, it is not automatically added to the Workbench. You have to manually add it. The step below shows you how to add the report to the Workbench.

1. Add ⇒ Add Current Report, in the Workbench. The report should now be under the Lesson 4 Reports folder in the Workbench, as shown in Figure 4-22.

   Close the report.

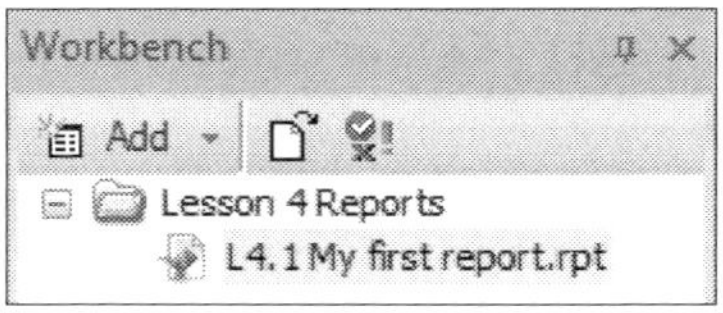

Figure 4-22 Report added to the Workbench

NEW Selecting A Data Source

In the previous exercise, you used the options in the **CREATE NEW CONNECTION** folder to create a connection to the ACT! database. That connection stays live until you close Crystal Reports.

When you reopen Crystal Reports any previous connections are automatically moved to the **MY CONNECTIONS** folder shown in Figure 4-23. If you right-click on the connection, you will see the shortcut menu shown in the figure.

The **PROPERTIES** option is used to view information about the data source of the connection.

The **RENAME CONNECTION** option is used to give the connection a more user friendly name.

The **OPTIONS** option opens the Database tab on the Options dialog box that you learned about in Lesson 2.

The Database Expert only has two folders (called Nodes): My Connections and Create New Connections. When you open a report or create a connection, the connection is automatically saved in the My Connections folder.

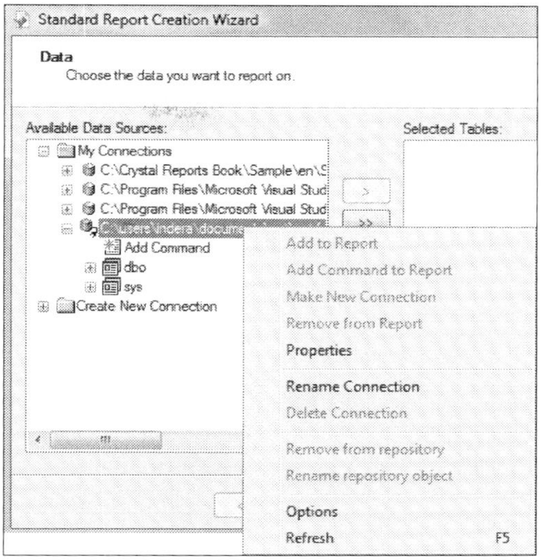

Figure 4-23 My Connections data source folder

Report Bursting Indexes

The Report Bursting Indexes command (Report ⇒ Report Bursting Indexes) is used to create indexes in reports that have saved data.

Figure 4-24 shows the **SAVED DATA INDEXES** dialog box, which is used to select the fields to create indexes for the next time the report data is refreshed.

After the fields are selected, the report should be refreshed so that the indexes can be created.

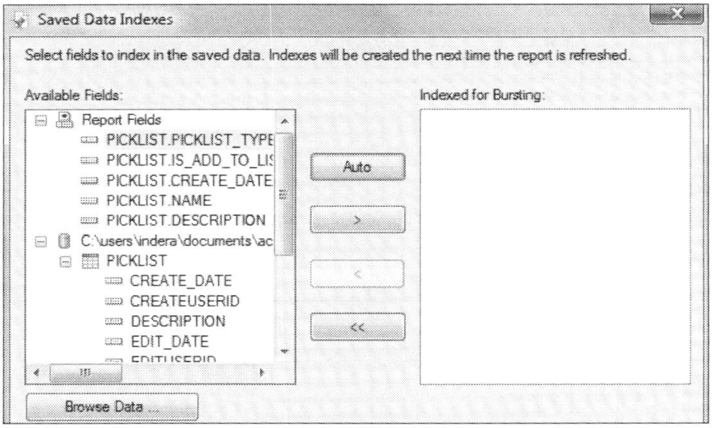

Figure 4-24 Saved Data Indexes dialog box

Clicking the **AUTO** button will automatically add all of the fields that are used in the report record selection criteria to the Indexed for Bursting list.

Exercise 4.2: Create An ACT! Table Report

When you connected to the ACT! demo database, you saw that there are a lot of tables in the database. One of the tables contains a list of all of the tables in the database and a description of the data in each table.

In this exercise, you will create a report to display all of the tables in the ACT! demo database. This will help you gain a better understanding of how the data is stored.

1. Click on the Report Wizard link on the Start Page or File ⇒ New ⇒ Standard Report.

2. Select the ACT! demo database connection, then add the ACT Tables table to the Selected Tables list and click Next.

3. Add the Display Name, Description and View Name fields to the Fields to Display list.

4. Click Finish. The report should look like the one shown in Figure 4-25. The report needs to be formatted better so that is it easier to read. You will learn formatting techniques in Lesson 7.

11/23/2009

DISPLAYNAME	DESCRIPTION	VIEWNAME
Activity	The ACT! Activity Record	ACTIVITY
Company	The ACT! Company Record	COMPANY
Company Activity	Links the Company record to	COMPANY_ACTIVITY
Company Contact	Links the Company record to	COMPANY_CONTACT
Company History	Links the Company record to	COMPANY_HISTORY
Company Note	Links the Company record to	COMPANY_NOTE
Company Opportunity	Links the Company record to	COMPANY_OPPORTUNITY
Contact	The ACT! Contact Record	CONTACT
My Record	Contact record of the current	MY_RECORD_CONTACT
Contact Activity	Links the Contact record to tl	CONTACT_ACTIVITY

Figure 4-25 L4.2 ACT Tables report

5. Save the report in your folder as `L4.2 ACT Tables report`.

As you can see, the data in the Description field is cut off. One formatting option to fix this is the **CAN GROW** option.

In the View Name column, notice that several of the table names have an underscore in the name. These tables are used to link other tables. These table names are actually pretty clever because the name is actually the two tables that can be linked together. For example, the Company History table contains the ID fields to link the Company and Company History tables.

Exercise 4.3: Create A Product List Report

In this exercise you will create a product list report that will print the Product ID, Product and Price fields.

1. Click on the Report Wizard link on the Start Page.

2. Select the ACT! demo database connection, then add the Product table to the Selected Tables list and click Next.

3. Add the Product ID, Product and Price fields to the Fields to Display list.

4. Click Finish because the report does not require any of the options on the other wizard screens.

   Your report should look like the one shown in Figure 4-26. As you can see the Product ID field needs to be wider so that the data does not overlap.

11/23/2009

PRODUCTID	PRODUCT	PRICE
{10D6D3E9-0518-4850-B9A:	Mini Core Replacement	100.00
{D55410C5-9F2B-47B9-A1C	ONE Component	2,500.00
{9DA1C71E-1631-4427-AC2	Service Contract	2,000.00
{E24C2E33-1778-4931-A55(	TechONE System	12,000.00
{339AF93C-9741-4D72-9AEI	TWO Component	4,000.00

Figure 4-26 L4.3 Product list report

NEW The **PRINT DATE SPECIAL FIELD** now displays the entire date automatically, as shown above in Figure 4-26, opposed to cutting it off as it did in Crystal Reports XI.

5. Save the report as `L4.3 Product list.`

Exercise 4.4: Create A Contact List Report

The fields that are needed to create this report are stored in two tables. This report will be grouped by the State field.

1. Open the Report Wizard, then select the ACT demo database connection.

2. Add the Contact and Contact Contact tables, then click Next.

Linking Tables

You will see the screen shown in Figure 4-27. The options on this screen are used to select the appropriate links for the tables that you have selected. Most of the time, the link that is automatically selected is the one that you need. Fields are automatically linked if they have the same name and compatible data type.

In other types of databases that I have used with Crystal Reports, the links that are automatically created do not have to be changed. I have noticed with ACT! databases, that I have to clear all of the links that are automatically created and create the links manually because too many links are created.

In this exercise, the tables should be linked by the Contact ID field.

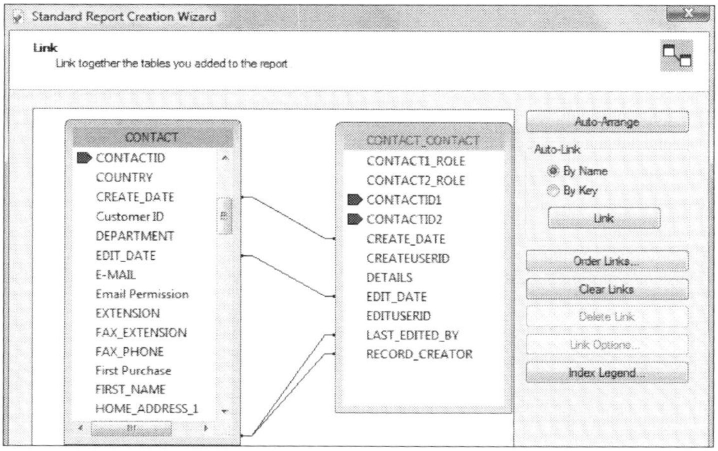

Figure 4-27 Link screen

You may need to make the dialog box wider to see both tables. To make the dialog box wider, place the mouse pointer on the right side of the dialog box and drag the border of the dialog box to the right. You can also make the tables longer if you want to see all of the fields in the table.

If you right-click on a field and select **BROWSE FIELD**, as shown in Figure 4-28, you will be able to see the first 500 unique values for the field that you selected. If you see more than one occurrence of the same value, it means that you have turned off the Select Distinct Data For Browsing option on the Database tab on the Options dialog box or on the Report Options dialog box.

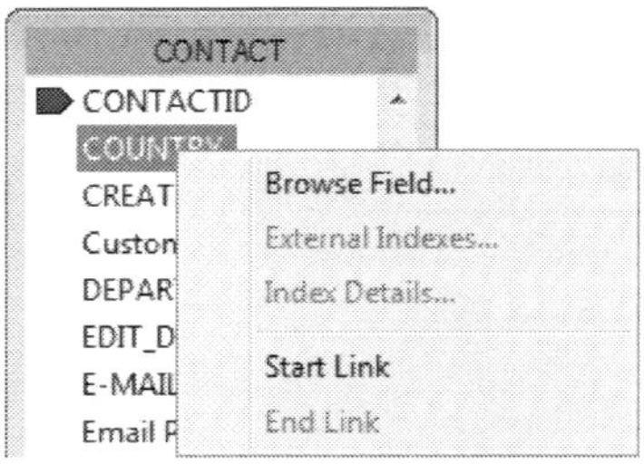

Figure 4-28 Link screen field shortcut menu

Index Legend

As you saw earlier in Figure 4-27, there are colored arrows next to some fields. If you click the **INDEX LEGEND** button, you will see the index that each colored arrow represents, as shown in Figure 4-29.

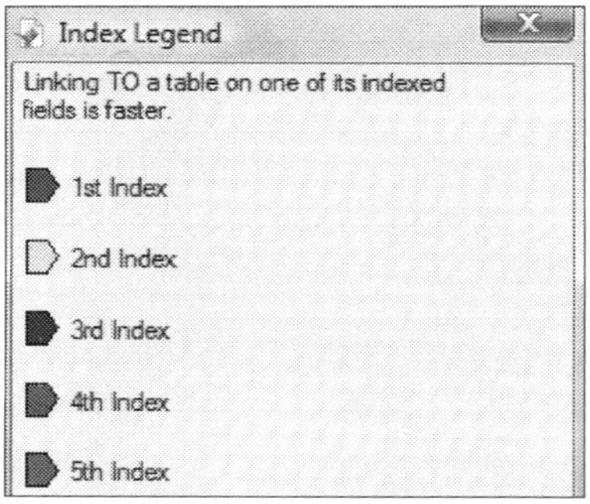

Figure 4-29 Index Legend dialog box

Change The Links

1. Click the Clear Links button, then click Yes when prompted to remove all links.

2. Drag the Contact ID field in the Contact table to the Contact ID1 field in the Contact Contact table. You will see blue line connecting the fields.

Add The Fields To The Report

1. Click Next on the dialog box shown earlier in Figure 4-27, then add the fields in Table 4-2 to the Fields to Display list. Figure 4-30 shows the order that the fields should be in. Click Next.

Contact	Contact Contact
State	Contact 1 Role
Contact ID	
First Name	
Last Name	
Home Phone	

Table 4-2 Fields to add to the report

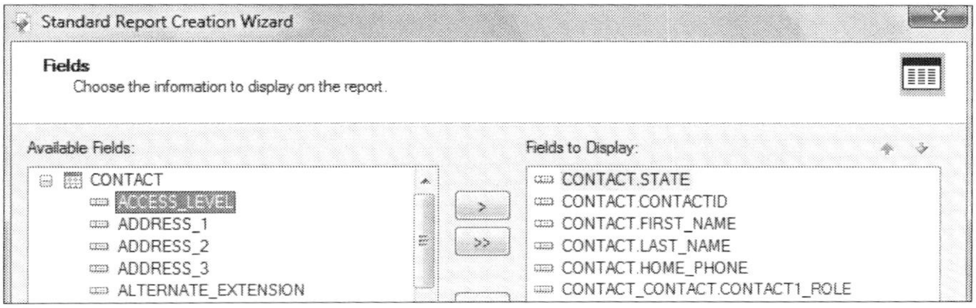

Figure 4-30 Fields selected for the report

Select The Grouping Options

This report would look better if it was grouped on the State field and within each State group, the contact names were sorted by last and first name. It would also be helpful if there was a count of contacts per state.

1. Add the State field to the **GROUP BY** list, then click Next.

2. Add the Contact ID field to the **SUMMARIZED FIELDS** list.

3. Open the drop-down list and select **COUNT**. Figure 4-31 shows the summary options that should be selected.

   This option will count the number of Contact ID's in each state. When you want a count of records, you should select a field that has unique values. Each contact is assigned a unique ID. Think of ID's as being the equivalent of social security numbers, where each persons social security number is unique.

   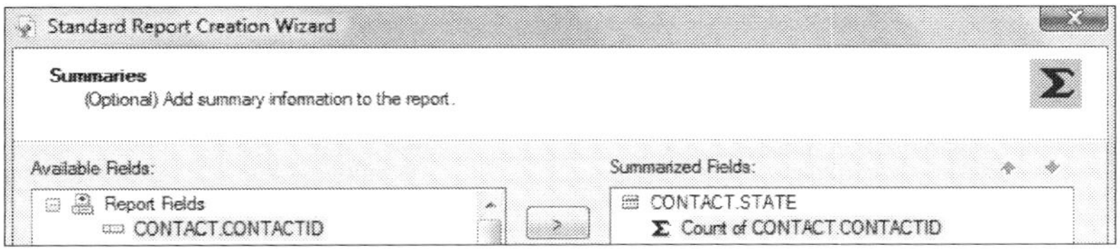

   Figure 4-31 Summary options

4. Click Next. Click Next again on the Group Sorting screen because you do not need to change any of the options.

Select The Chart Options

1. Select the **BAR CHART** option.

2. Type `Count of contacts per state` in the **CHART TITLE** field.

Figure 4-32 shows the chart options that should be selected.

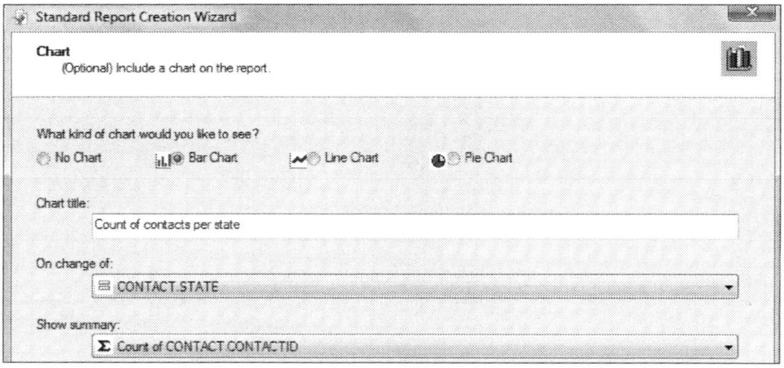

Figure 4-32 Chart options

Finish The Report

1. Click Finish because you do not need to select any other options.

Your report should look like the one shown in Figure 4-33.

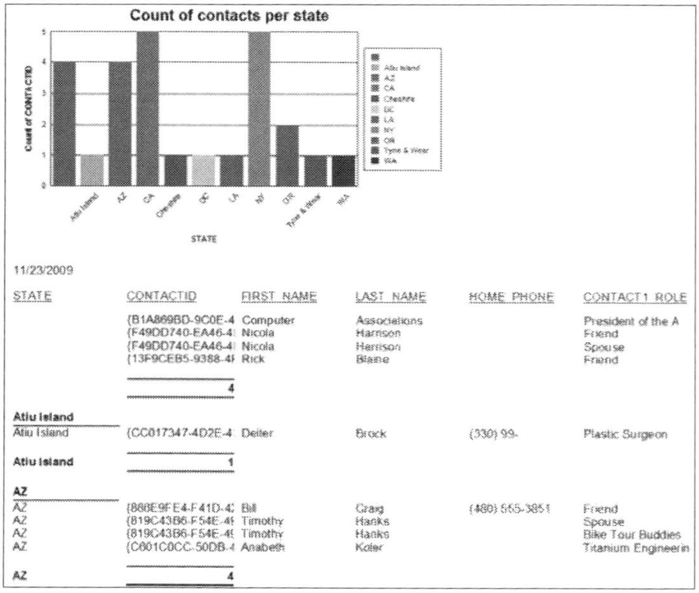

Figure 4-33 L4.4 Contact list report

2. Close the report and save it as `L4.4 Contact list by state.`

> If there is an existing report that has some of the data that you need to create another report, open the existing report and use the File ⇒ Save As option. Save the report with a new name and modify it as needed.

Report Processing Model

Reports in Crystal Reports are processed in three passes. The first pass reads all of the records, calculates the formulas and summary fields, suppresses fields and creates a temporary data file. This temporary file only contains the records needed for the report, not all of the records in the database. The second pass sorts records, calculates totals for groups, calculates running totals, generates charts, maps, cross-tabs, OLAP grids and subreports as needed. The second pass also formats the pages. The third pass calculates the total page count and Page N of M special fields if necessary.

Formulas can be placed in all sections of a report. Formulas are not processed in report section order. The processing model uses the following criteria to help determine the order to process formulas.

① Formulas that use database fields are processed while the records are being read in the first pass.
② There is no order to how formulas are processed in the same section of the report.
③ Formulas that only use variables are processed before records are read.
④ Formulas that use summary and group fields are processed after the records are read.
⑤ Cross-Tab summary fields are calculated in the first pass.

The link below provides more information on the processing model that Crystal Reports uses.
http://msdn2.microsoft.com/en-us/library/ms225477.aspx

If this report processing model seems complicated, remember the following:

① The first pass reads the records in the database, retrieves the records that match any selection criteria and calculates formulas where all of the fields in the calculation are fields in a table.
② The second pass selects data for groups and evaluates summary functions.
③ The third pass is mainly used to calculate the total page count (Page N of M) if needed.

CREATING REPORTS FROM SCRATCH

After completing the exercises in this lesson you will be able to:

- ☑ Create basic reports from scratch
- ☑ Use the Database Expert
- ☑ Use the Field Explorer
- ☑ Add and remove tables in the Field Explorer window
- ☑ Dock and undock explorer windows
- ☑ Understand relational databases
- ☑ Understand the different types of relationships
- ☑ Understand Linking, Join Types and Smart Linking techniques

> **Reminder**
>
> As you learned in the previous lesson, you will use the ACT! demo database. This database is used for the remainder of this book.

LESSON 5

The Database Expert

The Database Expert shown in Figure 5-1 is used to select the data source for the report.

Database ⇒ Database Expert, will open this dialog box.

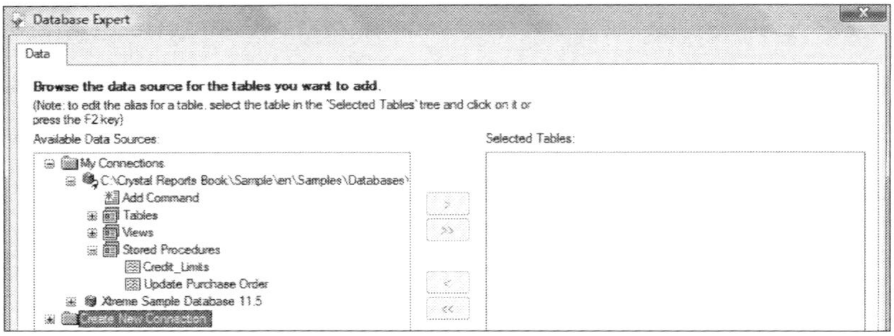

Figure 5-1 Database Expert dialog box

As you can see, this dialog box is very similar to the Data screen in the Report wizard that you used. Like the Data screen, the Database Expert has a Links screen.

Data Source Options

Each of the four data source options (Commands, Tables, Views and Stored Procedures) shown above in Figure 5-1 provide a different way to access data for the reports that you create. As the report designer, for the most part, you will not be required to create or maintain the data sources. You do however, need a good understanding of them so that you can select the best option, based on the requirements for the report. The only Data Source option that ACT! supports is tables.

Tables are probably the most used of the four data sources because accessing the tables does not require any code or programming skills, like the other three data source options require.

Explorers

As illustrated in Figure 5-2, Crystal Reports comes with three explorers that you can use to help create and manage reports.

The one that you will probably use the most is the Field Explorer. The explorers are discussed below.

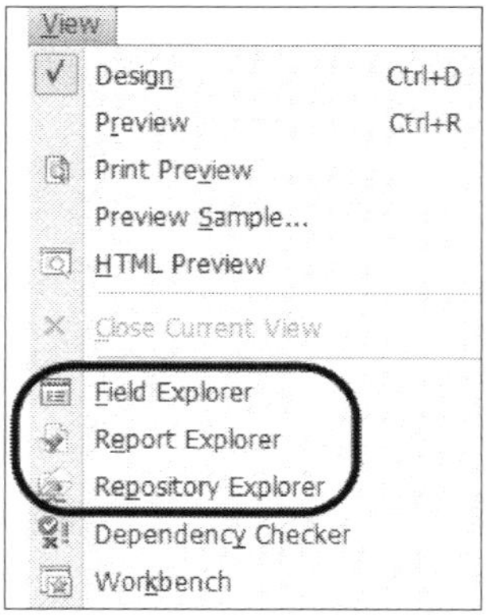

Figure 5-2 Explorer options illustrated on the View menu

The View menu shown above in Figure 5-2, has the options for the explorers. Buttons for the explorers are also on the Standard toolbar.

1. If the Field and Report Explorers are not visible in the Crystal Reports window, add them now.

   Figure 5-3 is how I have the explorer windows docked.

   Pay attention to the symbols (icons) that are next to each of the options in the Field Explorer. You will see them again when you learn how to create formulas.

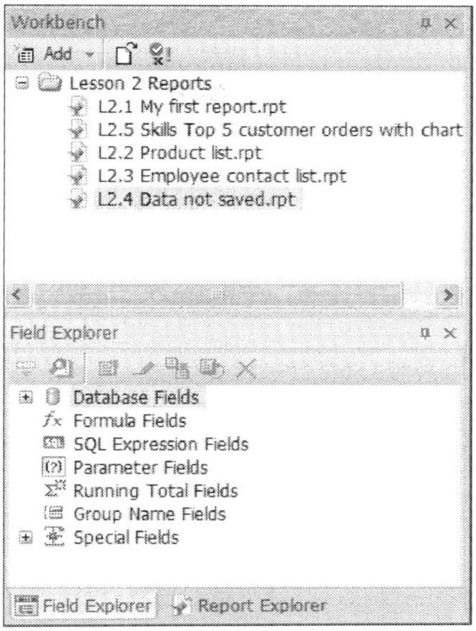

Figure 5-3 Field and Report Explorers illustrated

Field Explorer

The Field Explorer is used to add the seven types of fields shown above in Figure 5-3, to a report. Table 5-1 explains each of the field types.

Field Type	Description
Database	The fields in this folder come from tables and are usually placed in the details section of the report. This is the only field type in the Field Explorer that is stored in a database.
Formula	These are calculated fields that you create using the Formula Workshop. They are recalculated every time the report is run or previewed. (1)
SQL Expression	This type of field is written in a language called SQL. This field type queries (searches) the data to select records that meet the criteria in the query. They are stored on and run from a server. (1)
Parameter	This field type is one that you create. Parameter fields prompt the person running the report to provide information. The information gathered from the parameter fields is used to query the data to select records that meet the information in the parameter fields. Parameter fields allow the person running the report to produce several versions of the report from one report file. An example of parameter fields are the questions that you answer when you use an ATM machine to withdraw or deposit money. (1)

Table 5-1 Field types explained

Field Type	Description
Running Total	This is a formula field that sums (adds) the values in a numeric field (or column of data). Running Total fields can be placed in the details section of the report and will provide a total up to the current record. Running Total fields can be reset to zero. They can be used to create totals by group or for the entire report. Summary fields can only be placed in the group header and footer, report header and footer sections of the report. (1)
Group Name	This field type is automatically created for each group the report has. When a group is created, by default the group name field is added to the group header section of the report and will display the value in the field. You can customize the group name to display something other than the value in the field. (1)
Special Fields	These are system generated fields. Some of the more popular special fields include the page number, print date and Page N of M. Special Fields can be formatted like the other field types discussed in this table. [See Lesson 8, Special Fields] (1)

Table 5-1 Field types explained (Continued)

(1) This field type is not stored in a database.

Field Explorer Toolbar

Figure 5-4 shows the Field Explorer toolbar. Table 5-2 explains the buttons on the Field Explorer toolbar.

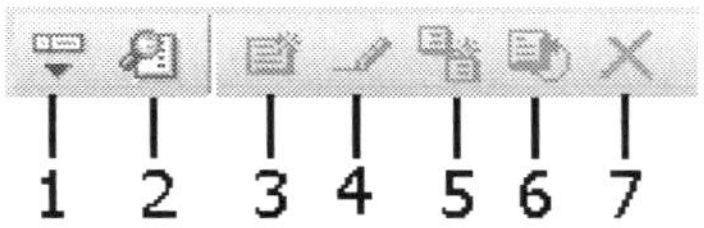

Figure 5-4 Field Explorer Toolbar

Button	Purpose
1	The **INSERT TO REPORT** button is used to add a field to the report.
2	The **BROWSE** button is used to view the data in the field that is selected.
3	The **NEW** button is used to create formula, parameter, SQL Expression or running total fields. (2)
4	The **EDIT** button is used to modify formula, parameter, SQL Expression or running total fields. (2)
5	The **DUPLICATE** button is used to create a copy of a formula, SQL Expression or running total field. This option does not duplicate parameter fields. (3)
6	The **RENAME** button is used to rename formula, parameter, SQL Expression or running total fields. (2)
7	The **DELETE** button is used to delete formula, parameter, SQL Expression or running total fields. (2)

Table 5-2 Field Explorer toolbar buttons explained

(2) Before clicking on this button, click on the category (below the toolbar) of the field type that you want to use.

(3)

Duplicating A Formula

If you need to create a formula that is similar to one that is already in the report, you can duplicate the formula, instead of creating the second formula from scratch.

Right-click on a formula field in the Field Explorer and select Duplicate. You can accept the default formula name or you can right-click on the duplicated formula and select **RENAME** to change the name.

Copying A Formula From One Report To Another

You can also copy a formula from one report to another. Open the report that has the formula that you want to copy and the report that you want to copy the formula to. Click on the formula field that you want to copy in the report layout, then Edit ⇒ Copy. Click on the tab of the report that you want to copy the formula to, then Edit ⇒ Paste.

Field Type Symbols And Naming Conventions

In Table 5-1 you read about several field types that can be added to a report. Four of these field types: Formula, SQL Expression, Parameter and Running Total, are fields that you create. Each of these field types must have a unique name. Crystal Reports will add a symbol to the beginning of the field name as discussed below. This is done to help you know what type of field it is when you are viewing the field in the design tab.

① **@ symbol** Is a formula field.
② **% sign** Is an SQL Expression field.
③ **? question mark** Is a parameter field.
④ **# sign** Is a running total field.

Do not use the field type symbols discussed above as part of a field name that you create.

Formula, SQL Expression, Parameter and Running Total fields must have a unique name within each field type. Therefore, it is possible to use the same field name for a parameter, formula and running total field in the same report. This is why understanding what the field type symbols represent is important.

Sort Fields In The Field Explorer

By default, the fields are displayed in the table in the order there were created. If you do not like the default order that the fields are displayed in the Field Explorer, you can sort the fields alphabetically by right-clicking on the table name and selecting **SORT FIELDS ALPHABETICALLY**, as illustrated in Figure 5-5. Figure 5-6 shows the fields after they have been sorted.

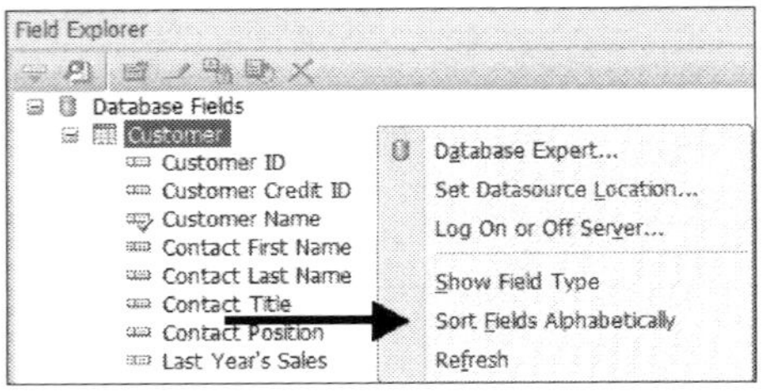

Figure 5-5 Fields in table before sorting

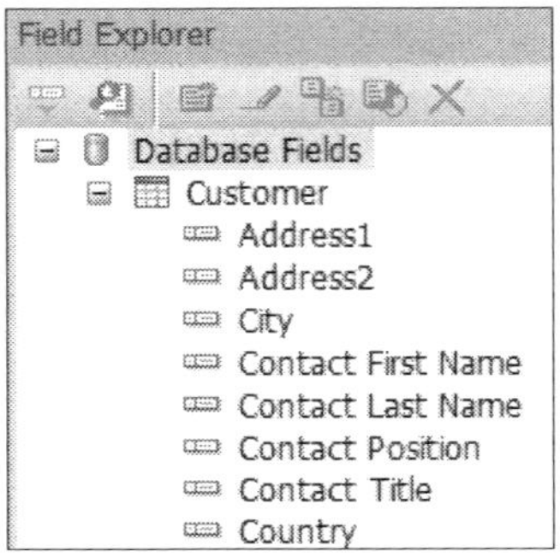

Figure 5-6 Fields in table after sorting

Repository Explorer

The Repository Explorer is used to save objects like images, queries and functions that you want to use in more than one report. The Repository Explorer can only be accessed through the Repository, which is stored in the Business Objects Enterprise. If your company does not have this enterprise system, this functionality is not available, regardless of the database being used.

Docking The Explorers

Docking explorers is not a requirement to complete the exercises in this book, but doing so will make the explorer windows easier to use. I find it easier to dock the explorers as shown earlier in Figure 5-3. I also dock the Workbench with the explorers. To accomplish this, you can follow the steps below.

1. Open two of the explorer windows, as shown in Figure 5-7.

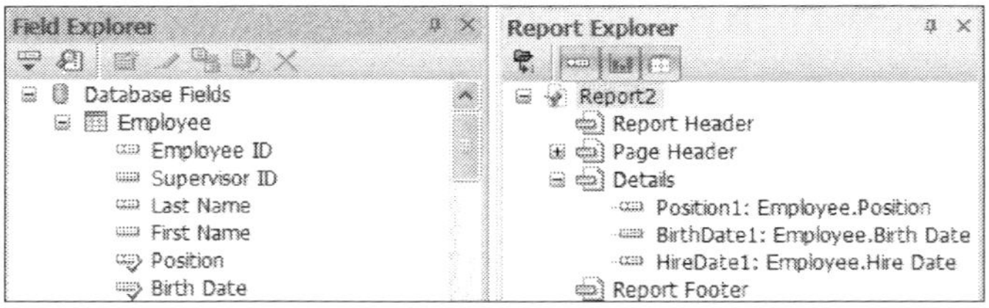

Figure 5-7 Two explorer windows opened in the workspace

2. With the left mouse button, drag the explorer window that you want to dock over to the explorer window that you want to dock it to, then release the mouse button when the window has a tab for the explorer window that you moved.

   The docked window will now contain the explorer window that you added, as shown in Figure 5-8.

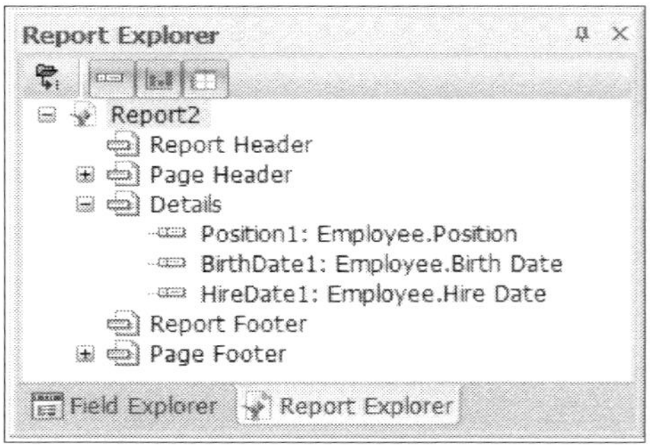

Figure 5-8 New window docked

As you saw earlier in Figure 5-3, I have the explorers docked below the Workbench. To do that, make the Workbench window smaller, then drag the explorer windows below it.

Docking Tips

Below are several tips that you may find useful when using the explorers. It could be me, but when I mistakenly move an explorer window, I have difficulty getting it back to where it was. This truly drives me nuts. I hope a solution is available soon. The reason that I am telling you this is so that if you have trouble getting the explorers exactly where you want them, you know that you aren't the only one that it happens to.

① To select the explorer that you want to use, click on the tab for it at the bottom of the explorer windows.
② If you double-click on an explorer's title bar, it will toggle between being in docked and free floating modes.
③ If you double-click on the title bar of a free floating explorer window, it will go back to where it was the last time that you used Crystal Reports.
④ In free-floating mode, the explorer window can be moved to a new location in the workspace.
⑤ The Workbench and Dependency Checker windows can also be docked with the explorers.

I prefer to keep the Workbench separate from the explorers because I use the Workbench frequently and like to always keep it open. If it was docked with the explorers, I would have to keep clicking on the tab to get to it.

The Workbench and Dependency Checker windows can also be docked together, as shown in Figure 5-9.

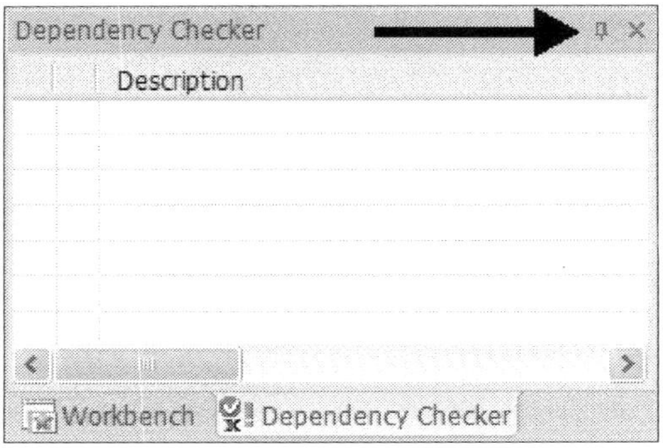

Figure 5-9 Workbench and Dependency Checker windows docked together

The Push Pin

If you click on the push pin illustrated in the upper right corner of Figure 5-9 above, you will open the toolbar shown in Figure 5-10. This toolbar will give you more space to work on reports.

To access one of the explorers from this toolbar, hold the mouse pointer over the icon and the corresponding explorer window will open.

To close the toolbar and return to the docked explorer windows, open an explorer window from the toolbar and click on the push pin.

Figure 5-10 Explorer toolbar

Explorer Shortcut Menu

If you right-click on the title bar of an explorer window you will see the shortcut menu shown in Figure 5-11.

The **UNDOCK** option removes the explorer window from the other windows that is it docked with. The **AUTOHIDE** option will display the toolbar shown above in Figure 5-10. The **CLOSE** option closes the explorer window.

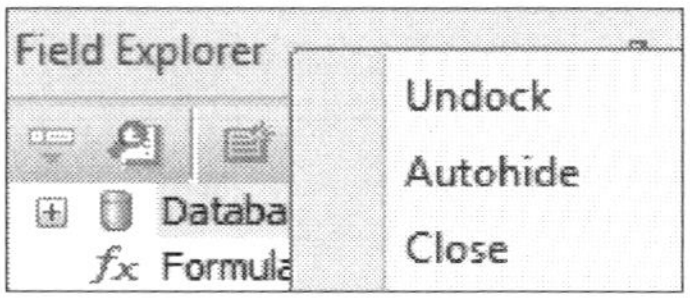

Figure 5-11 Explorer window shortcut menu

Exercise 5.1: Create Your First Report From Scratch

1. Click on the **BLANK REPORT** link on the Start Page. You will see the Database Expert dialog box. All of the wizards have this screen except for the OLAP Cube Report wizard.

2. Add the Contact table to the **SELECTED TABLES** list, then click OK. You will see an empty design tab.

How To Add The Fields To A Report

There are several ways to add fields in the Field Explorer to a report, as discussed below. If you are not familiar with the techniques discussed, take some time to try each of them and see which one you like the best.

① Drag the field to the report.
② Select the field. Click the **INSERT TO REPORT** button on the Field Explorer toolbar, then click in the report where you want to place the field.
③ Right-click on the field that you want to add to the report and select **INSERT TO REPORT** on the shortcut menu, then click in the report where you want to place the field.

> If you add a field to the report from the preview tab, the value in the field will be displayed instead of the field name.

Add The Fields To The Report

1. On the Field Explorer window click on the plus sign in front of the **DATABASE FIELDS** option, then click on the plus sign in front of the Contact table. You will see all of the fields in the table.

2. Drag the Company field to the **DETAILS** section. Notice that a field heading is automatically added to the page header section.

> If you add a field to a section other then the details section, a field heading will not automatically be added to the page header section. Field headings are only added automatically when the field is added to the details section.

As you add fields to the report you will see triangles called **GUIDELINES**, automatically being added to the beginning or end of the field. Text and date fields will have the guideline marker at the beginning of the field. Numeric fields will have the guideline marker at the end of the field. In Figure 5-12, the Customer Name and Order Date fields have the guideline markers at the beginning of the field. The Order ID and Unit Price fields have the guideline marker at the end of the field. These markers let you know visually where a field starts or ends on the report. Each field also has brackets around it to let you know how long the field is. You will learn more about guidelines in the next lesson.

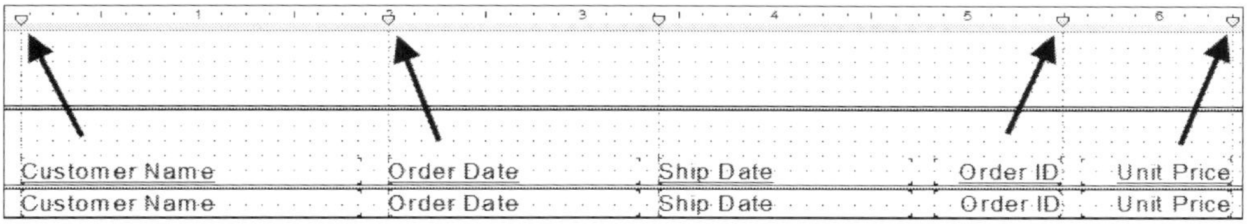

Figure 5-12 Guidelines illustrated

As a general rule, the brackets for one field should not be inside of the brackets for another field, unless you are combining objects and fields.

Overlapping fields, as illustrated in Figure 5-13, will cause the fields to print on top of each other as shown in Figure 5-14.

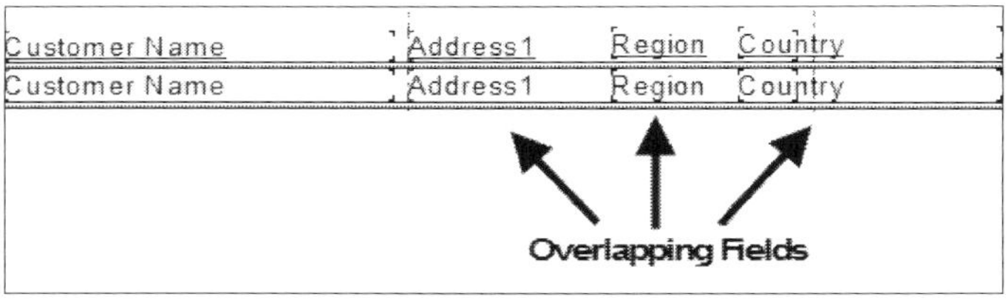

Figure 5-13 Fields overlapped in the design tab

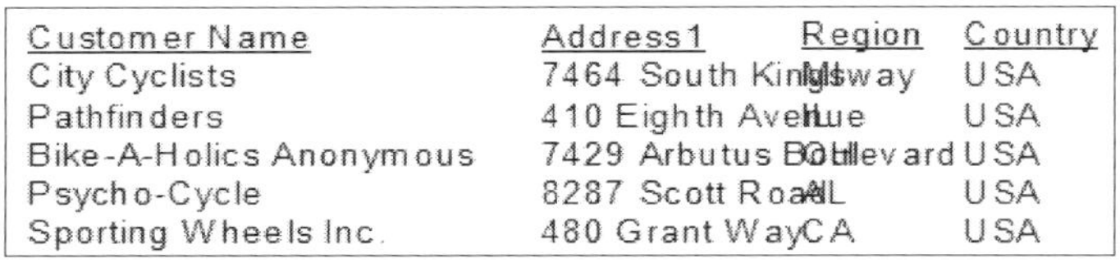

Figure 5-14 Overlapped fields shown in the preview tab

3. Add the following fields to the **DETAILS** section: Address 1, State and Zip Code. When you are finished, the report layout should look like the one shown in Figure 5-15.

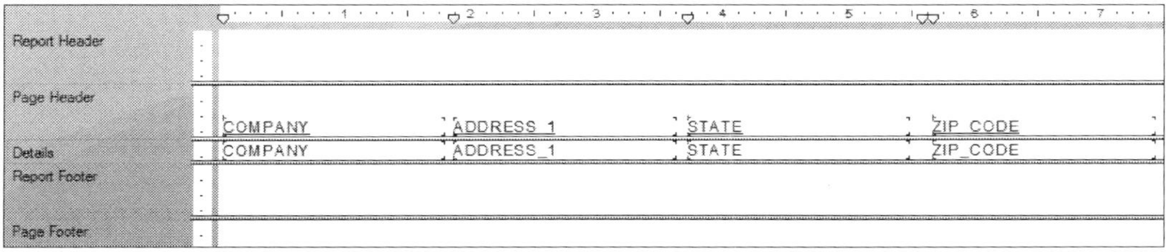

Figure 5-15 Report layout

> The green check marks illustrated in the Field Explorer in Figure 5-16 indicate that the field has been added to the report or is being used in a formula field that is being used on the report.

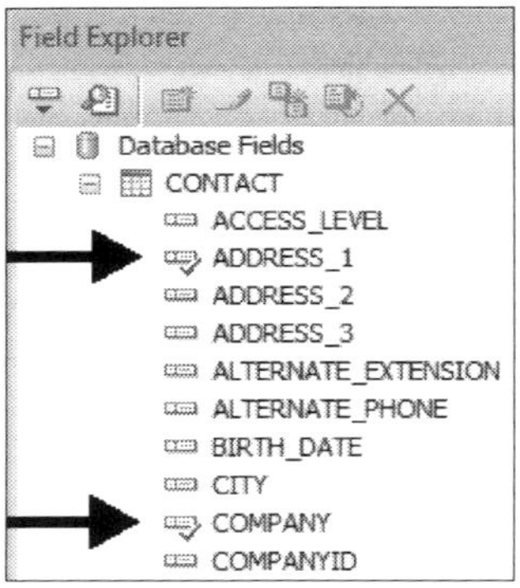

Figure 5-16 Checked fields illustrated

> **Find In Field Explorer Option**
>
> If selected, this option will highlight the field in the Field Explorer window. I am not sure of the benefit of this feature because if you have the tool tips option turned on, you can see which table the field is in by holding the mouse pointer over the field on the design window. This option is on the shortcut menu when you select a field.

4. Save the report in your folder. Type `L5.1 Contact information` as the file name. If prompted to generate the data to save, click Yes.

5. Preview the report. It should look like the one shown in Figure 5-17. Not bad for your first time creating a report from scratch. Close the report. If prompted to save the changes, click Yes.

COMPANY	ADDRESS 1	STATE	ZIP CODE
HAL's Consulting Corp	10 Countdown Loop	OR	97800
A1 Services-US Operations	2131 W. Tiny Rd.	NY	20122
Twelfth Dream	2010 Act Way	CA	94063
CH TechONE	13 East 54th St.	NY	10008
Modern Electric Supply	1919 Tecoma Dr.	FL	34655
Liberty Savings & Loan	100 E Bayard St	NY	13148
Mears Insurance	172 Edison Street	Cheshire	CH1 4PL
Django Consulting	14 East St		
Duke Industries	4075 Santa Monica Frwy	CA	90029

Figure 5-17 L5.1 Contact information report

Adding More Than One Field To The Report At The Same Time

There are two options that you can select from to add more than one field to the report at the same time.

① Click on a field, then press and hold down the **CTRL** key and click on the other fields that you want to add in the Field Explorer.
② Clicking on a field, then holding down the **SHIFT** key will let you select fields that are next to each other. If you click on the Address 1 field in the Contact table shown earlier in Figure 5-16 and hold down the Shift key and then click on the Birth Date field, all of the fields between these two fields will be selected.
③ Once you have selected all of the fields, drag them to the report.

Exercise 5.2: Create A Report Using Multiple Tables

In the previous exercise the report that you created was based on one table. Many of the reports that you will need to create will use two or more tables. The report that you will create in this exercise will use more than one table.

Select The Tables And Add The Fields To The Report

1. Open a blank report and add the Contact, Contact Note and Company tables to the report.

You can add more than one table at the same time by clicking on the first table that you want to add, then press and hold down the Shift key and select the other tables. You can also double-click on the table in the **AVAILABLE DATA SOURCES** section to add it to the Selected Tables list.

2. Click on the **LINKS** tab and make the dialog box larger. This will make it easier to see how the tables are linked.

The Database Expert calls the screen that you link tables on, the **LINKS** screen. The wizards call the same screen the **LINK** screen. They both do the exact same thing, so I don't know why they have slightly different names.

The **ORDER LINKS** button opens the dialog box shown in Figure 5-18. It is used to verify the order of how the tables are connected. Most of the time, the order that is automatically selected is what you need.

When you are using several tables it is a good idea to check the link order to make sure that the links are correct, because an incorrect linking order will produce an outcome different then what you expect.

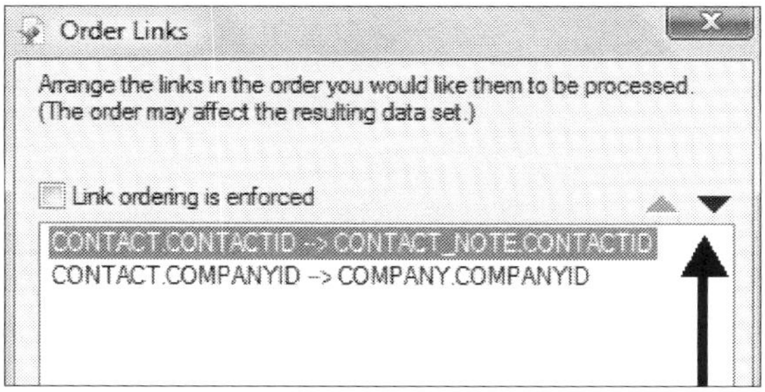

Figure 5-18 Order Links dialog box

If you need to rearrange the order of the links, click on the link that you need to move, then click the **UP** or **DOWN** arrow to move the link, as illustrated above in Figure 5-18.

If you are using a command or query as the basis of the report you do not have to create links because the links are created and stored in the command or query. Linking data in tables is an important concept to understand and will be covered in detail after you finish creating this report.

3. Click OK to close the Database Expert dialog box.

4. Add the following fields in the Contact table to the details section: First Name, Last Name and Company.

5. Add the Address 1 field in the Company table to the details section. Figure 5-19 shows the report layout.

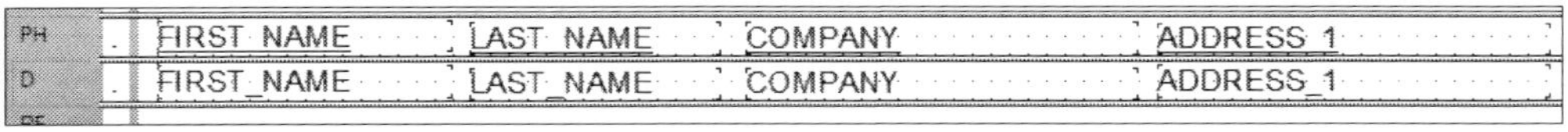

Figure 5-19 Fields added to the report

6. Save the report. Type `L5.2 Contact list` as the file name. Leave the report open to complete the next part of the exercise.

How To Add And Remove Databases And Tables

It is possible that during the report design process you may need to add or delete a database or table. You just realized that you do not need any fields from the Contact Note table and want to remove the table from the report. You can make changes like this on the design tab by following the steps below.

1. Right-click on the **DATABASE FIELDS** option in the Field Explorer. You will see the shortcut menu shown in Figure 5-20.

The **REFRESH** option shown in Figure 5-20 works the same as the Refresh button on the Navigation Tools toolbar. If you click on the **SHOW FIELD TYPE** option, the field type and field length if applicable, will be displayed at the end of the field as illustrated in Figure 5-21.

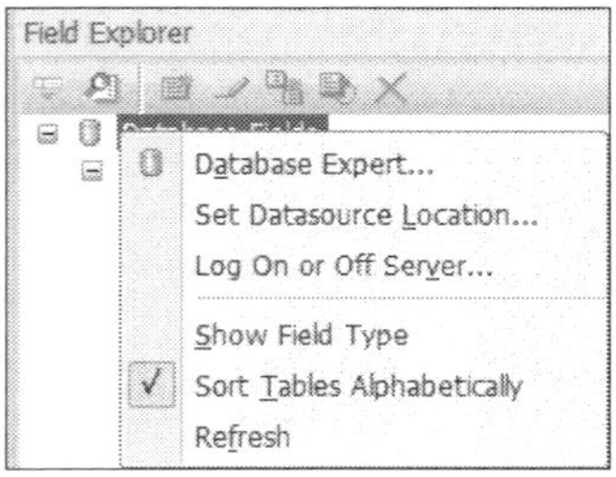

Figure 5-20 Field Explorer shortcut menu for databases, tables and fields

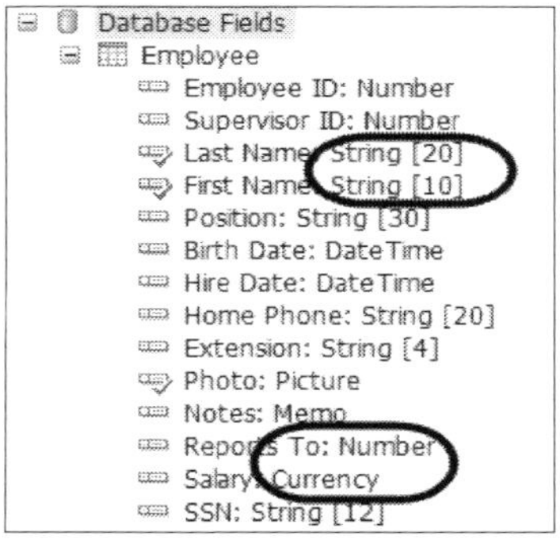

Figure 5-21 Field types and lengths illustrated

2. Select the **DATABASE EXPERT** option on the shortcut menu.

Other Ways To Open The Database Expert

① Right-click on a table in the Field Explorer and select Database Expert.
② Right-click on a field in the Field Explorer and select Database Expert.
③ Click the Database Expert button on the Expert Tools toolbar.

3. Click on the Contact Note table in the **SELECTED TABLES** list, then click the **<** button and click OK.

If you need to add a table, select it from the **AVAILABLE DATA SOURCES** list and add it to the Selected Tables list on the Database Expert dialog box.

4. Click OK to close the Database Expert dialog box, then preview the report. Click OK if prompted to refresh the report data. Your report should look like the one shown in Figure 5-22. Save the changes and close the report.

FIRST NAME	LAST NAME	COMPANY	ADDRESS 1
Allison	Mikola	CH TechONE	13 East 54th St.
Theodore	Barrett	Verge Records	4589 N. Taylor St.
Albert	Barry	Mercury Production Manager	66 Flash Rd.
Melissa	Pearce	CH TechONE	13 East 54th St.
Theodore	Barrett	Verge Records	4589 N. Taylor St.

Figure 5-22 L5.2 Contact list report

Relational Databases

Earlier in this lesson you learned a little about linking tables. The reason tables can be linked is because there is a relationship between them, thus the term "Relational Databases". Yes, this is a complicated topic and there are a lot of books on the concepts associated with relational databases and how to create them, so I won't bore you with the details, but please hear me out and don't skip this section.

If the databases that you will use out in the real world are created properly, you will not have to learn a lot about linking or relational databases, because Crystal Reports will create the links that you need. This doesn't mean that you do not have to learn anything about these topics. A good introduction to databases would be to read Chapter 25, "Understanding Databases" in the Crystal Reports User Guide. The more of that chapter that you understand, the easier it will be for you to create meaningful reports.

While databases are not the primary focus of this book, it is important that you understand a little more than the fundamentals that were covered in Lesson 3. Now you will learn how all of the components fit together. The reason that you need to understand databases is because they are the foundation for the reports that you will create and modify. If you have never created a database, or have very little experience creating them, the next few sections in this lesson will be your crash course in databases, relationships and linking. Figures 5-23 and 5-24 illustrate the layout of two tables.

Orders			
Order ID	Order Date	Order Amount	Cust ID
1000	1/2/2005	$263.99	48
1001	1/2/2005	$322.45	57
1002	1/3/2005	$196.00	3
1003	1/4/2005	$124.99	48

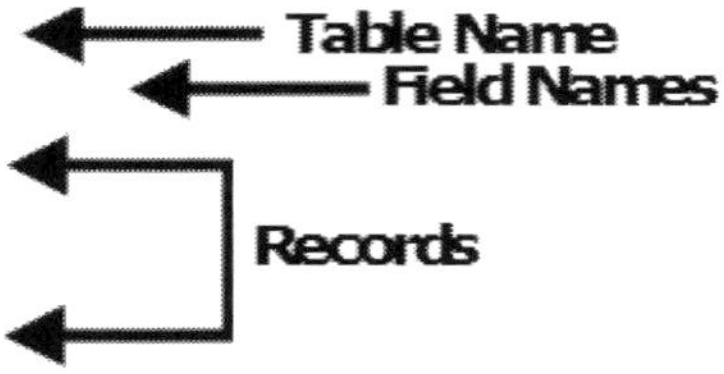

Figure 5-23 Orders table layout

Orders Detail		
Order ID	Product ID	Quantity
1000	43	4
1000	76	2
1001	76	3
1001	10	2
1003	10	1
1004	25	3

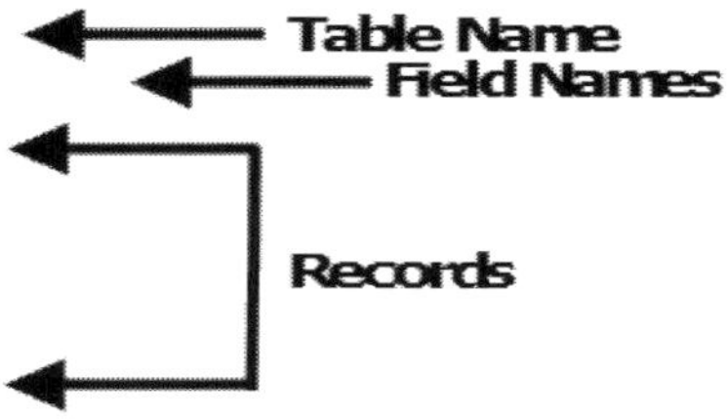

Figure 5-24 Orders Detail table layout

Primary Key Fields

Primary Key fields and ID fields are terms that are used interchangeably. I prefer to use the term ID field because primary key fields usually have "ID" as part of the field name.

> ID is short for identification. It is jargon that the programming community uses to reference a field that can be used to link the data in one table to the data in another table. I have to admit that ACT! databases have the strangest looking ID fields that I have ever seen.

All of the tables that you will use in the ACT! demo database have at least one ID field. Hopefully, you will find that this is also true out in the real world. The reason ID fields are used is because by design they provide a way for each record in the table to have a unique way to be identified.

I have taught several database classes and almost without fail, this topic causes a lot of confusion. For some reason, people want to create links on string (text fields). Please don't do that. It can cause you problems.

If you needed to create a report that showed all of the orders and what items were on each order, you would need a way to link the Orders and Orders Detail tables. Think of "linking" as having the ability to combine two or more tables "virtually" and being able to display the result of this "virtual linking" on a computer screen or on a printed report.

In Figures 5-23 and 5-24 above, the common ID field is the Order ID field. If you look at the data in the Orders Detail table, you will see that some records have the same Order ID number. That's okay. This means that some customers placed orders with more than one item. Each record in the Orders Detail table represents one item that a customer ordered. If you were to "virtually" join the data in the tables shown in Figures 5-23 and 5-24 above, it would look like the table shown in Figure 5-25.

This "virtual" join is what happens when tables are **LINKED**. If all of this data was stored in one table instead of two, at the very minimum, the Order Date and Order Amount fields would be repeated for every record that is in the Orders Detail table. Repetition of data is why this information is stored in two tables instead of one. It is considered poor table design to have the same information (other than fields that are used to join tables) stored in more than one table.

Orders				Orders Detail		
Order ID	Order Date	Order Amount	Cust ID	Order ID	Product ID	Quantity
1000	1/2/2005	$263.99	48	1000	43	4
1000	1/2/2005	$263.99	48	1000	76	2
1001	1/2/2005	$322.45	57	1001	76	3
1001	1/2/2005	$322.45	57	1001	10	2
1002	1/3/2005	$196.00	3			
1003	1/4/2005	$124.99	48	1003	10	1
				1004	25	3

Figure 5-25 Virtually joined tables

> Usually if you see a record in the Orders Detail table, like Order ID 1004 shown above in Figure 5-25, or any child table that is in a parent-child relationship, there is a problem with the data in at least one of the tables because all of the records in the child table should have at least one matching record in the parent table. Parent tables are used to get data from a child table.

Types Of Relationships

The Contact report that you just created required two tables. These tables are linked by a common field, the Company ID field. This field is what connects (joins) data from both tables and allows you to use data from both tables.

An ID field in the Contact table is how you find the matching record (known as a **ONE-TO-ONE RELATIONSHIP**) or records (known as a **ONE-TO-MANY RELATIONSHIP**, which is the most popular type of relationship) in another table. These are two of the most common types of relationships. The **MANY-TO-MANY RELATIONSHIP** is a third type of relationship. It is not used as much as the other two.

How Linking Works

More than likely, most reports that you create will require data from more than one table. Reports like the Product List report that you created, only used one table, so there is no linking involved. For reports that require two or more tables, the tables need to be linked. The tables are usually linked in the database. The links that you see on the Link screen are the same as the links in the database. When you create a report and need to view or modify the links, you can do so by opening the Database Expert and clicking on the Link tab. Even though most of the time the links that you need are created for you, it is important to understand what is going on behind the scenes, as they say.

The best way to understand the basic concept of linking tables is to look at the records or a portion of the records in the tables that need to be linked. When you create a report that you are not familiar with the data that is needed, you should take the time to look at the data in the tables. Figures 5-26 and 5-27 show the records in the Employee and Employee Addresses tables in another database. The field that these tables have in common is the Employee ID field, as shown below.

Employee : Table

Employee ID	Supervisor ID	Last Name	First Name	Position	Birth Date	Hire Date
1	5	Davolio	Nancy	Sales Representativ	12/8/1972	3/29/1991
2		Fuller	Andrew	Vice President, Sale	2/19/1969	7/12/1991
3	5	Leverling	Janet	Sales Representativ	8/30/1971	2/27/1991
4	5	Peacock	Margaret	Sales Representativ	9/19/1973	3/30/1992
5	2	Buchanan	Steven	Sales Manager	3/4/1975	9/13/1992
6	5	Suyama	Michael	Sales Representativ	7/2/1963	9/13/1992
7	5	King	Robert	Sales Representativ	5/29/1972	11/29/1992
8	5	Callahan	Laura	Inside Sales Coordi	1/9/1974	1/30/1993
9	5	Dodsworth	Anne	Sales Representativ	1/27/1976	10/12/1993
10	2	Hellstern	Albert	Business Manager	3/13/1968	3/1/1993
11	10	Smith	Tim	Mail Clerk	6/6/1973	1/15/1993
12	10	Patterson	Caroline	Receptionist	9/11/1979	5/15/1993
13	2	Brid	Justin	Marketing Director	10/8/1977	1/1/1994
14	13	Martin	Xavier	Marketing Associate	1/30/1975	1/15/1994
15	13	Pereira	Laurent	Advertising Speciali	12/9/1970	2/1/1994

Record: 1 of 15

Figure 5-26 Employee table data

Employee Addresses : Table

Employee ID	Address1	Address2	City	Region	Country	Postal Code
1	507 - 20th Ave. E.		Port Moody	BC	Canada	V3D 4F6
2	908 W. Capital Way	Suite 100	Coquitlam	BC	Canada	V3H4J7
3	722 Moss Bay Blvd.		Vancouver	BC	Canada	V6M 8S9
4	4110 Old Redmond Rd.		Richmond	BC	Canada	V5S 6H7
5	14 Garrett Hill		London		UK	SW1 8JR
6	Coventry House		London		UK	EC2 7JR
7	Edgeham Hollow	Apt #243	London		UK	RG1 9SP
8	4726 - 11th Ave. N.E.		New Westmins	BC	Canada	V7J 5G5
9	7 Houndstooth Rd.		Nottingham		UK	WG2 7LT
10	13920 S.E. 40th Street		Burnaby	BC	Canada	V2C 8H3
11	30301 - 166th Ave. N.E.	Apt #3D	North Vancouve	BC	Canada	V3K 2G9
12	16 Maple Lane		West Vancouve	BC	Canada	V3L 5S3
13	2 impasse du Soleil		Haguenau	Bas-Rhin	France	67500
14	9 place de la Liberte		Schiltigheim	Bas-Rhin	France	67300
15	7 rue Nationale		Strasbourg	Bas-Rhin	France	67000

Record: 15 of 15

Figure 5-27 Employee Addresses table data

Depending on the table structure, tables can have more than one field that they can be linked by. An example of this would be the Orders Detail table. This table has an ID field that would let you link it to the Orders table. There is a Product ID field in the Orders Detail table that would let you retrieve the Product Name from another table (the Product table) to print on the report, instead of printing the Product ID number. Displaying the product name on the report is more meaningful then displaying the Product ID field, which contains a number. If you are asking why the Product Name is not stored in the Orders Detail table, there are two reasons.

① The ID field takes up less space, thereby keeping the size of the Orders Detail table smaller.

② If a Product Name has to be changed for any reason, it only has to be changed in the Product table. Every place that the Product Name field is used on any report would automatically be updated with the revised product name. If the product name was stored in the Orders Detail table, every record in the Orders Detail table that had that product name would have to be changed, as well as, any other table that stored the product name. That would be a lot of extra work.

Join Types

Hopefully, you are still with me. Don't worry, the relational database "lecturette" is almost over. There are several types of links that can be created. These different types of links are called **JOIN TYPES**. Crystal Reports has several join types that you can select from. Each join type will return different results from the same tables, which you will see in Figures 5-28 to 5-31. **INNER** joins are the most common.

If you use any of the three **OUTER** join types discussed below, the order that the tables are added to the report is important. The four join types that are explained in Table 5-3 are the join types that are automatically created and are the most common. The other join types have to be created manually. They are covered later in this lesson.

The "matching" discussed in Table 5-3 is usually done on **ID** fields.

Join Type	How Records Are Selected
Inner	Records that have matching records in both tables, as illustrated in Figure 5-28.
Left Outer	Selects all records from one table (usually the left most table on the Links tab) and only matching records in the table on the right, as illustrated in Figure 5-29.
Right Outer	Selects all records from the right table and only matching records from the table on the left, as illustrated in Figure 5-30. This join type works the opposite of the Left Outer join type.
Full Outer	Selects all records from both tables whether or not there are matching records in the other table, as illustrated in Figure 5-31. Full Outer joins are also known as a **UNION** join type.

Table 5-3 Join types explained

In the Orders and Orders Detail tables, the Orders table is known as the **LEFT** table and should be added to the list of tables for the report first. The Orders Detail table is known as the **RIGHT** table and should be added to the list of tables after the Orders table. The reason the tables need to be added in this order is because for each record in the Orders table, there can be multiple records in the Orders Detail table that have the same ID. Earlier in this lesson you learned about the Order Links dialog box. If the tables were added incorrectly you can use the options on the Order Links dialog box to change the order.

Join Type Examples

When walking through these examples compare the data in the example to the data shown earlier in Figure 5-25. The examples in this section illustrate how the same data would be retrieved differently depending on the join type that is selected. This is why it is important to understand linking and join types.

In Figure 5-28, the record for Order ID 1002 in the Orders table would not be retrieved in an Inner join because there is no related record in the Orders Detail table. The arrows between the tables represent the flow of the data.

In Figure 5-29, the record for Order ID 1004 would not be retrieved from the Orders Detail table in a Left Outer join because there is no related record in the Orders table.

In Figure 5-30, the record for Order ID 1002 in the Orders table would not be retrieved in a Right Outer join because there is no related record in the Orders Detail table.

In Figure 5-31, all records would be retrieved in a Full Outer join whether there is a related record in the other table or not.

Orders			
Order ID	Order Date	Order Amount	Cust ID
1000	1/2/2005	$263.99	48
1001	1/2/2005	$322.45	57
1003	1/4/2005	$124.99	48

Orders Detail		
Order ID	Product ID	Quantity
1000	43	4
1000	76	2
1001	76	3
1001	10	2
1003	10	1

Figure 5-28 Inner join recordset

Orders			
Order ID	Order Date	Order Amount	Cust ID
1000	1/2/2005	$263.99	48
1001	1/2/2005	$322.45	57
1002	1/3/2005	$196.00	3
1003	1/4/2005	$124.99	48

Orders Detail		
Order ID	Product ID	Quantity
1000	43	4
1000	76	2
1001	76	3
1001	10	2
1003	10	1

Figure 5-29 Left Outer join recordset

Orders			
Order ID	Order Date	Order Amount	Cust ID
1000	1/2/2005	$263.99	48
1001	1/2/2005	$322.45	57
1003	1/4/2005	$124.99	48

Orders Detail		
Order ID	Product ID	Quantity
1000	43	4
1000	76	2
1001	76	3
1001	10	2
1003	10	1
1004	25	3

Figure 5-30 Right Outer join recordset

Orders			
Order ID	Order Date	Order Amount	Cust ID
1000	1/2/2005	$263.99	48
1001	1/2/2005	$322.45	57
1002	1/3/2005	$196.00	3
1003	1/4/2005	$124.99	48

Orders Detail		
Order ID	Product ID	Quantity
1000	43	4
1000	76	2
1001	76	3
1001	10	2
1003	10	1
1004	25	3

Figure 5-31 Full Outer join recordset

Tables Without A Link

If you added the Orders and Orders Detail tables to a report but did not link them, Crystal Reports would not know which record in the Orders table went with which record in the Orders

Detail table. The result would be that each order record would be displayed (matched) with each of the records in the Orders Detail table as shown in Figure 5-32. In total, 24 records would print on the report. When a report uses more than one table, this is usually not what you want.

Orders			
Order ID	Order Date	Order Amount	Cust ID
1000	1/2/2005	$263.99	48
1000	1/2/2005	$263.99	48
1000	1/2/2005	$263.99	48
1000	1/2/2005	$263.99	48
1000	1/2/2005	$263.99	48
1000	1/2/2005	$263.99	48
1001	1/2/2005	$322.45	57
1001	1/2/2005	$322.45	57
1001	1/2/2005	$322.45	57
1001	1/2/2005	$322.45	57
1001	1/2/2005	$322.45	57
1001	1/2/2005	$322.45	57
		.	
		.	
		.	
1003	1/4/2005	$124.99	48

Orders Detail		
Order ID	Product ID	Quantity
1000	43	4
1000	76	2
1001	76	3
1001	10	2
1003	10	1
1004	25	3
1000	43	4
1000	76	2
1001	76	3
1001	10	2
1003	10	1
1004	25	3
	.	
	.	
	.	
1004	25	3

Figure 5-32 Tables not joined recordset

The reports shown in Figures 5-33 and 5-34 have the same three fields: Customer Name, Product ID and Order ID.

The report shown in Figure 5-33 has the **LEFT OUTER** join between the Customer and Orders tables.

Customer Name	Product ID	Order ID
City Cyclists	2,201	1
Deals on Wheels	5,205	1,002
Deals on Wheels	102,181	1,002
Warsaw Sports, Inc.	2,213	1,003
Warsaw Sports, Inc.	5,402	1,003
Bikes and Trikes	402,002	1,004
SAB Mountain	1,101	1,005

Figure 5-33 Left Outer join report

The report shown in Figure 5-34 has the **RIGHT OUTER** join between the Orders and Orders Detail tables. As you can see, the output is completely different for these reports. Hopefully, these reports demonstrate why understanding table structures, types of relationships, linking and join types is important.

Customer Name	Product ID	Order ID
City Cyclists	2,209	1,387
City Cyclists	3,305	1,387
City Cyclists	302,201	1,387
City Cyclists	1,108	2,277
City Cyclists	2,207	2,277
City Cyclists	1,101	1,033
City Cyclists	1,105	1,033

Figure 5-34 Right Outer join report

Recursive Join

In addition to the join types discussed above, there is another join type called **RECURSIVE JOIN**. This type of join is not always obvious when looking at the table structures. A recursive join occurs when the same data is stored in two different ID fields in the same table. This is not the same as a parent/child (also known as a master/detail) relationship because this type of relationship does not require two tables like the Orders and Orders Detail tables that you read about earlier in this lesson.

An example of a recursive join is in the Employee table, discussed earlier. The Supervisor ID field in the Employee table contains the Employee ID of another record in the Employee table. This is because supervisors are also employees. Refer back to Figure 5-26. Seven employees have the number 5 in the Supervisor ID field (the second field from the left). This is because they all have the same supervisor, Steven Buchanan, whose Employee ID is number 5.

Recursive Join Functionality In ACT!

Fields that start with the word **PARENT** and end with ID, like the Parent Company ID field in the Company table in the ACT! demo database is an example of a field that could be used to create a hierarchical report.

The ParentGroup ID field in the Company table contains the Group ID of a different group in the Company table. The ParentGroup ID field contains the group that the subgroup is a member of. Recursive joins are used to create hierarchical reports, which you will learn how to create in Lesson 19.

Smart Linking

Smart linking is enabled by default. Crystal Reports uses this feature to create links based on an index or common fields in tables. You can change the default smart linking option on the Database tab of the Options dialog box. Some people turn this option off and always create the links manually to make sure that the correct join type is selected. The reason people turn this feature off is because tables are joined on fields that have the same name and data type, which may not be what you want.

View The Current Links

1. Open a blank report and add the Contact, Company and Company Opportunity tables.

2. Click on the Links tab and click the **CLEAR LINKS** button. Click Yes, when prompted if you are sure.

How To Manually Create Links

When you have the need to manually create links, follow the steps below.

1. Select a field in one table and drag it to a field in the other table. In this example, select the Contact field in the Contact table and drag it to the Create Date field in the Company table, then release the mouse button.

Fields that are used to link tables must have the same data type. You could not create a link between a date field and a string field. If there is something wrong with the link that you are trying to create, you will see a warning message similar to the one shown in Figure 5-35. This message lets you know that the link that you are trying to create is not valid.

2. Click OK to close the Visual Linking Editor message window, then click OK again.

Figure 5-35 Link error warning message

Manual Join Types

As discussed earlier, there are other join and link types that can be used to link tables. Table 5-4 explains the enforce join type options. Table 5-5 explains the link types.

Enforce Join Type	Description
Not Enforced	Selecting this option doesn't mean that the link will be included in the SQL statement. At least one field must be used to join tables in order for the linking criteria to be included in the SQL statement.
Enforced From	Selecting this option forces the link to the right table. When a field from the right table is used, but not one from the left table, the SQL statement requires that both tables be referenced.
Enforced To	Selecting this option forces the link from the left table, whether or not a field is used from the right table. This means that the SQL statement will include both tables.
Enforced Both	Selecting this option forces the link between the tables, regardless of where the fields that are used in the report are stored.

Table 5-4 Enforce Join types explained

Link Type	Description
Equal =	Creates a recordset where the link field has related records in the left and right tables.
Greater Than >	Creates a recordset where the link field from the left table is greater than the linked field in the right table.
Greater Than or Equal To >=	Creates a recordset where the link field from the left table is greater than or equal to the linked field in the right table.
Less Than <	Creates a recordset where the link field from the left table is less than the linked field in the right table.
Less Than or Equal To <=	Creates a recordset where the link field from the left table is less than or equal to the linked field in the right table.
Not Equal !=	Creates a recordset where the link field from the left table does not match the linked field in the right table.

Table 5-5 Link Types explained

Exercise 5.3: Create A Contact Opportunity Report

In this exercise you will create a report that displays contacts and their opportunities.

1. Open a blank report and add the Contact, Contact Opportunity and Opportunity tables. On the Links tab, clear all of the links.

2. Create the links in Table 5-6, then click Finish to close the Database Expert dialog box.

Link This Field	To This Field
Contact_ContactID	Contact_Opportunity_ContactID
Contact_Opportunity_OpportunityID	Opportunity_OpportunityID

Table 5-6 Links to create

3. Delete the Print Date field in the page header section, if it's there.

4. File ⇒ Page Setup. Select the Landscape option, then click OK.

Add The Fields

1. Add the Contact and Company fields in the Contact table to the details section. Make the fields smaller.

2. Add the Opportunity Name, Create Date, Days Open, Total, Status and Actual Close Date fields in the Opportunity table to the details section. Your report layout should look like the one shown in Figure 5-36. As shown, all of the fields currently do not fit on the report.

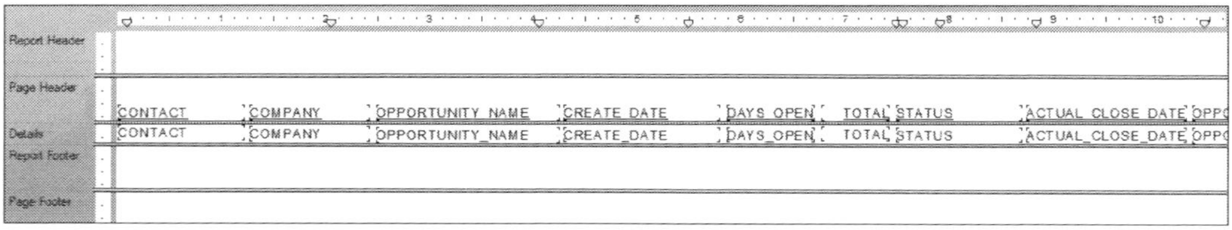

Figure 5-36 Contact opportunity report layout

3. Save the report. Type `L5.3 Contact opportunities` as the file name.

4. Preview the report. It should look like the one shown in Figure 5-37. Close the report.

CONTACT	COMPANY	OPPORTUNITY NAME	CREATE DATE	DAYS OPEN	TOTAL	STATUS	ACTUAL CLOSE DATE	OPP(
Amanda Form	A1 Services-US O	New Opportunity	10/30/2008 11:08:59AM	0	12,000.00	Closed - Lost	10/30/2009 7:00:00AM	{66D
Amanda Form	A1 Services-US O	New Opportunity	5/20/2007 7:28:29PM	96	12,000.00	Closed - Lost	8/23/2009 7:00:00AM	{6520
Amanda Form	A1 Services-US O	New Opportunity	5/20/2007 7:29:56PM	102	2,000.00	Closed - Lost	8/30/2009 7:00:00AM	{26E(
Amanda Form	A1 Services-US O	A1 Services US Operations-	5/15/2007 8:35:17PM	12	2,000.00	Open	12/31/9999 11:59:59PM	{6411
Mary Bailey	Liberty Savings & L	Liberty S&L-VT Operations	4/18/2008 8:36:20PM	132	12,000.00	Open	12/31/9999 11:59:59PM	{0E0E
Irene Murphy	Mears Insurance	New Opportunity	5/21/2007 3:06:48AM	389	12,000.00	Closed - Lost	6/12/2008 5:00:00AM	{FA8
Dan Minnick	Django Consulting	New Opportunity	5/21/2007 2:25:14AM	190	2,000.00	Closed - Lost	11/25/2009 8:00:00AM	{565E
Dan Minnick	Django Consulting	Django Consulting-Install Te	4/18/2008 7:54:13PM	256	12,000.00	Closed - Won	12/30/2008 6:00:00AM	{3D2

Figure 5-37 L5.3 Contact opportunities report

The reason that the information in the Contact, Company, Opportunity Name and Status fields is repeated, is because on some opportunities the contact ordered more than one item. As you can see, all of the reports that you have created so far in this book need to be edited and formatted so that they are more presentable. You will learn how to edit and format reports in the next few lessons.

EDITING REPORTS

As the title of this lesson indicates, you will learn editing techniques that you can use to make the reports that you create look better. After completing the exercises in this lesson you will be able to:

- ☑ Understand the editing and formatting options on shortcut menus
- ☑ Select objects
- ☑ Align objects
- ☑ Use guidelines
- ☑ Understand the purpose of the grid
- ☑ Resize objects

Shortcut Menus

Crystal Reports has several shortcut menus that you can use instead of selecting menu options or clicking on toolbar buttons. As you will see, you will spend a lot of time formatting and editing reports. A great time saver in my opinion to completing these tasks is using the options on the shortcut menus.

The options will change on the shortcut menu depending on the object that is right-clicked on.

In addition to the object shortcut menu, there is a general shortcut menu available when you right-click on an empty space in the design or preview window as shown in Figure 6-1. Several of the options on this shortcut menu are explained in detail later in this lesson. The options that aren't, are explained below.

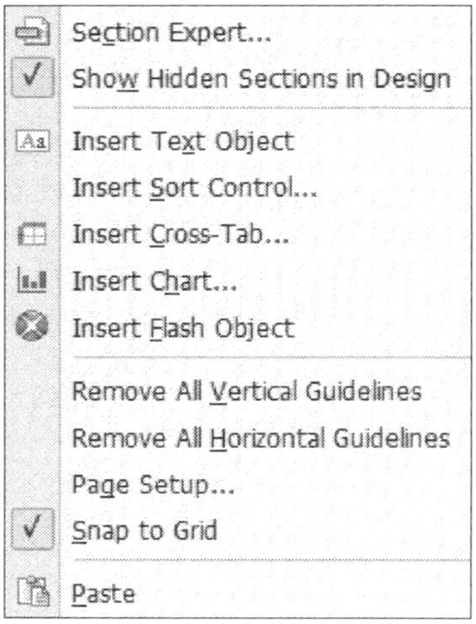

Figure 6-1 General shortcut menu

You can also open this shortcut menu by right-clicking on the design or preview tab.

① **Show Hidden Sections In Design** By default, this option is turned on. It is used to view hidden sections of the report in the design window. If this option is turned off (not checked), hidden sections have a small space between the sections, as shown in Figure 6-2. Suppressed sections have slanted lines as shown in Figure 6-3.

② **NEW** **Insert Sort Control** [See Lesson 14, Bind Sort Control]

③ **Insert Cross-Tab** Is used to add a cross-tab object to the report.

④ **Insert Chart** Is used to add a chart to the report.

⑤ **NEW** **Insert Flash Object** Is used to add a Flash (SWF) file to the report.

⑥ **Remove All Vertical Guidelines** This option will hide (not delete) vertical guidelines (1).

⑦ **Remove All Horizontal Guidelines** This option will hide (not delete) horizontal guidelines (1).

⑧ **Page Setup** [See Lesson 14, Page Setup Options]

(1) These options are not the same as clearing the **GUIDELINES** option on the Layout tab of the Options dialog box.

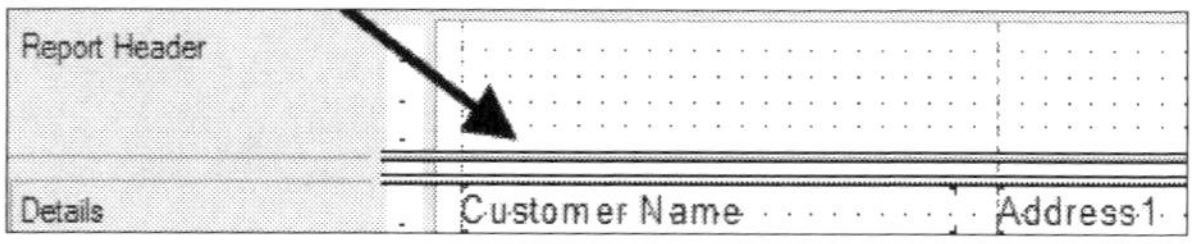

Figure 6-2 Page header section with the Show Hidden Sections In Design option turned off

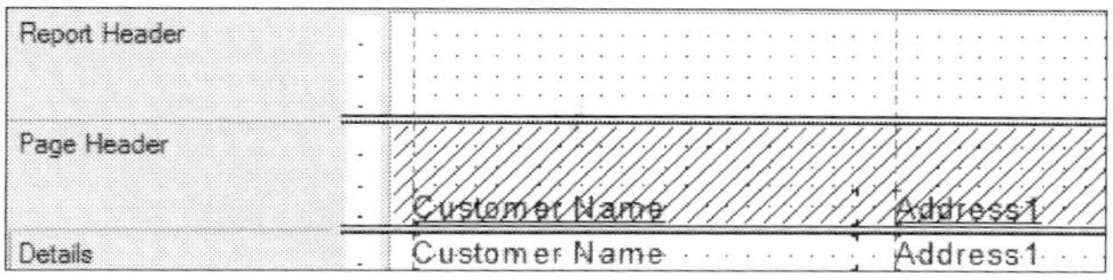

Figure 6-3 Page header section with slanted lines

Selecting Fields And Objects

A lot of the report editing that you will do requires fields and other objects to be selected. Often, you will have the need to apply the same changes to several fields or objects.

To select a single field or object, click on it with the left mouse button. When an object is selected you will see a blue frame around it, as illustrated in Figure 6-4. You will also see squares.

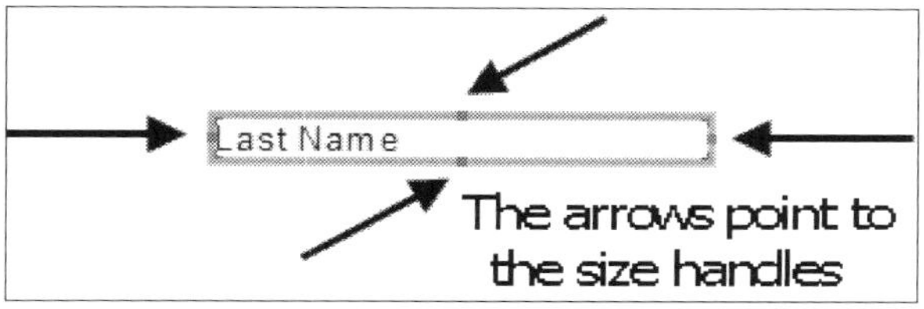

Figure 6-4 Field selected and size handles illustrated

These squares are called **SIZE HANDLES**. They allow you to change the size of the object to make it wider, longer, shorter or smaller. You will learn how to resize objects later in this lesson.

When I use the word "field", I am referring to a field in the details section of the report, or a field from a table or a calculated field that you create. "Objects" refer to items like the field heading, a text field or an image.

Selecting Multiple Fields And Objects

There are three ways to select the fields that you need, as discussed below.

① Click on one field or object. Press and hold down the **CTRL** or **SHIFT** key and click on the other fields or objects that you need to select.

② Draw what is called a **MARQUEE** or **LASSO** around the fields or objects with the mouse. To do this successfully, the objects need to be near each other, either side by side or up and down from each other. To use this technique, no objects can already be selected. Click outside of the first field or object. Hold the left mouse button down and draw around the objects that you need to select. You will see a frame being drawn. When you are finished selecting the objects and release the mouse button, you will see that several objects have been selected.

③ If you need to select all of the objects in one section of the report, right-click in the corresponding report section (page header, details, etc.) on the far left side of the design window and select the option, **SELECT ALL SECTION OBJECTS** as shown at the bottom of Figure 6-5.

The top of the shortcut menu lets you know which section of the report you are about to select all of the objects in. As shown in Figure 6-5, the objects that will be selected are in the page header section.

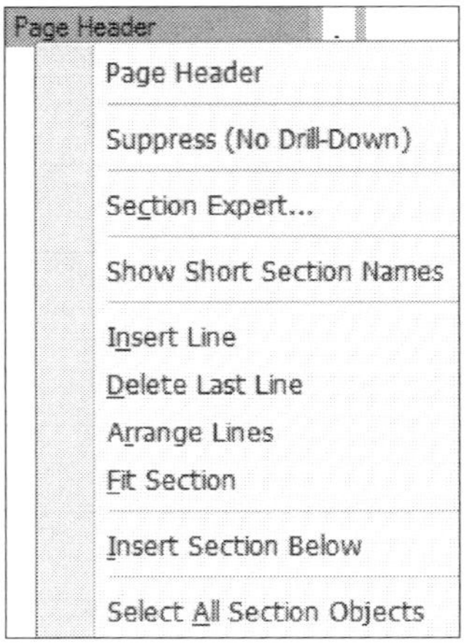

Figure 6-5 Report section shortcut menu

Exercise 6.1: Moving Objects

One of the tasks that you will do from time to time is rearrange fields and other objects on a report. This exercise will show you how to move fields and objects on a report.

1. Save the L4.3 report as `L6.1 Moving fields`. Make sure that you save the report in your folder.

2. On the design tab, drag the **PRICE** field in the details section to the right. Notice that the field heading also moved.

> Interestingly enough, when you have multiple objects selected, the last one that you select is the **MAIN OBJECT**. The main object is the one that the other selected objects emulate (follow). If you have multiple objects selected and you move the main object to a place in the report where it does not fit, none of the objects that are selected will be moved. If you move multiple objects to a location where some objects will fit, including the main object, the objects that will fit in the new location will be moved and those that will not fit, will not be moved.

Aligning Objects

In addition to moving objects, you will have the need to have multiple objects line up. The **ALIGN** option will help you line up several objects at the same time. Follow the steps below to learn how to align objects. Because everything on the report is currently aligned, you need to move an object to get it out of alignment to see how the align option works.

1. Drag the Price field heading to the right, as shown in Figure 6-6.

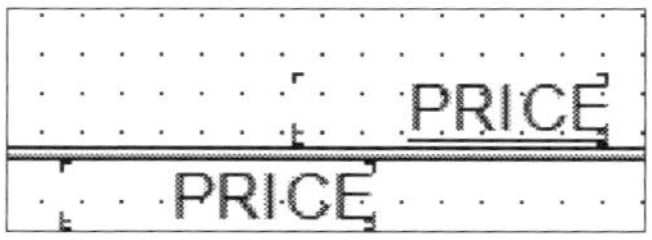

Figure 6-6 Field heading moved to the right

2. Select the Price field and heading, then right-click on the Price field.

In the step 2, you have to right-click on the object that has the alignment that you want duplicate. In this exercise you want to align the field heading with the field in the details section. If you right-clicked on the field heading in the step above and selected Align ⇒ Rights, the field in the details section would have been aligned on the right side with the field heading.

You can right-click on any object and select the **ALIGN** option. Just remember which object that you right-click on before selecting an align option, because you may get results different then what you expected. The alignment of the object that you right-click on will be applied to the other objects that are selected.

3. Align ⇒ Lefts, as shown in Figure 6-7. The field and heading should be where it was before you started this exercise.

   Table 6-1 explains the alignment options.

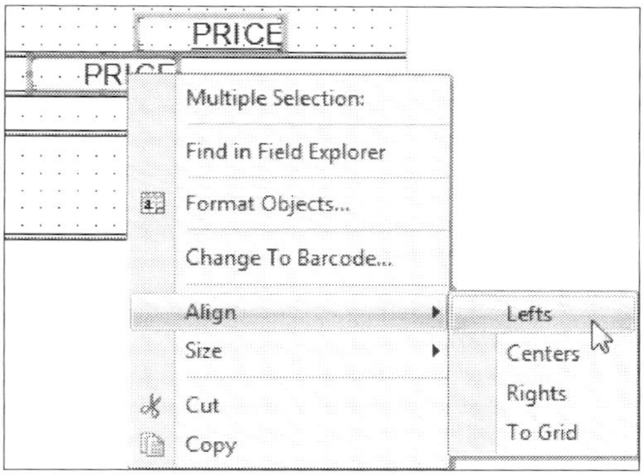

Figure 6-7 Alignment options illustrated

At the top of the shortcut menu if you see the words **MULTIPLE SELECTION**, as shown above in Figure 6-7, it means that multiple objects selected. When selecting multiple fields or objects, whatever change you make will be applied to all of the selected fields and objects as long as the change can be applied to the data type. Not all data types can have the same changes applied.

Align Option	How It Aligns
Lefts	Aligns on the left side of the object.
Centers	Aligns on the center of the object.
Rights	Aligns on the right side of the object.
To Grid	Aligns to the closest grid point of the object that you right-click on. You need to have the **GRID** option turned on to see how this feature works.

Table 6-1 Alignment options explained

Aligning Objects Horizontally

This type of alignment is very similar to the alignment options that you just learned about. The horizontal alignment option is useful when you manually add fields or objects to a report. If you rush and add fields to a report like I do, meaning that you just drop them on the report without paying attention to whether or not they are lined up properly, you will really appreciate this exercise. In order to demonstrate how this feature works, you need to rearrange objects on the report first.

1. Delete the Print Date field in the page header section.

2. Drag the Product ID and Price field headings up in the page header section, as shown in Figure 6-8.

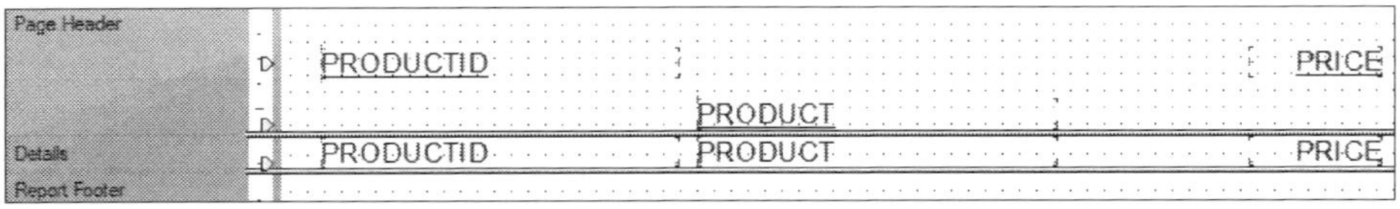

Figure 6-8 Field headings moved

3. Select the Product ID, Product and Price field headings, then right-click on the Product heading.

4. Align ⇒ Bottoms, as shown in Figure 6-9. The field headings should be back where they were before you started this exercise.

   Table 6-2 explains the horizontal alignment options on the shortcut menu.

   The alignment options shown in Figure 6-9 are only available when all of the selected objects are in the same section of the report.

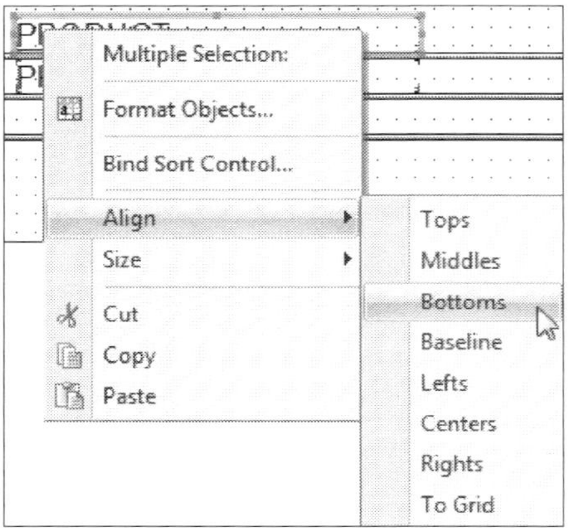

Figure 6-9 Horizontal alignment options

Align Option	How It Aligns
Tops	Aligns on the top of the object.
Middles	Aligns on the middle of the object.
Bottoms	Aligns on the bottom of the object.
Baseline	Aligns on the bottom of the text, not the bottom of the frame like all of the other alignment options discussed in this table. The baseline alignment option is useful when you are aligning objects that have a different font, font size or frame size.
Lefts	Aligns on the left side of the object.
Centers	Aligns on the center of the object.
Rights	Aligns on the right side of the object.

Table 6-2 Horizontal alignment options explained

Align Option	How It Aligns
To Grid	Aligns to the closest grid point of the object that you right-click on. You need to have the **GRID** option turned on to see how this works.

Table 6-2 Horizontal alignment options explained (Continued)

5. Click on a blank space on the report, then save the changes and leave the report open.

Guidelines

It may not always be easy to move or align objects. The guidelines feature helps you move and align objects easily. Guidelines let you move all objects that are anchored to the guideline at the same time. This means that you can move the field in the details section, the field heading in the page header section and all calculated or summary fields in other sections that are anchored to the guideline at the same time, without selecting them.

Guidelines are the **TRIANGLE BUTTONS** on the ruler at the top of the report, that are illustrated in Figure 6-10. The dotted lines that you see coming down from the guidelines in the page header and group header sections are **MARKERS** on the ruler. The reason you do not see the markers in the report header section in Figure 6-10 is because the section has a chart. The lines for the markers are behind the chart.

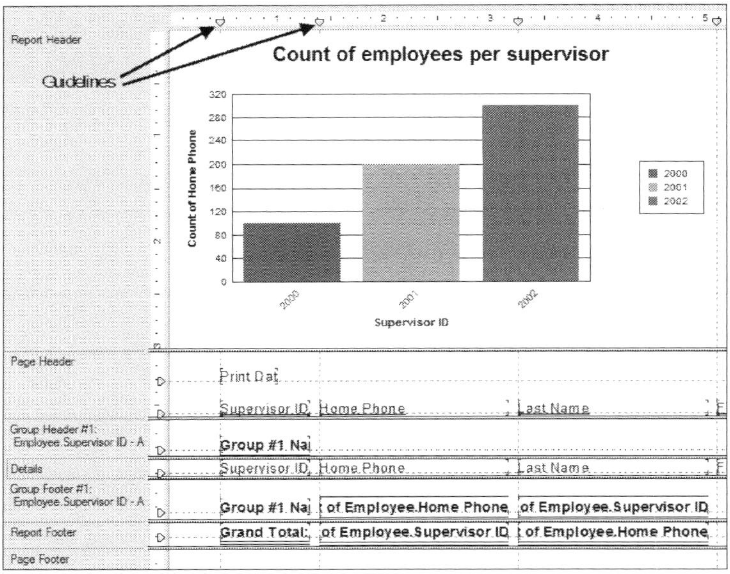

Figure 6-10 Guidelines illustrated

By default, the **VERTICAL GUIDELINE** option is enabled. To verify, File ⇒ Options ⇒ Click on the Layout tab. The **INSERT DETAIL FIELD HEADINGS** option should be checked.

If you moved the guideline that is anchored to the Last Name field shown above in Figure 6-10, all of the following objects would move at the same time: the field heading, the Sum of Employee.Supervisor ID field in the first group footer section and the Count of Employee.Home Phone field in the report footer section. Guidelines are automatically added to a report if any of the follow actions occur:

① A field is added to the details section.
② You right-click in a **REPORT SECTION** on the design tab, as shown earlier in Figure 6-5, then select **ARRANGE LINES**.
③ A summary field is added to the report.

You will see red marks on the side of objects that the guideline is on, if the object is anchored to a guideline. If you do not see the red marks, drag the object towards the guideline or drag the guideline towards the object.

How To Manually Add Guidelines

If the need arises to manually add guidelines, you can select one of the options below.

① Click on the horizontal ruler where you want to add a guideline.
② Click on the vertical ruler where you want to add a guideline.

> To remove a guideline, drag the triangle marker off of the ruler. Removing guidelines does not delete the objects attached to it.

Turning The Guidelines On

If you do not see the guidelines, View ⇒ Guidelines ⇒ Design, will turn the guidelines on (on the design tab), as shown in Figure 6-11.

The **PREVIEW** option will display the guidelines on the preview tab.

> By default, reports created with a wizard other then the **BLANK WIZARD** will have horizontal guidelines inserted automatically. You can manually add horizontal guidelines to reports created with the Blank wizard. The horizontal guidelines for all fields are at the top or bottom of the field or the baseline of the text in the field.

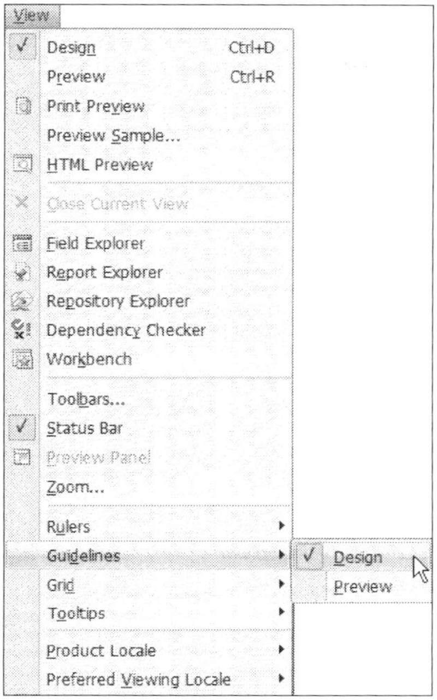

Figure 6-11 Option selected to turn the guidelines on

Using Guidelines To Move Objects

You can move all of the objects that are attached to the same guideline at the same time, by following the steps below.

1. Click on the guideline marker for the Product field on the L6.1 report and drag the marker to the right, to the 4 inch mark on the ruler, as illustrated in Figure 6-12.

   The field and field heading should have moved. If there were other objects anchored to this marker, like a total or summary field, they would have moved also.

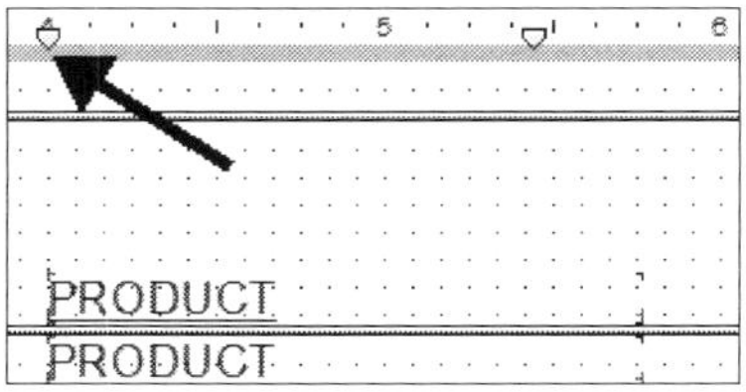

Figure 6-12 Product field marker moved

Guideline Issues

Depending on how much you use guidelines, you may notice that a few strange things happen with the guidelines. The ones that I have noticed are discussed in Table 6-3.

Issue	Solution
You delete objects from the report, but the guidelines stay.	Delete the guidelines that are no longer needed.
You moved an object, but the guideline did not move with it.	Move the object towards the guideline until the object snaps to the guideline.
You resized or moved an object and the object now appears to be attached to two guidelines.	Move the object away from the guideline that you do not want the object attached to and then resize the object and attach it to the guideline that you want.

Table 6-3 Guideline issues explained

Using The Grid

When you need to have greater precision over lining up objects on a report then the guidelines provide, you can turn on the **GRID** option. This option is not on by default. In addition to the grid option, turning on the **SNAP TO GRID** option provides additional precision. The Snap to grid option affects the guidelines.

View ⇒ Grid ⇒ Design, will display the grid on the design tab, as shown in Figure 6-13. The grid is the dot pattern in the background. When new fields or objects are added to the report manually, they are automatically placed on the closest grid position to where you release the mouse button. If you need to change any of the grid settings, they are located on the Layout tab on the Options dialog box.

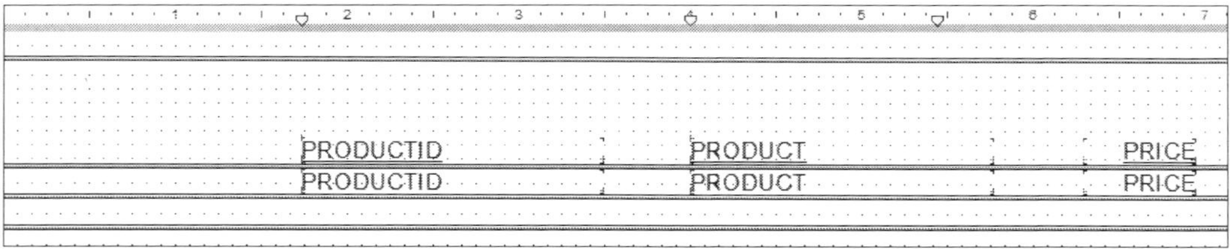

Figure 6-13 Report layout with the grid option turned on

Sizing Objects

When fields are added to a report, the size is the larger of the field or the field heading. It appears that Crystal Reports estimates the horizontal space needed for string fields. Sometimes this works and sometimes the data in a string field in the details section of the report gets cut off using this method. I suspect this happens because there is not enough space in the row to display all of the fields, so text fields are often truncated. This is what happened with the Product ID field on the report illustrated in Figure 6-14.

To fix this you need to resize the field. Depending on how close you placed the fields on the report, you may have to move the Product field to the right, before starting this exercise. To resize a field, follow the steps below.

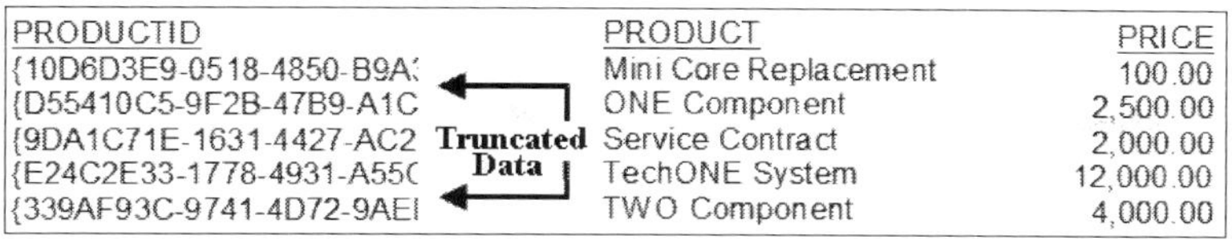

PRODUCTID	PRODUCT	PRICE
{10D6D3E9-0518-4850-B9A:	Mini Core Replacement	100.00
{D55410C5-9F2B-47B9-A1C	ONE Component	2,500.00
{9DA1C71E-1631-4427-AC2	Service Contract	2,000.00
{E24C2E33-1778-4931-A55(	TechONE System	12,000.00
{339AF93C-9741-4D72-9AEI	TWO Component	4,000.00

Figure 6-14 Truncated data illustrated

1. Click on the field that you need to resize. In this exercise, click on the Product ID field.

2. Place the mouse pointer on the right side of the field. The mouse pointer will change to a double arrow, as illustrated in Figure 6-15. Drag the **RESIZE HANDLE** that you saw earlier in Figure 6-4 to the right. You will see the color on the ruler change over the field, as illustrated in Figure 6-16. This may make it easier to see the size that you are adjusting the field to. Notice that the field heading was also resized.

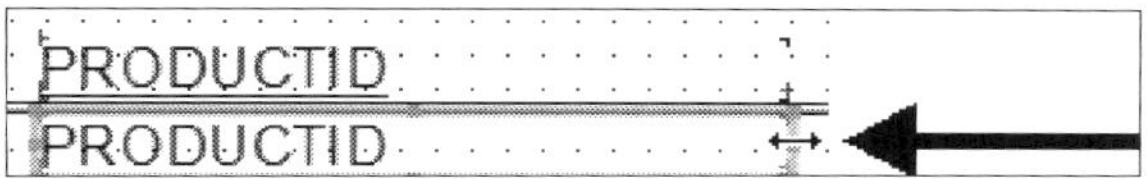

Figure 6-15 Mouse pointer in position to resize the field

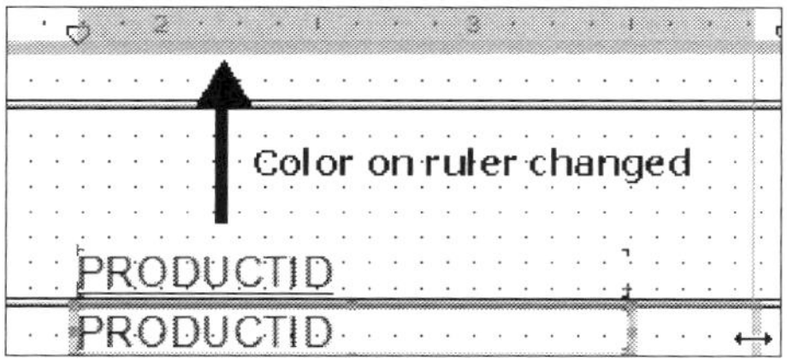

Figure 6-16 Color on ruler illustrated

3. Preview the report to see if you can now see all of the data in the Product ID field, as shown in Figure 6-17. Save the changes and leave the report open.

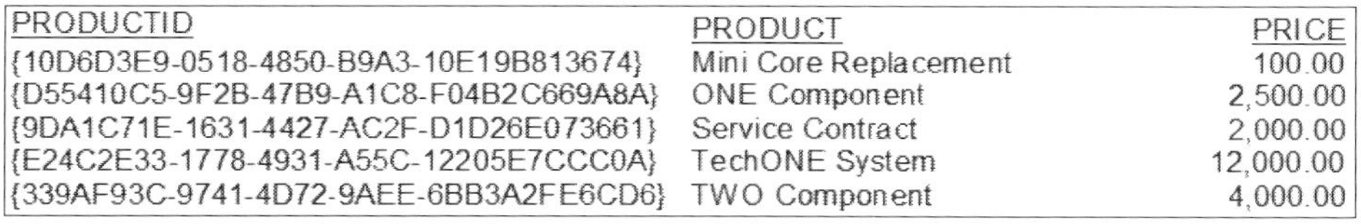

PRODUCTID	PRODUCT	PRICE
{10D6D3E9-0518-4850-B9A3-10E19B813674}	Mini Core Replacement	100.00
{D55410C5-9F2B-47B9-A1C8-F04B2C669A8A}	ONE Component	2,500.00
{9DA1C71E-1631-4427-AC2F-D1D26E073661}	Service Contract	2,000.00
{E24C2E33-1778-4931-A55C-12205E7CCC0A}	TechONE System	12,000.00
{339AF93C-9741-4D72-9AEE-6BB3A2FE6CD6}	TWO Component	4,000.00

Figure 6-17 Product ID field resized

> If the Product ID field is selected on the preview tab, click on a blank space in the report to deselect it. To keep this from happening, click on a blank space in the design tab before previewing the report.

> It is a good idea to scan through several pages of the report while previewing it to make sure that you do not see any data cut off (truncated) in the field that you are resizing. It is possible that the resized field may still not be wide enough.

4. Open the L5.3 report and resize the fields so that they fit on the report, then save the changes and close the report. Later, you will learn how to hide the time in date fields.

Object Size And Position Dialog Box

In addition to resizing a field manually, you can also use the Size and Position option on the shortcut menu by following the steps below.

1. Right-click on the field that you want to resize and select **SIZE AND POSITION**, as illustrated in Figure 6-18. In this exercise, right-click on the Product ID field in the L6.1 report.

   Notice that the options on the shortcut menu are different then the ones shown earlier in Figure 6-7.

   The options on the menu change, depending on how many objects are selected or the type of object that is selected.

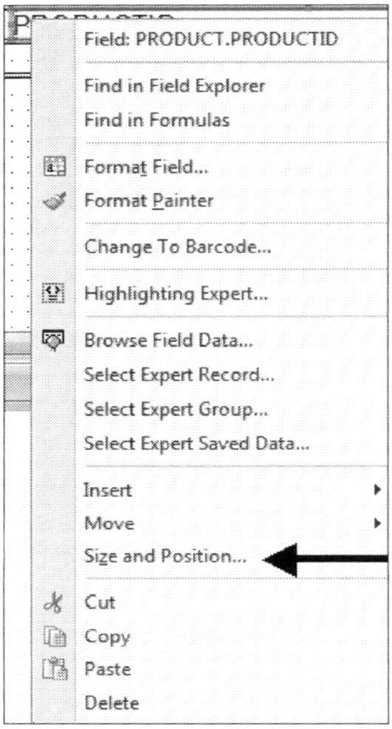

Figure 6-18 Object shortcut menu

2. Change the **WIDTH** to `1.0`, as shown in Figure 6-19, then click OK. Save the changes and leave the report open. This change will make the field shorter. If you enter a larger number in the width field, the selected field will be longer.

   If you do not have a need for this much field size precision, you will probably not have a need to use the options on this dialog box. I have been using Crystal Reports for years and other then writing this exercise, I have never used this dialog box.

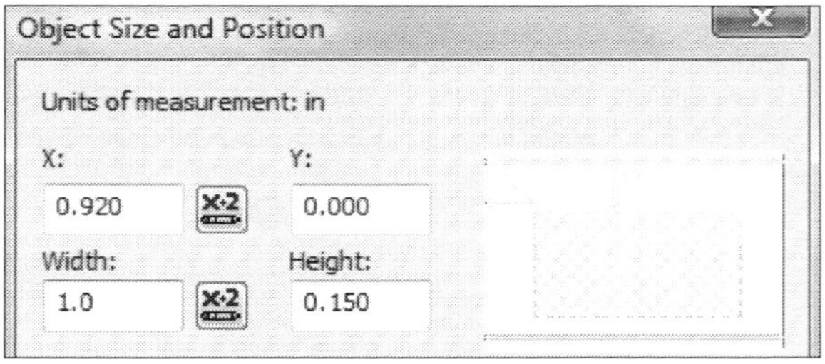

Figure 6-19 Object Size and Position dialog box

Nudging Objects

So far in this lesson you have learned how to move and resize objects using the mouse. You can also move and resize objects using the keyboard. This is helpful if you use a laptop and do not use a mouse. Using the keyboard to move or resize objects is known as **NUDGING** an object.

> If the **SNAP TO GRID** option is turned on, the arrow key will move the object one grid point each time an arrow key is pressed.

How To Move An Object By Nudging It

1. Without using the mouse, select the object that you want to move.
2. Use one of the four arrow keys on the keyboard to move the object in the direction that you need to reposition it.

How To Resize An Object Using The Nudge Feature

1. Without using the mouse, select the object that you need to resize, then press and hold down the **SHIFT** key.
2. Use the arrow key that points in the direction that you want to resize the object. If you used the nudging feature on a report, close the report but do not save the changes.

FORMATTING REPORTS

As the title of this lesson indicates, you will learn formatting techniques that you can use to make the reports that you create look better. Lessons 15 and 16 will teach you other ways to format reports. After completing the exercises in this lesson you will be able to:

- ☑ Add graphics to a report
- ☑ Use the Format Editor
- ☑ Use the Format Painter

LESSON 7

Formatting And Editing Overview

It can take an hour or more to create a report. You may struggle to write the formulas, make sure that the sorting and grouping options meet the report requirements and come up with an appropriate title for the report. You are pleased that you were able to accomplish all of these tasks and give a copy of the report to the person that requested it. You see them frown, but can't figure out why, especially because you checked the formulas by hand and know that the data is correct. You ask why they are frowning and they say, "Some of the fields are not lined up and there are too many fonts." As they say, "Perception is everything". Take from this what you will.

Crystal Reports provides a variety of options that you can use to make the reports that you design look better. You can draw boxes, apply templates, add color (probably best suited for reports that will be viewed as a web page or printed on a color printer) and more. You can also apply formatting conditionally to fields or sections of the report depending on whether the value in a field meets specific criteria. This type of formatting can be applied to any field that is on the report including summary and group name fields.

Earlier in this book you learned that everything on a report is an object, including charts, data fields, headings and formulas. I realize that this may take some getting use to. The good news is that each type of object has its own set of properties that you can modify. The options on the Standard, Formatting and Insert Tools toolbars contain many of the options that are covered in the next few exercises in this lesson.

Adding And Editing Text Objects

Text objects are used to add additional information to a report. Text objects include field headings, report titles or any text that you want to add to a report that is not automatically created based on a field in a table.

Exercise 7.1: How To Edit Text Objects

In this exercise you will learn how to edit text objects.

1. Save the L6.1 report as `L7.1 Text objects`.

The majority of the field headings on the report are clear and easy to understand. The one field heading that would be easier to understand is the one for the Product ID field. Most end-users (people that will use the report) would not understand the term "ID", so it would be better to change this field heading.

2. Right-click on the Product ID field heading in the page header section and select **EDIT TEXT**.

> You can also double-click on the Product ID field heading to change the text.

3. Select (highlight) the text shown in Figure 7-1. Type `Product #`, then click on a blank space on the report.

Figure 7-1 Text selected to change

You can also select a portion of the text in a field and change that. For example, you could select "ID" in Figure 7-1 and just change that.

Pressing the **ENTER** key does not end the editing session like it does in other software packages. Pressing Enter in Crystal Reports starts a new line in the text object. When you finish adding or editing text, click outside of the text object to end the editing session.

Make The Page Header Section Longer

The report that you have open does not have a report title. As you can see, there is not a lot of space in the page header section above the field headings to add the report title. The page header section needs to be longer. Follow the steps below to learn how to make a section of the report longer.

1. Click on the section bar below the page header section. The mouse pointer is in the right position when you see the double arrow illustrated in Figure 7-2. Drag the section bar down below the details section.

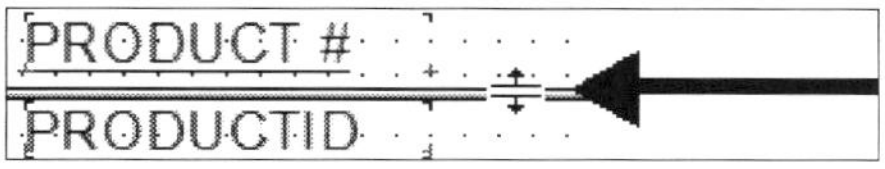

Figure 7-2 Mouse pointer in position to make the page header section longer

2. Move all of the field headings in the page header section down, then click on a blank space on the report.

The easiest way to move all of the field headings at one time is to select all of them first and then move them at the same time.

If you need to make a section in the report shorter, drag the section bar up.

How To Add A Text Object

1. Click the **INSERT TEXT OBJECT** button on the Insert Tools toolbar. The mouse pointer will change to a plus sign when placed over the report.

You can right-click on a blank space in the report and select **INSERT TEXT OBJECT**.

2. Click in the page header section and type `Product List Report` in the text object, then click on a blank space on the report.

When selecting fonts to use on a report, it is best to use the default fonts that come with Windows, otherwise the report will look different on computers that do not have the font that you selected. If you have to use a font that does not come with Windows, you should export the report to Adobe PDF format. Doing that will allow the report to be viewed and printed with the font that you selected.

How To Format A Text Object

Follow the steps below to learn how to format a text object.

1. Click on the object that you want to apply formatting to. In this exercise, click on the report title that you just created.

2. Click the **BOLD** button and change the font size to 14, then make the object longer and wider so that you can see all of the text.

3. Move the report title so that it is centered (left to right) across the page header section. The top of the report should look like the one shown in Figure 7-3. Save the changes and close the report.

Product List Report

PRODUCT #	PRODUCT	PRICE
{10D6D3E9-0518-4850-B9A3-10E19B813674}	Mini Core Replacement	100.00
{D55410C5-9F2B-47B9-A1C8-F04B2C669A8A}	ONE Component	2,500.00
{9DA1C71E-1631-4427-AC2F-D1D26E073661}	Service Contract	2,000.00
{E24C2E33-1778-4931-A55C-12205E7CCC0A}	TechONE System	12,000.00
{339AF93C-9741-4D72-9AEE-6BB3A2FE6CD6}	TWO Component	4,000.00

Figure 7-3 Modified page header section

> I use to find it difficult to center text like a report title across a page. I finally came up with the steps below to center a report title across the page.

① Make the report title object the width of the report, as shown in Figure 7-4.

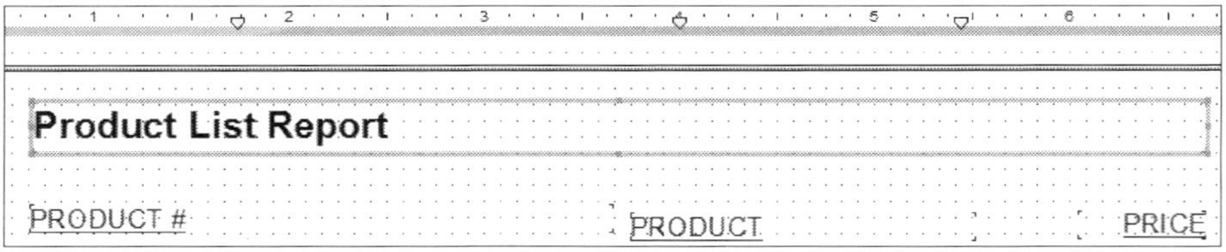

Figure 7-4 Text object resized to the width of the report

② Click the **ALIGN CENTER** button.

How To Import A Text File Into A Text Object

If there is text in a file that you want to add to a report, you can, by following the steps below.

1. Add a text object to the report, then double-click in the text object to start the edit mode.

2. Right-click in the text object and select **INSERT FROM FILE**, as shown in Figure 7-5.

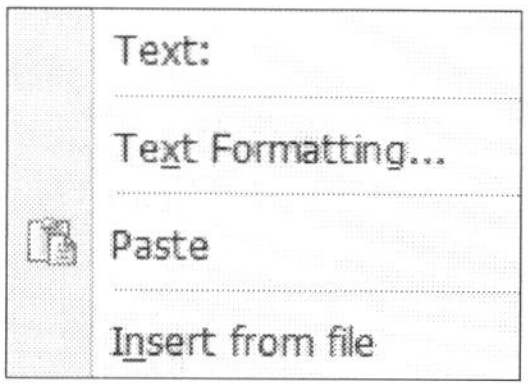

Figure 7-5 Text object shortcut menu

3. Find the file on your hard drive or in another location, then double-click on it. The content of the text file will be added to the text object. Save the changes.

Combining Text Objects And Database Fields

Text objects are more powerful then they may appear. If you have spent any time trying to get a text object and a field to line up side by side with spacing that looks right, but have had trouble doing so, you are in luck. Text objects can have data fields embedded in them. Text objects will automatically resize to accommodate the embedded field so that there is no extra space. The steps below explain how to embed a database field in a text object.

1. Add a text object to the report, then add the text to the object.

2. Drag a database field either from the report or from the Field Explorer into the text object, as shown in Figure 7-6, then release the mouse button. You will see a flashing cursor in the text object before you release the mouse button. This is where the database field will be added.

Figure 7-6 Database field being added to a text object

Combining Text Objects Tips

① You can edit the combined field or add more text or another database field to the text object.
② You can format part of a text object. If this is what you need to do, only select (highlight) the part that you want to format.
③ If you discover that you have added the wrong field to the text object, click on the database field in the text object, then press the **DEL** key.
④ I find it easier to drag the fields that I want to add to the report and format them there and then drag them into the text object instead of trying to format the fields inside of the text object.

Exercise 7.2: Adding Graphics To A Report

Some of the sample reports that come with ACT! have a logo.

This exercise will show you how to add any graphic file that is not stored in a table to a report.

There are two ways to access the Open dialog box shown in Figure 7-7.

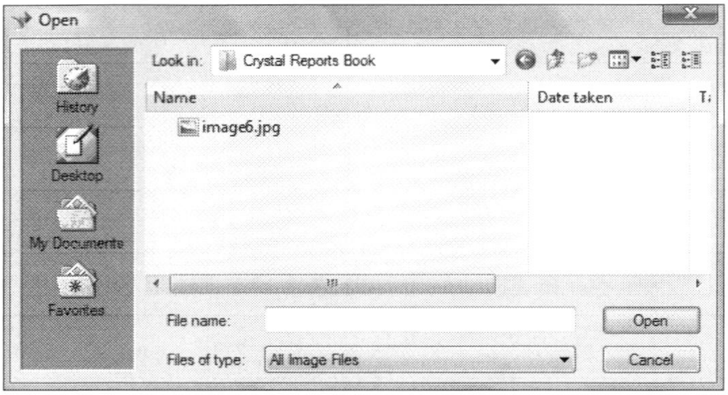

Figure 7-7 Insert Picture Open dialog box

① Click the **INSERT PICTURE** button on the Insert Tools toolbar.
② Insert ⇒ Picture.

1. Save the L6.1 report as `L7.2 Insert picture`.

2. Make the page header section longer by dragging the section bar (below the section) down. Move the field headings down in the page header section.

3. Open the Insert Picture dialog box shown above in Figure 7-7 and navigate to the folder or location where the graphic is, that you want to use. For this exercise, navigate to your folder. You may have to change the Files of type field at the bottom of the Open dialog box to **ALL FILES** to be able to see the image file.

4. Double-click on the file, image6.jpg.

   The mouse pointer should have changed to a shadow box (which is the actual size of the image), as shown in Figure 7-8.

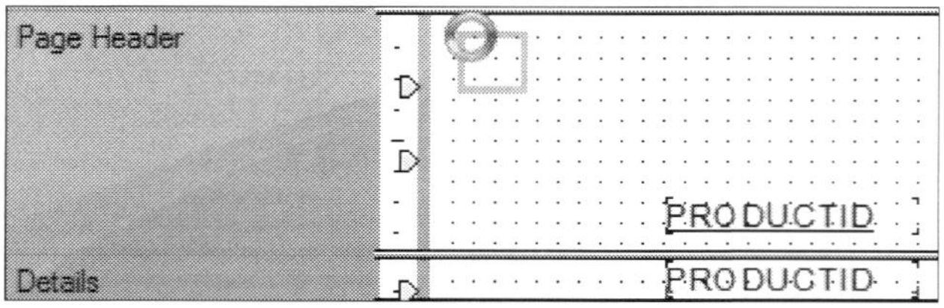

Figure 7-8 Mouse pointer in the Insert Picture mode

5. Click in the upper left corner of the page header section. You should see the image. Save the changes and leave the report open to complete the next part of the exercise.

How To Resize A Graphic

The image would look better if it were larger. Follow the steps below to resize the image.

1. Select the image if it is not already selected. Click on the lower right corner of the image and drag the mouse down and over to the right, until the image is large enough.

2. The report should look like the one shown in Figure 7-9. If the report had more pages you will see the image at the top of each page because it was placed in the page header section, which prints on every page. Save the changes.

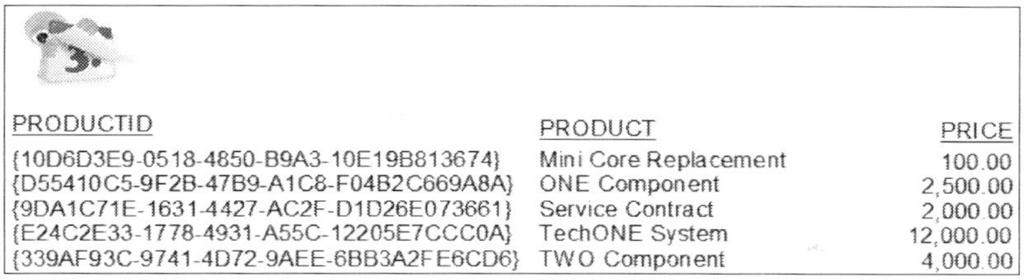

PRODUCTID	PRODUCT	PRICE
{10D6D3E9-0518-4850-B9A3-10E19B813674}	Mini Core Replacement	100.00
{D55410C5-9F2B-47B9-A1C8-F04B2C669A8A}	ONE Component	2,500.00
{9DA1C71E-1631-4427-AC2F-D1D26E073661}	Service Contract	2,000.00
{E24C2E33-1778-4931-A55C-12205E7CCC0A}	TechONE System	12,000.00
{339AF93C-9741-4D72-9AEE-6BB3A2FE6CD6}	TWO Component	4,000.00

Figure 7-9 L7.2 report with the logo added

Exercise 7.3: Adding Graphics From Fonts

In addition to being able to add graphic images to a report, you can also add graphics that are stored in fonts like the Wingdings font. Fonts that have graphics can be accessed from the Character Map application in Windows. These graphics have to be placed in a text object.
In this exercise you will add a graphic from a font to a report.

1. Save the L7.2 report as `L7.3 Graphics from fonts.`

2. Click the Start button (in Windows) ⇒ All Programs (or Programs) ⇒ Accessories ⇒ System Tools ⇒ Character Map.

3. Open the Font drop-down list on the Character Map dialog box and select **WINGDINGS**, if it is not already selected.

   You should see the dialog box shown in Figure 7-10.

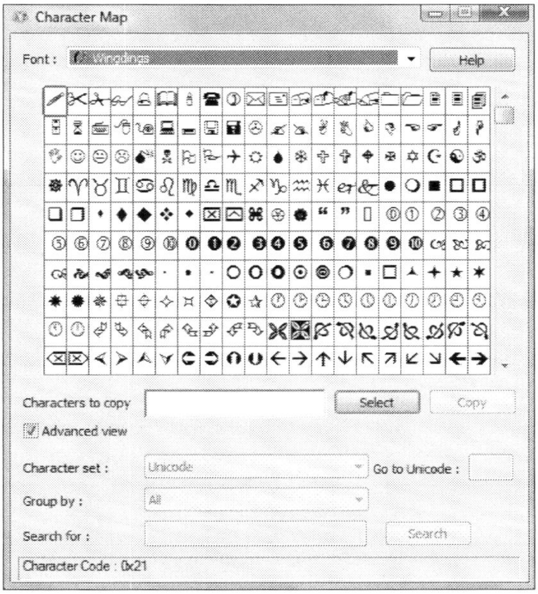

Figure 7-10 Character Map dialog box

4. Double-click on the document picture (the third picture from the right in the first row), then click the Copy button and close the dialog box.

5. Add a text object to the details section after the Price field, then press the CTRL+ V keys to paste the picture in the text object.

6. Click on a blank space on the report. Save the changes. The report should look like the one shown in Figure 7-11.

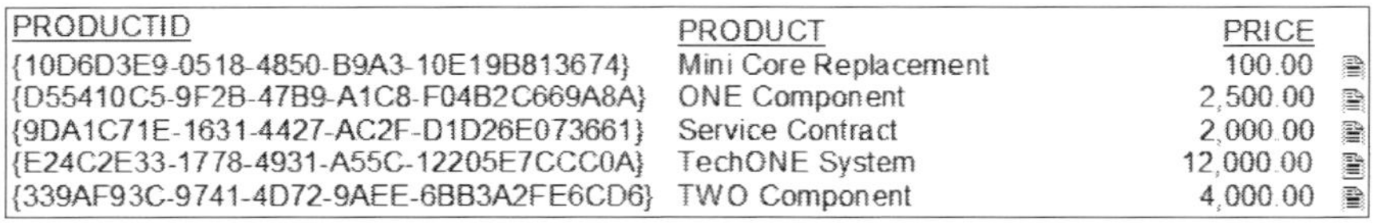

PRODUCTID	PRODUCT	PRICE
{10D6D3E9-0518-4850-B9A3-10E19B813674}	Mini Core Replacement	100.00
{D55410C5-9F2B-47B9-A1C8-F04B2C669A8A}	ONE Component	2,500.00
{9DA1C71E-1631-4427-AC2F-D1D26E073661}	Service Contract	2,000.00
{E24C2E33-1778-4931-A55C-12205E7CCC0A}	TechONE System	12,000.00
{339AF93C-9741-4D72-9AEE-6BB3A2FE6CD6}	TWO Component	4,000.00

Figure 7-11 L7.3 Graphics from fonts report

One reason to add an image next to each detail record is to create a hyperlink to another section of the report or to open a document or another report that has information that relates to the detail record.

The Format Editor

So far all of the formatting that you have learned about is considered basic formatting. For many reports that is all of the formatting that is required. When you need to create additional formatting, you can use the Format Editor. If the standard options on the Format Editor do not handle your needs, you can write conditional formulas. As you will see, many options on the Format Editor have a Formula button. Clicking on this button will let you create and apply conditional formatting to a field or object. The Format Editor provides a lot of options for changing how objects look on a report.

The options that are on the Format Editor dialog box will vary depending on the type of object that is selected. When you open the Format Editor, you will only see tabs that can be used for the field type that was selected before the dialog box was opened. Table 7-1 explains all of the tabs on the Format Editor. In the next few exercises you will learn how to use the Format Editor.

> If you need to make the same change to several objects, select all of the objects that need the same change, prior to opening the Format Editor.

There are three ways to open the Format Editor **AFTER** selecting at least one object in the report, as discussed below.

① Click the **FORMAT** button on the Expert Tools toolbar.
② Right-click and select **FORMAT <OBJECT TYPE>**. Depending on the object that is selected, you will see a different format option type. If the selected object is a graphic, you would see **FORMAT GRAPHIC**. The option for the Format Editor is always the first "Format" option on the shortcut menu. Notice that the icons to the left of the menu options shown in Figure 7-12 are the same icons that are on the buttons on the Expert Tools toolbar.
③ Format ⇒ Format <object type>.

Tab	Data Type	Purpose
Common	All	The options shown in Figure 7-13 can be used by most objects on a report. Table 7-2 explains the options on the Common tab.
Border	All	Add lines and drop shadows to fields.
Font	All except OLE & graphic objects	Select font, font size, font color, underlining, strike out and character spacing. Most of the options on this tab are also on the Formatting toolbar.
Hyperlink	All	Uses the selected object as a link to a web site, file, email address or a field on a web page.
Paragraph	String & Memo fields	Format paragraphs that are stored in string or memo fields.
Number	Number & currency	Apply formatting options that are only for number fields. (1)
Date & Time	Date & Time fields	Apply formatting options that are only for date and date/time fields. (1)
Picture	Graphic	Crop, scale, reset and resize graphic images.
Boolean	Boolean	Select how Boolean values will be displayed.

Table 7-1 Format Editor tab options explained

(1) Options on this tab support custom formatting.

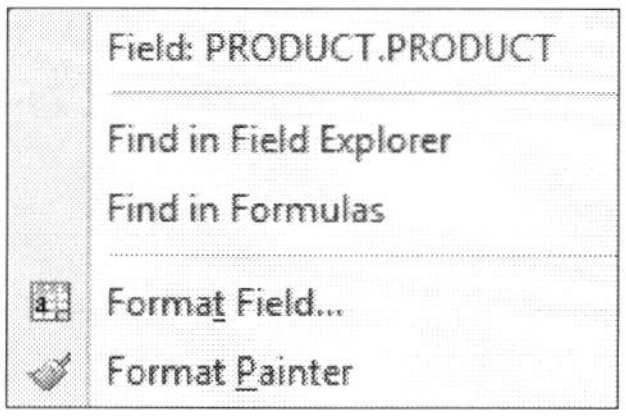

Figure 7-12 Format Editor menu option illustrated

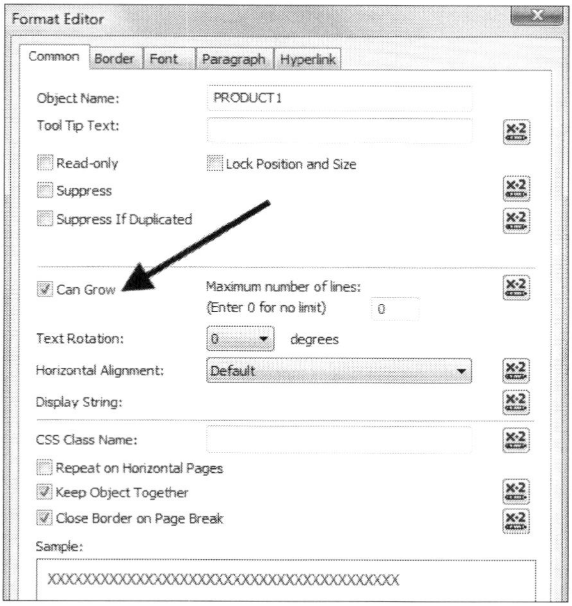

Figure 7-13 Common tab options

Option	Description
Object Name	This field is filled in by default. You can accept the default name unless you have a need to use it in a formula and want to use a shorter or more descriptive name. It is not mandatory to change the object name.
Tool Tip Text	Enter text in this field that you want displayed when the mouse pointer hovers over the field in the preview window.
Read-only	Prevents the object from having additional formatting applied.
Lock Position and Size	Prevents the object from being moved or resized.
Suppress	Hides the object.
Suppress If Duplicated	Hides the object if it has the same value as the one in the previous record.
Suppress Embedded Field Blank Lines	Suppresses the field if it does not have data. This prevents blanks lines from appearing on the report. This option is only for text fields which is why it is not visible in Figure 7-13 above.
Can Grow	Allows the field to expand vertically to accommodate more data.
Text Rotation	Change the angle of the field.
Horizontal Alignment	Contains the horizontal alignment types for the selected object.
CSS Class Name	If the field will be formatted with a style sheet, enter the CSS Class Name that should be applied to the object.
Repeat on Horizontal Pages	This option is mostly used with a cross-tab or OLAP grid that will print horizontally across more than one page.
Keep Object Together	Keeps the object from printing on more than one page. The object will be printed on the next page if it does not fit on the current page.
Close Border on Page Break	This option is used for fields that will print on more than one page and have a border. This option will print the bottom of the border of the object on the first page and print another border around the remaining data that prints on the next page.
	The Formula button opens the Formula Workshop, which is used to create a formula to use with the option. You can also attach an existing formula to the option. You would use a formula when you need to control when the option is turned on or off, based on a condition. For example, if you wanted to highlight the order amount field on records that were in a certain dollar amount range.

Table 7-2 Common tab options explained

Format A Text Object

1. Open the L7.1 report. Right-click on the report title, then select **FORMAT TEXT**.
   On the **BORDER** tab you will see the options shown in Figure 7-14. Table 7-3 explains the options on this tab.

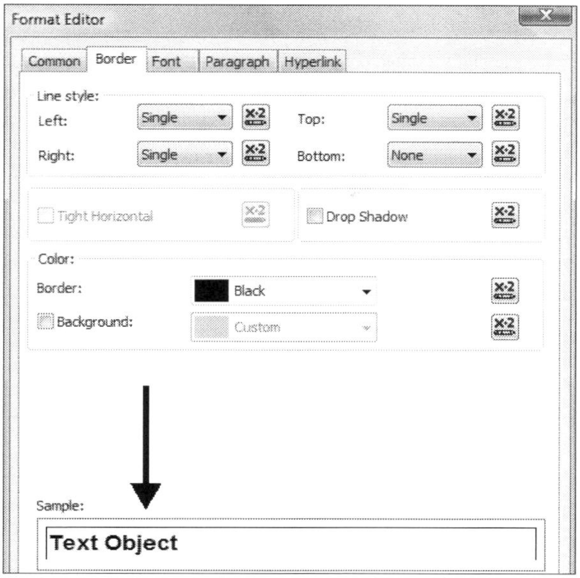

Figure 7-14 Border tab options on the Format Editor dialog box

Option	Description
Line Style	These four options are used to select the line style for each side of the object.
Tight Horizontal	Moves the border of the object closer to the object.
Drop Shadow	Adds the shadow effect to the lower right corner of the object.
Border Color	Select a color for the border and drop shadow.
Background Color	Select the color for the background of the object.

Table 7-3 Border tab options explained

2. Change the **LINE STYLE** to single for the Left, Right and Top options. Notice at the bottom of the dialog box in the **SAMPLE** section that you can see the options that you have applied to the object.

3. Check the **DROP SHADOW** and **BACKGROUND** options, then open the drop-down list across from the Background option and select **YELLOW**, as shown in Figure 7-15.

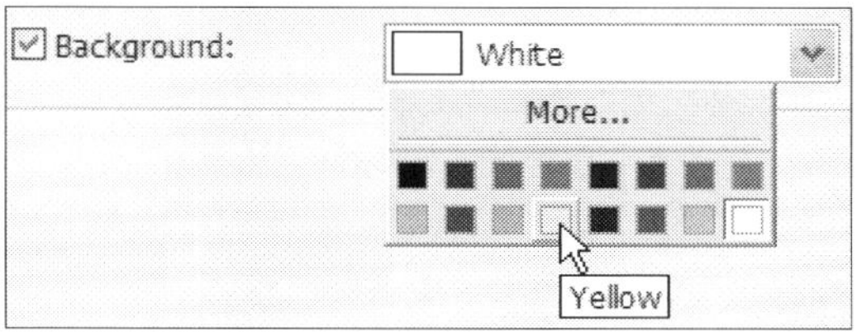

Figure 7-15 Background color options

If selected, the **MORE** option shown above in Figure 7-15 will open the Color dialog box, which is used to select additional colors or create a custom color.

4. Click OK to close the Format Editor. The report should look like the one shown in Figure 7-16. Save the changes.

Product List Report

PRODUCT #	PRODUCT	PRICE
{10D6D3E9-0518-4850-B9A3-10E19B813674}	Mini Core Replacement	100.00
{D55410C5-9F2B-47B9-A1C8-F04B2C669A8A}	ONE Component	2,500.00
{9DA1C71E-1631-4427-AC2F-D1D26E073661}	Service Contract	2,000.00
{E24C2E33-1778-4931-A55C-12205E7CCC0A}	TechONE System	12,000.00
{339AF93C-9741-4D72-9AEE-6BB3A2FE6CD6}	TWO Component	4,000.00

Figure 7-16 L7.1 report with formatting applied to a text object

The Can Grow Option

Earlier I mentioned that one reason data gets truncated is because there may not be enough room in the section of the report to accommodate all of the data. In the part of the exercise that you just completed there was enough room to make the field longer. If you have tried everything possible to get all of the data to fit but it won't, the **CAN GROW** option should fix the problem. This option will cause the data in the field to wrap to a new line, only when needed. Fields that have this option enabled, will only grow longer, not wider. Follow the steps below to learn how to turn this option on.

> The Can Grow option can only be used with string fields, text objects and memo fields.

1. Right-click on the object(s) in the report that you want to apply the Can Grow option to and select **FORMAT FIELD**. You will see the Format Editor dialog box.

2. On the **COMMON** tab, check the **CAN GROW** option, then click OK.

If you want to limit the maximum number of lines that a field can print on the report, enter it in the **MAXIMUM NUMBER OF LINES** field. For example, if you are applying the Can Grow option to a memo field that could have 500 characters or more of text, you may not want to have all of the text in the field print on the report. If this is the case, you would enter a number in the Maximum number of lines field so that only the first two or three lines of information in the field will actually print on the report. The Can Grow option, even when enabled will only be activated when needed. It does not force every record to expand to the number of lines entered in the field.

If you use the Can Grow option on a field and there is another field below it, it is possible that the field below will be overwritten. To prevent this, the following options are available.

① Put the field with the Can Grow option at the bottom of the section.

② Not as effective as the first option, but you can check the spacing to make sure that the field with the Can Grow option is not close to other fields.

3. Resize the field if needed. Save the changes.

Text Rotation

There may be times when some of the text on a report will look better if it is rotated. Figure 7-17 shows the degrees that text can be rotated. Select the text that you want to rotate, then select the degree rotation and click OK. Figure 7-18 shows the Product ID heading rotated 90 degrees.

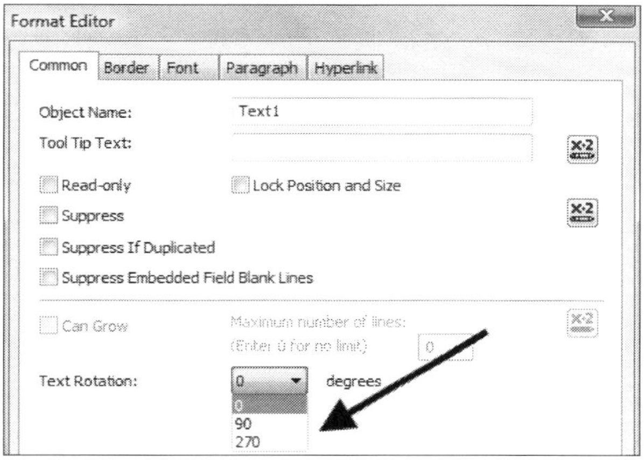

Figure 7-17 Text rotation options illustrated

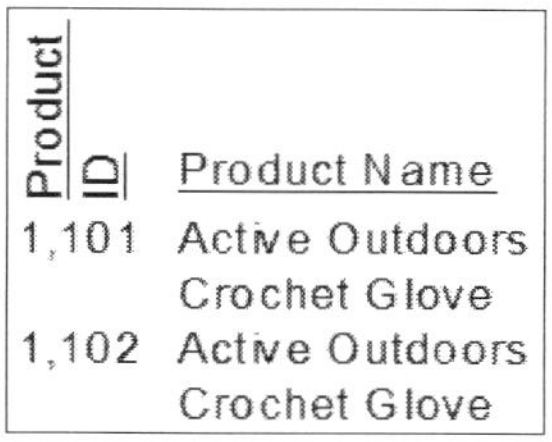

Figure 7-18 Product ID heading rotated 90 degrees

Figure 7-17 Text rotation options illustrated

Format Editor Paragraph Tab

When you are applying formatting to a text object, string or memo field, you will see the Paragraph tab shown in Figure 7-19.

The options on this tab are used to select how text fields that have multiple lines of data or text will be formatted.

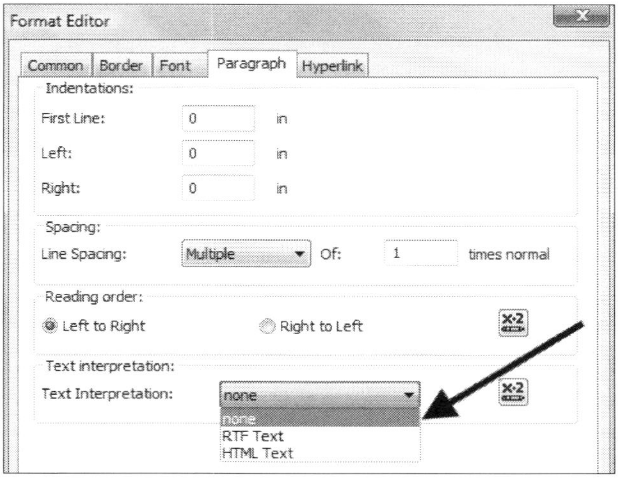

Figure 7-19 Paragraph tab options

The **TEXT INTERPRETATION** option illustrated in Figure 7-19 is not available for text objects. These options are helpful if the field has HTML (Hypertext Markup Language) formatting, which is used for web pages or RTF (Rich Text Format) formatting for text that may have special formatting from word processing or publishing software.

Format A Numeric Field

Sometimes numeric fields do not have any formatting and other times numeric fields need formatting. Follow the steps below to change the formatting of a numeric field.

1. Right-click on the numeric field in the details section that needs formatting and select **FORMAT FIELD**.

   You will see the dialog box shown in Figure 7-20.

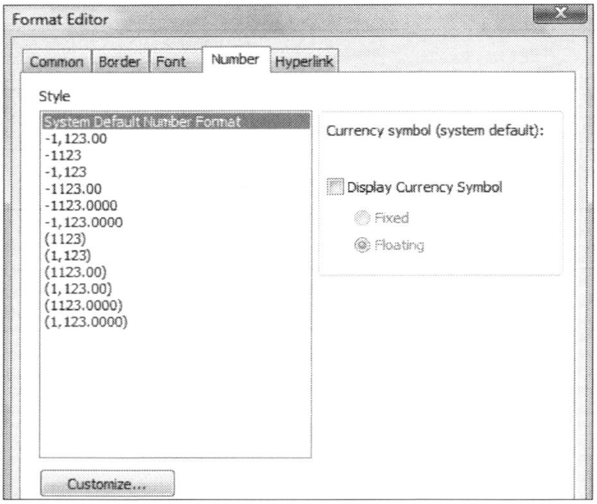

Figure 7-20 Number tab options

The Custom Style option has been removed from the Style drop-down list in Crystal Reports 2008.

2. Select the formatting style from the list. Click OK and preview the report.

A minus sign will only print if the number is negative.

If none of the options shown above in Figure 7-20 meet your needs to format currency or number fields, click the **CUSTOMIZE** button.

You will see the options shown in Figure 7-21 if the field that you are formatting is a currency field.

You will see the options shown in Figure 7-22 if the field that you are formatting is a number field.

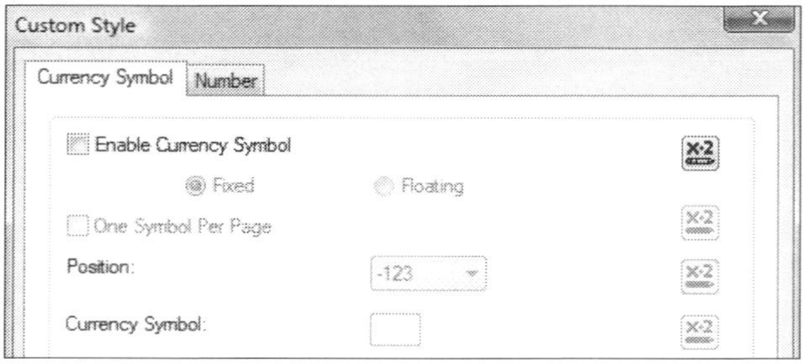

Figure 7-21 Currency symbol custom style options

Usually, the **DECIMALS** and **ROUNDING** options shown in Figure 7-22 are set to the same number of decimal places.

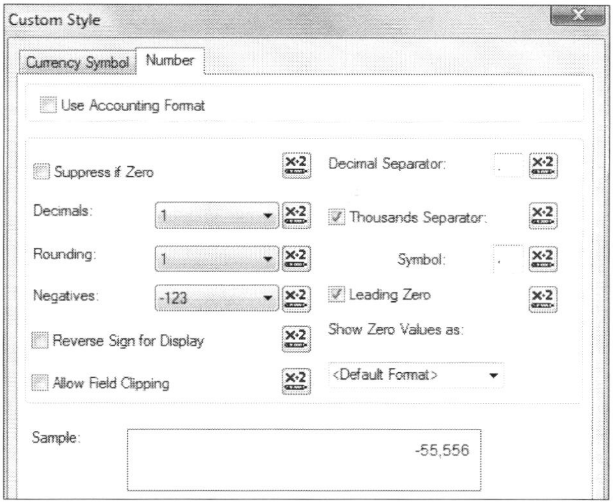

Figure 7-22 Number custom style options

If you think determining if a field is a string field or a numeric field based on the name is difficult or confusing, you can clear the **SHOW FIELD NAMES** option on the Layout tab of the Options dialog box. Clearing this option will display X's in string fields and 5's in numeric fields as shown in Figure 7-23.

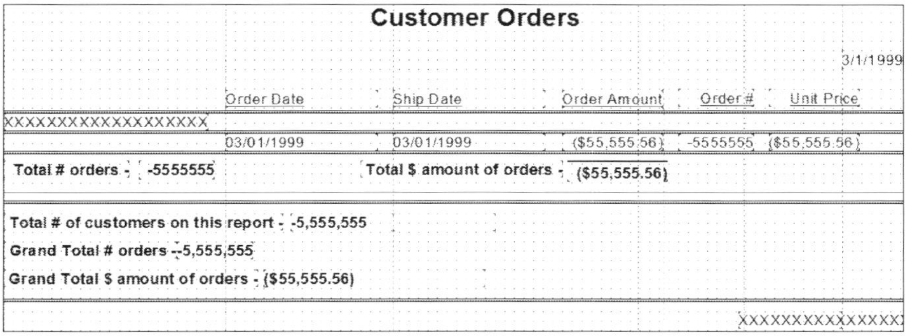

Figure 7-23 Fields without field names

Format A Date Field

Displaying the time as part of a date field is usually not needed on reports. To keep the time portion of the field from printing on the report, the field needs to be formatted. Follow the steps below to change the formatting of a date field.

1. Open the L5.3 report.

2. Right-click on the Create Date field and select Format Field.

   You will see the dialog box shown in Figure 7-24.

   If you click the **CUSTOMIZE** button you will see the dialog box shown in Figure 7-25.

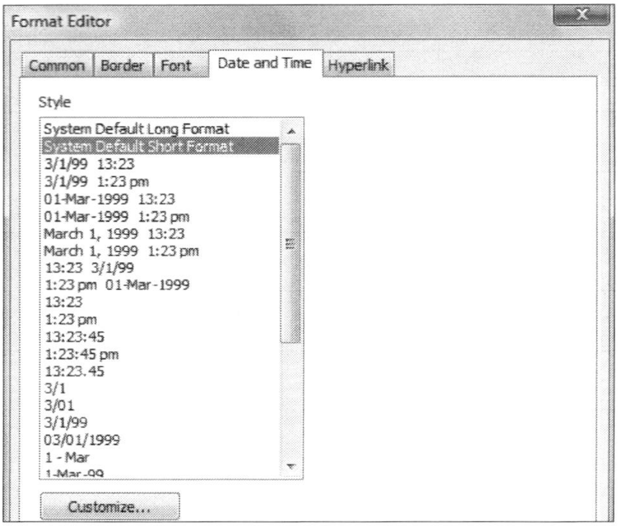

Figure 7-24 Date and Time tab options

The options on this tab are used to change the formatting for a date field or the date portion of a date/time field.

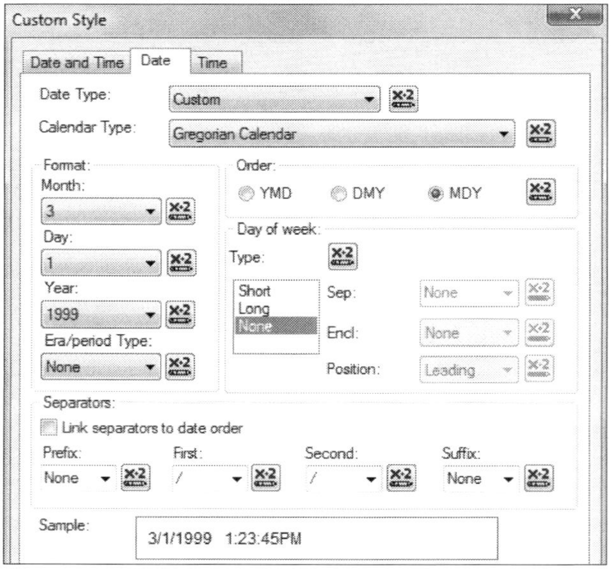

Figure 7-25 Date tab custom style options

3. Click on the option **3/1/99** on the Date and Time tab shown earlier in Figure 7-24, then click OK.

4. Select the same date format for the Actual Close Date field.

5. Resize the date fields, then move the fields to the left so that all of the fields fit on the page.

The options shown in Figure 7-26 are used to change the formatting for the time portion of a date/time field.

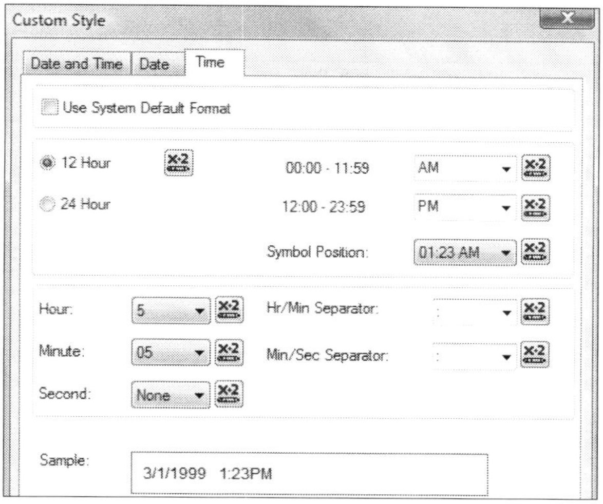

Figure 7-26 Time tab custom style options

6. The report should look like the one shown in Figure 7-27. You should not see the time on the Create Date and Actual Close Date fields like you did in Lesson 5, Figure 5-37. Save the changes and close the report.

CONTACT	COMPANY	OPPORTUNITY NAME	CREATE DATE	DAYS OPEN	TOTAL	STATUS	ACTUAL CLOSE DATE
Gareth Cram	Johnson Design & Buil	New Opportunity	5/21/07	360	12,000.00	Closed - Lost	5/14/08
Gareth Cram	Johnson Design & Buil	Johnson Design & Build-Edinborough :	5/21/07	191	4,000.00	Open	12/31/99
Jackie Jorgensen	Ace Pet Store Franchis	Ace Pet Store-Corporate Offices	5/20/07	105	2,000.00	Open	12/31/99
Jackie Jorgensen	Ace Pet Store Franchis	Ace Pet Store-Replacement Parts	10/30/08	87	600.00	Open	12/31/99
Jackie Jorgensen	Ace Pet Store Franchis	Ace Pet Store-SC for Corp Offices	5/15/07	197	4,000.00	Open	12/31/99
Jackie Jorgensen	Ace Pet Store Franchis	Ace Pet Store-New Opportunity	5/15/07	103	12,000.00	Closed - Won	8/31/07
James Finlay	Widget Corporation	New Opportunity	5/20/07	163	2,500.00	Closed - Won	10/30/08
James Finlay	Widget Corporation	Widget Corporation-Plant Expansion	5/20/07	-174	12,000.00	Open	12/31/99

Figure 7-27 L5.3 report with the date fields modified

Format A Graphic

Earlier in this lesson you added an image (graphic) to the L7.2 Insert Picture report. The image would look better if it had a border.

Resize The Image

1. Open the L7.2 report, then right-click on the image and select Format Graphic.

   Click on the **PICTURE** tab.

   You will see the dialog box shown in Figure 7-28.

   Table 7-4 explains the options on the Picture tab.

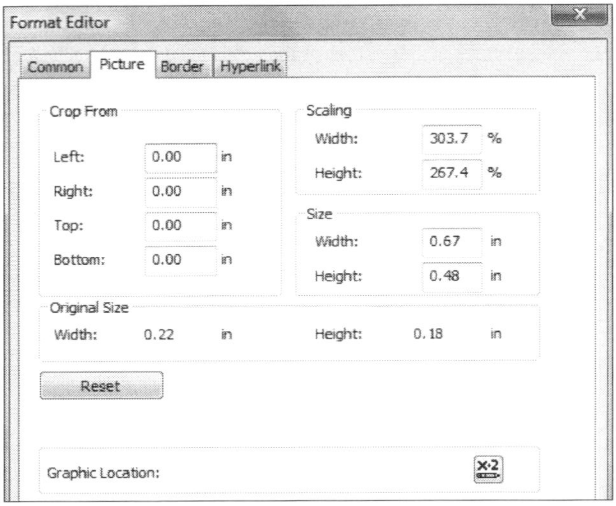

Figure 7-28 Picture tab options

Option	Description
Crop From	Removes part of the image. The part of the image that is removed is the part on the outside of the crop lines that are created when you enter the dimensions in any or all of the four crop options (left, right, top or bottom).
Scaling	Enlarge or reduce the image by a percent.
Size	Change the width and height of the image.
Reset	Removes all of the formatting that was applied to the image on the Picture tab. When you crop, scale or size an image, the original image file is not changed. It is only displayed differently on the report, based on the options that are selected.

Table 7-4 Picture tab options explained

2. Change the size **WIDTH** option to 2, then change the size **HEIGHT** option to 2 and click OK.

3. Move the field headings down in the page header section. Preview the report. Figure 7-29 shows the image before it was resized. Figure 7-30 shows the image after it was resized. Save the changes and leave the report open.

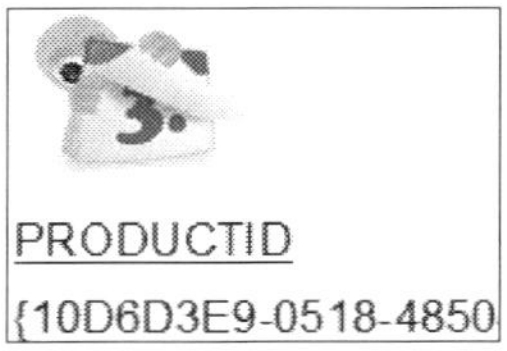

Figure 7-29 Image before resizing

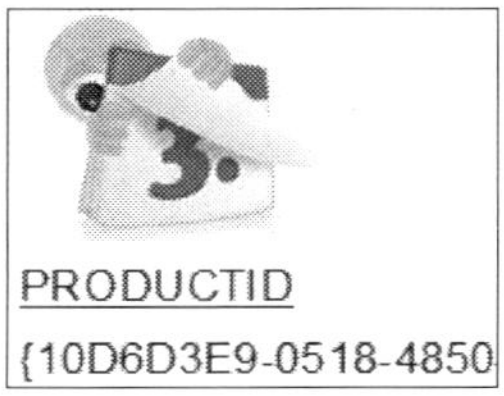

Figure 7-30 Image after resizing

Add A Border To The Image

1. Click on the image, then open the Format Editor and click on the Border tab.

2. Change all four **LINE STYLE** options to Dotted and click OK. The image should look like the one shown in Figure 7-31.

   Save the changes.

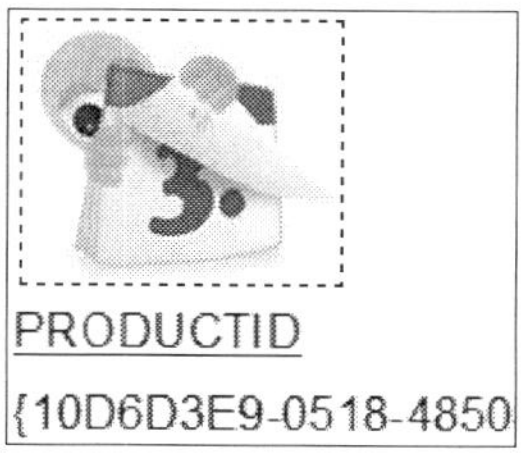

Figure 7-31 Border added to the image

Exercise 7.4: Format A Boolean Field

In this exercise you will change how the data in a Boolean field is displayed on a report.

1. Create a new report and add the following fields from the Contact table: Contact, Edit Date, Is Private and Is Imported.

2. Save the report as `L7.4 Boolean formatting`.

   The report should look like the one shown in Figure 7-32.

CONTACT	EDIT DATE	IS PRIVATE	IS IMPORTED
Lames Jawson	5/1/2009 11:14:10PM	True	False
Amanda Form	4/23/2009 6:15:14PM	True	False
William Buckley	5/1/2009 11:14:59PM	False	False
Allison Mikola	5/1/2009 11:18:13PM	False	False
Thomas Andrews	4/10/2009 6:07:23AM	True	False

Figure 7-32 L7.4 Boolean formatting report

The Is Private and Is Imported fields are Boolean fields. As you can see, they both are displaying true or false. You will format these fields so that they display Yes and No instead. Doing this does not change the data in the table.

3. Select both Boolean fields, right-click and select Format Objects.

4. On the Boolean tab open the **BOOLEAN TEXT** drop-down list and select Yes or No, as shown in Figure 7-33, then click OK.

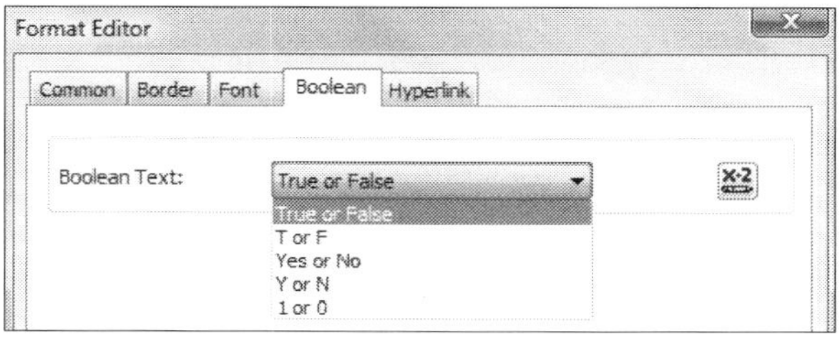

Figure 7-33 Boolean tab options

5. Preview the report. The value in the Boolean fields are now displayed as Yes or No, instead of True and False, as shown in Figure 7-34. Save the changes and close the report.

CONTACT	EDIT DATE	IS PRIVATE	IS IMPORTED
Lames Jawson	5/1/2009 11:14:10PM	Yes	No
Amanda Form	4/23/2009 6:15:14PM	Yes	No
William Buckley	5/1/2009 11:14:59PM	No	No
Allison Mikola	5/1/2009 11:18:13PM	No	No
Thomas Andrews	4/10/2009 6:07:23AM	Yes	No

Figure 7-34 Boolean fields displayed differently on the L7.4 report

The Format Painter

This is a pretty cool feature. It is used to copy the formatting from one object to several other objects with a mouse click. Formatting properties like the font, font size, font color and borders can be taken from a text object and applied to a numeric object. This is because this type of formatting is not specific to a data type. Usually, number specific formatting cannot be applied to other data types. There are three ways to start the Format Painter as discussed below, **AFTER** you have clicked on the object that has the formatting that you want to apply (copy) to other objects.

① Right-click on the object and select **FORMAT PAINTER**.
② Click the **FORMAT PAINTER** button on the Standard toolbar.
③ Format ⇒ Format Painter.

There are some things that the Format Painter cannot do, as discussed below.

① The Format Painter cannot copy a format that is created with the Highlighting Expert.
② Formatting cannot be copied from text objects or templates to fields in a table.
③ Formatted objects in the repository can be copied to reports. Formatting from reports cannot be copied to objects in the repository.
④ The Format Painter does not copy hyperlink properties.
⑤ The Format Painter will copy all formatting to other objects of the same data type. If formatting is copied from one data type to a different data type, only the formatting options that the objects have in common will be copied.

Change The Formatting Of An Object

In order to use this feature you need to change the formatting of an object.

1. Open the L7.2 report.

2. Change the font of the Product heading to Times New Roman, Bold and Size 10.

Apply The Formatting To Other Objects

1. With the Product heading selected, turn on the Format Painter. When you hold the mouse pointer over the Product ID heading, it will change to a **PAINT BRUSH**, as illustrated in Figure 7-35.

Figure 7-35 Mouse pointer in position to apply formatting

2. Click on the Product ID heading. The formatting from the Product heading should have been applied to the Product ID heading.

3. Close the report and discard the changes.

Using The Format Painter On Multiple Objects

If you need to apply the same formatting to more than one object, follow the steps below.

1. Select the object that has the formatting that you want to apply to other objects.

2. Turn on the Format Painter, then press and hold down the **ALT** key.

3. One by one, click on the objects that you want to change. The objects that you clicked on should all have the same formatting. If you tried to apply this formatting to the image, the mouse pointer would change to the symbol illustrated in Figure 7-36.

This symbol is used to let you know that the formatting cannot be applied to the object that you are holding the mouse pointer over.

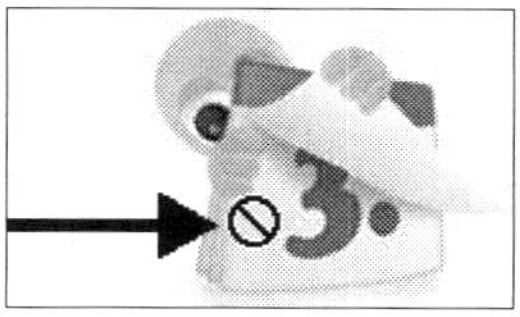

Figure 7-36 Symbol indicating that the formatting cannot be applied to the object

Exercise 7.5: Center Data Under A Heading

The contact information report that you created in Exercise 5.1 would look better if the following changes were made.

① Center the state field under the heading.
② Put a line under each detail record to make the report easier to read.

1. Save the L5.1 report as `L7.5 Modified contact information`.

2. Select the State field and heading, then click the **ALIGN CENTER** button on the Standard toolbar.

3. Make the State field and heading smaller. The data should now be centered under the heading. Save the changes.

4. Add the Country field after the Zip Code field.

5. Save the changes and leave the report open to complete the next part of the exercise.

How To Add Horizontal Lines To A Report

One way to make the data in the details section of a report easier to read is to place a line under the fields in this section. Like other objects, you can format lines that you add to a report. There are two ways to open the **LINE** tool, as discussed below.

① Click the **INSERT LINE** button on the Insert toolbar.
② Insert ⇒ Line.

Follow the steps below to add a line to the details section.

1. Move the details section bar down a little.

2. Select the **LINE** tool. The mouse pointer will change to a pencil. Draw a line under the fields in the details section.

> It is easier to draw a long line like this if you can see the entire width of the report. To do this, I often change the **ZOOM CONTROL** option to 75%.

Format The Line

Follow the steps below to learn how to format a line.

1. Right-click on the line in the details section and select **FORMAT LINE.**

   You will see the dialog box shown in Figure 7-37.

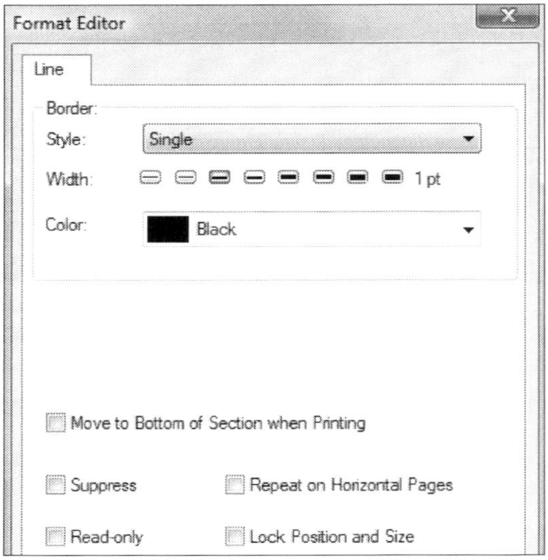

Figure 7-37 Format Editor line options

2. Open the **STYLE** drop-down list and select Single, if it is not already selected.

3. Click on the first button in the **WIDTH** section. You should see the word **HAIRLINE** at the end of the Width options.

> The **MOVE TO BOTTOM OF SECTION WHEN PRINTING** option shown above in Figure 7-37 is often used for lines in a section of the report that has a field with the Can Grow option turned on, like a Notes field. Checking this option will force the line to print at the bottom of the section, which is what you usually want. You can test how this option works by checking this option and making the section of the report longer that has the line and preview the report.

4. Click OK. The report should look like the one shown in Figure 7-38. Notice that the State field data is centered under the heading. Save the changes.

COMPANY	ADDRESS 1	STATE	ZIP CODE	COUNTRY
HAL's Consulting Corp	10 Countdown Loop	OR	97800	United States
A1 Services-US Operations	2131 W. Tiny Rd.	NY	20122	United States
Twelfth Dream	2010 Act Way	CA	94063	United States
CH TechONE	13 East 54th St.	NY	10008	United States
Modern Electric Supply	1919 Tecoma Dr.	FL	34655	United States
Liberty Savings & Loan	100 E Bayard St	NY	13148	United States
Mears Insurance	172 Edison Street	Cheshire	CH1 4PL	United Kingdom

Figure 7-38 L7.5 report with the details section modified

Exercise 7.6: Add Vertical Lines To A Report

In the previous exercise you learned how to add horizontal lines to a report. In this exercise you will learn how to add vertical lines to a report.

1. Save the L7.5 report as `L7.6 Vertical lines`.

2. Delete the horizontal line in the details section.

3. Insert ⇒ Line. Draw a vertical line in the details section after the Company field. Make sure that the line touches the section bar above and below the details section.

4. Right-click on the vertical line that you just created and select Copy, then right-click anyplace in the report and select Paste. The mouse pointer will have a picture of the line next to it.

5. Click at the end of the next field (the Address field) on the report.

6. Repeat steps 4 and 5 to place a vertical line after the other fields in the details section, then save the changes. The report should look like the one shown in Figure 7-39.

COMPANY	ADDRESS 1	STATE	ZIP CODE	COUNTRY
HAL's Consulting Corp	10 Countdown Loop	OR	97800	United States
A1 Services-US Operations	2131 W. Tiny Rd.	NY	20122	United States
Twelfth Dream	2010 Act Way	CA	94063	United States
CH TechONE	13 East 54th St.	NY	10008	United States
Modern Electric Supply	1919 Tecoma Dr.	FL	34655	United States
Liberty Savings & Loan	100 E Bayard St	NY	13148	United States
Mears Insurance	172 Edison Street	Cheshire	CH1 4PL	United Kingdom

Figure 7-39 L7.6 Vertical lines report

> You can also draw vertical lines through sections of the report. In the report that you just added vertical lines to, make the vertical lines longer by clicking on the line and dragging the top blue square on the line up, so that it is above the field heading in the page header section. The report should look like the one shown in Figure 7-40.

COMPANY	ADDRESS 1	STATE	ZIP CODE	COUNTRY
HAL's Consulting Corp	10 Countdown Loop	OR	97800	United States
A1 Services-US Operations	2131 W. Tiny Rd.	NY	20122	United States
Twelfth Dream	2010 Act Way	CA	94063	United States
CH TechONE	13 East 54th St.	NY	10008	United States
Modern Electric Supply	1919 Tecoma Dr.	FL	34655	United States
Liberty Savings & Loan	100 E Bayard St	NY	13148	United States
Mears Insurance	172 Edison Street	Cheshire	CH1 4PL	United Kingdom

Figure 7-40 L7.6 Vertical lines report with lines extended into the page header section

> If an object has the Can Grow option turned on, the object will grow but the vertical line will not grow by default, as shown in Figure 7-41. You will see breaks in the vertical line. To fix this, check the **EXTEND TO BOTTOM OF SECTION WHEN PRINTING** option shown in Figure 7-42.

COMPANY	ADDRESS 1	STATE	ZIP CODE	COUNTRY
HAL's Consulting Corp	10 Countdown Loop	OR	97800	United States
A1 Services-US Operations	2131 W. Tiny Rd.	NY	20122	United States
Twelfth Dream	2010 Act Way	CA	94063	United States

Figure 7-41 Can Grow option and vertical lines

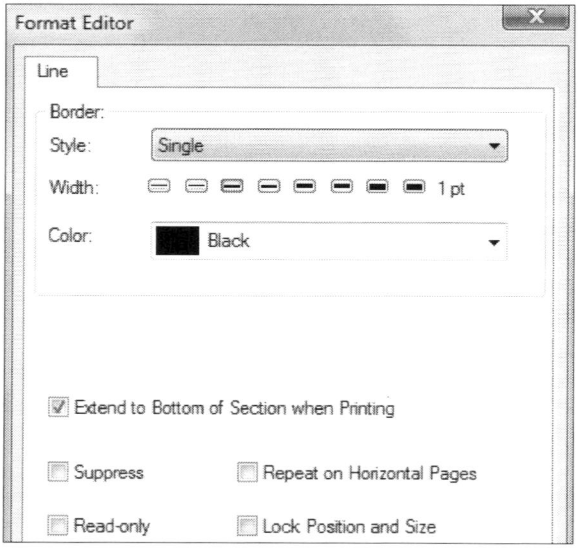

Figure 7-42 Format Editor options for a vertical line

USING SUBSECTIONS, SPECIAL FIELDS & THE REPORT EXPLORER

After completing the exercises in this lesson you will be able to:

- ☑ Use the Section Expert
- ☑ Add Special Fields to a report
- ☑ Understand how the Report Explorer works

LESSON 8

Subsections

As you saw in the L5.3 report, the report has a lot of fields. Crystal Reports allows you to split any section of the report into **SUBSECTIONS**. One reason that you would create subsections is to be able to spread the fields out so that they are easier to read. This allows fields to be in multiple rows.

Yes, you can make the section longer, but depending on the requirements of the report, creating subsections may be a better solution. One reason that comes to mind that this is a better solution is because you may need to apply conditional formatting to some fields in a section. When a section of the report is split, the subsections are labeled, A, B, C, etc, as shown in Figure 8-1.

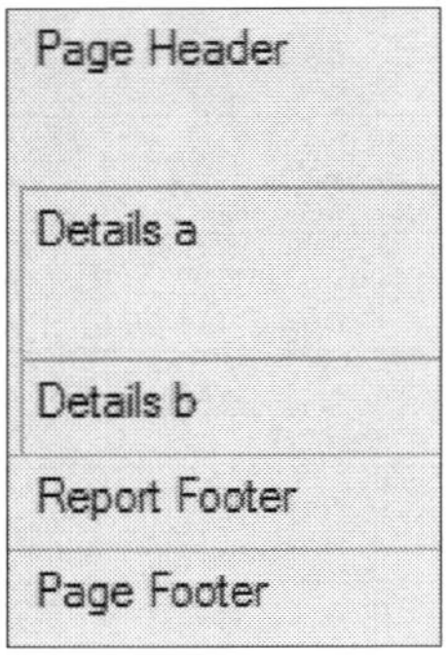

Figure 8-1 Details subsections

Exercise 8.1: How To Create Subsections

1. Save the L5.3 report as `L8.1 Subsections`.

2. Make the details section a little longer, then place the mouse pointer over the vertical ruler in the section that you want to split. In this exercise, place the mouse pointer over the edge of the vertical ruler in the details section. The mouse pointer will change to a vertical arrow, as illustrated in Figure 8-2.

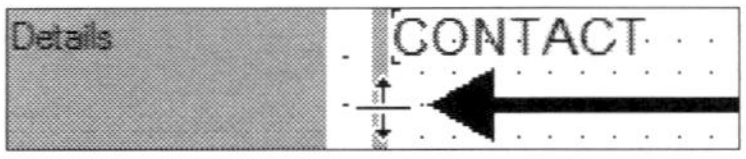

Figure 8-2 Mouse pointer in position to split a section

3. Press the left mouse button and hold it down until you see the gray line illustrated in Figure 8-3. This shows the start of the new section. Move the gray line to where you want to split the section, then release the mouse button. The details section should look like the one shown in Figure 8-4.

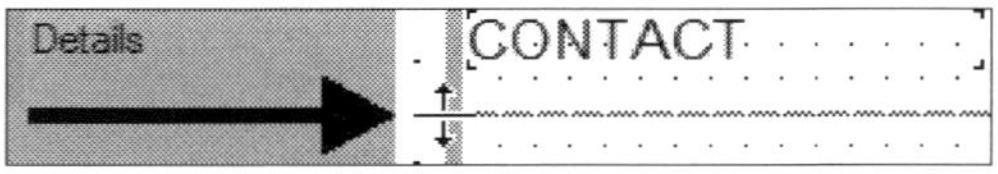

Figure 8-3 Gray line illustrated

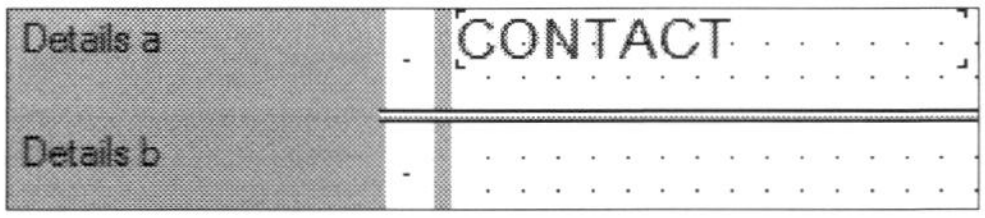

Figure 8-4 Details section split

4. Rearrange the fields in the details section as shown in Figure 8-5.

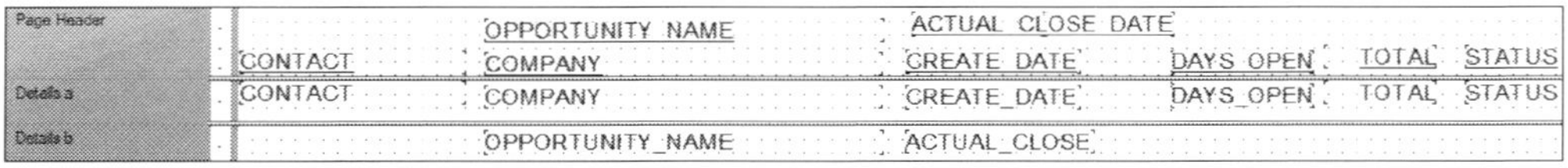

Figure 8-5 Fields rearranged in the details section

5. Change the orientation to portrait, then save the changes.

There are three other ways to add subsections to a report as described below.

① Use the Section shortcut menu. Right-click on the section on the left that you want to split and select **INSERT SECTION BELOW**.
② Click the Section Expert button on the Expert Tools toolbar.
③ Report ⇒ Section Expert.

Add Sections To The Report With The Section Expert

The benefit of using the Section Expert to add a new section to the report is that you can apply other options to the new section at the same time. These options are on the right side of the Section Expert. You will learn about the options on the Section Expert in Lesson 16.

1. Open the Section Expert, then click on the report section that you want to add a section to, as shown in Figure 8-6, then click the **INSERT** button. For this exercise, select the details section. You will see the section that you added, as illustrated in Figure 8-6.

Figure 8-6 Section added to the details section

2. Add a new section to the page header section, then click OK to close the Section Expert.

   The report layout should look like the one shown in Figure 8-7.

   Save the changes.

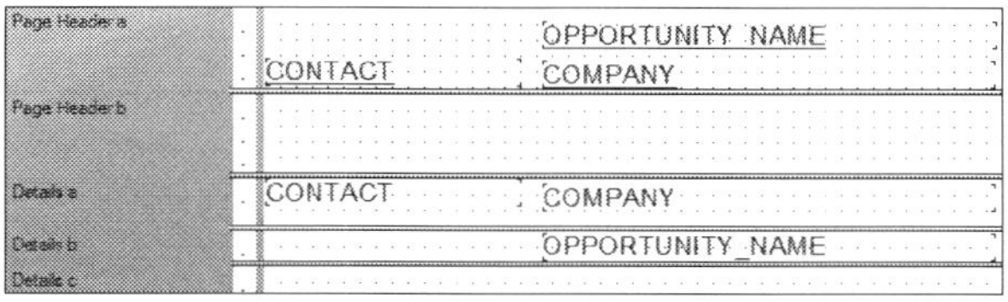

Figure 8-7 L8.1 Subsections report with new sections

Exercise 8.2: Add A Background Color To A Report Section

If you applied a background color to the page header section, all of the objects in the section would have the background. If there are other objects in the page header section besides the field headings, this may not be what you want. Fortunately, there is a solution for this.

If you only want the background color applied to the field headings and not the other objects in the page header section, you have to move the field headings to a new section.

1. Save the L6.1 report as `L8.2 Section background color`.

2. Move the fields closer together.

3. Open the Section Expert and select the Page Header section, then click on the Color tab.

4. Check the Background Color option, then open the drop-down list and select the color Gray. Click OK.

5. Select all of the field headings and change the color to white, then remove the underline and move the fields. (**Hint**: Use the Font tab on the Format Editor.)

6. Save the changes. The report should look like the one shown in Figure 8-8.

PRODUCTID	PRODUCT	PRICE
{10D6D3E9-051	Mini Core Replacement	100.00
{D55410C5-9F2	ONE Component	2,500.00
{9DA1C71E-163	Service Contract	2,000.00
{E24C2E33-177	TechONE System	12,000.00
{339AF93C-974	TWO Component	4,000.00

Figure 8-8 L8.2 Section background color report

Exercise 8.3: Add A Border To A Field

You have learned several formatting techniques that you can use to make reports look better. Another technique that you can use is to put borders around a field. Borders are often used to make a field stand out on the report. In this exercise you will add a border to the notes type field. ACT! has a notes field, but in the demo database the field does not have a lot of data. Instead, you will use fields on the History tab. To do that, you will have to add two tables to the report. In the previous lesson you learned about the Can Grow option. A notes field is a good field to use this option on.

Add Tables To The Report

1. Save the L8.1 report as `L8.3 Border around field`.

2. Open the Database Expert. Add the Contact History and History tables.

3. On the Links tab remove the links, then add the links in Table 8-1, as shown in Figure 8-9, then click OK.

Link This Field	To This Field
Contact.Contact ID	Contact History.Contact ID
Contact.Contact ID	Contact Opportunity.Contact ID
Contact History.History ID	History.History ID
Contact Opportunity.Opportunity ID	Opportunity.Opportunity ID

Table 8-1 Links to create

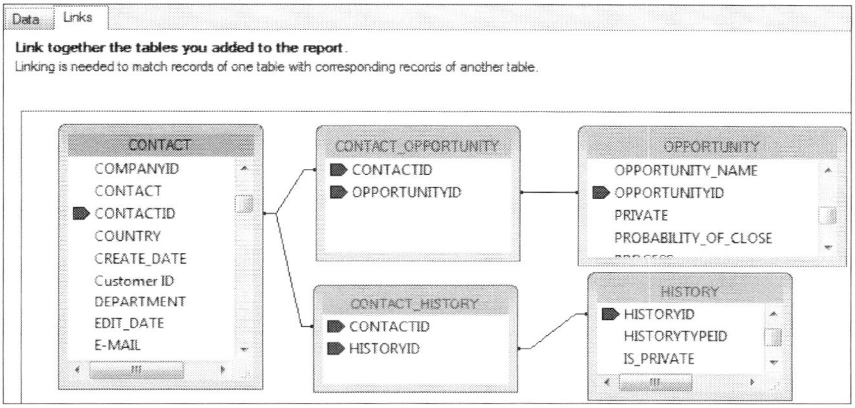

Figure 8-9 Tables and links added to the report

Create The Border

1. Make the details b and c sections longer.

2. Add the Create Date and Regarding fields in the History table to the details c section of the report. Make the Regarding field longer, as shown in Figure 8-10.

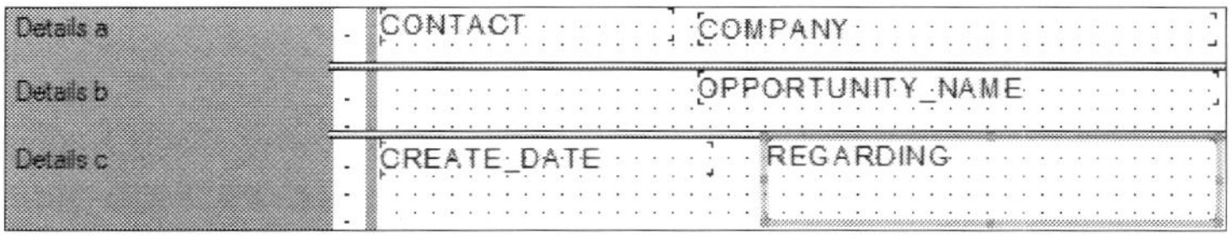

Figure 8-10 Fields added to the details section

3. Right-click on the Regarding field and select Format Field. On the Common tab check the **CAN GROW** option.

> It may be a good idea to check the **CLOSE BORDER ON PAGE BREAK** option on the Common tab on the Format Editor for fields that have a border because it is possible that the field could print on more than one page, especially a field that has the Can Grow option.

4. On the Border tab check the **DROP SHADOW** option.

5. Change the Line Style to **DOTTED** for the Left and Right options, then change the Top and Bottom Line Style options to **SINGLE**.

   You should have the options selected that are shown in Figure 8-11.

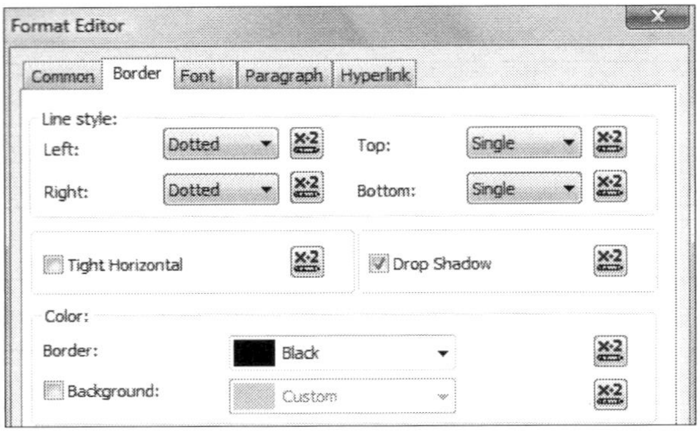

Figure 8-11 Border options

6. Add a line at the bottom of the details c section.

7. Save the changes. The report should look like the one shown in Figure 8-12. Close the report.

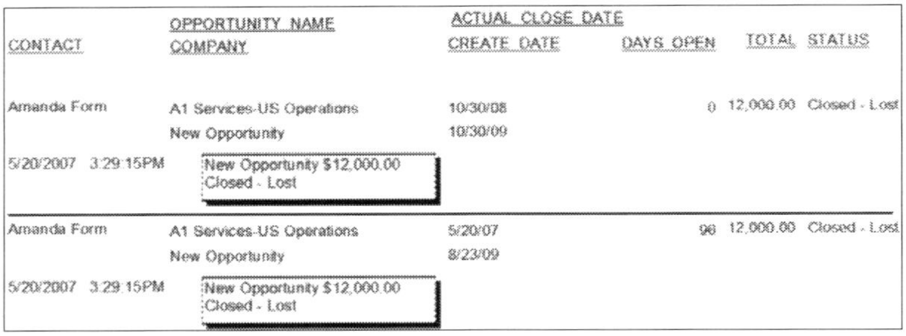

Figure 8-12 L8.3 Border around field report

Exercise 8.4: Adding Boxes To A Report

If you need to make something on a report stand out or you want to put a more decorative border around a field or heading then the border options that you learned about in Exercise 8.3, you can use the options on the Box tab on the Format Editor. In this exercise you will add a box to a field and a box to a report title. There are two ways to open the Box tool, as discussed below.

① Click the **INSERT BOX** button on the Insert toolbar.

② Insert ⇒ Box.

Add The Box

1. Save the L8.3 report as `L8.4 Box around objects`.

2. Remove the border from the Regarding field. Leave space in the details c section above and below the Regarding field.

3. Delete the line in the details c section.

4. Open the Box tool and draw a box around the Regarding field.

5. Right-click on the box and select Format Box. As you can see, the Box tab has many of the same options that the Line tab has. Table 8-2 explains the options that are different on the Box tab.

> If you have trouble selecting the box, open the Report Explorer and select it from there.

Box Option	Description
Fill Color	If checked, this option will let you apply a background color to the box.
Always Close Border	This option will close a box by adding additional lines if a box also prints on the next page of the report. The box at the bottom of the page will have a bottom line added to the border. The box at the top of the next page will have a line at the top of the box added automatically.
Extend to Bottom of Section when Printing	Checking this option will allow the box to extend to the bottom of the section as the field that it is being used for extends (grows).

Table 8-2 Box tab options explained

6. Select the **DOTTED** Border Style, then check the **FILL COLOR** option and select Silver as the color.

   Check the **EXTEND TO BOTTOM OF SECTION WHEN PRINTING** option. You should have the options selected that are shown in Figure 8-13.

   Leave the Format Editor open to complete the next part of the exercise.

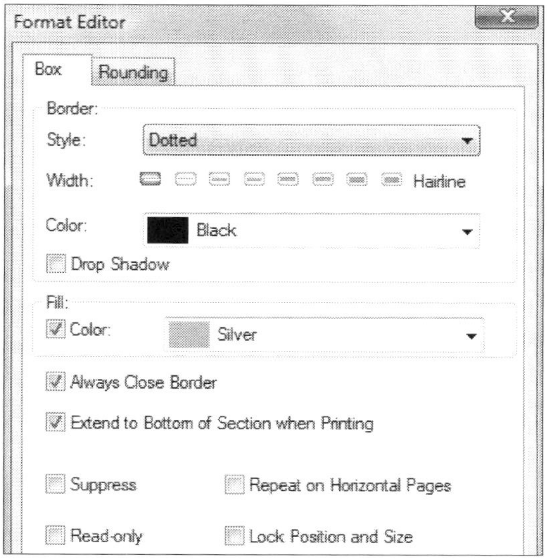

Figure 8-13 Box tab options

Use The Rounding Options

The options on the Rounding tab are used to make the corners of the box round.

1. On the Rounding tab change the **ROUNDING PERCENT** option to 50.

   You should have the options selected that are shown in Figure 8-14.

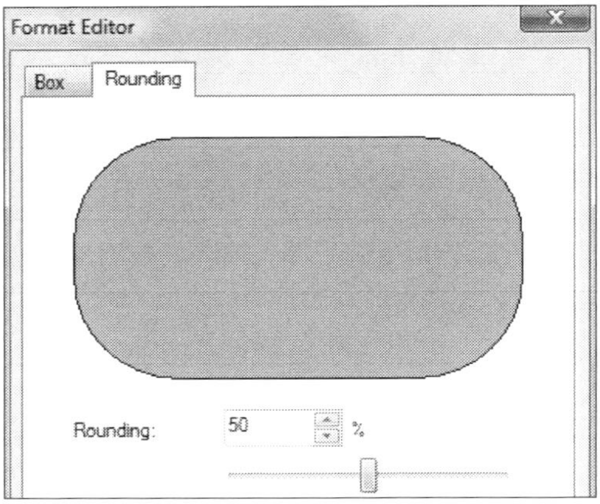

Figure 8-14 Rounding tab options

2. Click OK and save the changes. Leave the report open to complete the next part of the exercise.

> If you move the slider all the way to the right, the box will change to a circle.

Add A Box Around A Text Object

Just like you can place a box around a data field, you can place a box around a text object.

1. Add a text object to the report header section. Type `Contact Opportunities` in the text object.

2. Change the font size to 12. Make sure that there is some space above the text object.

3. Make the border of the text object smaller, so that it is close to the words in it.

4. Draw a box around the text object, then open the Format Editor for the box.

5. Accept the default options on the Box tab. Change the rounding percent to 100 on the Rounding tab. Click OK and save the changes. The report should look like the one shown in Figure 8-15. Close the report.

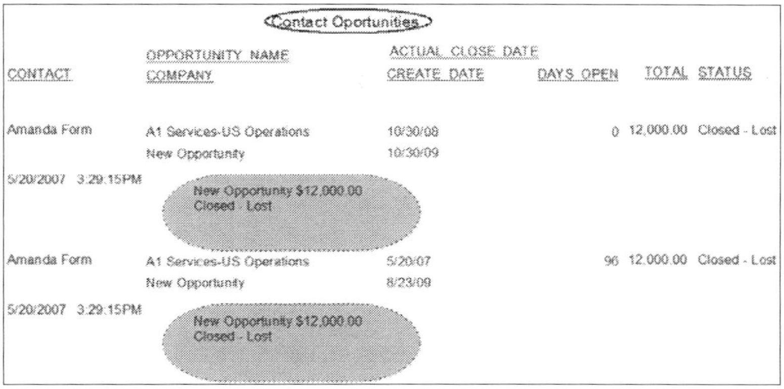

Figure 8-15 L8.4 Box around objects report

Deleting Objects From The Report Layout

There are three ways to delete one object or several objects from a report as discussed below. When deleting fields in the details section, the field heading in the page header section is also deleted.

① Right-click on the object(s) and select Delete.
② Select the object(s) and press the Delete key.
③ Select the object(s), then Edit ⇒ Delete.

Special Fields

Crystal Reports has 26 built-in fields that you can add to reports. You can drop and drag these fields from the Field Explorer to the report, just like you drop and drag fields from tables in the Field Explorer.

Figure 8-16 shows the Special Fields that you can add. Because these are system fields, the data in the field can change each time the report is run.

Table 8-3 explains the data that each of the Special Fields contains.

Special fields, like the fields from a table that are added to the details section, have headings automatically created in the page header section.

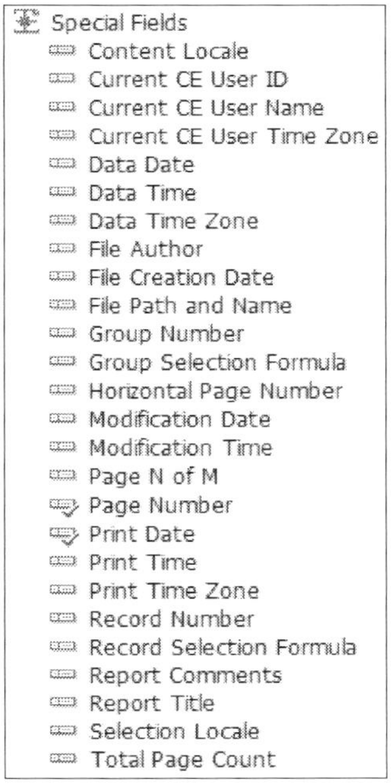

Figure 8-16 Special Fields

Special Field	The Field Will Print The . . .
Content Locale	Information in the **LOCATION** field. This data comes from the Regional & Language Options dialog box (which is part of Windows) shown in Figure 8-17. (1)
Current CE User ID	ID number of the Business Objects user. (1)
Current CE User Name	Name of the Business Objects user. (1)
Current CE User Time Zone	Time zone that the Business Objects user is in. (1)
Data Date	Date the data was last refreshed in the report.
Data Time	Time the data was last refreshed in the report.
Data Time Zone	Time Zone that the data was last refreshed in the report.
File Author	Information in the **AUTHOR** field. (2)
File Creation Date	Date the report was first created.
File Path And Name	File path and name of the report. (The location on the hard drive or server). For example: C:\Crystal Reports Book\L4.3 Product list.rpt.
Grouping Number	Number of each group in the group header or footer section. If the report does not have any groups, this field will print a "1". This number is created each time the report is run.
Group Selection Formula	Group selection formula if applicable.
Horizontal Page Number	Page number by objects like cross-tabs and OLAP grids that print on more than one page horizontally.
Modification Date	Date the report was last modified. This would be helpful during the report creation and modification process.
Modification Time	Time the report was last saved.
Page N of M	Page number and total number of pages in this format: Page 3 of 24. (3)
Page Number	Current page number.
Print Date	Date the report was printed. (1)
Print Time	Time the report was printed. (1)
Print Time Zone	Time zone the report was printed in. This data comes from the Date & Time Properties dialog box (which is part of Windows) shown in Figure 8-20. (1)
Record Number	System generated number that is a counter for each detail record. It is based on the sort order in the report.
Record Selection Formula	Record Selection formula that was created in the Record Selection Formula Editor.
Report Comments	Information in the **COMMENTS** field. (2)
Report Title	Information in the **TITLE** field. (2)
Selection Locale	NEW Contains the locale setting (the country) of the computer that the report is running on.
Total Page Count	Total number of pages in the report. (3)

Table 8-3 Special Fields explained

(1) This data comes from the computer that the report is run from.
(2) This data comes from the Summary tab on the Document Properties dialog box shown in Figure 8-19.

(3) The Page N of M and Total Page Count fields add to the processing time when the report is generated. If the report has hundreds of pages, you may notice a delay while the data is being processed, but it is bearable. If the report will contain hundreds or thousands of pages, it is best to leave the Page N of M field off of the report while you are designing it because Crystal Reports has to generate the entire report prior to displaying or printing these fields, which will take some time. Right before you put the report into production, add these fields to the report as needed.

To view the dialog box shown in Figure 8-17 or 8-18, open the Control Panel in Windows, then double-click on the **REGIONAL AND LANGUAGE OPTIONS** icon.
File ⇒ Summary Info, opens the dialog box shown in Figure 8-19.

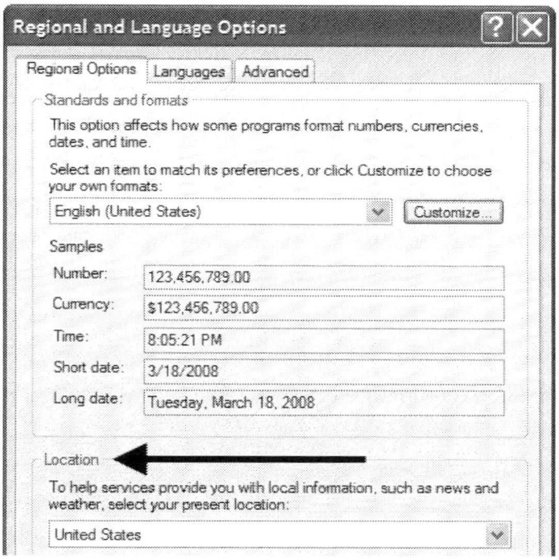

Figure 8-17 Location option illustrated in Windows XP

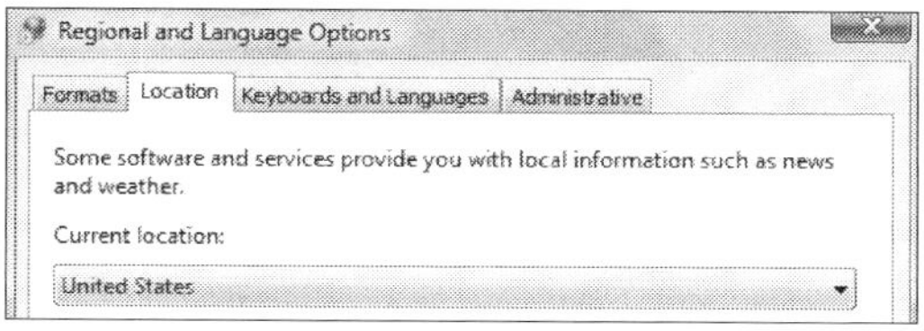

Figure 8-18 Location option in Windows Vista

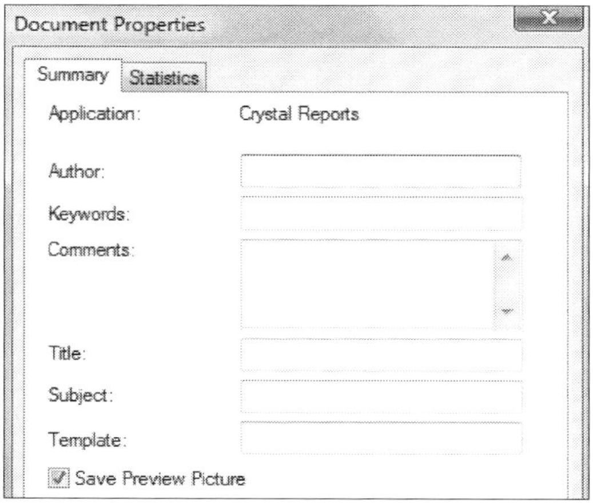

Figure 8-19 Summary tab options

To view the dialog box shown in Figure 8-20, open the Control Panel in Windows.

Double-click on the **DATE AND TIME** option, then click on the Time Zone tab in Windows XP.

In Windows Vista, the Time Zone options are on the Date & Time tab.

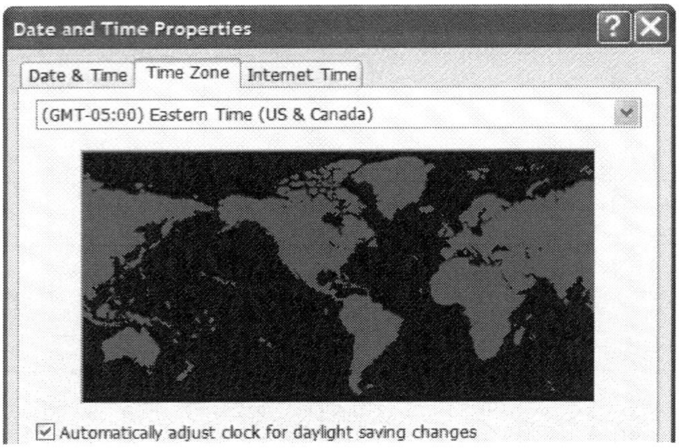

Figure 8-20 Time Zone options

Exercise 8.5: Add Special Fields To A Report

As you learned in Table 8-3 above, there are several Date and Time fields. To better understand what each of these fields will print, you will add all of them to one report in this exercise.

1. Save the L6.1 report as `L8.5 Date special fields`.
2. Make the report header section longer by dragging the section bar down to the fifth row of grid dots in the page header section.
3. Open the Special Fields section of the Field Explorer and drag the **DATA DATE** field to the upper right corner of the report header section.
4. Add the **DATA TIME** field to the upper right corner of the report header section and place it below the Data Date field.

Adding Text Objects

As you noticed, the headings were not created for the special fields that you added to the report header section. You have two options for using a text object with Special Fields, as discussed below. I tend to use the second option because I find it easier to move the objects when they are combined, but you can use either option.

① Create a text object. Enter a title for the field and place the text object next to the special field.
② Complete ① above, then press the **SPACE BAR** and drag the special field into the text object.

1. Create two text objects in the report header section.
   Type `Date the data was last refreshed:` in one of the text objects.
   Type `Time the data was last refreshed:` in the other text object.
   Make both text objects bold.

2. Rearrange the fields and text objects so that they look like the ones shown in Figure 8-21. Save the changes and leave the report open to complete the next part of the exercise.

> You may need to use the **ALIGN** options that you learned about in Lesson 6 to line up the objects that you just added to the report. This would be a good use of the Align ⇒ Baseline option, so that you can line up the text object and the corresponding field because the text object is bold and the field is not.

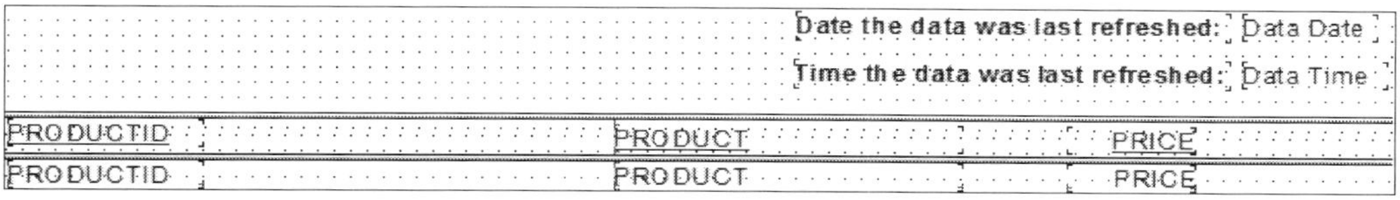

Figure 8-21 Fields and text objects arranged on the report

Add More Date And Time Special Fields

1. In the report header section, add the Special Fields and Text Objects in Table 8-4. Arrange the objects so that they look like the ones shown in Figure 8-22.

Special Field	Text For The Text Object
File Creation Date	Date the report was designed:
Modification Date	Date the report was last saved:
Modification Time	Time the report was last saved:
Print Date	Date the report was printed:

Table 8-4 Fields and text objects to add to the report

> You can select all of the special fields and then drag them to the report header at the same time.

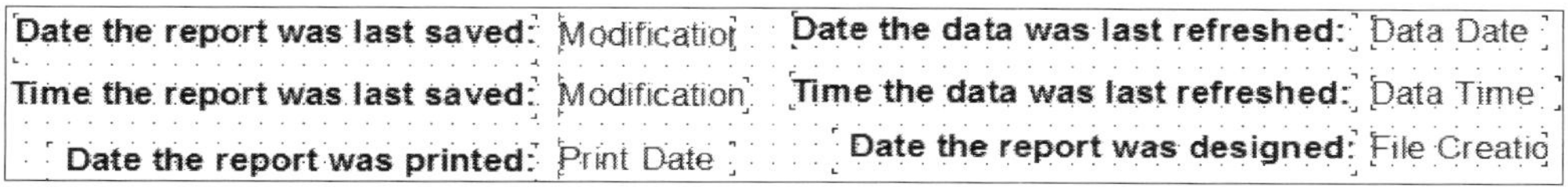

Figure 8-22 Special Fields and text objects arranged on the report

2. Save the changes. If prompted to refresh the data, click **NO**. Make any changes that are needed. The report should look similar to the one shown in Figure 8-23. Write down the dates and times that are displayed in the report. You can write them next to the headings in Figure 8-23.

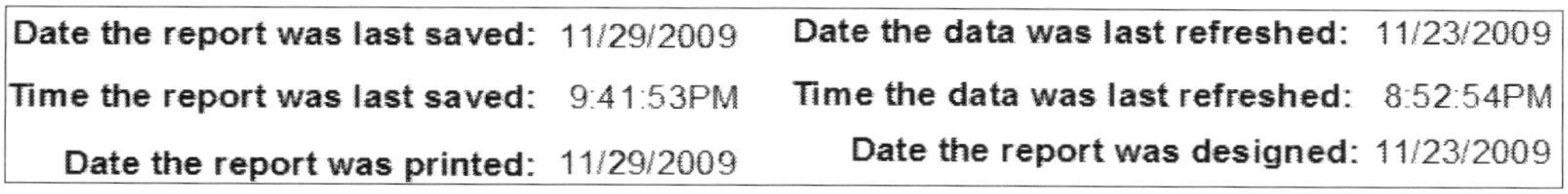

Figure 8-23 L8.5 report run on day one

3. Tomorrow, run this report twice as follows:

   ① Run the report without refreshing the data. Compare the dates and times to those that you wrote down in step 2 above. My report looks like the one shown in Figure 8-24. The only field that should have changed is the **DATE THE REPORT WAS PRINTED** field.

   ② Move the Print Date field and title to the upper left corner of the report and save the changes. Refresh the data and run the report. Compare the data to what you wrote down in step 2 above. My report looks like the one shown in Figure 8-25. The only field that should still have the same data is the **DATE THE REPORT WAS DESIGNED**, as shown in Figure 8-23 above.

Date the report was last saved:	11/29/2009	**Date the data was last refreshed:**	11/23/2009
Time the report was last saved:	9:41:53PM	**Time the data was last refreshed:**	8:52:54PM
Date the report was printed:	11/30/2009	**Date the report was designed:**	11/23/2009

Figure 8-24 L8.5 report run on day two without modifications

Date the report was printed:	**Date the report was last saved:**	11/30/2009	**Date the data was last refreshed:**	11/30/2009
11/30/2009	**Time the report was last saved:**	5:28:40PM	**Time the data was last refreshed:**	5:28:46PM
			Date the report was designed:	11/23/2009

Figure 8-25 L8.5 report run on day two with modifications

4. Save the changes and close the report.

Report Explorer

By default, the Report Explorer displays the following report sections, whether or not they are actually being used in the report: report header, page header, details, report footer and page footer. Figure 8-26 shows the Report Explorer window. At the top of the tree structure is the report name. Each of the branches in the tree represents one section of the report.

If you click on an object in the Report Explorer, the object will be displayed and highlighted in the design window. You may find it easier to locate the object that you need to edit or format in this window, then in the Field Explorer once it has been added to the report. Like the Field Explorer, the Report Explorer is used to view all of the fields on the report. The Report Explorer also displays all of the other objects that are on the report, like charts and images.

The icon next to a report section in the Report Explorer will change if the section has been suppressed (hidden) on the report. I find it hard to tell one icon from the next for the report sections. The field shortcut menus are the same as the ones in the Field Explorer.

Table 8-5 explains the buttons on the Report Explorer toolbar shown in Figure 8-27. The last three buttons on the toolbar are used to filter the object types, which means that you do not have to display all of the objects in the Report Explorer. This is helpful if you need to only see certain object types.

> The group header and footer sections are only displayed in the Report Explorer if they are being used.

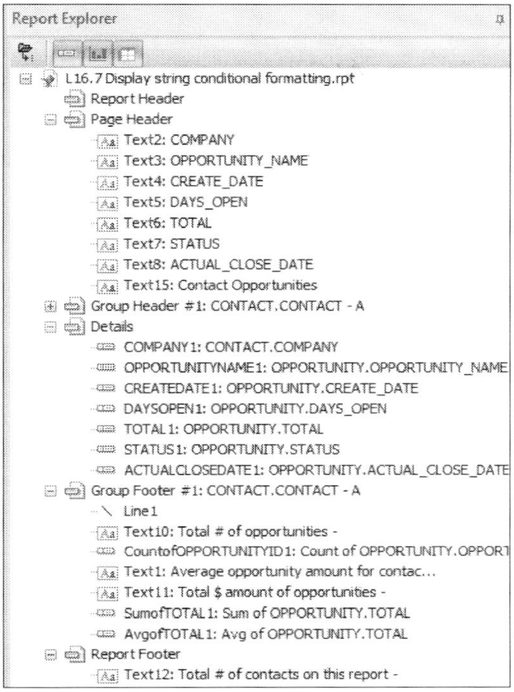

Figure 8-26 Report Explorer window

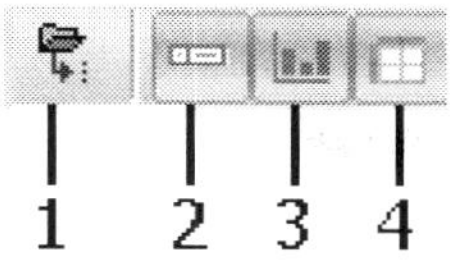

Figure 8-27 Report Explorer toolbar

Button	Purpose
1	The **EXPAND** button opens all of the sections in the Report Explorer that have a plus sign.
2	The **SHOW/HIDE DATA FIELDS** button will display or hide the data objects.
3	The **SHOW/HIDE GRAPHICAL OBJECTS** button will display or hide the lines, boxes, charts, maps and images (like photos or logos) in the Report Explorer.
4	The **SHOW/HIDE GRIDS AND SUBREPORTS** button will display or hide the cross-tabs, OLAP grids and subreports in the Report Explorer.

Table 8-5 Report Explorer toolbar buttons explained

You can delete objects in the Report Explorer, but you cannot add new objects in the Report Explorer.

If you right-click on an object in the Report Explorer, you will see the shortcut menu editing options shown in Figure 8-28. The shortcut menu options vary depending on the object that is selected. Figure 8-29 shows the shortcut menu if you right-click in the Report Explorer and an object is not selected.

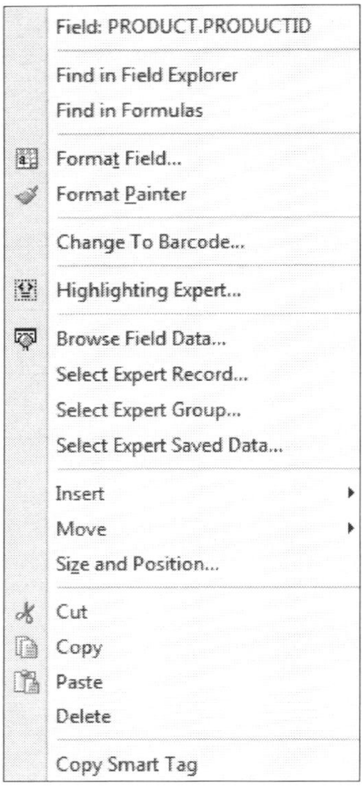

Figure 8-29 Report Explorer shortcut menu options when an object is not selected

Figure 8-28 Report Explorer shortcut menu editing options for a data field

If you need to make the same change to more than one field or object, select all of the fields and objects that require the change and then open the shortcut menu shown above in Figure 8-28.

The fields that you select should be the same data type, to make the best use of editing multiple fields. If you select multiple fields that have different data types, the shortcut menu options that you can use will be limited to those that work for all of the data types of the fields that you have selected.

Report Explorer Section Shortcut Menu

This shortcut menu has options that you can use to manage the sections of the report. Many of the options on the Report Explorer section shortcut menu shown in Figure 8-30 are the same as the options on the Report Section shortcut menu. Depending on the section that you right-click on in the Report Explorer, you will see different options on the shortcut menu.

Table 8-6 explains all of the options on the Report Explorer Section Shortcut menu, regardless of which section you right-click on.

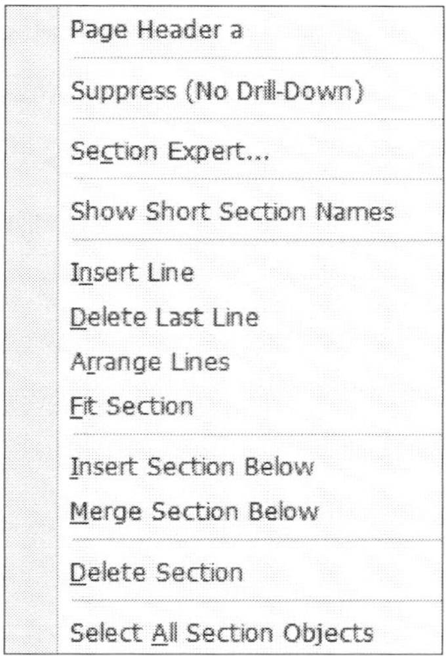

Figure 8-30 Report Explorer Section shortcut menu

Option	Description
Hide/Show (Drill-Down OK)	Hides the section when the report is printed. The section can be viewed on the preview window.
Suppress (No Drill-Down)	The section that this option is applied to will not be printed and cannot be viewed on the preview window.
Section Expert	Opens the Section Expert.
Show Short/Long Section Names	Toggles between displaying long and short section names.
Insert Line	Adds a guideline to the section that is selected.
Delete Last Line	Deletes the last guideline that was added to the section.
Arrange Lines	Spaces the guidelines in a section evenly.
Fit Section	Moves the bottom section bar up to the lowest object in the section.
Insert Section Below	Creates a new section below the selected section.
Merge Section Below	Combines the fields in the selected subsection with the subsection below it.
Delete Section	Deletes a sub section of the report. (4)
Hide Area	Hides a subsection of the report. (4)
Suppress Area	Suppress a subsection of the report. (4)
Don't Suppress Area	When selected, the subsection cannot be suppressed. (4)
Select All Section Objects	Selects all of the objects in the section. This is useful when you need to apply the same formatting or change to all of the objects in a section.

Table 8-6 Report Explorer section shortcut menu options explained

(4) This option is only available for a report section that has at least one subsection.

Custom Colors

If you create a custom color it can be saved. To create a custom color follow the steps below.

1. Open the Format Editor, then click on the Border tab or any tab that has a **COLOR** drop-down list field.

2. Open the Color drop-down list and select **MORE**, as illustrated in Figure 8-31.

   You will see the Color dialog box.

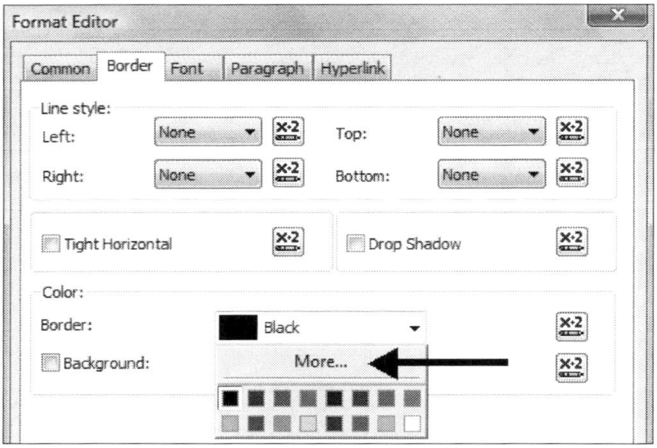

Figure 8-31 Color option illustrated

3. Use the options to create the custom color that you want.

   When you are finished, click the **ADD TO CUSTOM COLORS** button, shown in Figure 8-32.

   The color that you created should be in one of the custom color boxes on the left, as illustrated.

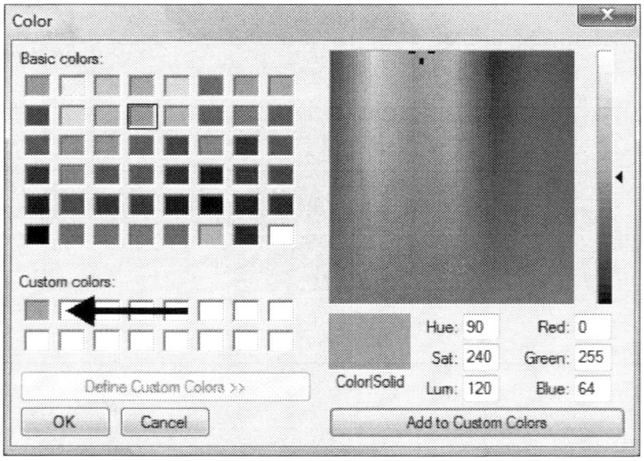

Figure 8-32 Color dialog box

4. Click OK twice to close both dialog boxes. Save the report. When you re-open the Color dialog box shown above in Figure 8-32, you will see the custom color that you created.

SELECTING RECORDS

After completing the exercises in this lesson you will be able to use the following techniques to control which records will appear on a report:

- ☑ Select, filter and query records
- ☑ Create report summary information
- ☑ Add summary information to a report

LESSON 9

Selecting Records Overview

So far you have learned to create a variety of basic reports. All of the reports that you created without a wizard retrieved almost all of the records in the tables. As you saw, many of the reports contained 500 or more detail records. Most of the time reports provide specific information, which means that all of the records in the tables selected should not be on every report that is created. For reports that use tables similar to the size of the ones in the ACT! demo database, this may not be a problem, but if the report is using tables or other data sources with thousands or millions of records (think credit card statements), the report will take a long time to run. Not only will you notice this on your computer, which may run out of memory, the network will also take a performance hit.

One way that Crystal Reports lets you narrow down the records that will appear on the report is through a selection process. One selection process uses the **SELECT EXPERT**. This tool is used to select which records will appear on the report by entering **CRITERIA** that a record must meet. Records that do not meet the criteria will not appear on the report. This process is also known as **FILTERING RECORDS** or **QUERYING THE DATABASE**. Other ways to select records include writing formulas and using functions.

In Lesson 4 when you used a wizard to create the L4.1 report, you created a filter on the Record Selection screen. [See Lesson 4, Figure 4-16] The Record Selection screen has similar functionality to the Select Expert that you will learn how to use in this lesson.

Examples of the types of information that can be retrieved when selecting records, filtering records or querying the database, include the following:

① Orders that were placed during a specific date range, like the month of June.
② Customers that purchased a specific product.
③ Orders that are over a certain dollar amount.
④ Products that need to be reordered.

Selecting, filtering or querying the database lets you ask a question about the data and then retrieve the records that meet the criteria that you specify. The records that are retrieved are known as a **RECORDSET**. The examples above are only asking one question. You can ask more than one question in the same query. You can ask the following types of multi-part questions.

① Orders that were placed during a specific date range and were more than $500.
② Customers that purchased a specific product and live in a specific state.
③ Orders that are over a certain dollar amount that were taken by a certain salesperson.
④ Customers that have a credit limit of $1,000 or more and have placed at least one order over $2,500, that shipped during a specific date range.
⑤ Orders that were placed or shipped during a specific date range.

In Lesson 5 you learned a little about SQL. Like SQL, the selection process produces the same results. Think of the Select Expert as an SQL code generator, without actually having to write code. The Select Expert creates the SQL code for you, which makes the Select Expert easy to use. The SQL code is what Crystal Reports uses to select records for the report.

In addition to selecting individual records, the Select Expert can also select groups. A group selection example would be to only display records in states that have an order total amount between $100,000 and $400,000.

The Select Expert provides two ways to select records as discussed below:

① Use the built-in **OPERATORS**. Table 9-1 explains the operators that are available. Not all of the operators listed in the table are available for all field types.
② **FORMULAS** let you write the SQL code. This is not a contradiction to what I said earlier about not having to write code to use the Select Expert, because writing code in the Select Expert is not mandatory.

Operator	This Operator Selects Records That . . .
Is Equal To	Are equal to (the same as) the value that you specify.
Is Not Equal To	Are not equal to the value that you specify. This operator works the opposite of the "Is Equal To" operator.
Is One Of	Match at least one of the values that you specify. If the criteria is NY, NJ or PA for the State field, any record that has one of these values in the state field would appear on the report.
Is Not One Of	Are not one of the values that you specify. This operator works the opposite of the "Is One Of" operator.
Is Less Than	Are less than the value that you specify. If you want to see products that have a reorder level of less then 10 items in stock, enter 10 in the criteria field and the report will display products with a reorder level of nine or less. (1)
Is Less Than Or Equal To	(Works similar to "Is Less Than"). The difference is that this operator will also select records that have the value that you specify. In the less than example above, the report would not display records with a reorder level of 10 items. The less than or equal to operator will. (1)
Is Greater Than	Are greater than the value that you specify. If you want to see all orders with an order amount over $500, enter $500 in the criteria field and the report will display records with an order amount of $500.01 or more.
Is Greater Than Or Equal To	(Works similar to "Is Greater Than"). The difference is that this operator will also select records that have the value that you specify. In the greater than example above, the report would not display records with an order amount of exactly $500. The greater than or equal to operator will.
Is Between	Fall between two values. If you want to see order amounts between $1,000 and $5,000 or orders between 6/1/08 and 6/15/08, this is the operator that you would use. This operator also selects records equal to the two values that you enter for the range.
Is Not Between	Are not in the range of values that you enter. This operator works the opposite of the "Is Between" operator. It will retrieve records outside of the range that you select.
Starts With	Begins with a specific character or set of characters. If you want to retrieve records of employees whose last name starts with the letter "M", use this operator. (2)

Table 9-1 Select Expert operators explained

Operator	This Operator Selects Records That . . .
Does Not Start With	Do not start with the character or set of characters that you specify. This operator works the opposite of the "Starts With" operator. (2)
Is Like	Meet the wildcard criteria that you specify. The wildcard characters that you can use are a ? (question mark) and an * (asterisk). (2)
Is Not Like	Do not meet the criteria that you specify with the wildcards. This operator works the opposite of the "Is Like" operator. (2)
Is In The Period	Meet the criteria of one of the functions explained in Table 9-2. These functions will save you a lot of time because you do not have to figure out what the formula should be. (3)
Is Not In The Period	Are not in the period that you select. This operator works the opposite of the "Is In The Period" operator. (3)
Is True	Have a value of true in the Boolean field. (4)
Is False	Have a value of false in the Boolean field. (4)
Formula	Is used to write the code for the records that need to be selected.

Table 9-1 Select Expert operators explained (Continued)

(1) This operator can also be used with a string field.
(2) This operator can only be used with a string field.
(3) This operator can only be used with date and date/time fields.
(4) This operator can only be used with a Boolean field.

In addition to the operators listed above in Table 9-1, there is another operator, **IS ANY VALUE**, which is the default operator that you see when the Select Expert is first opened. This operator does not apply any condition to the field that it is associated to. In reports that do not select any criteria, this is the operator that is used by default when the report is run.

The functions in Table 9-2 provide a date range. You can create the same criteria using the "Is Between" operator, but using these built-in functions is easier and does not require dates to be hard coded.

Function	When It Starts And Ends
Week To Date From Sun	From last Sunday to today
Month To Date	From the beginning of the current month to today
Year To Date	From the first day of the current year to today
Last 7 Days	From 7 days ago to today
Last 4 Weeks To Sun	From 4 weeks prior to last Sunday to last Sunday
Last Full Week	From Sunday of last week to Saturday of last week
Last Full Month	From the first day of last month to the last day of last month
All Dates To Today	From the earliest date in the table up to and including today
All Dates To Yesterday	From the earliest date in the table up to and including yesterday

Table 9-2 Is in the period criteria functions explained

Function	When It Starts And Ends
All Dates From Today	From today forward
All Dates From Tomorrow	From yesterday forward
Aged 0 To 30 Days	From 30 days ago to today
Aged 31 To 60 Days	From 31 days ago from today to 60 days ago
Aged 61 To 90 Days	From 61 days ago from today to 90 days ago
Over 90 Days	More than 90 days ago
Next 30 days	From today to 30 days in the future
Next 31 To 60 Days	From 31 days from today to 60 days in the future
Next 61 To 90 Days	From 61 days from today to 90 days in the future
Next 91 To 365 Days	From 91 days from today to 365 days in the future
Calendar 1st Qtr	From January 1 of the current year to March 31 of the current year
Calendar 2nd Qtr	From April 1 of the current year to June 30 of the current year
Calendar 3rd Qtr	From July 1 of the current year to September 30 of the current year
Calendar 4th Qtr	From October 1 of the current year to December 31 of the current year
Calendar 1st Half	From January 1 of the current year to June 30 of the current year
Calendar 2nd Half	From July 1 of the current year to December 31 of the current year
Last Year MTD	From the first day of the current month last year to the same month and day last year
Last Year YTD	From January 1 of last year to today's month and day last year

Table 9-2 Is in the period criteria functions explained (Continued)

Using The Select Expert

For the most part, using the Select Expert is point and click. The only time that you have to type is if the value that you want to use is not in the drop-down list. This sometimes happens because the drop-down list only displays the first 500 unique values in a field. Any field that has multiple values that are identical will only display the value once in the drop-down list. An example of this would be a date field because it is possible that multiple records have the same date in the same field.

If you want to create a customer order report and only want to display records for the Wheels Company, this company name may not appear in the drop-down list because there could be more than 500 companies in the table and this company name is near the end of the alphabet. This is an example of when you would have to type something in the Select Expert.

The other time that you would need to type something in the Select Expert is if you are using a value that you know is not one of the values for the field. For example, if you want to select records that have an order amount greater than $600. You may have to type 600 in the field if the Order Amount field does not have that value in any of the first 500 values that are in the drop-down list.

NEW The Select Expert is used to create criteria by record, group or saved data, as shown in Figure 9-1.

The **RECORD** option is used to create criteria for a field.

Select the **GROUP** option when you want the criteria based on a group name or summary field.

Figure 9-1 Select Expert submenu options

Select the **SAVED DATA** option when you want to filter data that has been saved with the report. This option does not cause data to be refreshed.

Unless stated otherwise, when opening the Select Expert to complete exercises in this book, select the Record option or just click on the button.

There are three ways to open the Select Expert, as discussed below:

① Right-click on the field that you want to create criteria for and select the **SELECT EXPERT** option that you need.
② Click the **SELECT EXPERT** button on the Expert Tools toolbar.
③ Report ⇒ Select Expert.

If you click on the field that you want to create the criteria for before you select option two or three above, the Select Expert will open with the field selected and you can start to create the selection criteria.

You can also use the Select Expert in the preview window.

The first eight exercises in this lesson will teach you how to create a variety of queries using the operators that you learned about earlier in Table 9-1. Hopefully, this will make you feel comfortable using the Select Expert.

Exercise 9.1: Using The Is Equal To Operator

In this exercise you will use the Select Expert to find contacts that are in CA.

1. Save the L7.5 report as `L9.1 State = CA`. Notice that there are 199 records in the report. The number of records is displayed in the Status bar.

2. Use one of the last two options discussed earlier to open the Select Expert to create criteria per record. You will learn how to use the first option in the next exercise. You will see the dialog box shown in Figure 9-2.

The reason that you see the Choose Field dialog box is because a field was not selected in the report prior to opening the Select Expert.

The **REPORT FIELDS** section at the top of the dialog box lists the fields that are currently on the report. Below that you will see all of the data sources that are connected to the report.

You can use any field in the Choose Field dialog box as a field for the selection criteria, whether or not it is being displayed on the report.

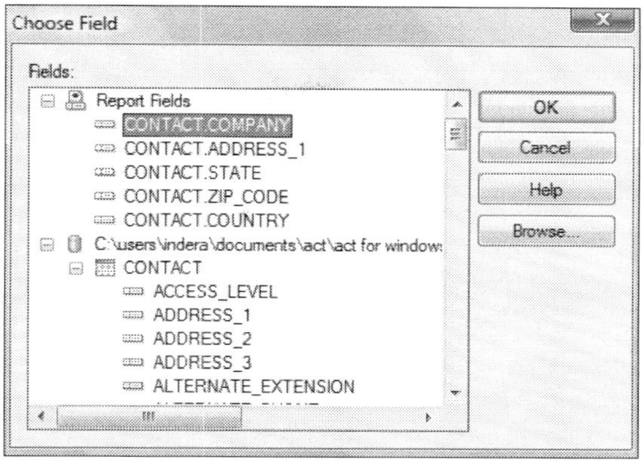

Figure 9-2 Choose Field dialog box

3. Click on the **CONTACT.STATE** field in the Report Fields section, then click OK. You will see the dialog box shown in Figure 9-3.

   Notice that the field that you selected is the name on the first tab. Multiple tabs means that there is more than one set of selection criteria for the report. The type of criteria that you are creating is in the Title bar.

Figure 9-3 Select Expert dialog box

The **NEW** button opens the Choose Field dialog box shown earlier in Figure 9-2.
The **DELETE** button deletes the tab that is selected.
The **BROWSE** button is used to view data in the field that is selected.
The **SHOW FORMULA** button will display the formula (in SQL) that was created by the selection criteria that you created.

4. Open the drop-down list and select **IS EQUAL TO**. You will see another drop-down list. This drop-down list is connected to the field that is selected. The values in the second drop-down list are from the State field in the table, as shown in Figure 9-4. As you learned earlier, drop-down lists that are connected to a field, only display the first 500 unique values in the field.

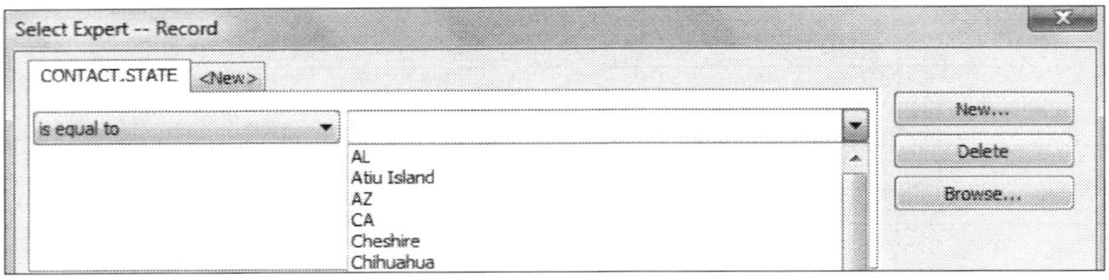

Figure 9-4 Data from the State field

5. Select **CA** from the drop-down list shown above in Figure 9-4. Figure 9-5 shows the criteria that should be selected. When the report is run, it will use this criteria to find records that have CA in the State field. Click OK and preview the report. You may see the message shown in Figure 9-6.

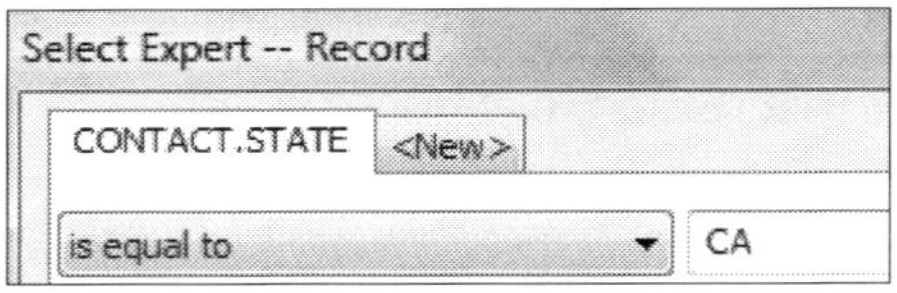

Figure 9-5 Record selection criteria

Figure 9-6 Change In Record Selection Formula message

The message in Figure 9-6 is asking if you want to use the data that is currently saved with the report or if you want to refresh the data. It also tells you the date and time the data was last refreshed. If you know that the data in the report is current or you want to use the data that is saved with the report, click the **USE SAVED DATA** button. If you are not sure, click the **REFRESH DATA** button. When in doubt, refresh the data.

If you were creating this report and using live data, you would probably select the Refresh Data option the first time that you run the report after creating the selection criteria. Keep in mind that refreshing data can take a little longer than using saved data if there are thousands of records in the table. Under certain conditions you may have to refresh the data, regardless of how long it takes. Don't worry, even with thousands of records, it only takes a few seconds. If the record selection criteria changes, Crystal Reports does not know if the database has to be re-queried. When this is the case, you will see the message shown above in Figure 9-6.

If you changed the selection criteria to include more records than the original selection criteria, you should refresh the data, so that the additional records that meet the criteria can be retrieved from the database. If you do not refresh the data when the modified selection criteria includes more records, the report will not display all of the records that should be on the report.

It is also possible that no records will be displayed on the report depending on the revised selection criteria, if the data is not refreshed.

6. Click the **REFRESH DATA** button. The report should look like the one shown in Figure 9-7. Notice that 26 records are displayed on the report. This means that there are 26 records in the Contact table in the state of CA. Save the changes and close the report.

COMPANY	ADDRESS 1	STATE	ZIP CODE	COUNTRY
Twelfth Dream	2010 Act Way	CA	94063	United States
Duke Industries	4075 Santa Monica Frwy	CA	90029	United States
Duke Industries	4075 Santa Monica Frwy	CA	90029	United States
Mad House;The	22 Acacia Ave.	CA	90266	United States

Figure 9-7 L9.1 State = CA report

Exercise 9.2: Using The Is One Of Operator

In the previous exercise you used the "Is Equal To" operator to find contacts in one state. In this exercise you will use the "Is One Of" operator to find contacts that are in OH or FL.

1. Save the L7.5 report as `L9.2 State = OH or FL`.

2. Right-click on the **STATE** field and select, **SELECT EXPERT RECORD**.

3. Open the drop-down list and select **IS ONE OF**, then open the next drop-down list and select **OH**.

> If you type in the first letter of the value that you are looking for in the drop-down list, the list will jump to the first value that starts with that letter that you type in. You can also type in the exact value that you want.

4. Open the same drop-down list that you just used and select **FL**.

   Figure 9-8 shows the criteria that should be selected. Click OK.

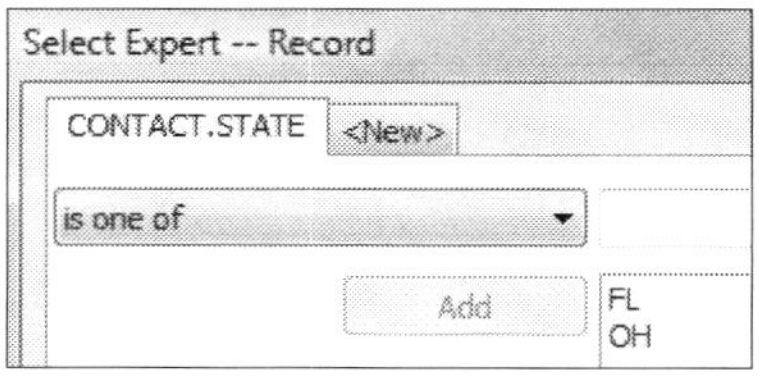

Figure 9-8 Record selection criteria

5. Preview the report. Click the **USE SAVED DATA** button. Your report should look like the one shown in Figure 9-9. Save the changes and close the report.

COMPANY	ADDRESS 1	STATE	ZIP CODE	COUNTRY
Modern Electric Supply	1919 Tecoma Dr.	FL	34655	United States
Golf Greens Extraordinaire	1800 Boca Club Drive	FL	33487	United States
MRP Enterprises	6161 Busch Blvd.	OH	43229-2508	United States
Dylan Inc.	1881 Easton Dr	OH	44325	
Golf Greens Extraordinaire	1800 Boca Club Drive	FL	33487	United States

Figure 9-9 L9.2 report

Exercise 9.3: Using The Is Greater Than Or Equal To Operator

In this exercise you will use the "Is Greater Than Or Equal To" operator to find all opportunities that were created on or after 6/24/2008.

1. Save the L5.3 report as `L9.3 Create Date GTE 6-24-2008`.
   The report should have 389 records. (GTE is an abbreviation for greater than or equal to that I made up).

2. Open the Select Expert to use with the Create Date field.

3. Select the "Is greater than or equal to" operator, then type 6/24/2008 in the next field.

   Figure 9-10 shows the criteria that should be selected.

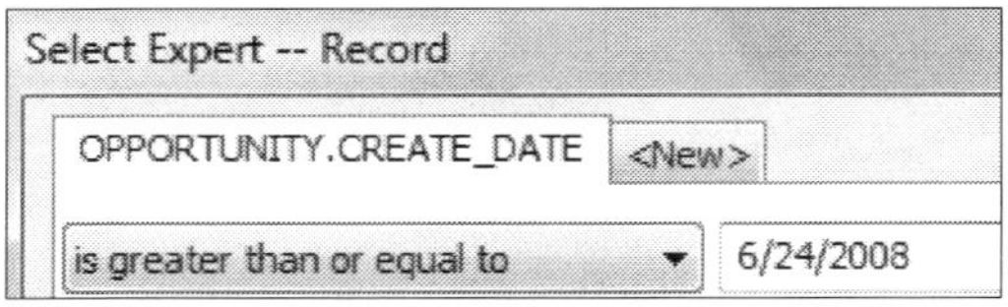

Figure 9-10 Record selection criteria

4. Click OK. Refresh the data. The report should look like the one shown in Figure 9-11. The report should have 37 records. Notice that there are fewer records then before the selection criteria was applied. Save the changes and leave the report open to complete the next exercise.

CONTACT	COMPANY	OPPORTUNITY_NAME	CREATE_DATE	DAYS_OPEN	TOTAL	STATUS	ACTUAL_CLOSE_DATE
Amanda Form	A1 Services-US Opera	New Opportunity	10/30/08	0	12,000.00	Closed - Lost	10/30/09
Ann Goodall	A1 Services of UK	A1 Services of UK-Update for UK Offic	10/30/08	92	4,000.00	Open	12/31/99
Jane Bellamy	Boomers Artworx	Boomer's Artworx-Headquarters	10/30/08	61	12,000.00	Open	12/31/99
Benny Lender	Best Lender Financing	Best Lender-SC on Banking Faciity	10/30/08	31	2,000.00	Open	12/31/99
Benny Lender	Best Lender Financing	New Opportunity	10/30/08	105	300.00	Closed - Won	2/12/10
Dorothy Gale	Rainbow Dreams Inc	Rainbow Dreams-Dorothy's Homestea	9/30/09	129	12,000.00	Open	12/31/99

Figure 9-11 L9.3 report

Exercise 9.4: Modify Selection Criteria

In the previous exercise you created criteria to find opportunities that have a create date greater than or equal to a specific date. In this exercise you will add to this criteria to select opportunities that have a gross margin that is at least $2,500.00.

Adding additional criteria via the Select Expert will reduce or increase the number of records that will appear on the report. As you have probably noticed, the report that you just added selection criteria to does not display the gross margin field. If you need to have additional fields on the report you can add them at anytime. If you need to create criteria for a field, but do not need to see the field on the report, you can create the criteria without adding the field to the report, which is what you will do in this exercise.

> Creating the criteria **IS GREATER THAN** 2499.99 will produce the same results as creating the criteria, **IS GREATER THAN OR EQUAL TO** 2500.00.

> Once you open the Select Expert and create the first set of criteria, you do not have to close it to add additional criteria. Click on the **NEW** tab to add more criteria.

1. Save the L9.3 report as
   `L9.4 Create Date GTE 6-24-08 and Gross Margin GT 2499.99.`

2. Open the Select Expert. Notice that you see existing criteria on the Select Expert dialog box. This is the criteria that you created in the previous exercise.

3. Click on the **NEW** tab, then select the Gross Margin field in the Opportunity table.

4. Open the drop-down list and select **IS GREATER THAN**, then type `2499.99` in the next drop-down list.

   Figure 9-12 shows the criteria that should be selected.

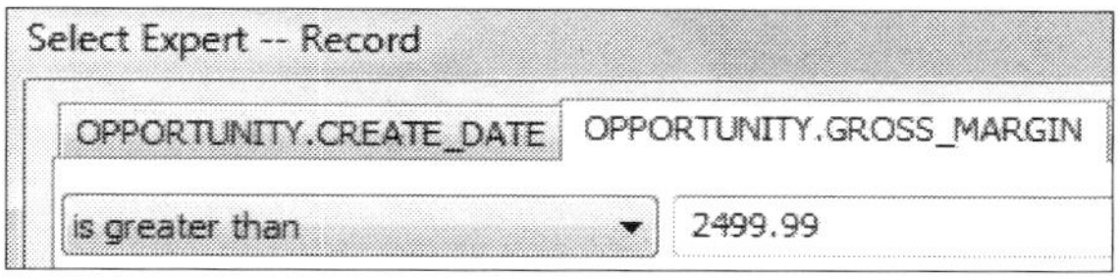

Figure 9-12 Record selection criteria

5. Click OK. Because you changed the selection criteria, you should refresh the data. The report should look like the one shown in Figure 9-13. The report should have 11 records. Save the changes.

CONTACT	COMPANY	OPPORTUNITY_NAME	CREATE_DATE	DAYS_OPEN	TOTAL	STATUS	ACTUAL_CLOSE_DATE
Amanda Form	A1 Services-US Opera	New Opportunity	10/30/08	0	12,000.00	Closed - Lost	10/30/09
Jane Bellamy	Boomers Artworx	Boomer's Artworx-Headquarters	10/30/08	61	12,000.00	Open	12/31/99
Dorothy Gale	Rainbow Dreams Inc	Rainbow Dreams-Dorothy's Homestea	9/30/09	129	12,000.00	Open	12/31/99
Hayleigh Frieda	American Dreams	American Dreams-Warehouse	10/30/08	31	12,000.00	Open	12/31/99
Melanie Daniels	Bodega's Bodacious Bi	Bodega's Birds-School Project	10/30/08	31	12,000.00	Open	12/31/99
Chris Burn	County Tennis Supplie:	County Tennis Supplies-UK	10/30/08	31	12,000.00	Open	12/31/99
Mitch Brenner	Bodega's Bodacious Bi	Bodega's Birds-Bodega Bay HQ	10/30/08	277	12,000.00	Closed - Won	1/29/10
Mitch Brenner	Bodega's Bodacious Bi	Bodega's Birds-Bodega Bay	10/30/08	31	12,000.00	Open	12/31/99
Gavin Dillerstone	Ace Pet Store Franchis	Ace Pet Store-Corporate Office	10/30/08	31	4,500.00	Open	12/31/99
Brandon Sloan	Sierra's Cafe	Sierra's Cafe-Cafe	9/30/09	19	12,000.00	Closed - Won	8/29/09
Rick Blaine	Beautiful Friendship Ba	New Opportunity	10/30/08	187	12,000.00	Closed - Lost	8/20/10

Figure 9-13 L9.4 report

Exercise 9.5: Using The Is Between Operator

In this exercise you will use the "Is Between" operator to find all of the opportunities that were created between 4/1/2007 and 6/30/2007.

1. Save the L5.3 report as
   `L9.5 Opportunities created between 4-1-2007 and 6-30-2007.`

2. Open the Select Expert to use with the Create Date field. Select the "Is between" operator, then open the top drop-down list on the right and select 4/1/2007. If the date is not in the drop-down list, you can type it in.

3. Type `6/30/2007` in the bottom drop-down list, as shown in Figure 9-14. Click OK.

   Preview the report, then refresh the data. The report should have 283 records.

   Save the changes and close the report.

Figure 9-14 Selection criteria

Exercise 9.6: Using Multiple Selection Criteria

In this exercise you will create a report that selects records that meet the following criteria: Country = United States, the Create Date is between 1/1/2008 and 12/31/2008 and the Actual Close Date is greater than 1/1/09.

☑ Table 9-3 contains the tables and fields for the report. The table names are in bold. You also need the Contact Opportunity table.
☑ Figure 9-15 shows the report layout.
☑ Figure 9-16 shows the selection criteria formula. Click the **SHOW FORMULA** button on the Select Expert dialog box to view the formula. Depending on the tab that is selected prior to clicking on the Show Formula button, the formula will be in a different order then what is shown. The Country tab was selected for this exercise.
☑ Figure 9-17 shows the report, which should have 62 records. Save the report as `L9.6 US opportunities with a close date GT 1/1/2009`.

Contact	**Opportunity**
Company	Create Date (5)
Opportunity Name	Total
Country	Actual Close Date (5)

Table 9-3 Tables and fields to add to the report

(5) Change the format of this field to MM/DD/YYYY on the report.

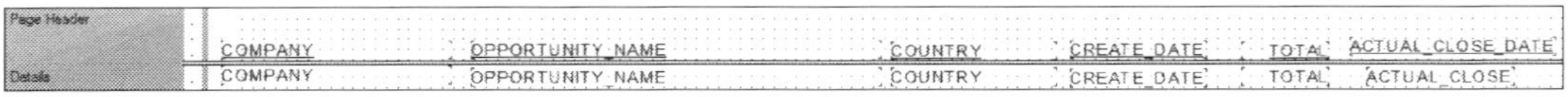

Figure 9-15 L9.6 report layout

> If the syntax in your formula looks different then what is shown in Figure 9-16 and your report looks exactly like the one shown in Figure 9-17, you are probably using the **BASIC SYNTAX** formula language instead of **CRYSTAL SYNTAX**. [See Lesson 15, Syntax]

```
{CONTACT.COUNTRY} = "United States" and
{OPPORTUNITY.CREATE_DATE} in DateTime (2008, 01, 01, 0, 0, 0) to DateTime (2008, 12, 31, 0, 0, 0) and
{OPPORTUNITY.ACTUAL_CLOSE_DATE} > DateTime (2009, 01, 01, 0, 0, 0)
```

Figure 9-16 Selection criteria formula

> The zeros at the end of the date/time fields in the formula shown above in Figure 9-16 represent the time in HH MM SS format (hours, minutes, seconds).

COMPANY	OPPORTUNITY_NAME	COUNTRY	CREATE_DATE	TOTAL	ACTUAL_CLOSE_DATE
Manxsys Financial	New Opportunity	United States	04/18/2008	12,000.00	03/18/2009
American Dreams	American Dreams-Allen Store	United States	04/18/2008	12,000.00	12/31/9999
American Dreams	American Dreams-Allen Additional Component	United States	04/18/2008	2,500.00	12/31/9999
Mandrake Think Tank	New Opportunity	United States	04/18/2008	12,000.00	03/18/2009
Yellow Jersey Bikes	YJBikes-Texas Operations	United States	04/17/2008	12,000.00	12/31/9999

Figure 9-17 L9.6 report

Using Wildcard Characters As Selection Criteria

Earlier in the lesson you learned that you could use the ? and the * as selection criteria using the "Is Like" and "Is Not Like" operators. Wildcard characters provide another way to retrieve records. Wildcards are characters that you can use to substitute all or part of the data in a field. You can also use wildcards to search for data that has a pattern. You can use these wildcard characters at the beginning or end of the search criteria.

① The question mark is used to replace one character in the data. If you entered t?n in the criteria field, the selection criteria would return records that have ten, tan, tune and ton, but not toon in the field.
② The asterisk is used to replace more than one character in the data. If you entered s*r in the criteria field, the selection criteria would return records that have star, start and sour, or any records that had the letter "s" come before the letter "r" in the field that the selection criteria is based on. This wildcard character selection criteria is more flexible, but often returns a lot of results that are not what you expected.

Viewing Formulas

Earlier in this lesson you created criteria that selected a create date greater than or equal to 6/24/2008. In another exercise you modified that criteria to only retrieve records that had a gross margin greater than $2,499.99. To view the formula, click the **SHOW FORMULA** button on the Select Expert. The formulas for the selection criteria are similar.

The bottom of Figure 9-18 shows the formula that was created for the selection criteria shown earlier in Figure 9-10. The bottom of Figure 9-19 shows the formula that was created for the report shown earlier in Figure 9-14. It also shows all of the criteria that must be met. At the end of the first line of the formula, you see the word **AND**. If you changed the "and" to **OR**, the report would look like the one shown in Figure 9-20. If you made this change and ran the report, you would see that there are 246 records in this report, compared to the 11 records in the report shown earlier in Figure 9-14.

NEW The **RECORD** and **GROUP SELECTION** options have been removed from the Select Expert dialog box.

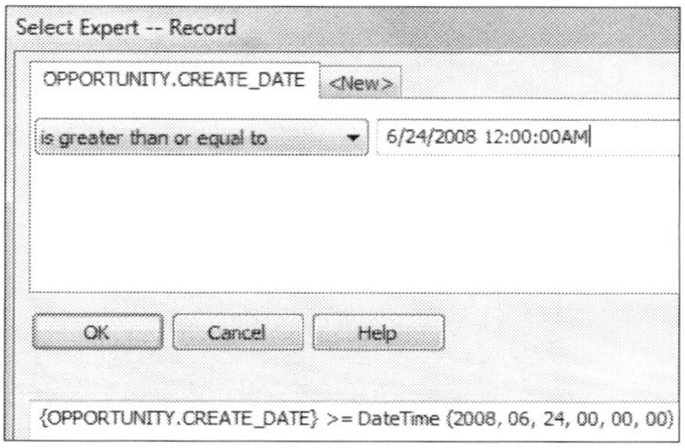

Figure 9-18 Formula for the selection criteria shown earlier in Figure 9-10

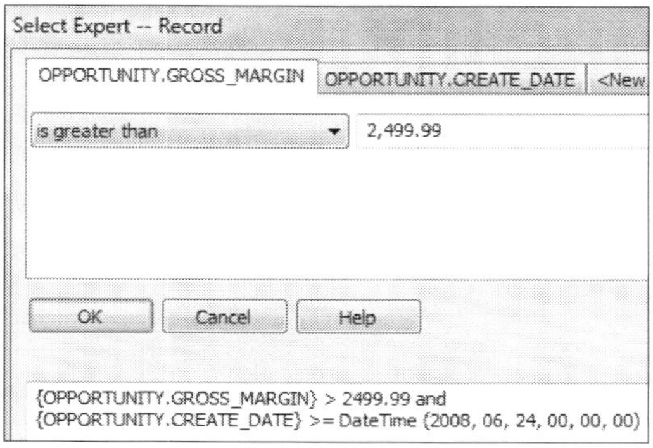

Figure 9-19 Formula for the selection criteria for the report shown earlier in Figure 9-13

CONTACT	COMPANY	OPPORTUNITY NAME	CREATE DATE	DAYS OPEN	TOTAL	STATUS	ACTUAL CLOSE DATE
Amanda Form	A1 Services-US Operal	New Opportunity	10/30/08	0	12,000.00	Closed - Lost	10/30/09
Jane Bellamy	Boomers Artworx	Boomer's Artworx-Headquarters	10/30/08	91	12,000.00	Open	12/31/99
Dorothy Gale	Rainbow Dreams Inc	Rainbow Dreams-Dorothy's Home	9/30/09	159	12,000.00	Open	12/31/99
Hayleigh Frieda	American Dreams	American Dreams-Warehouse	10/30/08	61	12,000.00	Open	12/31/99
Melanie Daniels	Bodega's Bodacious Bi	Bodega's Birds-School Project	10/30/08	61	12,000.00	Open	12/31/99
Chris Burn	County Tennis Supplie:	County Tennis Supplies-UK	10/30/08	61	12,000.00	Open	12/31/99
Mitch Brenner	Bodega's Bodacious Bi	Bodega's Birds-Bodega Bay HQ	10/30/08	277	12,000.00	Closed - Won	1/29/10

Figure 9-20 L9.4 report

As you have learned, a report can have more than one selection criteria. When this is the case, in order for records to appear on the report, they have to meet all of the selection criteria. That is because by default, Crystal Reports uses the logical **AND** operator on the Select Expert. If you need to create selection criteria where only one of the selection criteria options must be true in order for a record to appear on the report, you have to use the logical **OR** operator. To change the operator, you have to manually edit the selection formula that is created by the Select Expert.

How To Delete Selection Criteria

After you have created selection criteria you may decide that one or more of the criteria that you created is not needed. You do not have to delete everything and start over. The steps below will show you how to delete specific criteria on the Select Expert dialog box.

1. Open the report that has the selection criteria that you want to delete.

2. Open the Select Expert. Click on the tab that has the selection criteria that you want to delete, then click the **DELETE** button shown earlier in Figure 9-4.

3. Click OK to close the Select Expert and save the changes.

Understanding How Date/Time Fields Work In Selection Criteria

In Exercise 9.4, a date/time field was used as part of the selection criteria. You entered a date and the records that have a create date greater than or equal to 6/24/2008 were retrieved, even though you did not enter a time for the date that you selected. That is because Crystal Reports will use midnight as the time when a date is entered without a time. This is fine for selection criteria that only uses a date/time field once. If the selection criteria uses the **IS BETWEEN** operator for example (or any operator that requires that two dates be entered for the selection criteria), the records that are retrieved may not be exactly what you are expecting.

The first date in the selection criteria will be compared to midnight as the time, meaning that all records that have a time of midnight or later will be included. So far, so good. The problem is with the second date in the selection criteria. If a time is not entered for the second date, only records that have midnight as the time will be retrieved. This means that a record that has the same date as the second date field in the criteria, but the time is something other then midnight will not appear on the report. To include all records on the date in the second date field, you should enter 23:59:59 (or 11:59:59 PM) as the time. If you enter 17:00:00 (or 05:00:00 PM) as the time, for the second date, records that have a time that is greater than 5 PM will not be included on the report.

If you were going to modify the L9.6 report to show all of the opportunities that were created between 5/1/2007 and 5/15/2007 without an actual close date, Figure 9-21 shows what many people would enter as the selection criteria.

When the report is run with this selection criteria, no records will be retrieved.

This is incorrect because it does not account for records that have a time other than midnight on the Create Date field.

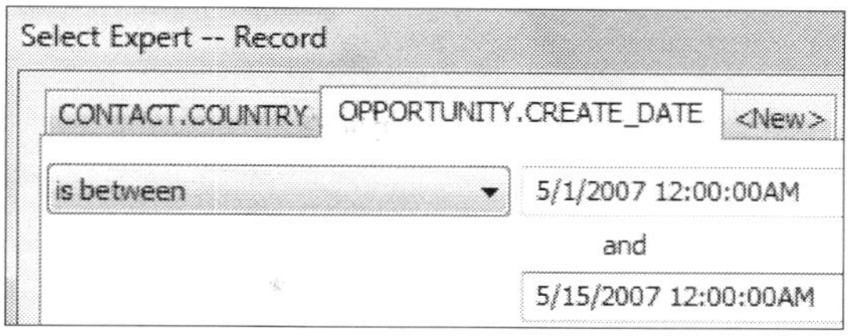

Figure 9-21 Incorrect selection criteria

If the selection criteria shown in Figure 9-22 was entered, the report would retrieve 11 records.

As you can see in Figure 9-23, the times on the Create Date field are different. Notice that there are 14 records that have a create date of 5/15/2007.

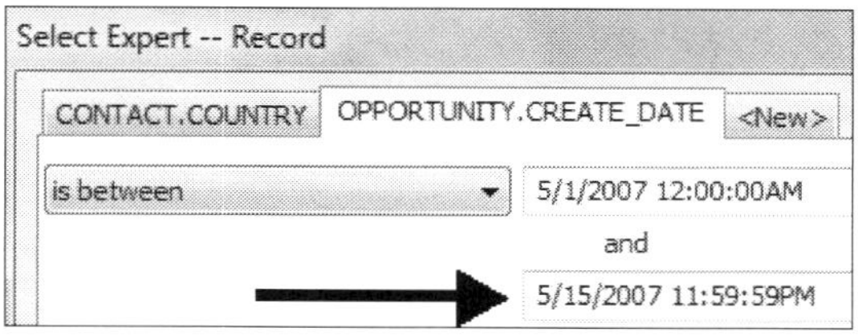

Figure 9-22 Correct selection criteria

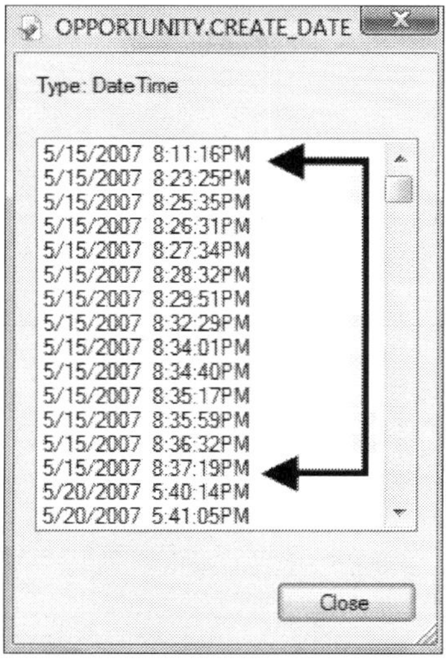

Figure 9-23 Ship Date field data

The **PASTE DATA** button has been removed from the Browse Data dialog box shown in Figure 9-23 when it is opened from the Field Explorer. This button is still available from the Select Expert.

If the second Create Date field has the time entered as 08:35:00 PM as shown in Figure 9-24, the last four records on the 15th, shown above in Figure 9-23 would not be displayed on the report because the time for these three records is after 8:35 PM.

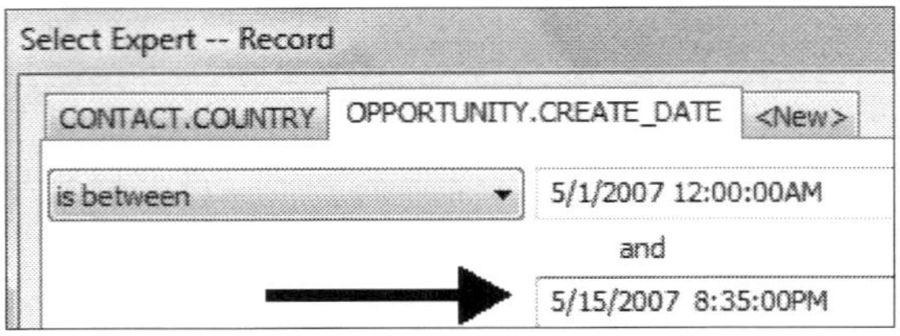

Figure 9-24 Criteria to show orders that were shipped between 5/1/2007 and 5/15/2007 by 8:35 PM

If you want to try this yourself, save the L9.6 report as `L9.6A Time Problem (Incorrect Criteria)` and delete all of the current selection criteria, then create the criteria shown earlier in Figure 9-21. Refresh the data and run the report. You will see that there are no records on the report.

Save the L9.6A report as `L9.6B Time Problem (Correct Criteria)`. Use the criteria shown earlier in Figure 9-22. You will see that there are 11 records on 5/15/2007. These are the records that you were expecting to appear on the report when you entered the criteria.

Save the L9.6A report as `L9.6C Time criteria with a specific time`. Use the criteria shown above in Figure 9-24. You will see that there are nine records. This is what you were expecting because the time on the Create Date criteria was 8:35 PM.

I don't know about you, but when I first figured this out it was somewhat scary. You have two options. You can always type in the time that you need on the second date field or you can type in the day after the last day that you want to include records for on the report. Instead of typing 5/15/2007 for the second date, you could type 5/16/2007 and let the time default to 00:00:00 AM. Doing this will produce the same result. Keep this in mind when you are creating reports on your own. In an effort to save time, when you create reports in this book that have similar selection criteria, you do not have to enter a time on the Select Expert dialog box.

Being able to enter a time is helpful for reports that are time sensitive. If you needed to create a report that displayed a list of medications that were dispensed to patients between 8 AM and 2 PM, you would enter the times as part of the selection criteria.

Report Criteria Summary

By now I think that you have figured out how important it is to understand how to create selection criteria to meet the requirements of the report. If the wrong criteria is created for the report, the output will not be what the user is expecting. This means that they could make decisions based on incorrect data and not know that the data is incorrect. If you aren't familiar with the data, it is a good idea to open the tables and look at the raw data.

Edit An Existing Formula

In Exercise 9.2, the criteria for the State field is that it has to contain one of two values. If you needed to add another value, you could use the Select Expert to add the value from the drop-down list or you could edit the formula that is at the bottom of the Select Expert dialog box.

If you type in the **FORMULA** field, Crystal Reports will disable the top portion of the Select Expert dialog box, as shown in Figure 9-25. Compare this to the Select Expert dialog box shown earlier in Figure 9-19, which displays criteria at the top and bottom of the dialog box.

In Figure 9-25 you do not see anything in the top portion of the dialog box. That is because I typed "PA" in the formula field at the bottom of the dialog box.

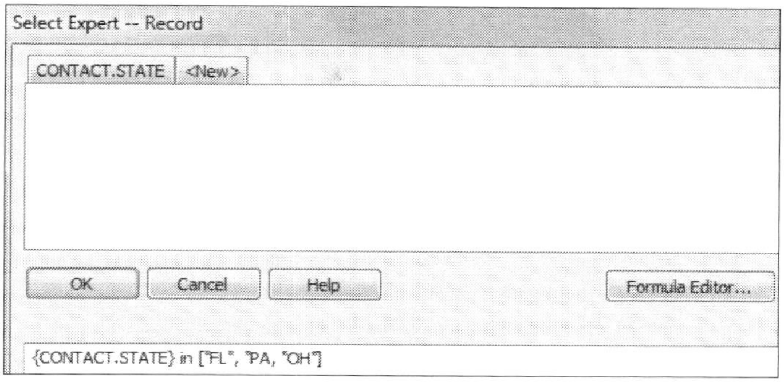

Figure 9-25 Top half of the Select Expert dialog box disabled

The reason Crystal Reports disables the top half of the Select Expert when you create or edit a formula at the bottom of the dialog box is because the formula can't be duplicated by the options that the Select Expert has in the top section of the dialog box.

Opening The Formula Editor From The Select Expert

If you can create or edit the formula at the bottom of the Select Expert shown above in Figure 9-25, you do not have to use the Formula Editor. If you cannot remember the function or need help creating the formula, there are two ways that you can open the Formula Editor from the Select Expert as discussed below. You will learn more about the Formula Editor in Lesson 15.

① Click the **FORMULA EDITOR** button shown above in Figure 9-25.

② Open the operator drop-down list, scroll to the bottom of the list and select the **FORMULA** option illustrated in Figure 9-26. The Select Expert will change, as shown in Figure 9-27, to let you create a formula.

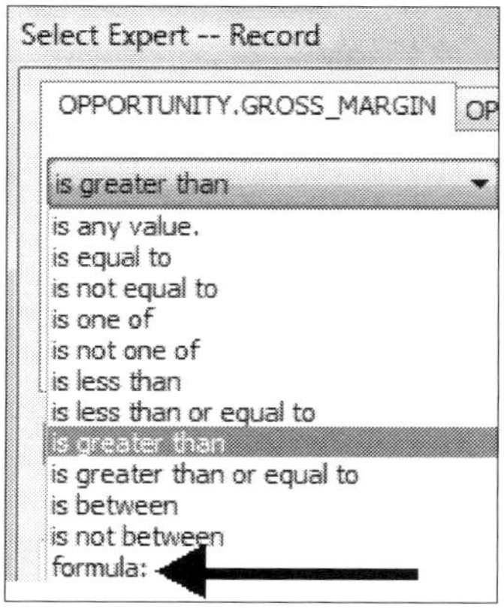

Figure 9-26 Formula option illustrated

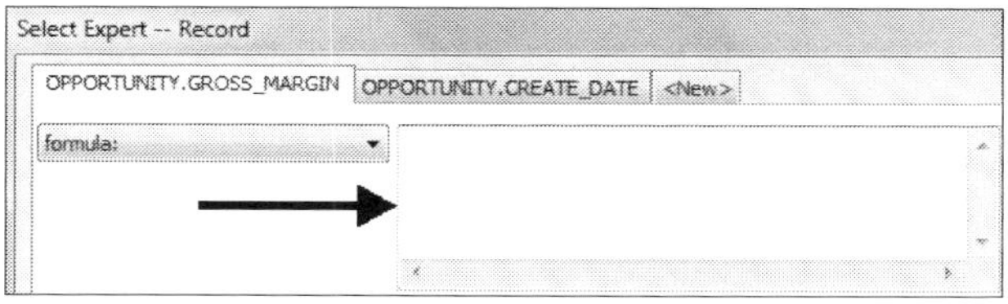

Figure 9-27 Select Expert with formula field

Record Selection Performance Considerations

The type of database that the report is using determines the record selection process that Crystal Reports uses. Databases that are stored on a database server or desktop databases that use an ODBC connection have more performance issues than desktop databases that are local or are on a network drive, as discussed below.

① If the database is on a server, Crystal Reports creates a WHERE clause and adds the clause to the query and sends the query to the database server. The query is run on the server and returns the records to Crystal Reports to use, to generate the report. If the database is on a server, performance improves if this record selection process is used.

② If the database is local or is a desktop database that is stored on a network drive (which is different then a database server), Crystal Reports runs the query that is created from the record selection criteria itself. Depending on the number of records, the report selection process can take some time.

> Making changes to a formula created with the Select Expert via the **SHOW FORMULA** button can really slow down the record selection process if the database is on a database server, especially if the underlying tables have a lot of records.

> The **USE INDEXES OR SERVER FOR SPEED** option if selected, will improve performance. If you want to use this option for the current report, it is on the Report Options dialog box. If you want this option to be the default for all reports that you will create going forward, select the option on the Database tab of the Options dialog box.

In Lesson 3 you learned about indexes. Using indexed fields will improve performance during the record selection process, especially when using tables that have a lot of records. When possible, you should use indexed fields for the record selection process because the fields index, stores all of the values that are in the field, in sorted order, which makes it faster to retrieve records.

Case Sensitive Considerations

When Crystal Reports is installed, case insensitivity is set as the default. This means that entering "new orleans" or "New Orleans" will retrieve the same records. When creating selection criteria on text fields, keep the following in mind.

① PC and SQL databases that are connected to via an ODBC connection usually ignores case sensitivity in Crystal Reports.

② Some databases and ODBC drivers may not support case insensitivity when used with Crystal Reports, even though the **DATABASE SERVER IS CASE-INSENSITIVE** option is turned on.

③ If the server that the database is stored on is set to be case sensitive, you cannot override it by turning on the **DATABASE SERVER IS CASE-INSENSITIVE** option on the Options dialog box. If you select the same option on the Report Options dialog box, you can turn the option on, only for the report that you are currently working with. If this is the case, you would have to convert the text field that you need to create the selection criteria for to all upper case and enter the criteria to support all upper case.

④ If the database is not stored on a server that is set to case sensitive and the database is set for case insensitivity, you can use the **DATABASE SERVER IS CASE-INSENSITIVE** option to control what the selection criteria returns.

> If you want the **DATABASE SERVER IS CASE-INSENSITIVE** option applied to reports that have already been created, you have to open each of the reports and select the option on the Report Options dialog box.

Document Properties

In Lesson 8 you learned about **SPECIAL FIELDS** and that they can be added to a report. You also learned that some of the special fields come from the Summary tab on the Document Properties dialog box. The next exercise will show you how to create summary information and save it, as well as, add the summary information to a report.

Exercise 9.7: How To Create Report Summary Information

1. Save the L9.1 report as `L9.7 State = CA with summary info.`
   Notice the name of the report on the tab.

2. File ⇒ Summary Info. Type your first name in the **AUTHOR** field.

3. Type `This report has summary information` in the **COMMENTS** field, then type `L9.7 State = CA` in the **TITLE** field. Figure 9-28 shows the options that should be filled in.

4. Save the changes.

The information that is entered on this tab is used for identification purposes. The options on this tab are properties of Windows files and are not specific to Crystal Reports. Other software packages have similar dialog boxes. For example, Microsoft Word has the Properties dialog box.

The **TEMPLATE** field shown in Figure 9-28 currently does not provide any use in Crystal Reports. It does not let you apply a template to the report or save the active report as a template. If the report is based off of a template, you could enter the template name in this field so that you will know which template the report is using.

The **SAVE PREVIEW PICTURE** option if checked, will let you view a thumbnail size picture of the first page of the report in the Open dialog box of Crystal Reports, as shown in Figure 9-29 or in Windows Explorer, as shown in Figure 9-31.

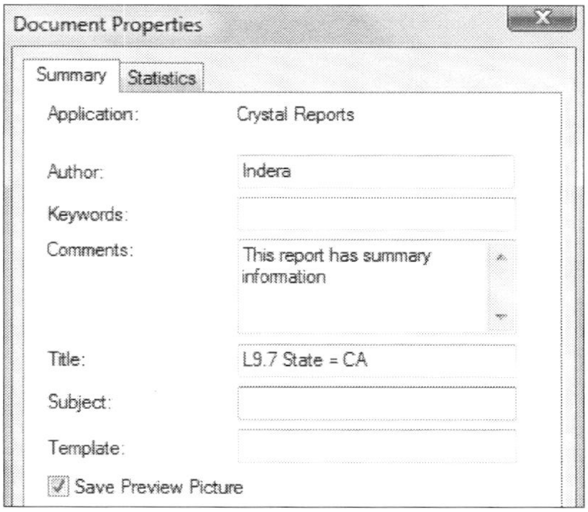

Figure 9-28 Summary tab options

> To view a thumbnail of the first page of the report on the Open dialog box, click the **PREVIEW** button illustrated in Figure 9-29.
>
> To view the Summary tab options on the Open dialog box in Crystal Reports, click the **PROPERTIES** button illustrated in Figure 9-30.
>
> To view a thumbnail of the first page of the report in Windows Explorer, open the **VIEWS** drop-down list in Windows Explorer and select Thumbnails in Windows XP or one of the icon options in Windows Vista. You will see similar options to those shown in Figure 9-31.

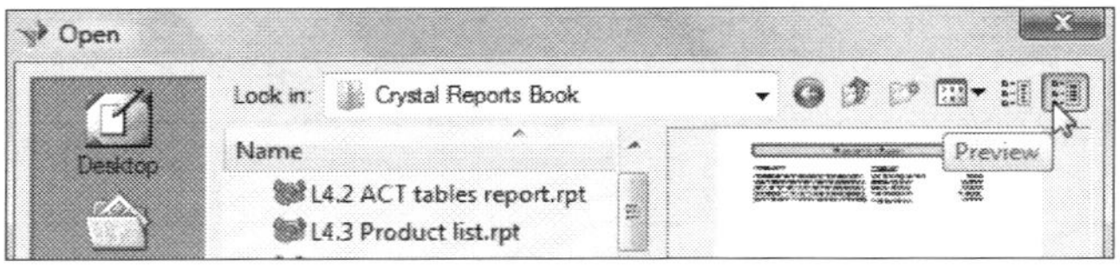

Figure 9-29 Thumbnail of a report in Crystal Reports

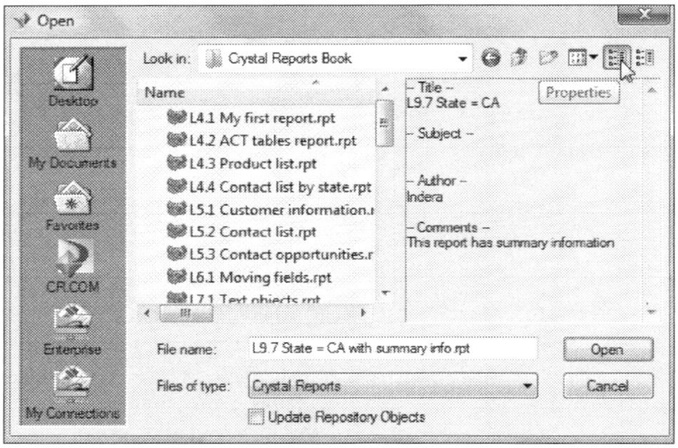

Figure 9-30 Summary options of a report in Crystal Reports

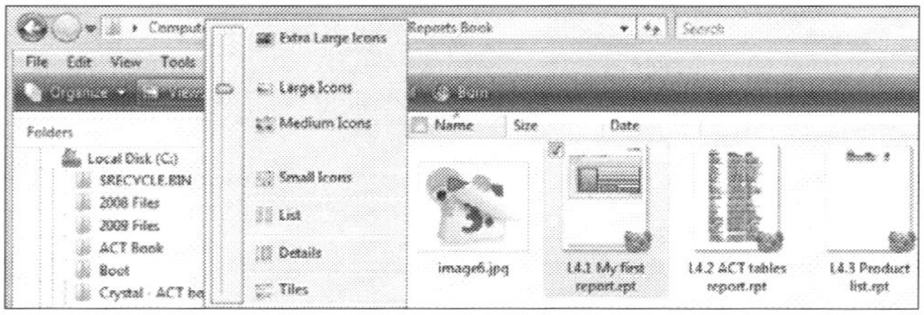

Figure 9-31 Thumbnail or icon view of reports in Windows Explorer

5. Look at the tab for the report. The text should have changed to what you entered in the Title field on the Summary tab. Leave the report open to complete the next part of the exercise.

Statistics Tab

1. Open the Document Properties dialog box and click on the Statistics tab.

The options shown in Figure 9-32 are **READ-ONLY**, which means that you cannot modify them manually.

The **REVISION NUMBER** is incremented each time the report is saved. If you are modifying a report that you did not create, the information on this tab may be helpful. The **TOTAL EDITING TIME** field displays how long the report has been open.

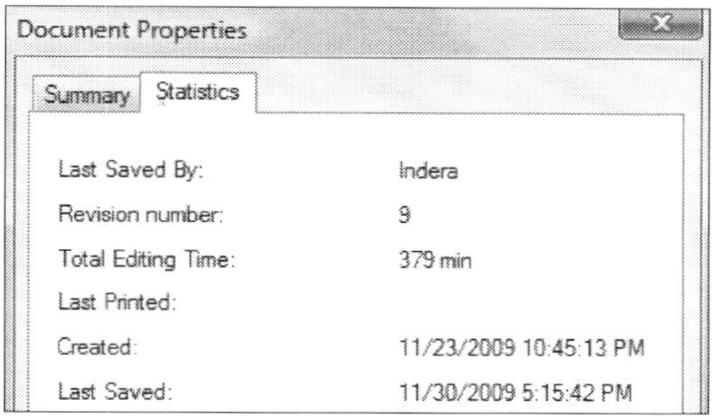

Figure 9-32 Statistics tab options

2. Close the Document Properties dialog box.

Add Summary Information To A Report

1. Add the **FILE AUTHOR** and **REPORT TITLE** Special Fields to the report header section of the L9.7 report. The report should look similar to the one shown in Figure 9-33. Save the changes and close the report.

Indera	L9.7 State = CA			
COMPANY	ADDRESS 1	STATE	ZIP CODE	COUNTRY
Twelfth Dream	2010 Act Way	CA	94063	United States
Duke Industries	4075 Santa Monica Frwy	CA	90029	United States

Figure 9-33 L9.7 report with summary information added

GROUPING, SORTING & SUMMARIZING RECORDS

After completing the exercises in this lesson you will be able to use the techniques listed below to control which records appear on a report and how they are organized.

- ☑ Grouping records
- ☑ Sorting records
- ☑ Create summary subtotals and group totals
- ☑ Organize the records that will appear on the reports

LESSON 10

Grouping And Sorting Overview

Sorting rearranges the order that records will appear on the report. Grouping takes sorting one step further by displaying records that have the same value in a field or a value that is in a range of values together. After all of the records in a group print, there are often totals or some type of summary information about the records in the group. You can sort records whether or not there are groups on the report. In Exercise 4.1 you created a report that grouped the data using a wizard.

Grouping Records

Grouping displays records together that meet specific criteria. Consider the following two examples:

① In the L9.2 State = OH or FL report, at a glance, it is hard to tell how many records are in OH versus how many are in FL. If the report was modified to print all of the records in the same state together, it would be easier to see how many records are in each state. This is known as grouping records.
② In the L9.6 US opportunities with a close date GT 1/1/2009 report, you cannot tell how many opportunities close on a particular day. If the records were grouped by the actual close date, you would be able to create a count summary field to show how many opportunities were closed by day. You could also have a total dollar amount by day, based on the total field of opportunities that were closed.

There are three main tasks that need to be completed when records in a report need to be grouped. The three tasks are listed below and are discussed in detail in this lesson.

① Select the fields to group on. [See Lesson 3, Report Design Process Step 4]
② Decide if the detail records in each group need to be sorted. [See Lesson 3, Report Design Process Step 4]
③ Decide if any fields in the details section of the report need summary information. [See Lesson 3, Report Design Process Step 2]

You learned about the group header and footer sections in Lesson 3. The name of the group is usually placed in the group header section. The summary information, which is not a requirement, is usually placed in the group footer section.

Being able to add this type of functionality to reports will make them much more useful in many cases, then the reports that were created in Lesson 9. Reports that have groups can also use the drill-down feature. In addition to creating the groups, Crystal Reports also provides summary functions including statistical, averaging and totals that you can add to a report.

Records are placed together because they have the same value in a field (or fields). This is how the group header and footer sections are automatically re-created each time the value in a field the report is grouped on changes. You will not see this in the design window. The process of creating another group each time the value changes is dynamic processing that happens behind the scenes, as they say. This is how you can create totals for a group. If you are shaking your head, after you complete the first exercise in this lesson, this should make more sense.

Grouping Tips

Below are some tips that I follow to help determine if a report needs a group and if so, which fields to group on.

① Reports that retrieve hundreds or thousands of records, probably would be easier to read, if nothing else, if there were one or two groups.
② If you need to provide a count or subtotal for a field.
③ If the report needs statistical information.

Insert Group Dialog Box

The options on the **COMMON** tab are used to create the groups. At a minimum, the field to group on (The first drop-down list shown in Figure 10-1.) and the sort order of the group (The second drop-down list shown in Figure 10-1.) have to be selected. Date and Boolean fields have an additional option that can be set. The **OPTIONS** tab will be discussed later. There are two ways to open the **INSERT GROUP** dialog box, as discussed below.

① Click the **INSERT GROUP** button on the Insert Tools toolbar.
② Insert ⇒ Group.

In addition to using the Insert Group dialog box to create and edit groups, you can also use the Group Expert to create and edit groups.

The **GROUP BY** field is the first drop-down list on the Common tab. It contains all of the fields that the report can be grouped by.

This list contains the fields that are on the report and the fields in tables that are connected to with the report. You can also use formula fields as the field to group on.

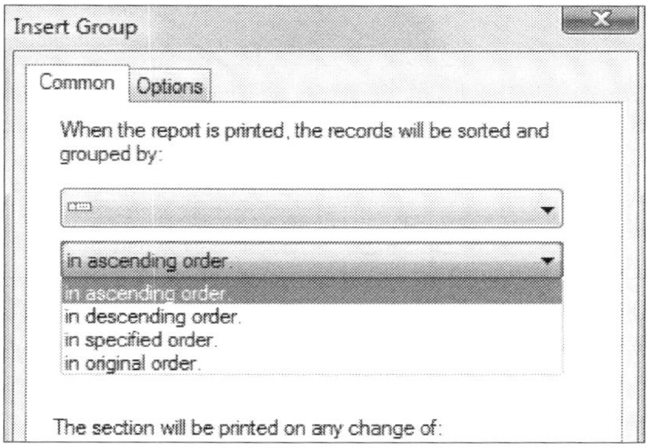

Figure 10-1 Insert Group dialog box

Memo fields will not appear in the group by drop-down list because they cannot be used as a field to group on.

The **GROUP SORT ORDER** field is the second drop-down list on the Common tab. The sort order determines the order that the groups will appear in, on the report. Table 10-1 explains the group sorting options. The first four options in the table are in the second drop-down list on the Insert Group dialog box.

Sorting Option	Description
In Ascending Order	Text fields will be sorted in A-Z order. Numeric fields will be sorted in low to high order. Date fields will be sorted in oldest to most recent date order.
In Descending Order	Text fields will be sorted in Z-A order. Numeric fields will be sorted in high to low order. Date fields will be sorted in most recent to oldest date order.
In Specified Order	This option is used to select the order of the groups. This is known as **CUSTOM GROUPING** and is discussed below. An example of a custom group would be to group customers by the amount of sales they placed last year. The option causes two tabs (Specified Order and Other) to appear on the Insert Group dialog box.
In Original Order	Leaves the data in the order that it is retrieved from in the database. It may be me, but I don't find this option very useful.
Use A Formula As Group Sort Order	Check this option if you want to allow the person running the report to be able to sort the groups in ascending or descending order.

Table 10-1 Group sorting options explained

Once a field is selected to be grouped on, it will appear under the text, **THE SECTION WILL BE PRINTED ON ANY CHANGE OF** at the bottom of the Insert Group dialog box.

The **DATE/TIME** option is only available when a date, time or date/time field is selected in the Group By drop-down list. Figure 10-2 shows the options for date/time fields.

Figure 10-2 Date/Time field options

The **BOOLEAN** option is only available when a Boolean field (for example a true/false or yes/no field) is selected in the group by drop-down list. The Boolean sort process does not work like the other sort options.

Boolean fields sort false before true, when the ascending sort order is selected. The groups are created when there are changes from yes to no, or from true to false in the Boolean field.

The exception to this is the **ON ANY CHANGE** option. Figure 10-3 shows the options for Boolean fields. Table 10-2 explains the Boolean field options.

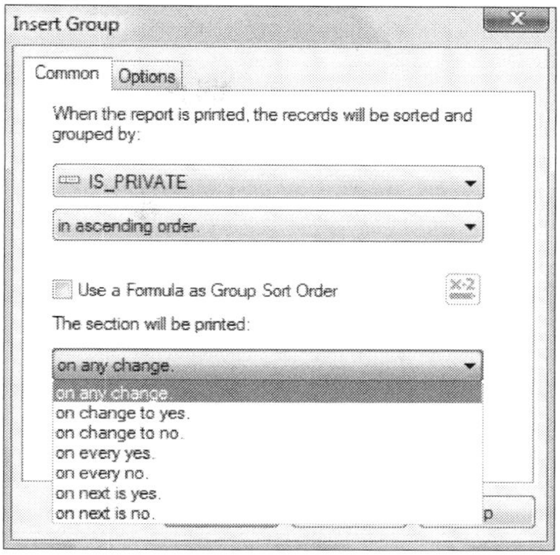

Figure 10-3 Boolean field options

Option	Description
On any change	This is the default option and will sort the values and place them next to each other.
On change to yes	Creates a new group each time a **True** value comes after a False value. (1)
On change to no	Creates a new group each time a **False** value comes after a True value. (1)
On every yes	Creates a group that always ends with a True value and includes any records in the middle that have a False value, back to the previous True value. (1)
On every no	Creates a group that always ends with a False value and includes any records in the middle that have a True value, back to the previous False value. (1)
On next is yes	Creates groups that always start with a True value and includes all records in the middle that have a False value until the next record with a True value is found. (1)
On next is no	Creates groups that always start with a False value and includes all records in the middle that have a True value until the next record with a False value is found. (1)

Table 10-2 Boolean field options explained

(1) The records are not sorted if this option is selected.

Custom Grouping

If the ascending and descending sort options are not sufficient, you can create custom groups by selecting the **IN SPECIFIED ORDER** option in the second drop-down list shown earlier in Figure 10-1. There are two custom group options available on the Insert Group dialog box: User defined sort order and User defined groups.

User Defined Sort Order

When you select this option, the **SPECIFIED ORDER** tab will appear on the Insert Group dialog box, as shown in Figure 10-4. The options on this tab are used to create the list of how the values in the groups will be sorted.

The **NAMED GROUP** drop-down list contains all of the values for the group field. Select the values in the order that you want the groups to appear in on the report, as shown at the bottom of Figure 10-5.

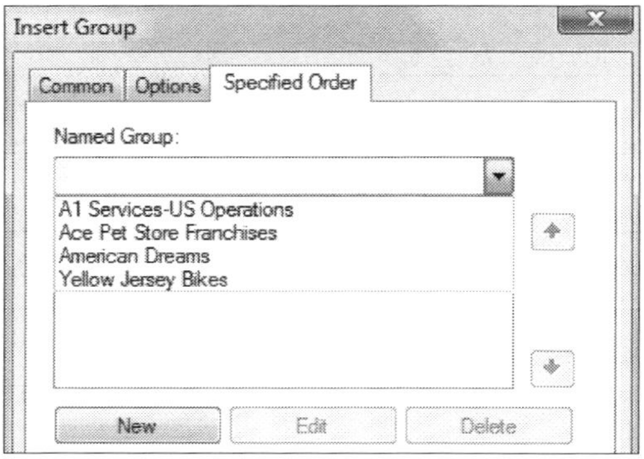

Figure 10-4 Specified Order tab

You can change the order of the values by clicking on the value that you want to move, then click the Up or Down arrow to the right of the list.

Once you add a value to the Named Group list, the **OTHERS** tab shown in Figure 10-6 will be available. The options on this tab are used to select what you want to happen to the group values that are not added to the Named Group list on the Specified Order tab. Table 10-3 explains the options on the Others tab.

> You do not have to order all of the group values. You can select just the ones that you need.

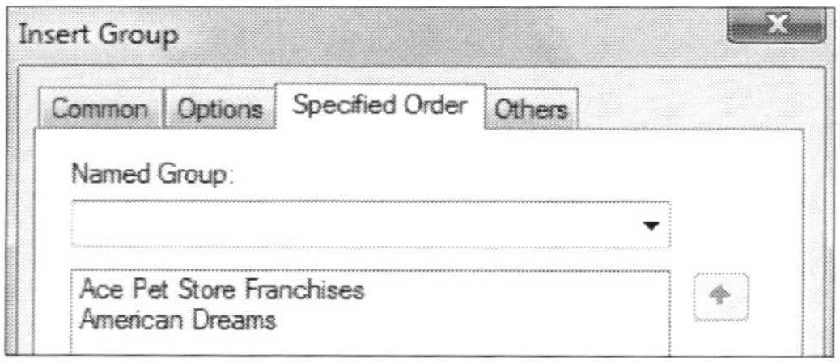

Figure 10-5 Values placed in a specific order

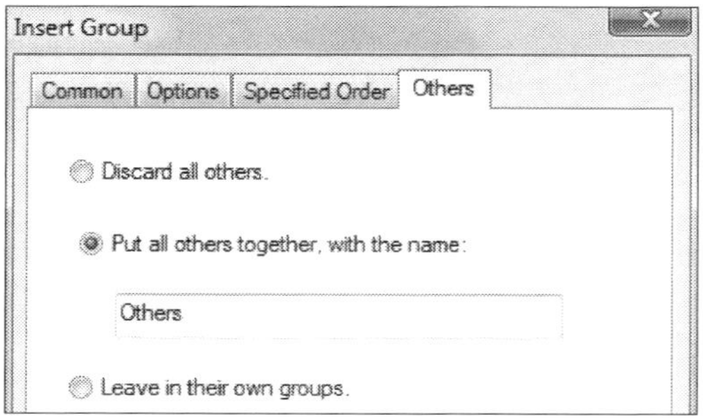

Figure 10-6 Others tab options

Option	Description
Discard all others	Selecting this option causes the group values (and their detail records) that are not selected on the Specified Order tab to not be displayed on the report.
Put all others together, with the name	Select this option to put all of the group values that are not selected on the Specified Order tab together under one group name that you type in the field.
Leave in their own groups	Selecting this option will print all of the group values that you selected on the Specified Order tab first on the report. The remaining group values will be printed after, in ascending order.

Table 10-3 Others tab options explained

Sorting Records

Sorting records is the second task that has to be completed. Like grouping, sorting is used to rearrange the order that records appear on the report. Data can be sorted by a database field, formula or SQL Expression. Data cannot be sorted by a memo field. The data can be sorted on more than one field, including fields that are not on the report. There are two types of sorting, as discussed below.

① You can sort the report as a whole. This option is for reports that do not have groups.

② You can sort the records within a group. After the groups for a report have been determined, you may decide that the report would be more meaningful if the detail records in the group were sorted. If you do not specify a sort order, the records in each group will print in the order that they are retrieved from the database.

The **RECORD SORT EXPERT** dialog box shown in Figure 10-7 is used to select the options to sort the records in the details section of the report.

The Sort Fields list shows how the detail records will be sorted within the group. Group field sorting is done before detail record sorting. This expert does not sort groups. You can sort in ascending or descending order on each field. There are two ways to open the dialog box, as discussed below.

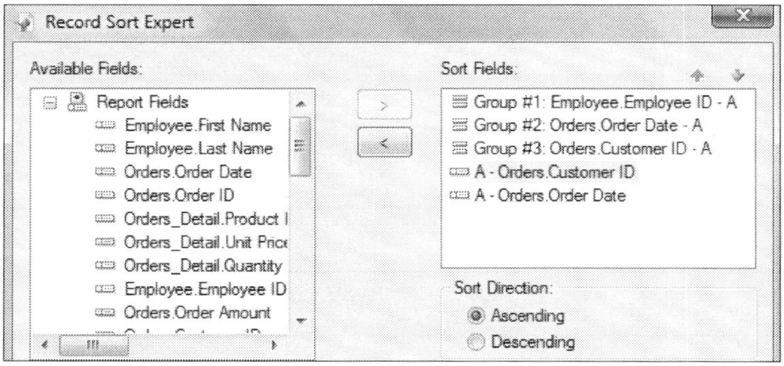

Figure 10-7 Record Sort Expert dialog box

① Click the **RECORD SORT EXPERT** button on the Expert Tools toolbar.
② Report ⇒ Record Sort Expert.

In addition to clicking on a field in the Available Fields list and clicking the arrow button to add it to the Sort Fields list, you can also drag fields to the Sort Fields list.

What I found interesting is that if you click on a group field on the Sort Fields list, all of the buttons become disabled on the dialog box. I suspect that this is because Crystal Reports is trying to protect you from changing the group order. Don't worry. If you need to change the order of the groups, you can change them on the design window by dragging them or you can use the Group Expert.

The order that fields are added to the **SORT FIELDS** list on the Record Sort Expert is the order that the records will be sorted in. If you discover that the fields are in the wrong order in the Sort Fields list, click on the field that is not in the correct place, then click the Up or Down arrow buttons to move the field to the correct location.

Summary Information

This is the third major task that has to be completed when groups are created. One reason that groups are created is to make the report easier to read. Another reason groups are created is to provide summary information for fields in the details section of the report.

These summary calculated fields are usually placed in the group footer section of the report. Summary fields can also be placed in the group header section. Students have asked me how is it possible that summary fields that are in the group header section contain accurate totals. The answer is somewhat beyond the scope of this book, but I will answer the question because it may help you understand and allow you to use summary fields in the group header section with confidence, when needed. Crystal Reports actually builds (processes) the entire report before it is printed. This means that values for summary fields, regardless of where they are placed on the report, are calculated before the report prints.

The two types of calculations that you can perform on text (string) data is counting records in a group and determining the frequency of records in the group. These summary calculations are often also placed in the report footer section to create what is known as a grand total or report total. Summary fields have similarities of **RUNNING TOTAL** fields which you will learn about in Lesson 19. Summary fields that are in the report header or footer section are not dependant on groups. You can create summary calculation fields in the report header and footer if the report does not have any groups. Summary fields in the report header and footer contain totals for all records on the report. Instead of having to manually count the number of orders on a report that each customer placed, a calculated field can be added to the report that would count the number of orders. Each summary field has to be created separately.

To create a group summary field, the report must have at least one group. If you select the option to create a summary field and the report does not have a group, you will be prompted to create a group. If you place the same summary field in different sections of the report, it will produce different total amounts, which is what should happen.

There are three ways to open the Insert Summary dialog box shown in Figure 10-8 **AFTER** you have selected the field that you need to create a summary calculation field for, as discussed below.

If the field that you need to create a summary calculation for is not on the report, you have to select option two or three below.

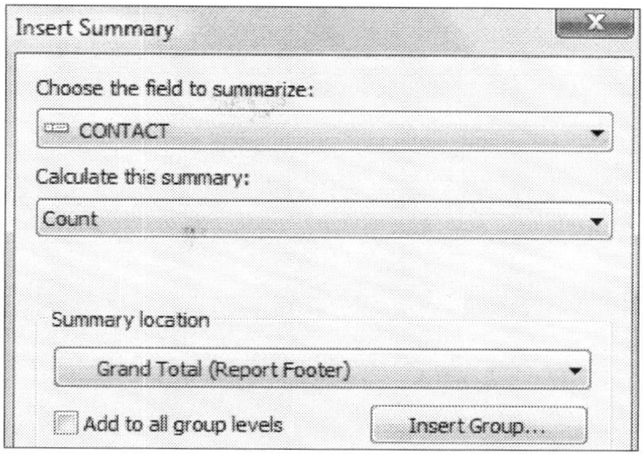

Figure 10-8 Insert Summary dialog box

① Right-click and select Insert Summary.
② Click the **INSERT SUMMARY** button on the Insert Tools toolbar.
③ Insert ⇒ Summary.

There are two types of summary calculations that you can create, as discussed below.

① The **Text** field summary calculation options are explained in Table 10-4. Text fields can only create the calculations in Table 10-4.
② The **Numeric** field summary calculation options are explained in Table 10-5. They can also be used with currency fields. Numeric fields can also create the calculations in Table 10-4.

Text Summary Calculation Options	
Calculation	**Description**
Count	Counts the detail records. By default, if the field that is being used to count on is **NULL**, it will not be included in the count. Select the **CONVERT DATABASE TO NULL VALUES TO DEFAULT** option on the Report Options dialog box if you need null values counted. Duplicate values in the field will also be counted. This may not be what you want.
Distinct Count	Counts all of the unique values in the selected field.
Maximum	Finds the highest value in the field.
Minimum	Finds the lowest value in the field.
Mode	Finds the most frequently used value in the field.
N^{th} Largest, N is:	Is used to select a number and calculate the Nth largest value in the selected field in the group. An example would be if you wanted to find out what the third largest (N^{th} largest) order amount (N) is in the group. (2)
N^{th} Most Frequent, N is:	Is used to select a number and calculate the Nth most frequently occurring value in the selected field. An example would be if you wanted to find out which product was ordered the most in the group, you would enter a 1 in this field. This is similar to the Mode function, but it is not limited to the frequent occurrences. (2)

Table 10-4 Text summary calculation options explained

Text Summary Calculation Options	
Calculation	**Description**
N^{th} Smallest, N is:	Is used to select a number and calculate the Nth smallest occurring value. An example would be if you wanted to find out what the fifth (N^{th} smallest) smallest order amount (N) is in the group. You would enter a 5 in this field. (2)

Table 10-4 Text summary calculation options explained (Continued)

(2) The N is a value.

Numeric Summary Calculation Options	
Calculation	**Description**
Average	Finds the average value of all of the values in the field.
Correlation With	Finds the relationship between the selected field and another field in the database or on the report.
Covariance With	Finds the difference (often called the variance) between the selected field and another field in the database or on the report.
Median	Finds the middle value of all the values in the field.
Mode	Finds the most frequently used value in the field.
P^{th} percentile, P is:	Is used to select a percent (the P is value) between 0 and 100 and calculates that percentile of the values in the field.
Population Standard Deviation	Calculates how far from the mean (the average) each value in the selected field deviates.
Population Variance	Divides the sum of the number of items in the population. The result is the population variance.
Sample Standard Deviation	Calculates the mean (the average) value for the data in the sample.
Sample Variance	Calculates the square root of the standard deviation of the sample.
Sum	Adds the values in the selected field to get a total.
Weighted Average With	Calculates the average, by the number of times the value is in the selected field. It will also let you adjust the average by selecting another field.

Table 10-5 Numeric summary calculation options explained

> Date and Boolean fields can only be used in the following types of calculations: count, distinct count, maximum, minimum, mode, N^{th} largest, N^{th} most frequent and N^{th} smallest.

In addition to the summary options that you learned about in Tables 10-4 and 10-5, the summary options in Table 10-6 are also available. They are located at the bottom of the Insert Summary dialog box.

Option	Description
Summary Location	This option is used to select the section of the report where you want to place the summary field. The good thing is that you are not limited to the options in the drop-down list. You can manually copy or move the summary field to another section of the report.
Add to all group levels	If checked, this option will add the summary field to all existing group levels on the report. This means that you no longer have to create the same summary field manually for every group section that needs the summary field.
Show as a percentage of	This option will calculate a comparison of the percent of one group that is part of a larger group. If selected, this option is used to select the group or total that you want the comparison to be based on. For example, this option can calculate the percent of sales for June compared to the sales for the entire year. The result would display what percent will tell you (out of 100%) the sales in June accounted for, compared to the sales for the entire year. This option is not available for all types of calculations. (3)
Summarize across hierarchy	On reports that have hierarchical groups (groups that have parent/child relationships), an identical summary field will be added to all subgroups under the primary hierarchical group. An example of a report that could have hierarchical groups would be one that displays a list of department managers (the parent group) and the employees (the child group) that are in each department.

Table 10-6 Summary options explained

(3)

> Percentage summaries cannot be placed in the report footer section.

If all of the summary calculation options seem a little confusing right now don't worry, you will only see options in the drop-down list that are available for the field type that you select to create the calculation for.

> Headings are not automatically created for group summary fields like they are for fields in the details section. By default, summary fields are usually placed in a section below the field it is summarizing. The exception would be if the summary field is placed in the group header section.

> Many of the exercises in this lesson will have you create a title for the report or a title for a field. When you see the phrase "Create a title", that means to add a text object to the report and type in the specified text. Report titles should be placed in the page header section unless stated otherwise. They should also be centered across the report.

Creating Groups

The reports that you modify in this lesson will show you how to apply a variety of group and sorting options effectively. The name of each exercise describes how the data will be grouped. You will also learn more formatting techniques. As you will see, the more data that you add to a report, the more the report needs to be formatted.

Exercise 10.1: Group Contact Information By State

In this exercise you will modify a report to include the following group and sorting options. These options also allow you to create totals for the group.

① Group the data by the state field and sort the group in ascending order.
② Sort the detail records in each group in ascending order by the Zip Code field.
③ Create a count of detail records in each group.

1. Save the L7.5 report as `L10.1 Contact info by state`.

2. Open the Insert Group dialog box. Open the first drop-down list and select the **STATE** field from the Contact table, then click OK.

Notice that a **GROUP HEADER** and **GROUP FOOTER** section have been added to the report, as illustrated in Figure 10-9.

If you also wanted to group this report on a second field, you would see a second set of group header and footer sections, as illustrated in Figure 10-10.

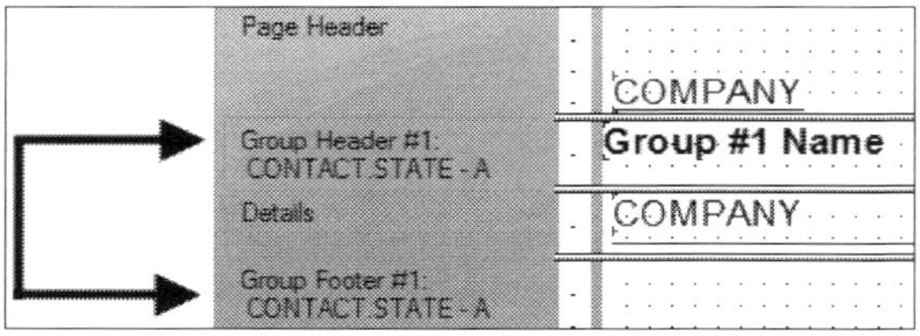

Figure 10-9 Group header and footer sections added to the report

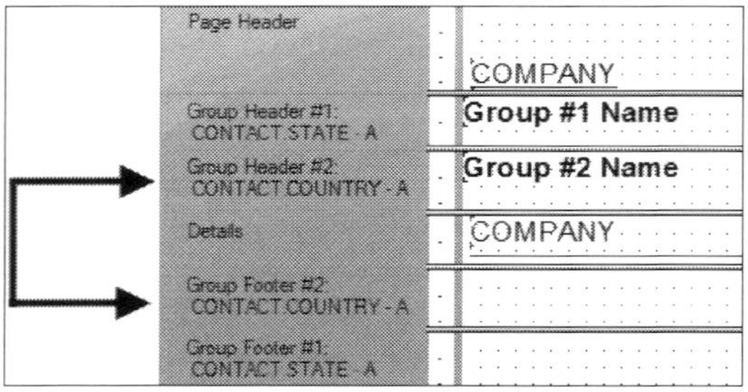

Figure 10-10 Two sets of group header and footer sections

> If you cannot see the entire group name on the left side of the design window, as shown above in Figure 10-10, you can drag the section bar below the group section down until you can see the full name. Keep in mind that doing this will cause additional space to be added to that section of the report when you preview or print it. A better solution would be to turn on the **SHORT SECTION NAMES** option, by following the steps below.

How To Turn The Short Section Names On

1. Right-click in the **REPORT SECTION** of the design tab. You will see the shortcut menu shown in Figure 10-11. Select the option **SHOW SHORT SECTION NAMES**. The report section should look like the one shown in Figure 10-12.

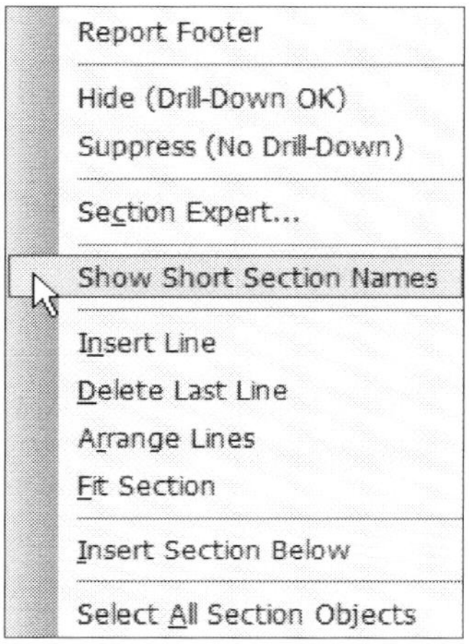

Figure 10-11 Report section shortcut menu

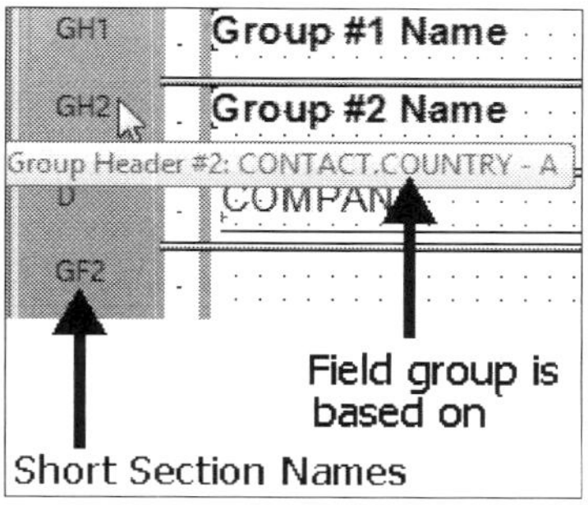

Figure 10-12 Report section with the short section names option turned on

> If you hold the mouse pointer over the **GROUP SECTION NAME**, as illustrated above in Figure 10-12, you will be able to see which field the group is based on and the order that the group is sorted in.

2. Save the changes. Page 2 of the report should look like the one shown in Figure 10-13. There is no group name at the top of the first page because those records do not have data in the group field. Depending on the needs of the report, you could opt to not display records where the state field is empty.

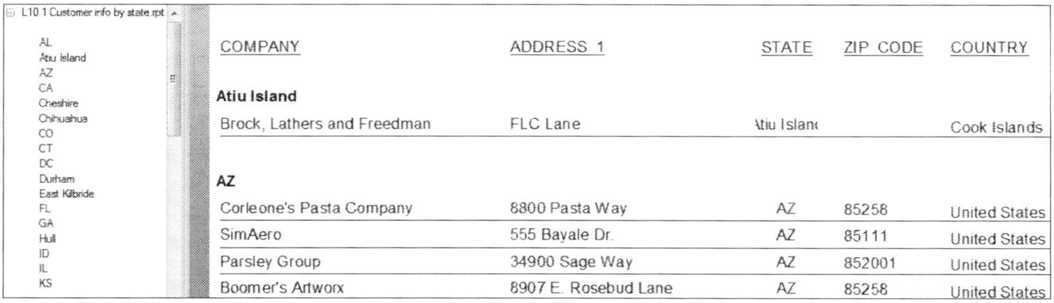

Figure 10-13 Contact information grouped by state

Notice that the group name is bold on the report. This makes it easier to know where each group starts. If you look in the group tree section on the left of Figure 10-13 above, you will see all of the groups that the report has. If you scroll down the list of groups and click on the **PA** group, that section of the report will be displayed, as shown in Figure 10-14.

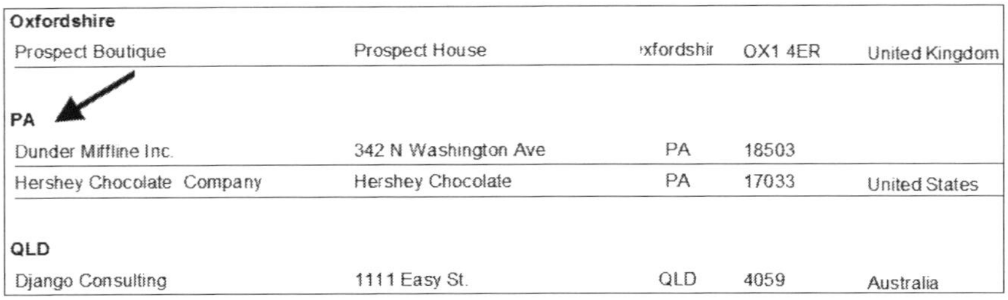

Oxfordshire				
Prospect Boutique	Prospect House	›xfordshir	OX1 4ER	United Kingdom
PA				
Dunder Mifflne Inc.	342 N Washington Ave	PA	18503	
Hershey Chocolate Company	Hershey Chocolate	PA	17033	United States
QLD				
Django Consulting	1111 Easy St.	QLD	4059	Australia

Figure 10-14 Contacts in PA

By default, group name fields are added to the group header section of the report. If at some point you decide that you do not want the group name to automatically be added to the group header section, you can turn the **INSERT GROUP NAME WITH GROUP** option off on the Layout tab on the Options dialog box. If you turn this option off and then need to add a group name to a specific report, you can, without turning this option back on.

Sort The Detail Records

As you can see in Figure 10-13 shown earlier, the detail records in each group are not sorted on any field. Unless you specify a sort order, the detail records will appear in the report based on the order they are retrieved from the database. In this part of the exercise you will sort the detail records by the Zip Code field.

1. Open the Record Sort Expert dialog box. Click on the Zip Code field in the **AVAILABLE FIELDS** list, then click the **>** button. Select the **ASCENDING** sort order if it is not already selected. Figure 10-15 shows the sort options that you should have selected. Click OK.

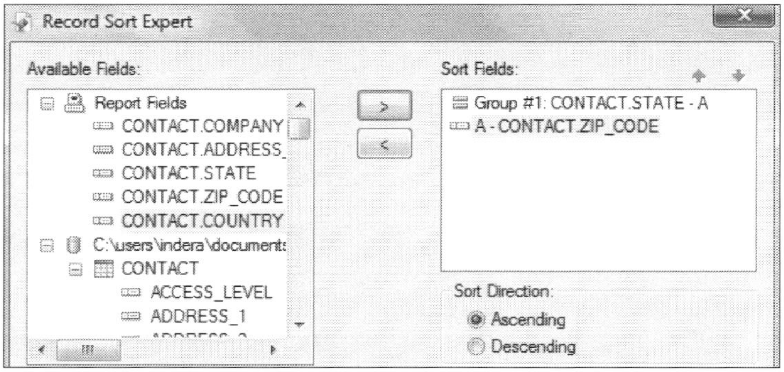

Figure 10-15 Report sort options

Notice that the group information for the report is the first entry in the **SORT FIELDS** list of the Record Sort Expert dialog box shown above in Figure 10-15. This is done to outline the sort order for the entire report. The first way that the report will be sorted is by group. Remember that the group is sorted in ascending order, which is denoted by the **A** at the end of the group field. If the field was sorted in descending order, you would see a **D** at the end of the field.

> If you need to sort a report by a persons name and the name is in two fields, you should sort on the last name field first and then sort on the first name field.

The detail records in each group will be sorted in ascending order by the Zip Code field. If you wanted to sort on other fields you can do that also, as shown in Figure 10-16.

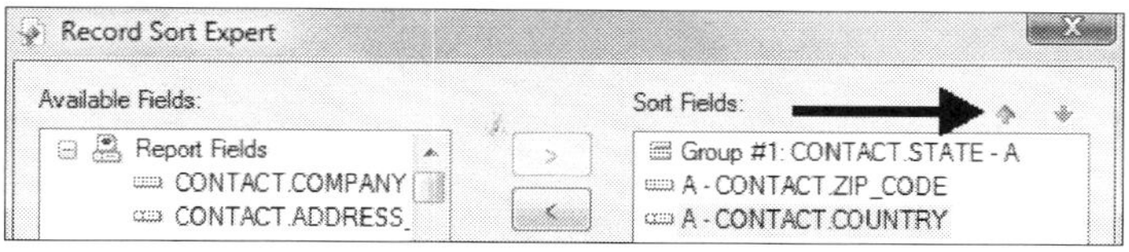

Figure 10-16 Second field in group to sort on

In this example, adding the Country field means that within each group, the detail records would be sorted by Zip Code first and then within each Zip Code in the group, the records would be sorted by Country. In reality, these sort options would produce strange results. It is shown here for illustration purposes only. A better way to sort on these two fields would be to sort on the Country field first because there are several Zip Codes within each Country.

If you wanted to sort on the Country field first you would click on the Country field and then click the **UP** arrow, as illustrated above in Figure 10-16. This would move the Country field up, as shown in Figure 10-17.

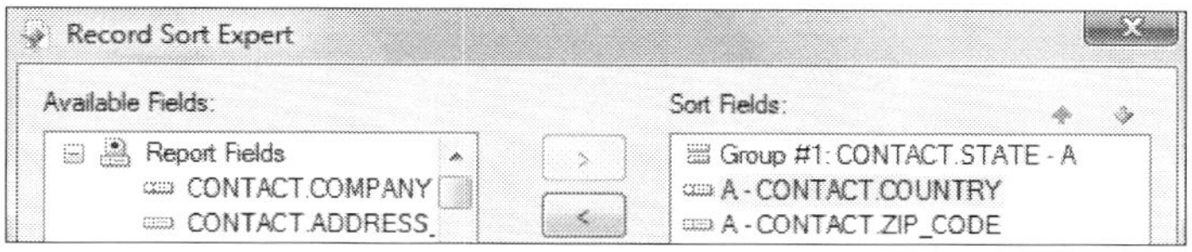

Figure 10-17 Sort order of the detail records changed

2. Save the changes. If prompted, click **YES** to generate (refresh) the data for the report. Preview the report. Go to the PA group. You should see the records shown in Figure 10-18. Notice the different order of the detail records in this version of the report, compared to the order of the detail records in the report shown earlier in Figure 10-14. Leave the report open to complete the next part of the exercise.

PA				
Hershey Chocolate Company	Hershey Chocolate	PA	17033	United States
Dunder Miffline Inc.	342 N Washington Ave	PA	18503	

Figure 10-18 Report with detail record sort order added

Count Summary Field Overview

As you learned earlier in this lesson, creating summary fields is the third step in the grouping and sorting process. In this part of the exercise you will create a summary field that will count the number of detail records in each group.

Create The Count Summary Field

1. On the Insert Summary dialog box open the first drop-down list and select the Contact ID field.

2. Open the second drop-down list and select **COUNT**. You should see the options that were discussed earlier in Table 10-4 for Contact ID field because it is a text (string) field.

> **ACT! Field Types**
>
> This is one of the things that bugs me about the table structure of ACT! databases. I was a programmer for more years then I will admit to and I have rarely seen an ID field set up as a string/text field, never mind the fact that the ID numbers are not sequential. If the ID fields were numeric, you could also use the options that were discussed earlier in Table 10-5.

> Notice that you can create a group from this dialog box. If you click the **INSERT GROUP** button, you will see the Insert Group dialog box that you saw earlier in Figure 10-1.

3. Open the **SUMMARY LOCATION** drop-down list and select the Group 1 option.

   Figure 10-19 shows the summary options that you should have selected.

   Click OK. The summary field should be in the group footer section.

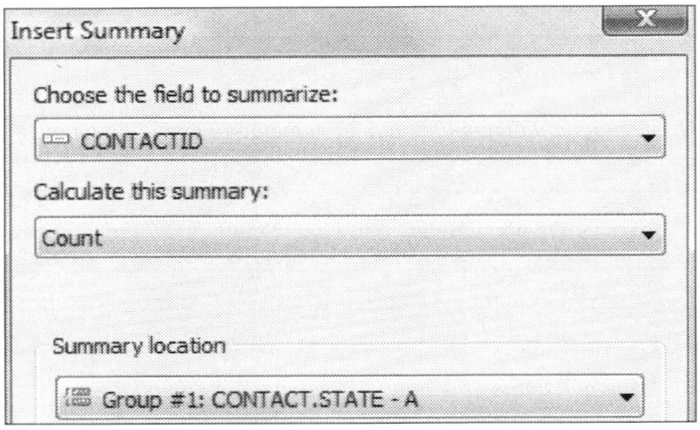

Figure 10-19 Summary options

4. Save the changes. Page 4 of the report should look like the one shown in Figure 10-20. The number in bold below the lines are the count field that you just created.

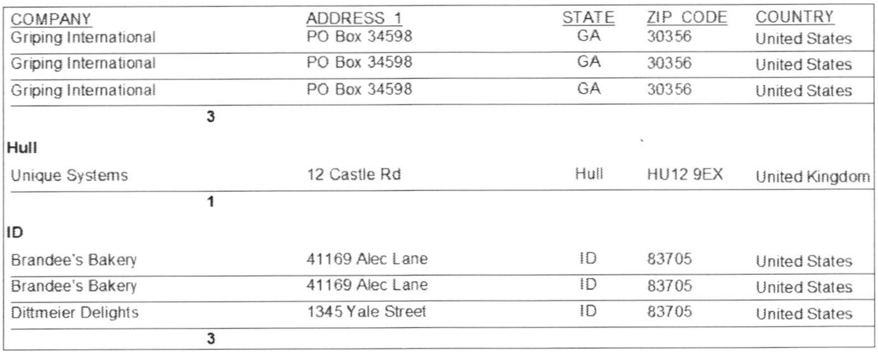

COMPANY	ADDRESS 1	STATE	ZIP CODE	COUNTRY
Griping International	PO Box 34598	GA	30356	United States
Griping International	PO Box 34598	GA	30356	United States
Griping International	PO Box 34598	GA	30356	United States
3				
Hull				
Unique Systems	12 Castle Rd	Hull	HU12 9EX	United Kingdom
1				
ID				
Brandee's Bakery	41169 Alec Lane	ID	83705	United States
Brandee's Bakery	41169 Alec Lane	ID	83705	United States
Dittmeier Delights	1345 Yale Street	ID	83705	United States
3				

Figure 10-20 L10.1 report with the summary field added

> When used with detail level fields, summary functions like Average and Count will not include records when the detail level field is null because null fields do not contain anything, which is different then an empty string or a zero.
>
> For example, if you were creating a summary field that counts on the city field and some records did not have any data in the city field and the database was set to use **NULL VALUES**, records that fall into this category would print on the report, but would not be included in the count summary calculation.
>
> Often, this may not be what you want to happen. If this is the case, checking the **CONVERT DATABASE NULL VALUES TO DEFAULT** option on the Report Options dialog box will convert the null values in the database (if the database supports null values) to an empty string for string fields or zero for numeric fields. Selecting this option will include records in the count or average summary calculation. If you want this to be the default option for all reports, check the same option on the Reporting tab on the Options dialog box.

Modify The Report

The report would look better if the following changes were made.

① Add a report title and page number.
② Change the Address1 heading to Address.
③ Delete the State field from the details section of the report. The field is not needed in this section because it is the field that the report is grouped on.
④ Create a title for the summary field that you created.
⑤ Create a grand total for the number of contacts that are displayed on the report. Place this field in the report footer section.
⑥ Rearrange the fields in the details section so that the report is easier to read.

Add A Report Title And Page Number

1. Make the page header section of the report longer, so that you will have room to add the report titles. Move all of the headings in the page header section down.

2. Create a report title and type `Contact Information Grouped By State` in the object. Make the font size 16 and make the title bold.

3. Create a second report title and type `Sorted By Zip Code` in the object. Change the font size to 14 and make the title bold.

4. Center both of these titles across the page.

5. Add the Page N of M special field above and to the right of the Country field. Right align the Page Number field.

Change The Field Headings And Delete Fields

1. Change the Address1 heading to `Address`.

2. Delete the State field, then move the other fields to the left.

Create A Title For The Summary Field

1. Create a title for the summary field in the group footer section and type `Total # of contacts in state -` in the object. Right align the title.

2. Move the summary field over and place the field title that you just created before it, then remove the bold from the summary field and left align the field.

3. Make the group footer section a little longer so that there will be more blank space on the report before the next group prints.

Create A Grand Total Summary Field

Grand totals are also known as **RUNNING TOTALS** because they keep a total for all of the detail records that are on the report. Earlier in this lesson you learned how to create group summary totals, which are also known as "subtotals". The difference between a group summary total and a running total is that a running total field cannot be summarized.

Another difference between group summary total fields and running total fields is that group summary total fields are automatically reset to zero each time a new group is started, as shown earlier in Figure 10-20. Running Total fields have the option of being reset to zero.

Grand or running total fields that are placed in the report footer section include all of the records in the report, regardless of which group the detail records are in. Earlier in this lesson, I stated that depending on the section of the report that the summary field is placed in, you will get different results. The summary field that you will copy to the report footer section in this exercise will demonstrate this.

1. Right-click on the summary field in the group footer section and select **COPY**.

2. Right-click in the report and select **PASTE**, then click in the report footer section where you want to place the field.

3. Create a title in the report footer section and type
   `Grand Total # of contacts on this report -` in the object.
   Place this title at the two inch mark, then move the grand total field to the right of the title.

> You could create another summary field by using the Insert Summary dialog box, just like the one you created for the group footer section and place it in the report footer section. I find it easier to copy the field and place the second field in the section that I need it in. You can also create a summary field by right-clicking on the field in the details section and selecting Insert ⇒ Summary or Insert ⇒ Running Total.

Rearrange The Fields

1. Move the fields in the details section to the right so that the Company field starts at the half inch mark.

2. Delete the line in the details section. The report layout should look like the one shown in Figure 10-21. Save the changes.

   Page 5 of the report should look like the one shown in Figure 10-22.
   The last page of the report should look like the one shown in Figure 10-23.
   The total number of pages in the report depends on the spacing that you have in each section of the report. Adjust the spacing if necessary, so that it is readable.

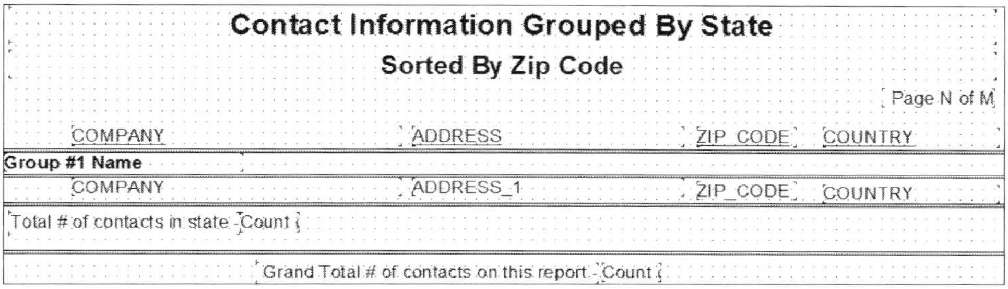

Figure 10-21 L10.1 report layout

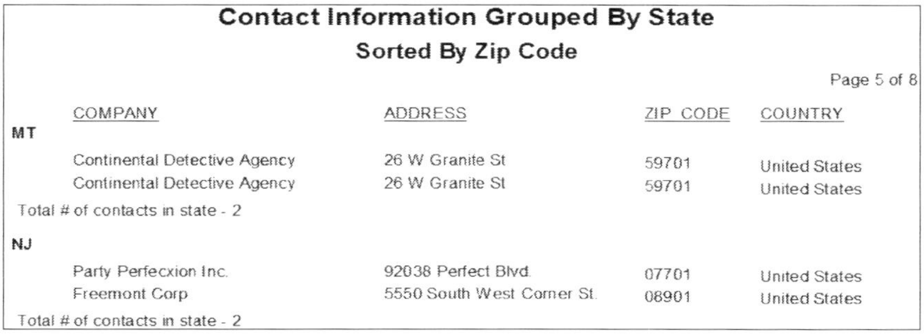

Figure 10-22 Page 5 of the L10.1 report

Figure 10-23 Last page of the L10.1 report

3. If you open the Field Explorer and click on the plus sign in front of the **GROUP NAME FIELDS** option, you will see the State group that you created, as illustrated in Figure 10-24.

   Close the report.

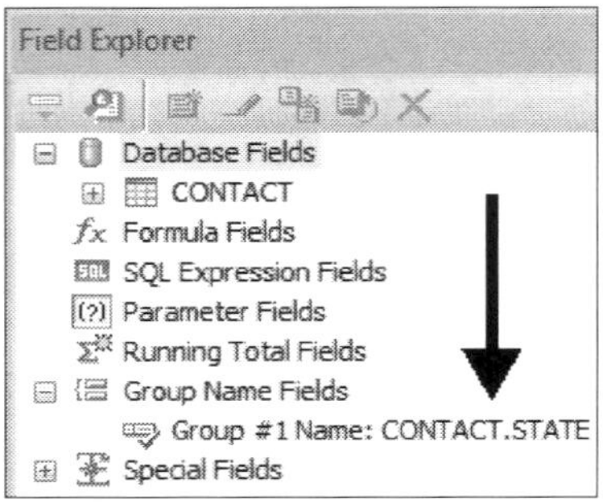

Figure 10-24 Group Name Fields section of the Field Explorer illustrated

You can drag the group name object from the **GROUP NAME FIELDS** section of the Field Explorer on to the report. If you prefer to keep the data in the group header or footer section visible, but not display it on the report, you can suppress the section.

Exercise 10.2: Group Opportunities By Contact

In this exercise you will modify a report to include the following group and sorting options.

① Group on the Contact field and sort the group in ascending order.
② Sort the detail records in each group in ascending order by Create Date.
③ Provide a count of detail records for each contact in each group.
④ Create a total amount per contact based on the total field. This will let the person reading the report know the total amount of the opportunities for each contact.

These options will create counts and totals for the group. The changes that you will make to the report will place all of the opportunities for each contact together. This will make the report more effective because you will be able to see all of a contacts opportunities in one place.

1. Save the L9.3 report as `L10.2 Opportunities by contact.`

2. Change the Create Date selection criteria to 1/1/2008.

3. On the Insert Group dialog box, open the first drop-down list and select the **CONTACT** field, if it is not already selected. Click OK. The report should look like the one shown in Figure 10-25.

CONTACT	COMPANY	OPPORTUNITY_NAME	CREATE_DATE	DAYS_OPEN	TOTAL	STATUS	ACTUAL_CLOSE_DATE
Albert Barry							
Albert Barry	Mercury Production Ma	Mercury Production Mgmt-Home Offic	4/18/08	-16	600.00	Open	12/31/99
Albert Barry	Mercury Production Ma	Mercury Productions Mgmt-Warehous	4/18/08	416	12,000.00	Closed - Won	6/17/10
Albert Barry	Mercury Production Ma	Mercury Production Mgmt-Home Offic	4/18/08	-16	2,000.00	Open	12/31/99
Alexander O'Brien							
Alexander O'Brien	Manxsys Financial	New Opportunity	4/18/08	334	12,000.00	Closed - Won	3/18/09

Figure 10-25 Opportunities grouped by contact

Sort The Detail Records

As you can see in Figure 10-25 above, the report is now grouped by contact. The detail records in each group are not sorted. Because opportunities are entered into the database in the order that they are received, they are often already in date order. There are exceptions to this, including opportunities that may get changed some how during the stages of the process.

Other exceptions that have to be accounted for include how the tables are linked and how the database sends the records to Crystal Reports. To be on the safe side, it is best to control the sort order. In this exercise that means that you should sort the records by the Create Date field to ensure that they are in date order, if that is the report requirement.

1. On the Record Sort Expert dialog box add the Create Date field to the Sort Fields list.

2. Select the Ascending sort order option, if it is not already selected.

   Figure 10-26 shows the sort options that should be selected.

   Click OK, then save the changes.

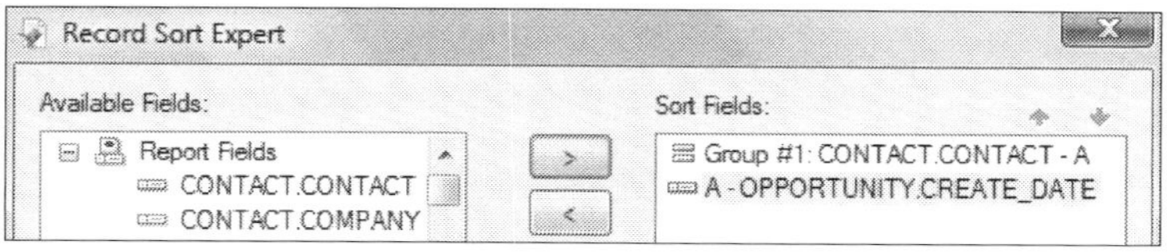

Figure 10-26 Sort options

Total Summary Fields Overview

In this part of the exercise you will create a summary field that will create a total dollar amount of the opportunities for each contact. You will also create a count to show the number of opportunities for each contact.

> The default summary type is **SUM** for numeric fields.
> The default summary type is **MAXIMUM** for Boolean, date and string fields.

Create The Total Summary Field

This summary field will create a total dollar amount of the opportunities for each contact.

1. On the Insert Summary dialog box, open the first drop-down list and select the Total field, then open the second drop-down list and select **SUM**.

2. Open the Summary Location drop-down list and select the Group 1 option. Click OK. The total summary field should be in the group footer section.

Create The Count Summary Field

This summary field will create a count of the number of opportunities for each contact.

1. On the Insert Summary dialog box, open the first drop-down list and select the Opportunity ID field in the Opportunity table, then open the second drop-down list and select **COUNT**.

2. Open the Summary Location drop-down list and select the Group 1 option. Click OK. The count summary field should be in the group footer section.

Create The Distinct Count Summary Field

The distinct count summary will only count the information in a field once. If there are 20 opportunities for one contact, the distinct count calculation will only count that contact once. This will let you create a count for the total number of contacts that are on the report.

1. On the Insert Summary dialog box, open the first drop-down list and select the Contact field if it is not already selected, then open the second drop-down list and select **DISTINCT COUNT**.

2. Open the Summary Location drop-down list and select the **GRAND TOTAL (REPORT FOOTER)** option if it is not already selected. The distinct count only needs to appear once, at the end of the report.

   Figure 10-27 shows the summary options that should be selected.

   Click OK. The distinct count summary field should be in the report footer section.

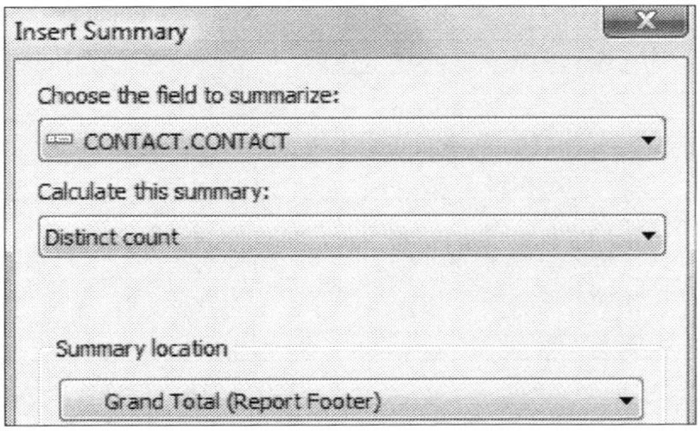

Figure 10-27 Distinct count summary options

3. Save the changes and refresh the data. The report should look like the one shown in Figure 10-28. The report needs a little work.

CONTACT	COMPANY	OPPORTUNITY_NAME	CREATE_DATE	DAYS_OPEN	TOTAL	STATUS	ACTUAL_CLOSE_DATE
Albert Barry							
Albert Barry	Mercury Production Ma	Mercury Productions Mgmt-Warehous	4/18/08	416	12,000.00	Closed - Won	6/17/10
Albert Barry	Mercury Production Ma	Mercury Production Mgmt-Home Offic	4/18/08	-16	2,000.00	Open	12/31/99
Albert Barry	Mercury Production Ma	Mercury Production Mgmt-Home Offic	4/18/08	-16	600.00	Open	12/31/99
	3				**14,600.00**		
Alexander O'Brien							
Alexander O'Brien	Manxsys Financial	New Opportunity	4/18/08	334	12,000.00	Closed - Won	3/18/09
	1				**12,000.00**		
Amanda Form							
Amanda Form	A1 Services-US Opera	New Opportunity	10/30/08	0	12,000.00	Closed - Lost	10/30/09
	1				**12,000.00**		

Figure 10-28 Opportunities by contact report

If you view the last page of the report, you will see the number 64. This is the distinct count summary field that you just created, which shows how many contacts are on the report. In the next part of this exercise you will create a title for this field.

Modify The Report

The report would look better if the following changes were made.

① Add a report title to the page header section.
② Create titles for the summary fields.

③ Create a grand total field and title for the total amount field and for the grand total count of order summary field.
④ Add currency symbols to monetary fields.
⑤ Add a line above all of the summary fields.
⑥ Rearrange the fields in the details section so that the report is easier to read.

1. Create a report title and type `Contact Opportunities` in the object. Make the font size 14 and the title bold. Center the title across the page.

> If a report has selection criteria, it is a good idea to incorporate the selection criteria in the report. Doing this lets the reader know what criteria the report is using. This report will print records for opportunities that were created after a specific date. How, or if you incorporate this information is up to you and the requestors of the report. Keep in mind that business decisions are based off of the data in reports, so providing as much helpful and useful information as possible, is a good thing.

2. Copy both of the summary fields in the group footer section and place them in the report footer section.

> If you select both fields before you select the **COPY** command, you can copy both fields at the same time.

3. Create the field titles in Table 10-7 for the summary fields. Make the titles bold. The section column in the table refers to the section in the report where the title should be placed.

Summary Field	Section	Title
Total	Group Footer	Total $ amount of opportunities -
Opportunity ID	Group Footer	Total # opportunities -
Contact	Report Footer	Total # of contacts on this report -
Total	Report Footer	Grand Total $ amount of all opportunities -
Opportunity ID	Report Footer	Grand Total # of opportunities -

Table 10-7 Field titles for Exercise 10.2

> If I know that the report needs several field titles with the same formatting, I create one and then copy it and just change the text. For me, this is quicker then using the Format Painter. Over time, you will find a process that works best for you.

> I usually right align titles for calculated fields, when the title is placed to the left of the calculated field. Doing this reduces the amount of white space between the title and the calculated field. When I do this, I also left align the calculated field to further reduce the space between the field and the title. The other option is to drag the calculated field into the text object.

4. Delete the Contact field in the details section, then remove the bold from the Group Name field.

Group Name objects can be formatted like any other object in the report.

5. Add a line at the bottom of the group footer section. Change the size of the line to 0.5 pt. Save the changes and leave the report open to complete the next part of the exercise.

Add A Line Above The Summary Fields

1. If necessary, move the summary fields in the group footer section down, so that you have room to add the line above the fields.

2. Right-click on the Total $ Amount summary field in the group footer section and select **FORMAT FIELD**. On the Border tab open the **TOP** drop-down list, select **SINGLE**. Leave the dialog box open.

The advantage of using the line option on the Border tab for a field is that if you move or resize the field, the line is automatically re-adjusted. You can also use the **LINE** tool to draw a line. If you use the Line tool and you move or resize the field, you will also have to move or resize the line.

Add The Currency Symbol

Crystal Reports supports currency fields, but the ACT! demo database does not use this data type for monetary fields, so you have to add the currency symbol manually to fields on a report, as needed.

1. On the Numbers tab, select the Display Currency Symbol option, then click OK.

2. Add the currency symbol to the other monetary fields on the report.

3. Rearrange the fields so that they look like the layout shown in Figure 10-29.

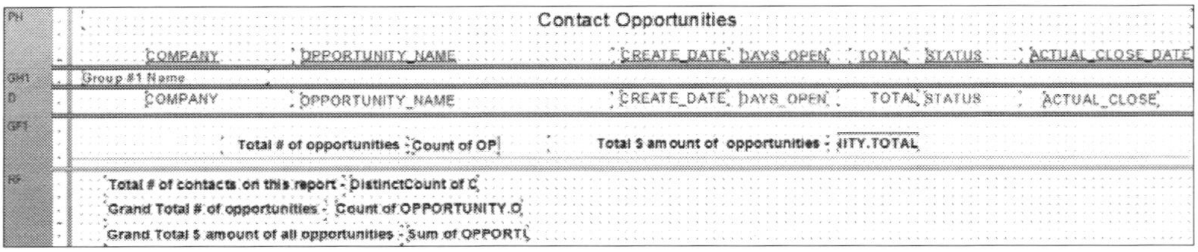

Figure 10-29 L10.2 report layout

4. Save the changes. Page 1 of the report should look like the one shown in Figure 10-30. The report footer section on the last page should look like the one shown in Figure 10-31.

If you see **###'s** in a field, make the field wider.

Contact Opportunities

COMPANY	OPPORTUNITY_NAME	CREATE_DATE	DAYS_OPEN	TOTAL	STATUS	ACTUAL_CLOSE_DATE
Albert Barry						
Mercury Production Ma	Mercury Productions Mgmt-Warehouse	4/18/08	416	$12,000.00	Closed - Won	6/17/10
Mercury Production Ma	Mercury Production Mgmt-Home Office Service	4/18/08	-16	$2,000.00	Open	12/31/99
Mercury Production Ma	Mercury Production Mgmt-Home Office Upgrade	4/18/08	-16	$600.00	Open	12/31/99
Total # of opportunities - 3		**Total $ amount of opportunities -**		**$14,600.00**		
Alexander O'Brien						
Manxsys Financial	New Opportunity	4/18/08	334	$12,000.00	Closed - Won	3/18/09
Total # of opportunities - 1		**Total $ amount of opportunities -**		**$12,000.00**		
Amanda Form						
A1 Services-US Opera	New Opportundy	10/30/08	0	$12,000.00	Closed - Lost	10/30/09
Total # of opportunities - 1		**Total $ amount of opportunities -**		**$12,000.00**		

Figure 10-30 Page 1 of the L10.2 report

Total # of contacts on this report - 64

Grand Total # of opportunities - 106

Grand Total $ amount of all opportunities - $ 714,500.00

Figure 10-31 Last page of the L10.2 report

5. Make any changes that are needed. Leave the report open to complete the next exercise.

Exercise 10.3: Group Opportunities By Contact With Averages

It may be useful to the reader of the report to know the average opportunity amount for each contact. The steps below will show you how to create an average summary field.

1. Save the L10.2 report as `L10.3 Opportunities by contact with averages.`

2. On the Insert Summary dialog box, open the first drop-down list and select the Total field, then open the second drop-down list and select **AVERAGE**. Open the Summary Location drop-down list and select the Group 1 option, then click OK. The total amount average summary field should be in the group footer section.

3. Move the average summary field below the Total $ amount of opportunities field.

4. Add the currency symbol to the average summary field.

5. Copy the average summary field and place the copy in the report footer section below the last Grand Total field.

6. Create a title for the Total average summary field in the group footer section and type `Average opportunity amount for contact -` in the object. Make the title bold.

7. Create a title for the Total average summary field in the report footer section and type `Average opportunity amount for all contacts -` in the object.

8. Make the title bold. Save the changes. The bottom of the last page of the report should look like the one shown in Figure 10-32. If you need to make any changes, make them now, then close the report.

COMPANY	OPPORTUNITY NAME

Total # of contacts on this report - 64

Grand Total # of opportunities - 106

Grand Total $ amount of all opportunities - $714,500.00

Average opportunity amount for all contacts -$6,740.57

Figure 10-32 L10.3 report with averages

Exercise 10.4: Group 2008 Opportunities By Status

In this exercise you will modify a report to include the following group and sorting options. These options also allow you to create totals for the group.

① Group on the Status field and sort the groups in ascending order.
② Sort the detail records in ascending order on the Create Date field.
③ Create a count of opportunities in each status group.
④ Create a total per contact in each status group.

This report currently only displays opportunities with a create date greater than 6/24/2008. All of the status options are printed. In order to get a count of detail records for each group and a total per contact, two groups need to be created. To get an accurate count of opportunities for each status in 2008, the existing selection criteria needs to be deleted and new criteria has to be created.

Create The Status And Contact Name Groups

1. Save the L9.3 report as `L10.4 2008 Opportunities by status`.

2. On the Insert Group dialog box, open the first drop-down list and select the **STATUS** field, then click OK.

3. On the Insert Group dialog box, open the first drop-down list and select the **CONTACT** field, if it is not already selected, then click OK. You should have two groups in the report layout similar to those shown earlier in Figure 10-10.

Sort The Detail Records

1. On the Record Sort Expert dialog box add the Create Date field to the Sort Fields list.

2. Select the Ascending sort order if it is not already selected. Figure 10-33 shows the sort options that should be selected. Click OK and save the changes. You do not have to generate data because you are not finished making changes to the report.

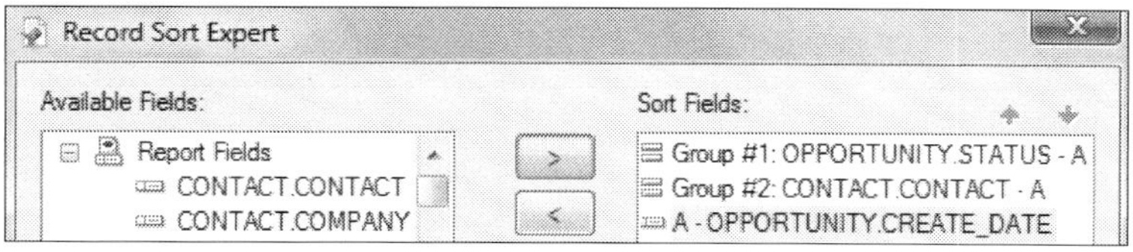

Figure 10-33 Sort options

3. Delete the Opportunity field, then move the fields after it to the left.

Change The Selection Criteria

The report that this one is based off of has selection criteria that needs to be changed. This report needs criteria to only display records from 2007 and 2008.

1. Open the Select Expert and change the current criteria to only include opportunities created in 2007 or 2008.

Create The Summary Fields

This report requires two summary fields: a count of opportunities and a total dollar amount of opportunities per contact. The count summary field will create a total number of opportunities per contact. It will also be copied to the report footer section to create a grand total number of opportunities on the report. The other summary field will create a total dollar amount per contact. It will also be copied to the report footer section to create a grand total opportunity amount on the report.

1. On the Insert Summary dialog box, open the first drop-down list and select the Opportunity ID field. Open the second drop-down list and select **COUNT**. Open the Summary Location drop-down list and select the Group 2 option. This will place the summary field in the contact group footer section. Click OK.

2. On the Insert Summary dialog box, open the first drop-down list and select the Total field, then open the second drop-down list and select **SUM**. Open the Summary Location drop-down list and select the Group 2 option, then click OK.

> Summary fields are available in the **REPORT EXPLORER** and **FORMULA WORKSHOP**. They are not available in the Field Explorer.

3. Save the changes and refresh the data. The report should look like the one shown in Figure 10-34.

CONTACT	COMPANY	CREATE DATE	DAYS OPEN	TOTAL	STATUS	ACTUAL CLOSE DATE
Closed - Lost						
Amanda Form						
Amanda Form	A1 Services-US Operations	5/20/07	96	12,000.00	Closed - Lost	8/23/09
Amanda Form	A1 Services-US Operations	5/20/07	102	2,000.00	Closed - Lost	8/30/09
Amanda Form	A1 Services-US Operations	10/30/08	0	12,000.00	Closed - Lost	10/30/09
	3			**26,000.00**		
Bella Minoal						
Bella Minoal	Jake Flakes Inc.	4/18/08	252	12,000.00	Closed - Lost	8/27/09
	1			**12,000.00**		
Carl Spackler						
Carl Spackler	Golf Greens Extraordinaire	5/21/07	31	2,000.00	Closed - Lost	6/19/10
	1			**2,000.00**		

Figure 10-34 L10.4 report

Modify The Report

The report would look better if the following changes were made.

① Add a report title to the page header section.
② Create titles for the summary fields.
③ Create a grand total field and title for the total amount and count of opportunity summary fields.
④ Rearrange the fields in the details section so that the report is easier to read.

1. Create a report title in the page header and type `2007 and 2008 Opportunities By Status` in the object. Change the font size to 14, then make the field bold.

2. Add a logo or image to the upper left corner of the page header section.

3. Delete the Contact and Status fields from the details section, then move the fields over to the left.

4. Remove the bold from the Group 2 Header field.

5. Remove the bold from the summary fields in the Group 2 Footer section.

6. Add the currency symbol to the summary total field.

7. Copy both of the summary fields in the Group 2 Footer section and place them in the Group 1 Footer and report footer sections.

8. Add a line under the totals in the Group 1 and 2 Footer sections. Change the line in the Group 1 Footer section to dotted. Change the size of the line in the group 2 header to 0.5.

9. Create the field titles in Table 10-8 for the summary fields. For now, place them in the page footer section.

Summary Field	Section	Title
Total	Group 1 Footer	Total opportunity amount for contacts -
Opportunity ID Count	Group 1 Footer	Total # opportunities for contacts -
Total	Group 2 Footer	Total opportunity amount for contact -
Opportunity ID Count	Group 2 Footer	Total # opportunities for contact -
Total	Report Footer	Total opportunity amount for all contacts -
Opportunity ID	Report Footer	Total # opportunities for all contacts -

Table 10-8 Field titles for Exercise 10.4

10. Copy the Group 1 Header field and place the copy in the Group 1 Footer section, then remove the bold from the field in the Group 1 Footer section.

11. Create a title in the Group 1 Footer section and type `Totals For:` in the object. Create a title in the report footer section and type `Report Grand Totals:` in the object. Make both objects bold.

12. Arrange the fields so that they look like the layout shown in Figure 10-35.

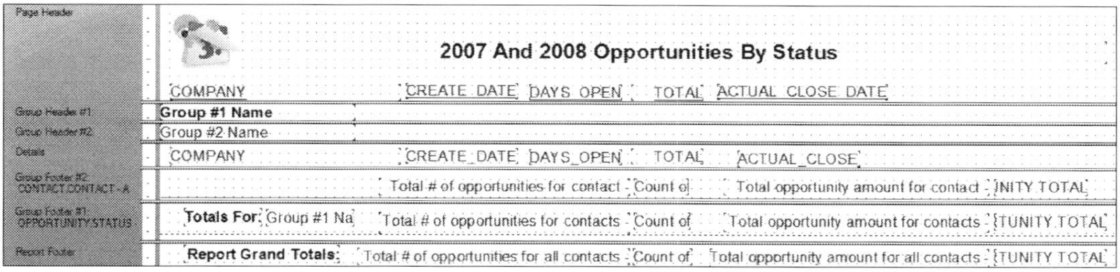

Figure 10-35 L10.4 report layout

13. Save the changes and refresh the data.
Page 1 should look like the one shown in Figure 10-36.
The bottom of page 4 should look like the one shown in Figure 10-37. Notice the totals for the status Closed-Lost. If this data is not on page 4, click on the Closed-Lost status for the company UR Powerful, in the group tree. The last page should look like the one shown in Figure 10-38.

2007 And 2008 Opportunities By Status

COMPANY	CREATE DATE	DAYS OPEN	TOTAL	ACTUAL CLOSE DATE	
Closed - Lost					
Amanda Form					
A1 Services-US Operations	5/20/07	96	12,000.00	8/23/09	
A1 Services-US Operations	5/20/07	102	2,000.00	8/30/09	
A1 Services-US Operations	10/30/08	0	12,000.00	10/30/09	
	Total # of opportunities for contact - 3			Total opportunity amount for contact -	$26,000.00
Bella Minoal					
Jake Flakes Inc.	4/18/08	252	12,000.00	8/27/09	
	Total # of opportunities for contact - 1			Total opportunity amount for contact -	$12,000.00
Carl Spackler					
Golf Greens Extraordinaire	5/21/07	31	2,000.00	6/19/10	
	Total # of opportunities for contact - 1			Total opportunity amount for contact -	$2,000.00

Figure 10-36 Page 1 of the L10.4 report

UR Powerful					
Captains of Industry	5/20/07	-252	12,000.00	3/21/08	
	Total # of opportunities for contact - 1			Total opportunity amount for contact -	$12,000.00
Totals For: Closed - Lost	Total # of opportunities for contacts - 42			Total opportunity amount for contacts -	$347,300.00

Figure 10-37 Page 4 of the L10.4 report

COMPANY	CREATE DATE	DAYS OPEN	TOTAL	ACTUAL CLOSE DATE	
Cadbury	5/20/07	195	2,000.00	12/31/99	
Cadbury	5/20/07	61	8,000.00	12/31/99	
Cadbury	5/21/07	196	2,000.00	12/31/99	
	Total # of opportunities for contact - 3			Total opportunity amount for contact -	$12,000.00
Totals For: Open	Total # of opportunities for contacts - 221			Total opportunity amount for contacts -	$1,595,000.00
Report Grand Totals:	Total # of opportunities for all contacts - 382			Total opportunity amount for all contacts -	$2,874,500.00

Figure 10-38 Last page of the L10.4 report

CREATING CUSTOM GROUPS

After completing the exercises in this lesson you will be able to create and use the following types of group functionality:

- ☑ Create percent calculations
- ☑ Create a custom group name
- ☑ User defined sort order
- ☑ User defined groups
- ☑ Use the Group Expert

LESSON 11

Custom Groups Overview

In the previous lesson you learned how to create basic groups. While the group functionality that you learned about will handle a large percent of your grouping needs, there will be times when you need to modify something about the group.

When you find that you cannot quite figure out how to use the group options that you learned about in the previous lesson to create the groups that you need, you can create what I call custom groups. That is the focus of this lesson.

Exercise 11.1: Group 2008 Opportunities By Month

In this exercise you will modify a report to include the following group and sorting options. These options also allow you to create totals and counts so that the records will be grouped by the month the opportunities were closed.

① Group on the Actual Close Date field.
② Sort the detail records in ascending order on the Actual Close Date field.
③ Provide a count of opportunities per month.

The goal of this exercise is to create a report that displays all of the closed opportunities created in 2008 and to have a subtotal for each month. In order to create a subtotal of opportunities for each month, the report needs to be grouped on the Actual Close Date field.

As you will see, when you group on a date or date/time field, the Insert Group dialog box will display the option, **THE SECTION WILL BE PRINTED**. This option is used to create the group by month, day, quarter, year and more.

Create The Actual Close Date Group

1. Save the L10.2 report as `L11.1 2008 Opportunities by month`.

2. Delete the group header and footer sections. Delete the data in the report footer section.

3. On the Insert Group dialog box, open the first drop-down list and select the **ACTUAL CLOSE DATE** field. Open the last drop-down list and select **FOR EACH MONTH**.

   Figure 11-1 shows the group options that should be selected.

   Click OK.

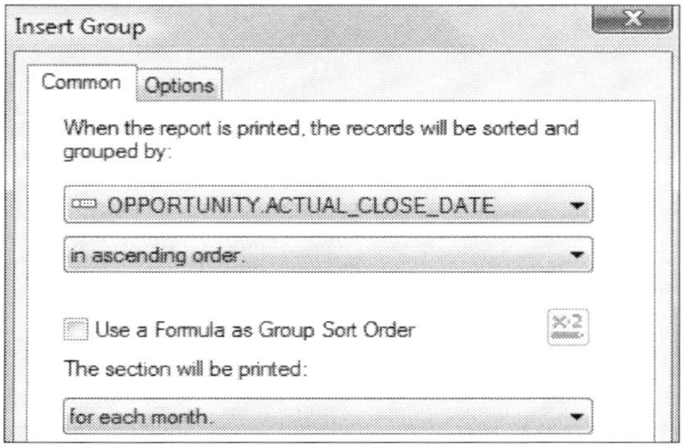

Figure 11-1 Group options

Sort The Detail Records And Create Selection Criteria

1. On the Record Sort Expert add the Actual Close Date field to the Sort Fields list.
2. Select the Ascending sort order if it is not already selected.
3. Delete the Create Date field, then click OK.
4. Create selection criteria to select all of the opportunities with an actual close date in 2008.
5. Delete the Create Date selection criteria, then save the changes.

Create The Summary Fields

The count summary field will create a total for the number of opportunities per month. It can also be copied to the report footer section to create a grand total amount of opportunities for the entire report, which you learned how to do in the previous lesson. The Total summary field will create a total dollar amount per month. It can also be copied to the report footer section to create a grand total opportunity amount.

1. On the Insert Summary dialog box, open the first drop-down list and select the Opportunity ID field, then open the second drop-down list and select **DISTINCT COUNT**. Open the Summary Location drop-down list and select the Group 1 option, then click OK.
2. On the Insert Summary dialog box, open the first drop-down list and select the Total field, then open the second drop-down list and select **SUM**. Open the Summary Location drop-down list and select the Group 1 option, then click OK.
3. Add a dollar sign to the Total summary field.
4. Delete the Status field from the report, then move the Actual Close Date field over.

How To Create Percent Calculations

Percent calculations are very useful when you have the need to show what percent each group on the report represents in comparison to the grand total value of the report. For example, on a report that shows the sales for an entire year, there could be a percent calculation by month on the Total field. This would tell the person that reads the report the percent of sales each month represents for the year. Another example on a yearly sales report would be the percent of sales each salesperson had per month, per year or both.

> You can only create percent calculations on summary fields that have a numeric value. This means that if you are creating a count summary of contacts based on the Contact field which is a text field, you can create a percent calculation, because the count summary field is a numeric value.

Each percent calculation on a report requires its own percent summary calculation field.
The process of creating a percent summary calculation starts off the same as the calculations that you have already learned how to create. The options to create percent calculations are at the bottom of the Insert Summary dialog box. To create a percent calculation check the

SHOW AS A PERCENTAGE OF option, then select the group or total that you want the percent comparison based on.

> If you need a total field and a percent calculation field that are based off of the same field, you have to create two summary calculation fields: one for the total amount and one for the percent.

In the previous part of the exercise you created the Total summary field. Now you will create the Total percent calculation field.

1. On the Insert Summary dialog box, open the first drop-down list and select the Total field, then open the second drop-down list and select **SUM**.

   Open the Summary Location drop-down list and select the Group 1 option, then check the **SHOW AS A PERCENTAGE OF** option.

   Figure 11-2 shows the summary options that should be selected.

   Click OK.

Figure 11-2 Insert Summary dialog box options

2. Move the percent summary field over to the right. On my report, it is currently on top of the total summary field that you just created.

3. Save the changes and refresh the data. The first page of the report should look like the one shown in Figure 11-3. Notice that the percent summary field is automatically formatted with a percent sign.

Figure 11-3 L11.1 report

How To Check Or Edit Summary Fields

Sometimes reports will have more than two or three summary fields and you may not remember what each summary field is calculating. If a summary field is not producing the output that you think it should, it is possible that you selected an option that you should not have. If either of these is the case, all is not lost. You do not have to delete the field and start over. You can follow the steps below.

1. Right-click on the percentage summary field and select **EDIT SUMMARY**. You will see the dialog box shown in Figure 11-4. You can make any changes that are necessary.

   The Edit Summary dialog box is almost identical to the Insert Summary dialog box. The difference is that you cannot change the location of the summary field.

   If you need to move a summary field from one section of the report to another, you will have to do it manually.

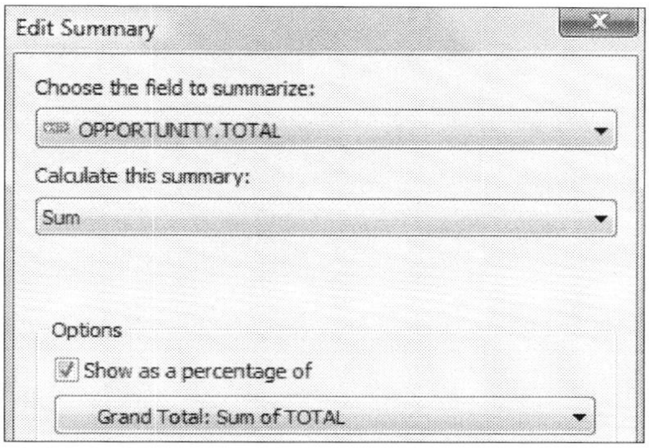

Figure 11-4 Edit Summary dialog box

Modify The Report

1. Create the titles shown in Figure 11-5 for the summary fields that you created.

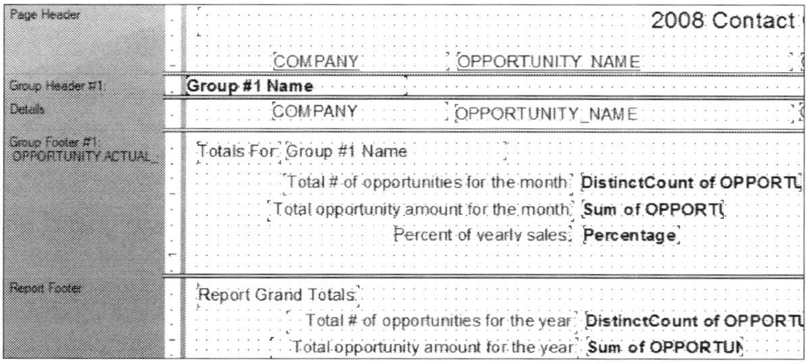

Figure 11-5 L11.1 report layout

When you preview the report you will see the months in the group tree section of the report. If you click on the 1/2008 group illustrated in Figure 11-6, you will see the orders that were placed in January.

The Percent of yearly sales field lets you know that the orders in January represent 8.72% of the total sales in 2008.

Figure 11-6 L11.1 report

How To Create A Custom Group Name

As you can see in Figure 11-7, the Actual Close Date group name displays the month number and year. The report would look better if the group name displayed the actual month name instead (January, February, March, etc.).

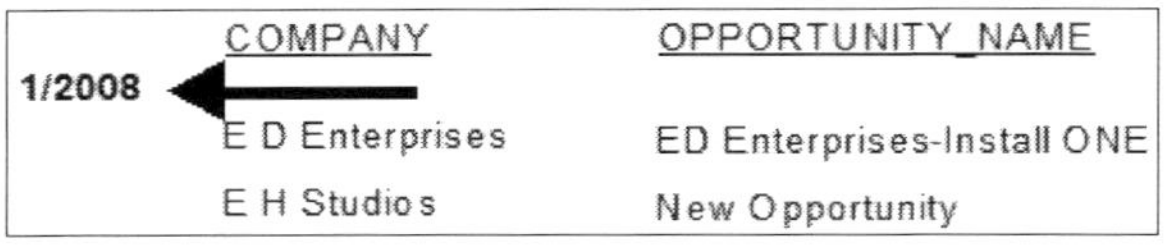

Figure 11-7 Actual Close Date group name illustrated

The Format Editor has an option that you can use to display the month name. You could create a formula to accomplish this task, but using the Format Editor is easier. The steps below will show you how to create a custom group name.

1. Right-click on the **GROUP 1 NAME** field in the group header section, then open the Format Editor. Click the **CUSTOMIZE** button on the Date and Time tab.
2. Open the **ORDER** drop-down list and select Date, as shown in Figure 11-8.

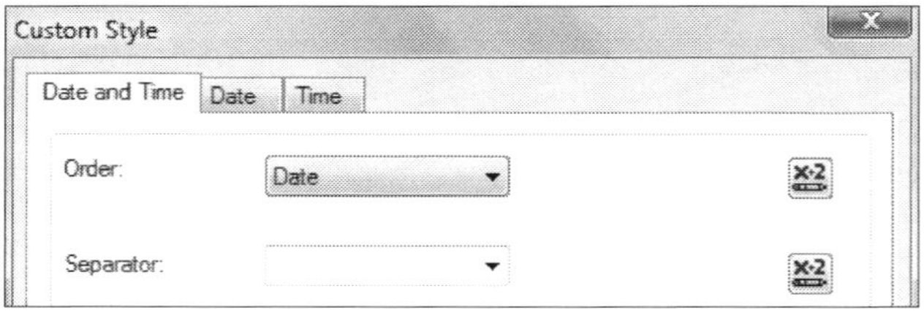

Figure 11-8 Date and Time tab options

3. On the Date tab open the Month drop-down list and select **MARCH**, then select **NONE** for the Day and Year options.

   Figure 11-9 illustrates the options that you should have selected.

   Click OK twice, to close both dialog boxes.

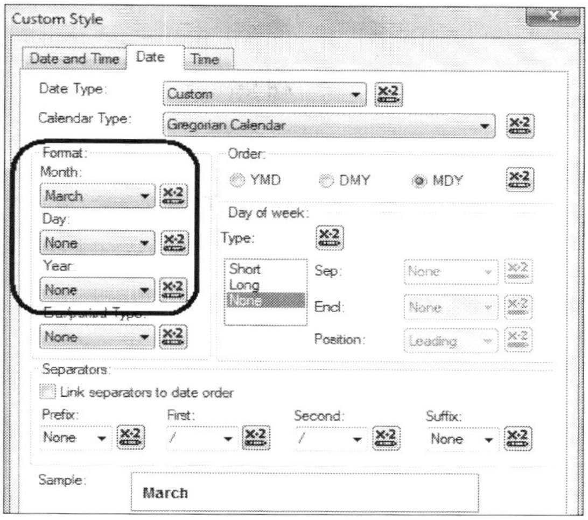

Figure 11-9 Date tab options illustrated

4. Format the Group Name field in the group footer section to have the same formatting as the one in the group header section.

   Save the changes. Go to the last page of the report. The totals for December and the report grand totals should look like the ones shown in Figure 11-10. Leave the report open to complete the next exercise.

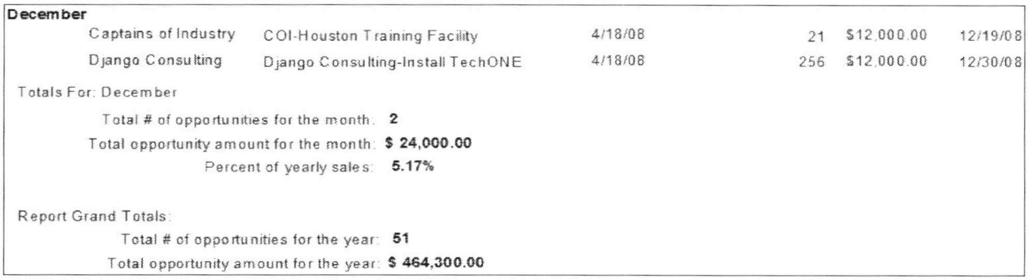

December

Captains of Industry	COI-Houston Training Facility	4/18/08	21	$12,000.00	12/19/08
Django Consulting	Django Consulting-Install TechONE	4/18/08	256	$12,000.00	12/30/08

Totals For: December

Total # of opportunities for the month: **2**

Total opportunity amount for the month: **$ 24,000.00**

Percent of yearly sales: **5.17%**

Report Grand Totals:

Total # of opportunities for the year: **51**

Total opportunity amount for the year: **$ 464,300.00**

Figure 11-10 Last page of the L11.1 report

Exercise 11.2: Create Selection Criteria On Summary Fields

In Lesson 9 you learned about record selection. **GROUP SELECTION** is similar. The difference is that group selection is done on summary fields, instead of fields in the details section. If a report is grouping the opportunities by state, each state would include an opportunity total amount.

In Exercise 11.1 you created a report that grouped the opportunities by month. At the end of each month are summary calculations for the total number of opportunities and total opportunity amount for the month. In this exercise you will learn how to create selection criteria on group summary fields. The report that you created in Exercise 11.1 displays data for every month in 2008. In this exercise you will use the Select Expert to modify that report to only display months where the total monthly amount is greater than $50,000.

1. Save the L11.1 report as `L11.2 2008 Monthly opportunity totals over 50K`.

2. Right-click on the Sum of Total field in the group footer section and select, Select Expert Group.

3. Open the drop-down list and select **IS GREATER THAN OR EQUAL TO**, then type `50000` in the second field. Notice that the field name on the tab does not display a table name. Instead, it displays information that lets you know that this is a summary field. Click OK.

4. Change the report title to `2008 Monthly Opportunity Totals Over $50,000`, then save the changes.

As shown in Figure 11-11, the first month displayed on the report is February. Notice that all of the groups are still visible in the group tree. If you click on the 06/2008 option in the group tree, you will not see the data for June. That is because the monthly total for June is less than $50,000. I don't know about you, but I would prefer that the only options that appear in the group tree are the ones that meet the criteria.

This happens because of the way Crystal Reports processes data, which currently cannot be changed. Remember that the group header information is processed before the totals for the summary calculations in the group footer are processed. This is why all of the months appear in the group tree.

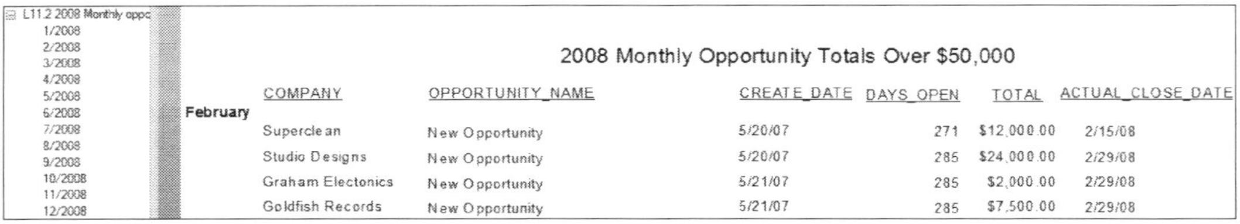

Figure 11-11 L11.2 report

User Defined Groups

Earlier you learned about the User defined sort order. In Exercise 11.1 you learned how to create a custom group name. Custom group names are used to rename existing group names. Custom groups must be based on a single field in the report. User defined groups are similar to custom group names. The major difference is that the user defined group name is free form. In addition to being able to create a free form group name, you can create custom groups. Below are examples of user defined groups.

① Orders placed between the first and the 15th of the month.
② Group customers based on their year to date sales (example Gold, Bronze and Silver levels).
③ Create sales territories and associate states to a territory (example Northeast, Southeast and Midwest).

There are four steps to creating a user defined group as discussed below:

① Select the field that you want to create the user defined group for, then select the option, **IN SPECIFIED ORDER** in the second drop-down list on the Common tab of the Insert Group dialog box. Once this option is selected, other tabs (the Specified Order and Others tabs) will appear on the dialog box.

② Type in the name for the first group name that you need in the **NAMED GROUP** drop-down list shown in Figure 11-12, then click the **NEW** button.

③ The **DEFINE NAMED GROUP** dialog box is similar to the Select Expert. One difference is that each tab on the Define Named Group dialog box is for the same field. User defined groups cannot use parameter fields and the formula cannot be modified. You would type in the criteria for the user defined group, as shown in Figure 11-13. The other difference is that these filters or selection criteria use the **OR** operand, meaning that the detail record can meet the criteria for filter 1 or filter 2 or filter 3.

④ Click OK and repeat steps 2 and 3 until you have created all of the user defined groups that the report needs.

> If checked, the **USE A FORMULA AS GROUP SORT ORDER** option as shown earlier in Figure 11-1 will not let you select a specified order that is based on a formula.

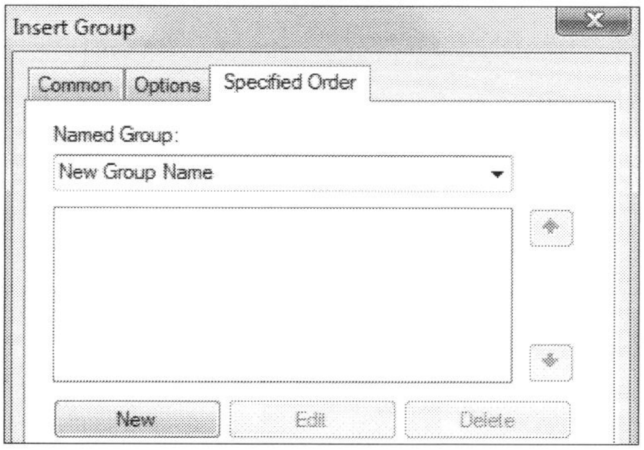

Figure 11-12 Specified Order tab options

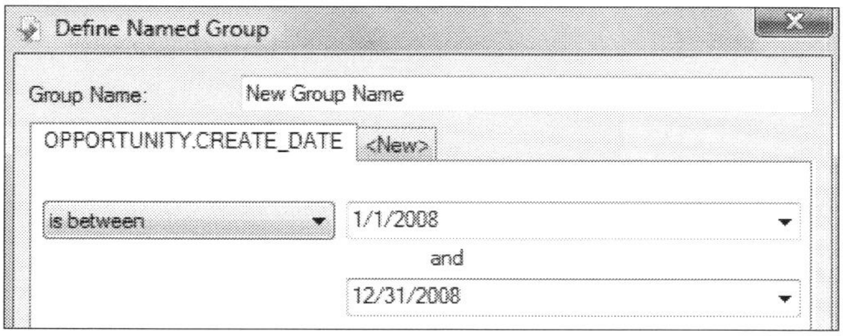

Figure 11-13 Criteria for a user defined group

If you wanted to group orders by specific date ranges like 1/1/10 to 1/15/10, 2/1/10 to 2/15/10 and 3/1/10 to 3/15/10, you would create three named groups, for example, Jan 10, Feb 10 and Mar 10. For each named group you would select the Create Date field, the operator "Is between" and the date range for the named group. The report would show the three groups and the detail records that have a create date that falls into one of the three date ranges.

If one group or all groups need additional criteria, click on the New tab and add the next piece of criteria for the group. You can only add criteria for the same field.

For example, if you also wanted to see opportunities for 1/15/10 to 1/25/10, you would add this criteria on the New tab, as shown in Figure 11-14.

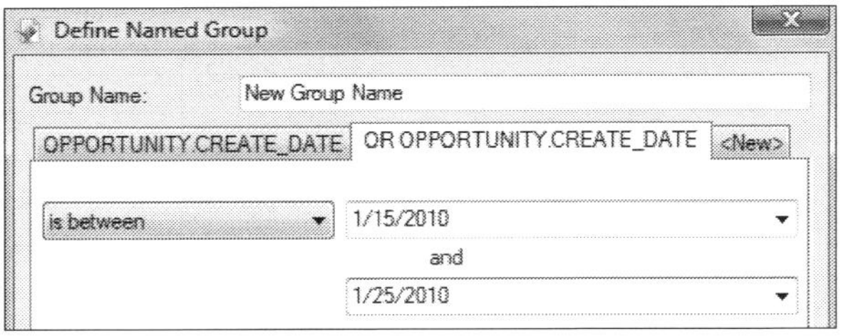

Figure 11-14 Additional criteria added to the named group

The criteria for each group name is joined using the **OR** operand. This means that as long as the record meets one of the sets of criteria for the group name, it will appear on the report.

The options on the Others tab, which you will learn about in the next exercise, are used to select what you want to do with the records that do not meet the criteria for any of the named groups.

Exercise 11.3: Create A User Defined Group Report

In this exercise you will modify the L10.1 report to include the following state user defined groups: AZ, CA and TX.

1. Save the L10.1 report as `L11.3 User defined groups`.

2. Right-click on the group header section and select **CHANGE GROUP**.

3. Select the **IN SPECIFIED ORDER** option in the second drop-down list. You should see the **SPECIFIED ORDER** tab.

4. Select AZ, CA and TX in the **NAMED GROUP** drop-down list. Make sure that the states are in the order shown in Figure 11-15.

   If they are not in the order shown, use the up and down arrow buttons to put the states in the order shown.

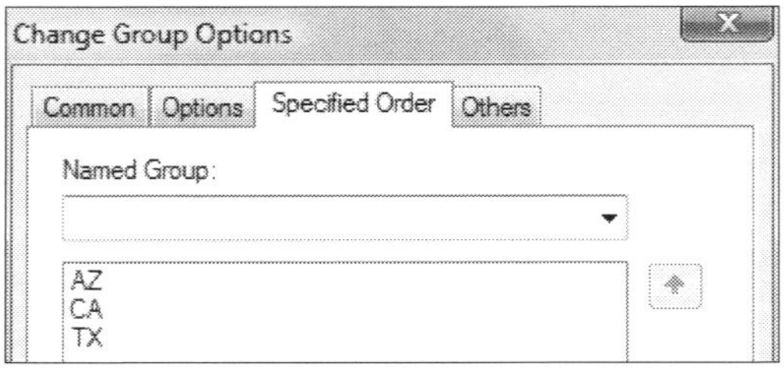

Figure 11-15 Change Group Options dialog box

5. On the **OTHERS** tab select the option **DISCARD ALL OTHERS**, as shown in Figure 11-16.

Selecting the Discard all others option means that records that are not in any of the groups listed on the Specified Order tab will not appear on the report.

The **PUT ALL OTHERS TOGETHER, WITH THE NAME** option, will put all of the other records that do not meet the criteria on the Specified Order tab in the report under a new group name that you enter on the field below the option. This group will appear at the end of the report.

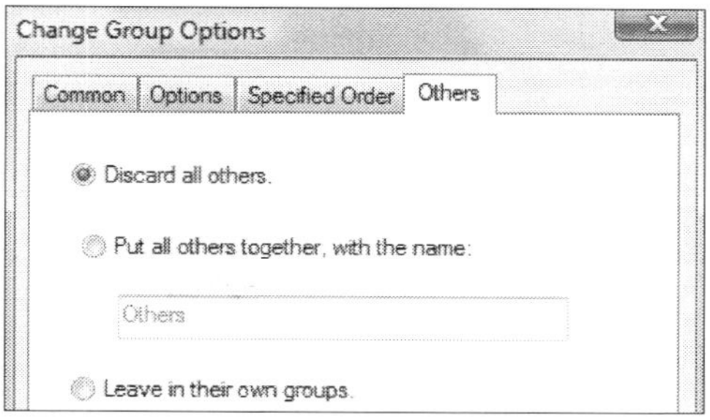

Figure 11-16 Others tab options

6. Preview the report. You should only see the AZ, CA and TX groups in the group tree, as shown in Figure 11-17. Save the changes and leave the report open to complete the next exercise.

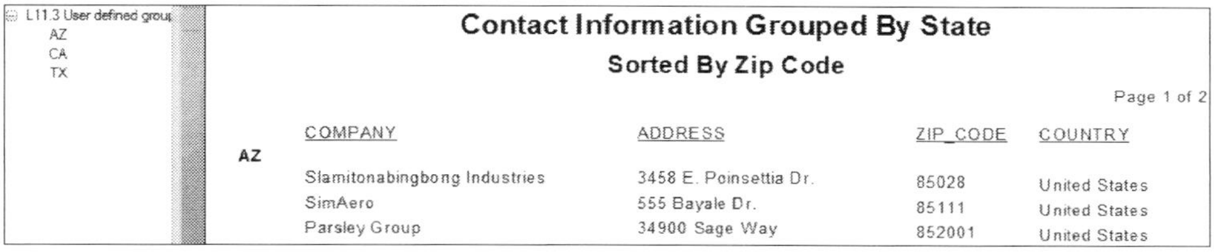

Figure 11-17 L11.3 User defined groups report

Exercise 11.4: Create A Custom Group Name Report

In the previous exercise, the User Defined Group report displayed the two character state name. In this exercise you will modify that report so that the state names are spelled out.

1. Save the L11.3 report as `L11.4 Custom group name`.

2. Right-click on the group header report section and select **CHANGE GROUP**, then click on the Specified Order tab and delete all of the Named Groups.

3. Click the **NEW** button, then type `Arizona` in the Group Name field.

   Open the drop-down list and select **IS EQUAL TO**, then select AZ from the second drop-down list. You should have the options selected that are shown in Figure 11-18. Click OK.

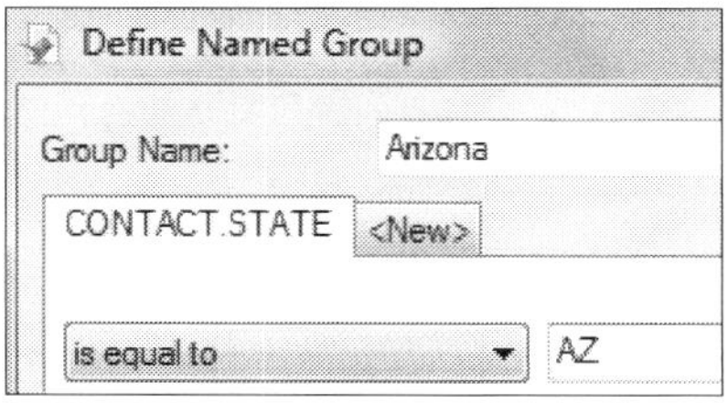

Figure 11-18 Defined Name Group options for AZ

4. Repeat step 3 above for CA and TX. Leave the Change Group Options dialog box open when you are finished.

5. On the **OTHERS** tab select the option **PUT ALL OTHERS TOGETHER, WITH THE NAME**, then type `Other States`, as shown in Figure 11-19.

   Click OK and save the changes.

   The report should look like the one shown in Figure 11-20. Notice that the state names are spelled out in the group tree and on the report.

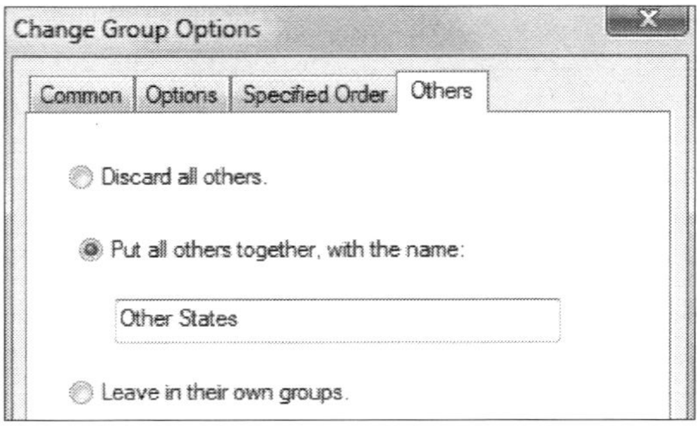

Figure 11-19 Others tab options

You should see a new group called **OTHER STATES** in the group tree. This group contains all of the records that meet the selection options for the report, but are not in AZ, CA or TX.

Figure 11-20 L11.4 Custom group name report

If you find that the majority of the reports with groups that you create, do not need the group name field that is automatically added to the header section, clear the **INSERT GROUP NAME WITH GROUP** option on the layout tab of the Options dialog box.

Using The Group Expert

All of the groups that you have created so far were created using the Insert Group dialog box.

You can also create groups using the Group Expert shown in Figure 11-21.

Figure 11-21 Group Expert

There are two ways to open the Group Expert as discussed below.

① Click the Group Expert button on the Expert Tools toolbar.
② Report ⇒ Group Expert.

> Memo fields cannot be used as a field to sort or group on from the Record Sort Expert or Group Expert dialog boxes. If you need to sort or group on a memo field, you have to create a formula.

One benefit of using the Group Expert is that you can create all of the groups for the report without having to re-open a dialog box to create each group.

Another benefit is if you need to see the data in a field, you can click the Browse Data button.

The **OPTIONS** button will open the Change Group Options dialog box shown in Figure 11-22. It is the same as the Insert Group dialog box.

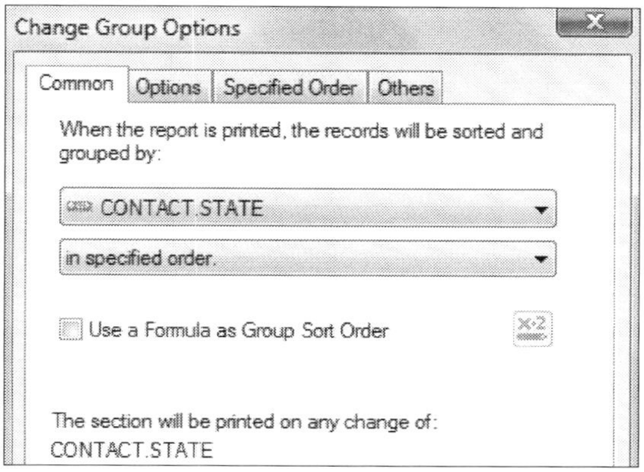

Figure 11-22 Change Group Options dialog box

REPORT WIZARDS

Lesson 4 provided an overview of how to create reports and charts using a wizard. In this lesson you will learn more about the wizards. In the last few lessons, all of the reports that you created were created from scratch. I figured that I would give you a break in this lesson from creating reports from scratch. After completing the exercises in this lesson you will be able to:

- ☑ Understand the options on the common wizard screens
- ☑ Know the types of reports that wizards can create
- ☑ Use the Mailing Label wizard

Report Wizard Overview

Now that you have used several report creation and modification features and were able to see the completed reports, many of the options on the wizard screens will hopefully make more sense. Selecting the wrong option in the wizard or not selecting an option that you need will cause you to have to fix the report manually. That's okay though, as wizards can be used as a starting point for a report that you can modify as needed.

I think that it is important to understand sorting, grouping and summary options before using a wizard to create a report. One reason that I think this is important is because many of the wizard screens are scaled down versions of an expert screen. This is why this lesson comes after lessons that had you create reports that demonstrate how to sort, group and summarize records.

Table 12-1 explains the type of report that each wizard creates. As you learn to use each of the report wizards, you will see that they have a core set of common screens. Table 12-2 illustrates the common screens and the screens that are unique to a specific report wizard.

Wizard	Type Of Report It Creates
Report	Creates a variety of reports because it is a generic report wizard. It is similar to creating a report from scratch.
Cross-Tab	Creates reports that look like spreadsheets. The Cross-Tab and Grid Style screens are used to create and format the Cross-Tab.
Mailing Label	Creates reports in a column layout, which can be used to create any size mailing label that you need.
OLAP Cube (1)	This wizard is similar to the Cross-Tab wizard because it displays the data in a grid, which is similar to a spreadsheet. While the output from a report created with the OLAP Cube wizard is similar to a Cross-Tab report, the process is different because of the requirements of working with OLAP data sources.

Table 12-1 Report Wizards explained

Screen	Report	Cross-Tab	Mailing Label	OLAP
Data	X	X	X	
Link	X	X	X	
Fields	X		X	
Grouping	X			
Summaries	X			
Group Sorting	X			
Record Selection	X	X	X	
Chart	X	X		X
Template	X			

Table 12-2 Report wizard screens

Screen	Report	Cross-Tab	Mailing Label	OLAP
Cross-Tab		X		
Grid Style		X		
Label			X	
OLAP Data (1)				X
Rows/Columns				X
Slice/Page				X
Style				X

Table 12-2 Report wizard screens (Continued)

(1)

OLAP Data And Reports

This functionality is not supported in ACT! databases.

You should be familiar with many of the wizard screens because in Exercise 4.1 you created a report using a wizard that selected options on every screen of the Report Wizard. This was done to demonstrate all of the options in the wizard. The reports that you create with wizards in this lesson will be more focused. Many of the reports that you will create in this lesson are reports that you have already created from scratch. The reason for this is two-fold:

① So that you will be able to determine which method (by wizard or by scratch) is better suited for a specific type of report.
② So that you can decide which way you like best.

The wizards are designed to make what may seem like a complicated task, a little easier to complete. What you may not realize is that there is often more going on behind the scenes of a wizard then you realize. By that I mean, wizards can have default options that you may not be aware of. In Exercise 12.4 you will see an example of this.

Unless you are very familiar with the data that is being used to create the report, you or the person using the report may not know that the data on the report is not 100% accurate. I personally try not to use wizards because of this. I may reconsider using wizards if there was documentation that thoroughly explains the inner workings and defaults that are set on wizard screens that you can't see.

Common Wizard Screens

As you saw above in Table 12-2, several of the report wizards use the same screens. The majority of reports that you will create with a wizard will be created using the standard wizard. This section will explain the purpose and features of the screens that provide the foundation for many of the wizards.

Some of the wizard screens including the Record Selection, Chart and Cross-Tab have less functionality than the "Expert" that it was taken from. If you find that there is a task that you can't complete using the wizard, check the options on the Expert toolbar to see if there is an option that will help you complete the task.

Data Screen

Figure 12-1 shows the Data screen. This is the first screen that many wizards use. This screen is used to select the data sources that are needed to create the report. The Data screen provides the same functionality as the Database Expert that you learned about in Lesson 5.

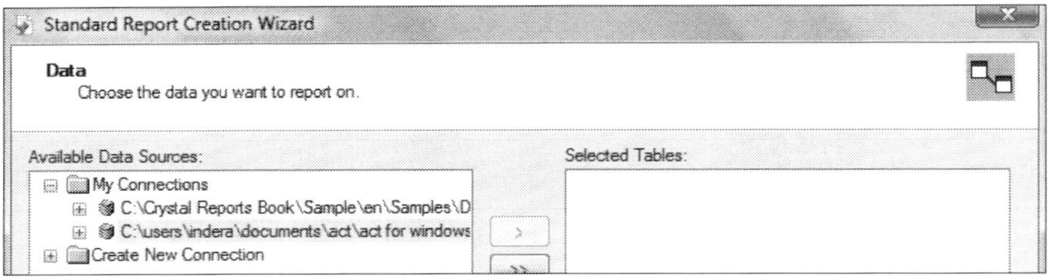

Figure 12-1 Data screen

Fields Screen

Figure 12-2 shows the Fields screen. This is where you select the fields that are needed for the report. The fields that you select on this screen will be placed in the details section of the report.

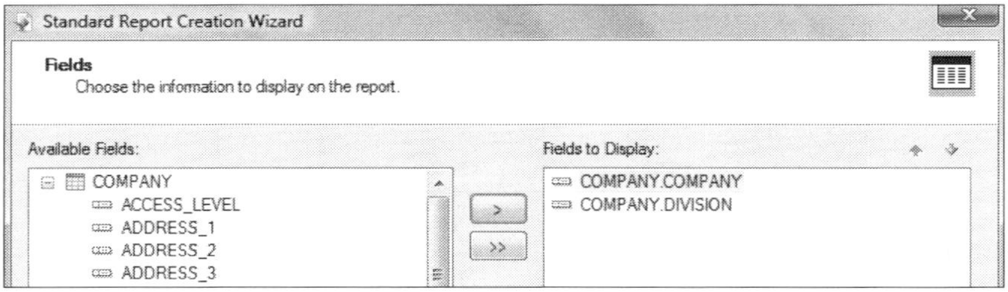

Figure 12-2 Fields screen

Grouping Screen

Figure 12-3 shows the Grouping screen. The options on this screen are used to select the fields to group on. Creating groups is optional. Grouping options if selected, will create the group header and footer sections of the report. This screen is the equivalent of the Insert Group dialog box.

Keep in mind that when you create a group using the wizard, the field(s) that are being grouped on, are automatically moved to the beginning of the report. The fields do not stay in the order that you add them to the report on the Fields screen.

You cannot sort the detail records on this wizard screen. If you need to sort records in a report that does not have a group, you will have to do that through the Record Sort Expert, after the report has been created with the wizard.

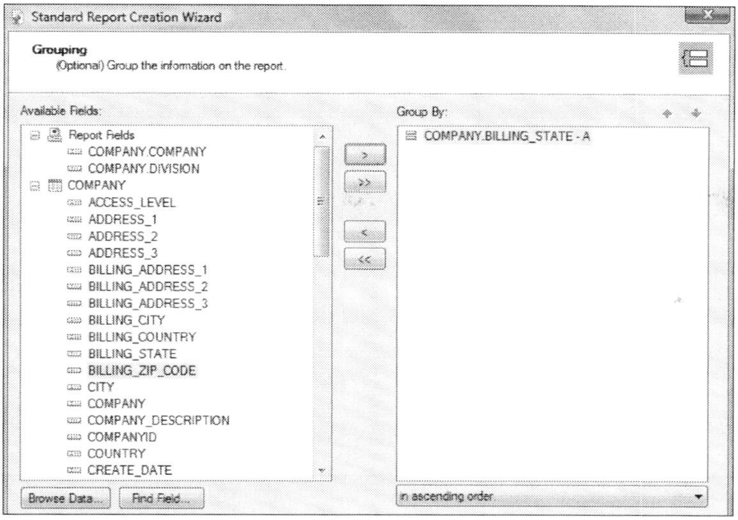

Figure 12-3 Grouping screen

Summaries Screen

The Summaries screen is only available if at least one field is being grouped on. By default, the numeric fields that are selected on the Grouping screen are automatically added to the **SUMMARIZED FIELDS** list as shown in Figure 12-4.

This may not be what you want. You can remove the field from the Summarized Fields list if there is no need to create a total for it.

The fields in the Summarized Fields list will automatically have grand total fields created and placed in the report footer section of the report. If you need to add a field to summarize on, select it here.

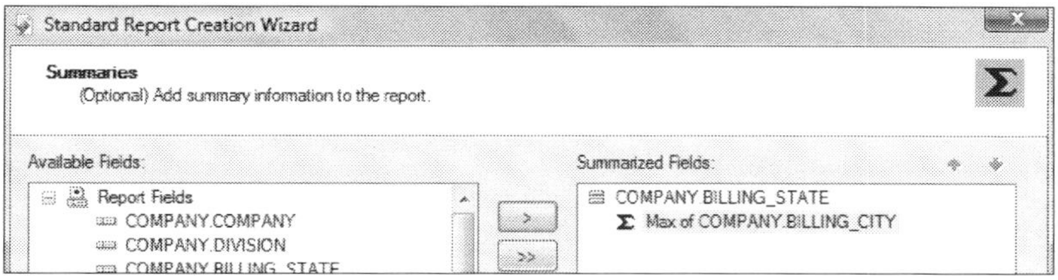

Figure 12-4 Summaries screen

Group Sorting Screen

The Group Sorting screen is only available if at least one field was selected on the Grouping and Summaries screens. Figure 12-5 shows the options that you can select as needed, to change the order of the groups based on the value from the selection on the Summaries screen. The Group Sorting screen is a scaled down version of the Group Sort Expert.

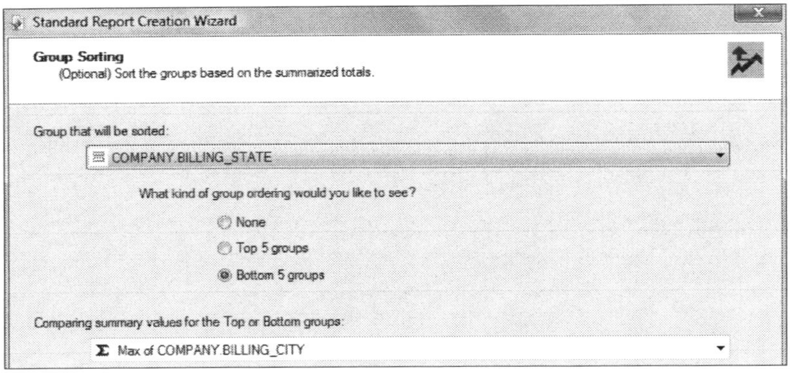

Figure 12-5 Group Sorting screen

There are three group ordering options that you can select from, as discussed below.

① **None** This is the default group ordering option. This option will leave the group order the way it is. Most of the time, this is the option that you want.
② **Top 5 Groups** This option will only select the five groups that have the highest value in the field that is being grouped on. The other groups will not appear on the report.
③ **Bottom 5 Groups** This option will only select the five groups that have the lowest value in the field that is being grouped on. The other groups will not appear on the report.

If the Top 5 groups or Bottom 5 groups option is selected, the **COMPARING SUMMARY VALUES FOR THE TOP OR BOTTOM GROUPS** option is enabled. This option is used to select the summarized field to base the sort on. The options available in the drop-down list come from the summary fields that you created on the Summaries screen.

Top and Bottom N reports, commonly known as Top N reports, are used to show the first N or last N records in a group. Instead of displaying all orders in a certain date range, you could only show the largest 10 orders in the date range. The wizard does not allow you to select the value of N. It always uses five. If you use the Group Sort Expert to create a Top or Bottom N report, you can select the value of N, by typing it in or by using a parameter field to get the value of N each time the report is run. You can use the Group Sort Expert to edit a Top N report that is created with a wizard.

Chart Screen

The options shown in Figure 12-6 are used to add a chart to the report. Adding a chart is optional. In order to add a chart, the report has to have at least one group.

Compared to the Chart Expert, the options and chart types on the Chart wizard screen are limited, which means that most of the time you will have to modify the chart after the wizard creates it.

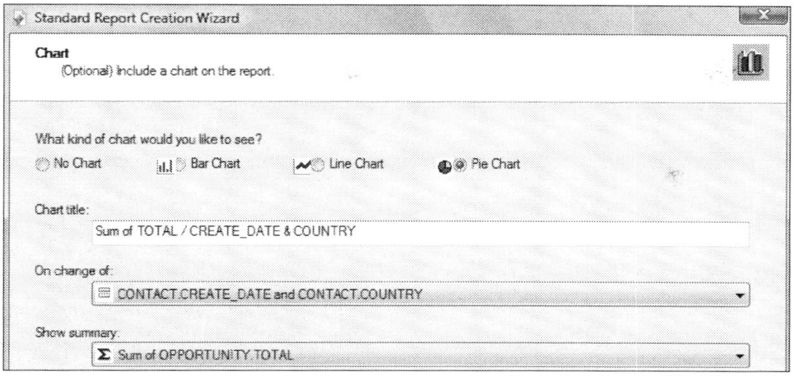

Figure 12-6 Chart screen

The other major drawback to creating a chart using a report wizard is that you have to create the chart from fields that will print on the report. The Chart Expert allows you to create a chart with fields that do not print on the report. Once you select a chart type in the wizard, the three options discussed below are available to help you customize the chart.

① **Chart Title** The information that you enter here will be printed at the top of the chart.
② **On Change Of** This option defaults to a field that the report is being grouped on.
③ **Show Summary** This option defaults to the summary field for the field that is in the On Change Of field.

Record Selection Screen

The options shown in Figure 12-7 are used to create selection criteria like you did in Lesson 9 when you learned how to use the Select Expert. Selecting options on this screen is optional. As you saw in Lesson 9, a formula is created when you use the Select Expert. A formula is created on the Record Selection screen if criteria is added. The difference is that you cannot see the formula that is created from the wizard screen.

You can view the formula after the report is created with the wizard by opening the Select Expert. This will let you edit the formula if necessary. Like the Select Expert, you can create as many filters as you need.

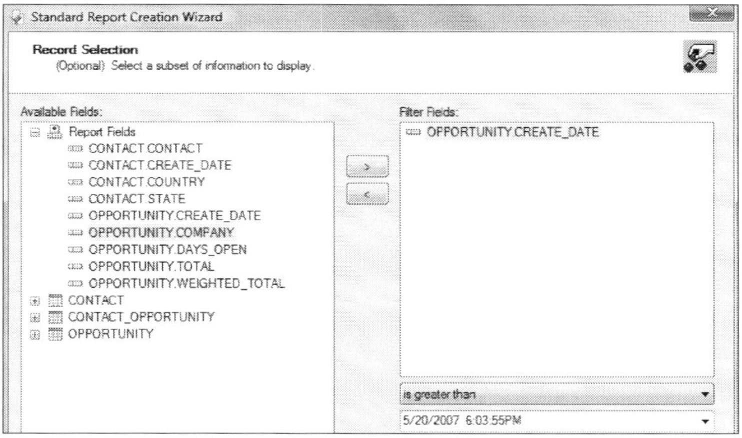

Figure 12-7 Record Selection screen

> The data in the drop-down list below the selection criteria shown above at the bottom of Figure 12-7 is the actual data in the field that you are creating the filter for. If the value that you want is not in the drop-down list, you can type it in.

Template Screen

The options shown in Figure 12-8 are used to apply a template (a pre-formatted style) to the report. Applying a template to a report is optional. You can also create your own templates. If there is a template that you want to use that is not shown in the Available Templates list, click the **BROWSE** button. This will let you navigate to the location where the template is that you want to use.

I would like to have the ability to preview the report before the wizard creates it. This would let you know how "close" you are to getting the output that you want. If you make a mistake or leave something out, you would not have to start all over again because you could click the Back button on the wizard screen and fix the mistake or add what you need, because you could see what the report would look like before clicking the Finish button.

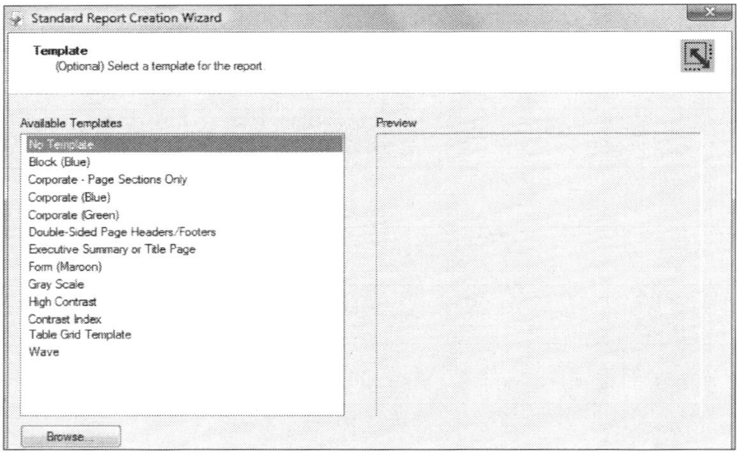

Figure 12-8 Template screen

Exercise 12.1: Create The State = OH Or FL List Report

As you learned in Lesson 4, list reports are one of the easiest types of reports to create. The report that you will create in this exercise is a list report that selects certain records. The L4.3 list report that you created displayed all of the product records. In this exercise you will select options on the wizard that will filter the data in the Contacts table to retrieve contacts that are in OH or FL.

1. Open the Report Wizard and add the Contact table, then click Next.

2. Add the following fields: Company, Address1, State, Zip Code and Country, then click Next.

3. Click Next on the Grouping screen because this report does not have any grouping requirements. Add the State field to the **FILTER FIELDS** list on the Record Selection screen.

4. Open the drop-down list and select **IS ONE OF**, then open the next drop-down list and select **OH** or you can type it in.

5. Open the same drop-down list that you just used and select **FL** or you can type it in.

   Figure 12-9 shows the filter options that should be selected.

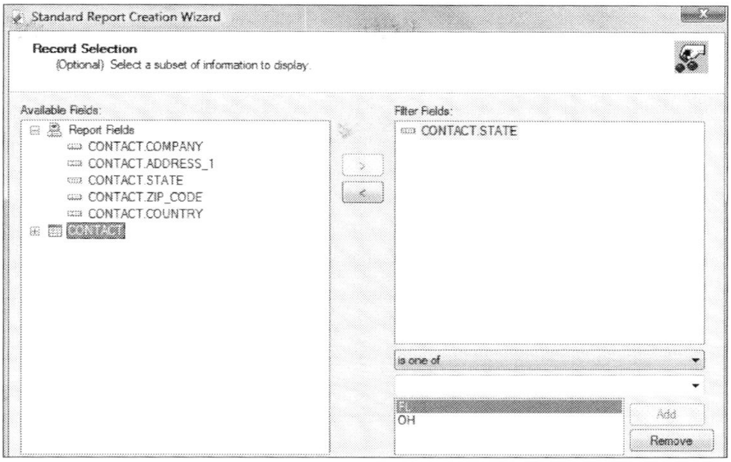

Figure 12-9 Record Selection screen options

6. The report does not require a template. Click **FINISH**. Your report should look like the one shown in Figure 12-10. Notice that a date field was automatically added to the report. Save the report as `L12.1 State = OH or FL list`, then close the report.

12/1/2009

COMPANY	ADDRESS_1	STATE	ZIP_CODE	COUNTRY
Modern Electric Supply	1919 Tecoma Dr.	FL	34655	United States
Golf Greens Extraordina	1800 Boca Club Drive	FL	33487	United States
MRP Enterprises	6161 Busch Blvd.	OH	43229-2508	United States
Dylan Inc.	1881 Easton Dr	OH	44325	
Golf Greens Extraordina	1800 Boca Club Drive	FL	33487	United States

Figure 12-10 L12.1 report

Exercise 12.2: Create The Create Date And Gross Margin Report

In this exercise you will create a filter that will select records that have a create date greater than or equal to 6/24/08 and has a gross margin greater than 2499.99. [See Exercise 9.4]

1. Open the Report Wizard and add the Contact, Contact Opportunity and Opportunity tables, then click Next.

2. Clear the links. Link the Contact table to the Contact Opportunity table by the Contact ID field. Link the Opportunity table to the Contact Opportunity table by the Opportunity ID field, then click Next.

3. Add the following fields: Company from the Contact table, Opportunity Name, Create Date, Total, Status and Actual Close Date fields from the Opportunity table, then click Next.

4. Click Next on the Grouping screen because this report does not have any grouping requirements. Add the Create Date field to the **FILTER FIELDS** list. Open the drop-down list and select **IS GREATER THAN OR EQUAL TO**, then type `6/24/2008` in the next field.

5. Add the Gross Margin field to the **FILTER FIELDS** list, then click on the field. Open the drop-down list and select **IS GREATER THAN**.

6. Type `2499.99` in the next drop-down list, then click **FINISH**. Your report should look like the one shown in Figure 12-11. Close the report.

12/1/2009

COMPANY	OPPORTUNITY_NAME	CREATE_DATE	TOTAL	STATUS	ACTUAL_CLOSE_[
A1 Services-US Ope	New Opportunity	10/30/2008 11:08:59AM	12,000.00	Closed - Lost	10/30/2009 7:00:0(
Boomers Artworx	Boomer's Artworx-Headquai	10/30/2008 10:48:41AM	12,000.00	Open	12/31/9999 11:59:5
Rainbow Dreams Inc	Rainbow Dreams-Dorothy's	9/30/2009 6:36:49PM	12,000.00	Open	12/31/9999 11:59:5
American Dreams	American Dreams-Warehou	10/30/2008 11:15:16AM	12,000.00	Open	12/31/9999 11:59:5

Figure 12-11 L12.2 report

7. Save the report as `L12.2 Create Date GTE 6-24-2008 and Gross Margin GT 2499.99`.

Exercise 12.3: Create A Group Summary Report

In Lesson 10 you learned how to create reports that had groups. In this exercise you will create a report that has a group using the wizard. The records will be grouped by the process and stage that the opportunity is in. In this exercise you will create a report that has a count summary field for the number of opportunities in each stage.

1. Open the Report Wizard and add the Opportunity, Process and Stage tables, then click Next. The reason that you are adding the Process table is so that you can print the description of the process.

2. Clear the links. Link the Opportunity table to the Stage table by the Stage ID field. Link the Process table to the Stage table by the Process ID, then click Next.

3. Add the following fields: Opportunity Name and Process fields from the Opportunity table. Add the Description field from the Process table. Add the Stage field from the Stage table, then click Next.

4. Add the Process and Stage fields to the Group By list, then click Next.

5. Add the Opportunity ID field to the Summarized fields list. Open the drop-down list and select Count.

6. Click Finish. Your report should look like the one shown in Figure 12-12. If you look in the group tree section you will see a list of the processes and stages in each process.

   As you can see, the fields are not in the order that you selected them in. This is one of my pet peeves with the wizard, when you add groups to a report. It moves the fields that are grouped on to the far left of the report.

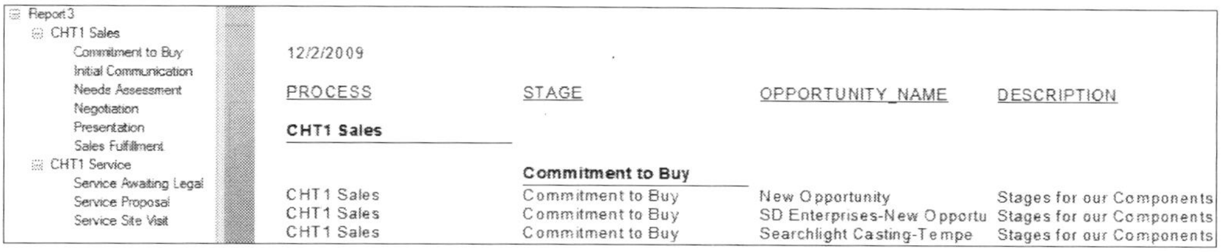

Figure 12-12 L12.3 summary report

7. Save the report as `L12.3 Product summary`, then close the report.

Exercise 12.4: Create A Top N Report

In previous exercises you created reports that grouped the data. By default, the groups are sorted on the value in the group field. For example, orders would be grouped by the values (the actual customer names) in the summary customer name field.

There is another way to sort groups on a report. In Lesson 9, you learned how to filter (select) which records would appear on the report. Just like you can filter the detail records, you can filter the groups. One way to explain Top N reports is that this sort method is sorting the groups on the value of a group summary field instead of the values in the group by field. Top N reports do not display all of the groups. They only display the groups that N has. Top N reports rank the groups based on the summary field values. For example, if N equals 7, only the seven highest groups based on the value of the summary field would be displayed on the report.

In this exercise you will create a report that will display the top five close dates in 2009 with the largest opportunity total. You will also create a pie chart that displays the top five close dates.

> The Group Sorting screen is used to limit the number of groups on the report to five by selecting the Top 5 or Bottom 5 group option. No more or no less. The Group Sorting Expert does not have a group number limitation.

> The grand totals that appear on a report when the top or bottom five group sorting option is used, are not the real totals for the detail records on the report. They are the totals for all records that meet the other report criteria before the top or bottom five group sort option is applied. This happens when the **INCLUDE OTHERS** option on the Group Sort Expert dialog box is not checked. If you do not want to use the Include Others option, create a running total field instead of the summary grand total field.

1. Open the Report Wizard, then add the Opportunity table, then click Next.

2. Add the following fields: Opportunity Name, Actual Close Date, Probability of Close, Status and Total, then click Next.

3. Add the Actual Close Date field to the **GROUP BY** list, then click Next.

4. Remove the Probability of Close field from the Summarized Fields list, then click Next.

5. Select the **TOP 5 GROUPS** option on the Group Sorting screen, then click Next.

6. Select the Pie chart option on the Chart screen.
   Type `Top 5 Actual Close Dates In 2009` in the Chart title field, then click Next.

7. Add the Status field to the Filter fields list on the Record Selection screen. Open the drop-down list and select Is equal to, then select Closed-Won.

8. Add the Actual Close Date field to the Filter Fields list on the Record Selection screen. Open the drop-down list and select **IS BETWEEN**, then type `1/1/2009` in the next drop-down list. In the last drop-down list, type `12/31/2009`. Figure 12-13 shows the options that should be selected.

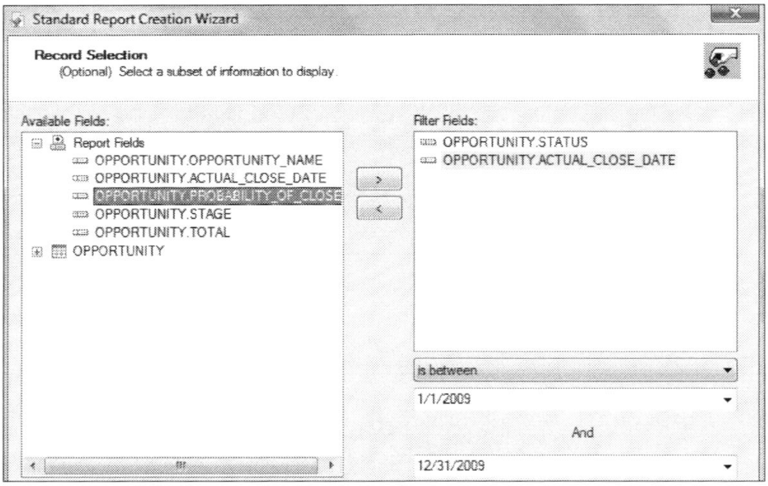

Figure 12-13 Record Selection options

9. Click Finish. Your report should look like the one shown in Figure 12-14. You will only see detail information for the top five close dates.

10. Save the report as `L12.4 Top 5 Actual Close Dates in 2009` and leave it open to complete the next exercise.

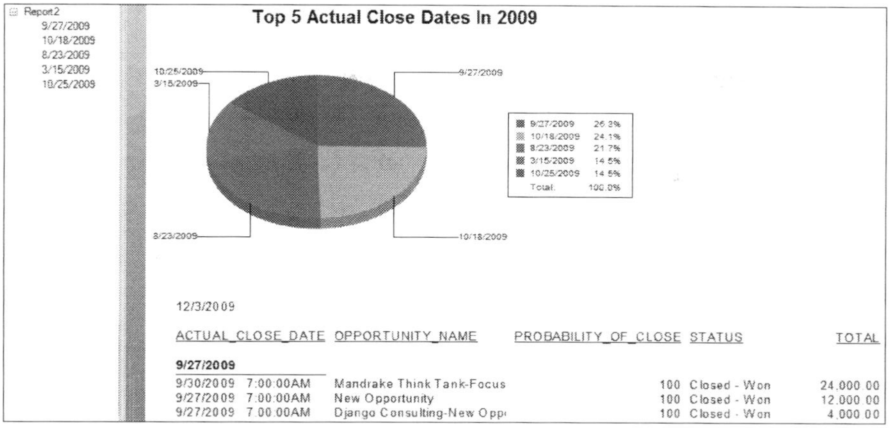

Figure 12-14 L12.4 report

Wizards Can Produce Unexpected Results

I created the report shown in Figure 12-15 with data in the sample database that comes with Crystal Reports. As you can see, one of the dates in the group tree is in May, even though the report should only display order days in June. If you click on that link, you will see orders for June. No, I did not lead you astray. This is one of the features of the wizards that do not work as intended and is why many report designers tend to stay away from the report wizards. There are options that are preset that you don't know about, that can produce unexpected results.

If you plan to use this wizard on a regular basis for something other then a basic report, hopefully you see how important it is to understand the data that the report should produce. That should lead you in the direction of how to fix any problem that the wizard creates.

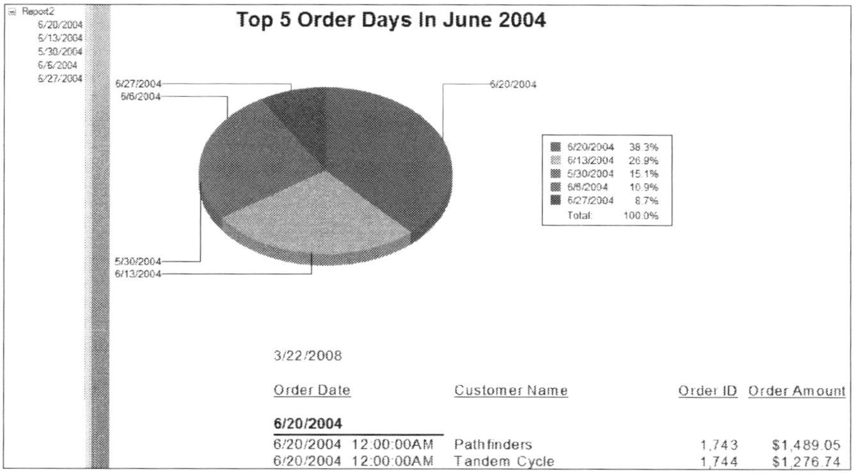

Figure 12-15 Top 5 order days in June 2004 report

Exercise 12.5: Fix The Top 5 Actual Close Dates Report

When I looked at the data in the L12.4 report, I noticed that some of the five groups on the report actually had more than one days worth of data. For example, the 10/25/2009 group at the end of the report, has records dated 10/30/2009 and 10/31/2009. Some groups actually had a weeks worth of data, even though I was expecting to only see data for one day in each group. Because the data is grouped on the Actual Close Date field, I realized that the wizard must have the group default set to weekly. I opened the Group Expert (which is a different expert then the Group Sort Expert) and sure enough, the option was set to weekly.

This is an example of how a wizard will produce unexpected results. What scares me is that I get the feeling that because the majority of people that use wizards use them without questioning the results, this is something that could easily be missed. What would be helpful on the wizard would be if the Group Sorting wizard screen had an option to select how you want the data to be grouped, by day, week, month, year etc. After looking at the options on the Group Sort Expert, I noticed that it did not have this option either, so because the Group Sorting wizard screen is a subset of the Group Sort Expert, it made a little sense.

Even though the wizard produces results that you may not want, I do not know about you, but I can do without this type of "help" from a wizard. The best advice that I can give you if you insist on using a wizard, is after the wizard creates the report, open each corresponding expert for a screen that you selected options on in the wizard and look at the options. While this is good advice, if you think for a minute, you will realize that even that advice would not have helped you detect this error because options from the Group Expert are not used in this wizard. The good news is that this report can be fixed by following the steps below.

1. Save the L12.4 report as `L12.5 Fixed Top 5 Actual Close Dates in 2009 report.`

2. Report ⇒ Group Expert, then click the **OPTIONS** button. You will see the Change Group Options dialog box. In the last drop-down list you will see that the option **FOR EACH WEEK** is selected. Open **THE SECTION WILL BE PRINTED** drop-down list and select **FOR EACH DAY**, as illustrated in Figure 12-16.

   As you can see, knowing about this option would allow you to create a variety of reports, just by changing this option.

   Click OK twice to close both dialog boxes.

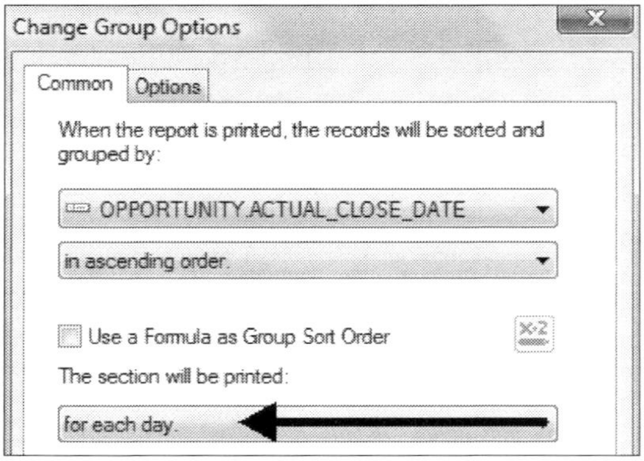

Figure 12-16 Change Group Options dialog box

3. Refresh the data and preview the report. It should look like the one shown in Figure 12-17. All of the detail records in each group should have the same date opposed to different dates, as shown in Figure 12-18. Notice that most of the top 5 dates have changed. Save the changes and close the report.

ACTUAL_CLOSE_DATE	OPPORTUNITY_NAME	PROBABILITY_OF_CLOSE	STATUS	TOTAL
10/18/2009				
10/18/2009 7:00:00AM	New Opportunity	100	Closed - Won	12,000.00
10/18/2009 7:00:00AM	COI-TX Headquarters	100	Closed - Won	24,000.00
10/18/2009 7:00:00AM	Willis Enterprises-Main Offic	100	Closed - Won	4,000.00
10/18/2009	**40,000.00**			
9/30/2009				
9/30/2009 7:00:00AM	Mandrake Think Tank-Focus	100	Closed - Won	24,000.00
9/30/2009 7:00:00AM	Cadbury-Chocolate Blending	100	Closed - Won	2,000.00
9/30/2009	**26,000.00**			
3/18/2009				
3/18/2009 5:00:00AM	New Opportunity	100	Closed - Won	12,000.00
3/18/2009 5:00:00AM	New Opportunity	100	Closed - Won	12,000.00
3/18/2009	**24,000.00**			

Figure 12-17 L12.5 Fixed Top 5 Actual Close Dates in 2009 report

ACTUAL_CLOSE_DATE	OPPORTUNITY_NAME	PROBABILITY_OF_CLOSE	STATUS	TOTAL
9/27/2009				
9/30/2009 7:00:00AM	Mandrake Think Tank-Focus	100	Closed - Won	24,000.00
9/27/2009 7:00:00AM	New Opportunity	100	Closed - Won	12,000.00
9/27/2009 7:00:00AM	Django Consulting-New Opp	100	Closed - Won	4,000.00
9/30/2009 7:00:00AM	Cadbury-Chocolate Blending	100	Closed - Won	2,000.00
9/27/2009	**42,000.00**			
10/18/2009				
10/18/2009 7:00:00AM	New Opportunity	100	Closed - Won	12,000.00
10/18/2009 7:00:00AM	COI-TX Headquarters	100	Closed - Won	24,000.00
10/18/2009 7:00:00AM	Willis Enterprises-Main Offic	100	Closed - Won	4,000.00
10/18/2009	**40,000.00**			
8/23/2009				
8/29/2009 7:00:00AM	A1 Services-SC	100	Closed - Won	2,000.00
8/28/2009 7:00:00AM	Spin Recording Studios-Aust	100	Closed - Won	12,000.00
8/29/2009 7:00:00AM	Sierra's Cafe-Cafe	100	Closed - Won	12,000.00
8/29/2009 7:00:00AM	American Dreams-N TX Offic	100	Closed - Won	10,000.00
8/23/2009	**36,000.00**			

Figure 12-18 Incorrect detail information before change

Exercise 12.6: Use The Mailing Label Wizard

This wizard is used to create a column layout report which many people use to print labels. You can use this wizard to create other types of columnar reports besides mailing labels. In this exercise you will learn how to create a report that can be used to print labels. The report will print labels for contacts that have an opportunity created in 2008, that are in the US. Many of the screens in this wizard are the same as the ones that you have used in the Report wizard.

1. Open the Mailing label report wizard and add the Contact, Contact Opportunity and Opportunity tables, then click Next.

2. Clear the links. Create a link between the Contact and Contact Opportunity tables on the Contact ID field. Create a link between the Contact Activity and Activity tables on the Opportunity ID field, then click Next.

3. Add the following fields: Contact, Address1, Address2, City, State and Zip Code, then click Next.

4. Open the **MAILING LABEL TYPE** drop-down list and select Avery 5163. Figure 12-19 shows the options that should be selected.

   The Mailing Label Type drop-down list has an option, **USER-DEFINED LABEL**, that is used to create a custom size label.

   After you select all of the options for the labels, look in the **NUMBER OF LABELS** section in the lower right corner of the dialog box to make sure that the selections that you made work with the labels that you will print.

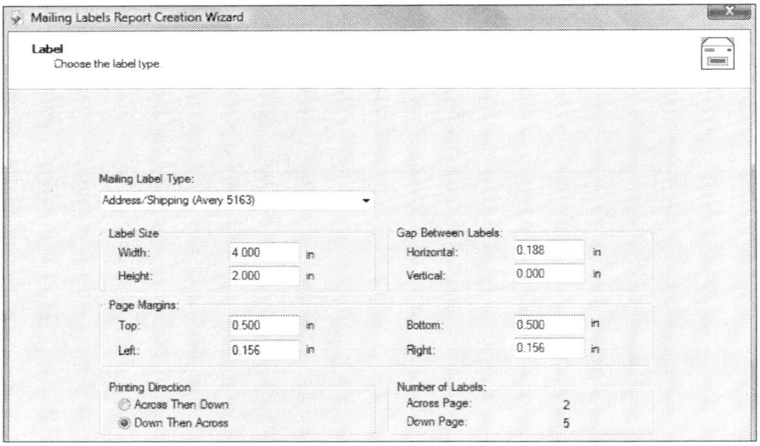

Figure 12-19 Label screen options

5. Click Next, then add the Country field (in the Contact table) to the Filter Fields list. Open the drop-down list and select **IS EQUAL TO**, then open the next drop-down list and select **UNITED STATES** or you can type it in.

6. Add the Create Date field (in the Opportunity table) to the Filter Fields list. Open the drop-down list and select **IS BETWEEN** and type `1/1/2008` in the first drop-down list, then type `12/31/2008` in the last drop-down list.

7. Click Finish. Your report should look like the one shown in Figure 12-20. The report should have 64 records.

Because the date criteria was for a month, you see duplicate contact names. More than likely, the labels would be printed daily, which means that you would not see duplicate contact names in the labels unless a contact had more than one opportunity created on the same day.

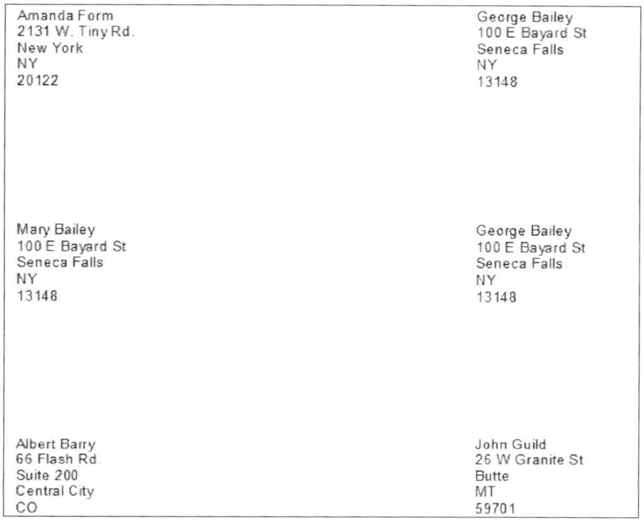

Figure 12-20 L12.6 labels report

8. Rearrange the fields as shown in Figure 12-21. You only have to make the changes on the left side and they will be duplicated on the right side.

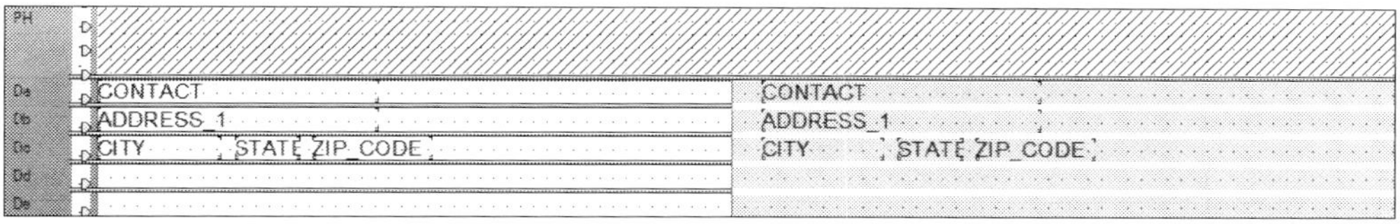

Figure 12-21 Modified label layout

9. Save the report as `L12.6 Contact labels for 2008`, then close the report.

CROSS-TAB REPORTS

After completing the exercises in this lesson you will be able to use the Cross-Tab wizard.

LESSON 13

Cross-Tab Reports Overview

As you saw in Lesson 12, Table 12-2, the Cross-Tab wizard has many of the same screens as the Report wizard. The major differences between the Report and Cross-Tab wizards are discussed below.

① There are no detail records in a cross-tab report.
② The functionality of the wizard grouping and summary screens are combined on one Cross-Tab wizard screen.
③ Cross-Tabs are most often placed in the report header or footer section, but they can be placed in other sections.

Cross-Tabs, like the Select Expert, are used to retrieve records that meet specific criteria. The cross-tab report takes the Select Expert one step further because it allows you to summarize the data that is in the detail section of reports. Cross-Tab reports are often used for comparison analysis. Examples of cross-tab reports are:

① Sales by sales rep by year.
② Sales by region.
③ Summarizing how many orders by year and by zip code, each sales rep has.
④ Sales of a specific product by sales rep, by month.
⑤ Summarizing how many customers by region purchased certain products by month or by year.

Cross-Tab reports often give new report designers difficulty. I suspect that this is because this type of report requires one to think in dimensions. Like spreadsheets, cross-tab reports have rows and columns. Each cell in a spreadsheet contains one piece of data. In a cross-tab object, the cell contains one piece of summary data (count, sum, average etc) that is the equivalent of the sub totals that are usually in group footer sections of the report.

Behind the scenes, cross-tab reports take the detail records that you are use to seeing, as well as, the groups and summarizes the detail data and places the result in a cell. Hopefully the following scenario will make the concept of cross-tab reports easier to understand.

Going From Standard Reports To Cross-Tab Reports

This scenario will use the first cross-tab example mentioned above; Sales by sales rep by year. The goal of this cross-tab report from a standard report perspective is to show sales for a year by sales rep.

The report shown in Figure 13-1 is a basic list report that sorts the sales, by sales rep and by year. It contains all of the data one would need to determine sales by sales rep, by year. Because there aren't any totals for the groups, it would take a while to manually do the math, especially if there were hundreds of sales reps. [See the L13 Cross-tab basic sort combined report in the zip file]

Yes, I know what you are thinking, modify the report to group the data by sales rep, then by year. Figure 13-2 shows that report.

Can you tell me how many saddles Robert King sold in total? Or can you tell me who had the lowest number of sales in 2004? Okay, I'll wait while you open the report shown in Figure 13-2 and get a calculator to add up the totals for the two sales reps. [See the L13 Cross-tab grouped report in the zip file] I can wait. I have patience <smile>.

Sales By Rep By Year

Last Name	First Name	Order Date	Order Amount	Customer Name
Davolio	Nancy	02/19/2003	$789.51	Belgium Bike Co.
Davolio	Nancy	02/19/2003	$58.00	Spokes for Folks
Davolio	Nancy	02/26/2003	$68.90	Mountain Madmen Bicycles
Davolio	Nancy	02/27/2003	$2,698.53	Pedals Inc.
Davolio	Nancy	02/27/2003	$1,079.70	Mountain Madmen Bicycles
Davolio	Nancy	02/27/2003	$1,529.70	Cycle City Rome
		.		
		.		
		.		
Last Name	First Name	Order Date	Order Amount	Customer Name
Suyama	Michael	02/14/2005	$5,893.20	Crazy Wheels
Suyama	Michael	02/19/2005	$6,005.40	Off the Mountain Biking
Suyama	Michael	02/19/2005	$7,685.25	To The Limit Biking Co.
Suyama	Michael	02/22/2005	$1,664.70	Bike-A-Holics Anonymous
Suyama	Michael	02/24/2005	$138.70	Tienda de Bicicletas El Pardo
Suyama	Michael	02/25/2005	$893.55	Whistler Rentals
Suyama	Michael	02/28/2005	$1,529.70	Belgium Bike Co.

Figure 13-1 Basic sorted report of sales by sales rep by year

Like the report shown above in Figure 13-1, the report in Figure 13-2 has all of the information that you need to answer these questions.

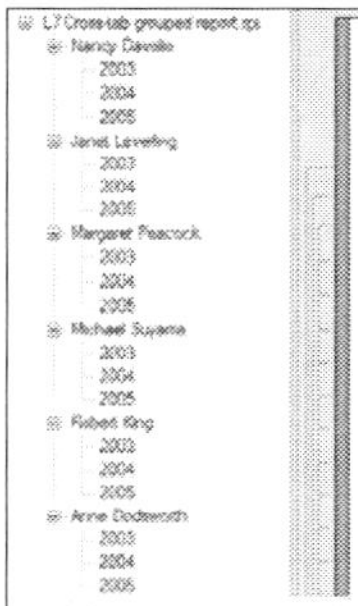

Sales By Rep By Year

Last Name	First Name	Order Date	Order Amount	Customer Name
Nancy Davolio				
2003				
Davolio	Nancy	02/19/2003	$789.51	Belgium Bike Co.
Davolio	Nancy	02/19/2003	$58.00	Spokes for Folks
Davolio	Nancy	02/26/2003	$68.90	Mountain Madmen Bicycles
Davolio	Nancy	02/27/2003	$1,079.70	Mountain Madmen Bicycles
Davolio	Nancy	02/27/2003	$2,698.53	Pedals Inc.
Davolio	Nancy	02/27/2003	$1,529.70	Cycle City Rome
Davolio	Nancy	12/02/2003	$41.90	City Cyclists
Davolio	Nancy	12/03/2003	$10,259.10	Piccolo
Davolio	Nancy	12/03/2003	$14,872.30	Cyclopath
Davolio	Nancy	12/04/2003	$29.00	Spokes 'N Wheels Ltd
Davolio	Nancy	12/07/2003	$890.61	Tienda de Bicicletas El Pardo
		.		
		.		
		.		
		.		
Davolio	Nancy	05/02/2005	$1,082.50	Warsaw Sports, Inc.
			$138,028.42	
			$660,756.95	
Janet Leverling				
2003				
Leverling	Janet	02/21/2003	$5,219.55	Tienda de Bicicletas El Pardo
Leverling	Janet	02/21/2003	$8,819.55	Bikes, Bikes, and More Bikes
Leverling	Janet	02/25/2003	$2,246.25	Folk och fä HB
Leverling	Janet	02/26/2003	$267.76	Hooked on Helmets
Leverling	Janet	02/26/2003	$61.35	Bike Shop from Mars

Figure 13-2 Data grouped by sales rep by year

The problem is that the data is spread out over several pages in the report which makes it difficult for comparison analysis. This same data in a cross-tab report will be in an easy to read format. With a cross-tab report you can quickly answer questions like how many sales Robert King had for three products and which sales rep had the lowest number of sales in 2004.

How To Create This Cross-Tab

Yes, I hear you grumbling and saying, "Great, I now see the advantages of creating a cross-tab report, but how do I get the data shown earlier in Figures 13-1 and 13-2 into cross-tab format?" Okay, here goes:

① Usually, the field down the left side of a cross-tab (that creates the rows) is the data element that there are more occurrences of. In this example, there are more sales reps than years. You can put the sales reps across the top of the cross-tab and still get the same results.

② The field that goes across the top (that creates the columns) represents the data element that there are less occurrences of.

③ The cells in the middle of the cross-tab are the sum (in this example, a count) of orders that the sales rep had for the year. This is the equivalent to grouping and sorting data.

④ The totals at the bottom of the cross-tab report display how many sales are for each year and a grand total number of sales for the entire report in the lower right corner of the cross-tab. These totals are automatically calculated in a cross-tab report.

⑤ I have saved the best for last - the placement of the fields on the Cross-Tab screen. The fields for the row and column were answered above. That leaves the field for the cells in the middle of the cross-tab report. Recall the original statement - Sales by sales rep, by year. You have already determined that the sales rep field (Employee Name field in the table), is what will be used for the rows. You have also determined that the Order Date will be used for the columns. The only field left is the sales (the orders). This is what goes in the Summary Fields section of the Cross-Tab screen. In this example, the cells represent a count of orders. The default calculation is Sum. You would change that to **DISTINCT COUNT** for the Order ID field.

Cross-Tab Screen

Now that you have a foundation of cross-tab reports, the options on the Cross-Tab and Grid Style screens will hopefully make sense. Figure 13-3 shows the Cross-Tab screen. Figure 13-4 shows the Grid Style screen.

The **AVAILABLE FIELDS** list is used to select the fields that are needed to create the report.

The **ROWS** section contains the field(s) that will be displayed down the left side of the report.

The **COLUMNS** section contains the field(s) that will be displayed across the top of the report.

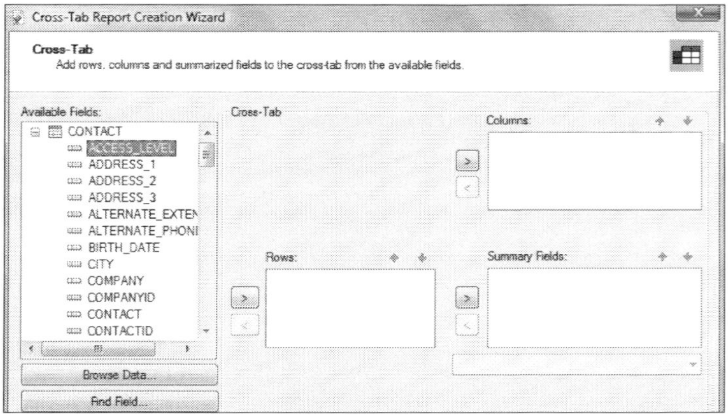

Figure 13-3 Cross-Tab screen

The **SUMMARY FIELDS** section contains the field(s) that will have the calculation (sum, count, average etc).

At least one field is required in the rows, columns and summary fields sections to create a cross-tab report.

Text fields cannot be printed in the cells of a cross-tab without selecting a summary type that works with a text field like count, distinct count, minimum or maximum.

The Grid Style screen contains options that are used to add formatting to the cross-tab, similar to templates.

Like other reports, you can format a cross-tab report manually.

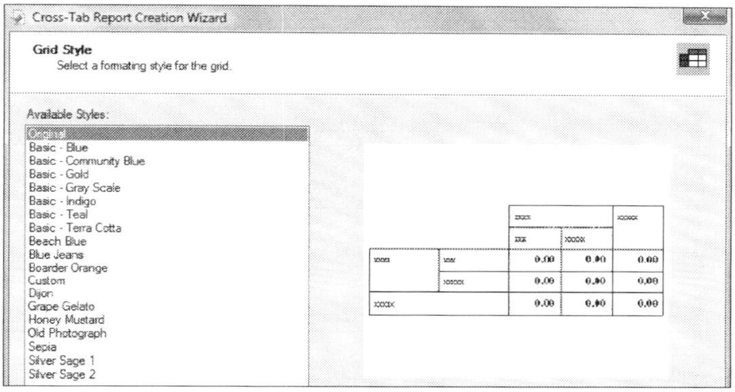

Figure 13-4 Grid Style screen

Exercise 13.1: Create A Cross-Tab Activity Report

In this exercise you will create a cross-tab report that shows the totals for three activity types: call, meeting and to-do by user.

1. Click on the Cross-tab report wizard link on the Start Page.
2. Add the Activity, Contact and Contact Activity tables, then click Next.
3. Clear the links. Create a link between the Activity and Contact Activity tables on the Activity ID field. Create a link between the Contact and Contact Activity tables on the Contact ID field, then click Next.
4. Click on the Contact field in the Contact table, then click the right arrow button next to the **ROWS** section.
5. Add the Activity Type field in the Activity table to the **COLUMNS** section.

You can click on the field in the Available Fields list and drag it to the section of the Cross-Tab screen that you need.

6. Add the Activity ID field in the Activity table to the **SUMMARIZED FIELDS** section.

7. Select **COUNT** from the drop-down list under the Summary Fields section.

   The Cross-Tab screen should have the options selected that are shown in Figure 13-5.

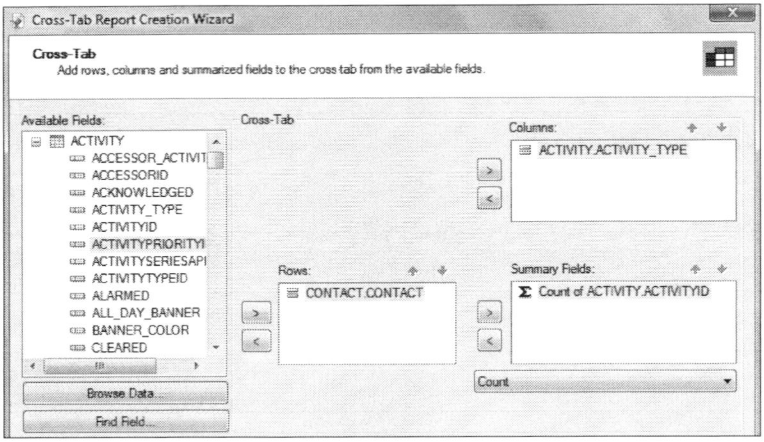

Figure 13-5 Cross-Tab screen options

8. Click Next, then select the **NO CHART** option, if it is not already selected and click Next.

9. This report needs to be filtered because you only want totals for three types of activities. Add the Activity Type field to the Filter Fields list, then open the drop-down list and select **IS ONE OF**.

10. Open the next drop-down list and select Call, Meeting and To-do.

    You should have the options selected that are shown in Figure 13-6.

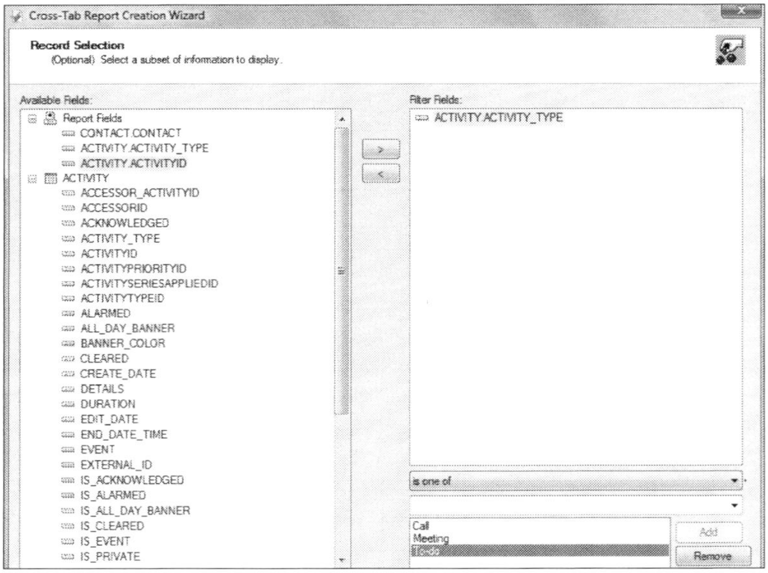

Figure 13-6 Record Selection options

11. Click Next. Click on the **ORIGINAL** grid style option if it is not already selected, then click Finish. Your report should look like the one shown in Figure 13-7. Save the report as `L13.1 Cross-Tab`, then close the report.

	Call	Meeting	To-do	Total
Albert Barry	0	2	0	2
Alexander O'Brie	1	3	0	4
Allison Mikola	0	397	210	607
Amanda Form	0	3	0	3
Andy Bosson	0	2	0	2
Andy Federici	1	1	0	2
Andy Harrison	0	1	4	5
Angela Ives	3	0	0	3

Figure 13-7 L13.1 Cross-Tab report

If you added the selection criteria shown in Figure 13-8, the report would look like the one shown in Figure 13-9.

Instead of having data for 23,594 records, there would only be 65 records in the cross-tab.

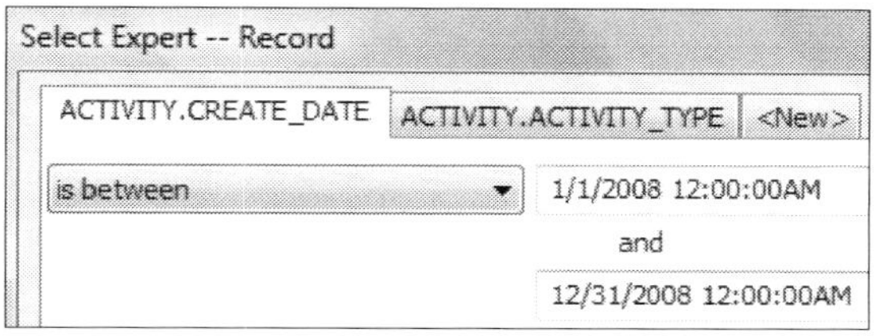

Figure 13-8 Create date selection criteria

	Call	Meeting	To-do	Total
Alexander O'Brie	0	1	0	1
Angela Ives	1	0	0	1
Ania Dawson	1	0	0	1
Anna Schmidt	0	1	0	1
Anthony Keltie	0	1	0	1
Ben Braddock	0	3	5	8
Brian David	0	1	0	1
Chris Burn	1	0	0	1

Figure 13-9 Modified cross-tab report

Exercise 13.2: Create An Opportunities Per Year Per Contact Cross-Tab Report

In this exercise you will create a cross-tab report that is similar to the sales per year, per sales rep report discussed earlier in this lesson.

1. Click on the Cross-tab report wizard link on the Start Page.

2. Add the Opportunity table, then click Next.

3. Click on the Contact field, then click the right arrow button next to the **ROWS** section and add the Actual Close Date field to the **COLUMNS** section.

4. Open the drop-down list under the Columns section and select **FOR EACH YEAR**. This will create a column for each year that there are opportunities in the Opportunity table.

5. Add the Total field to the Summary Fields section.

   You should have the options selected that are shown in Figure 13-10.

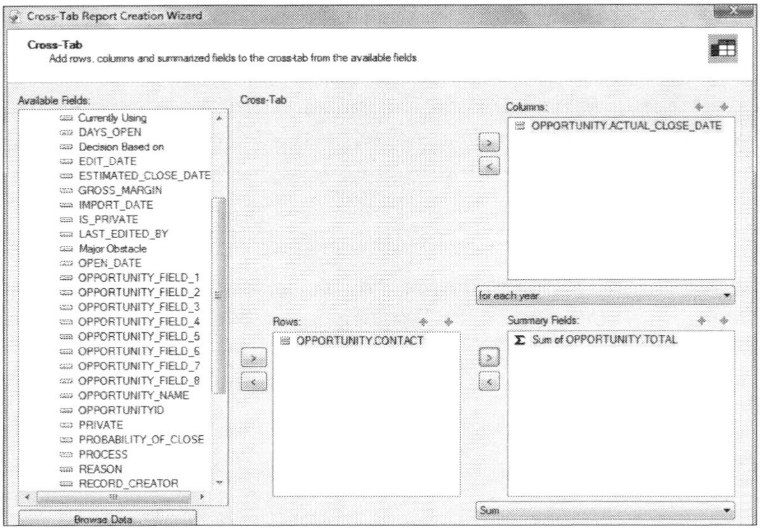

Figure 13-10 Cross-Tab screen options

If the Opportunity table had 10 years worth of data and you only wanted to show some of the years on the report, you would select the Actual Close Date field on the Record Selection screen and enter the date range for the years that you wanted to display on the report.

6. This cross-tab report does not need to select (filter) any records. Click Finish. Your report may look like the one shown in Figure 13-11. Leave the report open to complete the next part of the exercise.

	2007	2008	2009	2010	9999	Total
Albert Barry	0.00	0.00	0.00	########	2,600.00	14,600.00
Alexander O'Brie	0.00	0.00	########	0.00	0.00	12,000.00
Amanda Form	0.00	0.00	########	0.00	2,000.00	28,000.00
Andy Harrison	0.00	0.00	6,000.00	0.00	9,300.00	15,300.00
Angela Ives	0.00	0.00	########	300.00	0.00	12,300.00
Ania Dawson	0.00	0.00	0.00	0.00	########	18,500.00
Ann Goodall	0.00	0.00	0.00	0.00	########	23,500.00

Figure 13-11 Sales by year cross-tab report

> When you see fields cut off like they are in Figure 13-11 above, you should look at the **ALLOW FIELD CLIPPING** option on the Number tab on the Custom Style dialog box to make sure that the option is not checked. [See Lesson 7, Figure 7-22] If checked, the option causes the first digits in the field to be cut off until the remaining digits in the field can be displayed.

7. If the column totals are on the top and to the left, right-click on the border of the cross-tab and select Cross-Tab Expert. On the Customize Style tab, clear the **COLUMN TOTALS ON TOP** and **ROW TOTALS ON LEFT** options, then click OK.

Modify The Cross-Tab Report

As you can see, the grid is too small for the sales total amounts. This part of the exercise will show you how to modify the cross-tab report and add more selection criteria.

1. In the design window, select all four of the Total fields shown in Figure 13-12, then make the fields wider by dragging the right side border to the right.

   The border around the Cross-Tab will expand as you make the fields wider.

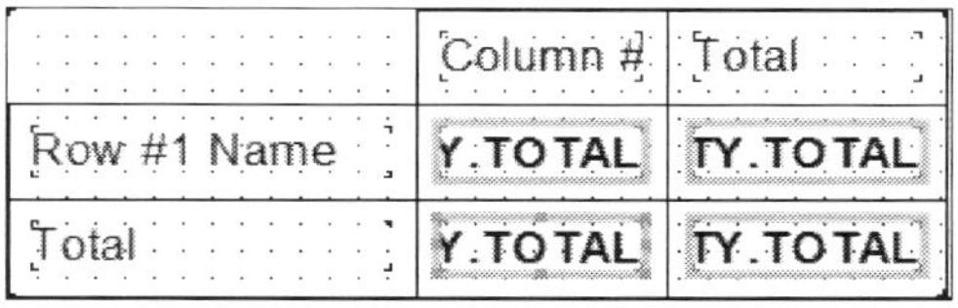

Figure 13-12 Total fields selected

2. Center the Column #1 Name and Total field headings.

3. Format the four Total fields to display a floating dollar sign.

Filter Data On The Cross-Tab

As you saw earlier in Figure 13-11, there is a column with 9999 as the year. This is not a valid date. In the real world, this data would have to be fixed. In this part of the exercise, you will create selection criteria to remove that column from the report.

1. Open the Select Expert, then create criteria for the Actual Close Date to not display record in the year 9999.

2. The report should look like the one shown in Figure 13-13. Save the report as `L13.2 Opportunities Per Year Per Contact Cross-Tab`.

	2007	2008	2009	2010	Total
Albert Barry	**$0.00**	**$0.00**	**$0.00**	**$12,000.00**	**$12,000.00**
Alexander O'Brie	**$0.00**	**$0.00**	**$12,000.00**	**$0.00**	**$12,000.00**
Amanda Form	**$0.00**	**$0.00**	**$26,000.00**	**$0.00**	**$26,000.00**
Andy Harrison	**$0.00**	**$0.00**	**$6,000.00**	**$0.00**	**$6,000.00**
Angela Ives	**$0.00**	**$0.00**	**$12,000.00**	**$300.00**	**$12,300.00**
Annette Sharkey	**$0.00**	**$7,500.00**	**$0.00**	**$0.00**	**$7,500.00**
Anthony Keltie	**$0.00**	**$24,000.00**	**$12,000.00**	**$0.00**	**$36,000.00**

Figure 13-13 L13.2 report

PRINTING AND EXPORTING REPORTS

You have created and modified a lot of reports in the previous lessons. So far, the reports that you have created have not been printed or shared with anyone. As the report designer, after you create the reports they are put into production so that other people can use them.

There are several ways that other people can use the reports, including: printing them if they have Crystal Reports installed, use a Crystal Reports viewer or export the reports to a file type that other people can use. Most users will not have Crystal Reports installed on their computer, so they will not be able to open the report file and print it like you can. After completing the exercises in this lesson you will be able to use the following printing, exporting options and techniques:

- ☑ Page Setup dialog box options
- ☑ Printer options
- ☑ Use the Set print date and time options
- ☑ Use the Preview Sample option
- ☑ Diagnose printing problems
- ☑ Report Options dialog box
- ☑ Export reports to a variety of file formats
- ☑ CrystalReports.com

You will also learn how to create bar codes and add sort controls to a report.

Printing Options

Crystal Reports has the majority of printing options for reports that you have already used in word processing and other software packages. As you learned, most people that run the reports that you create will not have Crystal Reports installed. Even if they do have Crystal Reports installed, do you think that every user will be able to set the printing and page setup options correctly without calling you? And if they can, you should still select the appropriate printing options so that the report will print as you intended it to.

NEW Page Setup Options

As shown in Figure 14-1, there are several options that you can select from to change the printed page layout to what is best suited for the report. The options shown are the defaults that are set when Crystal Reports is installed. The graphic at the bottom of the dialog box will change as the options are changed.

Table 14-1 explains the Page Setup options (File ⇒ Page Setup) that you may not be familiar with.

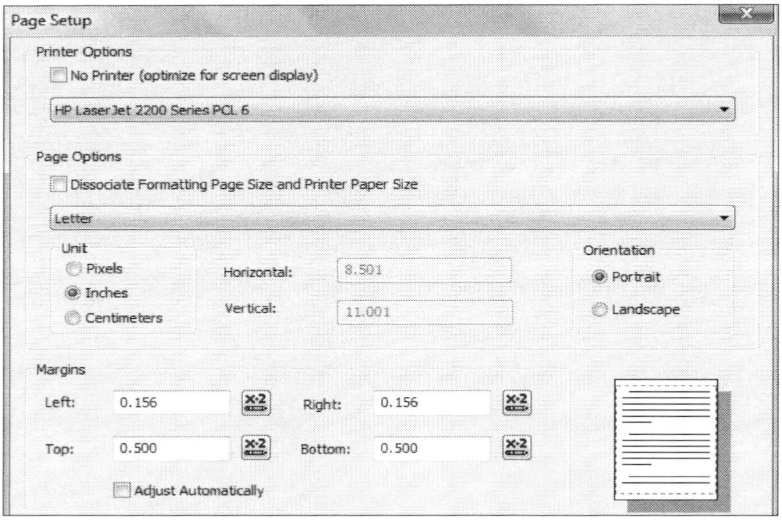

Figure 14-1 Page Setup dialog box

Setup Option	Description
No Printer	Select this option if the report will not be printed. This option will optimize the report to be viewed on a screen. It can also be used to resolve printing problems, as you will learn later in this lesson.
Dissociate Formatting Page Size . . .	NEW Select this option if you need complete control over how the report will print on the page.
Adjust Automatically	If checked, this option will cause the margins to change automatically, when the paper size or orientation is changed.

Table 14-1 Page Setup dialog box options explained

Page Orientation

As shown above in Figure 14-1, the default orientation is **PORTRAIT**. You can fit more fields across the page if the orientation is **LANDSCAPE**. Some of the reports that you have created may have had a field that was hanging off of the right side of the report. When you previewed the report, all of the data in the last field could not be displayed. If this happens select the Landscape orientation option.

Margins

If you have the need to change the margins based on a condition met in the report or from a condition set by a parameter field, click the Formula button next to the margin that you need to control as shown above in Figure 14-1 in the **MARGINS** section and type in the formula.

Paper Size

As shown earlier in Figure 14-1, the default paper size is **LETTER**. Some reports, in particular, financial reports may need to be printed on legal paper.

To change the paper size, open the Page Setup dialog box, then select the paper, envelope or post card size that you need, as shown in Figure 14-2.

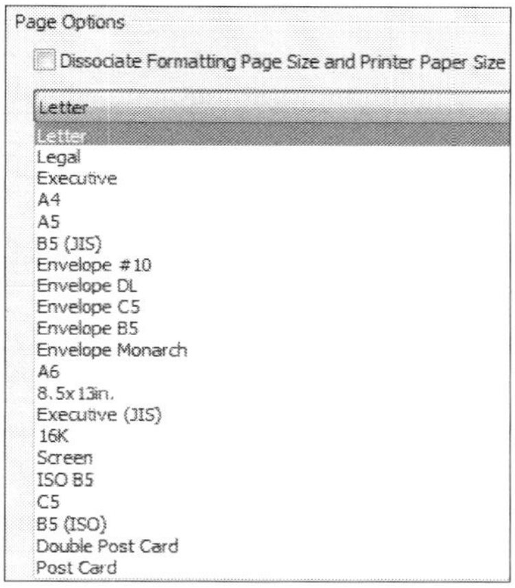

Figure 14-2 Page options

Exercise 14.1: Use The Adjust Automatically Option

You have read how to change the paper size, orientation and margins manually. As you read earlier in this lesson, when you change the paper size or orientation, the margins do not change. In this exercise you will learn how to make the margins change automatically when the paper size is changed.

1. Save the L5.3 report as `L14.1 Adjust margins automatically`.

2. Open the Page Setup dialog box and check the **ADJUST AUTOMATICALLY** option, then click OK and save the changes.

3. Change the Paper Size to Legal. Notice that the margins automatically changed. Click OK. Save the changes, then close the report.

Printer Options

The Print Setup dialog box shown in Figure 14-3 has options to select a printer and its options. These are the same options that you have probably used in other software packages.

File ⇒ Print, will open this dialog box.

If you have more than one printer installed, the default printer that you have selected in Windows will appear in the **NAME** drop-down list shown in Figure 14-3.

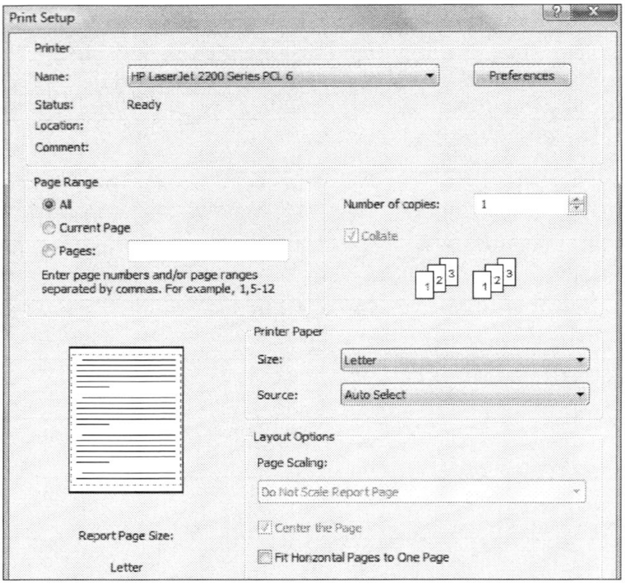

Figure 14-3 Print Setup dialog box

If the printer shown is not the one that you want to use, open the drop-down list and select the printer that you want.

The **PREFERENCES** button is used to select additional options for the printer that is selected.

Figure 14-4 shows the specific options for my default printer.

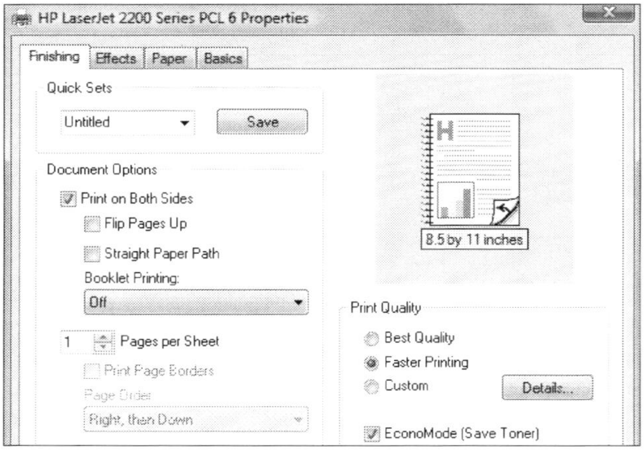

Figure 14-4 Specific printer options

Printing Problems

If you have an ink jet printer and have opened a document that was created by someone that has a laser jet printer, you may have noticed that sometimes the spacing is off. If so, the topics discussed in this section will be helpful. If you have experienced formatting issues (when it comes to printing a document) using other software, many of those problems are also found in Crystal Reports, as discussed below.

While the reports that you create may look good on your computer monitor and look good when you print them, that may not be the case when the reports go into production. This is because information like printer drivers and monitor resolution come from the options that are on the computer that the reports are created on. Technical people tend to install printer and video driver updates, while end-users do not. This can cause reports to print differently even if you have the same model printer as the person printing the report.

This information is saved with the report. This is why someone that does not have the same exact settings on their computer as you do, will sometimes get different printed or visual screen results when they run the report. The list below discusses several printing concepts that you should be aware of that can effect how the reports that you create, look on a computer monitor and how they look when printed.

① Crystal Reports uses information from the default printer driver when the report was created (meaning the one on your computer). The printer driver determines the character width and height of the information printed on a report.
② The video driver resolution and operating system used when the report was created can also effect the report when it is viewed on a different monitor.
③ It is important to note that some of the layout options of reports that you create come from the options on the Page Setup and Print Setup dialog boxes. The default margins from the Page Setup dialog box are used for the reports that you create.
④ The length of the report page comes from the type of printer that is selected, which is usually your default printer. This is important to know because each printer model has limits on how close to the edge of the paper it can print.

Okay, I can imagine that the information that you just read is cause for concern.
The suggestions below will help resolve many of the printing problems discussed above.

① Set the margins for the report instead of using the default printer driver margins.
② Use the **CAN GROW** option for fields that contain a lot of data, like memo fields. Putting memo fields in their own subsection of the report would also be helpful.
③ Select the computer monitor video resolution that most of the people that will view the report have. If this is not possible, consider exporting the report to PDF format, so that more people can view and print the report as intended.
④ Select the **NO PRINTER (OPTIMIZE FOR SCREEN DISPLAY)** option shown earlier in Figure 14-1. Selecting this option is best if the report will be printed on several different printer models. Doing this helps keep the formatting generic enough so that the report can be printed on a variety of printers. If you know that a report will be printed on a printer that is different from the printer that you have, select the No Printer option.
⑤ Use common True Type fonts, like Arial, Garamond and Times New Roman, that come standard on Windows based computers. If you need to use a non standard font, you should export the report to Adobe Acrobat PDF format, which you will learn about later in this lesson. Creating a PDF file is the best option to use if you have to use different fonts because this file type can be viewed and printed on any computer that has the free Adobe Acrobat Reader.

Report Viewers

If you do not have Microsoft Word or Excel, you can download the free viewers and use them to view reports that are exported to these formats. If the web pages listed below have changed and you can't find the files, search for the file name in parenthesis on Microsoft's web site.

Word 2003 Viewer - (wdviewer.exe)
office.microsoft.com/search/redir.aspx?AssetID=DC011320141033&Origin=HH100152641033&CTT=5

Excel 2003 Viewer - (xlviewer.exe) office.microsoft.com/downloads/2000/xlviewer.aspx

Exercise 14.2: Use The Set Print Date And Time Options

The Set Print Date and Time options are useful when you use the Print Date or Print Time special fields on a report and have the need to override these dates when the report is printed. The options on the dialog box are used to set these fields to a date or time, other then the current date or time.

1. Save the L8.5 report as `L14.2 Set print date`. Notice the date in the **DATE THE REPORT WAS PRINTED** field. It should be today's date.

2. Report ⇒ Set Print Date and Time. Select the **OTHER** option and type `1/1/2008` in the Date field, as shown in Figure 14-5.

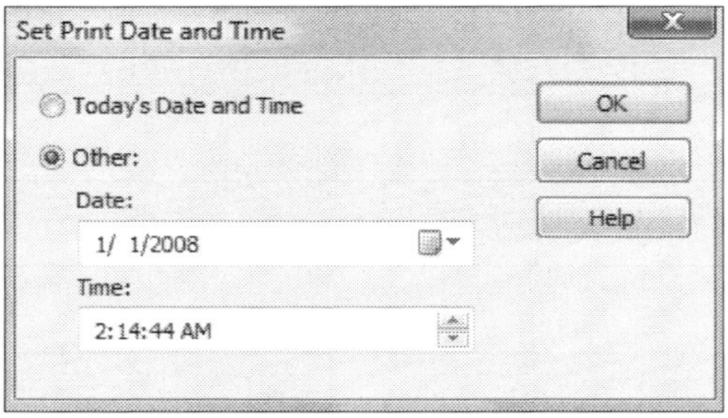

Figure 14-5 Set Print Date and Time dialog box

3. Click OK, then save the changes. You should see 1/1/2008 in the Date the report was printed field, as shown in Figure 14-6.

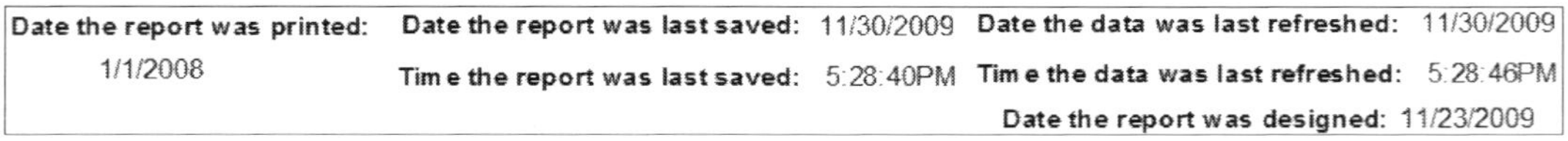

Figure 14-6 L14.2 report with the print date changed

4. Close the report. The 2008 date will print every time this report is run until you remove it from the Set Print Date and Time dialog box.

Exercise 14.3: Use The Preview Sample Option

If the report has hundreds or thousands of records and you do not want to see all of them when you are creating the report, you can specify the number of records that you want to see. The default for this is **ALL RECORDS**, which is why all of the records that met the criteria have appeared in every report that you have previewed so far.

1. Save the L10.4 report as `L14.3 Preview sample option`.
   Notice that there are 382 records.

2. View ⇒ Preview Sample. Select the **FIRST** option and type 125 in the **RECORDS** field.

   Figure 14-7 shows the options that should be selected. Click OK.

   The report will automatically re-open in the Preview window. Notice that there are 125 records being displayed in the report.

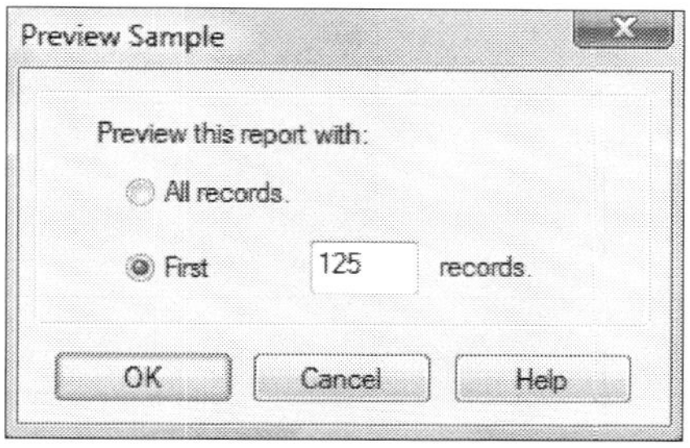

Figure 14-7 Preview Sample options selected

If you look in the group tree section, you will see that only two status options are included in the report, as shown in Figure 14-8. If you look at the group tree section in the original report shown in Figure 14-9, you will see that three status options are on the report. The Preview Sample option will stay in effect until it is removed.

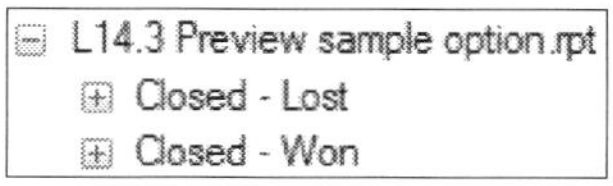

Figure 14-8 L14.3 Preview sample option report

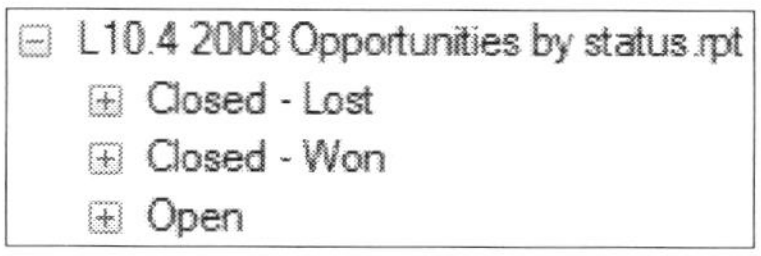

Figure 14-9 L10.4 report

> Keep in mind that when you select to preview a sample number of records, that they may not be the same first **N** number of records that will appear when you view all of the records. (N is the number that you enter on the Preview Sample dialog box shown earlier in Figure 14-7). In the exercise above, 125 records were selected to be previewed. If you preview the original report, some or all of the records that you see at the beginning of the report could be different.

3. Save the changes.

Report Options

The settings on the Options dialog box are global report options that are set. They are automatically applied to every report that you create.

There are also options that you can set on a report by report basis, as shown in Figure 14-10. (File ⇒ Report Options)
The options that are checked, are the default report options.

Many of the default options on this dialog box come from options that are checked on the Options dialog box.

Some default (checked) options, like the **DATABASE SERVER IS CASE-INSENSITIVE** is checked here because it is set as a global default on the Options dialog box.

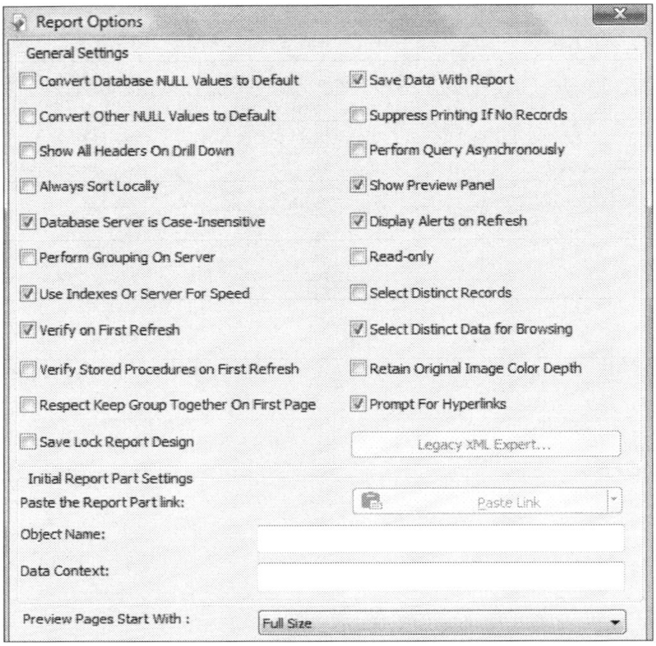

Figure 14-10 Report Options dialog box

Changes that you make on the Reporting tab on the Options dialog box will change the default options on the Report Options dialog box, shown above. The options selected on the Report Options dialog box override the corresponding option on the Options dialog box (when applicable), for the active report. This means that the options on the Report Options dialog box will always be applied to the report, while the options on the Options dialog box will only be applied if there is no corresponding option on the Report Options dialog box.

Report Export Overview

A report designer is not only responsible for creating and modifying reports, they can also be responsible for distributing the reports. There are several ways that an end-user can access and run reports that you create, as discussed below.

① Purchase and install Crystal Reports for every end-user that needs to run a report. This is probably not the best solution especially if there are hundreds or thousands of people in the company that need to run or print reports. This option could cost tens of thousands of dollars in hardware upgrades, software purchases, training and technical support.

② Hire someone to run reports all day, print them and send them via inter-office mail or email to end-users. This may sound good until you realize that end-users may not get the reports in a timely manner.

③ If the reports are part of a custom application that is being developed in a software package like Visual Basic or C++, the reports can be added to menu options or be attached to forms in the application. If this is the case, that's great, because your job is done.

④ Save the reports to a Crystal Reports Server or the Business Objects Enterprise.

⑤ Put the reports on www.crystalreports.com. You will learn about this service later in this lesson.

⑥ Use the free Crystal Reports viewer.

⑦ If none of the options discussed above are appropriate, all is not lost. There is another option. Exporting reports is cost effective and is something that a report designer can set up. The DBA would have to create a script that runs the exported report and place the exported report on a server. The only downside to this solution is that the reports will not necessarily have the most current data. If this is a problem, you will have to select one of the options above.

Export Format Options

Crystal Reports supports over 15 formats that reports can be exported to. Many of them are installed by default when Crystal Reports is installed. Exporting reports is a two step process, as discussed below.

① Select the **EXPORT** format. This option determines the format that the exported report will be saved in.

② Select the **DESTINATION**. This option determines where the report will be saved.

There are two ways to open the Export dialog box shown in Figure 14-11, as discussed below.

① Click the **EXPORT** button on the Standard toolbar.

② File ⇒ Export ⇒ Export Report.

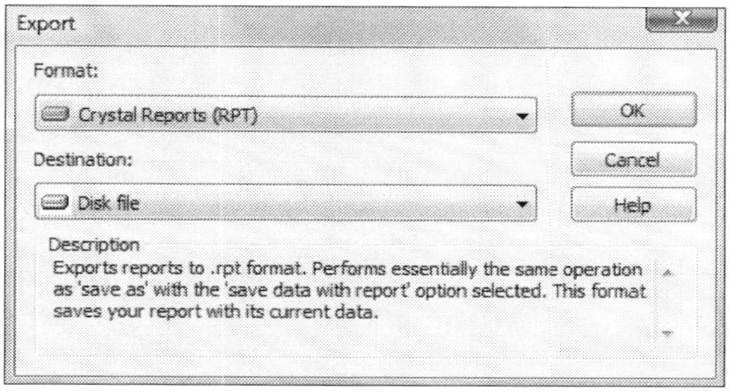

Figure 14-11 Export dialog box

Figure 14-12 shows the export format options. You may see the same or different options, then those shown.

Reports can be exported to more than one format if needed. Some export formats are better suited for certain types of reports then others. For example, some Word and Excel export format options are better suited for reports that may need to be edited by the end-user.

Table 14-2 explains the export format options. The software in brackets in the description column in the table is the most commonly used software to open the corresponding exported file format.

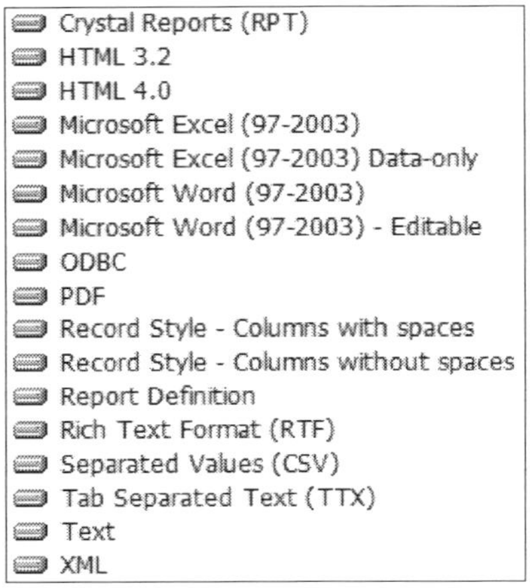

Figure 14-12 Export options

Some of the formats in the table do a better job of duplicating the report then others. I have noticed that sometimes reports that are exported to Excel get shifted a little. If the data does not need to be edited by the person using the exported report, the best format to use is PDF because it retains all of the formatting that you see when the report is viewed in Crystal Reports.

Format	Description
Crystal Reports (RPT)	This format can only be read by Crystal Reports or a report viewer from Crystal Reports Server, the Report Application Server (RAS) or a program that was created in Visual Basic, C++ or another application development tool that supports a runtime viewer. [Crystal Reports]
HTML 3.2	Select this option if you want to display the report on the Web. This format can be read by web browsers that use HTML v3.2 or higher. By today's standards, browsers that cannot use anything higher than HTML v3.2 are considered obsolete. [Web browser or HTML Editor] (1)
HTML 4.0	Select this option if you want to display the report on the Web. This format can be read by web browsers that use HTML v4.0 or higher. This format has better formatting capabilities then the HTML v3.2 format. [Web browser or HTML Editor] (1)
Excel (97-2003)	Select this format if you want to export the report to a spreadsheet and keep as much of the formatting as possible. This format will not include any formulas from the report, just the result of the formula. [Microsoft Excel]
Excel (97-2003) Data Only	Select this format if you want to export the report to a spreadsheet. Don't select this format if the report has charts or maps that you also need to export. Any data that is suppressed will not be exported. [Microsoft Excel]
Word (97-2003)	This format will create an RTF document, which requires Microsoft Word or the viewer. RTF stands for Rich Text Format. [Microsoft Word]

Table 14-2 Export format options explained

Format	**Description**
Word (97-2003) - Editable	This format will create an RTF document. It allows the user to edit the report in Microsoft Word. [Microsoft Word]
ODBC	This format allows the report to be exported to any ODBC database.
PDF	This format will create a PDF file, which is one of the most popular export formats because it can be read by both PC and MAC computers. If you want the report to retain its look after it is exported, select this format. [Adobe Acrobat or the free reader] (2)
Record Style - Columns with spaces	Select this format when you want to export the data to an ASCII fixed length format, with spaces. (3)
Record Style - Columns without spaces	Select this format when you want to export the data to an ASCII fixed length format, without spaces. (3)
Report Definition	This format produces a report that contains a description of the reports design. This includes the sections, selection criteria, object formats, groups and more. [Notepad] (4)
Rich Text Format (RTF)	This RTF export option retains the formatting of the report including graphics. Select this option if the report will be opened in a word processor other than Word. [Microsoft Word]
Separated Values (CSV)	This format is similar to the two ASCII Record Style formats discussed above. The difference is that in this format the fields are separated by commas. This is often called a "Comma Delimited" file. CSV stands for Comma Separated Values. [Microsoft Excel]
Tab Separated Text (TTX)	This format is similar to the Separated Values format because it separates the fields. The difference is that the fields are separated by tab spaces. [Notepad]
Text	This format creates a plain text file. [Notepad] (5)
XML	This format will create an XML data file from the data in the report. Style sheets can be applied to the XML file, so that the data can be used in another application or on the web. XML stands for Extensible Markup Language. [Web browser]

Table 14-2 Export format options explained (Continued)

(1) Left justified is the only justification that will work.
(2) The drill down feature and hyperlinks will not work with this report format.

(3) This format is often used to move data into older applications.
(4) This report format is usually for technical people. It does not export the data in the report. It exports information about the report.
(5) Text (TXT) reports do not retain any formatting like bold, italic or underline.

Export Destination Options

In addition to selecting an export format, a destination for the report also has to be selected. The destination options that are available by default are discussed in Table 14-3. Some of the options may not be installed. You may have other options in addition to the ones in the table.

Option	Description
Application	Select this option when the export format is the Adobe Acrobat Reader or a Windows based application like Word or Excel. Selecting this option causes the application that is associated with the export format to open after the report is exported. Exported files that use this destination option are automatically saved in the TEMP directory. You can move the file to another location. If you want to change the default location, you have to modify the path in the ExportDirectory key in the registry. The path to this key is HKEY_CURRENT_USER\Software\Business Objects\Suite 12.0\ Crystal Reports\ Export, as illustrated in Figure 14-13.
Disk File	This option lets you select a folder, either on a hard drive or on a server (which is also known as a Network drive), where the exported report will be placed. This destination option does not automatically open the application associated with the export file type.
Exchange Folder	This option allows the exported report to be placed on a public or private Exchange mail server.
Lotus Domino	This option will export the report to a Lotus Domino database. This requires that the form already be created in the Lotus database before the export is run. (6)
Lotus Domino Mail	This option is used to send the exported report as an attachment to a Lotus email message. (6)
MAPI	This option is used to send the exported report as an attachment to a MAPI compliant email. To use this option, email software like Outlook has to be installed and configured on your computer.

Table 14-3 Destination options explained

(6) To use this option, the appropriate Lotus mail client software must be installed and configured on your computer.

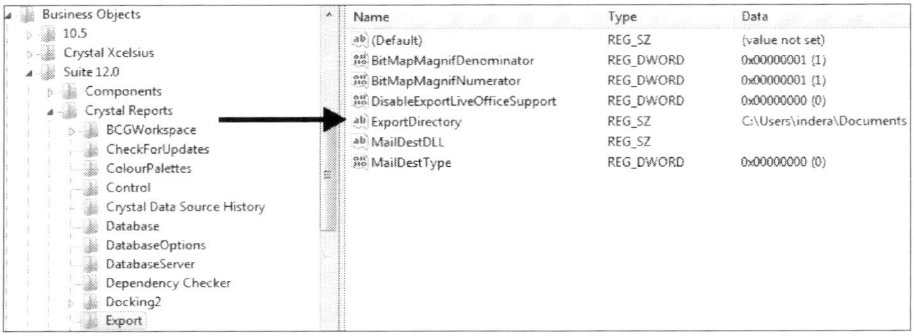

Figure 14-13 Path in the registry to change the default application export folder

Export Formatting Tips

I have found that by making sure that the export format tips listed below are followed, the exported file, regardless of the format, will look more like the report does in Crystal Reports.

① Make sure that all of the data fields in the same column have the same alignment (left or right). This is especially important for number and currency fields. If the fields in the same column have a different alignment option, some fields may appear in a different column in the exported report.

② All objects in the same column should be attached (snapped) to the same guideline.

③ Remove any space that is not needed in each section of the report by moving all of the objects in each section up, as much as possible.

Report Export Formats

Some of the exercises in this lesson will show you how to create some of the more popular report export formats. To demonstrate the differences between the export format output options, you will export the same report to create all of the export formats covered in this lesson.

The L11.1 report is the report that you will use to create all of the export reports in this lesson. You should open this report and then open the Export dialog box shown earlier in Figure 14-11, prior to starting each exercise, unless instructed otherwise. Save each exported report in the Crystal Reports Book folder.

Exercise 14.4: Create An Adobe Acrobat PDF Export File

This export file type will create a PDF (Portable Document Format) file of the report. End-users that need to open reports in this file type will need to have the Adobe Acrobat Reader installed.

This software is free and can be downloaded from http://get.adobe.com/reader/. You do not have to download and install any of the other software that is on the web page for the Acrobat Reader software to work. This export file type can also be opened and viewed with Adobe Acrobat, which is the full version of the software that lets you create PDF files.

1. Select the PDF format, then open the Destination drop-down list and select **DISK FILE** if it is not already selected. Click OK.

> If you select the **APPLICATION** destination option, you will get the same PDF export file. The difference is that the Application option will not let you select where the export file will be saved initially. Once the report is exported you can save it to a different location. The exported file will automatically be stored in your temp folder. Usually the files are not automatically deleted from these folders, so you may want to check the folder from time to time and delete the files that you do not need.

The dialog box shown in Figure 14-14 is used to select whether you want to include all or some of the pages from the report in the PDF export file that you are about to create.

If you were going to send each sales rep their stats for the month from the report, you would enter the corresponding page numbers in the From and To fields in the dialog box. If the report has **PARAMETER FIELDS**, you would not have to do this to get a specific sales reps stats.

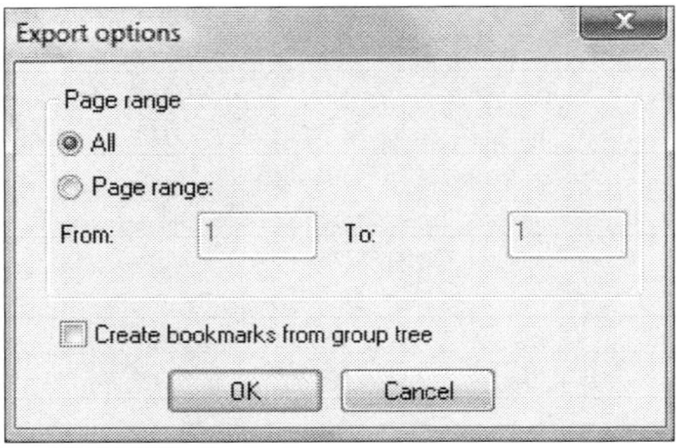

Figure 14-14 Export Options dialog box

The **CREATE BOOKMARKS FROM GROUP TREE** option if checked, will create bookmarks (similar to hyperlinks) in the PDF file for each group in the group tree. This will make it easier for the person reading the PDF version of the report to find specific information.

2. Check the Create bookmarks from group tree option.

   Click OK to include all of the pages. You will see the dialog box shown in Figure 14-15. This dialog box is used to select where you want to save the export file.

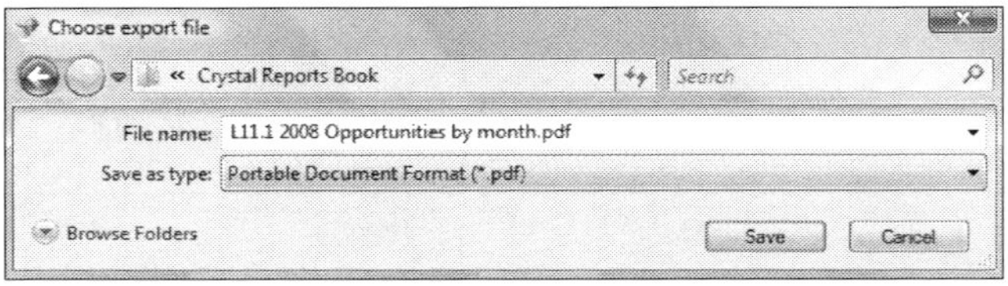

Figure 14-15 Choose export file dialog box

3. Navigate to your folder, as shown above in Figure 14-15 and type `L14.4 2008 Contact opportunities by month exported PDF file` as the file name, then press Enter or click the Save button.

   You will see the dialog box shown in Figure 14-16. This dialog box lets you know that the export file is being created and how many records will be exported.

Figure 14-16 Exporting Records dialog box

When the export is complete, you can open the PDF file in either the Adobe Acrobat Reader or Adobe Acrobat. The exported PDF file should look similar to the one shown in Figure 14-17. The bookmarks shown in Figure 14-17 are the groups on the report.

Like the report, you can click on the group and the corresponding section of the report will be displayed.

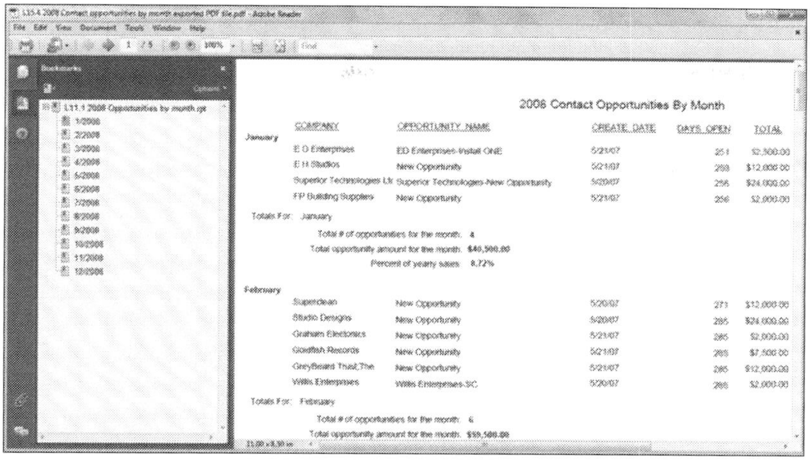

Figure 14-17 L14.4 exported PDF file

4. Close the PDF report.

Exercise 14.5: Create An Excel (97-2003) Export File

This export file type will create an Excel file of the report. To view this exported file type, Microsoft Excel or the free Excel viewer needs to be installed. As you read in Table 14-2, there are two Excel export formats. The Excel export format options provide a different output of the data.

1. Select the first Excel (97-2003) format, then open the Destination drop-down list and select **APPLICATION**.

   Figure 14-18 shows the options that should be selected. Click OK.

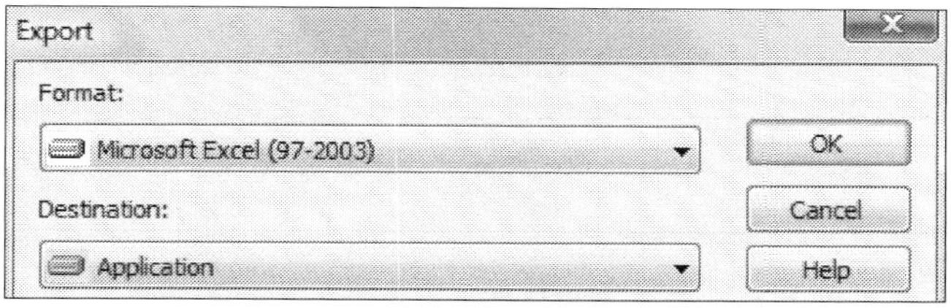

Figure 14-18 Export format options

   You will see the dialog box shown in Figure 14-19. As you can see, there are several options that you can select, which will determine how the data will be formatted in Excel. Table 14-4 explains the options.

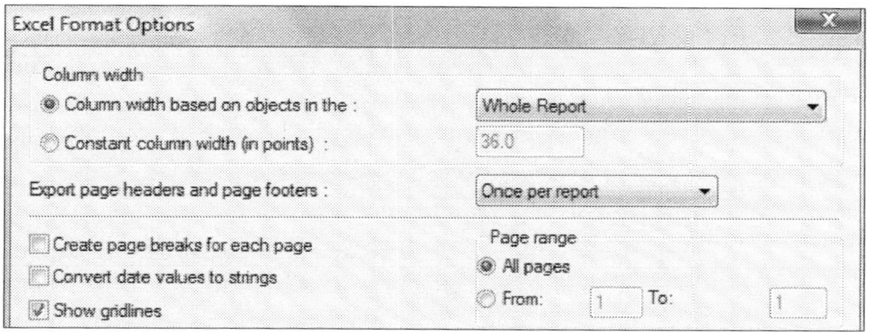

Figure 14-19 Excel (97-2003) Format Options dialog box

Option	Description
Column Width	These options are used to select the column widths in Excel. ① The **COLUMN WIDTH BASED ON OBJECTS IN THE** option is used to select the column width in Excel based on a section in the report. ② The **CONSTANT COLUMN WIDTH (IN POINTS)** option is used to select a free form column width.
Export page headers and page footers	This option is used to select whether or not the information in the page header and footer sections on the report will be exported to Excel. If the page header and footer information is exported, the options in the drop-down list determine where the information will be placed in the Excel file. ① **ONCE PER REPORT** causes the header information to only print at the top of the first page and the footer information to only print at the bottom of the last page. ② **ONCE PER PAGE** causes the header and footer information to print on each page of the report.
Create page breaks for each page	If selected, page breaks will be added to the exported Excel file in the same place they would appear in Crystal Reports. This may cause the report to break someplace other then at the end of the printed page. If you want the page breaks to happen automatically in Excel, do not check this option.
Convert date values to strings	If selected, this option will keep the date formatting in Crystal Reports when the report is exported to Excel. If this option is not checked, the formatting for the date fields when the report is exported will come from the date formatting options in the copy of Excel that the exported file is opened with. This means that if different people have different date settings in their copy of Excel, the dates in the exported file will appear differently.
Show Gridlines	If selected, this option forces gridlines in the exported copy of the report.
Page range	These options are used to select how many pages of the report will be exported.

Table 14-4 Excel (97-2003) export format options explained

2. Select the **SHOW GRIDLINES** option that is shown above in Figure 14-19, then click OK. You will see the records being processed/exported. When the export is complete, Excel will open and you will see the report shown in Figure 14-20.

3. Scroll down to the row that has the Total # of opportunities for the month for January and click in the cell that is illustrated in Figure 14-21. If you look in the Formula Bar at the top of the spreadsheet window, you will not see the summary calculation (formula).

One reason to use this export format is if you do not want the end-user to be able to change or see the formulas. For other end-users, it would be helpful if the formulas that are used in the report were also exported.

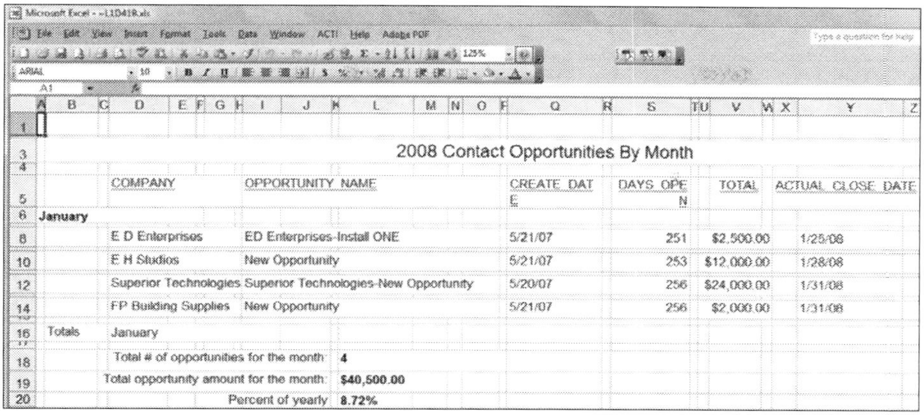

Figure 14-20 L14.5 exported Excel file

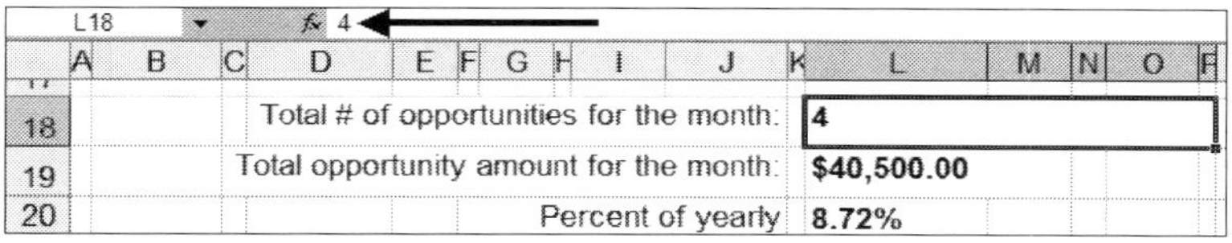

Figure 14-21 Formula Bar illustrated

4. Save the exported file as `L14.5 2008 opportunities by month exported file`, then close the spreadsheet.

ODBC Export Format

If you select the ODBC export format, the destination option is not enabled on the Export dialog box. This is because this format exports the data from the report to a table. When you click OK on the Export dialog box, you will see the dialog box shown in Figure 14-22. You may be prompted to install the DLL. Select the ODBC format that you want to export the report to, then click OK. You will then see the dialog box shown in Figure 14-23. Enter the name for the table that you will export the data to, then click OK. The table will be created in the format that you selected and the data will be exported to it.

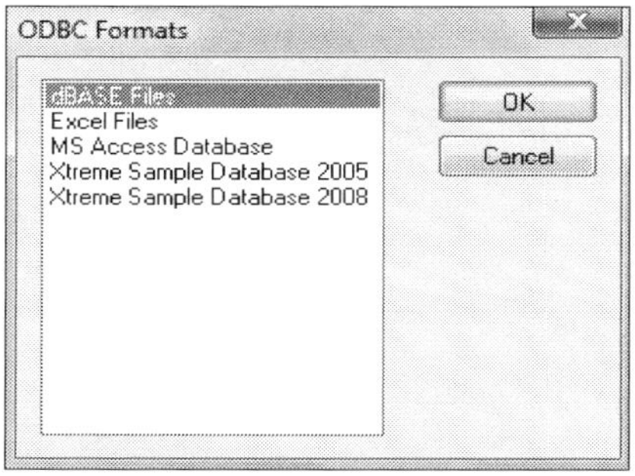

Figure 14-22 ODBC database format options

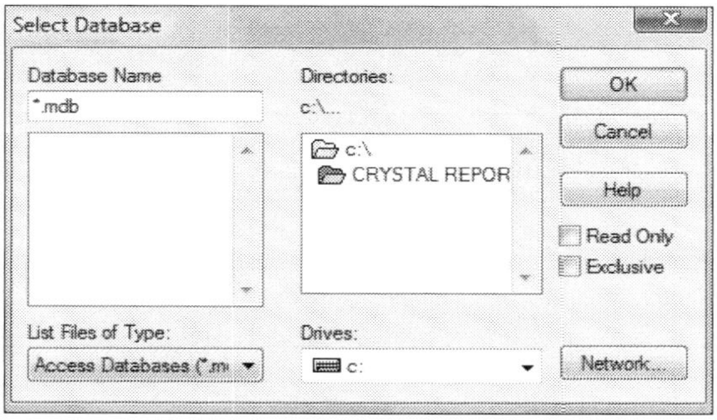

Figure 14-23 ODBC table name options

Text Export Format

Selecting this export format will prompt you to select the **CHARACTERS PER INCH** and the **NUMBER OF LINES PER PAGE** that you want for the exported file, as shown in Figure 14-24.

To me, the characters per inch option is similar to selecting the font size.

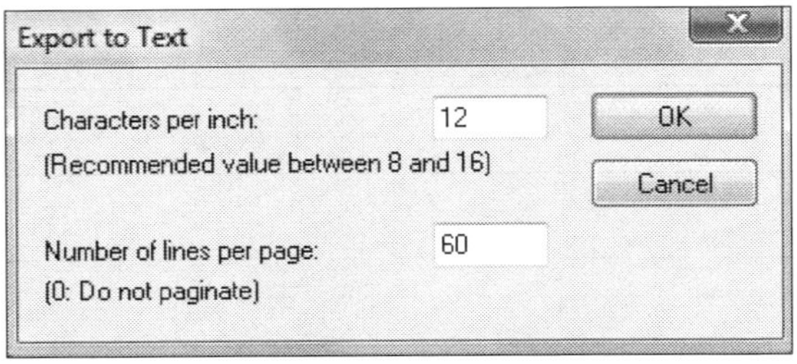

Figure 14-24 Export To Text dialog box

NEW XML Export Format

The XML export options have been modified. This export format is similar to the HTML export format that you read about earlier in this lesson, because it is also web based. Like the HTML format, the XML (which stands for Extensible Markup Language) export format requires you to create a folder to store the XML files in. XML uses **TAGS** that will format the data or content for the report.

Figure 14-25 shows the XML options. If you need to customize or add an XML export format, you can use the Manage XML Exporting Formats dialog box (File ⇒ Export ⇒ Manage XML Exporting Formats) shown in Figure 14-26.

The people that will view a report in XML format will need software that recognizes XML files.

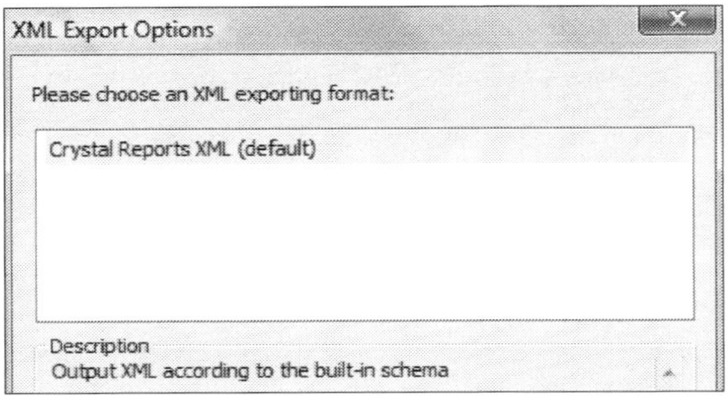

Figure 14-25 XML export options

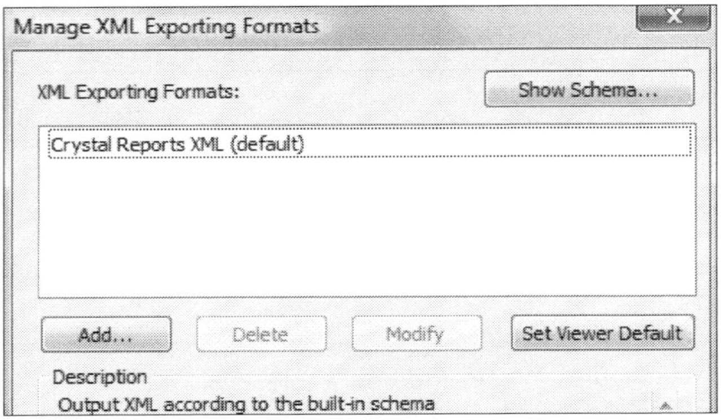

Figure 14-26 XML Export Formats

NEW Bar Codes

Crystal Reports now supports basic bar code creation and printing. Currently, the bar codes that can be produced are very basic. Usually bar codes print a UPC or ISBN code. The two formats currently supported, do not have this functionality. To access the bar code utility, follow the steps below.

1. Open the report that has the field that you want to use to create the bar code from.

2. Right-click on the field that has the data that you want converted to a bar code and select **CHANGE BAR CODE**.

   You will see the dialog box shown in Figure 14-27.

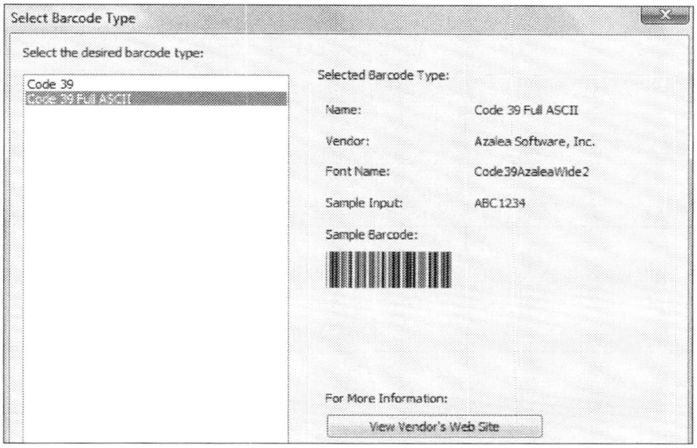

Figure 14-27 Select Barcode Type dialog box

3. Select the type of bar code that you want and click OK. The data in the field will be changed to a bar code, as shown in Figure 14-28.

Figure 14-28 Product ID field changed to a bar code

NEW Exercise 14.6: Bind Sort Control

In Lesson 2 you read that this control will allow the person running the report to be able to sort the report on their own. In Lesson 10 you learned how to sort the records. This will handle a lot of the users requirements of needing a report sorted more than one way. You could create parameter fields that will allow the user to select a sort order. The advantage of Bind Controls is that the data does not have to be refreshed.

In this exercise you will add two bind controls to a report to allow the user to sort the report in more than one way. Bind controls can only be used on fields that are sorted or grouped on in the report.

1. Save the L5.1 report as `L14.6 Bind Control`.

2. Sort the report on the State and Zip Code fields.

3. Insert ⇒ Sort Control.

   You will see the dialog box shown in Figure 14-29.

Figure 14-29 Sort Control dialog box

4. Select the State field, then click OK.

5. The mouse pointer will change to a cross-hair. Draw a box over the State heading, then click on a blank space on the report. Resize the text object so that it is smaller.

6. Right-click on the Zip Code heading and select Bind Sort Control. Select the Zip Code option, then resize the control.

7. Save the changes. The report should look like the one shown in Figure 14-30.

Figure 14-30 Bind controls added to the report

8. Click on the down arrow for the State field. The report should be sorted in descending order by state. Click on the up arrow on the Zip Code field. The report should be sorted in ascending order by Zip Code.

It is not a requirement that the control be placed on a field heading. You can place the control any place on the report. The reason that I place them there is so that there are no extra fields on the report when it is printed.

If you placed the controls in the report header, they would be visible on the first page of the report, as shown in Figure 14-31.

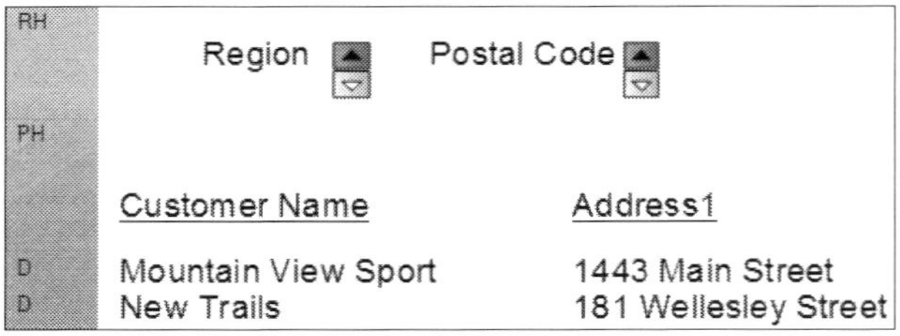

Figure 14-31 Bind Controls in the report header section

Crystalreports.com

This is a way to share reports on the Internet. You may have seen information about it on the Start page of Crystal Reports. It is easy to use and it is secure.

You can share up to 10 reports with three users including yourself, for free. If you need to share more than 10 reports or give more than three people access, there is a professional plan that you or your company can purchase.

FORMULAS AND FUNCTIONS

After completing the exercises in this lesson you will be able to:

- ☑ Understand the difference between formulas and functions
- ☑ Know what the formula rules are
- ☑ Select a Syntax Editor
- ☑ Use the Formula Workshop and know the purpose of its toolbar buttons
- ☑ Customize the Formula Editor window
- ☑ Use the Workshop Tree
- ☑ Understand the formula evaluation order
- ☑ Create numeric formulas
- ☑ Create string formulas
- ☑ Use functions in string formulas
- ☑ Create date formulas
- ☑ Use the Truncate function

LESSON 15

Formulas And Functions Overview

Formulas and functions are some of the most powerful features in Crystal Reports. Ironically, many people that are first learning Crystal Reports think that formulas and functions are one of the most dreaded features because there is math and logic involved <smile>. If you fall into this category, hopefully this lesson will help you overcome some of the fear.

In Lesson 3 as part of the report design process, you learned that not all fields that are needed for a report exist in tables. In Lesson 10 you learned how to create summary fields which are not stored in tables. While summary fields provide a quick way to create totals, that is about as far as they go.

For example, summary fields will not let you add two fields together, nor can you multiply a field in a table by a constant value, like calculating the sales tax for an order. When you have exhausted all other math related options, it is time to turn to formulas and functions. Formulas are created in the Formula Workshop, which you will learn about later in this lesson.

Actually, you have two options for creating formulas: The Formula Workshop and writing SQL Expressions. This type of field is what would be placed in the SQL Expression Fields section of the Field Explorer. If you are already freaking out about creating formulas, for now you should focus on using the Formula Workshop, because you would need to learn the version of SQL that works with the database that you are using for the reports that you are creating or modifying.

While creating SQL Expressions is more efficient than creating formulas in the Formula Workshop, SQL Expressions are evaluated (processed) on the server and sent back to Crystal Reports. The SQL for some types of databases is limited and can have fewer options than Crystal Reports has. For example, if you have to create a formula that needs to process or refer to (as in lookup) a record, other than the current record, you would have a problem if the database does not have any analytical functionality. I'm not saying this to scare you away from learning SQL, merely pointing out something that you may not be aware of.

What Is The Difference Between Formulas And Functions?

One of the questions that I am asked a lot is, "What is the difference between formulas and functions?" Formulas are calculations or some type of data manipulation that you create. Functions are built-in formulas or procedures that have already been created. If there is a built-in function that meets your needs, use it because there is no point reinventing the wheel, as they say. If you have created or used formulas or functions in spreadsheet software, you are already familiar with the basics of using them.

Formula Overview

Formulas are used to create new fields. If you need to include data on a report that is not stored in tables, many times you will need to create a formula to get the data. An example of this would be the line item total on an order report. Line item information is not stored in an Order Detail table, but the price and quantity ordered are stored in the table. These are the fields that you would use to create the formula to calculate the line item total. A line item total is sometimes referred to as the "Extended Price". If there is a built-in function that has the calculation that you need, you can use that. Formulas allow you to create the following types of calculations, comparisons, manipulations and much more.

① Solve math problems
② Convert data from one format to another
③ Compare or evaluate data
④ Combine two or more text fields into one field
⑤ Combine text and data fields

You may be thinking or asking why all of this information is not stored in tables. There are many reasons including the following, why data that falls into these categories is not stored in tables.

① It would take a lot of hard drive or server space to store all of the data for these fields.
② Applications that share data have slightly different data needs, which means that some tables would have empty fields.
③ Some data is only needed once or the data changes constantly, so it is more efficient to calculate it when it is needed.
④ The more data that has to be written (added or changed) to a table, the slower the application will run. This "slowness" is often referred to as a performance issue.

Syntax Rules

Formulas have rules (also known as syntax rules) that have to be followed. Basically, the rules require that items be placed in a certain order, so that the formula will work. Table 15-1 provides the rules for Crystal Syntax, that if followed, will make learning how to write formulas easier. The items listed below are the parts of the formula.

Item	Syntax
//	The double slash is used to add comments to a formula. This is helpful when you need to document the formula. (1)
Case Sensitive	Formulas are not case sensitive.
Hard Returns	Pressing the Enter key to continue the formula on another line to make the formula easier to read is acceptable. The one time that this will cause an error is if there is a hard return between quotation marks in a formula.
Operators	Placing a space before or after an operator is acceptable, but is not required. Many people include spaces to make the formulas easier to read. The spaces are ignored when the formula is executed. The operators are similar to the ones that you learned about in Lesson 9. The difference is that symbols are used in formulas instead of words. = < > + - are some of the operators that you can use when creating formulas.
Fields	They must be surrounded by braces. For example, {Table.Field Name}.
Functions	Each function requires at least one argument. Each argument must be followed by a comma, except the last one. Arguments must be entered in this format: FunctionName (Argument 1, Argument 2).
Numbers	Numbers must be entered without any formatting. 5600 or 56000 is correct. 5,600 or 56,000.00 is incorrect.
Text	Text must be entered inside of quotation marks. Examples: "Help" would be printed as Help. ' "Help" ' would be printed as "Help". Notice the difference in the output when different types of quotes are used.

Table 15-1 Syntax rules explained

(1) Comments should be added to formulas to explain the purpose of the formulas and to provide documentation. If the comment needs more than one line, each line must start with two slashes, otherwise Crystal Reports will treat the line as part of the formula, which will generate a syntax error. You may think that you will remember what the formula does six months from now, but it may take you a minute or so to remember. I have learned that it is easier to add comments to formulas and give them a descriptive name when they are first created.

Formulas cannot be stored in the Repository.

Functions Overview

Functions are prewritten, built-in formulas or procedures. Software that supports functions have built-in functions, plus allow you to create your own. Functions have been thoroughly tested and from what I can tell, they are error free in Crystal Reports. However, this does not mean that if there is bad data in a table that you won't have a problem with the function. If you do not follow the syntax rules or fill in the arguments correctly when using the function, you will get an error.

Crystal Reports has over 300 functions that you can use. Sum, Average, Count and Distinct Count are functions that you have already learned how to use. Many of the Special Fields that you have learned about are also functions, as are the Document Properties that you learned about. You also read about the Date Range functions. [See Lesson 9, Table 9-2] This lesson covers some of the more popular functions that you may have a need to use. For more information on functions, you can type functions on the Index tab of the Help window in Crystal Reports. You will see a list of functions. Select the function that you want to learn more about.

Syntax

You can select the syntax language that you want to use. If you are already familiar with one, by all means continue to use it. If you have used a previous version of Crystal Reports, you may already be familiar with Crystal Syntax. You can create formulas and incorporate functions in both languages and both can be used in the same report. The good thing is that you do not have to be a programmer to create formulas or use functions in the Formula Workshop. Each language has its own rules for control structures, functions and other syntax. In order to create a formula, you need to select one of the following languages:

① **Crystal Syntax** This language has been included in every version of Crystal Reports and is the default language that is selected when Crystal Reports is installed. The formulas that you viewed at the bottom of the Select Expert dialog box are written in Crystal Syntax, unless you changed the default language to Basic Syntax prior to working on the exercises in this book. Some say that Crystal syntax is more user-friendly than Basic syntax. The exercises in this book use Crystal Syntax.

② **Basic Syntax** If you have developed applications in Visual Basic, you will find this syntax language familiar. The main difference that you will notice between Visual Basic and Basic Syntax is that the Basic Syntax language has extensions for creating reports. Figures 15-1 and 15-2 show the same formula using different syntax editors.

```
// This formula combines the Supplier ID and Supplier Name fields
ToText ({Supplier.Supplier ID},0 )+ " - " +{Supplier.Supplier Name}
```

Figure 15-1 Formula using Crystal Syntax

```
'This formula combines the Supplier ID and Supplier Name fields
formula = ToText ({Supplier.Supplier ID},0)+ " - " + {Supplier.Supplier Name}
```

Figure 15-2 Formula using Basic Syntax

Statements

Depending on the environment that you work in, you may hear the term "Statement" and have a different interpretation of what a statement is then the context that I will present it in. That's fine, I just don't want you to think that either interpretation is incorrect. You may have also heard the term **EXPRESSION**. I believe that the terms statement and expression mean the same thing, but some will argue that there is a difference. Formulas in Crystal Reports and other software tools as well, consider a statement a combination of fields, operators, functions and other variables that provide an answer or value. I think of statements in Crystal Reports as sentences. Formulas have at least one statement.

Control Structures

This is how Crystal Reports processes a formula. The process starts at the beginning of the formula and moves from one statement to the next. Control structures evaluate expressions or conditions. The result of this evaluation is known as the **RETURN VALUE**. Formulas must return a value. The result of the last statement executed in the formula contains the result value. It is important to note that the last statement executed may not be the last physical line of code in the formula.

Types of control structures include **WHILE DO/DO WHILE**, **SELECT CASE STATEMENTS** and **IF STATEMENTS**, which are also known as If Then Else or Nested If statements. You will learn how to create If statements in the next lesson.

Formula Workshop Overview

The Formula Workshop shown in Figure 15-3 is the tool that you will use to create and manage formulas. You can also work with record and group selection formulas in the Formula Workshop. Notice that it does not have any menus. Depending on how you open the Formula Workshop, you will either see the Formula Editor or the Formula Expert. If you do not like the toolbars at the top of the window, you can move them. Each section of the Formula Workshop is explained below.

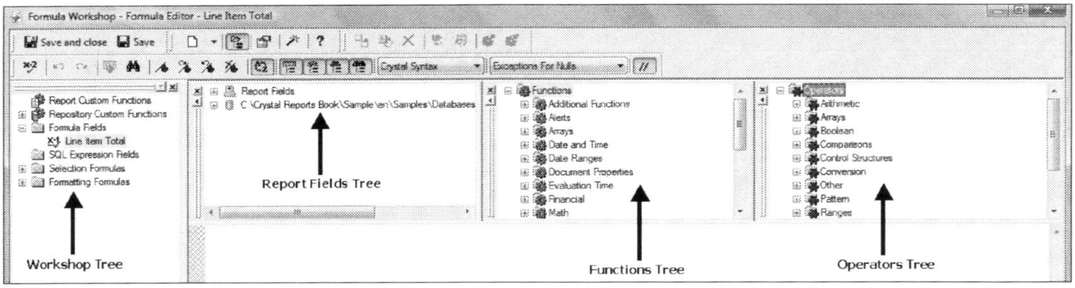

Figure 15-3 Formula Workshop

General Toolbar

Figure 15-4 shows the General toolbar. Table 15-2 explains the buttons on the General toolbar.

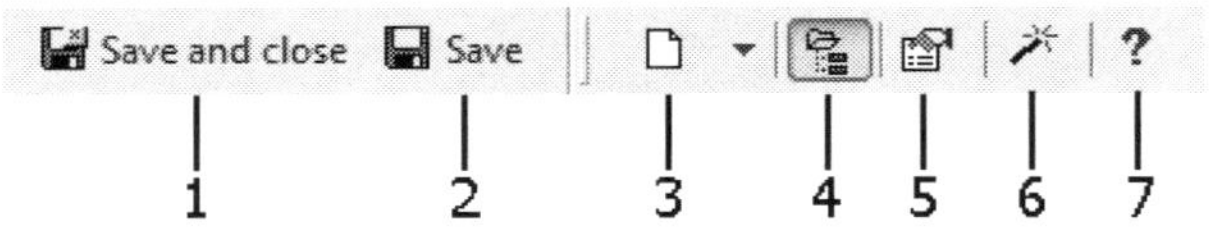

Figure 15-4 General toolbar

Button	Purpose
1	Closes the Formula Workshop after prompting you to save changes if necessary. (2)
2	Saves the formula and leaves the Formula Workshop open. (2)
3	The New button is used to create a new formula based on the category selected from the drop-down list shown in Figure 15-5. If a formula is open prior to clicking this button, the syntax is checked and the current formula is saved.
4	The Show/Hide Workshop Tree button displays or hides the Workshop Tree.
5	The Toggle Properties Display button toggles between displaying the Custom Function Editor and Custom Function Properties dialog box. Custom functions and formulas (where possible) are displayed in the selected mode until this button is clicked again.
6	The Use Expert/Editor button toggles between the Formula Editor and the Formula Expert. Use the Formula Expert to create a formula based on a custom function. This button is not available when creating a custom function.
7	Opens the online help for the Formula Workshop, Formula Editor or Formula Expert, depending on which is currently displayed or where the cursor is.

Table 15-2 General toolbar buttons explained

(2) When you save the changes, the formula, custom function or SQL Expression is checked for errors.

The **RECORD SELECTION FORMULA** option is used to create a formula to select data that will appear on the report based on records.

The **GROUP SELECTION FORMULA** option is used to create a formula to select which groups will appear on the report.

NEW The **SAVED DATA SELECTION FORMULA** option is used to create a formula to filter the data that has already been saved with the report.

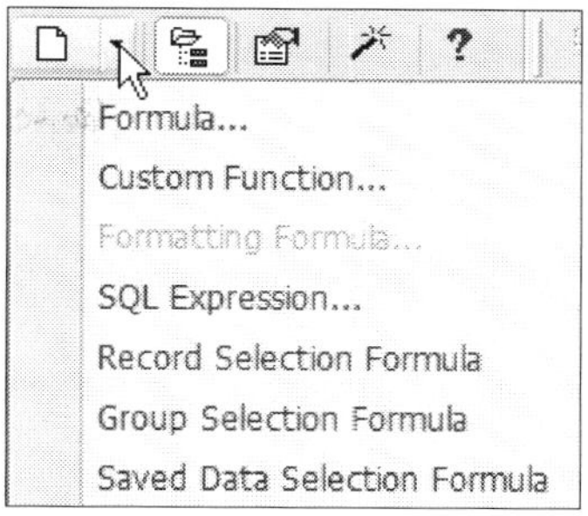

Figure 15-5 New button options

Workshop Tree Toolbar

Figure 15-6 shows the Workshop Tree toolbar. Table 15-3 explains the buttons on the Workshop Tree toolbar.

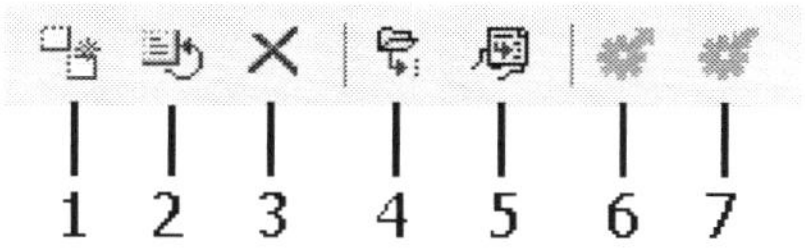

Figure 15-6 Workshop Tree toolbar

Button	Purpose
1	Duplicates the formula selected in the Formula Fields section of the Workshop tree.
2	Renames the selected formula, custom function, or SQL Expression.
3	Deletes the selected formula, custom function, or SQL Expression.
4	Expands the selected node(s) in the Workshop Tree.
5	The Show Formatting Formulas button displays or hides all of the report objects in the Formatting Formulas folder or only the objects that have a formatting formula.
6	The Add To Repository button opens the Add Custom Function To Repository dialog box so that you can select the repository to add the custom function to.
7	The Add To Report button adds the selected repository custom function to the report.

Table 15-3 Workshop Tree toolbar buttons explained

Expression Editor Toolbar

Figure 15-7 shows the Expression Editor toolbar. Table 15-4 explains the buttons on the Expression Editor toolbar.

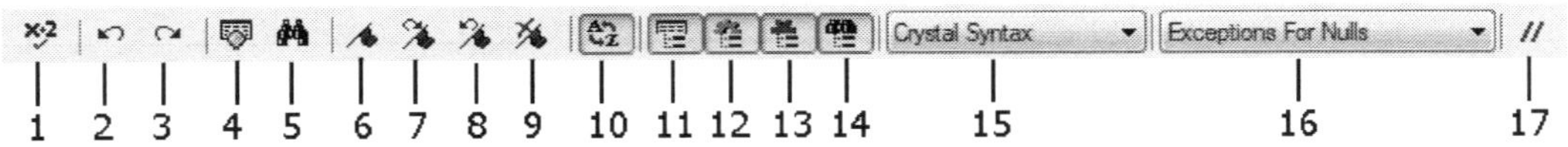

Figure 15-7 Expression Editor toolbar

Button	Purpose
1	The Check button tests the syntax of the formula or custom function and identifies syntax errors.
2	The Undo button undoes the last action made to the formula.
3	The Redo button redoes the last action made to the formula.
4	The Browse Data button is used to view the data in a field in the Report Fields window. (3)
5	The Find or Replace dialog box shown in Figure 15-8 searches the formula, fields, functions or operators for words or expressions. You can also replace text in formulas using this dialog box. The **EDIT TEXT** option is where you type in the formula.
6	The Bookmark button inserts a bookmark in the current line of the selected formula. Click the button again to remove the bookmark. Bookmarks are used to mark a line of code as important. The bookmark feature is helpful in long formulas when you have to go from one part of the formula to another.
7	The Next Bookmark button places the cursor at the next bookmark in the formula.
8	The Previous Bookmark button places the cursor at the previous bookmark in the formula.
9	The Clear All Bookmarks button deletes all bookmarks in the current formula.
10	Sorts the options in the Report Fields, Functions and Operators trees in alphabetical order or returns them to their original order.
11	Displays or hides the Report Fields tree. (3)
12	Displays or hides the Functions tree.
13	Displays or hides the Operators tree.
14	Displays or hides the formula search results, as shown in Figure 15-9.
15	Is used to select **CRYSTAL SYNTAX** or **BASIC SYNTAX** as the formula syntax editor.
16	This option is used to select **EXCEPTIONS FOR NULLS** or **DEFAULT VALUES FOR NULLS** as the method for dealing with null values in the data. Fields in a formula that have a null value will return invalid data or generate an error. Selecting the Default values for nulls option will replace data that has a null value, with the default value for the field type. String fields are changed to an empty string. Numeric fields are changed to zero. If you don't know how or do not want to write code to test for nulls or check for errors, select this option.

Table 15-4 Expression Editor toolbar buttons explained

Button	Purpose
17	Add comments to a formula. Commented lines are not evaluated as part of the formula. I type the // into the Formula section when writing the formula because I find it faster then clicking this button.

Table 15-4 Expression Editor toolbar buttons explained (Continued)

(3) This button is not available for custom functions.

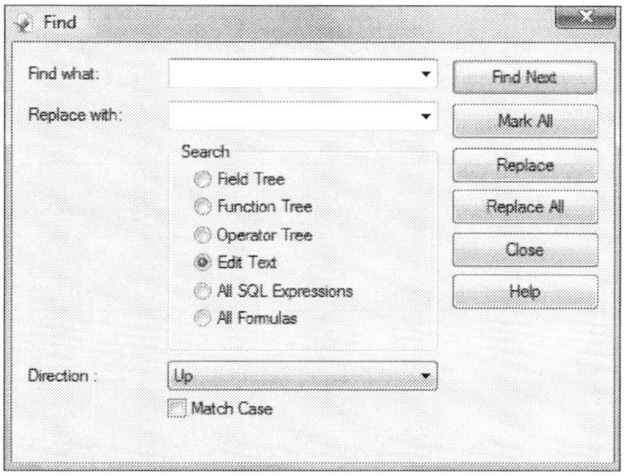

Figure 15-8 Find dialog box

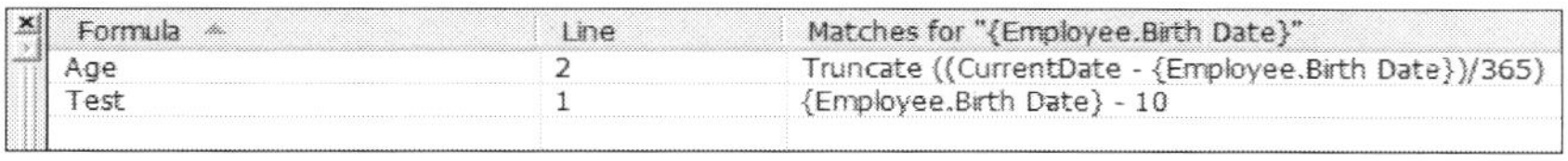

Figure 15-9 Find Results window

> The **SEARCH** options change depending on the field type or object that is selected prior to clicking the Find and Replace button.

The **FIND IN FORMULAS** shortcut menu option is used if you need to find out if a field is used in a formula. Right-click on the field either in the report or in the Field Explorer and select Find in formulas. If the field is being used in a formula, the Formula Workshop will open and display all of the formulas that use the field, as shown above in Figure 15-9.

How To Open The Formula Workshop

Like many other tools in Crystal Reports, there is more than one way to open the this tool. The Formula Workshop is no exception. This tool has more ways that it can be opened then most tools in Crystal Reports.

① Click the **FORMULA WORKSHOP** button on the Expert Tools toolbar.

② Report ⇒ Formula Workshop.

③ Right-click on a formula or SQL Expression field in the design (or preview) window and select Edit.

④ Right-click on a formula or SQL Expression field in the Field Explorer and select New or Edit.

⑤ Click on a formula or SQL Expression field and click the **NEW** button on the Field Explorer toolbar.

⑥ Click the **FORMULA** button on any tab of the Format Editor dialog box.

⑦ Open the Select Expert, click the Show Formula button, then click the **FORMULA EDITOR** button.

Workshop Tree

This section of the Formula Workshop contains all of the formulas that are in the report and includes formulas that are in the repository that can be used in the report. Items under the Selection Formulas folder are the ones that you have created with the Select Expert.

As you saw earlier in Figure 15-3, the Workshop Tree contains several sections called **NODES** or **CATEGORY** folders that formulas can be saved in. In addition to being able to create formulas, you can also rename and delete formulas, just like you can in the Field Explorer. Each of the categories in the Workshop Tree are explained below.

① **Report Custom Functions** If you create a function or copy a function from the repository into the report, this is where it would be stored. The functions in this category can be used by any formula in your report. Custom functions are used just like the built-in functions that come with Crystal Reports.

② **Repository Custom Functions** The functions stored in this category are stored in the repository. To use a repository custom function, it has to be added to the report so that it will become a report custom function.

③ **Formula Fields** The formulas in this category are server based and are the same ones that are in the Field Explorer in the Formula Fields, Parameter Fields, Running Total Fields and Group Name Fields sections.

④ **SQL Expression Fields** The formulas in this category are the same expression fields that are in the SQL Expression Fields section of the Field Explorer. If you create a new expression or modify an existing expression, the SQL Expression Editor will open in the Formula Workshop instead of the Formula Editor. The options in the Report Fields Tree, Functions Tree and Operators Tree will change and display the options that are available for the type of database that the report is using. It has been reported that the SQL Expression Editor may not reflect all of the operators and functions that are really available for certain database types.

⑤ **Selection Formulas** The formulas in this category are created when you use the Select Expert or the selection formula options on the Report menu. You can also create selection formulas in the Formula Workshop. If you click on the Group Selection option, the **GROUP SELECTION FORMULA EDITOR** will open. If you click on the Record Selection option, the **RECORD SELECTION FORMULA EDITOR** will open.

NEW If you click on the Saved Data option, the **SAVED DATA SELECTION FORMULA EDITOR** will open. The only difference that you will notice with these editors is that the title bar of the Formula Workshop will change as shown in Figure 15-10. Compare this title bar to the one shown earlier in Figure 15-3.

Figure 15-10 Record Selection Formula Editor title bar

⑥ **Formatting Formulas** This category has a folder for each section of the report. All of the objects from each section of the report are listed here. Formatting formulas like changing the color, font or font size for objects in the report are stored in this category.

Formula Editor

The Formula Editor is in the Formula Workshop. The contents of each of the trees in the Formula Editor change to show the options that are available for the type of database that the report is based on. The Formula Editor is used to create formulas by double-clicking on the functions, operators and fields that you need to include in the formula. The Formula Editor can create at least 90% of the formulas that you need. The Formula Editor contains the three trees discussed below. You may want to open some of the categories (nodes) in each tree to become familiar with the options.

① The **Report Fields Tree** displays all of the fields that are on the report, including groups, summary fields, running totals, parameters, formulas and the tables that the report uses. This tree is similar to the Field Explorer. You can use any of these fields in a formula.
② The **Functions Tree** contains built-in functions. The functions are divided into categories, which makes it easier to find the function that you need.
③ The **Operators Tree** contains the operators (logical and mathematical) that you can use to create formulas. The operators are grouped by type to make them easier to find. Operators use symbols instead of words.

> When you first open the Formula Workshop, you will not see the Formula Editor. You can do either of the following to open the Formula Editor.

① Select an option in a folder under the Formula Fields, SQL Expression Fields or Selection Formulas in the Workshop Tree.
② Select one of the formula or function options on the New button drop-down list shown earlier in Figure 15-5.

> If you open the Formula Editor using the **FORMULA EDITOR** button on the Select Expert, Crystal Syntax is the only programming language that you can use.

Formula Section

In addition to the three trees, the blank section below the trees is where you type in the formula. Depending on the field selected in the Workshop Tree, the Formula Editor can change to a different editor, because each formula type has its own editor. By default, the font is automatically color coded as follows:

① Green is used for comments that you type in.
② Blue is used for reserved words like functions.

③ Black is used for constants and variables.

You can use the **AUTO COMPLETE** feature in the Formula text window by typing in the first few letters of the function that you need and then press the **CTRL** + **SPACE BAR** keys. You will see a list that has functions that start with the letters that you typed in, as shown in Figure 15-11. If you type in enough letters to only display the function that you want, the drop-down list will not be displayed. Instead, the function will be filled in for you. If you press the CTRL + Space bar keys before typing any letters, you will see all of the functions in the list.

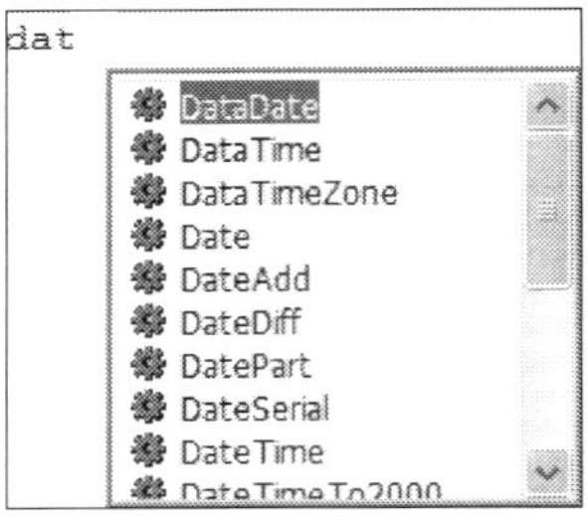

Figure 15-11 Auto complete list

Customizing The Formula Editor

You can customize the Formula Editor by doing any or all of the following:

① You can resize any of the tree sections by dragging the bar illustrated in Figure 15-12.
② Close a tree by clicking on the button to the left of the section that you want to close.
③ Expand a tree by clicking on the button to the left of the section that you want to expand.
④ Make the Formula section longer or shorter by dragging the section bar above it, up or down.

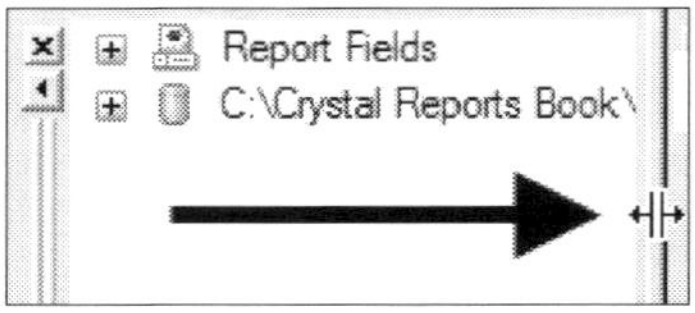

Figure 15-12 Mouse pointer in position to resize a tree

Formula Expert

The Formula Expert shown in Figure 15-13 is used to create custom functions. The functions that you create in the Formula Expert can be used in other reports if they are saved in the repository. By design, the Formula Expert will help you create a formula without having to use the Crystal Reports syntax programming language. While this may sound appealing to those that are new to Crystal Reports or do not want to write code, the Formula Expert only creates formulas that use one custom function. You cannot use the math operators or the Crystal Reports syntax programming language in the Formula Expert.

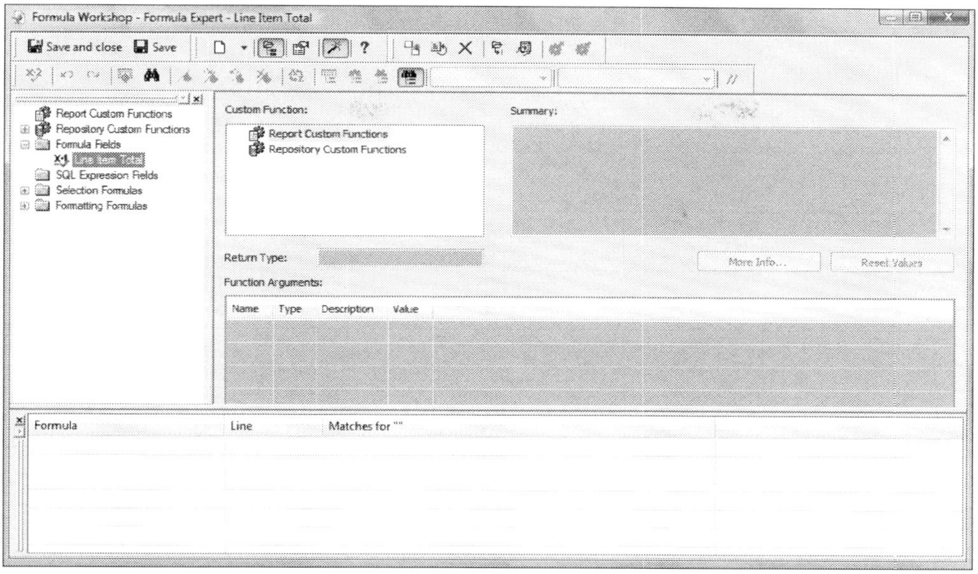

Figure 15-13 Formula Expert

Formula Editor Versus Formula Expert

The main difference between the two is that formulas created in the Formula Editor are saved with the report that they are created in and can only be used in that report. Formulas created in the Formula Expert can be saved as a **CUSTOM FUNCTION** in the repository and can be used in any report. Creating custom functions and using the repository are beyond the scope of this book.

If you find yourself creating the same formula in several reports, copy it to the Formula Expert and save it as a custom function. I often also save the custom functions that I create in a word processing document because I find it easier to get to them that way, instead of logging into the repository. If you work from home, you will understand what I mean. Many will say that this is not a good technique. There are valid reasons not to save custom functions in a document. I will leave it up to you to decide what works best for you in the environment that you will create reports in.

Formula Evaluation Order

Many of the formulas that you will create will use more than one operator. The order that the formula is written in from left to right may not be the order that the formula is calculated or evaluated in. Some operations are processed first, regardless of where they are in the formula. This is known as the **ORDER OF PRECEDENCE**. The formula evaluation order is:

① The portion of the formula that is in parenthesis.

② Exponential.

③ Multiplication and division. (4) (5)
④ Integer division.
⑤ MOD.
⑥ Addition and subtraction. (4)

(4) If the operators (3 and 6 above) are on the same level, they are evaluated from left to right. See the examples below.

Example #1: 3 + 4 / (2 + 19) = 3.19
Example #2: 3 + (4 / 2) + 19 = 24

The first example calculates the (2+19) first, then divides that by 4 and then adds 3.
The second example calculates the (4/2) first, then adds 3 and then adds 19.

(5) In Crystal syntax, percents are evaluated at the same level as multiplication and division.

> You may find it helpful to write the formula on paper and use data in the tables to test the formulas to see if you get the results that you are expecting from the formula. As you saw in the examples above, the same data and operators can produce different results.
>
> I have noticed in the workplace and in classes that I teach that this is one area where many people have a lot of trouble. I think this is because they are not willing to write out the formula and test it prior to opening the Formula Workshop. Yes, I am fully aware that doing this takes more time up front, but experience shows that the more time you spend "preparing", the less time you will spend debugging reports in the future. Trust me, a year from now, you will not remember why you wrote a formula the way that you did <smile>. Keep the following in mind when creating formulas:
>
> ① Formulas must have an equal number of left and right parenthesis.
> ② Arguments must be the same data type.

Formula Naming Conventions

The naming conventions for formulas is free form. You should use as descriptive a name as possible, one that will make sense to you a year from now. The name that you select is what you will see when the formula field is added to the report. Formula names can be up to 256 characters. You can use upper and lower case letters, spaces and the underscore. You should not use characters like the slash, dollar or percent sign in the formula name.

The company that you work for may have naming conventions. You should check to find out. One convention that many companies have is that they do not want spaces in object names. When this is the case, most companies use the underscore in place of spaces in object names.

Create Numeric Formulas

The exercises in this section will teach you how to create numeric formulas.

Exercise 15.1: Create A Formula Field

In this exercise you will modify a report that has product details for opportunities. You will create a formula that will calculate the amount for each item. This is known as the line item amount. The formula is Price * Quantity. This will allow the report to have the correct total amount per opportunity.

1. Save the L15 Formula field report (in the zip file) as `L15.1 Formula field for line item totals.`

2. Click on the **FORMULA FIELDS** option in the Field Explorer, then click the **NEW** button on the Field Explorer toolbar.

3. Type `Line Item Total` in the dialog box shown in Figure 15-14, then click OK.

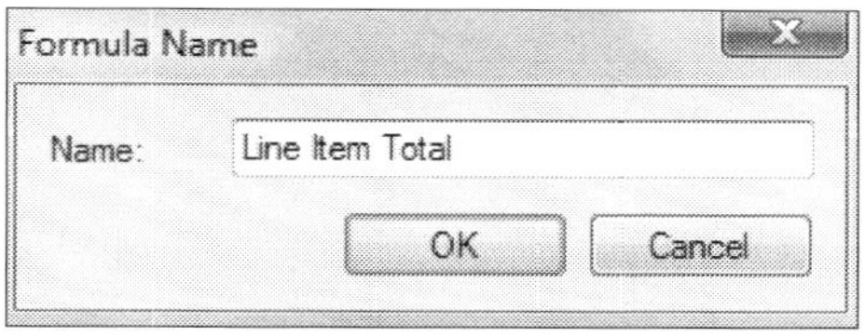

Figure 15-14 Formula Name dialog box

4. In the Report Fields tree, double-click on the Price field in the Product table.

   You should see the field in the Formula section of the Formula Editor, as shown at the bottom of Figure 15-15.

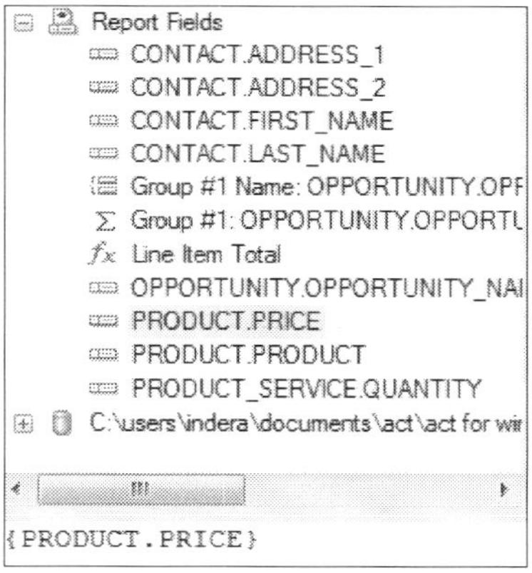

Figure 15-15 Field added to the Formula section

> In addition to double-clicking on a field you can also drag the field to the Formula section.

5. Type a * after the Price field, then double-click on the Quantity field in the Product Service table.

> You can use the **MULTIPLY** Arithmetic operator illustrated in Figure 15-16 instead of typing the operator.

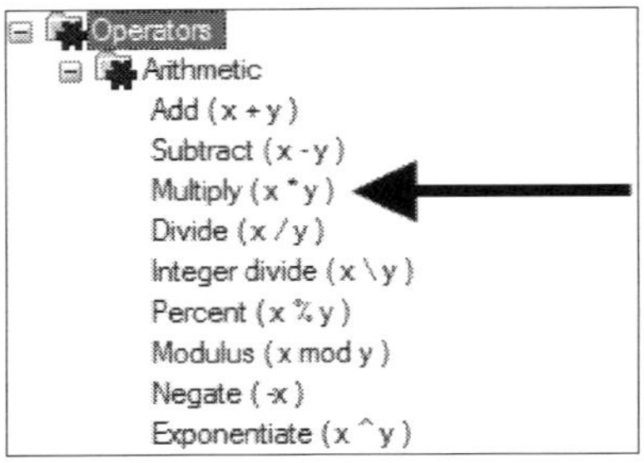

Figure 15-16 Multiply arithmetic operator illustrated

6. Add a blank line above the formula and type the following comment.
   `// This formula calculates the Line Item Total.`
   Your formula should look like the one shown in Figure 15-17.

```
// This formula calculates the Line Item Total
{PRODUCT.PRICE}*{PRODUCT_SERVICE.QUANTITY}
```

Figure 15-17 Line Item Total formula

Notice that the comment line is a different color then the formula line. This is one way to know that you have entered the comment correctly. Comments do not have to go above a formula.

7. Click the **CHECK (X+2)** button on the Expression Editor toolbar.

   You should see the message shown in Figure 15-18.

Figure 15-18 No errors found message

The message shown above in Figure 15-18 means that Crystal Reports did not find a syntax error. This does not mean that the formula will produce the results that you are expecting.

If you do not see the message shown above in Figure 15-18, there is an error in your formula. Check to make sure that your formula looks like the one shown earlier in Figure 15-17.

Figure 15-19 shows one error message that you could see. If there is an error, the flashing insertion bar will be in the location in the formula where Crystal Reports thinks the error is. The part of the formula where the syntax checker stopped understanding the formula will also be highlighted, as illustrated in Figure 15-19. You are not required to fix the error immediately. You can save the formula as is and work on something else. Just don't forget to come back and fix it.

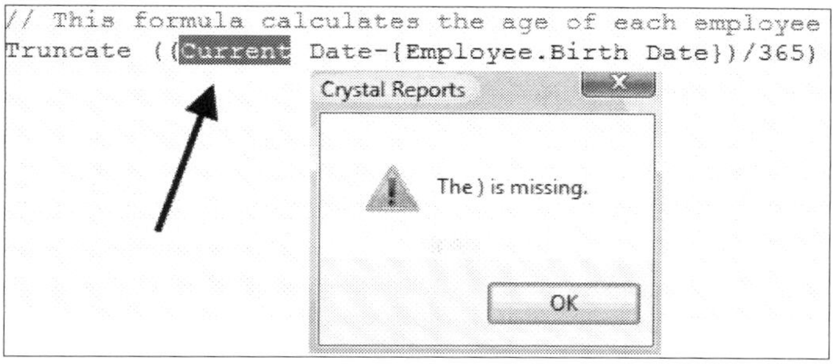

Figure 15-19 Formula error message

8. Click OK, then click the **SAVE AND CLOSE** button.

> If you need to work on another formula, click the **SAVE** button instead of the Save and close button. Doing this will leave the Formula Workshop open. When you save a formula it becomes a field, which you can add to the report or use in another formula.

Using Formula Fields In Reports

You can use formula fields in reports, just like you use fields from a table. Formula fields can be placed in any section of the report. You can create counts and summary fields that are based on formula fields. You can also use formula fields as selection criteria.

Add The Line Item Formula Total Field To The Report

In this part of the exercise you will add the formula field that you just created to the report.

1. Add the Line Item Total field to the report after the Price field. (**Hint**: The field is in the Field Explorer in the Formula Fields section.) The report should look like the one shown in Figure 15-20.

LAST_NAME	ADDRESS_1	ADDRESS_2	PRODUCT	QTY	PRICE	Line Item Total
Goodall	Unit 34	Holystone Ind Estate	ONE Component	3	$2,500.00	7,500.00
				Order Total	**$2,500.00**	
Ives	67a Station Road		TechONE System	1	$12,000.00	12,000.00
				Order Total	**$12,000.00**	
Ives	67a Station Road		Mini Core Replacement	3	$100.00	300.00
				Order Total	**$100.00**	
Goodall	Unit 34	Holystone Ind Estate	Service Contract	2	$2,000.00	4,000.00
				Order Total	**$2,000.00**	

Figure 15-20 L15.1 report

2. Save the changes and leave the report open to complete the next exercise.

As you can see, the order total for each contact is not correct. That is because the order total field is adding the values in the Price field. The order total field should be adding the values in the Line Item Total formula field.

Exercise 15.2: Create A Sales Tax Formula

Many items that you buy require sales tax to be collected. This exercise will show you how to create a sales tax formula. You will create a formula that calculates 6% of the line item total. If all items were taxable, you could create a sales tax formula that used the order total times the sales tax rate. In this exercise, you will modify a report and create a sales tax formula that will use the Line Item Total field instead of the Total field.

> In the real world, the product table would have a field that is used to signify if each product is taxable or not. In that case, you would have to create a conditional formula that checked the field to see if the product is taxable. If it is taxable, then calculate the sales tax for that product.

1. Save the L15.1 report as `L15.2 Sales tax formula`.
2. Create a formula field and name it `Line Item Sales Tax`.
3. Double-click on the Line Item Total field in the Report Fields tree in the Formula Workshop, then type `*.06` at the end of the field.
4. Check the formula to make sure that the syntax is correct. Your formula should look like the one shown in Figure 15-21. Save the formula and close the Formula Workshop.

```
{@Line Item Total}* .06
```

Figure 15-21 Line Item Sales Tax formula

5. Add the Line Item Sales Tax field to the end of the details section, then format the field to have a dollar sign.
6. Change the field title for the Line Item Sales Tax field to `Sales Tax`. Your report should look similar to the one shown in Figure 15-22. Save the changes.

FIRST_NAME	LAST_NAME	ADDRESS_1	ADDRESS_2	PRODUCT	QTY	PRICE	Line Item Total	Sales Tax
Ann	Goodall	Unit 34	Holystone Ind Estate	ONE Component	3	$2,500.00	7,500.00	$450.00
					Order Total	**$2,500.00**		
Angela	Ives	67a Station Road		TechONE System	1	$12,000.00	12,000.00	$720.00
					Order Total	**$12,000.00**		
Angela	Ives	67a Station Road		Mini Core Replacement	3	$100.00	300.00	$18.00
					Order Total	**$100.00**		

Figure 15-22 L15.2 report

Exercise 15.3: Use A Formula Field As Selection Criteria

Earlier you learned that you can use a formula field as selection criteria. In this exercise you will use the Line Item Total formula field to only display line items that have an amount between $1,000 and $5,000.

1. Save the L15.1 report as `L15.3 Formula field used as selection criteria`.

2. Create the selection criteria for the Line Item Total formula field. The report should look like the one shown in Figure 15-23. There should be 194 records on the report. Save the changes and close the report.

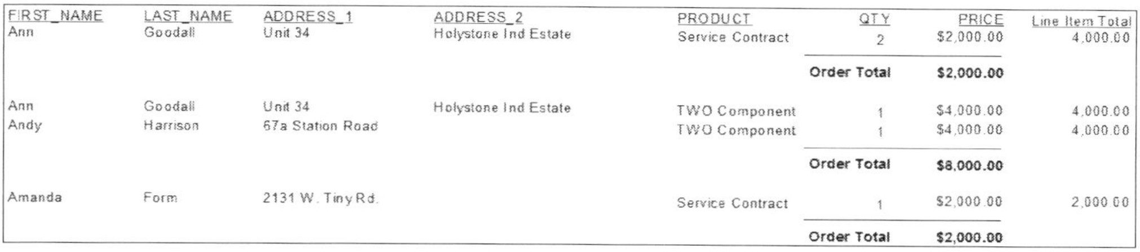

FIRST_NAME	LAST_NAME	ADDRESS_1	ADDRESS_2	PRODUCT	QTY	PRICE	Line Item Total
Ann	Goodall	Unit 34	Holystone Ind Estate	Service Contract	2	$2,000.00	4,000.00
					Order Total	$2,000.00	
Ann	Goodall	Unit 34	Holystone Ind Estate	TWO Component	1	$4,000.00	4,000.00
Andy	Harrison	67a Station Road		TWO Component	1	$4,000.00	4,000.00
					Order Total	$8,000.00	
Amanda	Form	2131 W. Tiny Rd.		Service Contract	1	$2,000.00	2,000.00
					Order Total	$2,000.00	

Figure 15-23 L15.3 report

Create String Formulas

The exercises in this section will teach you how to create formulas that use String fields or literals. The most used string formulas are used to convert date and numeric fields to text, select specific portions of a field and trim fields. A common string formula that is used is one that will concatenate (combine) the first and last name fields. Names are usually stored in two or more fields in a table. There are several string formula operators and functions that you can use, as explained in Tables 15-5 and 15-6.

Operator	What It Does
+ or &	These are known as concatenation operators. They are used to combine text fields. The plus sign requires that all arguments be string fields. The plus sign allows for custom formatting. Crystal Reports will automatically convert every argument to a string when the ampersand (&) operator is used. This means that you can use fields with different data types if you use the ampersand.
[ ]	Subscript operators are used to select specific characters from a text field.
" " or ' '	Quotes will treat the text inside of them as a literal. If a string or text field contains numeric data and you need to use it in a formula, you have to put the numeric data in quotes.
If Then Else	This operator allows different actions to be taken based on a condition. (6)

Table 15-5 String operators explained

Date/Time literals must be in one of these formats: #6/24/2005# or #June 24, 2005#.

Keep in mind that while the + (plus sign) operator is used to join text and data fields, it does not add a space between the fields that are being joined. You have to type + " " + to add a space between the fields that you are joining. There is a space between the quotes in the syntax above.

Function	What It Does
Is Null	This function checks to see if a field has a value. It is often used with the If...Then...Else operator. If the function is used alone, it returns a value of True or False (Boolean). (6)
Length (str)	This function counts the number of characters in a string. It can be used to determine if a value in a field is a certain length. (6)
Lower Case (str)	This function converts the text to all lower case letters. Use **LOWERCASE** for Crystal Syntax. Use **LCASE** for Basic Syntax.
Picture (str, picture)	This function is used to format a string field. This is similar to the "mask" feature found in some database software packages.
To Text	This function is used to convert non text fields like Date, Number and Currency to a text string. This function can have multiple arguments, as shown in Figure 15-24. The only argument that requires a value is X.
Trim (str)	This function removes spaces before and after the data in a string argument. Use **TRIMLEFT** if you only want to remove spaces to the left of the string argument. Use **TRIMRIGHT** if you only want to remove spaces to the right of the string argument.
Upper Case (str)	This function converts the text to all upper case letters. Use **UPPERCASE** for Crystal Syntax. Use **UCASE** for Basic Syntax.

Table 15-6 String functions explained

(6) You will learn how to use this operator in Lesson 16.

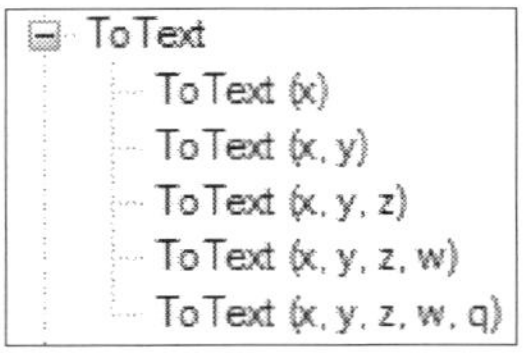

Figure 15-24 To Text functions

Exercise 15.4: Combine Two String Fields

Earlier in this lesson you modified an opportunity report. That report would look better if the first and last names were closer together. This produces the same result as dragging one field into another. One reason that you would write code to combine the name fields is if you only needed to combine fields when a certain condition was met. Another reason to write code to combine fields is if there is a possibility that at least one of the fields is null.

1. Save the L15.1 report as `L15.4 Combine string fields`.
2. Create a formula field and name it `Full Name`, then add the First Name field from the Contact table to the Formula section.
3. Click after the First Name field and type `+ " " +` This will add a space after the First Name. Make sure that there is a space between the quotes.

4. Add the Last Name field to the formula.

5. Add a blank line above the formula and type `// This formula combines 2 fields`, then check the formula for errors. The formula should look like the one shown in Figure 15-25. Save the formula and close the Formula Workshop.

```
//This formula combines 2 fields
{CONTACT.FIRST_NAME}+ " " +{CONTACT.LAST_NAME}
```

Figure 15-25 String formula

Add The Full Name Formula Field To The Report

1. Delete the First and Last name fields in the report, then add the Full Name field in place of the two fields that you just deleted.

2. Change the field heading to `Contact`.

3. Move all of the other fields to the left. The report should look like the one shown in Figure 15-26. Save the changes and leave the report open to complete the next exercise.

Contact	ADDRESS_1	ADDRESS_2	PRODUCT	QTY	PRICE	Line Item Total
Ann Goodall	Unit 34	Holystone Ind Estate	ONE Component	3	$2,500.00	7,500.00
				Order Total	$2,500.00	

Figure 15-26 L15.4 report

Exercise 15.5: Use The Subscript Operator

The subscript operator is used to extract specific characters in a field based on their position in the field. In Exercise 15.4 you learned how to combine the first and last name fields. If you needed to modify that formula to only display the first letter of the first name, you would use the subscript operator. The subscript [1] means to select the first character in the field from the left. Subscript [3] means to select the third character in the field from the left. In this exercise, you will add the subscript operator to an existing formula.

1. Save the L15.4 report as `L15.5 Subscript`.

2. Modify the Full Name formula so that it looks like the one shown in Figure 15-27.

```
// This formula combines 2 fields and only uses the first letter
// of the First Name field
{CONTACT.FIRST_NAME} [1] + " " +{CONTACT.LAST_NAME}
```

Figure 15-27 Subscript formula

3. Make the Full Name field and heading smaller, then move the other fields to the left.

4. Save the changes. The report should look like the one shown in Figure 15-28. Notice that only the first letter of the first name is displayed. Close the report.

Contact	ADDRESS_1	ADDRESS_2	PRODUCT	QTY	PRICE	Line Item Total
A Goodall	Unit 34	Holystone Ind Estate	ONE Component	3	$2,500.00	7,500.00
				Order Total	$2,500.00	

Figure 15-28 L15.5 Subscript report

Exercise 15.6: Combine A Text And Numeric Field

In the reports that you have created with totals, you created a text object for the title of the summary field. If you had trouble either getting the text object and total field to line up or getting the two fields to be close together, this exercise will show you how to combine these fields using a formula, which means that you will not have to align the field and text object.

> If the numeric field that you will use needs to be formatted, you should not combine it with a text field because text fields cannot be formatted with numeric formatting options.

1. Save the L10.1 report as `L15.6 Combine text and numeric fields`.

2. Create a formula field and name it `Total Field`.

3. Add the comment `This formula combines text with a numeric field`.

4. Type `"Total # of contacts in state - "` in the Formula section.

5. Open the **STRINGS** operators node and drag the **CONCATENATE (X&Y)** operator illustrated on the right in Figure 15-29 to the formula.

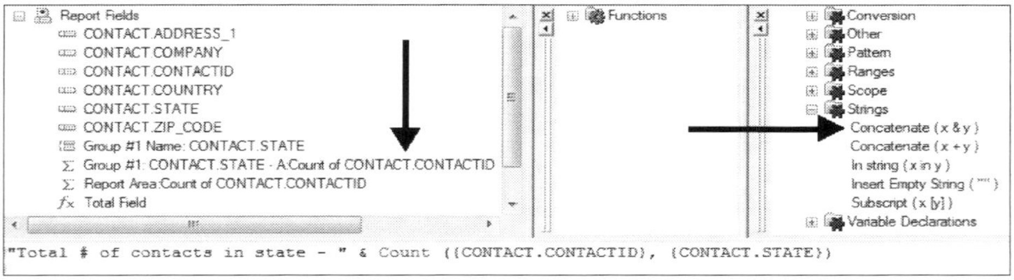

Figure 15-29 Formula Workshop options

6. Add the Group 1 Contact ID field illustrated above in Figure 15-29 to the formula, then check the formula for errors. Save the formula and close the Formula Workshop.

Add The Total Formula Field To The Report

1. Delete everything in the group footer section.

2. Add the Total Field formula field to the group footer section. The bottom of page 1 in the report should look like the one shown in Figure 15-30. Notice that there is a decimal point in the number. You cannot format the number. Save the changes and close the report.

	Circle Photography	Unit 43 Dobson Ind Est	TS14 5QY	United Kingdom
	Superior Technologies Ltd	52 Billingham Road	TS45 9QA	United Kingdom
Total # of contacts in state - 35.00				
AL				
	Finch Legal Aid	2570 S Alabama Ave	36461	United States
Total # of contacts in state - 1.00				
Atiu Island				
	Brock, Lathers and Freedman	FLC Lane		Cook Islands
Total # of contacts in state - 1.00				

Figure 15-30 L15.6 report

Use Functions In String Formulas

You may have the need to combine data that is stored in different data types or format data differently then it is stored in the table. The next two exercises will show you how to incorporate functions in string formulas.

Exercise 15.7: Use The Picture Function

The phone numbers in the Contact table are stored in several formats, as shown in Figure 15-31.

Notice that there are also international phone numbers in the table. When you want to print US phone numbers, they will look better if they all printed like this **(704) 555-5555**. In this exercise you will use the Picture function to format phone numbers in the Contact table.

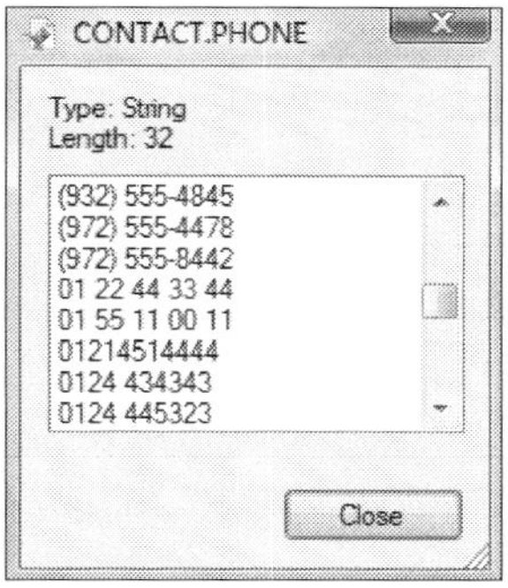

Figure 15-31 Phone numbers stored in the table

1. Create a new report. Add the Contact table, but do not add any fields to the report. Save the report as `L15.7 Picture function`.

2. Create a formula field and name it `Contact Phone`, then add the comment `This formula formats the Phone Number field` to the formula.

3. Display the Contact table in the Report Fields tree.

4. Open the **ADDITIONAL FUNCTIONS** category in the Functions tree, then open the **SAMP1** category and double-click on the **PICTURE** function illustrated in Figure 15-32.

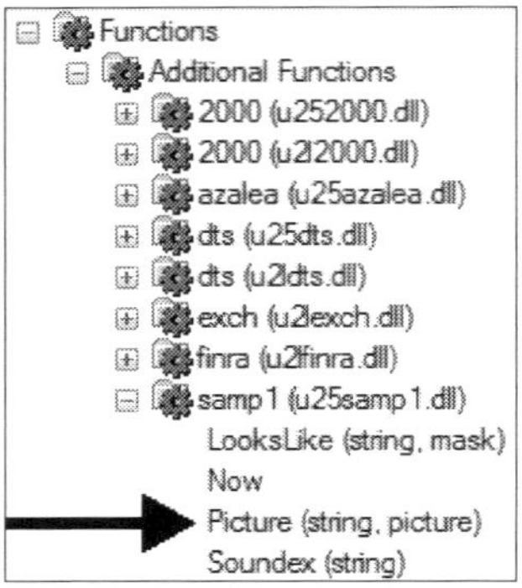

Figure 15-32 Picture function illustrated

5. Double-click on the Phone field in the Report Fields tree, then click after the comma in the formula and type `"(XXX)XXXXXXX"`. Your formula should look like the one shown in Figure 15-33. Save the formula and leave the Formula Workshop open to complete the next part of the exercise.

```
// This formula formats the Phone Number field
Picture ({CONTACT.PHONE},"(XXX)XXXXXXX")
```

Figure 15-33 Phone number formula

> The brackets { } in a formula are used for data fields. The parenthesis ( ) are used to control the order that the formula is evaluated in.

In Figure 15-31 shown earlier, you saw some of the phone number formats that are stored in the Contact table. All of the phone numbers will not work with the mask that you just created in the formula. In order to be able to accommodate international phone numbers, the formula would have to be modified to also use the **LENGTH** function and have another mask to accommodate phone numbers of a different length. This is known as conditional formatting, which you will learn how to do in the next lesson.

Use The ToText Function

The ToText function is one of the more popular functions. It is used to convert dates, numbers and more to a string/text field. In this part of the exercise you will combine the Last Years Purchases and Contact fields. Yes, I know that is a strange combination, but there are very few numeric fields in the ACT! demo database. In order to combine a numeric and string field, you have to convert the numeric field to text. The **TOTEXT** function is used to do this.

1. Create a formula field and name it `Contact & Purchase`, then add the comment `This formula combines the Contact and Last Years Purchases fields.`

2. Open the Strings category in the Functions tree and double-click on the ToText (x,y) function.

3. Click inside of the parenthesis and add the Last Yrs Purchases field before the comma.

4. Click after the comma in the formula and type a zero. The zero means that the number should not display any decimal places, if there are any in the field.

5. Click outside of the formula on the right and type + " - " +, then add the Contact field. Your formula should look like the one shown in Figure 15-34. Save the formula and close the Formula Workshop.

```
// This formula combines the Contact and Last Years Purchases fields
ToText ({CONTACT.Last Yrs Purchases},0 )+ " - " +{CONTACT.CONTACT}
```

Figure 15-34 Contact and Purchase formula

6. Add both of the formula fields to the details section of the report.

   The report should look like the one shown in Figure 15-35.

   Save the changes and close the report.

Contact & Purchase	Contact Phone
1,252 - Lames Jawson	((50)3) 555-2232
	((21)2) 546-7890
	((65)0) 780-1202
	((21)2) 555-2485
	((72)7) 555-4578
	(315)-988-6700
	(012)4 434343

Figure 15-35 L15.7 report

The reason that there are phone numbers without names and purchase amounts is because more than likely, the Last years purchase field is empty for the record. I say that because most records have the contact name filled in.

As you can see, phone numbers that already had formatting were re-formatted. You will run into problems like this when data is allowed to be entered inconsistently and if there are no data entry rules.

Using The Ampersand To Concatenate Strings

In the exercise that you just completed, you used the ToText function and the plus sign operator to concatenate string fields. The benefit of using the ToText function with the plus sign is that you can control the formatting. If you do not need to control the formatting, use the ampersand operator instead of the plus sign.

Formatting Strings With A Mask

In Exercise 15.7 you formatted a phone number field with the Picture function, which used a mask to format the field. Masks use characters including x, d, m and y as placeholders for the data, which determines how the data will be formatted when it is converted to a string. Table 15-7 lists some of the mask placeholders that are used the most for date fields. Table 15-8 provides placeholder examples for the date 6/1/09.

Placeholder	Description
d	Day of the month in numeric format without a leading zero.
dd	Day of the month in numeric format with a leading zero if necessary.
dddd	Name of the day spelled out.
M	Month in numeric format without a leading zero.
MM	Month in numeric format with a leading zero if necessary.
MMMM	Name of the month spelled out.
y	Last two digits of the year.
yyyy	Four digit year.

Table 15-7 Placeholder options

Mask	Displays
dd, MM, yy	01, 06, 09
MMMM dd yyyy	June 01 2009
dddd MMMM d, yyyy	Wednesday June 1, 2009
M, d, yy	6, 1, 09

Table 15-8 Mask examples

Date Functions

Table 15-9 provides an overview of some of the date functions. The exercises in this section will show you how to create some of the more popular date formulas using functions.

Function	Description
ChrW(x)	Returns the character that represents the Unicode value of (x).
CurrentDate	Uses the system date on your computer.
DateAdd	Is used to increment a date field by intervals, including days, weeks, months and years.
DateDiff	Calculates the difference between the start and end dates in the function. (7)
Day	Extracts the day from a Date or Date/Time field and returns a whole number.
Month	Extracts the month from a Date or Date/Time field and returns a whole number.
ToText	Is used to format any or all parts of a date field. This function is also used to convert a date field to a text value.
Year	Extracts the year from a Date or Date/Time field and returns a whole number.

Table 15-9 Date functions explained

(7)

> The DateDiff function has arguments that you can use to determine how you want to calculate the difference between two date fields. For a full list of arguments, type `DateDiff` on the Index tab of the Help application. The most common arguments are:
>
> **D** will calculate the difference in days.
> **M** will calculate the difference in months.
> **YYYY** will calculate the difference in years.

Exercise 15.8: Create A Date Formula To Calculate The Days To Close Time

In this exercise you will create a formula to find out how long it is between the day an opportunity record is created and when the opportunity was closed. I am sure by now that you have seen the Days Open field and are wondering what the difference is between that field and the formula field that you will create in this exercise. The Create Date field contains the date the opportunity record was created. I am not 100% sure, but the Open Date field is when the initial contact was made or will be made. I noticed that in the demo database, that some dates in the Open Date field are in the future.

1. Save the L9.3 report as `L15.8 Calculate days to close`.
2. Create a formula field and name it `Days to close`.
3. Open the Date & Time function node.
4. Expand the **DATEDIFF** function node, then double-click on the first DateDiff function.
5. Type `"d"` before the first comma in the formula.
6. Add the Create Date field (in the Opportunity table) to the formula after the first comma, then add the Actual Close field to the formula after the second comma. Your formula should look like the one shown in Figure 15-36. Check the formula for errors, then save the formula and close the Formula Workshop.

```
DateDiff ("d",{OPPORTUNITY.CREATE_DATE} ,{OPPORTUNITY.ACTUAL_CLOSE_DATE} )
```

Figure 15-36 Days to close formula

Add The Days To Close Formula Field To The Report

1. Delete the Opportunity Name and Days Open fields, then move the fields starting with the Create Date field to the left.
2. Change the Actual Close Date heading to Close Date.
3. Delete the existing selection criteria, then create criteria that the status is Closed-Lost or Closed-Won.
4. Sort the report by Create Date in ascending order.

5. Add the Days to close formula field to the end of the report and format it so that it does not have any decimal places. The report should look like the one shown in Figure 15-37. Save the changes and close the report.

CONTACT	COMPANY	CREATE_DATE	TOTAL	STATUS	CLOSE_DATE	Days To Close
Gavin Dillerstone	Ace Pet Store Franchis	5/15/07	12,000.00	Closed - Won	11/27/09	927
Jackie Jorgensen	Ace Pet Store Franchis	5/15/07	12,000.00	Closed - Won	8/31/07	108
Colleen McCarthy	Ace Pet Store Franchis	5/15/07	12,000.00	Closed - Won	4/14/08	335
Angela Ives	A1 Services of UK	5/15/07	12,000.00	Closed - Won	4/13/09	699
Kristi Cameron	American Dreams	5/15/07	10,000.00	Closed - Won	8/29/09	837

Figure 15-37 L15.8 report

A zero in the Days to close field means that the opportunity was closed within 24 hours of when it was created. Depending on the time the opportunity was created, the Actual Close Date could be the next day and still have a zero in the Days to close field because the opportunity was closed in less than 24 hours. Remember that the fields used in this formula are Date/Time fields.

Exercise 15.9: Calculate The Contacts Age

One of the more popular date functions will allow you to calculate a persons age if you have their date of birth. In this exercise you will create an contact birthday list report. You will create a formula to calculate the age of the contacts. In the Formula Overview section earlier in this lesson, I listed four reasons why certain types of data are not saved in a table. A persons age is a good example of the type of data that should not be saved in a table. The reason is because the age changes every year. This would mean that the field would have to be updated once a year on each persons birthday. This is why it is best to calculate the age, each time the report is run.

1. Create a new report and add the following fields from the Contact table: Contact, Title, Department and Birth Date.

2. Remove the time from the Birth Date field, then save the report as `L15.9 Calculate age formula`.

3. Create a formula field and save it as `Age`.

4. Add the Current Date function from the Date and Time category to the Age formula, then type a – (minus sign).

5. Add the Birth Date field to the formula and check the formula for errors. Save the formula and close the Formula Workshop.

Modify The Report

1. Add the Age formula field to the report after the Birth Date field.

2. Sort the report in ascending order by the Last Name, then First Name field. The report should look like the one shown in Figure 15-38.

CONTACT	TITLE	DEPARTMENT	BIRTH DATE	Age
George Agen	Advanced Technician		06/24/1959	18,426.71
Ashley Allan	VP of Sales		05/30/2002	2,745.79
Charlie Allnut	Captain			
Ernst Anderson	Vice President of US Operati	Sales	06/22/1964	16,601.79
Gracie Anderson	Music and Lighting Coordinat	Drums and Space	01/04/1968	15,310.71
Thomas Andrews	President/CEO			

Figure 15-38 Age field added to the report

Notice that not all of the contacts have a birth date. Depending on your needs you may want to exclude records if the birth date field is blank or you could contact the people and get their birth date.

Modify The Age Formula

As you can see, the formula did not return the age in the format that you expected. The age shown on the report is in days, not years. This is because the Current Date function calculates in days. The formula will have to be modified so that the age is displayed in years.

1. Right-click on the Age formula field in the report and select Edit Formula.

You may be thinking that the only thing that you have to do is click after the Birth Date field and type /365 and the age would be converted to years. Just adding this to the formula will not calculate the age in years. Instead, you will see the message shown in Figure 15-39.

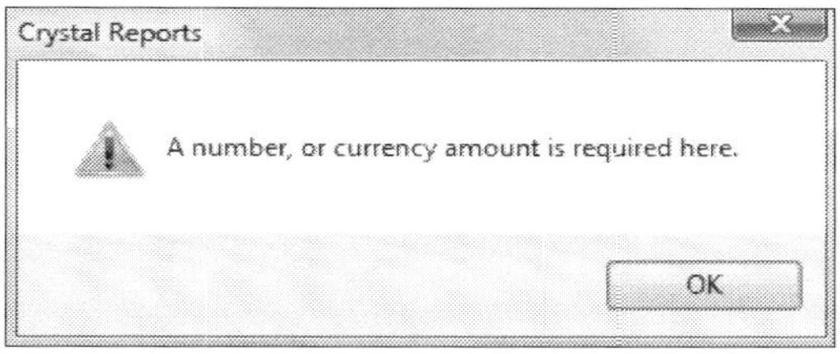

Figure 15-39 Calculation warning message

The reason that you see this message is because you are trying to divide the Birth Date field which is a Date/Time field by 365, which is a numeric field. As you learned earlier, arguments must be the same data type to use them in a formula. This is not the case in this formula.

Another reason that this formula will not work is because of the formula evaluation order. The evaluation order must be forced in this formula. The way to force it is by adding parenthesis around the portion of the formula that has to be evaluated first. The order needed is to force the Birth Date to be subtracted from the Current Date **BEFORE** the division takes place.

2. Type parenthesis around the formula, then type `/365` after the last parenthesis and check the formula.

Use The Truncate Function

When you previewed the report you saw that the age field has a decimal place, as shown earlier in Figure 15-38. The decimal place represents part of the year. This is not what you want. The Truncate function will remove that portion of the field.

1. Add the comment `This formula calculates the contacts age.`
2. Expand the Math function node, then expand the Truncate function node.
3. Click at the beginning of the formula, then double-click on the Truncate (x) function.

> **TRUNCATE(X)** truncates a field. **TRUNCATE (X, #PLACES)** determines how many decimal places to keep before truncation occurs.

4. After the truncate function, you will see parenthesis. Delete the right parenthesis and add it to the end of the formula. Your formula should look like the one shown in Figure 15-40. Check the formula for errors, then save and close the formula.

```
// This formula calculates the contacts age
Truncate ((CurrentDate-{CONTACT.BIRTH_DATE})/365)
```

Figure 15-40 Age formula

5. Sort the report by last name, then by first name.
6. Format the Age field so that it does not have any decimal places. The report should look like the one shown in Figure 15-41.

CONTACT	TITLE	DEPARTMENT	BIRTH DATE	Age
George Agen	Advanced Technician		06/24/1959	50
Ashley Allan	VP of Sales		05/30/2002	7
Charlie Allnut	Captain			
Ernst Anderson	Vice President of US Operations	Sales	06/22/1964	45
Gracie Anderson	Music and Lighting Coordinator	Drums and Space	01/04/1968	41
Thomas Andrews	President/CEO			

Figure 15-41 L15.9 report

> You may see a different age for some or all of the contacts. This will happen if you run the report after a contacts birthday has past. For example, I ran the report shown above in Figure 15-41 in December 2009. I ran the report shown in Figure 15-42 in January 2010 a month later. Notice that the age for some of the contacts has changed. That is because some people had a birthday since I ran the report shown above.

CONTACT	TITLE	DEPARTMENT	BIRTH DATE	Age
George Agen	Advanced Technician		06/24/1959	50
Ashley Allan	VP of Sales		05/30/2002	7
Charlie Allnut	Captain			
Ernst Anderson	Vice President of US Operati	Sales	06/22/1964	45
Gracie Anderson	Music and Lighting Coordinat	Drums and Space	01/04/1968	42

Figure 15-42 L15.9 report run a month later

> If you need to use the same formula in more than one report, you can copy it from one report and paste it in another report.

Run-Time Errors

No one likes to talk about errors, but they do happen. Earlier in this lesson you learned about syntax errors and that if a formula passes the syntax checker, errors can still occur. These errors occur when the report is run (previewed). Run-time errors usually occur when a data type being used is not what the formula expected.

Examples of run-time errors include null values in a field or formula that returns zero (Divide By Zero). You can debug these errors using the **CALL STACK**. If you get a run-time error, you will see the error message in the Formula Workshop which will display the formula that triggered the error.

The call stack shown on the left of Figure 15-43 shows the formula that has the error. You will also see all of the fields in the formula and the values in the field of the record that was being processed when the run-time error occurred.

The value in the field is displayed after the field name, as illustrated. Being able to see the data may help you figure out what caused the error.

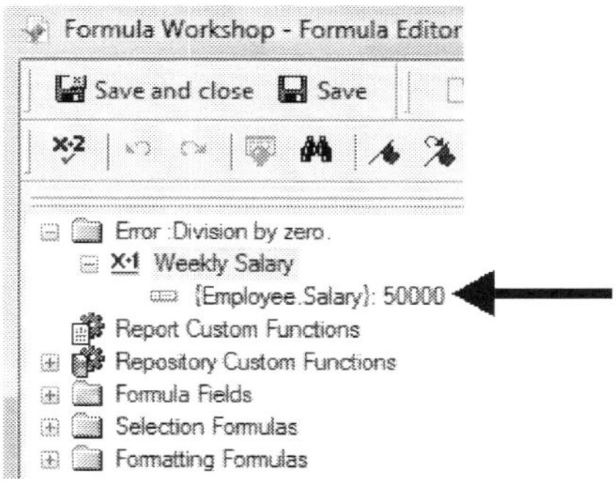

Figure 15-43 Run-time error call stack illustrated

CONDITIONAL FORMATTING

After completing the exercises in this lesson you will be able to use the following tools and techniques to format fields and sections in a report.

- ☑ Highlighting Expert
- ☑ Apply conditional formats to fields
- ☑ Create If Then Else statements
- ☑ Suppressing fields and sections
- ☑ Section Expert

LESSON 16

Conditional Formatting Overview

In Lesson 7 you learned basic formatting techniques. In Lesson 15 you learned that data could be formatted or manipulated using formulas and functions. The techniques covered in those two lessons will handle a large percent of your report formatting needs. What you may have noticed is that the formatting that you have learned to create so far is applied to every detail (or group) record. There will be times when the report does not need or require the same formatting to be applied to every detail record.

There are formatting techniques that you can use that will give you the option of applying the formatting only if a condition is met. This is known as **CONDITIONAL FORMATTING**. Examples of conditional formatting include the following:

① Highlighting records when the data in one field is greater than a constant value.
② Highlighting records with a specific color that have data missing in a field.
③ Check the value or length of a field and apply different formatting, depending on the value or length of the field.
④ Print a background color on every other detail record on the report.
⑤ Formatting one field with a border based on the value in another field.

The formatting techniques that you learned in Lesson 7 are known as **ABSOLUTE FORMATTING** because they are applied to every occurrence of the object. Conditional formatting starts off as absolute formatting, but goes a step further by setting up criteria to determine when the formatting should be applied.

> Conditional formatting is created using the Format Editor. Conditional formatting overrides absolute formatting that is created with the Format Editor. You can set the "on" and "off" properties conditionally.

There are two types of properties that conditional formatting can be applied to. The property type determines the type of conditional formula that has to be created.

① **On-Off** properties like the Can Grow option or any option that has a check box on the Format Editor. On-off properties require **BOOLEAN** formulas.
② **Multiple choice** properties like the border line style option, which is a drop-down list, on the Line tab of the Format Editor. Multiple choice properties require If Then Else or Select Case statements.

Highlighting Expert Overview

The Highlighting Expert is used to easily create and apply font, background and border conditional formatting to fields on a report without having to write any code. It is a scaled down version of the Format Editor. The downside is that it does not provide a lot of options. The Highlighting Expert is used to bring attention to certain values on the report by changing at least one of the following:

☑ Font style
☑ Font color

☑ Background color
☑ Border style

> Conditional formatting that is created by the Highlighting Expert cannot be modified in the Formula Editor.

An example of when to use the Highlighting Expert would be if you wanted to highlight the order amount if it is more than $1,000.

Like many of the other experts, there are three ways to open the Highlighting Expert dialog box, shown in Figure 16-1.

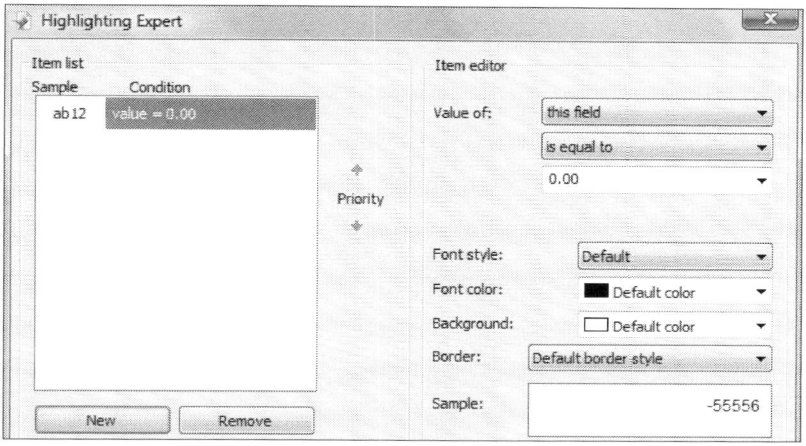

Figure 16-1 Highlighting Expert dialog box

① Right-click on the field that needs to meet a condition and select Highlighting Expert.
② Click the Highlighting button on the Experts toolbar.
③ Format ⇒ Highlighting Expert.

As shown above in Figure 16-1, the Highlighting Expert has the following two sections:

① **Item List** Displays the conditional formatting formulas created by the Highlighting Expert for the field that is selected. The **CONDITION** column displays the formula that will create the formatting.
② **Item Editor** Is used to create and view the conditional formatting formulas. The **SAMPLE** section that will let you see the highlighting that will be applied.

Item List Section Options

① The **PRIORITY** buttons are used to change the order that the highlighting will be applied. Priority is important when there are multiple conditions set for the same field. For example, if you want to set the background of a date field to green if it is greater than 1/1/07 and another condition to place a border around the same date field if the date is greater than 6/24/08. If the date is 1/24/09, which of the two formatting conditions should be applied to the date field? If the greater than 1/1/07 is the first condition, all of the records that are greater than 1/1/07 would have a green background applied, even if the date is greater than 6/24/08. In some instances, multiple conditions can conflict. This is why setting a priority is important. It is how Crystal Reports resolves the conflicts.
② The **REMOVE** button will delete the highlighting criteria that is displayed in the Item List.

Item Editor Section Options

① The **VALUE OF** drop-down list contains the fields, formulas and functions that are on the report or that are connected to the report, as shown in Figure 16-2.

These are the fields that you can use to create the conditions for.

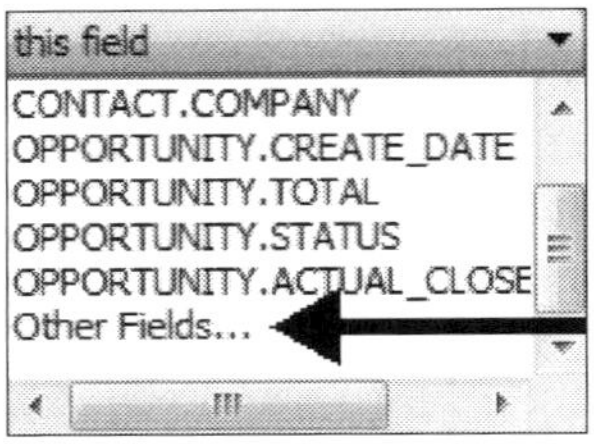

Figure 16-2 Field selection drop-down list

The **THIS FIELD** option in the Value of field lets you use the field that was selected before the Highlighting Expert was opened. Selecting a different field then the one that was selected prior to opening the Highlighting Expert means that you want to apply the formatting to the field selected prior to opening the Highlighting Expert, but you want the condition to be set based on the value in a different field.

The last option in the drop-down list, **OTHER FIELDS** opens the Choose Field dialog box, which is used to select another field from any data source connected to the report to use to create highlighting criteria for.

② The **COMPARISON** drop-down list is the second field in the Item Editor section.

It contains the selection criteria options shown in Figure 16-3. You can use these operators to select which records will be highlighted.

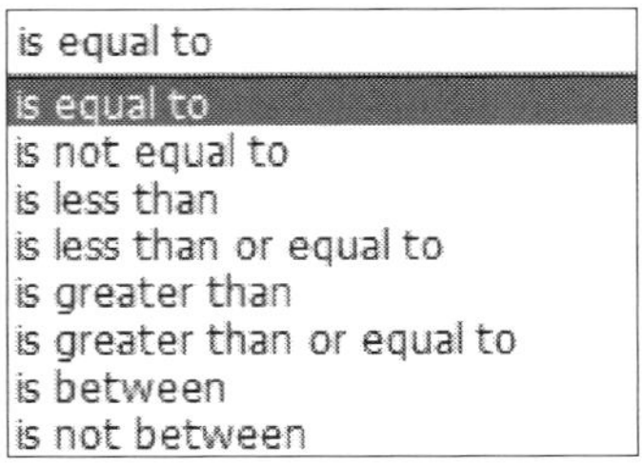

Figure 16-3 Comparison drop-down list operators

③ The **COMPARE TO** drop-down list is the third field from the top. It displays the values in the field that you select in the Value of drop-down list. This is like the Browse Data window. You can also type in the value that you want.

The Highlighting Expert does not work with **PARAMETER FIELDS**. The Highlighting Expert can only compare data in a table to set the conditional formatting.

The Highlighting Expert is similar to the Select Expert. One difference that I noticed is that the Highlighting Expert does not have as many operators as the Select Expert.

Create Reports That Highlight Data

The first two exercises in this lesson will show you how to highlight data using the Highlighting Expert.

Exercise 16.1: Use The Background Highlighting Option

In this exercise you will modify a report to highlight the background of the Days to close field for opportunities that were not closed in 365 days or less.

1. Save the L15.8 report as `L16.1 Highlight days to close conditionally.`

2. Right-click on the Days to close formula field and select **HIGHLIGHTING EXPERT**, then click the **NEW** button on the Highlighting Expert dialog box.

3. Open the Comparison drop-down list and select **IS GREATER THAN**, then type `365` in the next field.

4. Select **GRAY** as the background color.

   You should have the options selected that are shown in Figure 16-4.

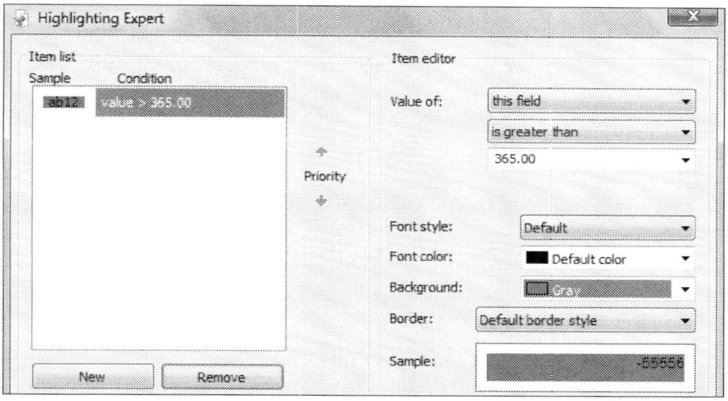

Figure 16-4 Highlighting options

5. Click OK, then save the changes. The report should look like the one shown in Figure 16-5. Close the report.

CONTACT	COMPANY	CREATE DATE	TOTAL	STATUS	CLOSE DATE	Days To Close
Gavin Dillerstone	Ace Pet Store Franchis	5/15/07	12,000.00	Closed - Won	11/27/09	927
Jackie Jorgensen	Ace Pet Store Franchis	5/15/07	12,000.00	Closed - Won	8/31/07	108
Colleen McCarthy	Ace Pet Store Franchis	5/15/07	12,000.00	Closed - Won	4/14/08	335
Angela Ives	A1 Services of UK	5/15/07	12,000.00	Closed - Won	4/13/09	699
Kristi Cameron	American Dreams	5/15/07	10,000.00	Closed - Won	8/29/09	837
Gavin Dillerstone	Ace Pet Store Franchis	5/20/07	4,000.00	Closed - Won	7/30/10	1167
Kristi Cameron	American Dreams	5/20/07	2,500.00	Closed - Won	4/18/08	334
Mitch Brenner	Bodega's Bodacious Bi	5/20/07	12,000.00	Closed - Won	8/30/09	833
Jane Bellamy	Boomers Artworx	5/20/07	7,500.00	Closed - Won	3/30/10	1045
Jane Bellamy	Boomers Artworx	5/20/07	12,000.00	Closed - Lost	7/29/10	1166

Figure 16-5 L16.1 report with conditional field background highlighting

Exercise 16.2: Use One Field To Highlight Another Field And Set A Priority

More than one highlighting condition can be created for a field. You can also use one field to highlight another field. In this exercise you will create two conditions for the same field and set a priority for the conditions. You will create the following conditions:

① Make the quantity bold if it is greater than or equal to three.
② Italicize the quantity if the price is greater than $3000.

Create The Quantity Is Greater Than Condition

1. Save the L15 Formula Field report as `L16.2 Use multiple conditions to highlight a field.`
2. Delete the group information.
3. Right-click on the Quantity field and open the Highlighting Expert, then click New.
4. Open the Comparison drop-down list and select **IS GREATER THAN OR EQUAL TO**, then type a `3` in the next field.
5. Select the bold font style. Leave the Highlighting Expert dialog box open to complete the next part of the exercise.

Create The Price Is Greater Than Condition

1. Click New, then open the Value Of drop-down list and select the Price field.
2. Open the Comparison drop-down list and select **IS GREATER THAN**, then type `3000` in the next field.
3. Select the bold italic font style, then select red as the font color. Leave the Highlighting Expert dialog box open to complete the next part of the exercise.

Set The Priority

There could be a lot of records that meet both of the conditions that you just created. Unless it doesn't matter which order the conditions are applied to the field, you should set a priority. In this exercise, the most important criteria is for the Price field.

1. Click on the Price condition in the **ITEM LIST**, then click the (Priority Up) button.

   You should have the options selected that are shown in Figure 16-6.

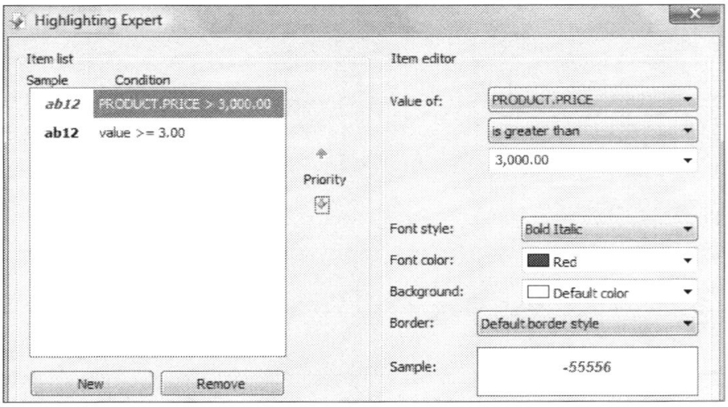

Figure 16-6 Highlighting conditions

2. Click OK and save the changes. The report should look like the one shown in Figure 16-7. Close the report.

FIRST NAME	LAST NAME	ADDRESS 1	ADDRESS 2	PRODUCT	QTY	PRICE
Amanda	Form	2131 W. Tiny Rd.		TechONE System	1	$12,000.00
Amanda	Form	2131 W. Tiny Rd.		TechONE System	1	$12,000.00
Amanda	Form	2131 W. Tiny Rd.		Service Contract	1	$2,000.00
Amanda	Form	2131 W. Tiny Rd.		Service Contract	1	$2,000.00
Mary	Bailey	100 E Bayard St		TechONE System	1	$12,000.00
Irene	Murphy	172 Edison Street		TechONE System	1	$12,000.00
Dan	Minnick	14 East St		Service Contract	1	$2,000.00
Dan	Minnick	14 East St		TechONE System	1	$12,000.00
Dan	Minnick	14 East St		Mini Core Replacement	8	$100.00

Figure 16-7 L16.2 Use multiple conditions to highlight a field report

Highlighting Expert Limitations

Despite being relatively easy to use, the Highlighting Expert is one feature in my opinion that could be improved. You should be aware of the following two facts about the Highlighting Expert.

① Formulas created by the Highlighting Expert override formulas in the Formula Editor.

② Formulas created by the Highlighting Expert are not stored in the Formula Editor. This means that you cannot see the formulas created by the Highlighting Expert and can easily forget that they exist.

> Any formula that you can create with the Highlighting Expert can be created in the Formula Editor. It is easier to maintain formulas if they are all in the same place. Take from this what you will.

If...Then...Else Statements

This is one of the most used lines of programming code. This statement is used to set different options based on what you need to happen when the data is evaluated. The syntax below is for an If Then Else statement:

If **EXPRESSION/CONDITION** Then **TRUE STATEMENTS**
Else
FALSE STATEMENTS

Parts Of The If Then Else Statement Explained

① The **Expression/Condition** must evaluate to true or false.

② The **True Statements** will execute if the Expression/Condition is true.

③ The **Else** part of the statement is optional. If the Else clause is not included and the Expression/Condition is false, nothing will happen, which may be what you want. By "nothing happens", I mean that the If statement will default to the value for the data type. For example, if Field A is greater than 95, then textfield5 = "Great Job". If the variable "textfield5" was not declared to have a specific default value, the default value for a text field data type is " " (null), which is what would be displayed if Field A is not greater than 95.

④ The **False Statements** will execute if the Expression/Condition is false.

The plain English translation of an If Then Else statement is: **IF** Choice A meets this condition, **THEN** do X, **ELSE** do Y. Walk through the examples in Table 16-1 to gain a better understanding of If Then Else statements. Fill in the column on the right based on the numbers in the Choice A column.

If Choice A is greater than 25,
then Field B = 100, else Field B = 0.

Choice A	What Does Field B=
26	
1	
25	

Table 16-1 If Then Else examples

It may help to understand If...Then...Else statements if you think of them as a true or false test question. In the example above, the test question can be worded as "Is Choice A greater than 25?" There are two possible answers:

① Yes, it is (True). If it is, Field B would be set to 100.

② No, it isn't (False). If it isn't, Field B would be set to 0.

How Did You Do?

Table 16-2 contains the answers for the second column in Table 16-1. The third column in the table explains the answer.

Choice A	Field B=	Reason
26	100	The answer is 100 because 26 is greater than 25.
1	0	The answer is 0 because 1 is less than 25.
25	0	The answer is 0 because 25 is not greater than 25.

Table 16-2 If Then Else answers for Table 16-1

To complicate If statements even more, there can be multiple true and false statements in the same If Then Else statement. When this is the case, they have to be enclosed in parenthesis, otherwise Crystal Reports will stop processing the statement after the first semi-colon, which often will produce a syntax error. Statements with multiple true and false statements are known as **NESTED IF STATEMENTS**.

> Each statement except the last one in an If Then Else statement must end in a semi-colon.

Conditional Formatting Tips

As you will learn, you may not always need to apply the formatting that you create. This type of formatting is known as **CONDITIONAL FORMATTING**. The options on the Format Editor and Section Expert if checked, turn on what is known as **ABSOLUTE FORMATTING**, which means that the format will be applied to all values in the field. Absolute Formatting is not on if the option is not checked. This also applies to drop-down lists and text fields on these dialog boxes.

When you create a formula for an option, this is known as conditional formatting because the formula will turn the option on and off. Boolean formulas are used for on-off options in conditional formatting. When creating conditional If...Then...Else statements, keep the following in mind:

① **CHECK BOX** formatting options are either on or off. This means that you do not have to type the entire If...Then...Else statement. Crystal Reports will turn the format option on if the test returns a true value. If the formula returns a false value, the formatting is not turned on. This is when you would create a Boolean formula.
② **DROP-DOWN LIST** and **TEXT BOX** formatting options can have more than one choice. For this type of conditional formatting you have to type the entire If...Then...Else statement to specify what you want to happen if the test is true and if the test is false.

Conditional Formatting Warnings

You should be aware of the following when creating conditional formatting:

① If a field has formatting that is created with the Highlighting Expert and with conditional formatting, the Highlighting Expert formatting takes precedence. If the conditional formatting does not change the formatting created by the Highlighting Expert, the conditional formatting will be applied.
② Conditional formatting overrides absolute formatting even if the result of the conditional formatting is false.
③ Keep in mind that Crystal Reports does not require the "Else" part of an If Then Else statement.
④ If absolute and conditional formatting are applied to a field and the If Then Else statement for the conditional formatting does not have an Else clause and the conditional formatting does not return a "True" value, neither the conditional formatting or the absolute formatting is applied.
⑤ In addition to If Then Else statements you can also use **SELECT CASE** statements as long as the formatting property is in the Functions tree.

As you can see, it can be difficult to apply both absolute and conditional formatting to the same field. Even with the best intentions and code, you can get unexpected results. There are two things that you can do to help ensure that you get the output that you need when you have to combine absolute and conditional formatting. I have found the second option below to be more effective, but if the first option fits your needs, you should use it.

① Use the "Else" clause on If statements or the **DEFAULT** clause on Select Case statements.
② Use the "Else" clause with the **DEFAULTATTRIBUTE** function. To do this, select the default (absolute) option on the Format Editor dialog box and use the DefaultAttribute as the Else part of the If statement. For example, if you need to set the default value for a field to green on the Format Editor, use the following If Then Else statement.

This formula will display weekly salaries that are less than or equal to $750 in red and the other salaries in green.

```
If {Employee.Salary}/52 <= 750
  Then crRed
    Else
      DefaultAttribute
```

Exercise 16.3: Use The If Then Else Statement And IsNull Function

You have created a formula to combine two name fields. The formula that you created in that exercise is fine as long as there is data in both name fields. Unless the fields are required to be filled in on a data entry form, you cannot be 100% sure that they will contain data. In Lesson 3, you learned about null values in fields. The second address field is an example of a field that can have null values because all addresses do not require two fields.

If the Contact table only had a few records, you could manually check to see if the first two address fields contained data before creating the formula. If the table had two million records, checking them manually probably is not a good idea and could be quite time consuming. There are two options discussed below that you can use to prevent a formula from failing, if a field is null (empty).

① The **ISNULL** function is used to test a field to see if it is null. If it is, you can make a decision on what to do. To make this decision you need to use the If Then Else statement with the IsNull function.

② Turn on the **CONVERT DATABASE NULL VALUES TO DEFAULT** option on the Options dialog box. Turning this option on will convert null values to zero for numeric fields or blank for string fields. "Blank" is different than Null.

> While Crystal Reports supports the **CONVERT DATABASE NULL VALUES TO DEFAULT** option, not all databases support it. If you want to use this option, you need to make sure that the database that you are working with supports it. If you can't or don't want to confirm whether or not a database supports this feature, you can use the **ISNULL** function. I personally find it easier to use the IsNull function all the time, so that I can "see" what is going on.

In this exercise you will create a formula that will combine two contact address fields and check the Address2 field to see if it is null. The majority of the time, the second address field will be the one that will not have data. On the rare occurrence that the first address field is null, you would want the formula to fail so that the field would be blank on the report. Hopefully, people reading the report will notice this and fix the data. You can also write code that will print a message in the combined address field if either of the address fields is empty.

> The **ISNULL** function has to be placed inside the If Then Else statement because the check that it will perform on the Address2 field is the first part (the test question) that the If Then Else statement evaluates. In "plain" English, the formula that you will create is:
>
> **If** the Address2 field does not have any data
> **then** set the Full Address field (the name of the formula) to only display/print the Address1 field
> **else** set the Full Address field to display/print the Address1 field and the Address2 field.

1. Save the L16.2 report as `L16.3 If Then Else Statement.`

2. Create a formula field called `Address.`

3. Open the **CONTROL STRUCTURES** category in the Operators tree and double-click on the **IF X THEN Y ELSE Z** statement illustrated in Figure 16-8.

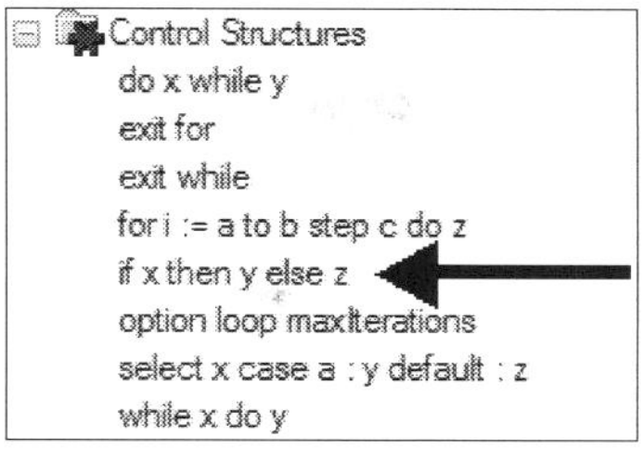

Figure 16-8 If Then Else statement illustrated

4. Open the **PRINT STATE** category in the Functions tree, then double-click on the **ISNULL** function illustrated in Figure 16-9.

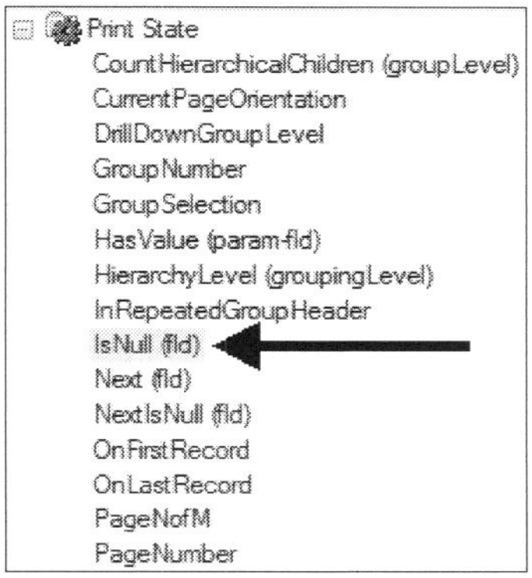

Figure 16-9 IsNull function illustrated

5. With the flashing insertion point between the parenthesis in the formula, double-click on the Address2 field in the Reports Field tree. This is the question part of the **IF** statement.

6. Click after the word **THEN** in the formula and double-click on the Address1 field, then press Enter. The word **ELSE** should be on the next line. This is the "true" part of the question, meaning that this is what you want to have print if the Address2 field is null.

7. Click after the word **ELSE** and add the Address1 field, then type + " " +.

8. Add the Address2 field. If you want to add a comment to the formula, you can. Check the formula for errors. The formula should look like the one shown in Figure 16-10.

```
//Formula to check if the Address 2 field is null
if IsNull ({CONTACT.ADDRESS_2}) then {CONTACT.ADDRESS_1}
else {CONTACT.ADDRESS_1}+ " "+{CONTACT.ADDRESS_2}
```

Figure 16-10 If Then Else and IsNull formula

9. Save the formula and close the Formula Workshop.

10. Delete the address fields, then add the Address formula field after the Last Name field.

11. Page 2 of the report should look like the one shown in Figure 16-11. Compare this to page 2 of the L16.2 report. Save the changes and close the report.

FIRST NAME	LAST NAME	Address	PRODUCT	QTY	PRICE
Lucy	Connor	Acorn Close Hale	TechONE System	2	$12,000.00
Lucy	Connor	Acorn Close Hale	Service Contract	1	$2,000.00
Theodore	Barrett	4589 N. Taylor St. Suite 50	TechONE System	1	$12,000.00
Theodore	Barrett	4589 N. Taylor St. Suite 50	Service Contract	1	$2,000.00
Theodore	Barrett	4589 N. Taylor St. Suite 50	ONE Component	3	$2,500.00

Figure 16-11 L16.3 If Then Else Statement report

Exercise 16.4: Use The Length Function

The Length function will check the number of characters in a field. Based on the length, you can assign different actions. For example, if a field has 10 characters you can display one message and if the same field in another record has 12 characters, you can display a different message.

In Exercise 15.7 you created a formula to format a phone number field. What you saw was that all of the phone numbers were not the same length. This caused some of the phone numbers to not be formatted properly. Using the Length function on the phone number field will allow you to use different formatting options based on the number of characters in the field. If you look at the data in the Phone field you will see that phone numbers are 10 or more characters long.

In this exercise you will modify the report to check the number of characters in the Phone number field for each record and format the field based on the number of characters in the field. This exercise does not cover all options for the phone field. In the real world, the current data in the phone field would have to be modified so that it is consistent.

Create A Formula For 11 Character Phone Numbers

In this part of the exercise you will create a formula that checks for 11 characters and creates the formatting for 11 character phone numbers.

1. Save the L15.7 report as `L16.4 Length function`.

2. Open the Contact Phone formula field and delete the formula, then open the **CONTROL STRUCTURES** category in the Operators tree and double-click on the If x then y else z statement.

3. Open the **STRINGS** category in the Functions tree, then double-click on the **LENGTH(STR)** function illustrated in Figure 16-12.

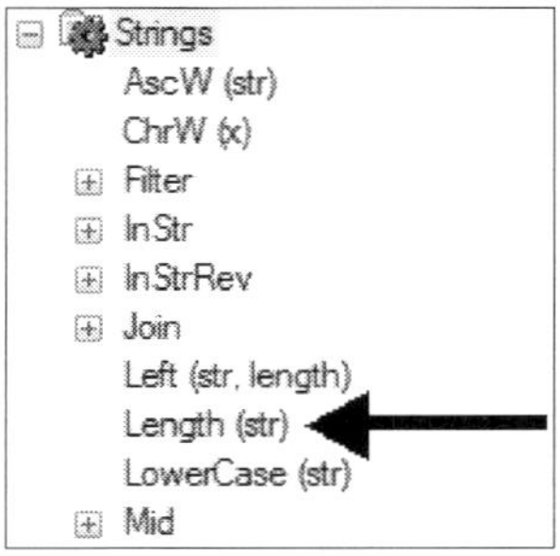

Figure 16-12 Length function illustrated

4. With the flashing insertion point between the parenthesis in the formula, add the Phone field, then click outside of the parenthesis on the right and type `=11` before the word "then".

5. Click in front of the word **ELSE** and press Enter. Open the **ADDITIONAL FUNCTIONS** category in the Functions tree and open the **SAMP1** category, then double-click on the **PICTURE** function.

6. Double-click on the Phone field in the Report Fields tree, then click after the comma in the formula and type `"(XXX)XXX-XXXX"`.

7. Click in front of the word **ELSE** and press Enter. Leave the Formula Workshop open to complete the next part of the exercise.

Create A Formula For 15 Character Phone Numbers

In this part of the exercise you will create the formula that checks for 15 characters and creates the formatting for phone numbers that have 15 characters. Most of the formula is the same as the one that you created for 11 characters. It is easier to copy the formula and change what's needed, then it is to create it again from scratch.

1. Copy the 11 character formula and paste it below the word **ELSE**.

2. Change the second =11 to `=15`, then change the Picture to `XX-XXX-XXXXXX`.

In this exercise if the phone number is not 11 or 15 characters, you just want the phone number printed without any formatting. You have complete control over which lengths you want to provide formatting for and which ones you don't.

3. Add the Phone field after the last **ELSE** in the formula. Your formula should look like the one shown in Figure 16-13. Check for syntax errors.

```
// This formula formats the Phone Number field
if Length ({CONTACT.PHONE})=11 then
Picture ({CONTACT.PHONE},"(XXX)XXX-XXXX" )
else
if Length ({CONTACT.PHONE})=15 then
Picture ({CONTACT.PHONE},"XX-XXX-XXXXXX" )
else
{CONTACT.PHONE}
```

Figure 16-13 Phone number formula

4. Delete the Contact & Purchase field from the report, then add the Contact field in its place.

5. Move the Contact Phone formula field over to the right, then add the Phone field to the report.

6. Save the changes. The report should look like the one shown in Figure 16-14.

   With both phone fields on the report, you can see which phone numbers met the formatting criteria and which ones did not.

CONTACT	PHONE	Contact Phone
Lames Jawson	(503) 555-2232	(503) 555-2232
Amanda Form	(212) 546-7890	(212) 546-7890
William Buckley	(650) 780-1202	(650) 780-1202
Allison Mikola	(212) 555-2485	(212) 555-2485
Thomas Andrews	(727) 555-4578	(727) 555-4578
Mary Bailey	315-988-6700	315-988-6700
Irene Murphy	0124 434343	(012)4 4-34343

Figure 16-14 L16.4 report

Exercise 16.5: Use Nested If Statements In Formulas

In the previous exercise the formula that you created contained more than one If statement. This type of If statement is known as a **NESTED IF** statement. There can be as many If statements in a formula as needed. In this exercise you will create a Nested If statement to give contacts a different discount on their next opportunity based on the total amount of their last opportunity.

1. Save the L5.3 report as `L16.5 Nested If Statement`.

2. Delete the Opportunity Name, Create Date, Days Open, Status and Actual Close Date, then move the Total field over to the left.

3. Change the page orientation to portrait.

4. Create a formula field and name it `Order Discount`, then add the If Then Else statement to the formula.

5. Add the Total field, then type `>=10000`.

6. Click after the word **THEN** and type `"10% discount"`.

7. Copy the formula and paste it twice.

8. Change the second line of code to `>=5000`, then change the discount to `15%`.

9. Change the last line of code to `>=2500`, then change the discount to `20%`.

10. Click after the last **ELSE**, press Enter and type `"25% discount"`. Your formula should look like the one shown in Figure 16-15.

```
if {OPPORTUNITY.TOTAL}>=10000 then "10% discount" else
if {OPPORTUNITY.TOTAL}>=5000 then "15% discount" else
if {OPPORTUNITY.TOTAL}>=2500 then "20% discount" else
"25% discount"
```

Figure 16-15 Order Discount formula

11. Save the formula and close the Formula Workshop. Add the Order Discount formula field to the report after the Total field. The report should look like the one shown in Figure 16-16. Save the changes and close the report.

CONTACT	COMPANY	TOTAL	Order Discount
Amanda Form	A1 Services-US Operations	12,000.00	10% discount
Amanda Form	A1 Services-US Operations	12,000.00	10% discount
Amanda Form	A1 Services-US Operations	2,000.00	25% discount
Amanda Form	A1 Services-US Operations	2,000.00	25% discount
Mary Bailey	Liberty Savings & Loan	12,000.00	10% discount
Irene Murphy	Mears Insurance	12,000.00	10% discount
Dan Minnick	Django Consulting	2,000.00	25% discount

Figure 16-16 L16.5 report

Because the Order Discount field is evaluated for each record, it will only match one of the If statements when the statement is set up correctly. If the Total is $3,000, the formula will stop processing after the third statement. If the Total is $6,500, the formula will stop processing after the second statement.

The order that you place the criteria values in is very important. If the statements were in a different order, the formula would not return the correct result because it is possible that the total would meet the criteria of another statement. For example, if the >=2,500 portion of the statement was above the >=10,000 portion of the statement and the total is $6,500, the formula would stop processing after the first If statement because $6,500 is >=2,500. That is not the outcome that you want though. You really want the $6,500 amount to receive a 15% discount.

The rule of thumb is to put the criteria in high to low order. The option after the last else statement is the "catch all" statement. Sometimes you may need to print a message on the report because the data is outside of the range of data that you need to report on. In the example above, the customer would receive a 25% discount off of their next order if their last order was less than $2,500. In this example, the company is going to offer larger discounts to people that placed smaller orders in hopes of having them place a larger order the next time that they order.

Suppressing Fields And Sections

There are times when there is no need to print the same data over and over on a report. Sometimes not repeating the same data makes the report easier to read. There are also times when you will need to suppress a section of the report. Like the Highlighting Expert, the suppression of fields and sections in a report can be based on a condition. These conditions are created using Boolean formulas.

Exercise 16.6: Suppressing Fields

In this exercise you will learn how to suppress fields by creating a conditional formula for a field that has a total greater than $11,000.

1. Save the L16.5 report as `L16.6 Suppress total GT 11000`.

2. Right-click on the Total field and select Format Field.

   On the Common tab, check the **SUPPRESS** option illustrated in Figure 16-17.

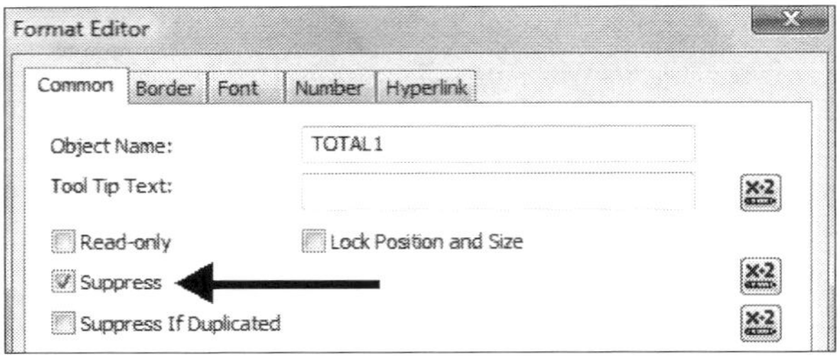

Figure 16-17 Common tab on the Format Editor

> The default color for the Formula button is blue, which means that the option does not have a formula. If the button is red, it means that the option does have a formula. You will also notice that the pencil is in a different position when the option has a formula.

3. Click the **FORMULA** button across from the Suppress option on the Format Editor. Create a formula to suppress the total if it is greater than $11,000. Add a comment that explains what the formula does. Save the changes and close the Formula Workshop.

4. Notice that the button across from the **SUPPRESS** option on the Formula Editor has red text. Close the Formula Editor. Notice that the Total field is not enabled on the design tab. This lets you know that this field will not always print because of the suppression criteria. The report should look like the one shown in Figure 16-18. If your report does not look like the one shown, make sure that your formula looks like the one in Figure 16-19. Save the changes and close the report.

CONTACT	COMPANY	TOTAL	Order Discount
Amanda Form	A1 Services-US Operations		10% discount
Amanda Form	A1 Services-US Operations		10% discount
Amanda Form	A1 Services-US Operations	2,000.00	25% discount
Amanda Form	A1 Services-US Operations	2,000.00	25% discount
Mary Bailey	Liberty Savings & Loan		10% discount
Irene Murphy	Mears Insurance		10% discount
Dan Minnick	Django Consulting	2,000.00	25% discount
Dan Minnick	Django Consulting		10% discount
Dan Minnick	Django Consulting	800.00	25% discount
Dan Minnick	Django Consulting	4,000.00	20% discount

Figure 16-18 L16.6 Suppress total GT $11000 report

```
// This formula will suppress the total field if it is > $11,000
{OPPORTUNITY.TOTAL}>11000
```

Figure 16-19 Suppression formula

Comparison Conditional Formatting

You can use one field for the comparison criteria and a different field to apply the conditional formatting to. You will learn how to do this in the next three exercises.

Exercise 16.7: Compare Contact Averages

In Exercise 10.3 you created a report that printed the average order amount for each contact and the average opportunity amount for all of the contacts on the report. In this exercise you will modify that report to display a message if a contacts average opportunity amount is greater than the average opportunity amount for all contacts on the report. If the average opportunity amount is less, no message will print. In order to print a message based on a condition, the formula has to be on the **DISPLAY STRING** option on the Format Editor.

> If you open the Formula Workshop from the Format Editor dialog box, you cannot create a different type of formula. You also cannot modify or delete existing formulas.

1. Save the L10.3 report as `L16.7 Display string conditional formatting`.
2. Right-click on the Average Opportunity Amount field in the group footer section and select Format Field.
3. On the Common tab click on the Formula button across from the **DISPLAY STRING** option, then add the If Then Else statement to the Formula section.
4. After the word **IF**, add the Group 1 Avg Total field, then type `>=` after the field.
5. Add the Report Area:Avg of Total field, then press Enter.
6. Click after the word **THEN** and add the ToText(x) function. (It's under the Strings category.)
7. Add the Group 1 Avg Total field inside of the ToText(x) function. Click outside of the parenthesis and type `+ " ** Above report average"`, then press Enter.
8. Copy the ToText portion of the formula up to the plus sign and paste it after the **ELSE** clause, then type `+ " "` at the end of the formula. Your formula should look like the one shown in Figure 16-20.

```
if Average ({OPPORTUNITY.TOTAL}, {CONTACT.CONTACT})>= Average ({OPPORTUNITY.TOTAL})
then ToText (Average ({OPPORTUNITY.TOTAL}, {CONTACT.CONTACT})) +" ** Above report average"
else ToText (Average ({OPPORTUNITY.TOTAL}, {CONTACT.CONTACT})) +" "
```

Figure 16-20 Customer average comparison formula

9. Save the changes and close the Formula Workshop, then click OK to close the Format Editor.
10. Make the Average Opportunity field in the group footer section wider, then preview the report. Page 1 should look like the one shown in Figure 16-21. Notice that there is no message next to the first average. That is because the average amount is less than $6,740.50, which is the average opportunity amount for the report.

    Save the changes and leave the report open to complete the next exercise.

> If the average amount field is not lined up, this is one of the rare times that I will modify a report on the preview tab. To line up the Average Opportunity field, left align it and then drag it in the direction needed to line it up with the field above.

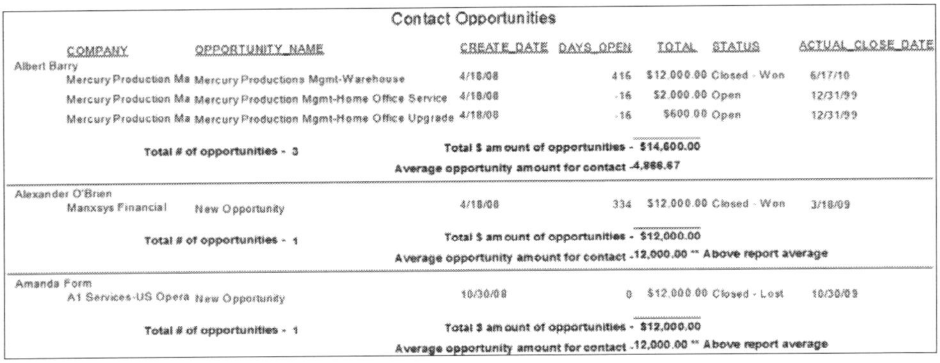
Contact Opportunities

COMPANY	OPPORTUNITY_NAME	CREATE_DATE	DAYS_OPEN	TOTAL	STATUS	ACTUAL_CLOSE_DATE
Albert Barry						
Mercury Production Ma	Mercury Productions Mgmt-Warehouse	4/18/08	416	$12,000.00	Closed - Won	6/17/10
Mercury Production Ma	Mercury Production Mgmt-Home Office Service	4/18/08	-16	$2,000.00	Open	12/31/99
Mercury Production Ma	Mercury Production Mgmt-Home Office Upgrade	4/18/08	-16	$600.00	Open	12/31/99

Total # of opportunities - 3 Total $ amount of opportunities - $14,600.00
Average opportunity amount for contact -4,866.67

Alexander O'Brien						
Manxsys Financial	New Opportunity	4/18/08	334	$12,000.00	Closed - Won	3/18/09

Total # of opportunities - 1 Total $ amount of opportunities - $12,000.00
Average opportunity amount for contact -12,000.00 ** Above report average

Amanda Form						
A1 Services-US Opera	New Opportunity	10/30/08	0	$12,000.00	Closed - Lost	10/30/09

Total # of opportunities - 1 Total $ amount of opportunities - $12,000.00
Average opportunity amount for contact -12,000.00 ** Above report average

Figure 16-21 Page 1 of the L16.7 report

Exercise 16.8: Font Color Conditional Formatting

In the previous exercise you compared the opportunity average amount to the average amount for the report. It may be helpful to change the color of contacts that have an average less than the report average.

1. Save the L16.7 report as `L16.8 Font color conditional formatting`.

2. Right-click on the Average Opportunity Amount field in the group footer section and select Format Field. On the Font tab click on the Formula button across from the **COLOR** option.

> The comments that you see in the Formula section are colors that you can use.

The formula that you need to create to change the font color is the opposite of the formula that you created in the previous exercise. Rather than type it in again, you can copy the formula that you created in the previous exercise and change it as needed.

3. Open the **FORMATTING FORMULAS** folder in the Workshop Tree. Under the Avg Of Opportunity.Total section, you should see the **DISPLAY STRING** formula illustrated in Figure 16-22.

   Click on the Display String formula and select (highlight) the formula up to the first ToText function, then press the **CTRL** + **C** keys.

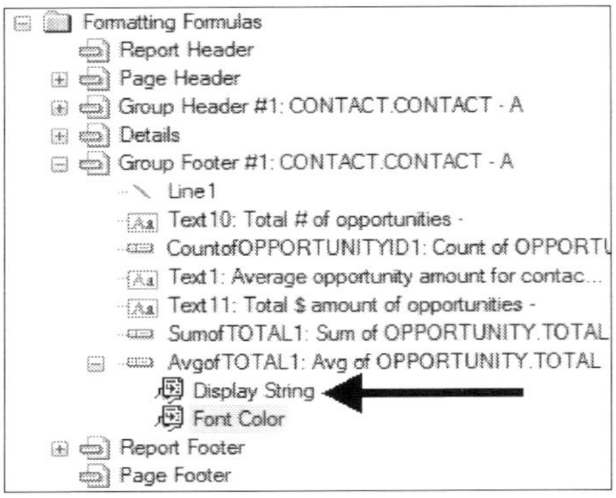

Figure 16-22 Formatting Formulas folder

4. Click on the Font color formula in the Workshop Tree and scroll to the end of the comments and paste the formula in by pressing the **CTRL** + **V** keys.

5. Change the >= to <=, then type `crRed` after the word **THEN**. Save the changes and close the Formula Workshop. Click OK to close the Format Editor.

6. Preview the report. You should see the contact average dollar amounts in red. If you do not see the color red on the first page of the report, compare your font color formula to the one shown in Figure 16-23. Save the changes and close the report.

```
//
if Average ({OPPORTUNITY.TOTAL}, {CONTACT.CONTACT})<= Average ({OPPORTUNITY.TOTAL})
then crRed
```

Figure 16-23 Font color formula

Exercise 16.9: Suppress Currency Formatting

Every detail record on the L16.7 report prints the dollar sign for the Total field. The report may look better if the dollar sign only printed for the first detail record for the contact. In this exercise you will create conditional formatting to suppress the dollar sign on records other then the first one for each contact.

1. Save the L16.7 report as `L16.9 Suppress currency formatting`.

2. Right-click on the Total field in the details section and select Format Field. Click on the Customize button on the Number tab, then click on the **CURRENCY SYMBOL** tab.

3. Click the Formula button across from the **ENABLE CURRENCY SYMBOL** option, then add the If Then Else statement to the Formula section.

4. Click after the word **IF** and add the **ONFIRSTRECORD** function, which is under the Print State category. Type the word `or`, then press the space bar.

5. Add the Contact field, then type <> `Previous`. Add the Contact field again, then press Enter.

6. Delete the word **ELSE** and add the **CRFLOATINGCURRENCYSYMBOL** function. (**Hint:** You can copy this function from the comments above in the formula.)

7. Type two left parenthesis in front of the first Contact field and one parenthesis after the field.

8. Type two left parenthesis in front of the second Contact field and three after the field. You can add a comment to the formula.

9. Save and close the formula. Click OK twice to close both dialog boxes. The report should look like the one shown in Figure 16-24.

As you can see, the dollar sign for the Total field only prints on the first detail record for each contact. If your report does not look like the one shown, compare your formula to the one in Figure 16-25. Save the changes and close the report.

Contact Opportunities

COMPANY	OPPORTUNITY NAME	CREATE DATE	DAYS OPEN	TOTAL	STATUS	ACTUAL CLOSE DATE
Albert Barry						
Mercury Production Ma	Mercury Productions Mgmt-Warehouse	4/18/08	416	$12,000.00	Closed - Won	6/17/10
Mercury Production Ma	Mercury Production Mgmt-Home Office Service	4/18/08	-8	2,000.00	Open	12/31/99
Mercury Production Ma	Mercury Production Mgmt-Home Office Upgrade	4/18/08	-8	600.00	Open	12/31/99

Total # of opportunities - 3 Total $ amount of opportunities - $14,600.00

Average opportunity amount for contact -4,866.67

Figure 16-24 L16.9 report

```
// This formula will suppress the dollar sign on all detail records
if OnFirstRecord or
(({CONTACT.CONTACT}) <> Previous (({CONTACT.CONTACT})))
then crFloatingCurrencySymbol
```

Figure 16-25 Dollar sign suppression formula

Formula Wrap Up

So how did you do creating If Then Else statements? Hopefully you did okay. The reason that I am asking is because if you can understand and create If Then Else statements, you are on your way to becoming a Crystal Reports power report writer. If you are curious about other statements that you can use, check out the following in the Help file: For Loop and my favorite, the Select Case statement.

Select Case Statement

The Select Case statement is similar to the If Then Else statement. I personally find Select Case statement easier to read and understand, especially easier then Nested If statements. For example, Figure 16-26 shows a nested If statement.

```
if {Orders.Order Amount} >=10000 then "10% discount" else
if {Orders.Order Amount} >=5000 then "15% discount" else
if {Orders.Order Amount} >=2500 then "20% discount" else
"25% discount"
```

Figure 16-26 Nested If statement

The following Select Case statement provides the same logic as the Nested If statement shown above in Figure 16-26. For whatever reason, I find this easier to read and understand.

```
Select {Orders.Order Amount}
    Case Is >= 10000:
          "10% discount"
    Case Is >= 5000:
          "15% discount"
    Case Is >= 2500:
          "20% discount"
    Default:
          "25% discount"
```

Boolean Formulas

In Lesson 3 you learned that Boolean fields have values of true/false or yes/no. **BOOLEAN EXPRESSIONS** return a value of true or false. In Lesson 7 you learned how to format a Boolean field. Earlier in this lesson I said that one way to understand If Then Else statements is to think of them as a true or false question. A Boolean formula is the test question portion of an If Then Else statement. Boolean formulas do not have to be created on Boolean fields. The value that a Boolean formula returns is either true or false. You can then format the result of the Boolean formula like you did in Exercise 7.4.

You could create a formula that would suppress the salary if it was greater than $50,000. A Boolean formula could have been used to accomplish the same result. Figure 16-27 shows the formula. The difference would be the values printed in the salary field. Instead of printing the salary for some records and leaving the field blank, the values true or false could be printed, as shown in Figure 16-28.

```
{Employee.Salary} > 50000
```

Figure 16-27 Boolean formula

First Name	Last Name	Address1	Region	Salary > 50K
Steven	Buchanan	14 Garrett Hill		False
Robert	King	Edgeham Hollow		False
Anne	Dodsworth	7 Houndstooth Rd.		False
Michael	Suyama	Coventry House		False
Bas-Rhin				
Justin	Brid	2 impasse du Soleil	Bas-Rhin	True
Xavier	Martin	9 place de la Liberté	Bas-Rhin	False
Laurent	Pereira	7 rue Nationale	Bas-Rhin	False
BC				
Andrew	Fuller	908 W. Capital Way	BC	True

Figure 16-28 Report using a Boolean formula

NEW The Section Expert

The Section Expert has been modified. A new tab has been added and the page and orientation options were moved to the new tab. So far, all of the formatting techniques that you have learned were to change individual objects on the report. You can use the Section Expert to format an entire section of the report, similar to how the Format Editor is used to format fields. You can also create formulas for many of the options on the Section Expert which is shown in Figure 16-29.

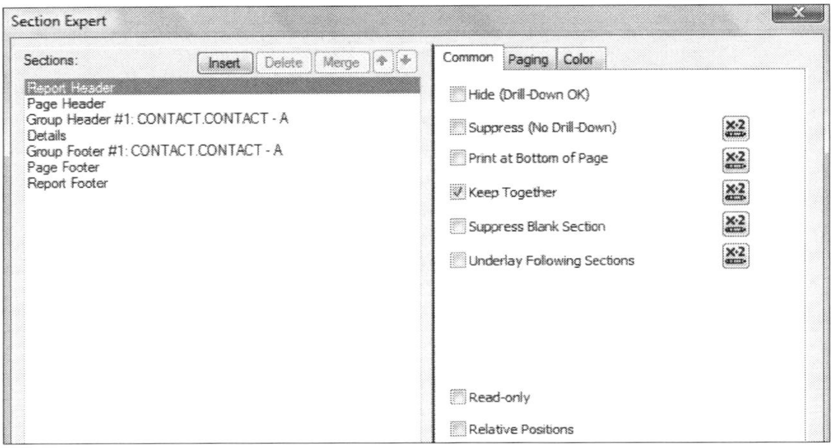

Figure 16-29 Section Expert

With section formatting, you can make the following types of changes to a report.

① Force each group to start at the top of a new page.
② Change the line spacing in the details section to something other than single spacing.
③ Create page breaks.
④ Conditionally suppress a section of the report.

There are three ways to open the Section Expert as discussed below.

① Right-click on the section name on the left side of the design window and select Section Expert.
② Click the Section Expert button on the Experts toolbar.
③ Report ⇒ Section Expert.

> The advantage to using the first option above to open the Section Expert is that the section will already be selected on the left side of the Section Expert dialog box when it is opened. Table 16-3 explains the formatting section options on the Common tab. Table 16-4 explains the options on the Paging tab. Table 16-5 explains the section options that are only available for a specific section of the report.

Option	Description
Hide (Drill-Down OK)	Hides the objects in the section when the report is printed. The section can be viewed on the preview window. If the report section that this option is applied to is part of a higher level group and the group is drilled-down on, the objects in the section will be visible on the drill-down tab. This option is not available for subsections.
Suppress (No Drill-Down)	The section that this option is applied to will not be printed, does not allow drill-down and cannot be viewed on the preview window, even if a higher level section is drilled-down on. This option is also available for subsections.
Print at Bottom of Page	Forces the section to be printed as close to the bottom of the page as possible, even if the detail records stop printing half way down the page.
Keep Together	Keeps the section together on the same page when printed. This option is sometimes confused with the Keep Group Together option on the Group Expert dialog box. These options produce different results.
Suppress Blank Section	Prevents the section from printing when all of the objects in the section are blank.
Underlay Following Sections	Causes the section to print in the same location that the section below it will print. This option will allow charts or images to print next to the section that follows.
Read-Only	Suppresses formatting in the section and prevents any formatting to the section. This option is similar to the **LOCK FORMAT** and **LOCK SIZE AND POSITION** options on the Format Editor and Formatting toolbar.
Relative Positions	Locks an object next to another object like a cross-tab or OLAP grid. If the cross-tab grows, the object will be repositioned so that it remains aligned with the grid object.
Background Color	This option is on the Color tab. It is used to select a color for the background of the section. This is different then the formatting that objects in the section have. You learned how to use this option in Exercise 8.2.

Table 16-3 Common tab section formatting options explained

Option	Description
New Page Before	Forces a page break before the section prints. (1)
Reset Page Number After	Resets the page number back to one after the section has printed. This option also resets the Total Page Count special field.
New Page After	Forces a page break after the section prints. (1)
Orientation	Is used to select how the report will print on the page as shown in Figure 16-30. Figure 16-31 shows the options on the Paging tab for the details section.

Table 16-4 Paging tab options explained

(1) This option is often used to force each group to start on a new page.

Formatting options that are not available for the section of the report that is selected are not enabled. For example, in Figure 16-30, the **NEW PAGE BEFORE** option is not enabled for the report header section.

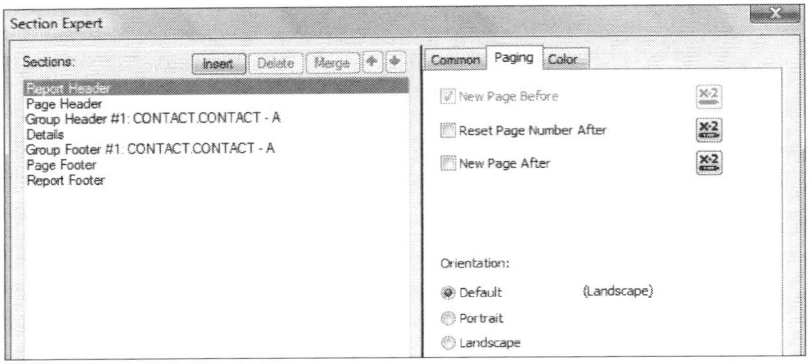

Figure 16-30 Paging tab options for the report header section

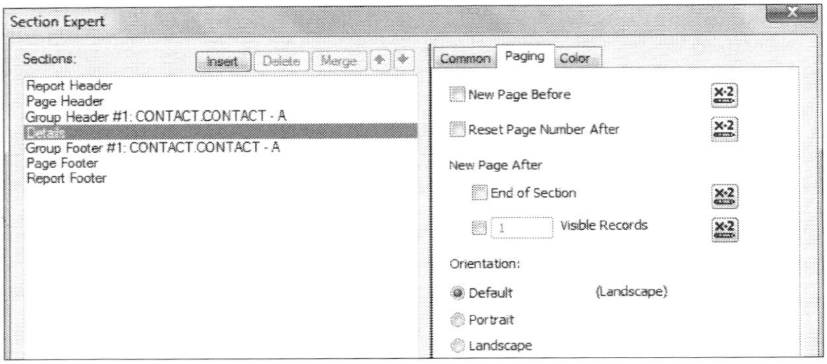

Figure 16-31 Paging tab options for the details section

Section	Option	Description
Page Footer	NEW Clamp Page Footer	If checked, this option will remove white space from the bottom of the report.
Page Footer	Reserve Minimum Page Footer	Select this option when you need to remove space in the page footer section to gain more space on the printed page.
Details	Format With Multiple Columns	Displays data in columns similar to a newspaper layout. When checked, a new tab named **LAYOUT** will open, as illustrated in Figure 16-32. The options on the Layout tab are used to select the size of the columns.

Table 16-5 Section specific formatting options explained

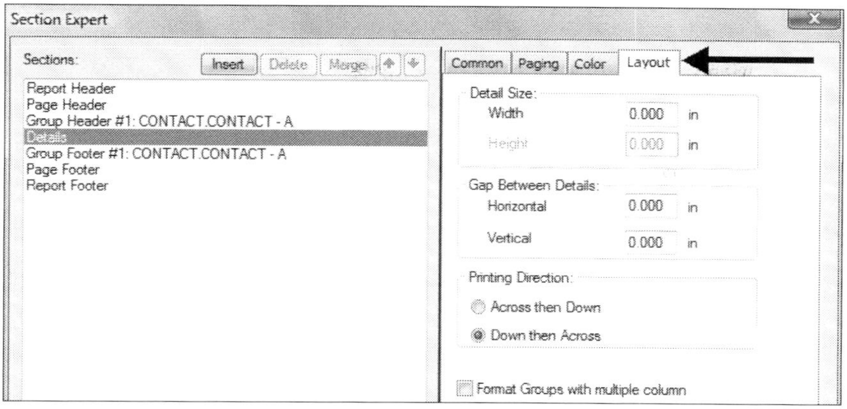

Figure 16-32 Layout tab illustrated

Exercise 16.10: Create Page Breaks

Page breaks are one of the most used section formatting techniques. While the concept appears straight forward, it can be tricky and can produce unexpected results. In this exercise you will add a page break to a report that prints orders by month. The objective is to force a page break when the month of the actual close date changes in the group header section of the report.

1. Save the L11.1 report as `L16.10 Report with a page break`.
2. Open the Section Expert, then click on the group header section. On the Paging tab check the **NEW PAGE BEFORE** option.
3. Preview the report. You should notice that the first page of the report is blank. More than likely, having the first page break occur before the detail records for the first group are printed on the report, is not what you had in mind. Save the changes and leave the report open to complete the next exercise.

Exercise 16.11: Conditionally Format The Page Break

As you saw in the previous exercise, selecting the **NEW PAGE BEFORE** option did not accomplish what you thought it would. In this exercise you will fix this problem. The problem with only selecting this option is that it causes a page break before any data prints.

Hopefully you are asking yourself what is different about the first group of data. You may have looked through the functions to see if there is a function that you can use. If you have looked for a function, you won't find any that are specifically for sections on a report or for page breaks. You could create your own formula, but what would you write? You may have to think outside of the box on this one.

In case you are thinking that you could use the **NEW PAGE AFTER** option for the group header section, this option would cause the detail records to start on a different page, but the group header information would remain on the previous page, as shown in Figure 16-33.

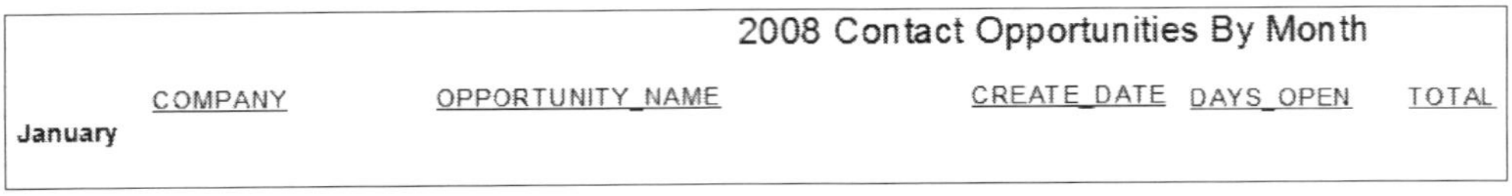

Figure 16-33 New Page After option turned on for the group header section

I know what you are thinking: Use the **NEW PAGE AFTER** option on the group footer section. That will give you the desired output of having each group start on a new page. The downside is that if the report has data in the report footer section, it will not print on the same page as the last group footer section of information. The information in the report footer section will be forced to a new page. If the report that you are creating does not have data in the report footer section or you want the information in the report footer section to print on a page by itself, using the New Page After option on the group footer section will work.

In Exercise 16.9 you used a function called **ONFIRSTRECORD**. You could write code to see if the group contains the first record in the report. If it does, do not force a page break. This will work because only one group per report will contain the first record on the report. It just so happens that the first record is in the first group, which is the group that currently has a page break before it. Creating a formula to not force a break on the first record will cause the formatting (in this case a page break) to be turned off, on the first group. This is what you want to have happen.

1. Save the L16.10 report as `L16.11 Conditional page break`.

2. Open the Section Expert, then click on the group header section. On the Paging tab click on the Formula button across from the New Page Before option.

3. Type `Not` and press the space bar, then add the OnFirstRecord function, or you can type the function in.

4. Save and close the formula, then click OK to close the Section Expert. Preview the report. Save the changes and close the report.

The first group (January), should be on page 1 of the report instead of on page 2, like it was in the previous exercise. If you look at the last page of the report, you will see that the report footer information is not on a page by itself.

Using The New Page After Option To Format A Page Break

Earlier, the idea of using the New Page After option was discussed as a way to force a page break. Adding the **NOTONLASTRECORD** function to the New Page After option on the group footer section will force each group to start on a new page, just like the exercise that you just completed.

Exercise 16.12: Resetting Page Numbers

Depending on the type of report that you create, you may have the need to have the page number reset after a certain condition has been met. A report that you may need this for is one that will be distributed to more than one person. An example of this would be a report like the contact opportunities that you created in Lesson 10, Exercise 10.2. Resetting the page number to one when opportunities for a different contact prints, would allow the report to be distributed to each contact and have the page numbers make sense to each contact. Can you imagine receiving a report that started on page 75? You may think that the report was missing pages. Using the **RESET PAGE NUMBER** section formatting option would prevent that from happening. In this exercise you will learn how to use this option.

1. Save the L10.2 report as `L16.12 Reset page number`.

In addition to creating the page break, the report needs a page number field and the selection criteria needs to be deleted.

2. Add the Page Number special field to the page footer section.

3. Delete the selection criteria.

No contact has enough detail records to create a second page in the report, so we will have to fake it a little.

4. Drag the section bar below the details section down to the end of the page footer section. This will cause a second page for some contacts.

Create The Page Break

1. Create a page break formula that does not cause a page break on the first record of the report, for the group header section.

2. Check the **RESET PAGE NUMBER AFTER** option on the Section Expert Paging tab, for the group footer section. The first page of the report should start on page 1. The page number is at the bottom of the report.

3. In the group tree, click on the contact Albert Berry. If you scroll down to the bottom of the page you will see that the page number is 1. If you go to the next page, it will be page 2, even though it is the third physical page of the report. This is what should happen. Save the changes and leave the report open to complete the next exercise.

Exercise 16.13: Use The Change Group Dialog Box Options

If you look at the second page for any group in the report that you just modified, you will notice that the group header information (the Contacts name) only prints on the first page of each group. The report would look better if the group name printed on every page. Options on the **CHANGE GROUP** dialog box are used to force the group header information to print on every page.

1. Save the L16.12 report as `L16.13 Repeat group header option`.

2. Right-click on the group header section on the left side of the design window and select **CHANGE GROUP**.

3. On the Options tab check the **REPEAT GROUP HEADER ON EACH PAGE** option shown in Figure 16-34.

   This option will cause the group header information to print on every page of the report.

   Click OK.

   If you go to any page on the report after the first page of a group, you will see the group header information, just like it is on the first page of each group.

Figure 16-34 Change Group Options dialog box

4. Save the changes and leave the report open to complete the next part of this exercise.

NEW The **NEW PAGE AFTER VISIBLE GROUPS** option shown above in Figure 16-34 will force a page break after a specific number of groups have printed.

How The Change Group Options Work

If checked, the **CUSTOMIZE GROUP NAME FIELD** option is used to create the name for the group as you want it to appear in the group header section, or a different section if you copy or move the group header field to it.

Do not check this option if you only want to display the data that is in the field that is being grouped on.

The **USE A FORMULA AS GROUP NAME** option is used to create a formula that will control what appears in the Group Name field. This option is very helpful if you need to change what prints in the group name field based on data that appears in the report or data in a table that is connected to the report.

The **REPEAT GROUP HEADER ON EACH PAGE** option will cause the group header section to be printed at the top of each page. This will let you know which group the details records and totals are for.

> The purpose of the **KEEP GROUP TOGETHER** option shown above in Figure 16-34 is to force all records that are in the same group print on the same page. If this option is checked and the first group on the report does not fit on the first page, the group will start printing on the second page and the first page of the report will be blank. If this happens, clear the **RESPECT KEEP GROUP TOGETHER ON FIRST PAGE** option on the Report Options dialog box.
>
> The Keep Group Together option if checked, will cause all of the group sections (the group header, group footer and detail section for the group) to be printed on the same page. If all three sections will not fit on the current page, they will start printing on the next page. This is different then the **KEEP TOGETHER** option on the Section Expert, which only causes the section that the option is applied to, to print on the same page. [See Table 16.3, earlier in this lesson] These options are best suited for reports that do not have a lot of detail records in each group. Groups that have a lot of records may require more than one page, which may result in the report having breaks in unexpected places.

Use The InRepeatedGroupHeader Function

Prior to changing the group options in the previous part of the exercise, it was easy to tell which was the first page for each group in the report. For this report, that is not exactly true because each group starts on page 1, but pretend that the page numbers are not reset. To help make reading the report easier, adding text on the pages in the group, other than the first page would resolve this issue.

The **INREPEATEDGROUPHEADER** function is used to add conditional formatting to a group header or footer when the group prints on more than one page.

1. Add a text object to the right of the Name field in the group header section and type `(Continued)` in the object. Change the font size of the text object to 8.

2. Right-click on the text object and select Format Text, then click the Formula button across from the Suppress option. Type `Not InRepeatedGroupHeader` in the Formula section.

3. Save the formula and close the Formula Workshop. Save the changes. Go to page 3 of the report. You should see (Continued) next to the contacts name, as shown in Figure 16-35. If you do not see it, make the details section longer.

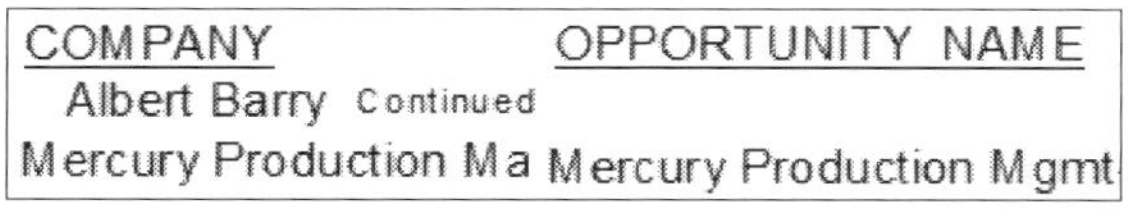

Figure 16-35 Page 3 of the L16.13 report

Exercise 16.14: Suppress A Section Of The Report

There will be times when you need to permanently hide a section of a report. Often, this is done (on a second copy of an existing report) when you do not want some users to see certain information on a report. An example that comes to mind is the opportunities by contact report that you modified in Exercise 16.12. Because the goal of the report in Exercise 16.12 was to distribute the sections of the report to the appropriate contact, there is no reason to display the Report Total information in the report footer section. You will learn how to suppress a report section in this exercise.

1. Save the L16.12 report as `L16.14 Report footer suppressed`.

2. Open the Section Expert and check the **HIDE (DRILL-DOWN OK)** option for the report footer section.

> You can also turn the suppression options on or off by selecting them on the Section shortcut menu.

3. On the last page of the report you should not see the report totals at the end of the report. Save the changes and close the report.

Using The Suppress (No Drill-Down) Option

In Lesson 8 you learned how to add sections to a report. In the exercise that you just completed, you learned how to suppress a section of the report. If you have the need to create a report that uses more than one address field, often they are placed on separate rows in the details section. The second address field is often blank, which means that a blank row will print for the records when the second address field is blank, as illustrated in Figure 16-36.

When combined, the Suppress (No Drill-Down) section option and adding a section with conditional formatting will allow you to suppress a section of the report based on a condition.

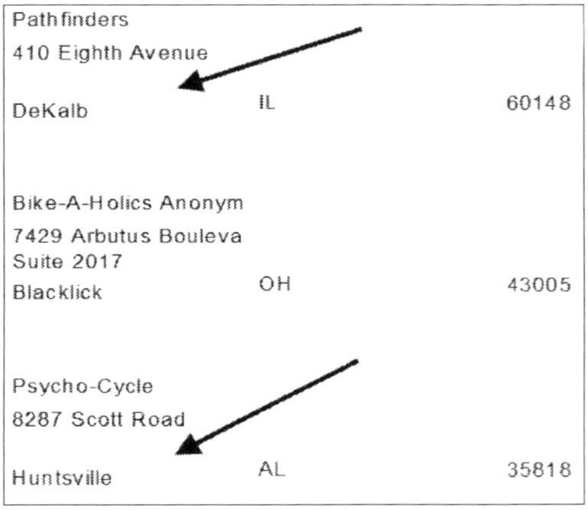

Figure 16-36 Blank row illustrated

You can combine these options and place the second address field in a section by itself, they conditionally hide the section if the second address field is blank.

Remember that if you suppress a field in a section that has other objects, the entire section will be suppressed if the condition is true. Often, this is not what you want.

If you move the second address field to its own section of the report as shown in Figure 16-37, you can suppress the section if the address field is blank. This will cause the report to print like the one shown in Figure 16-38 instead of the one shown above in Figure 16-36.

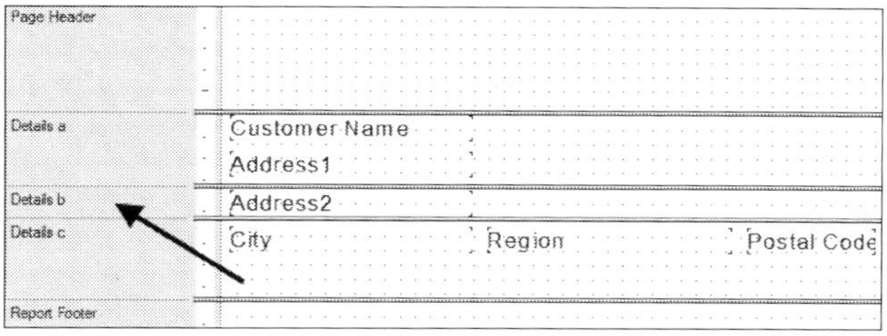

Figure 16-37 Address 2 field in a section by itself

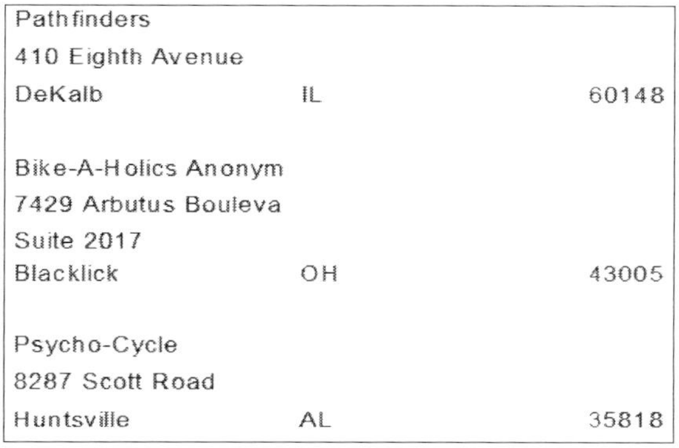
Pathfinders
410 Eighth Avenue
DeKalb IL 60148

Bike-A-Holics Anonym
7429 Arbutus Bouleva
Suite 2017
Blacklick OH 43005

Psycho-Cycle
8287 Scott Road
Huntsville AL 35818

Figure 16-38 Report with the Address 2 field suppressed

Exercise 16.15: Suppress A Group

Depending on the amount of data that is displayed on a report, not all users may need to view all of the records. In this exercise you will modify a report to only print groups of data that meet specific criteria. You will modify a report to only print groups that have a group total average amount that is less than $5,000.

1. Save the L10.3 report as
   `L16.15 Suppress group if amount LT 5000K`.
   (LT is my abbreviation for less than.)

2. Change the Create Date selection criteria to only include opportunities in 2008.

3. Change the Total # of opportunities summary field in the group footer section to Distinct count.

4. Change the Grand Total # of opportunities summary field in the report footer section to Distinct count.

5. Change the format on the two distinct summary fields that you just modified to be whole numbers with no cents.

Add The Suppression Criteria

1. Open the Section Expert and add the formula shown in Figure 16-39 to the Suppress (No Drill-Down) option for the group header, details and group footer sections.

```
// This formula will suppress groups on the report where
// the average total amount of the contact is less than $5,000
//
// This formula is used on the group header, details
// and group footer sections suppress (no drill-down) option
Average ({OPPORTUNITY.TOTAL}, {CONTACT.CONTACT}) < 5000
```

Figure 16-39 Suppress group formula

Notice that the Formula Workshop displays the format option Suppress (No Drill-Down) in the title bar as shown in Figure 16-40.

Formula Workshop - Format Formula Editor - Suppress (No Drill-Down)

Figure 16-40 Formula Workshop title bar

2. Save the formulas and close the Formula Workshop. Save the changes. The report should look like the one shown in Figure 16-41. Some of the groups (contacts) that you should not see are Albert Barry, Andy Harrison and Angela Ives. Compare it to the L10.3 report.

   Figure 16-42 shows the grand totals for the report. The report has suppression criteria to not display a group if the average opportunity amount is less than $5,000.

Contact Opportunities

COMPANY	OPPORTUNITY_NAME	CREATE_DATE	DAYS_OPEN	TOTAL	STATUS	ACTUAL_CLOSE_DATE
Alexander O'Brien						
Manxsys Financial	New Opportunity	4/18/08	334	$12,000.00	Closed - Won	3/18/09
Total # of opportunities - 1		Total $ amount of opportunities -		$12,000.00		
		Average opportunity amount for contact -		$12,000.00		
Amanda Form						
A1 Services-US Opera	New Opportunity	10/30/08	0	$12,000.00	Closed - Lost	10/30/09
Total # of opportunities - 1		Total $ amount of opportunities -		$12,000.00		
		Average opportunity amount for contact -		$12,000.00		
Bella Minoal						
Jake Flakes Inc	Mixing Room	4/18/08	252	$12,000.00	Closed - Lost	8/27/09
Total # of opportunities - 1		Total $ amount of opportunities -		$12,000.00		
		Average opportunity amount for contact -		$12,000.00		

Figure 16-41 L16.15 report

Total # of contacts on this report - 57
Grand Total # of opportunities - 92
Grand Total $ amount of all opportunities - $681,500.00
Average opportunity amount for all contacts - $6,883.84 ←

Figure 16-42 L16.15 report totals

Remember that records that are suppressed are still included in the total fields on the report. Some people consider this a flaw so to speak, of how data is processed. To correct this problem, running total fields should be used instead of summary fields in the group and report footer sections. In Lesson 19 you will learn how to fix this report so that the contacts whose averages are less than $5,000 are not counted in any total amount field on the report.

Exercise 16.16: Use The Color Tab Section Expert Options

One of the more popular uses of the Color tab on the Section Expert is to add a color background to every other detail record on the report. If you have ever seen what is known as "green bar" computer paper, you understand the color effect that you will create in this exercise.

1. Save the L7.5 report as `L16.16 Add color to rows.`

2. Delete the line object in the details section.

3. Open the Section Expert, then click on the details section. Click on the Color tab.

4. Click the Formula button, then type the formula shown at the bottom of Figure 16-43.

```
// This formula will print a silver background for all
// even number rows in the Details section of the report.
//
// RecordNumber mod 2 will return 0 for even row numbers
// and 1 for odd number row numbers
//
// DefaultAttribute is the default row color
//

If RecordNumber mod 2 = 0
then crSilver
Else DefaultAttribute
```

Figure 16-43 Row color formula

You can change this formula to create a background pattern different then every other row as you will see in the examples in the next section.

5. Save the formula and close the Formula Workshop. The report should look like the one shown in Figure 16-44. Save the changes and close the report.

COMPANY	ADDRESS 1	STATE	ZIP CODE	COUNTRY
HAL's Consulting Corp	10 Countdown Loop	OR	97800	United States
A1 Services-US Operations	2131 W. Tiny Rd.	NY	20122	United States
Twelfth Dream	2010 Act Way	CA	94063	United States
CH TechONE	13 East 54th St.	NY	10008	United States
Modern Electric Supply	1919 Tecoma Dr.	FL	34655	United States
Liberty Savings & Loan	100 E Bayard St	NY	13148	United States
Mears Insurance	172 Edison Street	Cheshire	CH1 4PL	United Kingdom
Django Consulting	14 East St			Australia

Figure 16-44 L16.16 Add color to rows report

> Some of the options on the Format Editor and Section Expert will be displayed with comments when they are opened in the Formula Workshop, as shown in Figure 16-45. The comments that you see are for the four line style options for the Border tab on the Format Editor. The options in the comments let you know what values you can use in your formula. The row color formula that you just created had a list of colors at the top of the formula that you could select from to use as the background color.

```
// This conditional formatting formula must return one of the following Line Style Constants:
//
// crSingleLine
// crDoubleLine
// crDashedLine
// crDottedLine
// crNoLine
//
```

Figure 16-45 Default comments for the line style option

How The Row Color Formula Works

Now that you have created a row color formula, knowing how it works will be helpful because you can modify the formula to meet other needs.

RECORDNUMBER is a special field that counts records in the details section.

MOD divides one number by another number and returns the remainder, instead of the result of the division.

The code **IF RECORDNUMBER MOD 2=0** means to divide the record number by 2. If the remainder is zero, meaning that if the record number is evenly divisible by two, apply the color to the background of the detail row.

> If the report section that you are applying the background row color formatting to has background formatting for objects, you should use **NOCOLOR** for the Else clause instead of using the color white because NoColor produces a result that is similar to being transparent, which is what you want. Using the color white will cause the background color applied to individual fields to produce results that are not always visually appealing.
>
> If the report section does not have any fields with background color formatting, using the **DEFAULT ATTRIBUTE** is acceptable.

Row Color Examples

Example #1 The formula If RecordNumber mod 5 = 0 will shade every fifth row as shown in Figure 16-46.

Customer Name	Order #	Order Date	Order Amount	Ship Via	First Name	Last Name
City Cyclists	1	12/2/03	$41.90	UPS	Nancy	Davolio
Deals on Wheels	1002	12/2/03	$5,060.28	Pickup	Janet	Leverling
Warsaw Sports, Inc.	1003	12/2/03	$186.87	UPS	Margaret	Peacock
Bikes and Trikes	1004	12/2/03	$823.05	Pickup	Margaret	Peacock
SAB Mountain	1005	12/3/03	$29.00	Loomis	Janet	Leverling
Poser Cycles	1006	12/3/03	$64.90	Purolator	Margaret	Peacock
Spokes	1007	12/3/03	$49.50	Parcel Post	Anne	Dodsworth
Clean Air Transportation Co.	1008	12/3/03	$2,214.94	Purolator	Margaret	Peacock
Extreme Cycling	1009	12/3/03	$29.00	Loomis	Margaret	Peacock
Cyclopath	1010	12/3/03	$14,872.30	UPS	Nancy	Davolio
BBS Pty	1011	12/3/03	$29.00	Purolator	Margaret	Peacock
Piccolo	1012	12/3/03	$10,259.10	Loomis	Nancy	Davolio
Pedals Inc.	1013	12/3/03	$1,142.13	Parcel Post	Margaret	Peacock
Spokes 'N Wheels Ltd.	1014	12/4/03	$29.00	Purolator	Nancy	Davolio
Cycle City Rome	1015	12/4/03	$43.50	UPS	Anne	Dodsworth
SAB Mountain	1016	12/4/03	$563.70	FedEx	Janet	Leverling

Figure 16-46 Mod 5 = 0 output

Example #2 The formula If RecordNumber mod 3 in [1,2] will shade the first two rows out of every three rows, as shown in Figure 16-47. Figure 16-48 shows the formula.

Customer Name	Order #	Order Date	Order Amount	Ship Via	First Name	Last Name
City Cyclists	1	12/2/03	$41.90	UPS	Nancy	Davolio
Deals on Wheels	1002	12/2/03	$5,060.28	Pickup	Janet	Leverling
Warsaw Sports, Inc.	1003	12/2/03	$186.87	UPS	Margaret	Peacock
Bikes and Trikes	1004	12/2/03	$823.05	Pickup	Margaret	Peacock
SAB Mountain	1005	12/3/03	$29.00	Loomis	Janet	Leverling
Poser Cycles	1006	12/3/03	$64.90	Purolator	Margaret	Peacock
Spokes	1007	12/3/03	$49.50	Parcel Post	Anne	Dodsworth
Clean Air Transportation Co.	1008	12/3/03	$2,214.94	Purolator	Margaret	Peacock
Extreme Cycling	1009	12/3/03	$29.00	Loomis	Margaret	Peacock

Figure 16-47 Mod 3 in [1,2] output

```
If RecordNumber mod 3 in [1,2]
then crSilver
Else DefaultAttribute
```

Figure 16-48 Mod 3 in [1,2] formula

Example #3 The formula If RecordNumber mod 10 in [3,5] will shade the third and fifth rows out of every ten rows, as shown in Figure 16-49.

Customer Name	Order #	Order Date	Order Amount	Ship Via	First Name	Last Name
City Cyclists	1	12/2/03	$41.90	UPS	Nancy	Davolio
Deals on Wheels	1002	12/2/03	$5,060.28	Pickup	Janet	Leverling
Warsaw Sports, Inc.	1003	12/2/03	$186.87	UPS	Margaret	Peacock
Bikes and Trikes	1004	12/2/03	$823.05	Pickup	Margaret	Peacock
SAB Mountain	1005	12/3/03	$29.00	Loomis	Janet	Leverling
Poser Cycles	1006	12/3/03	$64.90	Purolator	Margaret	Peacock
Spokes	1007	12/3/03	$49.50	Parcel Post	Anne	Dodsworth
Clean Air Transportation Co.	1008	12/3/03	$2,214.94	Purolator	Margaret	Peacock
Extreme Cycling	1009	12/3/03	$29.00	Loomis	Margaret	Peacock
Cyclopath	1010	12/3/03	$14,872.30	UPS	Nancy	Davolio

Figure 16-49 Mod 10 in [3,5] output

Exercise 16.17: Create Odd And Even Page Headers

As more and more word processing mail merge documents are being converted to reports, the need for odd and even page headers and footers is becoming more popular in reports. Some of these documents have header and footer information similar to the pages in this book. Documents that fall into this category are also often printed on printers that support duplex printing.

In the previous section you learned that the MOD function can be used with a special field to determine an action based on the current record number. Creating odd and even page headers is similar. The difference is that for the page header, you need two page header sections and each one requires its own conditional MOD formula. These formulas are for the page number and determine if the current page number is odd or even. Each page of the report only needs the odd page header information or the even page header information. Therefore, each page header section has to be suppressed when the other page header section prints.

> Even page numbers have a remainder of zero. Odd page numbers have a remainder of one.

1. Save the L7.5 report as `L16.17 Odd even page headers`.
2. Delete the line in the details section, then delete the Country field.
3. Add a page header section.
4. In the first page header section add a text object, then type `This is the right page header and should have an odd page number` in the object.
5. Add the Page Number field to the right corner of the Page Header a section, then place the text object to the left of the page number field.
6. Copy everything in the Page Header a section to the Page Header b section. Make sure that the field headings in both page header sections are lined up with the fields in the details section.
7. In the second page header section change the text object to `This is the left page header and should have an even page number`. Move the Page Number field to the left corner, then place the text object to the right of the page number field. The report layout should look like the one shown in Figure 16-50.

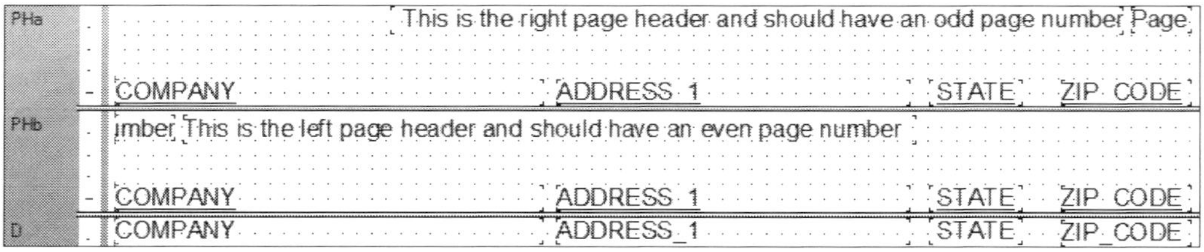

Figure 16-50 L16.17 report layout

8. Add the following formula `PageNumber mod 2 = 0` to the Page Header a Suppress (No Drill-Down) option on the Section Expert. You are adding this to the right page header section so that the left page header section will be suppressed when the right page header information is printed. Because the report does not have any groups, you do not have to check the Suppress (No Drill-Down) option.

9. Add the following formula `PageNumber mod 2 = 1` to the Page Header b Suppress (No Drill-Down) option on the Section Expert.

10. Save the changes. The report should look like the one shown in Figures 16-51 and 16-52. Close the report.

This is the right page header and should have an odd page number 1

COMPANY	ADDRESS 1	STATE	ZIP CODE
HAL's Consulting Corp	10 Countdown Loop	OR	97800
A1 Services-US Operations	2131 W. Tiny Rd.	NY	20122

Figure 16-51 L16.17 report - odd page number

2 This is the left page header and should have an even page number

COMPANY	ADDRESS 1	STATE	ZIP CODE
Boomer's Artworx	8907 E. Rosebud Lane	AZ	85258
VoiceComUSA	2700 Victory Blvd	NY	10314

Figure 16-52 L16.17 report - even page number

CREATING CHARTS

Crystal Reports has an expert that you can use to create charts. There are 16 types of charts that you can create, including pie, bar and line. In this lesson you will learn how to create many of the chart types using the Chart Expert.

LESSON 17

Charts Overview

In addition to being able to format data in reports, charts are used to present data in a graphical format which often makes the data easier to understand by visually displaying the relationship between the data. Charts also allow data to be presented in formats that text-only reports cannot do as well. For example, charts can show trends over time, relationships or how one set of data compares to another set of data.

In previous lessons you created basic charts using a report wizard. As you saw, the chart options were very limited. When you need to create or modify charts that require more detail than the wizards provide, you should use the Chart Expert. It is very easy to get carried away when creating charts. Try to create charts that present the data in a meaningful way. Remember that sometimes, less is more.

There are four ways to open the Chart Expert as discussed below.

① Click the **INSERT CHART** button on the Insert Tools toolbar.
② Insert ⇒ Chart.
③ Right-click on an existing chart and select Chart Expert.
④ Click on an existing chart, then Format ⇒ Chart Expert.

Chart Considerations

There are two areas that need to be addressed before you start to create the chart: The chart type and the source of the data for the chart. You will select the chart type on the Type tab on the Chart Expert, which is discussed below. Changing the chart type is easy. If you are not sure which chart type is the most appropriate, with a few mouse clicks, you can try out a few chart types and variations to see which is the best one for the data. Charts should enhance the ability to understand the data and make it easy to see the differences. The data source for the chart comes from one of the following: records in the details section of the report, a cross-tab, an OLAP grid or summary data.

I teach a technical writing class and one of the assignments has students create three charts to visually present data. Overall, the students do a good job on the charts. However, it is easy to tell which students have never created a chart before for at least one of the reasons listed below.

① The wrong chart type was selected. Newsflash: Bar charts are not the best option for all types of data, especially data that shows trends or needs to show how data has changed over time.
② The values on the X and Y axes are backwards. Dollar amounts, quantity, percents, usually go on the Y axis and time, dates and categories usually go on the X axis.
③ Not understanding the data that the chart will use.

The Chart Expert

This is the tool that is used to create and edit charts. It has wizard like characteristics because you click on the tabs to accomplish different tasks associated with creating and editing a chart. The biggest benefit of using the Chart Expert instead of the chart options on a wizard is that you have a lot of the chart options available from the beginning and the chart does not have to be based on data that will be printed on the report, like the wizards require. The options on each tab are covered in detail in this lesson because not understanding what all of the options are or not knowing where they are, will take you longer to create a chart. As you read about the Chart Expert, you may gain a better understanding of the options if you have the Chart Expert open.

The six tabs on the Chart Expert (Type, Data, Axes, Options, Color Highlighting and Text) contain options for a variety of features that you can use to make the chart as effective as possible. Keep in mind that not all of these tabs are available for all chart types. The tabs and options are discussed below.

You do not have to create a chart from an existing report. You can select the fields that you need on the Chart Expert.

Type Tab

The options on this tab are used to select what the chart will look like. There are 16 chart types that you can select from as shown on the left side of Figure 17-1. Many of these chart types have variations that you can select, which gives you more chart options. Each chart type is explained later in Table 17-1.

There are additional chart types, which Crystal Reports refers to as templates.

You will learn about the other chart types in the next lesson.

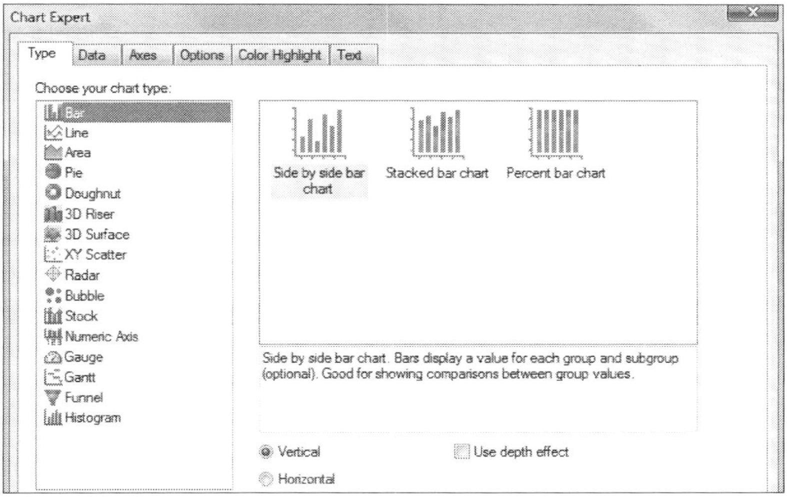

Figure 17-1 Chart Expert Type tab options

In previous lessons you created a pie and bar chart using a wizard. If you have created charts in spreadsheet software, you are probably familiar with many of the chart types in Crystal Reports. When selecting the chart type, the most important consideration should be to select the chart type that will best display the data that will be presented in the chart. This is the first thing that you have to do. When you select the chart type on the left you will see variations of the chart on the right. Click on the chart style (variation) on the right that you want to use. Under the chart variations you will see a description of the chart type.

Chart Type Options

At the bottom of the Type tab shown above in Figure 17-1, you will see the first two options discussed below for the bar, line, area and histogram chart types. Most chart types also have the third option below.

① **Vertical** This is the default option. The elements will start at the bottom of the chart, as shown on the percent bar chart on the right side of Figure 17-1 above.
② **Horizontal** If selected, this option will change the direction of the elements on the chart. The bars will start on the left, instead of the bottom, as shown in Figure 17-2.
③ **Use Depth Effect** If checked, this option will display the chart in 3D format, as shown in Figure 17-3.

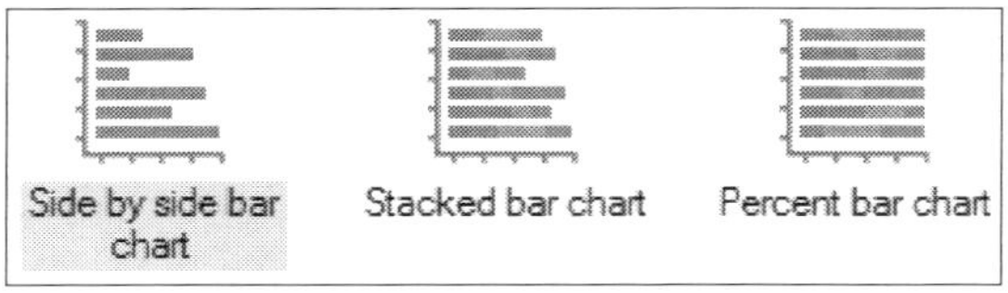

Figure 17-2 Horizontal bar chart options

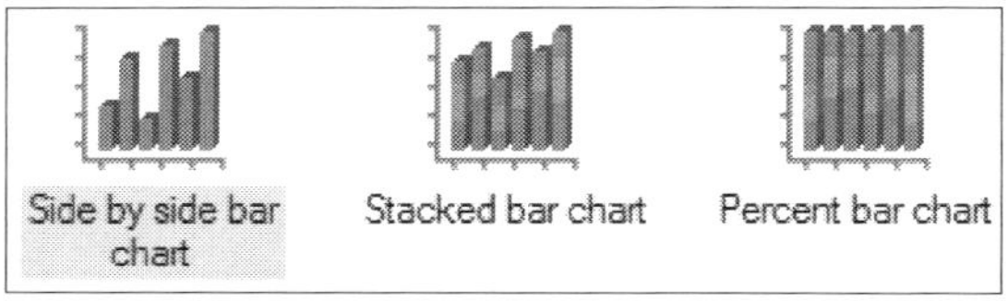

Figure 17-3 Use depth effect options

Chart Types

Chart Type	Description
Bar	Bar charts, as shown in Figure 17-4 show differences between items and relationships between grouped data. This is probably the most used chart type. Stacked bar charts show each item as a percent of the total.
Line	Line charts show trends and changes over a period of time. The markers on the bottom three line chart types indicate the exact values. In Figure 17-5, the data is represented with lines. A good use of **3D LINE CHARTS** is when the data lines cross each other often. This makes a line chart easier to read. (1)
Area	Area charts show how the data has changed over a period of time. Figure 17-6 shows how the four types of income (mail order, store, kiosk and Internet) make up the total income and how the income changes over the months. Area charts are almost identical to stacked line charts. The difference is that area charts are filled in below the trendline. Area charts are probably best suited for a few groups of data. (1)

Table 17-1 Chart types explained

Chart Type	Description
Pie	Pie charts only show information for one point in time. Figure 17-7 shows the various types of income for July. Each slice of the pie represents the percent for the item. The Multiple pie chart type will create a chart for each group. (2)
Doughnut	This chart type is similar to pie charts. The difference is that there is a hole in the center, which contains the grand total of the data presented in the chart. (2)
3D Riser	This is the 3D version of bar charts that shows data values side by side, separately or stacked. It can display several groups of data in shapes like a pyramid or octagon.
3D Surface	This is the 3D version of area charts. This chart type uses three sets of data. The surface of the chart has a curve and shows trends in relation to time.
XY Scatter	XY Scatter charts show how two values are related (like month of year and order amount) and how a change in one value affects the other value, as shown in Figure 17-8. This chart type is used to show the correlation between the items. The X and Y axis must display numeric data. If data like dates or months can be converted to numeric data, it can be used in this chart type.
Radar	Radar charts compare sets of data relative to a center point and shows how far the data value is from the standard (the center point value). The values that are often used are group subtotals. The data from the X axis is usually plotted in a circle and the Y values are plotted from the center of the circle out.
Bubble	This chart type is similar to XY Scatter charts because it plots individual points. The difference is that bubble charts use different size plot points based on the data value. The larger the data value, the larger the size of the plot point.
Stock	This chart type is similar to bar charts. The difference is that the bars in stock charts do not have to touch the bottom of the chart. This type of chart is often used to display the minimum and maximum of stock prices, where each bar represents a different stock. Stock charts plot the first and last trade of the day or the high and low values for each element.
Numeric Axis	This chart type does not use a fixed X axis value or interval like many other chart types do. You can use a date/time field or numeric value for the X axis. This chart type is another way to create bar, line and area charts.
Gauge	This chart type looks like a gauge in a car as shown in Figure 17-9. The needle in the chart points to the value that is being represented. If there is more than one value or group being represented, a gauge chart is created for each value or group. Multiple needles in one gauge means that there is more than one "On change of" value.
Gantt	This type chart is primarily used to display project management data like the start and end dates of tasks on a project plan. Gantt charts only work with date and date/time fields.

Table 17-1 Chart types explained (Continued)

Chart Type	Description
Funnel	This chart type is similar to stacked bar charts because each bar on the funnel shows each item as a percent of the total. The difference is that the bars are in the shape of a funnel. The height of the bar represents the percent of the data. The width of the bar does not represent anything.
Histogram	This chart type places the data into buckets, based on the range that the data falls into and displays a count of the records in each bucket, as shown in Figure 17-10. Usually, you will not see more than eight bars on a histogram chart, regardless of how many ranges (buckets) there really are.

Table 17-1 Chart types explained (Continued)

(1) This chart type requires at least two sets of data.
(2) This chart type only uses one value because it shows how the whole (100%) is divided.

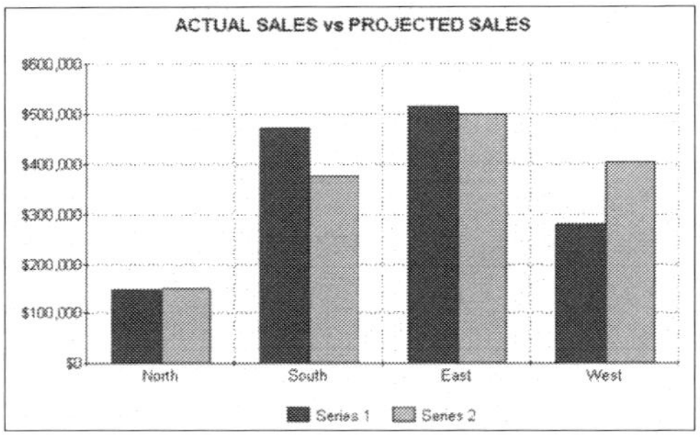

Figure 17-4 Bar chart

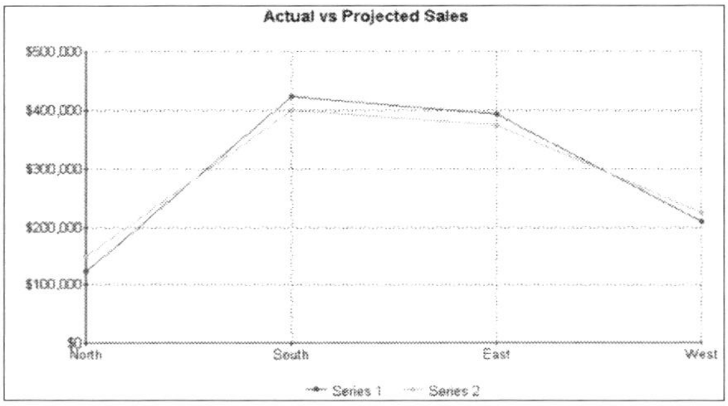

Figure 17-5 Line chart

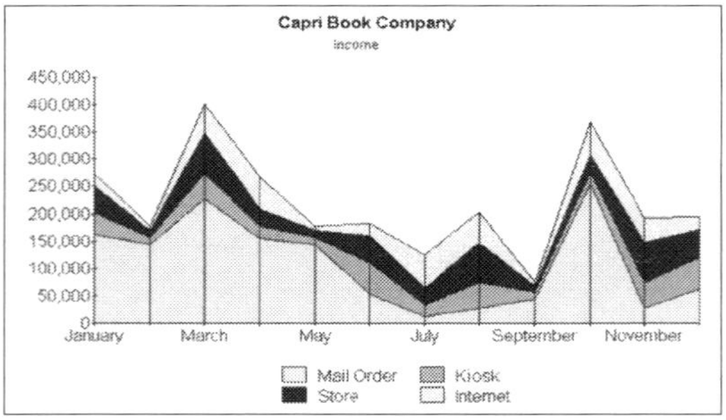

Figure 17-6 Area chart

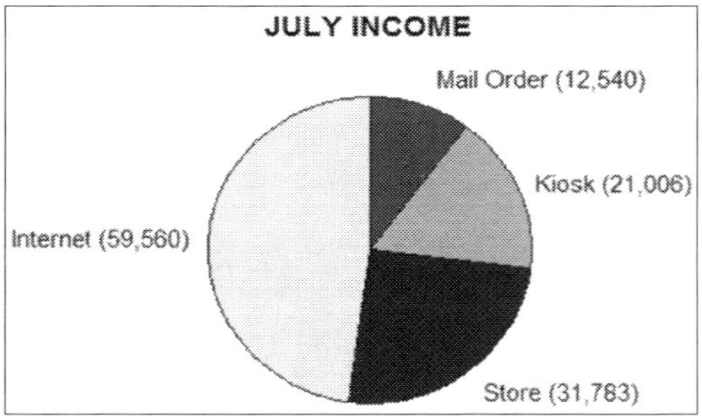

Figure 17-7 Pie chart

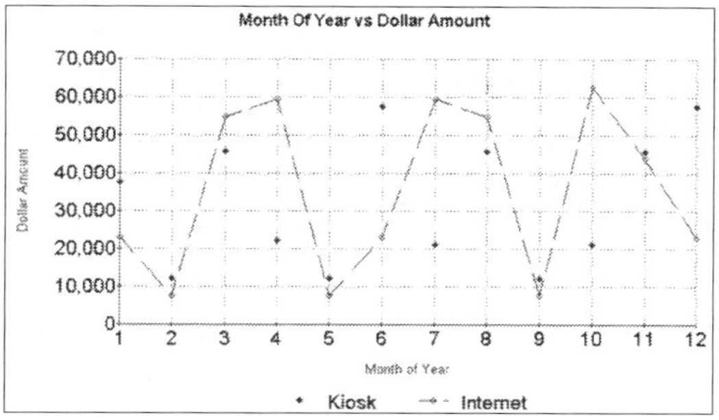

Figure 17-8 XY Scatter chart

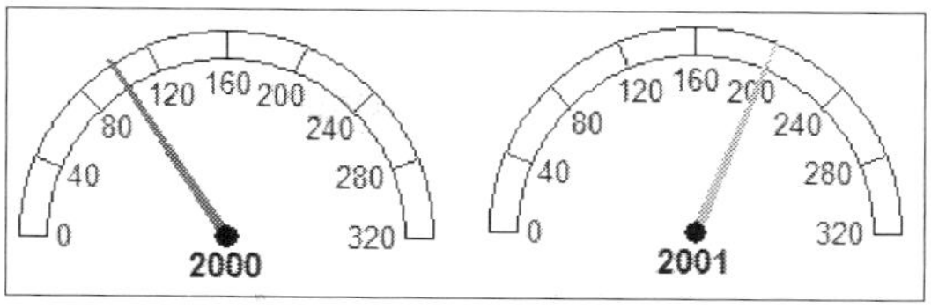

Figure 17-9 Gauge chart

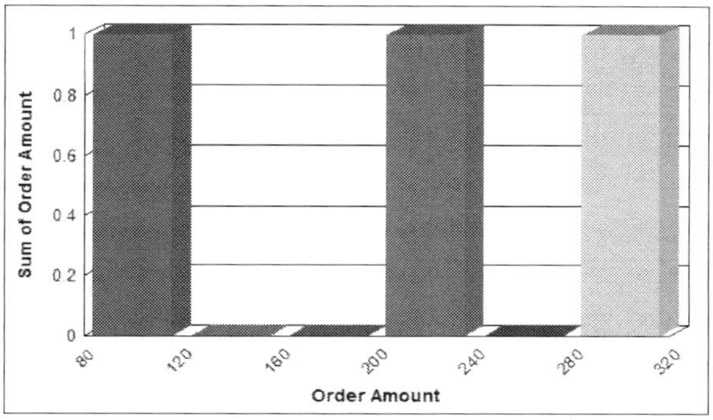

Figure 17-10 Histogram chart

It would be very helpful and a big time saver to me if at least one of the tabs on the Chart Expert would display the chart with the options that are selected, similar to what you see when you use the Chart Options dialog box to modify the chart. You will learn how to use the Chart Options dialog box in the next lesson.

Data Tab

The options on this tab are used to select the source of the data for the chart. This is the second area that needs to be addressed before you create the chart. There are four ways (called layout options) to chart data, as discussed below. Depending on the chart type that was selected, not all of the data layout options will be available.

Each layout type works independently of the others. You can only select one layout type. If you select one and make changes on that screen, then select a different layout type and make changes, the only information that will be saved, will be the layout that you changed last.

All four layout options have the **ON CHANGE OF** drop-down list field. The options in this list are how you decide when a new element (bar, slice of pie, point on a line, etc) will be added to the chart. This option lets Crystal Reports know that when the value in the field(s) listed below this option changes, you want a new element of the chart to be created.

The options in the Placement section including the **PLACE CHART** drop-down list shown in Figure 17-11, is used to select where the chart will be placed in the report. The **ONCE PER REPORT** option places the chart in the report header or footer section.

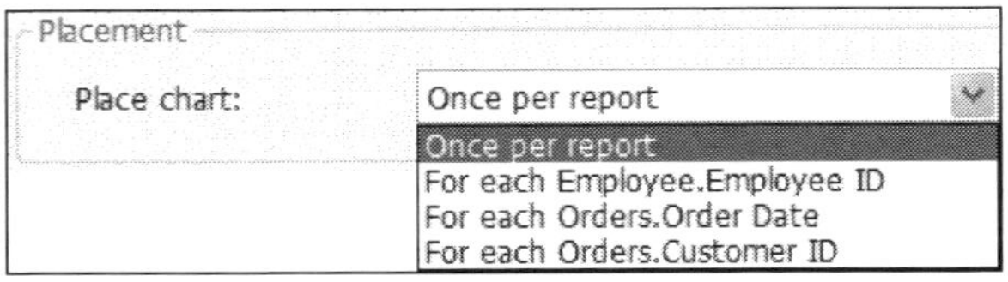

Figure 17-11 Place chart drop-down list options

If the report has groups, you will see the options similar to those shown above in Figure 17-11 in the drop-down list. The reason that you see three **FOR EACH** options is because the report has three groups. Charts are placed at least one section in the report above the data that is displayed on the chart. Advanced, group, cross-tab and OLAP charts cannot be placed in the details section of a report.

When you are working on exercises that use the options on the Advanced tab, you will see this instruction: **ADD THE FIELD TO THE FIRST LIST BOX**. This means to add the field to the list that is under the On Change Of option.

Advanced Layout Options

This layout option is always available. Out of the four layout options, this is probably the most complex because it is used to create a chart that is not based on data that will print on the report. If you created a report using the Blank Report option and have not added any fields to the report, the options on this tab are used to select the fields for the chart. This is how you would create a report that only has a chart. If you need to a create a chart based on records in the details section of the report, click on the Advanced layout option on the Data tab. You will see the options shown in Figure 17-12.

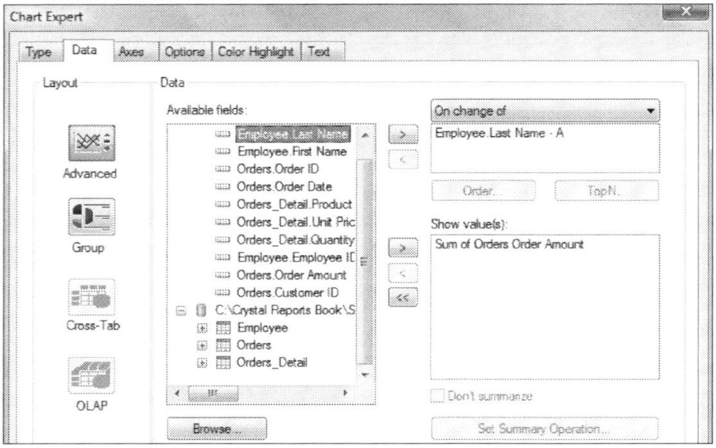

Figure 17-12 Chart Expert Data tab - Advanced options

If the report already has groups defined, you can still create an advanced chart because the options on this tab are not affected by the groups that are on the report.

The **AVAILABLE FIELDS** section of the Data tab contains the fields that are already on the report, including the summary and running total fields, as well as, all of the fields in the tables connected to the report. This section is only available if the On Change of option is selected in the drop-down list on the right.

Summary and running total fields can only be added to the **SHOW VALUE(S)** list.

The **ON CHANGE OF** option is used to select up to two fields to group the data in the chart on. This group is not a real group like the ones that you learned how to create earlier in this book. When the value in the field changes, a new element is created. Each element on the chart represents one group.

If you wanted to create a chart that displayed the orders by sales rep, you would add the sales rep (Employee Last Name) field to the list box below this drop-down list.

The Order Amount field would be added to the Show Value(s) list to get a total for each sales rep. Figure 17-13 shows this report.

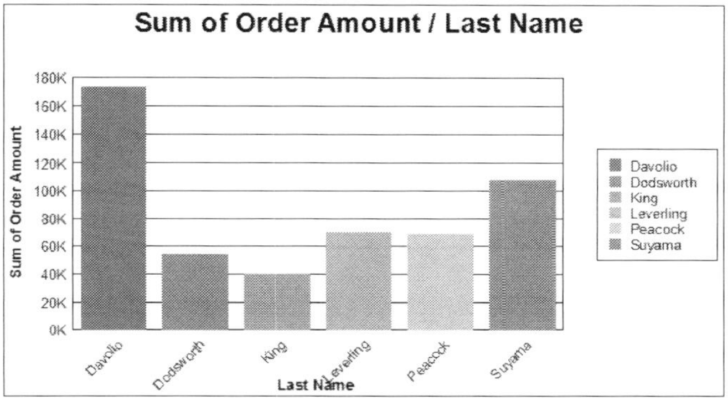

Figure 17-13 Sales reps orders chart

The On Change Of option works like the group option because it summarizes the values in the group. The difference is that the groups in the chart do not have an effect on the report. If you select multiple fields to group on, the data from each group will be displayed side by side or stacked, based on the chart type that is selected. If the order date was added to the Evaluate option, as shown in Figure 17-14, the report would look like the one shown in Figure 17-15.

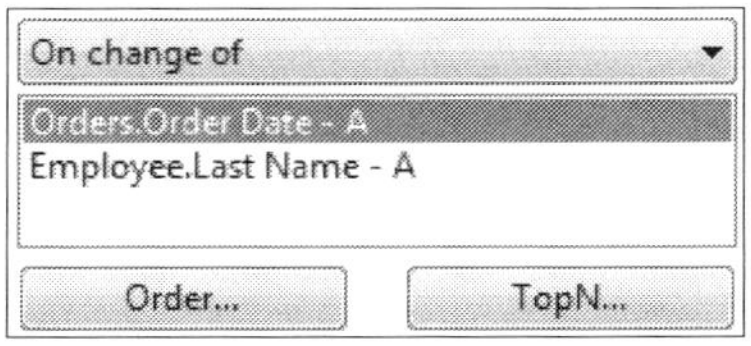

Figure 17-14 On change of options

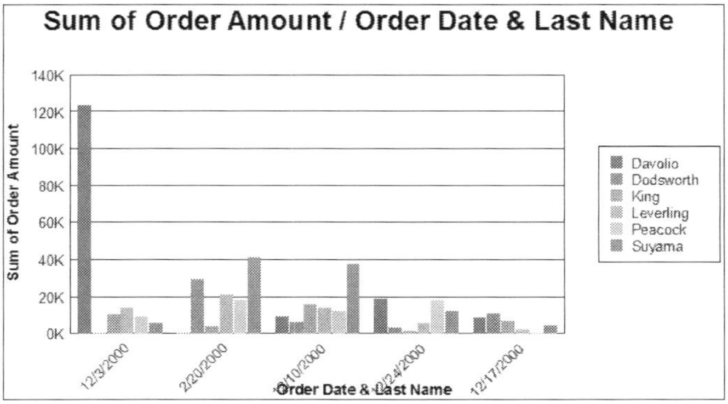

Figure 17-15 Sales reps orders chart with additional options

The first field below the On change of drop-down list is the primary group and determines how the data is grouped. The second field below the drop-down list creates the elements in the primary group. In the example shown above in Figure 17-14, the order date field is the primary group. The Employee last name field is the secondary group. Putting the fields in this order groups the records by date. Each element in the date group is a different sales rep.

The **FOR EACH RECORD** option in the On change of drop-down list will cause a new element to be added to the chart for every record that would print on the report. If this option is selected, only one field can be added to the box below this drop-down list. If there is not a lot of data in the table for the field that you select, it is okay to select this option because the chart will be legible. If there are a lot of records, more than likely it would be hard to read the chart if this option is selected. If this option is selected, fields that are added to the **SHOW VALUE(S)** list will not be summarized, the actual value in the field is what will appear in the chart.

You can reduce the records that are used to create the chart by using the Select Expert. If you realize that you need to do this, you can create the selection criteria after the chart has been created. You will learn how to do this later in this lesson.

Gantt charts have to use the **FOR EACH RECORD** option. A start and end date must be added to the Show value(s) list.

The **FOR ALL RECORDS** option creates a chart with only one element, which is a grand total for all of the records that are on the report. You cannot add any fields to the box below the On change of drop-down list if this option is selected.

The **SHOW VALUE(S)** list contains the field(s) that the chart will create a summary for. The actual value or the value from the summary calculation will be used as an element on the chart. Which value is used is determined by the option selected in the evaluation option drop-down list. Table 17-2 explains the type of summary value that each evaluation option creates. If you add more than one field to this list, the chart will plot a separate line or bar for example, for each field in this list. Each chart type allows at least one field in the Show Value(s) list. In the Orders by sales rep example, if you add the Order Amount field to the Show value(s) list, a total (summary) for each sales rep would be created.

Option	Show Value Summary Type
On change of	Summary for each group.
For each record	Actual value for each record.
For all records	One summary value for the entire report.

Table 17-2 Evaluation options explained

Summary Calculations

Table 17-3 explains the default type of summary calculations that are applied to different field types. You can change the type of calculation as needed.

Field Type	Default Calculation Type
Number	Summary
Currency	Summary
All others	Count

Table 17-3 Default summary calculations

You can change the summary calculation type by following the steps below.

① Click on the field that you want to change the calculation for in the Show value(s) list.
② Click the **SET SUMMARY OPERATION** button shown earlier at the bottom of Figure 17-12. You will see the Edit Summary dialog box.
③ The options in the **CALCULATE THIS SUMMARY** drop-down list are the ones that are available for the data type of the field that you are changing. Select the type of calculation that you want.

The **ORDER** button on the Data tab will open the Chart Sort Order dialog box shown in Figure 17-16.

The options on this dialog box work the same way that the options on the Insert Group dialog box that you learned about in Lesson 10. These options are used to select the sort order for the element in the chart.

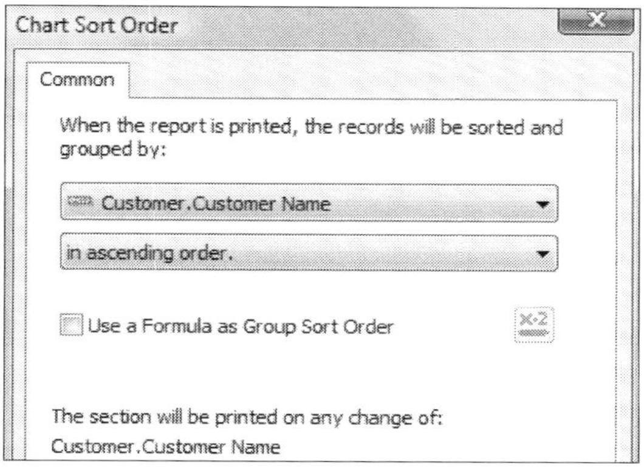

Figure 17-16 Chart Sort Order dialog box

In the orders by sales rep example, if you selected the Order Amount field and then clicked the Order button you would be able to select how you wanted the total order amount for each rep to be displayed. If you were creating a bar chart and wanted to see the sales reps in order from high to low based on sales, you would select **DESCENDING**.

The **TOP N** button will open the Group Sort Expert shown in Figure 17-17. The options on this dialog box are similar the ones on the **OTHERS** tab on the Change Group Options dialog box. [See Lesson 11, Figure 11-16] If you only wanted to include the top or bottom N records, groups or percents, you would select the options here.

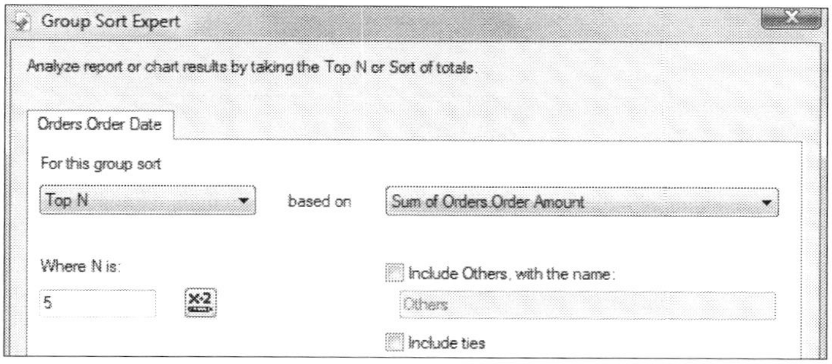

Figure 17-17 Group Sort Expert

The options selected above in Figure 17-17 will display the five sales reps that had the lowest number of sales.

If you want to include groups that are not part of the group sort, you can by checking the appropriate **INCLUDE** options on the right side of the Group Sort Expert dialog box. If checked, the **INCLUDE TIES** option will include groups that have the same summarized value if they meet the other selection criteria. Notice that you can also create formulas if the chart requires it.

Group Layout Options

The group layout options create a chart that is based off of fields in a group header or footer section of the report. This chart layout type is only available if both of the conditions discussed below have been met.

① The chart must be placed in the report header or footer or in a group header or footer section that is on a higher level then the data in the group that the chart will be based on.

② The report has to have one group that has a summary or total field.

The options shown in Figure 17-18 are used to select how the data in the group will be displayed in the chart. The options are explained below.

The options below the **ON CHANGE OF** drop-down list are the fields (that have a summary or total field) that are in a lower level then the section of the report that the chart has been placed in.

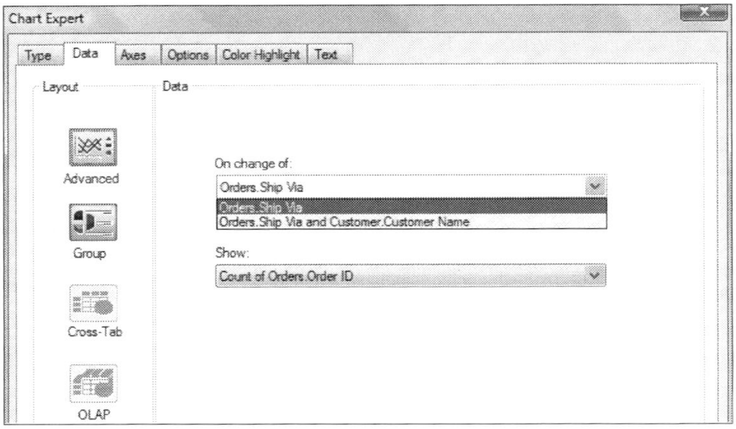

Figure 17-18 Chart Expert Data tab - Group options
(On Change Of options for the two groups below the chart)

This option is used to select the group that the chart will be based on.

The example report that is used in this discussion has two groups: the Ship Via group and the Customer Name group. Both of these groups have summary fields.

If you put the chart in the report header or footer section, the On Change Of drop-down list will have the options shown above in Figure 17-18.

If the report has three groups with a summary or total field and you place the chart in the first group section, you would see the summary or total fields for the two groups below it. Just by looking at the options in Figure 17-19, you do not know if the chart is in a report or group section.

If you put the chart in the first group header or footer section or the report header or footer section and there is only one group below it that has a summary or total field, you would only see one option in the On Change Of drop-down list, as shown in Figure 17-19. These are the summary fields in the group header or footer section in the report.

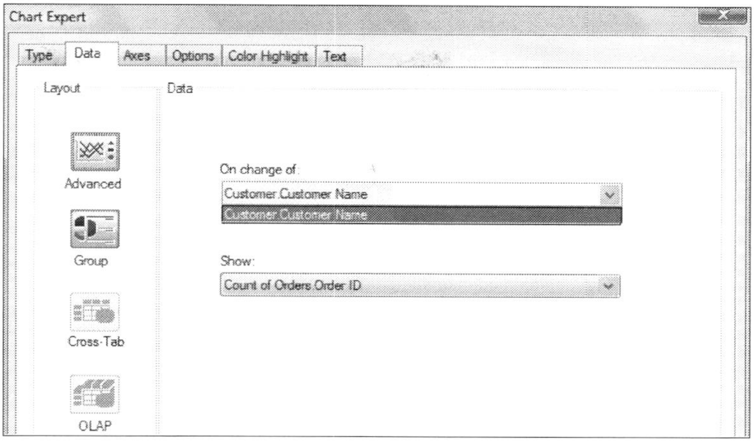

Figure 17-19 On Change Of options for one group below the chart

The fields in the **SHOW** drop-down list are the summary and subtotal fields in the group that is selected in the On Change Of field. This is how you select the summary field in the group that will be used in the chart.

Cross-Tab Layout Options

This layout option is only available if the report has a cross-tab object in the same or corresponding section of the report that the chart is placed in. By corresponding section, I mean if the cross-tab that the chart will be based on is in the Group 2 footer section, the chart can be placed in the Group 2 header or footer section. The options shown in Figure 17-20 are used to create a chart based on the data in the cross-tab.

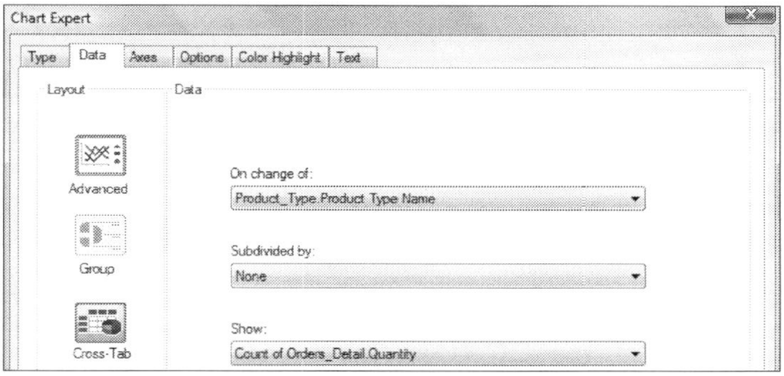

Figure 17-20 Chart Expert Data tab - Cross-Tab options

Earlier you learned that cross-tab charts cannot be placed in the details section. If you move the cross-tab object to a different section after a cross-tab chart has been created, the report will automatically be moved to the new section also.

> If the report has more than one cross-tab object, you have to select the cross-tab object that you want to create the chart for before you open the Chart Expert.

The options in the **ON CHANGE OF** drop-down list are the first fields in the Rows and Columns sections of the Cross-Tab Expert or Wizard, regardless of how many fields each of these sections have. [See Exercise 13.1] The field selected in this drop-down list is the first (or only) element that will be used as the primary X axis value.

Selecting a field in the **SUBDIVIDED BY** drop-down list is optional, which is why the default option is **NONE**. The only field that is available in the Subdivided By drop-down list is the one that was not selected in the On Change Of drop-down list. Selecting a field will create a second X value, which will add a second series of data to the chart. This will let you create a chart that does a side by side comparison.

Figure 17-21 shows a line chart with the first field in the Row section and the first field in the Column section from the cross-tab selected.

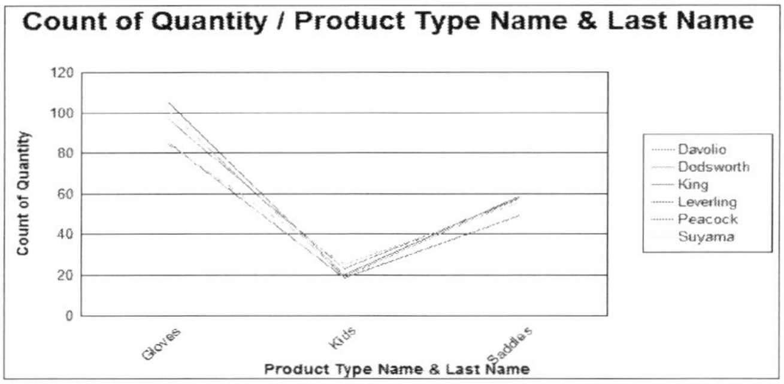

Figure 17-21 Line chart with the row and column fields selected

The options in the **SHOW** drop-down list are the fields that are in the Summary Fields section of the Cross-Tab window. They are the fields that you select from to summarize the report on, like the Show Value list on the Advanced Layout screen.

OLAP Layout Options

These options are not available with ACT! databases.

Axes Tab

Depending on the chart type that is selected, you may not see the Axes tab shown in Figure 17-22.

You will see this tab if the chart type selected uses the X and Y axis. For example, bar, line and area charts use the X and Y axis. Pie, Doughnut and Gantt chart types do not.

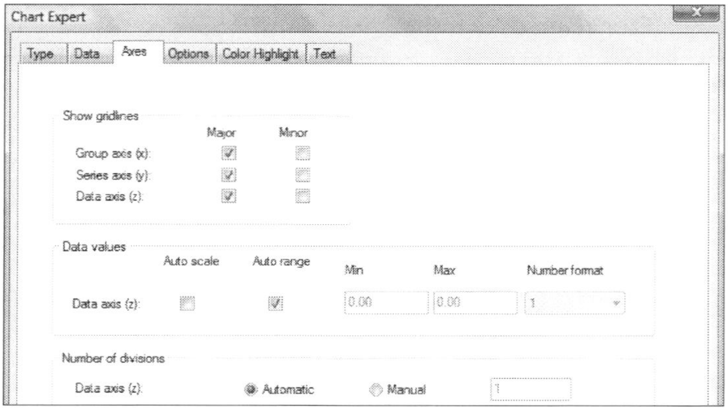

Figure 17-22 Chart Expert - Axes tab

The options on this tab are used to select how the chart will display the data values that you see across the bottom of the chart (the X axis) and on the left side of the chart (the Y axis). If you are creating a 3D chart, you can also select the data values for the Z axis. If the chart that you are creating needs to display order totals by month, the months would be placed on the X axis because the report is grouped by month and the totals would be placed on the Y axis because they represent the quantity, as shown in Figure 17-23. If you were creating the same chart, but selected a 3D layout, the chart would look like the one shown in Figure 17-24, which also includes the data axis (the Z axis).

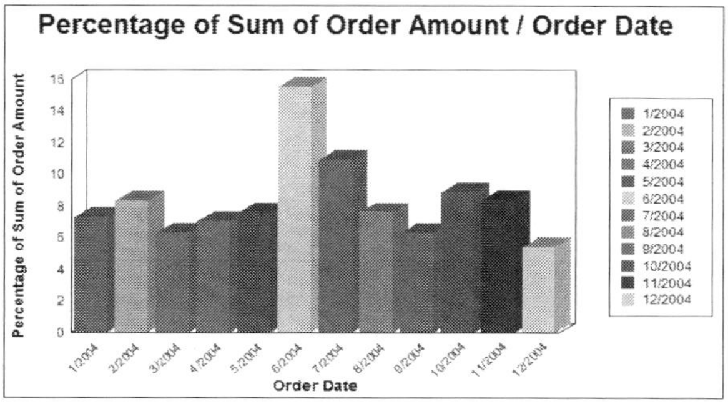

Figure 17-23 Bar chart with X and Y axis data

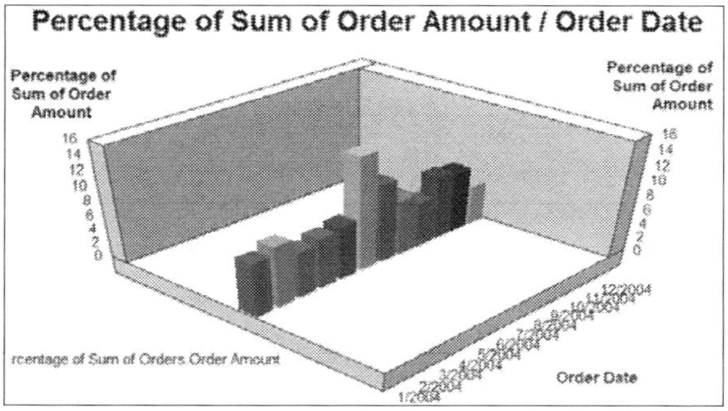

Figure 17-24 Bar chart with X, Y and Z axis data

Show Gridlines Options

You will see two or three axis options in this section depending on whether the chart is two or three dimensional.

The **Group Axis** option corresponds to the **ON CHANGE OF** field on the Data tab.
The **Series Axis** option will only appear for three dimensional chart types.
The **Data Axis** option corresponds to the **SHOW** field on the Advanced layout section of the Data tab.

Some chart types will have a gridline on the Group axis whether you select the option or not.

If checked, the major and minor options will add gridlines to the chart.

The **MAJOR** option will place the gridlines (with labels) on the axis, as shown in Figure 17-25.

The **MINOR** option can only be used with numeric labels and will place the gridlines between the labels on the axis.

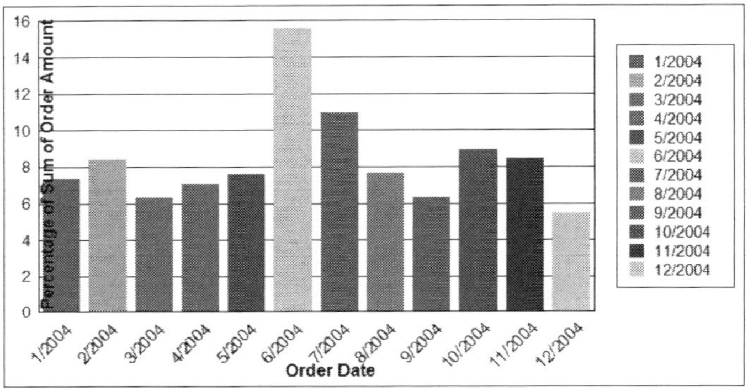

Figure 17-25 Bar chart with major gridlines added

Data Values Options

The options in this section of the Axes tab let you customize the **VALUES** on the Data axis.

The **AUTO RANGE** option is the default and lets Crystal Reports use the chart values to set the starting and ending values for the Data axis. If you want to customize the values, clear this option and enter the Min, Max and Number formats that you want. If you change the data value options and then recheck this option, the changes that you made will still be in effect, even though the options are not enabled.

MIN is the lowest value that you want to see on the axis. Usually this is zero, but you may have the need to use a different starting value.

MAX is the highest value that you want to see on the Axis. This value is usually larger than the largest value of the data on the axis.

The danger in changing the max value in my opinion is that you would be basing the change on the current values being displayed on the chart. If the report is run later and for whatever reason has a larger value than the value that you entered in the max field, the chart would not display the largest value.

The **NUMBER FORMAT** option is only available if the Auto Range option is not checked.

The options in the drop-down list shown in Figure 17-26 are used to select the format for the numbers that will be displayed on the chart.

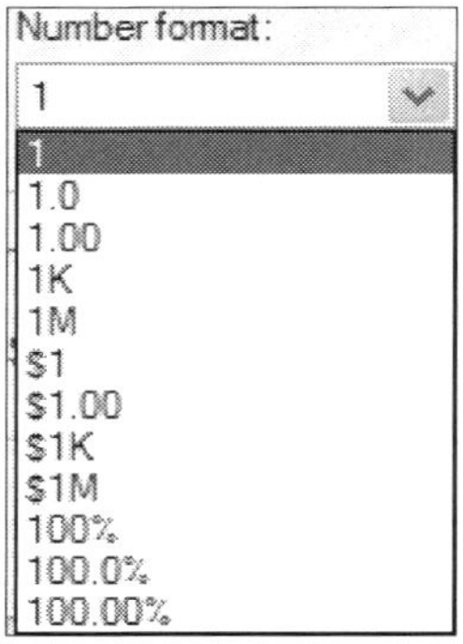

Figure 17-26 Number format options

If checked, the **AUTO SCALE** option is used to select the starting numeric value that the chart will use.

Number Of Division Options

The options in this section are used to customize the number of gridlines (intervals) and labels that the data axis will have. Select the **MANUAL** option if you want to set the intervals.

Options Tab

Figures 17-27 to 17-29 show various versions of the Options tab. The options are different depending on the chart type that is selected.

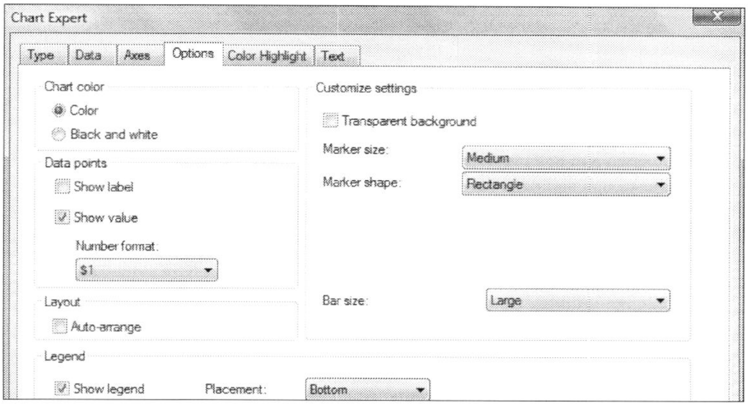

Figure 17-27 Options tab for a bar chart

NEW The **AUTO-ARRANGE** layout option resets the chart to its original size and position.

The options in the **CUSTOMIZE SETTINGS** section are used to select the size and shape for the legend in some chart types or the shape of the markers for bar and line charts.

The **MARKERS** are the points on a chart that are connected by lines. This option is often used in line charts, as you saw earlier in Figure 17-5.

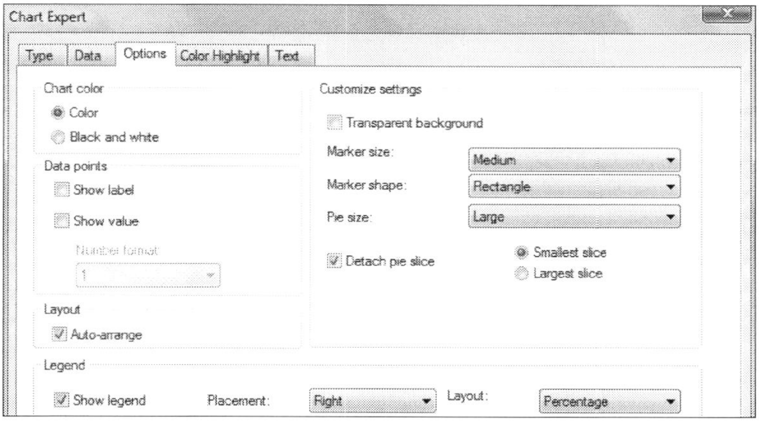

Figure 17-28 Options tab for a pie chart

The last size option in this section is used to select the size of the element. For example, the size of a slice of the pie chart or the size of the bar as shown in Figures 17-28 and 17-29.

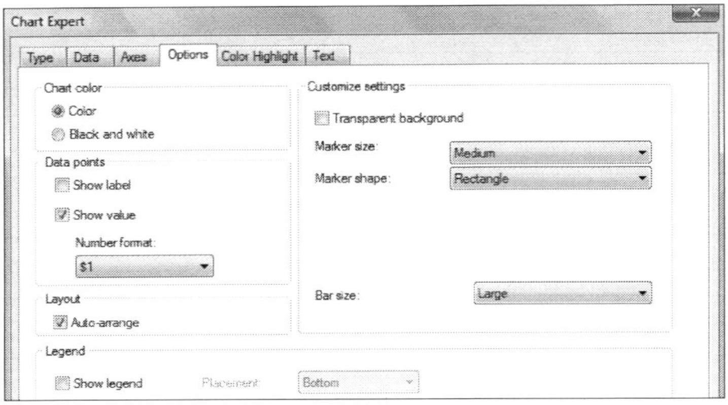

Figure 17-29 Options tab for a histogram chart

The options in the **DATA POINTS** section are used to select whether or not labels and values (the actual data) are displayed with the elements. Each element (slice) in the pie chart shown earlier in Figure 17-7 has a label and value. The value is in parenthesis for illustration purposes.

The options in the **LEGEND** section are used to turn the legend on and off, as well as, select where you want the charts legend placed. The legend is the color coded key that lets you know what the elements on the chart are referencing.

The area chart shown earlier in Figure 17-6 has the legend at the bottom of the chart. In Figure 17-28 shown earlier, the legend will be placed on the right side of the chart. Notice in Figure 17-29 above that the legend options are not enabled. That means that the chart type cannot have a legend. There are also times when a chart looks better without a legend.

Color Highlight Tab

The options on this tab are used to conditionally format the colors for the elements on a chart.

The options shown in Figure 17-30 should look familiar because they are similar to the options on the Highlighting Expert.

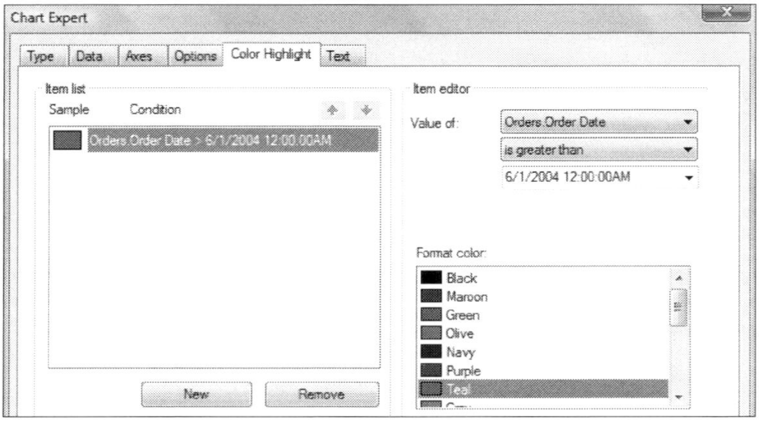

Figure 17-30 Color Highlight tab options

The difference between them is that the Highlighting Expert works with objects on the report and the options on the Color Highlight tab work with elements on a chart. The options shown will change the color of the field to Teal if the order date is greater than 6/1/2004.

The conditional formatting that you apply to an element does not change if the data for that element changes. For example, if you apply conditional formatting to the bottom section (for example, the mail order section) of the area chart shown earlier in Figure 17-6 and the data changes and the mail order element is no longer on the bottom, the formatting for the mail order element does not change. The new data that is in the bottom section of the area chart will change.

In my opinion, conditional formatting usually looks better on charts that are using data that is grouped.

Text Tab

The options on this tab are used to add text to a chart.

As shown in Figure 17-31, the **AUTO TEXT** option is checked for all of the title fields and the text fields are not enabled.

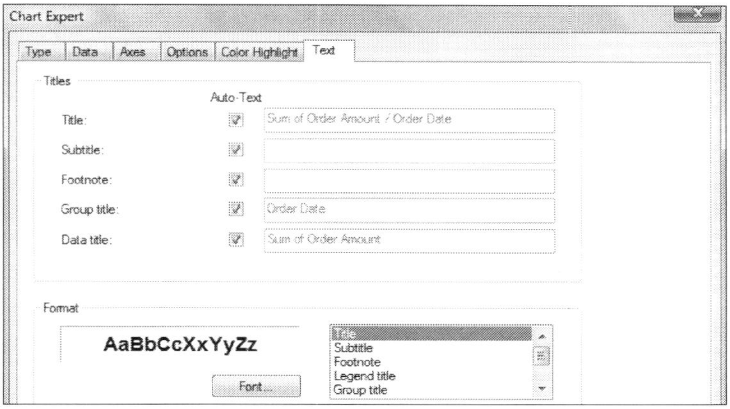

Figure 17-31 Text tab chart options

This is because Crystal Reports automatically creates many of the titles based on the field names that the chart is being created from. You saw this when you created charts with the wizards in Lesson 12.

To change a title, clear the check mark next to the title that you want to change and type in the title that you want. It is not a requirement to have titles.

You can change the font of a title by clicking on the title that you want to change in the **FORMAT** section and then click the Font button. Figure 17-32 shows the font options.

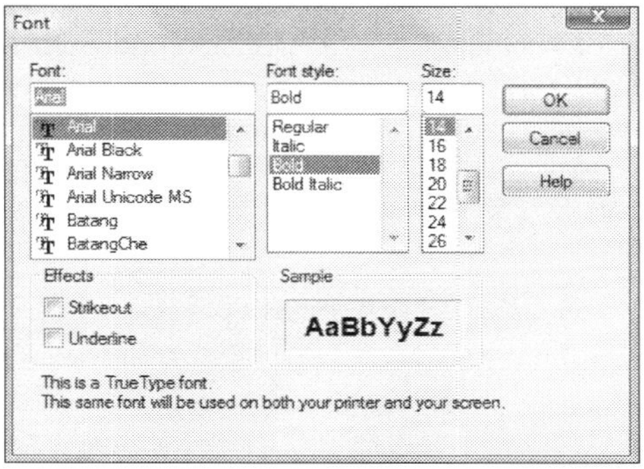

Figure 17-32 Font options

Parts Of A Chart

Charts can contain all or any of the options discussed below. It is important that you understand these options. These options can be added or deleted as needed. Figure 17-33 illustrates many of the parts of a chart that have already been discussed in this lesson. The parts of the chart illustrated are explained below.

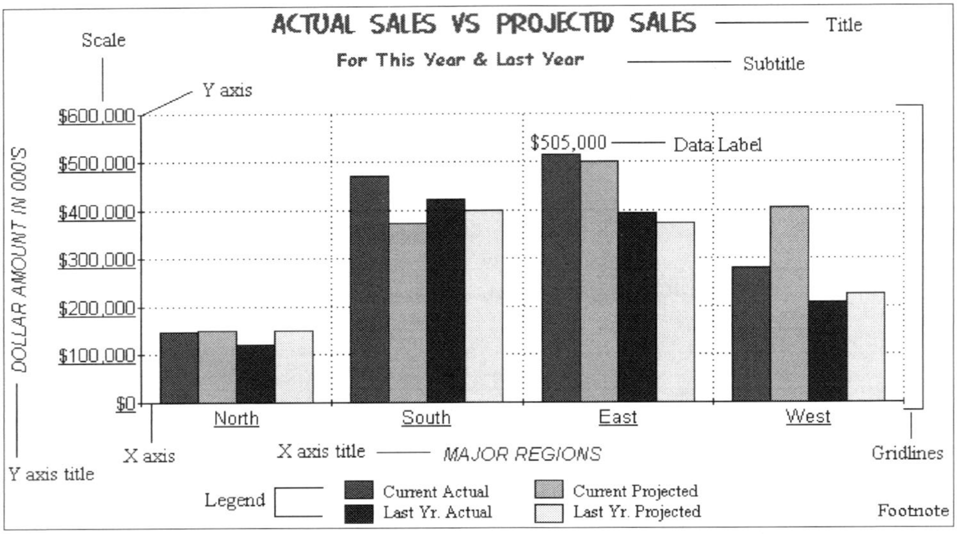

Figure 17-33 Parts of a chart illustrated

Title and **Subtitle** are a description of what type of data the chart is displaying.

X and **Y Axis** represent the vertical (Y) axis and horizontal (X) axis of the chart. The X axis often represents quantities or percents.

Gridlines make the chart easier to read if the values are close in range. You can have horizontal and vertical gridlines.

Scale shows the unit of measurement. The scale range is taken from the data that is displayed on the report. The scale is automatically created for you, but you can change it. Crystal Reports uses the Auto Scale and Auto Range options on the Chart Expert Axes tab to create the scale.

The **Legend** is used to help make the chart easier to read. Legends are color coded representations of different data elements on the chart.

Adding A Chart To A Report

The way that charts are added to the report has changed from the previous version of Crystal Reports. This applies to the Insert ⇒ Chart option and Insert Chart button options. When either of these options are selected, you will see a shadow box like you see when you add an image to a report. Click in the section of the report that you want to place the chart in. If you select a section that the chart cannot be placed in, the cursor will change to a circle with a line through it. If this happens, you have to start the insert chart process over. Once you select a section of the report where the chart will be placed, one of two things will happen:

① The Chart Expert will automatically open.
② A bar chart will be added to the report with several options already selected. If this happens and the default options are not what you need, right-click on the chart and select Chart Expert on the shortcut menu.

The way that the above options are determined is not random. The scenarios below explain under what conditions the Chart Expert will or will not automatically open.

① If a chart is added to the report header or footer section of a report that has a group with a summary field, a bar chart based on the group will automatically be added to the report. The Chart Expert will not automatically open.
② If a chart is added to the report header or footer section of a report that does not have a group or a group that does not have a summary field, the Chart Expert will open automatically.
③ If a report has a cross-tab or OLAP object and it is not selected prior to inserting a chart, the Chart Expert will automatically open.
④ If a report has a cross-tab or OLAP object selected prior to inserting a chart, a bar chart based on the data in the cross-tab or OLAP object will be added to a new section of the report.

Like summary fields on the report, the section of the report that a chart is placed in determines the data that will be used to create the chart. If the chart is placed in the report header or footer section, the chart will contain data from the entire report. If the chart is placed in the group header or footer section, the chart will only contain data for the group.

Tips For Creating Charts

1. Unless stated otherwise, if the exercise does not create a new report, place a chart object in the report header section of the report and open the Chart Expert after step 1 in each exercise.
2. When creating a new report which requires more than one table, make sure that the links are correct before creating the report.

When you view a chart on the design window, you may see fields that you did not select. You will see real data on the preview tab. The chart in the design window does not represent data in the tables that the chart is using. I am telling you this because I do not want you to think that you are losing your mind when you see a chart in the design window that doesn't display what you may be expecting.

Exercise 17.1: Create A Bar Chart

1. Save the L12.5 report as `L17.1 Bar chart`.

2. Delete the existing chart. Select the Side by side bar chart type, then select the Group data layout option on the Data tab, if it is not already selected.

3. Select the Actual Close Date field from the On Change Of drop-down list if it is not already selected, then select the Total field in the Show drop-down list.

4. On the Axes tab, add a major gridline to the Group axis option.

5. On the Options tab, select the Show value Data Points option, then change the Number format to $1.

6. Place the legend at the bottom of the chart.

   You should have the options selected that are shown in Figure 17-34.

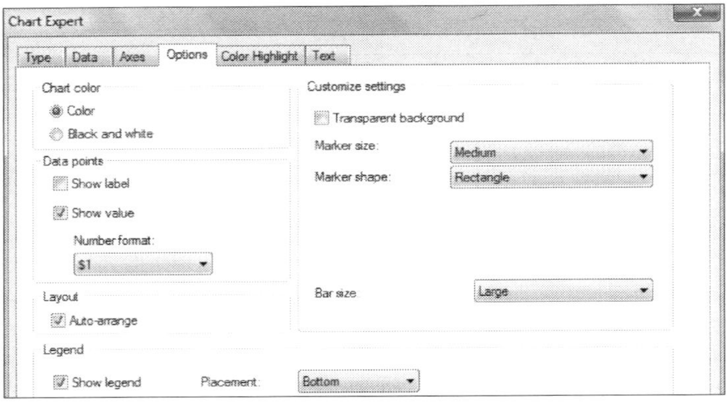

Figure 17-34 Options for the bar chart

7. On the Text tab, change the Title to `Bar Chart`.

   Save the changes.

   The chart should look like the one shown in Figure 17-35. The chart looks good, but with a few changes, it would look better. In the next lesson you will learn how to modify a chart.

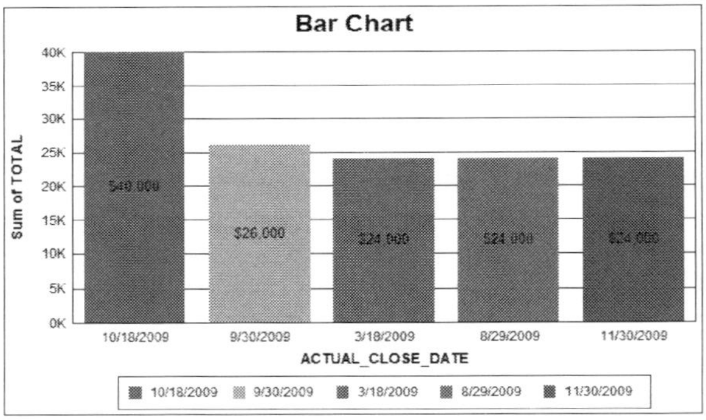

Figure 17-35 Bar chart

Exercise 17.2: Create A Line Chart

In this exercise you will create a line chart that displays opportunities by month.

1. Save the L16.10 report as `L17.2 Line chart`.

2. Select the Line chart type with markers at data points, then select the Group layout option.

3. Select the Sum Total field in the Show drop-down list.

4. Place the legend on the right side of the chart. Select the large **MARKER SIZE** and the **DIAMOND** Marker shape.

5. Change the Title to `Line Chart`.

   Save the changes.

   The chart should look like the one shown in Figure 17-36.

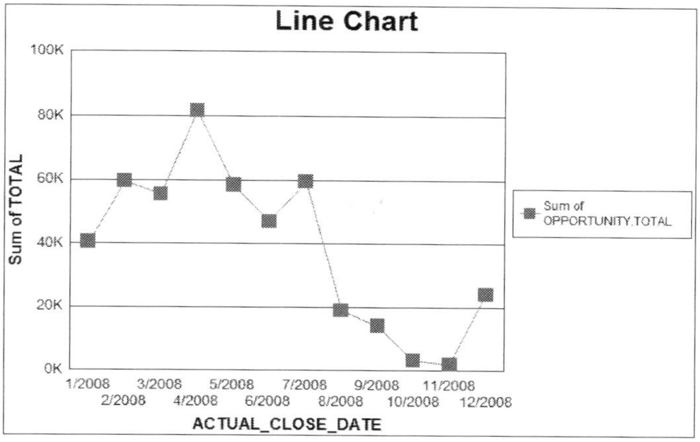

Figure 17-36 Line chart

Exercise 17.3: Create An Area Chart

As mentioned earlier, you can add a chart to a report that does not have any data. You will learn how to do that in this exercise by creating a report that charts the sum of last years purchases by state.

1. Create a new report and add the Contact table, then save the report as `L17.3 Area chart`.

2. Place a chart object in the report header section. The Chart Expert should open automatically. Select the Stacked Area chart type, then check the Use depth effect option.

3. Add the State and Contact fields from the Contact table to the first list box on the Data tab, then add the Last Yrs Purchase field to the Show value(s) list. The options on the Data tab should look like the ones shown in Figure 17-37.

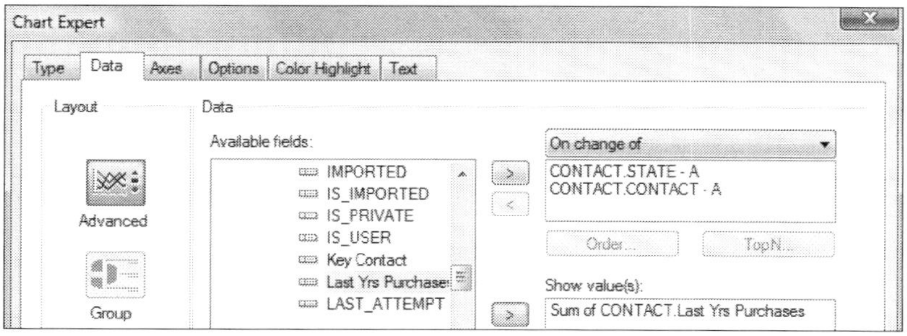

Figure 17-37 Area chart data tab options

4. Add a major gridline to the Group axis option, then change the option to display the legend at the bottom of the chart.

5. Change the Subtitle to `Area chart`. Delete the Group title, then click OK.

6. Change the font size of the title to 10.

Add The Selection Criteria

In addition to being able to create a report that does not have any other information besides a chart, you can also select the records that you want the chart to be based on.

1. Open the Select Expert, select the State field.
2. Select the **IS ONE OF** value, then add the following states: CA, TX, NY and PA.

   Click OK and save the changes.

   The chart should look like the one shown in Figure 17-38.

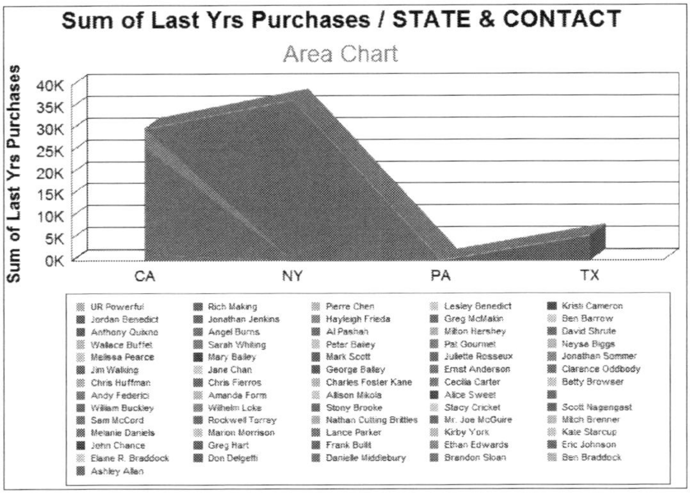

Figure 17-38 Area chart

Exercise 17.4: Create A Pie Chart

In this exercise you will create a pie chart that displays the opportunity totals for 2008, by quarter.

1. Save the L11.1 report as `L17.4 Pie chart`.
2. Open the Group Expert. Click the Options button, then change the For each month option to For each quarter.
3. Select the Pie chart type, then check the Use depth effect option.
4. Check the Show label and Show value options. Change the Number format to 1, if it is not already. Select **BOTH** for the Legend layout option.
5. Change the Title to `Pie Chart`, then change the title font size to 10.
6. Add the Footnote `2008 Opportunities By Quarter`, then make the footnote italic. Save the changes.

   The chart should look like the one shown in Figure 17-39. The number under the date on each slice of the pie is the number of opportunities for that quarter.

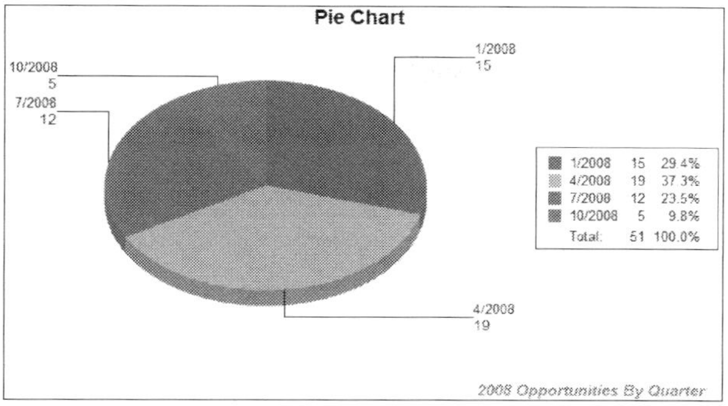

Figure 17-39 Pie chart

Exercise 17.5: Detach A Slice Of A Pie Chart

One way to emphasize a slice of a pie chart is to pull it away from the rest of the chart. This is sometimes referred to as "Exploding" a slice of a pie chart.

1. Save the L17.4 report as `L17.5 Explode a slice of the pie chart.`
2. Open the Chart Expert. On the Options tab check the option **DETACH PIE SLICE**, then select the **LARGEST SLICE** option.
3. Change the Title to `Explode a slice of a pie chart.`

   Save the changes.

   The chart should look like the one shown in Figure 17-40.

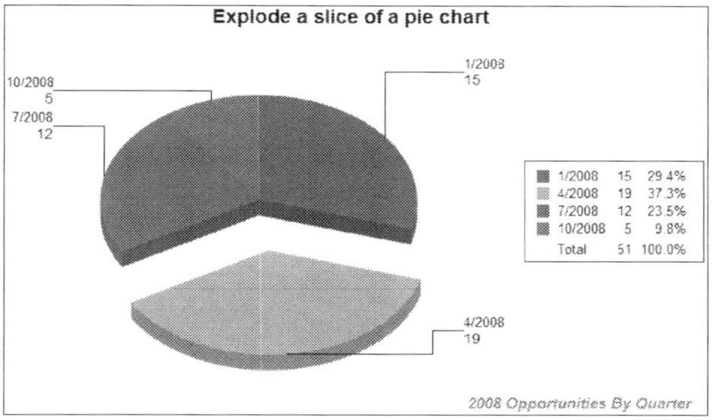

Figure 17-40 Explode a slice of the pie chart

Exercise 17.6: Create A Doughnut Chart

In this exercise you will modify the pie chart that you created in Exercise 17.4 so that it will be a doughnut chart.

1. Save the L17.4 report as `L17.6 Doughnut chart.`
2. Select the Doughnut chart type.

3. Change the Title to `Doughnut Chart.`

   Save the changes.

   The chart should look like the one shown in Figure 17-41.

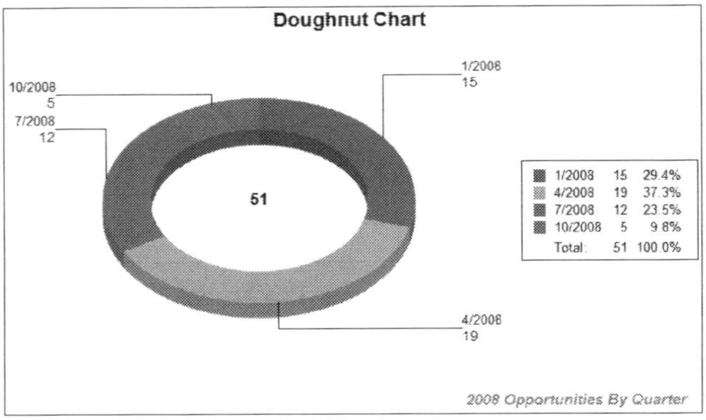

Figure 17-41 Doughnut chart

You can detach a slice of a doughnut chart, just like you can in a pie chart.

Exercise 17.7: Create A 3D Riser Chart

In this exercise you will create a chart that shows last years sales for three states that are over a certain dollar amount. In order to do that, the report will need selection criteria.

1. Save the L17.3 report as `L17.7 3D Riser chart.`

2. Use the Select Expert to create the criteria shown in Figure 17-42, then refresh the data.

```
{CONTACT.Last Yrs Purchases} >= 5000.00 and
{CONTACT.STATE} in ["CA", "NJ", "NY"]
```

Figure 17-42 Selection criteria

3. Select the 3D Riser bar chart type.

4. Display major gridlines for all axes. Show minor gridlines for the Data axis. Clear the Auto Scale option, if it's selected.

5. Change the Title to `3D Riser Chart.`
   Change the Subtitle to `Last Years Purchases >= 5,000`. Save the changes.
   The chart should look like the one shown in Figure 17-43.

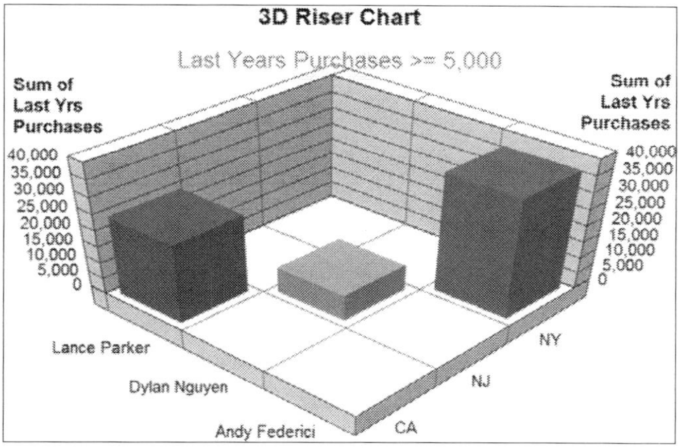

Figure 17-43 3D Riser chart

Exercise 17.8: Create An XY Scatter Chart

In this exercise you will create a chart that plots the number of closed opportunities in 2008 by month and total dollar amount.

1. Save the L11.1 report as `L17.8 XY Scatter chart`.
2. Select the XY Scatter chart type, then select the Advanced layout option.
3. Add the Create Date field to the first list box, then add the Opportunity ID and Total fields to the Show value(s) list.
4. Change the summary type of the Opportunity ID field to Distinct count.
5. Change the Marker shape to **DIAMOND**.
6. Change the Title to `XY Scatter Chart`.

   Change the title font size to 10.

   Add the Subtitle `Opportunities Closed in 2008 By Month`.

   Save the changes.

   The chart should look like the one shown in Figure 17-44.

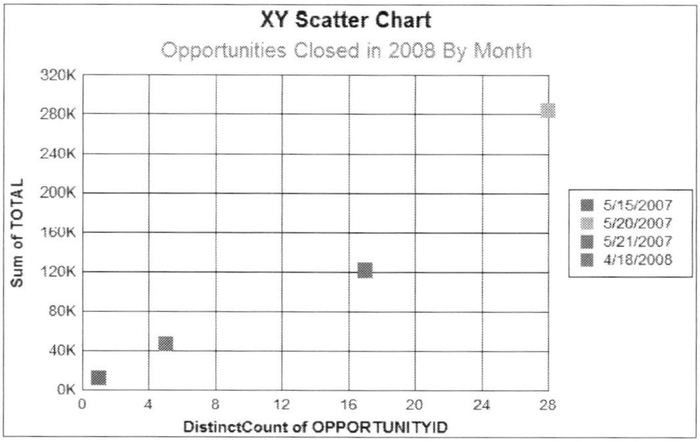

Figure 17-44 XY Scatter chart

As you can see, the markers are not diamond shaped. This option does not seem to work on the Chart Expert. You will learn how to fix this in Exercise 18.3. If your report has diamond markers, there was a software update that fixed this after this book was published.

Exercise 17.9: Create A Radar Chart

In this exercise you will create a chart that plots the opportunity totals in 2008 by quarter.

1. Save the L17.4 report as `L17.9 Radar chart.`
2. Delete the pie chart.
3. Select the Radar chart type, then select the Group layout option, if it is not already selected.
4. Select the Sum of Total field from the Show drop-down list.
5. Check the Show value option, then select the circle Marker shape.
6. Change the Title to `Radar Chart` and the font size to 10.

   Add the Subtitle `Sum of 2008 opportunities by quarter.`

   Save the changes.
   The chart should look like the one shown in Figure 17-45. This is a good example of not selecting the appropriate chart type for the data. This chart is somewhat hard to read.

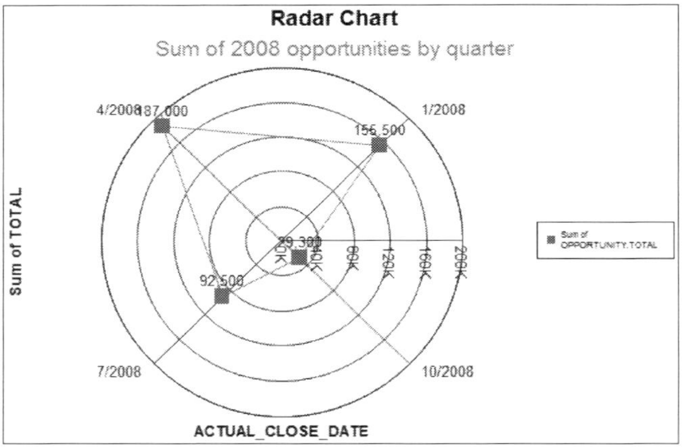

Figure 17-45 Radar chart

Exercise 17.10: Create A Bubble Chart

In this exercise you will create a chart that plots the opportunities between 5/15/2007 and 12/31/2008. Even though the Bubble chart is similar to the XY Scatter chart, the Bubble chart requires three fields in the Show value(s) list.

1. Save the L12.2 report as `L17.10 Bubble chart.`
2. Change the Create Date selection criteria to between 5/15/2007 and 12/31/2008, then delete the Gross Margin criteria and refresh the data.
3. Select the Bubble chart type.

4. On the Data tab add the Create Date field to the first list box, then add the Total field to the Show value(s) list.

5. Add the Opportunity ID field to the Show value(s) list. Change the summary type to Count.

6. Add the Total field to the Show value(s) list again. Change the summary type to Average.

7. Add a major gridline to the Group axis option.

8. Display the Title and change the font size to 10.

   Add the Subtitle `For opportunities between 5/15/2007 and 12/31/2008.`

   Save the changes and refresh the data.

   The chart should look like the one shown in Figure 17-46.

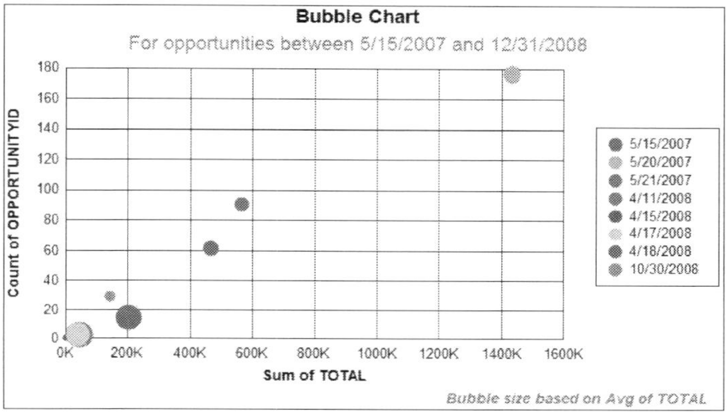

Figure 17-46 Bubble chart

If the Auto Scale option was selected instead of the Auto Range option and the Number Format option was changed to 100%, the chart would look like the one shown in Figure 17-47.

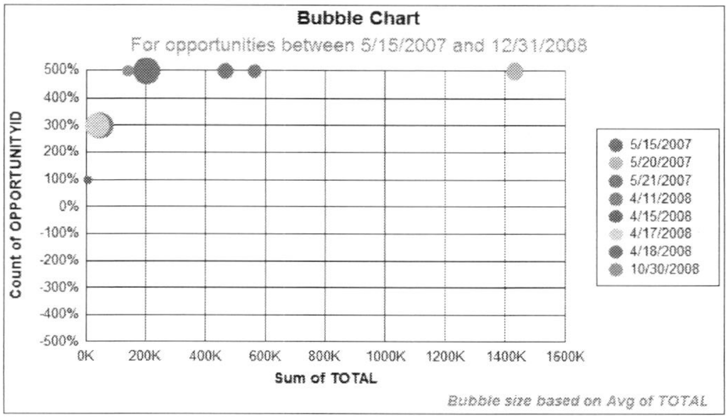

Figure 17-47 Bubble chart with options changed

Exercise 17.11: Create A Gantt Chart

In Lesson 15 you created a report that calculated how many days it took to close the opportunity. Gantt charts require a start and end date. In this exercise you will use the create date as the start date and the actual close date as the end date.

The L15.8 Calculate days to close report currently only has criteria for the status. The Gantt chart would not be readable if all of the records that are currently on the report were displayed on the chart. To make the chart readable, you will select a few contacts to display on the chart.

1. Save the L15.8 report as `L17.11 Gantt chart`.

2. Create selection criteria that limits the report to the following contacts: Amanda Form, Bruce Baker, Ethan Edwards and Liz Dittmeier.

3. Add a chart object to the report header section. Select the Gantt chart layout and the Use depth effect option.

4. Select the **FOR EACH RECORD** option from the drop-down list on the Data tab, then add the Contact field to the first list box.

5. Add the Create Date and Actual Close Date fields to the Show value(s) list.

6. Add the Title `Gantt Chart`, then change the font size to 10.

   Add the Subtitle `Days to close`.

   Save the changes.

   The chart should look like the one shown in Figure 17-48.

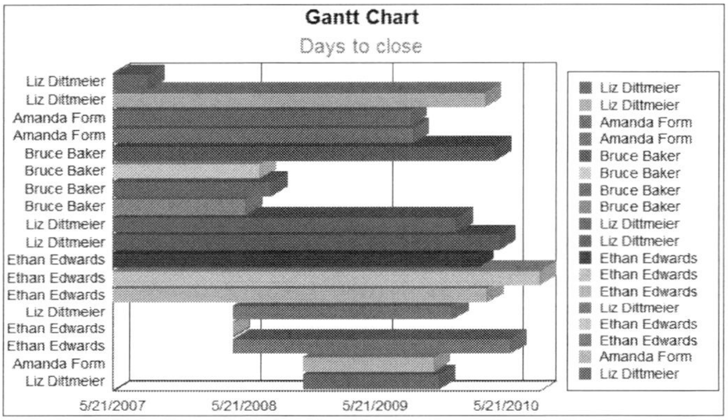

Figure 17-48 Gantt chart

Exercise 17.12: Create A Funnel Chart

In this exercise you will create a chart that will display the daily opportunity totals for the top five close dates in 2009.

1. Save the L12.5 report as `L17.12 Funnel chart`.

2. Delete the existing chart and add a chart object to the report header section.

3. Select the Funnel chart type, then select the Advanced layout option.

4. Add the Actual Close Date field to the first list box, then add the Total field to the Show value(s) list.

5. Change the Legend layout option to **BOTH**.

6. Change the Title to `Funnel Chart`, then change the font size to 10.
   Add the Subtitle `With total opportunity amounts by day`.
   Add the Footnote `For the top 5 close dates in 2009`.
   Save the changes. The chart should look like the one shown in Figure 17-49.

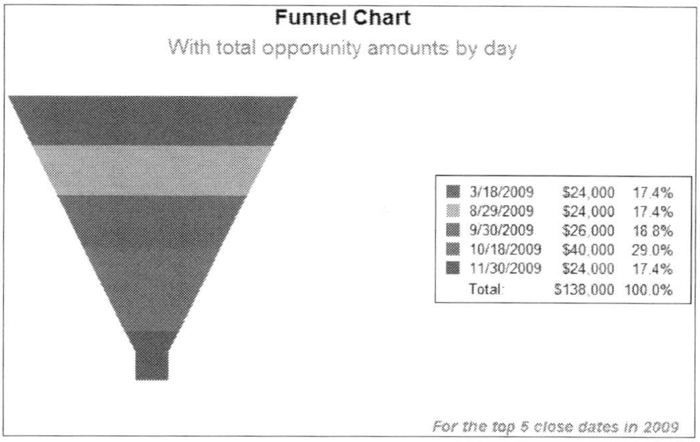

Figure 17-49 Funnel chart

Exercise 17.13: Create A Color Highlighting Chart

In this exercise you will create a chart that will change the color of the bars on the chart to red if the days to close the opportunity is greater than or equal to 261 days or yellow if the days to close the opportunity is between 100 and 260 days. To reduce the number of close dates to something that will make the chart readable, you will add selection criteria to the report.

1. Save the L15.8 report as `L17.13 Highlighted chart`.
2. Change the status selection criteria to only show Closed-Won opportunities.
3. Add selection criteria to the report so that only opportunities with an actual close date in the first three months of 2008 will appear on the report.
4. Select the Side by side bar chart type and the Use depth effect option.
5. On the Data tab add the Opportunity ID field to the first list box, then add the Days to close formula field to the Show value(s) list.
6. Change the Title to `Color Highlighting Chart`, then change the font size to 10.
   Add the Subtitle `Yellow = 100-260, Red = 261+`.
   Add the Footnote `Opportunities closed and won 1st quarter in 2008`.
   Delete the Group title.
   Change the Data title to `Days to close`.
   Leave the Chart Expert open to complete the next part of the exercise.

Add The Color Highlighting To The Chart

In this part of the exercise you will create the criteria that will change the colors of the bars on the chart to red or yellow depending on the value in the Days to close field.

1. On the Color Highlight tab, click the New button.

2. Open the first drop-down list and select the Days to close field. Open the second drop-down list and select Is greater than or equal to. Type `261` in the last field.

3. Select Red as the Format color, then click the New button.

4. Open the first drop-down list and select the Days to close field, then open the second drop-down list and select Is between. Type `100` in the first field and `260` in the last field.

5. Select Yellow as the Format color.

   Click OK, then save the changes.

   The chart should look like the one shown in Figure 17-50.

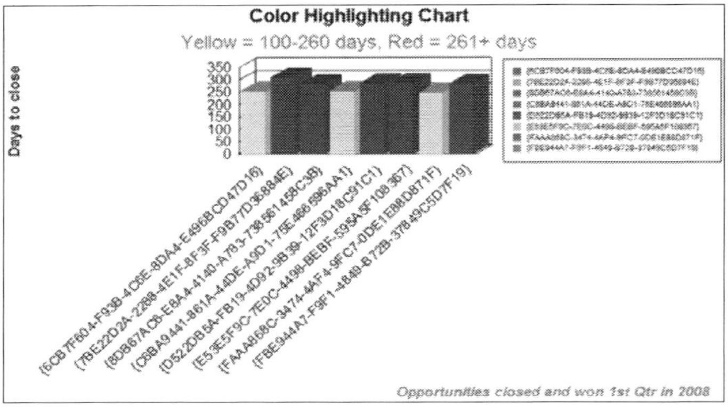

Figure 17-50 Highlighted chart

As you can see, the Opportunity ID field is very long and makes the chart look unprofessional. One way to fix this is to truncate the field. The formula shown in Figure 17-51, will display the Opportunity ID field, as shown in Figure 17-52. To get this to work, remove the Opportunity ID field from the Data tab on the Chart Expert and add the formula field in its place.

```
Mid ({OPPORTUNITY.OPPORTUNITYID}, 2, 8 )
```

Figure 17-51 Formula to truncate the Opportunity ID field

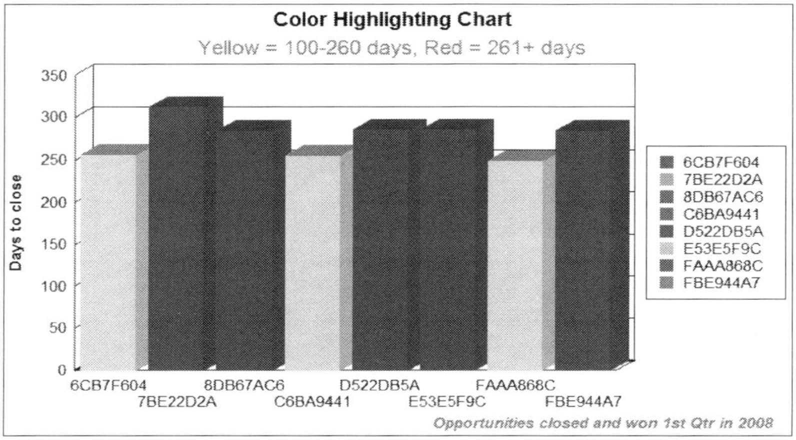

Figure 17-52 Truncated Opportunity ID field

FORMATTING AND EDITING CHARTS

In this lesson you will learn basic chart formatting and editing techniques.

LESSON 18

Formatting And Editing Charts Overview

There are a variety of techniques available to format and edit charts as a whole or individual parts of a chart, like the legend and axis titles. The majority of these options are in one of two places: the Chart Options dialog box or the Format Series dialog box. Other options are on the Chart menu.

Some of the formatting techniques that you will learn are resizing a specific element on the chart, add color to the background of a chart and how to apply a template to a chart.

Zooming In And Out

Depending on the level of formatting intricacy, you may find it helpful to zoom in or out on the chart while you are modifying it. There are two ways to access the Zoom In option from the preview window as discussed below. Once you select the Zoom In option, the mouse pointer will change to a magnifying glass with a plus sign.

① Right-click on a blank space on the chart and select Zoom In.

② Click on a blank space on the chart, then Chart ⇒ Zoom In.

> The Zoom options only work with bar and line charts.

The zoom feature in charts does not work the same way in Crystal Reports that it does in other software packages where you can click on the chart to zoom in or out. Instead, once you select the Zoom In option, you have to draw a box on the portion of the chart that you want to zoom in on. To zoom out, right-click on the chart, select Zoom Out, then click anyplace on the chart.

When you are finished zooming in or out, you have to select the option **SELECT MODE** from the shortcut menu or from the Chart menu. Doing this will change the mouse pointer back to the default, so that you can continue working.

> After changing the mouse pointer back to the default, I was expecting the chart to go back to its original size. I didn't find that to be the case. To put the chart back to its original size, I clicked the Undo button once for each time that I zoomed in on the chart.

The **PAN** option is only available when a chart has been zoomed in on. This option is used to scroll left or right on the chart.

Resizing Charts

Charts and objects have the same sizing handles that images have. Like images, you can drag the chart to another section of the report or to a different location in the section that it is currently in. You can resize the chart manually or you can use the options on the Size and Position dialog box. There are two ways to open the Size and Position dialog box, as discussed below.

① Right-click on a blank space on the chart and select **SIZE AND POSITION**.

② Click on a blank space on the chart, then Format ⇒ Size and Position.

There are two options for resizing charts. You can resize the entire chart or you can resize individual elements on the chart. When you want to resize the entire chart, make sure that individual elements on the chart are not selected.

> You can place the mouse pointer anyplace on the highlighted border of the chart to resize the chart in any direction that you need.

Exercise 18.1: Use The Chart Expert Shortcut Menu Options

If you right-click on a chart in a group section on the preview tab and select the Chart Expert option, you will see the shortcut menu shown in Figure 18-1.

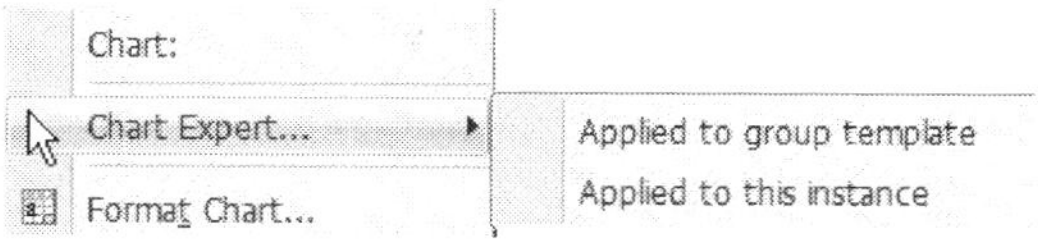

Figure 18-1 Chart Expert shortcut menu options

The **APPLIED TO GROUP TEMPLATE** option is used to apply the changes that you are about to make on the Chart Expert to all charts in all of the groups in the report.

The **APPLIED TO THIS INSTANCE** option is used to only apply the changes that you are about to make to the group chart that you have selected. Remember that the preview window displays every occurrence of a chart that is in a group section.

Add Charts To The Report

The report that you will modify already has one group for the months. You need to create another group so that you can see how the options on the Chart Expert shortcut menu work. The group that you will create will be for the company name.

1. Save the L11.1 report as `L18.1 Group chart changes`.

2. Insert ⇒ Group. Open the first drop-down list, select the Company field, then click OK.

3. Copy the three summary fields and headings in the group footer 1 section to the group footer 2 section and save the changes.

Add Two Charts To The Report

1. Add a bar chart to the group header 1 section, as shown in Figure 18-2.

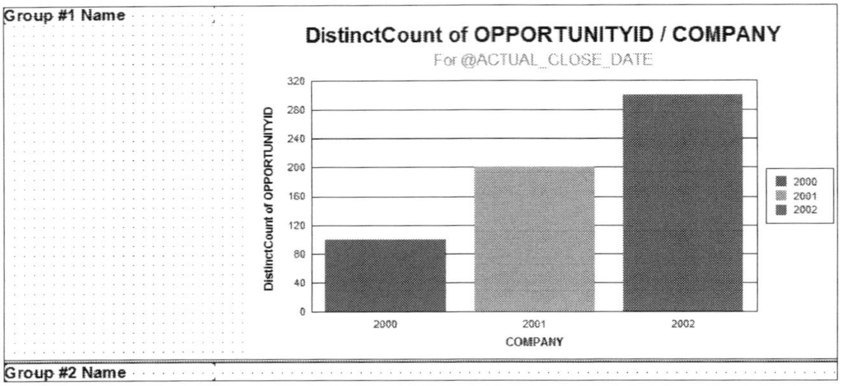

Figure 18-2 Chart added to the group header 1 section

2. Make the Group 1 Name field smaller, then move the chart closer to the Group 1 Name field.

3. Open the Chart Expert and select the side by side bar chart if it is not already selected.

4. Change the Title to `Monthly Total Amount By Actual Close Date`, then change the title font size to 10.

   Delete the Subtitle.

   Change the Data title to `Number of opportunities.`

   Save the changes.

   The chart should look like the one shown in Figure 18-3.

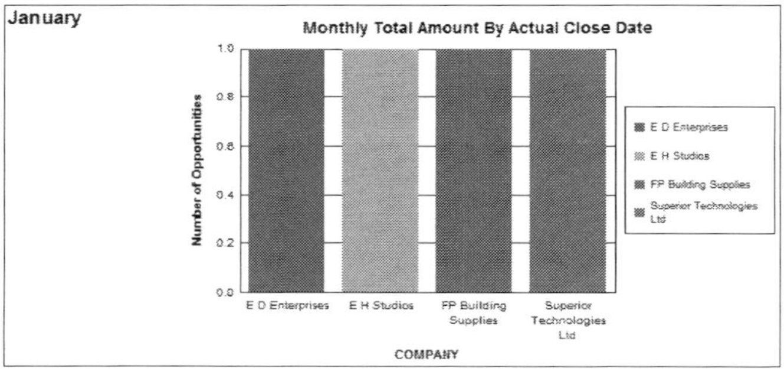

Figure 18-3 Monthly opportunities by actual close date chart

Yes, I know that the scale for the number of opportunities is strange. That is because each company only had one opportunity for the month.

5. Add a side by side horizontal bar chart with depth effect to the group header 2 section.

6. Add the Company field to the first list box on the Data tab.
   Add the Opportunity ID field to the Show value(s) list, then change the summary type to Distinct count. Add the Total field to Show value(s) list.

7. On the Options tab check the Show value option.

8. Add the Title `Company Totals By Actual Close Date`, then change the title font size to 10.

9. Save the changes.
   The chart should look like the one shown in Figure 18-4.

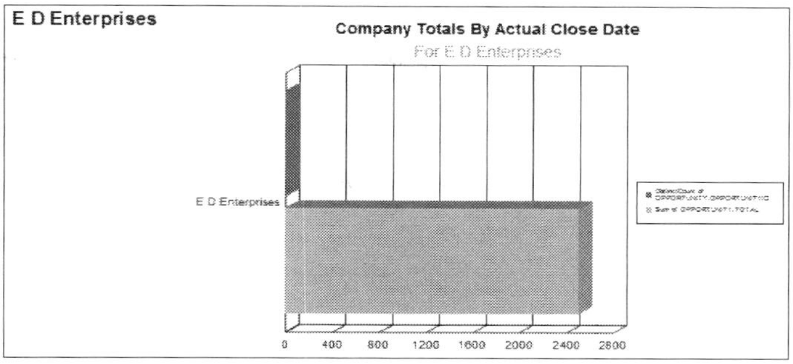

Figure 18-4 Company totals by actual close date chart

Modify The Group Header 1 Chart

In this part of the exercise you will modify one of the group charts on the preview tab and apply the change to all charts in the group.

1. Right-click on the chart for January in the group header 1 section and select Chart Expert ⇒ Applied to group template.

2. Change the location of the legend to the left of the chart. Click OK and save the changes. When you look at all of the charts in the group header 1 section (the charts for January, February, March etc.), you will see that the legend is now to the left of the chart.

Modify The Group Header 2 Chart

In this part of the exercise you will modify the chart for a particular company from the preview tab.

1. Right-click on the chart for EH Studios on page 2. Select Chart Expert ⇒ Applied to this instance.

2. On the Options tab check the Show label option, then change the **BAR SIZE** to small.

   Save the changes.

   The chart for EH Studios should look like the one shown in Figure 18-5.

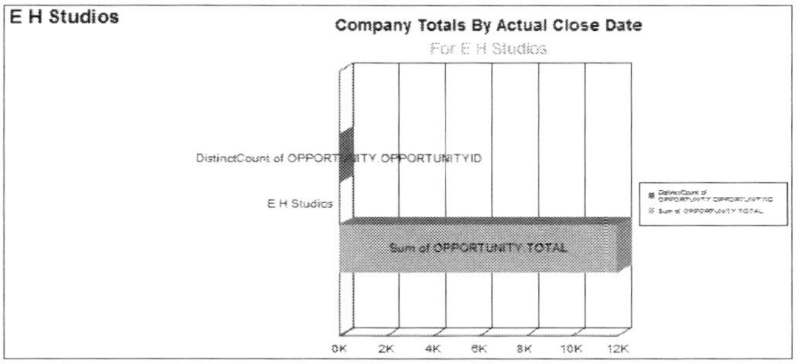

Figure 18-5 Modified chart for EH Studios

Notice the values on the bars and the size of the bars. The chart for ED Enterprises on page 1 should still look like the one shown above in Figure 18-4. This chart was not changed.

More Chart Types

As mentioned in the previous lesson, there are more chart types in addition to the ones on the Type tab on the Chart Expert. If you want to apply a different chart type, follow the steps below.

1. Right-click on the chart in a report that you want to change and select **LOAD TEMPLATE.**

   You will see the dialog box shown in Figure 18-6.

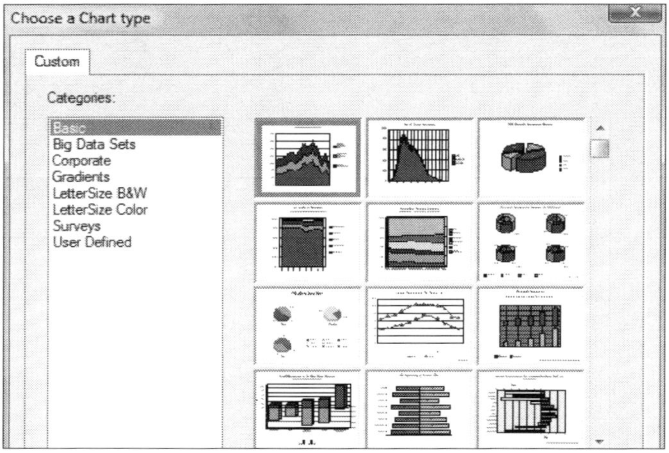

Figure 18-6 Choose a Chart type dialog box

> You will not see the Load Template option if the **CUSTOM CHARTING** option was not installed when Crystal Reports was installed. If this is the case, you can run the setup again and install this option.

2. Click on a category on the left to view the chart types, then select the chart type that you want to use on the right and click OK. Customize the chart as needed.

Trendlines

Trendlines are added to a chart to better illustrate trends in data. They are often applied to bar charts.

To add trendlines to a bar chart, select one of the options below. You will see the Trendlines dialog box shown in Figure 18-7.

Select the type of trendline that you want from the **AVAILABLE TYPES** list and move it to the Show Trendlines list.

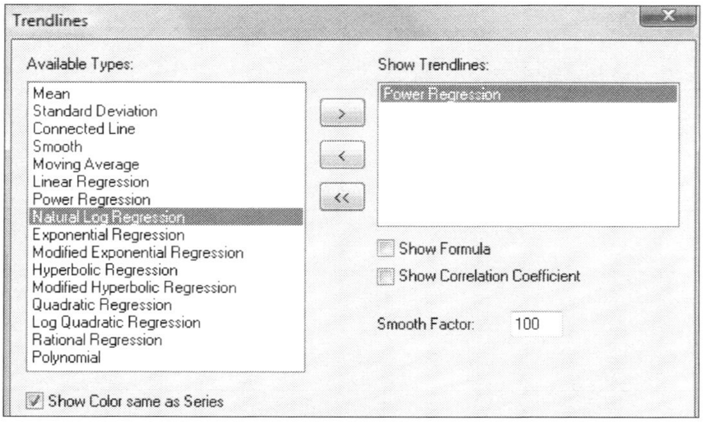

Figure 18-7 Trendlines dialog box

All trendline types are not available for every chart type.

① Right-click on a bar in the chart and select Trendlines.
② Click on a bar in the chart, then Chart ⇒ Trendlines.

Exercise 18.2: Use The Underlay Following Sections Option

The Underlay option is used to place the content in one section of the report next to the content in the section below it. In this exercise you will apply this option so that the chart will print next to the data that it represents. This is often used with charts that are in the group header section of a report so that the records in the details section will print next to the chart.

The **UNDERLAY FOLLOWING SECTIONS** option on the Section Expert is better suited for reports that do not have a lot of fields in the details section. If you cannot get the chart and the fields in the details section to fit, you can select the landscape print option to have more space across the page. You will modify a report and apply the Underlay option to the group header section.

1. Save the L18 Chart in group footer report (in the zip file) as `L18.2 Chart with underlay option`.

2. Delete the group name field in the group header 1 section.

3. Drag the chart in the group footer 1b section to the group header 1 section and place it as far left as possible.

4. Resize the chart so that it ends at the 3.5 inch mark on the ruler.

5. Change the chart title to `Chart With Underlay Option`.

6. Move the fields in the details and group footer 1a sections over to the right so that they start to the right of the chart as shown in Figure 18-8.

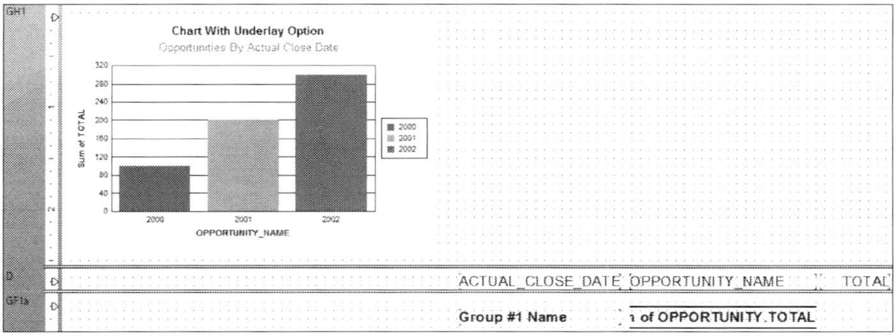

Figure 18-8 Modified details and group footer layout

7. Open the Section Expert and apply the **UNDERLAY FOLLOWING SECTIONS** option to the group header 1 section.

8. Delete the group footer 1b section. Save the changes. The report should look like the one shown in Figure 18-9.

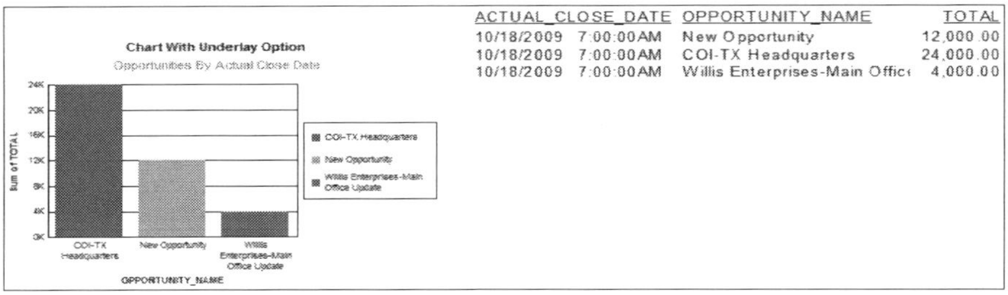

Figure 18-9 Chart with the Underlay option applied

If there is information in the group header section that you do not want to include in the underlay, create another group header section and place the chart in the new group header section as shown in Figure 18-10. You would still apply the underlay option to the group header section with the chart. The report would look like the one shown in Figure 18-11. Notice that the information in the first group header section (The Group #1 Name field) did not move.

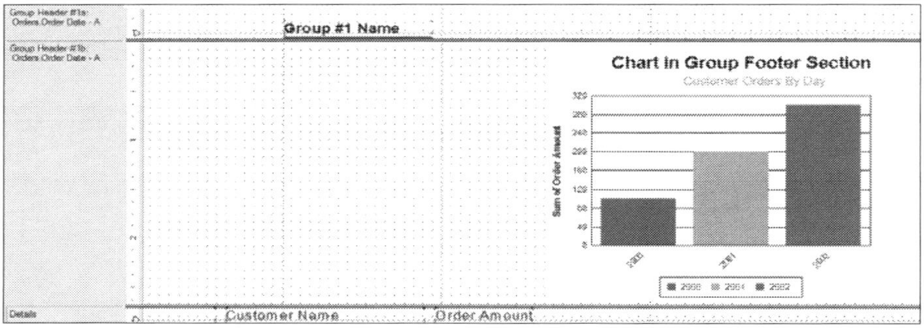

Figure 18-10 Sample report layout for the chart in its own group header section

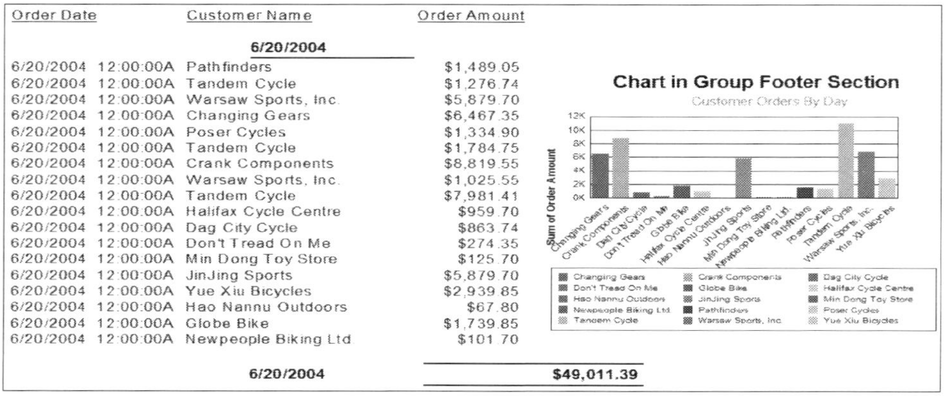

Figure 18-11 Sample report

Chart Options Dialog Box

The options on this dialog box pick up where the options on the Chart Expert leave off. I would like to see the following dialog boxes added to the Chart Expert: Chart Options, Choose A Chart, Series options and Chart Format. I think that would make creating and modifying charts easier because all of the chart options would be in one place.

Depending on the chart type, you will see slightly different options on the Chart Options dialog box. The options are used to change the overall look of the chart. What I like most about the Chart Options dialog box is that you can see what your changes will look like without having to preview the report. This is very helpful when you need to experiment with several options. To open the dialog box, right-click on the chart and select Chart Options.

> If you click on the Help button on any tab on the Chart Options dialog box, you will see detailed information for all of the options on the tab.

Many of the settings on the Chart Options dialog box are the same as the ones on the Chart Expert. One difference that you will notice is that the settings have more options on the Chart Options dialog box then they do on the Chart Expert.

Appearance Tab

The options on this tab effect the general look of the chart. Figures 18-12 to 18-14 show the appearance options for three types of charts.

Use Depth If checked, this option will display the chart in 3D format.

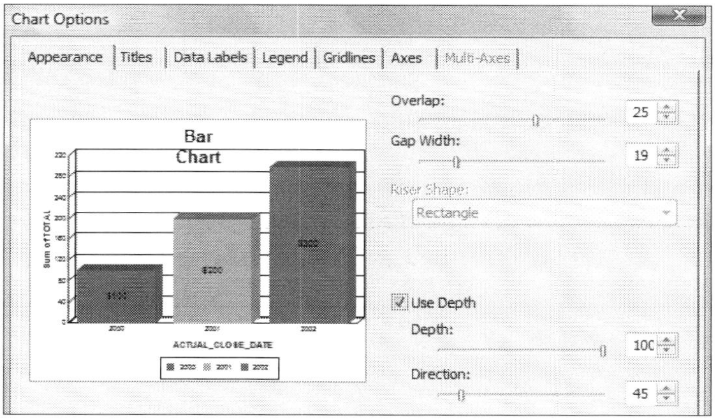

Figure 18-12 Bar chart appearance tab options

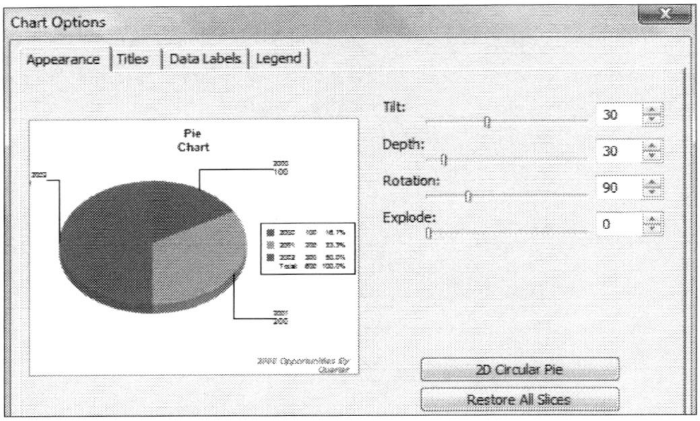

Figure 18-13 Pie chart appearance tab options

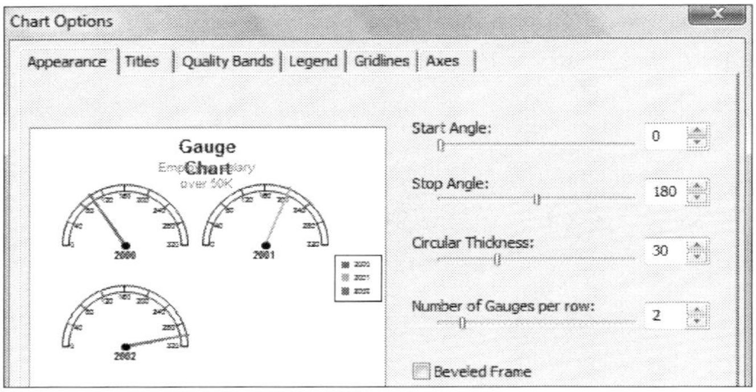

Figure 18-14 Gauge chart appearance tab options

Titles Tab

The options shown in Figure 18-15 are used to add or modify the titles on the chart.

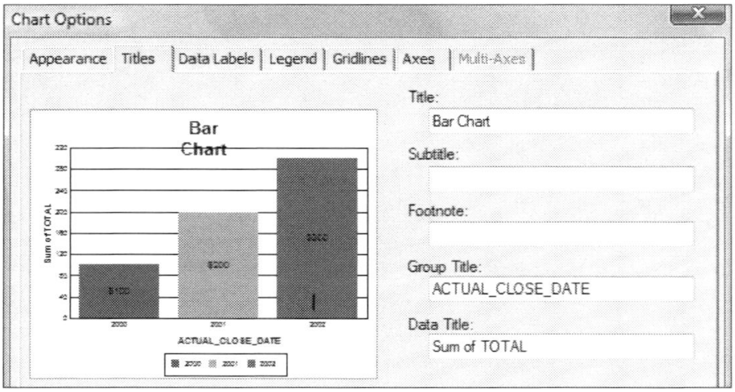

Figure 18-15 Titles tab options

Data Labels Tab

The options shown in Figure 18-16 are used to add data labels to the chart, change the location of the labels and what the label will display.

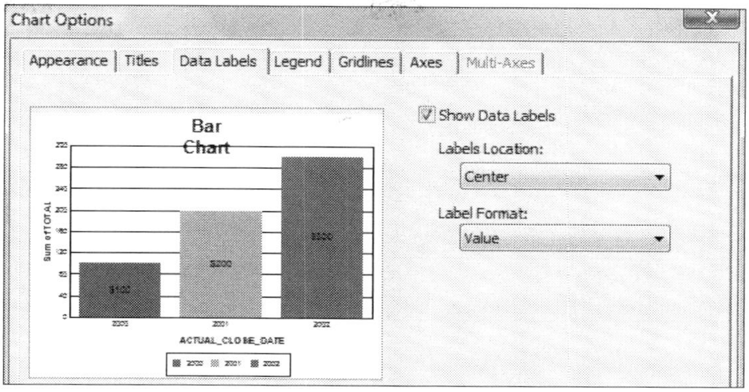

Figure 18-16 Data Labels tab options

Legend Tab

The options shown in Figure 18-17 are used to modify the legend, add a frame around the legend, change the color of the items and swap the location of the series and groups.

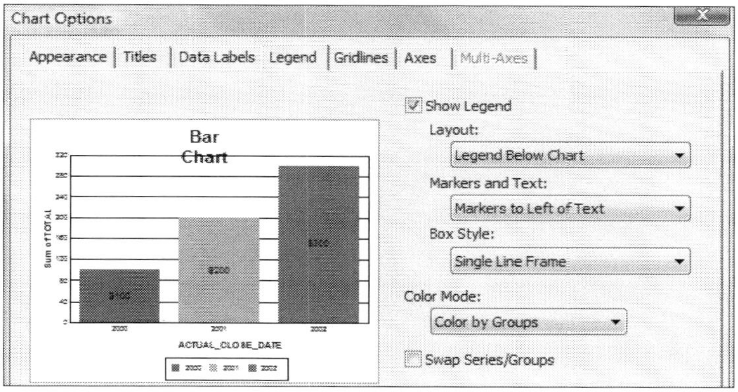

Figure 18-17 Legend tab options

Gridlines Tab

The options shown in Figure 18-18 are used to add and remove major and minor gridlines for the group and data axis.

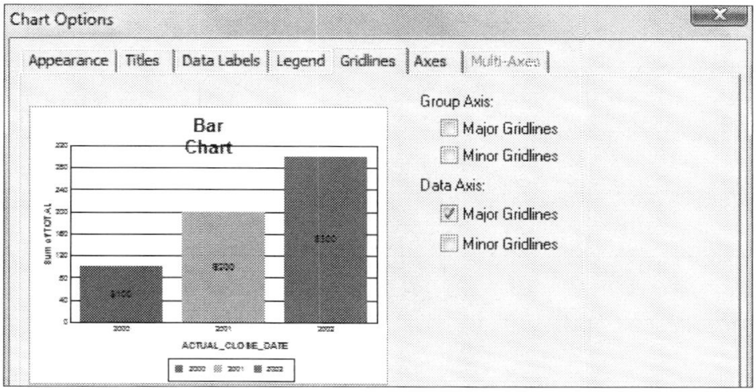

Figure 18-18 Gridlines tab options

Axes Tab

The options shown in Figure 18-19 are used to select how the group axes line will be displayed on the chart.

The axis line may not be visible after selecting the option if it is the same color as the frame of the chart.

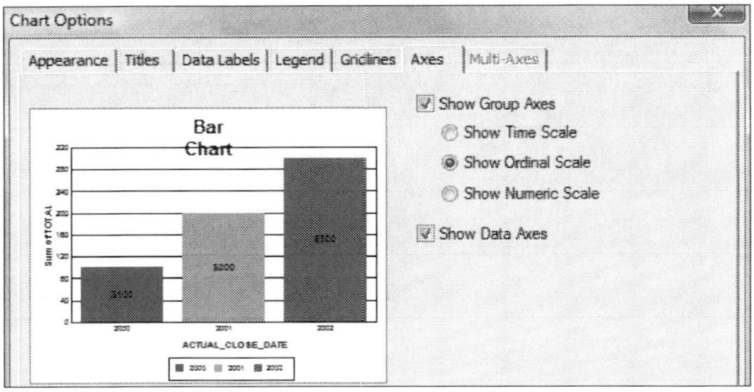

Figure 18-19 Axes tab options

Multi-Axes

The options shown in Figure 18-20 are used to add a second set of data to the report. The L17.8 XY Scatter chart that you created will enable these options. To enable this tab, check the **DUAL AXES** option on the Axes tab.

This chart is currently plotting data for only one year. If you want to plot data for another year, select it from the Secondary (Y2) Axis list.

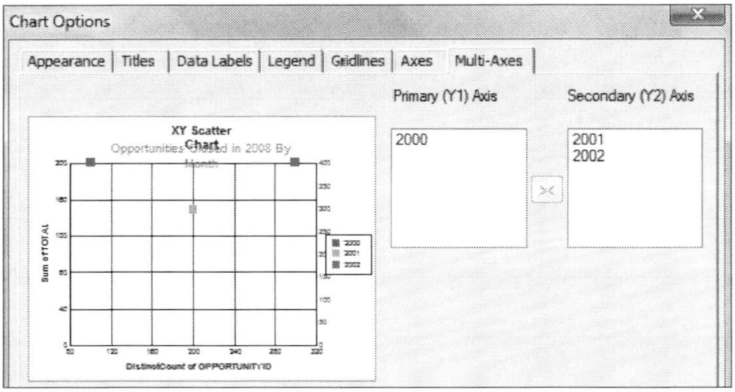

Figure 18-20 Multi-Axes tab options

Edit X Axis Labels

If the labels across the X axis (at the bottom of the chart) are hard to read, right-click on the specific label on the preview window and select the **EDIT AXIS LABEL** option shown in Figure 18-21. You will see the dialog box shown in Figure 18-22. Make the changes to the label, then click OK.

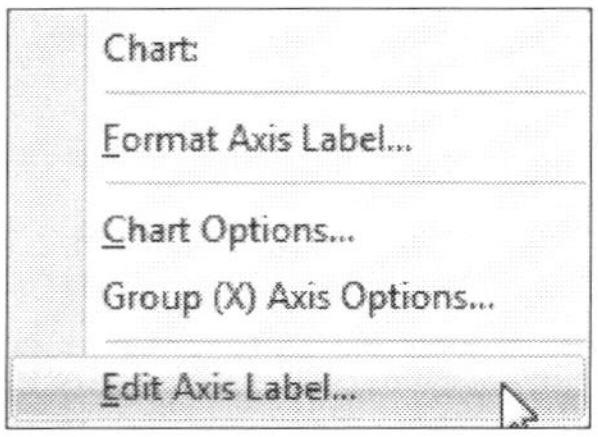

Figure 18-22 Label Aliasing dialog box

Figure 18-21 Axis label shortcut menu

Modify Parts Of The Chart Manually

So far, almost all of the chart modification techniques that you have learned have been selecting or changing options on a dialog box. You can also move or resize elements like the title or legend on the chart manually. Doing this allows you to have greater control over what the chart will look like.

If you make changes to the chart and then decide that you do not like them, you can use the **AUTO ARRANGE CHART** option. This option will reset the chart to its default size, formatting and placement settings. You have to select the entire chart, not a specific element, for this option to appear on the chart shortcut menu.

Exercise 18.3: Move Labels On A Chart

In many of the charts that were created in the previous lesson, one or all of the axis labels are displayed on top of the values for the axis. Moving the axis labels would make the charts easier to read. In Exercise 17.8 you learned that the marker option on the Chart Expert does not work. You will learn another way to change the markers in this exercise.

1. Save the L17.8 report as `L18.3 Move labels on a chart.`

> Moving labels is easier to do in the preview window because you can see the live data in the chart.

2. Select the Sum of Total label on the left and drag the label to the left so that there is a little more space.

3. Right-click on the chart title and select Chart Options, then click on the Titles tab.
   Change the Title to `Move Labels On A Chart.`
   Change the X-Axis to `Number of opportunities.`
   Change the Data title to `Total monthly opportunity amount.`

4. On the Appearance tab change the **SIZE** to 50, then change the **SHAPE** to Diamond.

   Save the changes.

   The chart should look like the one shown in Figure 18-23.

   Compare this chart to the one shown in Exercise 17.8. The markers now have the diamond shape.

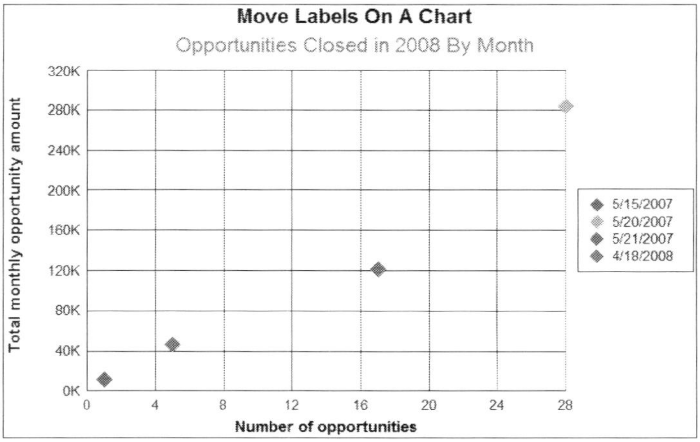

Figure 18-23 Labels modified on a chart

Customizing 3D Charts

The Appearance tab options are used to tilt and rotate 3D charts. If you want or need more 3D chart formatting options, right-click on a chart like the 3D Surface or 3D Riser chart and select **3D VIEWING ANGLE**. You will see the dialog box shown in Figure 18-24.

You can scroll through the list of viewing angles to find one that you like. If clicked, the **ADVANCED OPTIONS** button displays additional options that are used to customize the viewing angle even more, as shown in Figure 18-25.

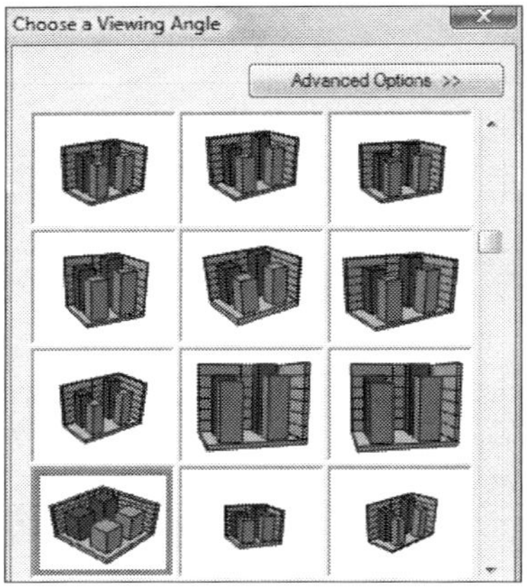

Figure 18-24 Choose A Viewing Angle dialog box

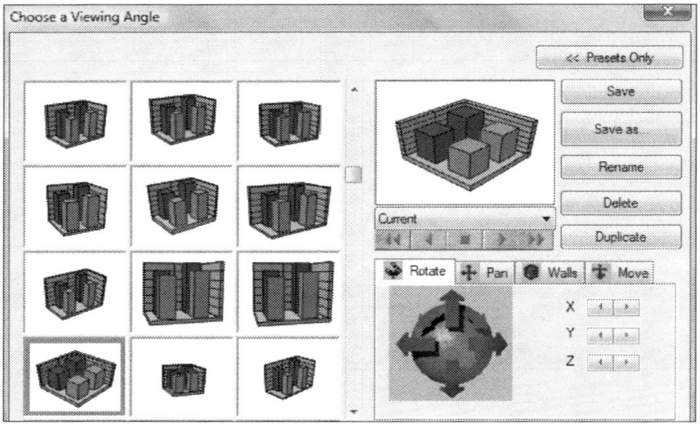

Figure 18-25 Advanced viewing angle customization options

You can also view the Preset Viewing Angles on the left by clicking on the forward and backward (VCR style) buttons that are to the left of the Duplicate button.

Another way to view them is by opening the drop-down list under the chart thumbnail. The options on the **ROTATE**, **PAN**, **WALLS** and **MORE** tabs are used to customize additional 3D options.

> If you make any manual changes to a viewing angle, you will be prompted to save the changes with a new viewing angle preset name when you click OK. Entering a name on this dialog box will let you save a new viewing angle or replace an existing one. You do not have to do this to apply the changes that you have selected on the Choose a Viewing Angle dialog box. If you want to apply the changes to the chart without saving them as a viewing angle, click the Cancel button on the **ENTER 3D VIEWING ANGLE PRESET NAME** dialog box and the changes will still be applied to the chart.

Customizing Individual Elements On The Chart

Each element on a chart can be customized. For example, you can change the color of the report title or change the color of individual bars or slices of the chart. You have learned about the Format Editor and how you can use it to customize fields on the report. Each of the elements on a chart also has a Format dialog box that has additional formatting options.

Figures 18-27 to 18-31 show the Format dialog boxes for some of the more popular chart elements. You can open these dialog boxes by selecting either of the options discussed below.

① Right-click on the chart element that you want to modify and select the Format option on the shortcut menu shown in Figure 18-26.

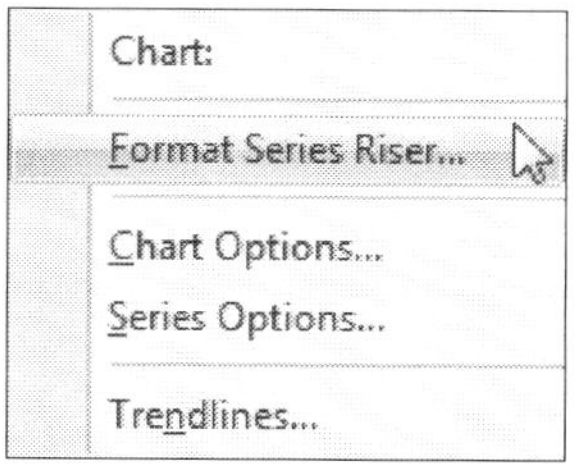

Figure 18-26 Bar element shortcut menu

> The name after the word Format on the shortcut menu will change depending on the type of element that is selected.

② Click on the chart element that you want to modify, then Chart ⇒ Format.

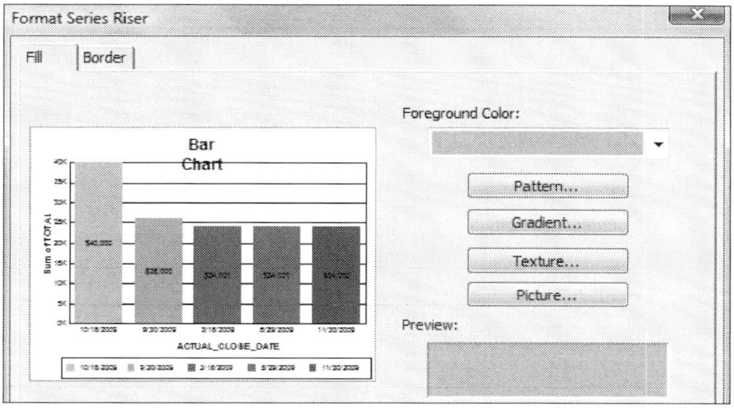

Figure 18-27 Bar chart format fill tab options

The **GRADIENT** button on the Fill tab (shown above in Figure 18-27) will open the dialog box shown in Figure 18-28.

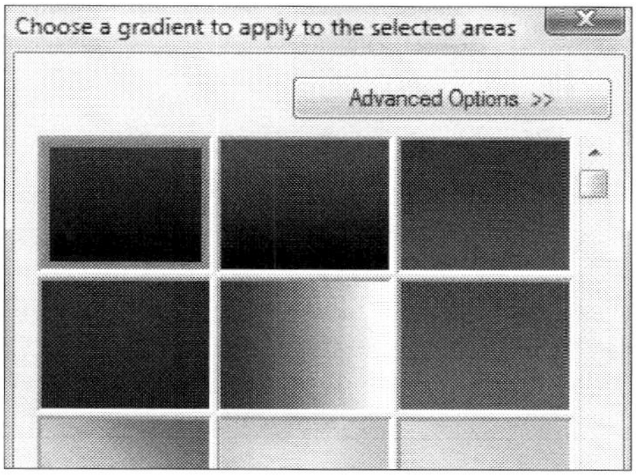

Figure 18-28 Bar chart gradient options

Selecting the options on the border tab shown in Figure 18-29 will place a dotted border around the chart.

You have to select a color. I think the Color option should default to black instead of transparent, like it does on the Format Gridlines dialog box shown in Figure 18-30.

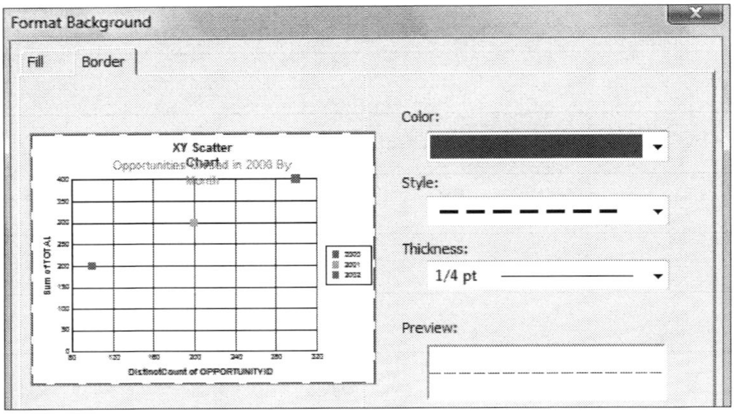

Figure 18-29 XY Scatter chart format border tab options

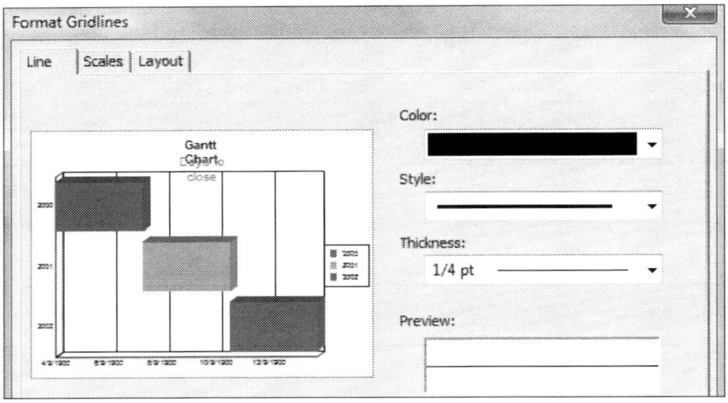

Figure 18-30 Format Gridlines options

To open this dialog box, right-click on a data label on the chart and select **FORMAT DATA LABEL.**

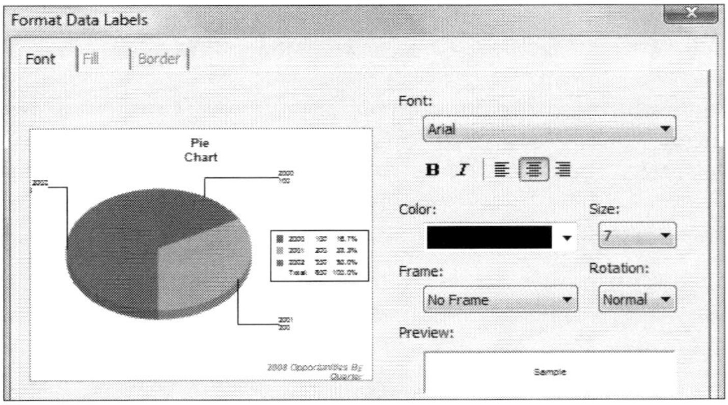

Figure 18-31 Format Data Label options

Exercise 18.4: Apply Color To Chart Elements

This is probably one of the most used formatting options. In this exercise, you will apply color to parts of a chart.

1. Save the L18.1 report as `L18.4 Add color to charts`.

2. Click on the second bar (so that it is selected) on the chart in the group header 2 section, then right-click on it and select Format Series Riser. Change the **FOREGROUND** color to Yellow. (It's on the first row.)

3. Click the Pattern button, then select the next to last option in the first row, as illustrated in Figure 18-32.

   Click OK twice to close both dialog boxes.

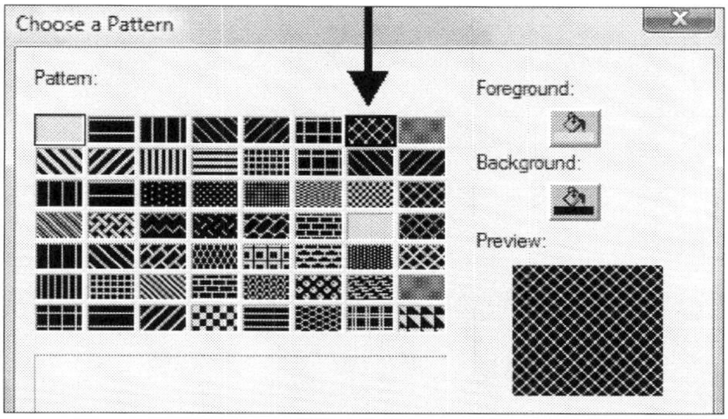

Figure 18-32 Pattern option illustrated

4. Change the chart in the group header 1 section to a pie chart.

5. Open the Chart Options dialog box for the pie chart and make the following appearance changes: Tilt 45 and Explode 15, then click OK.

6. Right-click on the pie chart and select Format Background.

7. Click the Gradient button, then select the fourth option in the first column. (It's yellow) Click OK twice to close both dialog boxes.

> If you click the **ADVANCED OPTIONS** button on the **CHOOSE A GRADIENT TO APPLY TO THE SELECTED AREAS** dialog box, you will see options that are used to create your own gradients, as shown in Figure 18-33. Compare this to the default options that were shown earlier in Figure 18-28.

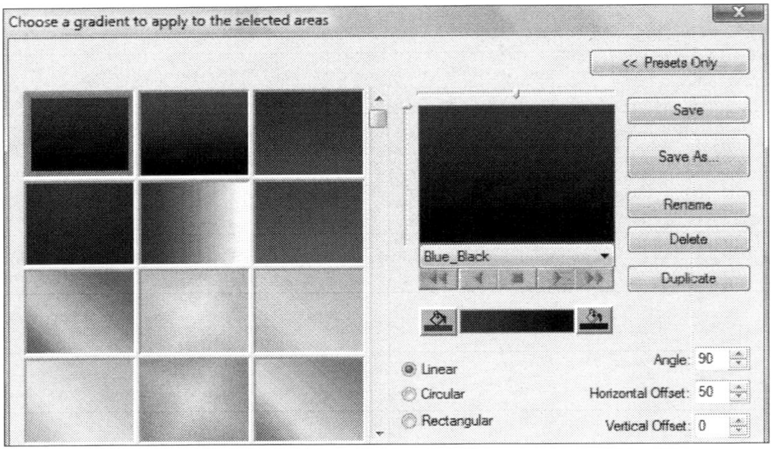

Figure 18-33 Gradient options

8. Save the changes.

   The pie chart should look like the one shown in Figure 18-34.

   The bar chart should look like the one shown in Figure 18-35.

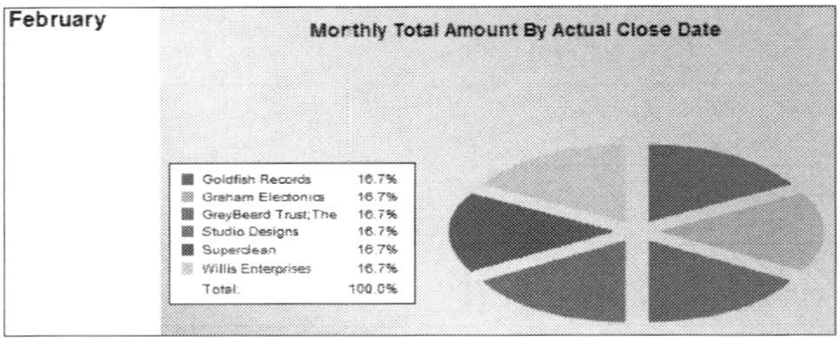

Figure 18-34 Format options applied to pie chart

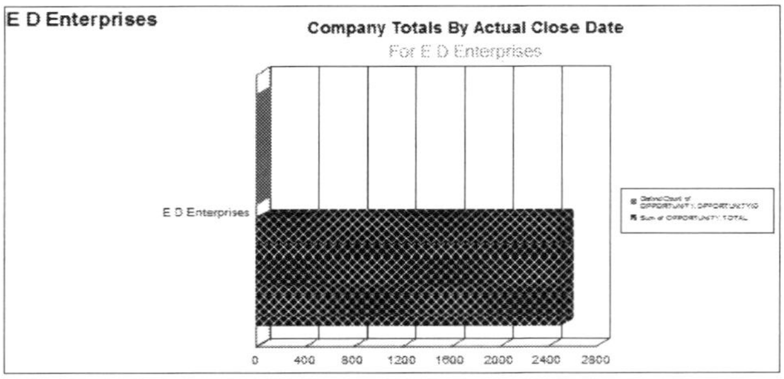

Figure 18-35 Format options applied to bar chart

Modifying Charts On The Preview Tab

If you modify a chart on the preview tab, in particular, a chart that is in the group header or footer section, by default the changes that you make will only be applied to that instance of the report. This does not happen when a chart is modified in the design window. Changes made to charts on the design tab will be applied to all instances of the chart.

In Exercise 18.2 you modified a chart that was in the group footer section that displays data for the top five close dates in 2008. Because the chart is grouped by date, the chart in the group footer section will appear five times on the report, once for each of the close date groups.

If you selected the chart for the second close date on the report and made changes to it from the preview tab, the changes that you make would only be applied to that instance of the chart. The charts for the other four dates would not be changed. If you decide that you do want to apply the changes that you made to the one instance of the chart, to all of the charts in the same group, select one of the two options listed below. They work the same as the Applied to group template option that you learned about earlier in Exercise 18.1.

① Right-click on the chart that you made changes to on the preview tab and select Apply Changes To All Charts.
② Click on the chart that you made changes to on the preview tab, then Chart ⇒ Apply Changes To All Charts.

Chart Templates

If you have formatted a chart that has several options that you would like to use on other charts, you can save the options as a template, like the ones you saw earlier on the Choose A Chart Type dialog box. You can save a chart as a template by selecting one of the options below, then type in a name for the template.

① Right-click on the chart and select Save As Template.
② Click on the chart, then Chart ⇒ Save As Template.

To apply the template to another chart, click on the **USER DEFINED** category on the Choose A Chart Type dialog box shown earlier in Figure 18-6.

By default, chart templates that you create are saved in the following location on your hard drive: C:\Program Files\Business Objects\Common\4.0\ChartSupport\Templates\User Defined folder.

If you want to change the location that the chart templates that you create are saved in, you can change the ChartSupportPath registry key, which is in this location. HKEY_LOCAL_MACHINE\Software\Business Objects\Suite12.0\Crystal Reports\

ADDITIONAL CRYSTAL REPORTS FUNCTIONALITY

Believe it or not, this book only covers a little more than half of the functionality that Crystal Reports has to offer report designers. You may be thinking that you have learned enough in the first 18 lessons to create all of the reports that you need. The cross-tab and drill-down reports that you will create in this lesson build on what you have already learned in previous lessons. Other topics are being introduced for the first time. Many of the reports that you learn how to create in this lesson are known as or referred to as "Non standard report types".

In this lesson you will learn how to:

☑ Use the Cross-Tab Expert
☑ Apply conditional formatting to a cross-tab object
☑ Create Running Totals
☑ Create Hierarchical Groups
☑ Use the Group Sort Expert
☑ Add a watermark to a report

LESSON 19

Cross-Tab Expert Overview

In Lesson 13 you learned how to create a cross-tab report using a wizard. In this lesson you will learn more about cross-tab reports by learning how to use the Cross-Tab Expert. Cross-Tab reports are used to summarize large amounts of data in columnar format, in a relatively small amount of space. Cross-Tab reports do not have to be the only object on the report. You can add a cross-tab object to a report that has standard data. In addition to using the Cross-Tab wizard, there are three ways to add a Cross-Tab object to a report as discussed below.

① Right-click on a blank space on the report and select Insert Cross-Tab, then click in the report section that you want to place the cross-tab in.
② Click the Insert Cross-Tab button on the Insert Tools toolbar.
③ Insert ⇒ Cross-Tab.

The Cross-Tab Expert has three tabs: Cross-Tab, Style and Customize Style. Many of the options on the first two tabs are on the Cross-Tab wizard.

Figure 19-1 shows the Cross-Tab tab.
Table 19-1 explains the buttons that are not on the Cross-Tab wizard.
Figure 19-4 shows the Style tab. The options on this tab are the same as the ones on the wizard.
Figure 19-5 shows the Customize Style tab. Tables 19-2 to 19-4 explain the options on this tab.

Cross-Tab Tab

The options shown in Figure 19-1 are used to select the fields that will be used to create the cross-tab.

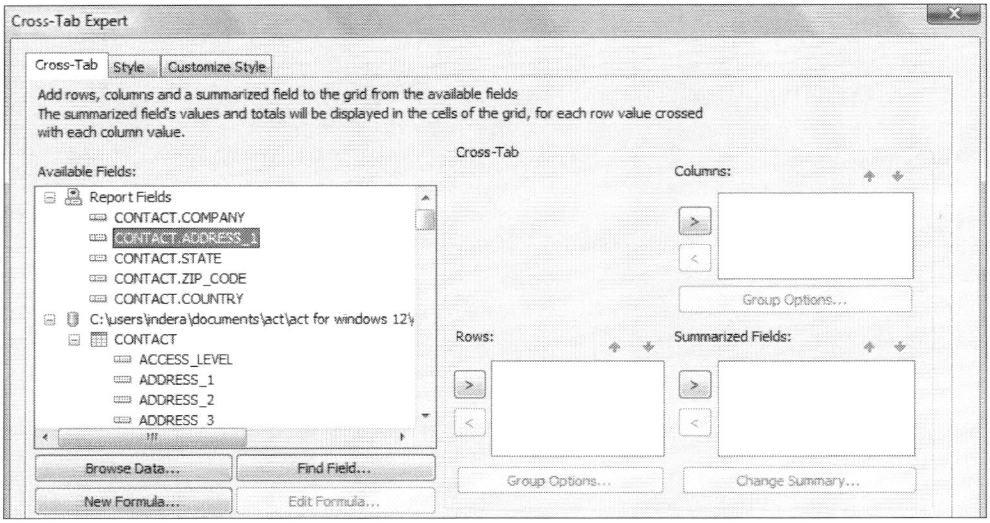

Figure 19-1 Cross-Tab options

Button	Description
New Formula	Opens the Formula Workshop.
Edit Formula	Opens the Formula Workshop so that you can edit an existing formula. You can edit a formula that has been added to the cross-tab or a formula that is listed in the Available Fields list.
Group Options	Opens the Cross-Tab Group Options dialog box shown in Figure 19-2. It is similar to the Insert Group dialog box. After you click on a field in the Rows or Columns section, this button will be enabled and you can change the group options for the field.
Change Summary	Opens the Edit Summary dialog box shown in Figure 19-3. It works the same way that the Insert Summary dialog box works and is used to change the summary type that was selected when the field was added to the Summarized Fields section.

Table 19-1 Buttons on the Cross-Tab tab explained

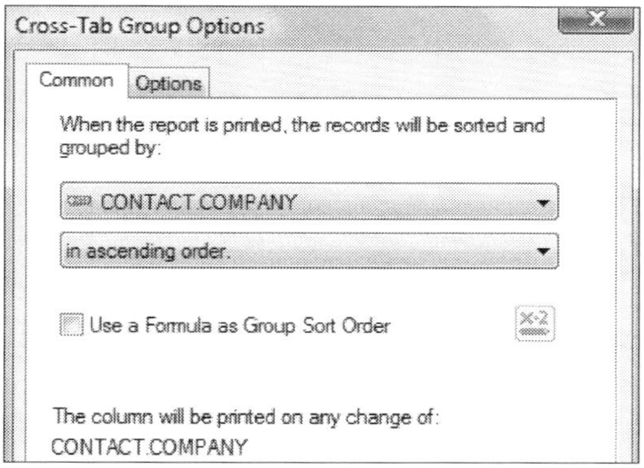

Figure 19-2 Cross-Tab Group Options dialog box

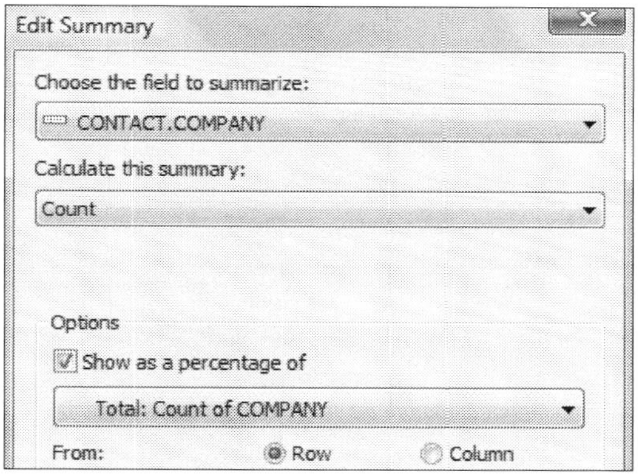

Figure 19-3 Edit Summary dialog box

Cross-Tab Tips

① It is best not to place any other objects in the same report section as the cross-tab because they will probably be overwritten.
② When more than one field is added to the rows, columns or summarized fields sections on the Cross-Tab Expert, the values will be stacked in the cell.
③ If you want the cross-tab to capture all of the data in the report, place the Cross-tab object in the report header section.
④ It is better to position fields so that there are more rows than columns. Doing this will help keep the cross-tab from being forced to print on more than one page.

Style Tab

The options shown in Figure 19-4 are the templates that you can use to format the entire cross-tab object at one time. These are the same styles that are on the Cross-Tab wizard.

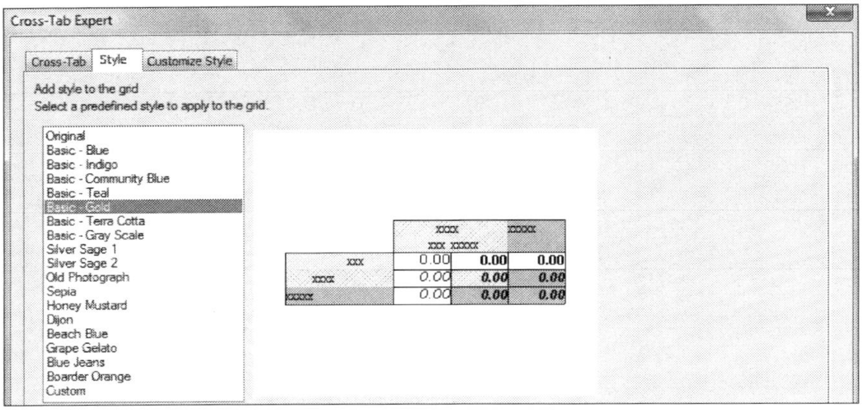

Figure 19-4 Style tab options

Customize Style Tab

The options shown in Figure 19-5 are used to apply formatting to a specific section of the cross-tab like a row or to the entire cross-tab object. Each field in the Rows and Columns sections represent a group. The options in the Grid Options section are applied to the entire cross-tab. The options in the Group Options section can be applied to each field.

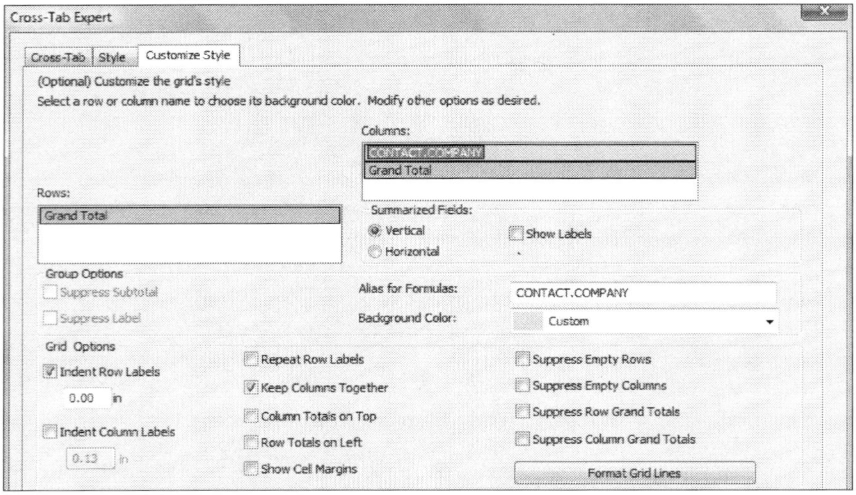

Figure 19-5 Customize Style tab options

Option	Description
Vertical/Horizontal	These options determine how the summarized fields will be displayed. There has to be at least two summarized fields to select one of these options. The **VERTICAL** option will stack the summarized fields in the same cell. You will see how this works when you complete the cross-tab exercise in this lesson. The **HORIZONTAL** option will place the summarized fields side by side.
Show Labels	If checked, this option will display the summarized field name in the row or column header.

Table 19-2 Summarized Field options explained

Option	Description
Suppress Subtotal	This option is only available if there are two or more fields in the Rows section or two or more fields in the Columns section. This option cannot be used on grand total fields. If checked, this option will suppress the subtotal for the row or column that is selected.
Suppress Label	This option is only available if the Suppress Subtotal option is checked. If checked, this option will suppress the Group By fields label.
Alias for Formulas	This option is used to enter a different name for the field that is used on the cross-tab. The name entered in this field can be used in conditional formatting formulas instead of the name in the table.
Background Color	This drop-down list box is used to select a background color for the row or column of data.

Table 19-3 Group Options explained

Option	Description
Indent Row Labels	Determines how much the row labels will be indented.
Indent Column Labels	Determines how much the column labels will be indented.
Repeat Row Labels	This option is only available if the Keep Columns together option is checked. This option will force the row labels to be repeated on other pages when the width of the cross-tab requires more than one page.
Keep Columns Together	Prevents a column from being split across two pages.
Column Totals on Top	Forces column totals to print at the top of the column.
Row Totals on Left	Forces row totals to print on the left of the cross-tab object.
Show Cell Margins	Adds white space on all four sides of the cell.
Suppress Empty Rows	If checked, rows that do not have data will not appear in the cross-tab.
Suppress Empty Columns	If checked, columns that do not have data will not appear in the cross-tab.

Table 19-4 Grid Options explained

Option	Description
Suppress Row Grand Totals	If checked, the grand total row will not appear in the cross-tab.
Suppress Column Grand Totals	If checked, the grand total column will not appear in the cross-tab.
Format Grid Lines button	Clicking this button will open the Format Grid Lines dialog box shown in Figure 19-6. Table 19-5 explains the options on this dialog box.

Table 19-4 Grid Options explained (Continued)

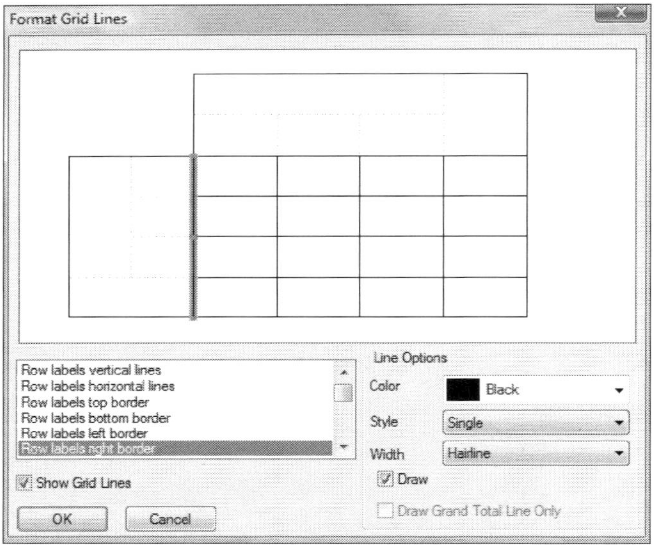

Figure 19-6 Format Grid Lines dialog box

Option	Description
Grid Line	Selects the grid line in the list box that you want to modify. The grid line(s) that you select will be highlighted in the grid at the top of the dialog box.
Show Grid Lines	Displays or hides the grid lines.
Color	Is used to select a color for the grid lines.
Style	Is used to select a style for the grid lines.
Width	Is used to select a width for the grid lines.
Draw	Is used to select a specific grid line to hide.
Draw Grand Total Line Only	If checked, this option will only display/print grid lines on grand total rows or columns.

Table 19-5 Format Grid Lines dialog box options explained

Cross-Tab Shortcut Menu

Like many features in Crystal Reports, the cross-tab object has its own shortcut menu. The **PIVOT CROSS-TAB** option is used to move the rows to where the columns are and the columns to where the rows are on the cross-tab.

Formatting Formulas

You can create conditional formatting formulas in a cross-tab using the Format Editor, similar to how conditional formatting formulas are created for other fields. In addition to being able to use the **CURRENTFIELDVALUE** and **DEFAULTATTRIBUTE** functions, cross-tabs can also use the **GRIDROWCOLUMNVALUE** function. This function is used to create a formula that depends on the value in a row that is related to the current cell. An advantage to using the GridRowColumnValue function is that you can use the Alias field name instead of the real field name. The examples below demonstrate how these functions can be used in a cross-tab or OLAP grid.

Example #1 The formula below will set the current field (cell) to yellow if it is greater than or equal to 25.

If CurrentFieldValue >= 25 Then crYellow Else DefaultAttribute

Example #2 The formula below will set the current field (cell) to yellow if it is greater than or equal to 100 and the Product Name is "Gloves".

If GridRowColumnValue {Product.Product Name} = "Gloves" and CurrentFieldValue >= 100 Then crYellow Else DefaultAttribute

You can use the **HIGHLIGHTING EXPERT** to format data fields in a cross-tab.

Exercise 19.1: Use The Cross-Tab Expert

In this exercise you will recreate the cross-tab report that you created in Exercise 13.1. You will enhance the report by adding the following:

① Indenting the row labels.
② Modifying the grid lines.
③ Applying conditional formatting to change the background of cells that meet a specific condition.
④ Create a formula to calculate the total dollar amount of opportunities per product, per contact.

Create The Product Type Selection Criteria

The Cross-Tab wizard has a Record Selection screen that is used to create selection criteria. If you use the Cross-Tab Expert, you have different options. You can create a formula or create the selection criteria using the Select Expert.

1. Open a new report, then add the following tables to the report: Opportunity, Opportunity Product Service and Product Service, then click Next.

2. Create the following links. Link the Opportunity and Opportunity Product Service tables on the Opportunity ID field. Link the Product Service and Opportunity Product Service tables on the Product Service ID field.

3. Open the Select Expert. Select the Actual Close Date field. Select the Is between operator. Enter the range `6/1/2009` to `12/31/2009`.

4. Select the Name field in the Product Service table. Select the "Is one of" operator, then add the One Component, TechOne System and Service Contract products, then click OK.

Create The Cross-Tab

1. Add a cross-tab object to the report header, then right-click on the cross-tab object and select Cross-Tab Expert.

2. Add the Contact field in the Opportunity table to the **ROWS** section, then add the Name field in the Product Service table to the **COLUMNS** section.

3. Add the Quantity field in the Product Service table to the **SUMMARY FIELDS** section. Click the **CHANGE SUMMARY** button and change the summary type to Count, then click OK.

Customize The Cross-Tab

The Customize Style tab has several options that you can use to change the appearance of the cross-tab.

1. On the Customize Style tab clear the **COLUMN TOTALS ON TOP** and **ROW TOTALS ON LEFT** options.

2. Check the Indent Row Labels option, then type `.25` in the box below it.

3. Click the Format Grid Lines button. Select the **COLUMN LABEL BOTTOM BORDER** option in the list on the left, then select Dashed from the Style drop-down list. Click OK to close the Format Grid Lines dialog box, then click OK to close the Cross-Tab Expert.

4. Save the report as `L19.1 Cross-Tab`.

   The report should look like the one shown in Figure 19-7.

   Leave the report open to complete the next part of the exercise.

	ONE Component	Service Contract	TechONE System	Total
Amanda Form	0	1	2	3
Andy Harrison	0	1	0	1
Anthony Keltie	0	0	1	1
Bella Minoal	0	0	1	1
Brandon Sloan	0	0	1	1
Buck Turgidson	1	0	0	1
Chris Burn	1	1	0	2

Figure 19-7 Cross-Tab report

Add Another Row Of Data To The Cross-Tab

In this part of the exercise you will create a formula that will calculate the total of each product that each contact purchased.

1. Open the Cross-Tab Expert, then click the New Formula button.

2. Type `Line Item` as the formula name, then type the formula shown below.
   `{Product_Service.Unit_Price} * {Product_Service.Quantity}`

3. Save the formula, then click on the formula field in the Available Fields list on the Cross-Tab Expert and add it to the Summarized Fields section. Click OK.

4. Format all four formula fields in the Cross-Tab to display a dollar sign.

   Save the changes.

   The cross-tab should look like the one shown in Figure 19-8.

	ONE Component	Service Contract	TechONE System	Total
Amanda Form	0 $0	1 $2000	2 $24000	3 $26,000
Andy Harrison	0 $0	1 $2000	0 $0	1 $2,000
Anthony Keltie	0 $0	0 $0	1 $12000	1 $12,000
Bella Minoal	0 $0	0 $0	1 $12000	1 $12,000
Brandon Sloan	0 $0	0 $0	1 $12000	1 $12,000
Buck Turgidson	1 $5000	0 $0	0 $0	1 $5,000
Chris Burn	1 $2500	1 $2000	0 $0	2 $4,500

Figure 19-8 Second row of data added to the cross-tab

Exercise 19.2: Create Conditional Formatting In Cross-Tabs

Creating conditional formatting in cross-tabs is not that much different then creating conditional formatting in other types of reports. In this exercise you will create conditional formatting on the quantity cells in the TechOne System column to change the background color to yellow if the quantity is greater than or equal to 2. It would be helpful to quickly be able to see which contacts purchased the most of this particular product.

1. Save the L19.1 report as `L19.2 Conditional formatting Cross-Tab`.

2. In the first column of the cross-tab, right-click on the detail Quantity field and select Format Field.

3. On the Border tab click the Formula button across from the Background option, type the formula shown below, then click the Save and close button.

```
If GridRowColumnValue("Product_Service.Name") = "TechOne
System" and CurrentFieldValue >= 2 Then crYellow Else
DefaultAttribute
```

4. Click OK and save the changes. The TechOne System quantity for the first contact should have a yellow background.

Cross-Tab Printing Issues

Cross-Tab objects can have printing issues, in particular cross-tab objects that require more than one page to print horizontally. The Cross-Tab Expert has the Repeat Row Labels and Keep Columns Together options, that you learned about earlier in Table 19-4, that you can use to resolve some printing issues. If there are horizontal printing issues, the options discussed below can help resolve them.

① **Horizontal Page Number** This special field counts the number of horizontal pages in a report. This field will not work if the cross-tab is in a section of the report that will not print page footers.
② **Repeat Horizontal Pages** This option is on the Common tab on the Format Editor dialog box. If checked, this option will force objects in the page header or page footer section to print on every horizontal page.
③ **Relative Positions** This option is on the Common tab on the Section Expert. Use it to control an object that is to the right of a cross-tab object. If checked, this option will cause the object next to the cross-tab to stay in the same relative position, regardless of how much the cross-tab grows.

Running Total Fields

Running total fields are similar to the summary fields that you have already learned to create. While running total fields are similar to summary fields, they provide more options which allows you more flexibility over the total fields that you create. There are four differences between running total and summary fields, as discussed below.

① Running total fields only calculate data that is displayed.
② Running total fields can be placed in the details section of the report, which would display a total up to the current record.
③ Running total fields are only evaluated/calculated during the **WHILE PRINTING RECORDS** pass of the report is taking place. Crystal Reports uses a multi pass system. This means that records in the "Others" group will not be counted in grand totals.
④ Running total fields are calculated at the detail level (record by record) and summary fields are calculated by group. If a running total field is placed in the group header section, it will only include a total for the first record in the group because the other records in the group have not been processed at this point.

Top N reports do not have to include records that do not meet the Top N criteria. Records that do not meet the Top N criteria can be placed in the "Others" group. It is important to note that records in the "Others" group will be included in any grand totals on the report, whether or not the records in the "Others" group are printed on the report.

The "Others" group is something that needs to be addressed during the report design phase. You have to find out if the people requesting the report want grand totals only for the records that meet the Top N requirements or all records including those in the "Others" category. Figure 19-9 shows the Create Running Total Field dialog box. If you only want report or grand totals for the records that meet the Top N condition, you have to use a running total field instead of a summary field.

You have probably figured out that there are a lot of good reasons to use running total fields instead of summary fields. You have also probably realized that selecting the appropriate type of total field (summary or running total) requires some thought. The other item that you have to consider is where the running total field will be placed on the report. Table 19-6 explains what the running total field will calculate depending on which section of the report it is placed in. The output will change depending on the **EVALUATE** option that is selected.

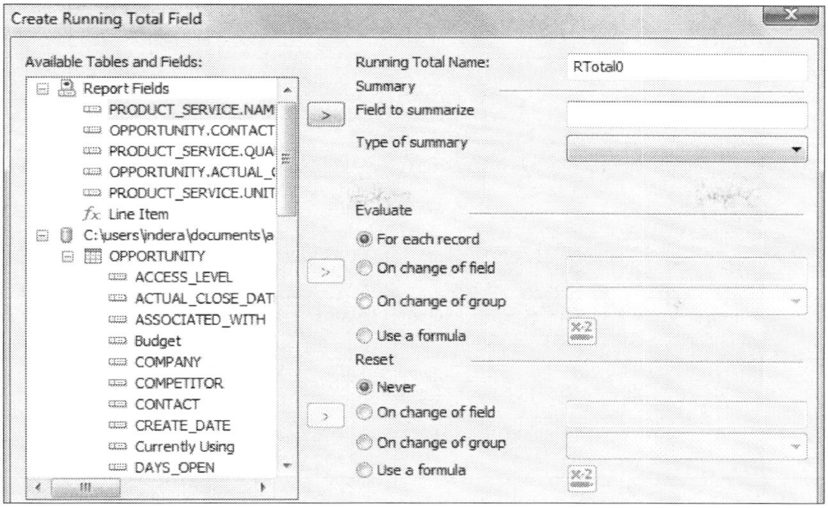

Figure 19-9 Create Running Total Field dialog box

Section	Which Records Will Be Calculated
Report Header	The first record on the report.
Page Header	All records up to the first record that will be printed on the current page.
Group Header	All records up to the first record of the current group.
Details	All records up to the current detail record.
Group Footer	All records up to the last record in the current group.
Page Footer	All records up to the first record on the next page.
Report Footer	All records on the report.

Table 19-6 Running total field output options explained

Like other dialog boxes that you have used, the Available Tables and Fields list contains the fields and formulas that you can use to create running total fields. The options in the **SUMMARY** section at the top on the right are used to enter a name for the running total field, select a field from the Available tables and fields list and select the type of summary. The options in the **TYPE OF SUMMARY** field drop-down list are the same as the ones for summary fields. The name of this field can be misleading because a running total field does more than create totals. Like summary fields, it can provide counts, averages, percents and more.

The options in the **EVALUATE** section are used to select when you want the running total field to be incremented. The **FOR EACH RECORD** option is most like a summary field calculation because the running total field is incremented after each detail record is processed.

The **ON CHANGE OF FIELD** option performs the running total field calculations when the value in the field is different then the value from the previous record. This is useful when the field that the running total field is using can have several records that have the same value and you only want to count the value once. This is like the Distinct Count summary type. If you are using a field like the Order ID field and the report uses the Orders and Orders Details tables, most of the time you should select the Order ID field from the parent table, which in this example is the Orders table.

When selecting this evaluation option, give some thought to the data that is in the field that you are using because records other then the first one that has the same data will not increment the running total field because this option excludes records. The key to using this option successfully is to select a field that has a lot of unique values in it.

> If you are going to use the **ON CHANGE OF FIELD** option, make sure that the records are sorted correctly, otherwise you will end up with unexpected results.

The **ON CHANGE OF GROUP** option can only be used on a report that has a group. This option will evaluate (increment) the running total field when the group changes.

If you need the running total field to be incremented based on a condition, select the **USE A FORMULA** option and click the Formula button next to the field. Then create a formula that the records must meet in order for the running total field to be incremented. An example of this would be if the report needed a total of orders that were not shipped in three days. The formula would check the Delay in days to ship formula field. If it was greater than three, add the order total to the running total field. If you needed a count of how many orders were not shipped that had an Delay in days to ship amount greater than three, you would create another running total field, use the count summary type and use the same formula for this running total field.

The options in the **RESET** section are used to select when you want the running total field to be reset to zero. If you were using the running total field to get group totals, you would select the **ON CHANGE OF GROUP** option, then select the field and select the group from the drop-down list. You could also create a formula that determined when to reset the running total field.

> You should use a running total field on reports that suppress records if there is a group selection formula. Report grand totals are calculated **BEFORE** the group selection formulas that have suppression are calculated.

There are three ways to open the Create Running Total Field dialog box, as discussed below.

① Right-click on the field in the details section that you want to create a running total for and select Insert ⇒ Running Total.

② Right-click on the Running Total Fields category in the Field Explorer, then select New.

③ Click on the Running Total Fields category in the Field Explorer, then click the New button on the Field Explorer toolbar.

Exercise 19.3: Create Two Running Total Fields

In this exercise you will create two running total fields. You will create one to get a total amount of opportunities that have been open for more than 90 days. The second running total field will count the number of opportunities that have been open for more than 90 days.

1. Save the L15 Formula field report as `L19.3 Running total fields.`

2. Delete the two address fields, then move the other fields over to the left.

3. Create the Line Item formula field that you created earlier in Exercise 19.1 and add it to the report after the Price field.

Create The Total Amount Running Total Field

In this part of the exercise you will create a running total field that will only count the Unit Price amount if the Number of days open is greater than 90 days.

1. Right-click on the Line Item formula field in the report and select Insert ⇒ Running Total.
2. Type `Total amount` in the Running Total Name field, then select the Sum Type of summary, if it is not already selected.
3. Select the **USE A FORMULA** Evaluate option, then click the Formula button.
4. Double-click on the Days Open field in the Opportunity table, then type `> 90` as the criteria.
5. Highlight the formula and press the Ctrl + C keys. This will let you paste the code into the next formula that you create. Click the Save and close button, then click OK and save the changes.

Create The Opportunity Count Running Total Field

In this part of the exercise you will create a running total field to get a count of the number of opportunities that have been open for more than 90 days.

If you preview the report you will see duplicate values in the Name field. This means that some opportunities have more than one item. If this were live data, often the products that are in stock will ship immediately and the ones that are not, will be delayed. Whatever the case is, you only want to count each opportunity once. Therefore, using the Count summary option would not work. You would have to use the Distinct Count option on the Opportunity ID field.

1. Open the Create Running Total Field dialog box and type `Opportunity count` in the Running Total Name field.
2. Select the Opportunity ID field as the Field to summarize, then select the Distinct count Type of summary.
3. Select the Use a formula Evaluate option, then click the Formula button.
4. Paste the formula in by pressing the Ctrl + V keys. Click the Save and close button, then click OK and save the changes.

> You could get the same results without a formula if the report was sorted on the Opportunity ID field and you selected the **ON CHANGE OF FIELD** Evaluate option.

Add The Running Total Fields To The Report

1. Drag the Opportunity count and Total amount running total fields to the report footer section and create field headings for them.

2. Format the Total amount field to have a floating dollar sign.

3. Add the record number special field to the report footer section, then create a heading for it. This will display the total number of detail records on the report create a title for the field.

4. Save the changes. The totals on the last page of the report should look like the ones shown in Figure 19-10.

   As you can see, there is a rather large difference in the number and amount of the opportunities that have been open for more than 90 days versus the number of opportunities that are printed on the report.

FIRST NAME LAST NAME PRODUCT

Total # records on the report 401

Total # of opportunities open > 90 273

Total $ amount of opportunities open > 90 $ 2,257,800.00

Figure 19-10 Running totals report

> Some of the data on the report will be different because you did not run the report on the same day that I did.

Running Total And Summary Field Limitation

The one limitation that both field types have is that they will not produce the correct result if the report suppresses data because by default, both fields will calculate the suppressed records that will not be printed on the report. This happens because both fields perform calculations without taking into account conditional formatting formulas that the suppress option may have.

In Exercise 16.15 you modified a report and added a formula to the Suppress (No Drill-Down) option on three sections of the report. This was done because the report requirement was to only display groups that met a condition. You have to follow the same process for a running total field. The reason that you have to do this is because you only want running total fields to include records that will actually appear on the report. To fix the L16.15 report, add the same formula to the running total fields.

Running Total Field Limitation

The two limitations of running total fields are discussed below.

① The calculation types are limited to the ones summary fields use.
② Summary functions and shared variables cannot be used.

Hierarchical Group Reports

A hierarchical group is a special type of parent-child, one-to-many relationship. It shows the relationship between records that are in the same table. If it helps, think of the parent field as the field that is displayed in the group header section and the child fields will be displayed in the details section of the report. In Lesson 5 you learned about **RECURSIVE JOINS**. This type of join is required to create hierarchical reports. [See Lesson 5, Recursive Joins]

Hierarchical groups are useful when you need to create a report where two fields in the same table relate to each other. This is what Crystal Reports refers to as a hierarchical group. This is how you can create organizational charts. An Employee table lists the employees that work for the company. It also contains who each employee reports to. Remember that the person that has someone reporting to them is also an employee.

In this example, the people that have someone reporting to them are the "parent" portion of the relationship. Employees that do not have anyone reporting to them are the "child" portion of the relationship. The Hierarchical Group Options dialog box shown in Figure 19-11 is used to create a hierarchical group report.

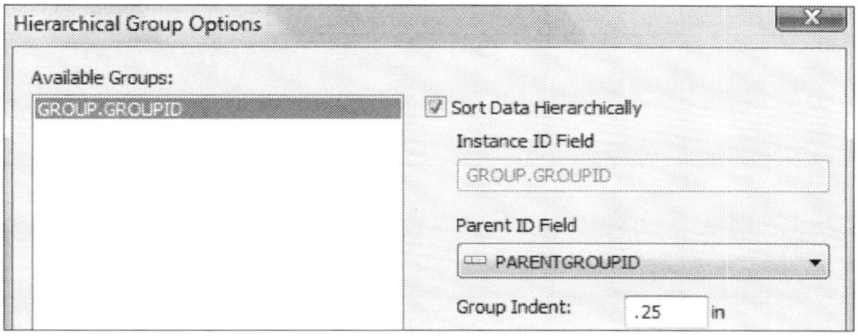

Figure 19-11 Hierarchical Group Options dialog box

The **AVAILABLE GROUPS** list contains all of the groups that the report has. The hierarchical report must be created using one of the groups that are listed in this section.

Once you select a group, check the **SORT DATA HIERARCHICALLY** option to indicate that you want to apply hierarchical sorting to the group that is selected.

The **INSTANCE ID FIELD** contains the field that will be used as the child field.

The **PARENT ID FIELD** contains the fields that can be used as the parent field. The parent record (in this example, the supervisor) will print first and then the employees that report to the supervisor will print below. All of the fields in this drop-down list are the same data type as the group field.

The **GROUP INDENT** option is used to select how much the child records should be indented. Using this feature is optional. If the columns do not contain a lot of data and the Group Indent option is greater than zero, it is possible that some data will not line up properly with the field headings.

One way to fix this is to make the Group Indent number smaller. Another option is to resize some of the fields on the report. Leaving this option set to zero means that the child records will not be indented, which will make it difficult to see who reports to who.

Hierarchical Report Requirements

To create a hierarchical report, the following three requirements must be met.

① The table must have two fields that represent the same data. This allows the data in one field to point to another record in the same table.
② The parent and child fields must have the same data type.
③ The report must be grouped on the child field.

Exercise 19.4: Create A Hierarchical Group Report

In this exercise you will create a report that shows each group and its subgroups.

1. Create a new report and add the Group table, but do not add any fields to the report.

2. Create a group on the Group ID field. Use the Options tab to display the group name instead of the Group ID.

3. Report ⇒ Hierarchical Grouping Options. You will see the Hierarchical Group Options dialog box. Check the Sort Data Hierarchically option, then select the ParentGroup ID field from the Parent ID Field drop-down list.

4. Change the Group Indent option to `.25`. You should have the options shown earlier in Figure 19-11. Click OK.

5. Add the Group Description and Has Subgroups fields to the group header section, then create headings for these fields in the page header section.

6. Apply the Can Grow option to the Group Description field.

7. Format the Has Subgroups field so that it displays Yes or No.

8. Save the report as `L19.4 Hierarchical report`.

   The report should look like the one shown in Figure 19-12.

Group Name	Description	Has SubGroup
Database Users	Contacts who are Users of this database	No
Recently Edited Contacts	Contacts edited within the last 30 days	No
Upcoming Opportunities	Contacts with Opportunities estimated to close within the next 30 days	No
TechONE Seminar	Invitations	No
Friends	ID/Status =(Contains) Friend	No
Customers	ID/Status=Customer	Yes
Customers-TWO Component	Opp Prod= (Contains) TWO Component;ID/Status= (Contains) Customer	No
Customers-ONE Component	Opp Prod= (Contains) ONE Component;ID/Status= (Contains) Customer	No

Figure 19-12 Hierarchical report

Optional Hierarchical Report Options

If the Hierarchical report needs summary or grand totals, use the Insert Summary dialog box.

If you select the summary field and then open the Insert Summary dialog box, you will see the **SUMMARIZE ACROSS HIERARCHY** option illustrated in Figure 19-13.

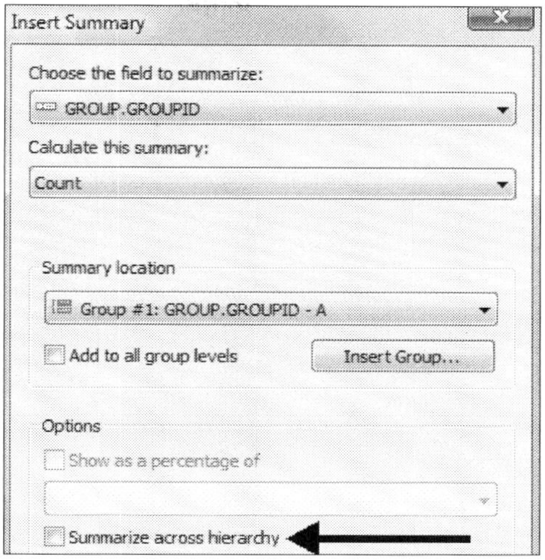

Figure 19-13 Hierarchy option illustrated

The Group Sort Expert

You have already used the Group Sort Expert to create and modify Top N reports. In addition to being able to create and modify Top N reports, the Group Sort Expert is used to sort groups in ways other than ascending or descending order. You can sort groups based on values in a summary field in the group.

For example, in Exercise 10.2, you created a report that grouped the opportunities by contact. You also created two summary fields for the contact group; one for the contact total dollar amount of opportunities and one for the total number of opportunities. If someone needed to see the opportunities in high to low or low to high order based on the total dollar amount of the contact, you could sort the contact group on the Total summary field. If you sorted the Total summary field in ascending order, the contacts with the lowest total dollar amount would appear at the beginning of the group.

In Exercise 11.1 you created a report that grouped the opportunities closed in 2008 by month. If you wanted to show the months with the highest monthly totals at the beginning of the report, you would sort the month group in descending order on the Total summary field.

Figure 19-14 shows the Group Sort Expert dialog box. When you open the dialog box you will see a tab for each group that the report has. You can sort on as many of the summary values in the groups as needed.

Keep in mind that the sorting starts with the first tab and works its way across the tabs.

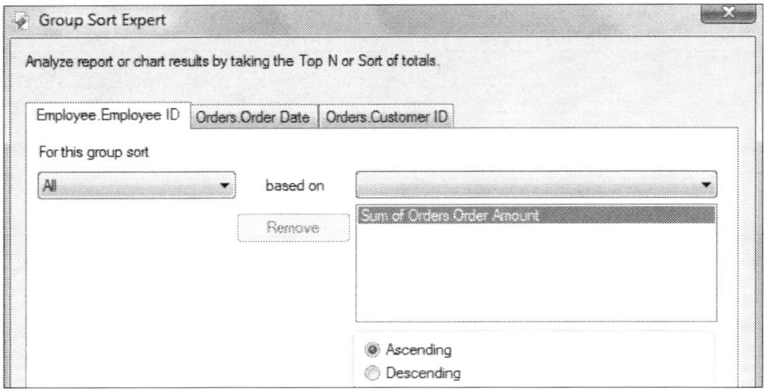

Figure 19-14 Group Sort Expert dialog box

In addition to the Top N, Bottom N, Top Percentage and Bottom Percentage options, the **FOR THIS GROUP SORT** drop-down list has the following options:

NO SORT, which is the default and will use the sort options that were set up when the group was created.

The **ALL** option will include all of the groups and not suppress any groups like the Top N, Bottom N, Top Percentage and Bottom Percentage options will.

The options in the **BASED ON** drop-down list are the summary fields that are in a group section of the report.

To create a Top or Bottom N report, the report must have the two items discussed below, before opening the Group Sort Expert.

① The report must have at least one group.
② The group that you want to use for the Top N report must have a summary field in it.

The way that you know that the report has both of the options discussed above is that you can open the Group Sort Expert. Reports that do not meet the criteria will not have the Group Sort Expert option enabled.

There are two ways to open the Group Sort Expert, as discussed below.

① Click the Group Sort Expert button on the Expert Tools toolbar.
② Report ⇒ Group Sort Expert.

Exercise 19.5: Sort On The Contact Group By Total Field

In this exercise you will change the sort order of the groups to show the groups that have contacts with the lowest total order amounts at the top of this report. You will also sort the groups by the number of opportunities in descending order. This sort will happen within the opportunity amount sort. This is helpful if two or more contacts have the same opportunity total amount.

1. Save the L10.2 report as `L19.5 Group sorted on two fields.`

2. Open the Group Sort Expert and select the All option from the drop-down list.

3. Select the Total summary field if it is not already selected, then select the ascending option.

4. Select the Opportunity ID count field from the drop-down list on the right, then select descending and click OK. Save the changes. The report should look like the one shown in Figure 19-15. As you look through the report, you should see the contacts with the lowest total amounts at the beginning of the report.

Contact Opportunities

COMPANY	OPPORTUNITY NAME	CREATE DATE	DAYS OPEN	TOTAL	STATUS	ACTUAL CLOSE DATE
Joanne Lisle						
Picture Frame Ltd	Picture Frame Ltd-Framing Facility	9/30/09	148	$0.00	Open	12/31/99
Total # of opportunities - 1		Total $ amount of opportunities -		$0.00		
Angela Ives						
A1 Services of UK	A1 Services of UK-Replacement Parts for Portat	10/30/08	168	$300.00	Closed - Won	4/15/10
Total # of opportunities - 1		Total $ amount of opportunities -		$300.00		
Sean Duffy						
Circle Photography	Circle Photography-Office Replacements	4/18/08	227	$400.00	Open	12/31/99
Total # of opportunities - 1		Total $ amount of opportunities -		$400.00		

Figure 19-15 Group sorted on two fields report

As the report designer, it may be obvious to you how a report is sorted and grouped. Unlike the reports that you have created earlier in this book that have groups, reports that have groups that are sorted by a value in a summary field, may not be as easy for the reader to figure out how the report is grouped and sorted, just by looking at it.

If you look at the report shown above in Figure 19-15, you will see the group name (the company name field) in the group header section. Many people will think that this is how the report is sorted even though the report is sorted by the values in the total summary field. You should do something to make sure that the person reading the report is aware of how the report is sorted or grouped. There are three options that I select from to help clarify how a report presents data. You can use any of the options below or come up with a different solution.

① Add how the report is grouped and sorted as a subtitle on the report. For example, Grouped by (field name) and sorted by summary (field name), where you fill in the (field name).
② Add how the report is grouped and sorted to the page or report footer section.
③ Add the summary value to the group header section.

Creating Group Selection Formulas

Group selection formulas are used to filter groups that do not meet a condition. The formulas can be created by using the values in a group summary field or by using the values in the Group Name field. To use a Group Name field you have to use the Group Name function. The only time that you need to use this function is if the report has custom group names.

To create a group selection formula, select a summary field on the Select Expert instead of a detail field. In Exercise 19.5 you modified the report to sort the groups in ascending order. If you only wanted to see groups (in this example, contacts) that have a total summary amount less than $10,000 and are in the USA, you would create two selection criteria options; one on the Total summary amount, which is a group summary field and one on the Country field.

Exercise 19.6: Create A Group Selection Formula

1. Save the L19.5 report as `L19.6 Group selection formula.`

2. Right-click on the Total summary field in the group footer section and select the Select Expert Group option. Select the "Is less than" operator, then type `10000` in the next drop-down list. This is the group selection formula.

3. Click on the New tab, then select the Country field. Select the "Is equal to" operator, then select the United States in the drop-down list. Click OK.

4. Open the Select Expert for records and delete the Create Date criteria. Click OK and save the changes. The report should look like the one shown in Figure 19-16.

Contact Opportunities

	COMPANY	OPPORTUNITY NAME	CREATE DATE	DAYS OPEN	TOTAL	STATUS	ACTUAL CLOSE DATE
Jon Ritter							
	Parsley Group	Boomer's Artworx-SC for Phoenix	5/20/07	209	$2,000.00	Open	12/31/99
	Total # of opportunities - 1		Total $ amount of opportunities -		$2,000.00		
Al Pashah							
	Making Technology Co	Boomer's Artworx-Phoenix Expansion	5/20/07	209	$4,000.00	Open	12/31/99
	Total # of opportunities - 1		Total $ amount of opportunities -		$4,000.00		
Ben Barrow							
	Making Technology Co	Ace Pet Store-Corporate Offices	5/20/07	123	$2,000.00	Open	12/31/99
	Making Technology Co	Making Technology-Testing ONEComponent	5/21/07	432	$2,500.00	Closed - Won	7/25/08
	Total # of opportunities - 2		Total $ amount of opportunities -		$4,500.00		

Figure 19-16 Group selection formula report

As you may expect, group selection formulas will suppress groups that do not meet the selection criteria. What I find interesting is that the summary field group totals are the same as if there were no suppressed groups. This is because there is a difference between suppressing groups and filtering records. Keep this in mind when creating group selection formulas.

Multi-Column Reports

In Lesson 12 you used the Mailing Label Report wizard, which can be used to create multi-column labels. You can use the options on the Layout tab shown in Figure 19-17, on the Section Expert to create multi-column reports.

The options on the Layout tab are used to create columns like the Mailing Label wizard does. Unlike word processing software that often has a "Number of columns" option, the Layout tab does not. You create the columns by using the **DETAIL SIZE** and **GAP BETWEEN DETAILS** options.

The **FORMAT GROUPS WITH MULTIPLE COLUMN** option if checked, will cause the group headers and footers to have the same width as the details section.

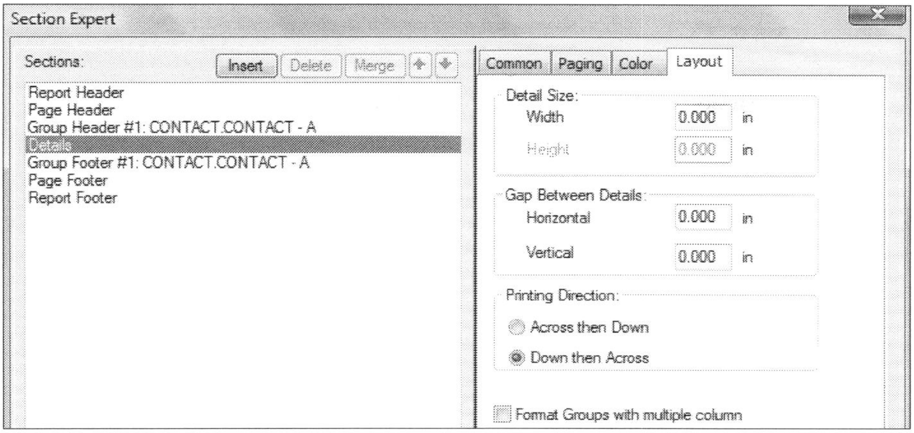

Figure 19-17 Layout tab options

Summary Reports

The majority of reports that you have created in this book contained detail level records. This is the type of report that many people are use to seeing. Detail level reports provide a lot of information. There are times when this is too much information and someone will want to only see summary information. There are two main ways to create summary reports, as discussed below.

① Use the Hide or Suppress report section options.
② Use a Parameter field.

Drill-Down Reports

Drill-down reports initially look like summary reports. The difference is that drill-down reports do not use the Suppress (No Drill-Down) option. Keep in mind that the only data that will print or be exported when using the drill-down feature is what is displayed on the selected preview tab.

Drill-Down Report Problems

There are two problems that you may encounter when designing reports that will use the drill-down feature, as discussed below.

① Problems with the group headers.
② Problems with the column headings.

What I have noticed on reports that have at least three groups is that when you drill-down, you will see more headers than you probably want or need. When you drill-down on the top level group (group 1), you will see the headers for the second group. This may not be what you want when you drill-down to the third level.

Using the Hide (Drill-Down OK) option on the Section Expert doesn't work well to resolve the heading problem. The **DRILLDOWNGROUPLEVEL** function is used to control when group headers are suppressed. This function is used for printing. The original preview window will return a zero when this function is used. If you are drilling down on group 2, the function will return a 2.

When you drill-down on the first group, you usually do not have a need to see the headers for the second group. To prevent this from happening, you would use the formula shown below to conditionally suppress the second level group headers. You would place this formula on the Suppress (No Drill-Down) option. In this example you would place it on the group 2 header. When this formula is applied, the group 2 header will not appear when you drill-down on the first level. The group 2 header will appear when you drill-down on the third level, which is what you want to have happen.

```
DrillDownGroupLevel = 1
```

Column Heading Problems

On the first preview tab you will see column headings but no detail records if you use the Hide or Suppress option on the Section Expert. This happens when the column headings are in the page header section. When you drill-down to the detail level, the data in the page header section does not appear. Yes, I was confused when I realized this.

The number of groups on the report determines the solution. If the report only has one group, move the column headings to the group header section. Decide if they look better above or below the group name field if you plan to keep the group name field on the report.

If the report has more than one group, create a second details section and move the detail fields to the second section, then move the column headings to the first detail section and select the **SUPPRESS BLANK SECTION** option on the Section Expert.

Exercise 19.7: Drill-Down Report

In this exercise you will modify a report so that the field headings are displayed when the report is drilled down.

Add The Summary Report Functionality

1. Save the L10.2 report as `L19.7 Drill-Down report`.

2. Delete the Status field, then move the Actual Close Date field left.

3. Suppress the field headings.

4. Hide the details section.

5. Change the report title to `Summary Of Opportunities`.

6. Remove the bold from all of the objects in the group footer section.

7. Remove the line from the Total summary field.

8. Save the changes. The layout should look like the one shown in Figure 19-18. The report should look like the one shown in Figure 19-19.

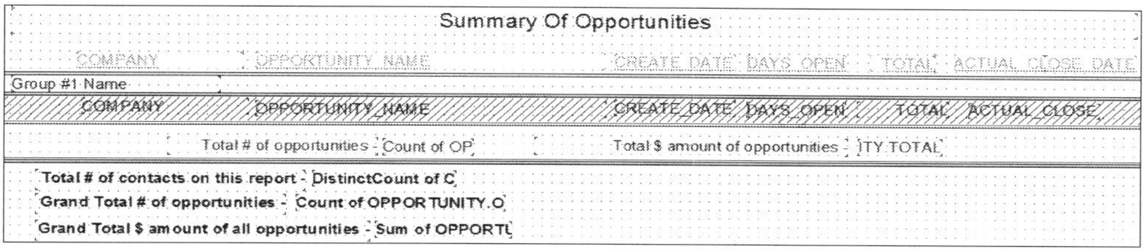

Figure 19-18 Report layout

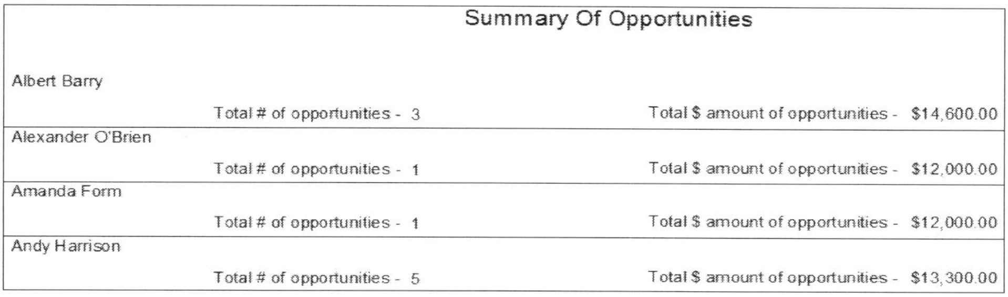

Figure 19-19 Drill-Down report

9. Double-click on the first contact name in the report preview mode, which is a group header field. You should see the tab shown in Figure 19-20. Notice that there are no field headings on this tab. The tab name has the contacts name.

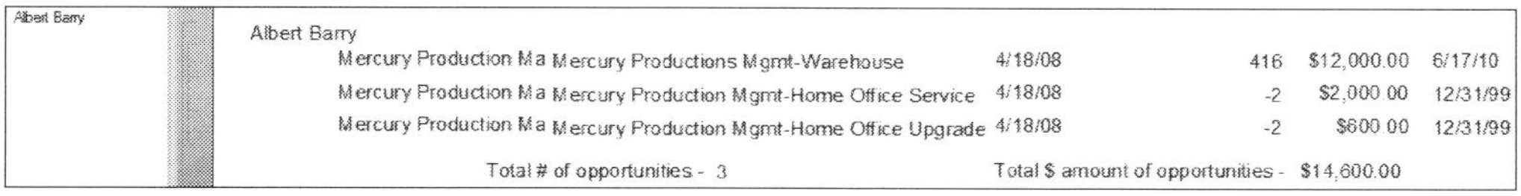

Figure 19-20 Detail records tab

Modify The Summary Report

In this part of the exercise you will move the field headers to the group header section so that they will appear on the drill-down tabs.

1. Make the group header section longer, then drag the field headings to the group header section below the group field, as shown in Figure 19-21.

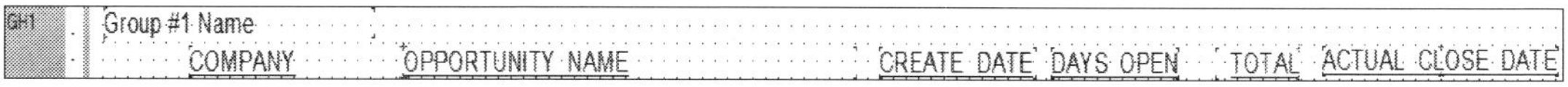

Figure 19-21 Field headings moved to the group header section

2. Select all of the field headings, then open the Format Editor. Clear the suppress option on the Common tab, then click OK.

3. Save the changes. If you double-click on the first contact name, the new tab should display the field headings, as shown in Figure 19-22. Like the full report, you can print the data on the detail records drill-down tab.

Albert Barry

COMPANY	OPPORTUNITY NAME	CREATE DATE	DAYS OPEN	TOTAL	ACTUAL CLOSE DATE
Mercury Production Ma	Mercury Productions Mgmt-Warehouse	4/18/08	416	$12,000.00	6/17/10
Mercury Production Ma	Mercury Production Mgmt-Home Office Service	4/18/08	-2	$2,000.00	12/31/99
Mercury Production Ma	Mercury Production Mgmt-Home Office Upgrade	4/18/08	-2	$600.00	12/31/99

Total # of opportunities - 3 Total $ amount of opportunities - $14,600.00

Figure 19-22 Field headings displayed on the drill-down tab

Exercise 19.8: Add A Watermark To A Report

In Exercise 18.2 you learned how to use the Underlay option. In this exercise you will use the Underlay option to add a watermark to a report.

1. Save the L5.3 report as `L19.8 Watermark report`.

2. Create another page header section. Move the field headings to the new page header section.

3. Add the draft_watermark logo from the zip file to the page header a section.

   Place the logo in the center of the section, then make it larger, as shown in Figure 19-23.

Figure 19-23 Logo added to the first page header section

4. Open the Section Expert for the page header a section. Select the Underlay Following Sections option, then click OK.

   Save the changes and preview the report. It should look like the one shown in Figure 19-24.

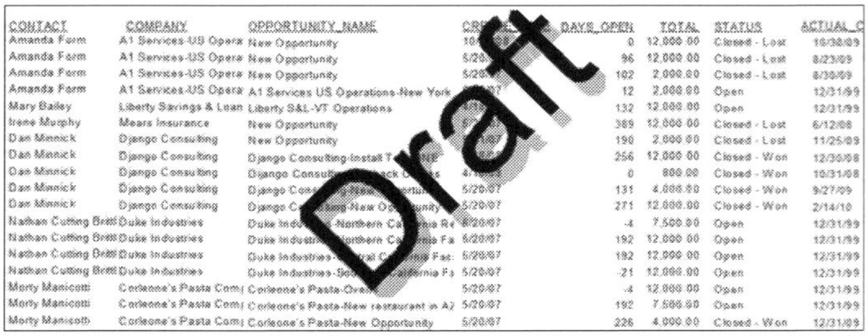

Figure 19-24 Watermark added to the report

The End!

If you are reading this paragraph, I hope it means that you have completed all of the exercises in this book. If so, congratulations because you have covered a lot of material. If some topics seem a little fuzzy right now, that is to be expected. Hopefully you have gained some valuable Crystal Reports skills and techniques. As you have probably figured out, unless you are creating a basic list report, there are a lot of options and features at your disposal to create reports that people will "like" to use. I hope that you enjoyed the book.

INDEX

D

E

F

G

H

I

J

L

Q

R

S

T

U

V

W

X

Y

Z

Made in United States
Orlando, FL
10 November 2026

90510183R00249